WHO'S WHO IN DICKENS

WHO'S WHO IN DICKENS

ALEX J. PHILIP AND LAURENCE GADD

STUDIO EDITIONS
LONDON

"A Dickens Dictionary" was originally published by
Simpkin Marshall,
London, 1928

This paperback edition published 1992 by Studio Editions Ltd.
Princess House, 50 Eastcastle Street
London W1N 7AP, England

ISBN 1 85170 928 2

Printed and bound in Finland

CONTENTS

PREFACE TO THE SECOND EDITION.

In this the second edition of " A Dickens Dictionary " the work has been divided into two parts. The second part, while incorporating the 'originals' in the first edition, has been compiled afresh by Lieut. Col. Gadd, who alone is responsible for the opinions expressed in certain identifications. Possibly no two authorities can be found to agree on all the 'orginals': so it seemed best to leave the responsibility with the one, and as Col. Gadd has kept himself very closely in touch with the work of Dickens enthusiasts for the last twenty years or more it naturally fell to him to give the final conclusion in any doubtful or debatable case.

The opportunity has been taken to correct as far as possible the Dictionary portion of the book, and in this direction too, I have to acknowledge very gratefully Col. Gadd's assistance.

Gravesend, ALEX. J. PHILIP.
Oct., 1928.

Introduction to the First Edition.

Two extremes have been the fashion at different times and with different people: on the one hand it has been asserted that all Dickens' characters and places had originals on which they were founded, and prototypes have been found or imagined; on the other hand it has been stated, on what should be good authority, that with a few notable exceptions the novelist had no real people or scenes in his mind's eye when he drew the exquisite pictures which are caricature and human nature at the same time. To me it appears that neither of these rather wholesale statements is correct. It is quite obvious to any one who "feels" as he reads that Dickens was not an imaginative writer. It is impossible to imagine his having written a story from his own fancy: even his fairy stories, the tales of the spirits, the goblins, and sprites are not even fanciful; each one is a moral, a sentiment, or a thought masquerading very heavily in a flimsy disguise. The characters are evidently founded on the men and women and children of all classes, of various nations, and of innumerable dispositions which jostled him in the street, and the field-path, in the village inn, and in the hotel, and at every point of his varied life. An almost infallible memory made possible what might otherwise appear improbable. From this it follows that each character was protrayed from a vivid and permanent picture in the author's mind; but it is equally certain that each of these mind pictures was a very composite photograph, the characteristics of many men entering into the making of one portrait. Even those characters which are admittedly based upon actualities, such as Harold Skimpole, cannot be attributed to one original—in this case alone at least two men entered into the making of one minor character. It is therefore useless to hope to identify in the world of names and addresses all those people who have sat consciously or unconsciously to the facile pen of the great writer.

The case is somewhat different with regard to the localities and the houses which enter so largely into the novels. It is impossible to point to any novelist in the English language in which locality and local colour play so important a part. And the thin disguise covering the identity of some of the scenes leaves no doubt that the place, and the one place only, is being described, although the one place may be typical of a whole class. But even places and houses are sometimes composite, as were the characters, instancing Jasper's Gatehouse, which is neither of the gatehouses in Rochester, but is all three of them. That real places entered into even the apparently minor scenes of the novels is evident from Dickens telling his daughter, many years after the publication of *Pickwick*, that a certain spot was where the redoutable nimrod lost his whip. The scene was a picture drawn with a fine sweep on large canvas and touched in with the inimitable individuality of the author.

In estimating the probability, or otherwise, of originals having existed for this character or that place, it is necessary to probe the psychology of the writer as expressed in his works—in short, as Mr. Micawber would say, to feel with him and think with him, to allow ourselves to be carried along on the stream of the story. An array of facts, with a counter array of facts on the negative side, are of little value in the analysis of the thoughts of a man whose brain probably teemed with plots and plans and characters and incidents. And there is probably no better example of the development, the expansion, and the growth of Dickens's thought than that expressed in *Pickwick*. One can see there the young author feeling his feet, and as he gains assurance, allowing his satire freer play, pointing his wit more broadly and indicating more clearly the places and people who were held up to kindly ridicule or roundly abused for their betrayal of their trust or the public good. To indicate the way in which this development made itself felt it is necessary only to lightly sketch the salient features of the topography of the work.

Rochester is avowedly Rochester, but there is nothing against Rochester in *Pickwick*—when it is treated disparagingly it becomes "Dulborough." Muggleton, however, and the people and places in connection with it are disguised most thoroughly, and yet it is probable that the picture is nothing more than a humorous caricature of Gravesend. Farther on in the book the place names are more obvious. Ipswich, Bath, and Bury are named, although the mention of the Mayor of Ipswich must have given rise to a great deal of chaff to that individual in the flesh. But the name of "Boz" was by that time a household word, and the famous young writer could do many things he would not have ventured on a few months previously. In the same way the disguise of Justice Stareleigh was so thin that Gazlee was immediately recognised. But Mr. Wardle has not yet been identified with the certainty that could be desired.

The allusion to the identity of Mr. Wardle reminds me that I have been informed that a farm "Dingle Dell," corresponding in every respect to the Manor Farm, Dingley Dell, and owned by an English Yeoman, the prototype of Wardle, existed in the early part of the nineteenth century, some where between Gravesend and Rochester. This is an old family tradition which may or may not be founded on fact—there is an illimitable fund of anecdote and story to be gleaned from Kentish family tradition—but as I have been unable to verify it by a search through early directories and local papers, I have been obliged to omit from my "originals."

One peculiar feature of Dickens and his work seldom sufficiently allowed for is the fact that he was a novelist by intention. Some writers write to please themselves, or because they have a mission, or it may be for the sake of the pounds shillings and pence which so many thousands of words represent, while the motives of others are a conglomeration of all three. Dickens, however, was or appears to have been, actuated by the singular idea of amusing and interesting his readers, the people. This solicitude for the people was revealed in his politics and his political writings, and was due possibly to the histrionic strain that manifested itself in his amateur theatricals and in his lectures. I can think of no closer simile than that of an actor acting—acting and conscious meanwhile that he is acting. The knowledge lends itself to the highest art, while it inflicts an enormous strain on the actor or writer, and above all, it produces a mind which cannot be measured by the ordinary rules of thought nor gauged by the limitations of ordinary ideas. The conscious artist has an eye for his public and posterity, for the superficial and for the heart of things. His art is not to produce the perfect work to satisfy the arbitrary canons of his own taste, but to draw forth the acclamations of his readers. It is this that has led to the otherwise incomprehensible state of affairs when Dickens is condemned as a mountebank, and lauded as a wit, praised as a humorist and sneered at as a caricaturist of the small beer of humanity: read and re-read as a transcendental limner of the everlasting traits of human nature; and thrown aside as the originator of the gutter press. And he is not only a great artist but a bold man who will dare to throw down the gauntlet to posterity in the firm faith that no matter how much the dogs may snarl and snap in the arena the work of his genius will endure.

The reason just mentioned gives the clue to the cause of hiding Rochester under the guise of Cloisterham so late in the day that he could have written about Heaven without offending his readers; and for depicting Uptown so vaguely that it may have been Rochester, Chatham, Strood or Gravesend. Possibly Dickens desired to arouse curiosity regarding Pip's village in the marshes, and the identification may have been intentionally simplified, while sufficient alteration was made to cause a momentary doubt. Joe Gargery's forge, too, has been the subject of a good deal of controversy; and even quite recently the church in the marshes has been subjected to a searching review of the "higher criticism" kind with interesting results.

Possibly none of Dickens's works give so much evidence of conscious art as his unfinished romance, the *Mystery of Edwin Drood.* I do not want to appear to labour this idea of intentional genius, but few people are aware of its existence. The "small" man limited by his capacity, and striving with heart-sickness to cross the narrow border line between clever facility and genius, apes genius, and because he has it not he falls away even from that position of brilliance he might have occupied had he limited the cravings of his ambition to the ability of his mental gifts. From this cause come most failures in life. Most successes in life are due to unconscious genius, but they are the mediocrity of genius. The world-genius who demands with a fling of defiance a universal admiration of his gifts and succeeds in fixing the eyes of the world in the dimension of time is a genius of the transcendental order. Bacon as Bacon does not possess it, but Shakespeare whether as himself or as Bacon is the age-long embodiment on the conscious possession of genius with the power of grasping by personal force a commensurate recognition. Dickens is of this plane and of this class. Many of his admirers will say that I have belittled the genius of the writer when I endeavour to show that he was aware of his lustrous possession, and wrote with an eye to its proper setting and perpetuation. This is not true. I have added courage to his genius.

One sometimes wonders where the vivid compelling charm of Dickens lies in his works. Obviously it is not in the beauty of the language; sometimes his construction is ungrammatical, and in other cases it is harsh and forced. There is none of that limpid poetry in prose that gives a fascination to the writings of some authors who have nothing more to put into them. There are, in fact, very few elaborately drawn scene pictures, and few of the characters are dressed in a point to-point fashion with the finicky taste and detail of a court tailor or dressmaker. Human nature on the whole, however, is the same to-day as it was yesterday; woad and a girdle of grass are only names for coats and dresses. Hate, greed, and the lust of body and mind, with their body servants of cant, hypocrisy and duplicity are the same now as they were a hundred or a thousand years ago with, perhaps, a freer leaven of love and good feeling. One at least of the irresistible attractions of the master's works is to be found in his portrayal of people as they were. The character may be a composite one, in fact each character usually is, but because it is true it is complete. Imagination sees only the broad outlines of human nature, with the result that a man is a devil or an "angel" according to the immediate requirements of the creator of the character. The student of human nature, however, sees that the human character is a piece of machinery much more complex than the mechanism of the body.

It may be said with truth, therefore, that although Dickens drew his characters from the flesh, he portrayed life as it was, with the inevitable advantage that life always appeals to life.

There are characters in the novels which at first sight appear all black. But on a closer acquaintance the tar-brush is found to be streaked with lighter shades. Sikes is capable of affection, and of remorse, and of fear. The wickedness of Jonas Chuzzlewit is the result of his cupidity and his cowardice. Pecksniff cherished his two daughters. Magwitch had a lasting gratitude for Pip. Uriah Heep and his mother loved one another. Steerforth was not all rogue. On the other hand, David made many errors. Agnes was too indulgent to her father; and a weaker writer would have made her the unconscious instrument or unintentional reward of her father's deliverance instead of leaving that release from the bondage of Heep to the accident of Micawber's impecuniosity. There is just that difference between melodrama and tragedy. The delineator of life as it stands is a realist, but the realist can only describe with the faithfulness of a journalist the minutiae of filth and indecency, separating the garbage from the profitable refuse with the care of a rag-picker. There are other rooms in the house than the scullery? There are other things in the garden than the manure? But for some inexplicable reason the writer who includes in his word-picture the rose and the thorn, the dead leaves and the new shoots is a caricaturist. On these lines Dickens was a caricaturist.

There are certain recognised methods of discovering the history of localities, and in the same way there are methods of conducting the search for for Dickens' originals. All the work our author can put forth is based on the knowledge he has assimilated and moulded by the fingers of his genius; therefore we may look for prototypes with some hope of discovering the individuals, and with the certainty of learning the nature of the world in the early Victorian era and feeling that change which overtook England, and the outward appearance and the superficial nature of the men and women who inhabited it, with those great changes of the forty years of the growth of steam.

Places have changed and the difficulties of identification are immeasurably increased, which, together with the disguise, more or less thin, which Dickens often spread over both scenes and characters sometimes make it impossible to identify a place with certainty. There will be found amongst other identifications in the following pages suggestions as to the originals of Muggleton, Dingley Dell, the Manor House, and the *Ship*. Some are doubtful, others are more probable. The *Ship* can only be the *Ship and Lobster*; Joe's forge can be only the forge at Chalk: but probably it will be impossible to demonstrate beyond doubt that Gravesend is the Muggleton of Pickwick. It does not find a legitimate place in this book to describe the finding of the most likely house in which Dickens' honeymoon was spent, but it is most interesting as an example of the way in which such things "come about."

At least two routes have been mapped out as that taken by "Little Nell" and her grandfather. And while I do not doubt for a moment that Dickens travelled with the people of his brain along a well remembered road and met with well defined curiosities of humanity which he had fallen in with on other roads, I do not think that either route can be pointed to with certainty. And I think it extremely likely that many roads of real life were pressed into the service of the one. No doubt it is a sign of the truth that so many places live on the memories of the great novelist, and although the fifthy-five inns and hotels of *Pickwick* have dwindled to a paltry dozen, the only result so far has been to increase the interest of those remaining.

With the exception of Bath it is rather curious that Dickens' books deal in a great measure with East and South East England, a part of England which still appears to enjoy the greatest popularity with the Londoner.

There are endless phases of the novelist's works, but even if I were able it would not be desirable to deal here with more than those two which are responsible for the existence of the book. Of these, the first is the belief that it will assist the study of Dickens to be the re-creation of the material aspect of the country and town as it was in his day. Quite apart from the possible value of the work as a book of reference, I would fain hope that it will show that Dickens' novels may be relied upon for this purpose. The second reason for the compilation of the book is a similar one regarding the people of the period. It would be easy to write a vivid description, a life-like picture, of the Victorian era from Dickens' works. Our doubt of the works ; and the accusation of exaggeration, which has been so often levelled against them ; are due to our own ignorance of life at that time. The incident of the coachman cutting at Jonas with his whip when that ill-fated man was engaged on his second great crime seems unreal and impossible, until it is remembered that the coachman was king of the road, and so literally did he realize this position that he demanded *pourboire* with the effrontery of a footpad, and met a refusal with the same methods of foul language and fisticuffs. Even the children's games, some of them still seen in the poorer London districts, were real, and were played by the many girls and boys who then made walking in the London byways somewhat hazardous. The rhyme of the Deputy Winks—

" Widdy Widdy wen !
I—ket—ches—I'm—out—ar—ter—ten.
Widdy Widdy wy !
  Then—E—don't—go—then—I—shy—
Widdy Widdy wake—cock warning ! "

was in part a warning note in a rough and tumble boys' game, although I must confess myself quite unable to give any explanation of its meaning or the origin of its use.

Here are two minute details, but the thousands of pages of Dickens' novels teem with many more thousands of incidents or unconsidered trifles which either are or will become priceless gems of folklore and its study.

GRAVESEND, ALEX. J. PHILIP.
December, 1908.

the firm [illegible] the [illegible] street, the only readers [illegible] with the description [illegible] in a great measure [illegible] which [illegible]

There are endless [illegible] able it would not be desirable to deal [illegible] are responsible for the [illegible] be [illegible] the industrial [illegible] the country and town [illegible] from the [illegible] that [illegible] purpose. The second reason [illegible] [illegible] [illegible] often [illegible] the [illegible] [illegible] London [illegible] rhyme of the [illegible]

[illegible]

which [illegible] [illegible] or the [illegible]

[illegible]

[illegible]

A
DICKENS DICTIONARY

A DICKENS DICTIONARY.

Synopses of the Various Works

In Chronological Order.

Sketches by Boz. (Published in volume form **1836.**)

A series of papers of a humorous character dealing with life and scenes, chiefly in the Metropolis, as they were, for the most part, at the time of publication and the earlier part of the nineteenth century. They first appeared in the *Monthly Magazine* and the *Morning and Evening Chronicle.* They are arranged in sections, opening with Our Parish and continuing successively with Scenes, Characters, and Tales.

Sunday under three Heads. (Published **1836.**)

Sunday—As it is: As Sabbath Bills would make it: As it might be made.

Posthumous Papers of the Pickwick Club. (Published in volume form **1837.**)

After the first chapter the Club scarcely reappears until its interment at the end of the book. The narrative has no plot, and chronicles the doings of the Corresponding Members of the Club, the central figure of which is Mr. Pickwick. Mr. Pickwick, accompanied by Tupman, Snodgrass and Winkle, makes an excursion, in the interests of research, into Kent. They meet Jingle, and through this chance acquaintanceship they encounter the first "real" adventure to the party. On this occasion they encounter Mr. Wardle, and accept his invitation to the Manor Farm, Dingley Dell. During their too great enthusiasm for sport, rather greater than their skill, Winkle wings Tupman. Tupman retires and is nursed by Miss Wardle, when he falls under the spell of her charms. Jingle again turns up and cleverly puts Tupman out of court and elopes with Miss Wardle. They are pursued by Mr. Wardle, who is accompanied by Mr. Pickwick. They elude their pursuers on the road, but are discovered at the *White Hart Inn* in the Borough, where Jingle is induced to relinquish his claims on the lady for a monetary consideration. Here Mr. Pickwick finds Sam Weller and attaches him to his service. In announcing the change to his landlady, Mr. Pickwick falls into the greatest adventure in the book, viz., the breach of promise case Bardell *v.* Pickwick. During the progress of the preliminaries of the case Mr. Pickwick and his friends make other excursions: to Eatanswill; to Bury St. Edmunds; to Dingley Dell again; to Ipswich; and back again to Dingley Dell. Mr. Pickwick loses his case and Mrs. Bardell is awarded £750 damages. Mr. Pickwick refuses to pay, and in the interval that elapses between the finding of the jury and his commitment to prison he and his friends visit Bath. The Bath visit is full of interest, the most important event being Mr. Winkle's adventure with Mrs. Dowler in the sedan-chair. Mr. Pickwick enters the Fleet Prison and Sam arranges for his own arrest so that he may still attend his master. Jingle and Trotter are found in a state of destitution in the prison. Mr. Pickwick befriends them and assists them to emigrate. As Messrs. Dodson and Fogg are unable to get their costs from Mr. Pickwick they imprison Mrs. Bardell. Mr. Pickwick is prevailed upon by the plight of his late landlady to pay the costs in the case and in return obtains a release. During this time Winkle has succeeded in marrying Arabella Allen. Snodgrass and Emily Wardle are married at the house at Dulwich, to which Mr. Pickwick retires. Sam and Mary accompany him.

Mudfog Papers. (Published **1837.**)

Public Life of Mr. Tulrumble. First Meeting of the Mudfog Association for the Advancement of Everything.

Second meeting of the Mudfog Association for the Advancement of Everything. (**1838.**)

Pantomime of Life. (**1838.**)

Mr. Robert Bolton. (**1838.**) Some particulars concerning a lion. (**1838**

Familiar epistle from a parent to a child. (**1838.**)

Adventures of Oliver Twist. (Published in volume form **1838.**)

The object of this book was to show "the principle of good surviving through every adverse circumstance." Oliver is born in a workhouse and named Oliver Twist by the Parish Beadle. His mother dies without revealing anything of her history, and Oliver becomes a workhouse brat, at first farmed out and then returned to the workhouse. He is apprenticed to an undertaker named Sowerberry. He fights, and beats, Noah Claypole, the other apprentice; this calls down the wrath of the powers and Oliver runs away to London. On the road he falls in with the Artful Dodger, who shares his food with him and then takes him to Fagin. The first time Oliver goes out with Fagin's boys on the "pinching lay" he is arrested for a theft he did not commit. He is only released on the testimony of the Bookstall Keeper. Mr. Brownlow, the old gentleman whose pocket had been picked, takes him home with him and has him cared for. When on an errand for his benefactor he is recaptured by Fagin's gang. He is then forced to take part in the housebreaking expedition to Mrs. Maylie's house at Chertsey. He raises the alarm, however, but is wounded, and is found next morning at the Maylie's house. His story is credited, and with the assistance of Dr. Losberne the Bow Street runners are deceived. Fagin and Monks hunt out Oliver's sanctuary and plan his recapture. But Nancy who has been stricken with remorse, reveals everything to Rose Maylie. Nancy is murdered by Bill Sikes for this. Sikes accidentally hangs himself over the Folly Ditch in his attempt to escape, and the gang is broken up. Fagin is executed. Charlie Bates turns over a new leaf and becomes a farmer. Claypole turns evidence and becomes a paid informer with the assistance of Charlotte. It transpires that Monks and Oliver are half-brothers, and the former has been endeavournig to make the boy a criminal, to prevent his inheriting under their father's will. Rose Maylie turns out to be the sister of Oliver's mother. Monks goes abroad with the portion that has been given him, but dies in prison in a state of poverty. Rose marries Harry Maylie, who takes a country parish. Mr. Brownlow again takes Oliver under his protection. Bumble and his wife are left inmates of the workhouse, where they had so long lorded it over the former inmates.

Sketches of Young Gentlemen. (Published **1838.**)

The Bashful Young Gentleman—The Out-and-out Young Gentleman—The Very Friendly Young Gentleman—The Military Young Gentleman—The Political Young Gentleman—The Domestic Young Gentleman—The Censorious Young Gentleman—The Funny Young Gentleman—The Theatrical Young Gentleman—The Poetical Young Gentleman—The Throwing-off Young Gentleman—The Young Ladies' Young Gentleman.

Life and Adventures of Nicholas Nickleby. (Published in volume form **1839.**)

Like *Oliver Twist*, *Nicholas Nickleby* contains a purpose, viz., the exposure of "farming" schools where young children were taken for a small fee and were underfed and cruelly treated, which at that time were remarkably common in Yorkshire. Nicholas, his mother, and his sister Kate, come to London relying on the assistance of Ralph Nickleby, when the death of Nicholas' father leaves them almost penniless. Ralph is a miserable miser, but he secures the post of usher in one of the Yorkshire schools for Nicholas; and places Kate with Madame Mantalini. Nicholas is unable to adapt himself to the conditions of the school and leaves the place, accompanied by the poor drudge Smike, after soundly thrashing Squeers the schoolmaster. Nicholas and Smike travel to London, assisted by John Browdie. There they are befriended by Newman Noggs and Nicholas becomes tutor to the Kenwigses children. As Ralph Nickleby threatens to do nothing more for Kate and her mother unless Nicholas leaves London, he and Smike go to Portsmouth. They there meet Mr. Vincent Crummles, the head of a mediocre theatrical company, " and go on the stage " with some success. An urgent letter from Newman Noggs recalls them to London. In the meantime Kate has gone from the Mantalini establishment and entered the household of the Wititterly's. She is molested by Hawk and Verisopht, clients of Ralph Nickleby. Nicholas overhears a conversation in a public place in which Sir Mulberry Hawk disparages Kate, and thrashes him. Nicholas, Kate, and their mother then decline to have anything more to do with Ralph, and Nicholas secures a berth with the Cheeryble brothers. Squeers recaptures Smike, but John Browdie again befriends him and he escapes. Ralph and Squeers concoct a plot to get Smike from his protectors by putting forward Snawley as Smike's father, but they are frustrated. Nicholas falls in love with Madeline Bray, and Frank Cheeryble with Kate Nickleby. Ralph and Gride endeavour to ruin Madeline by forcing her to marry Gride, who wants her property. At the last moment Nicholas prevents this. Smike dies. Ralph discovers that he has been persecuting his own son, and this, together with the failure of his other schemes and monetary losses, preys on his mind until he hangs himself. Gride's old woman servant robs him and is in turn robbed by Squeers, who is eventually landed in prison. Through the intercession of the Cheeryble brothers Frank marries Kate, and Nicholas weds Madeline. The end of the story, so far as the other characters are concerned, is quickly told. Dotheboys' Hall School is broken up. Newman Noggs recovers himself. Lord Verisopht dies at the hands of Hawk, who flies to the Continent. Vincent Crummles has come to London and then goes to America. Lillyvick returns to the bosom of the Kenwigses family; his wife, formerly Miss Petowker, leaves him in favour of a half-pay captain.

The Old Curiosity Shop. (Published in volume form **1841.**)

This, Dickens's fourth novel, first appeared in *Master Humphrey's Clock* (1840-1.) The central figure is that of Little Nell. She is first seen in her Grandfather's shop—the Old Curiosity Shop—where she appears to be responsible for the whole household management, although she is only a child. Her grandfather, with a feverish desire to accumulate a fortune for his little grand daughter, is secretly visiting the gaming tables. He loses more than he wins and borrows money from Quilp, the evil dwarf. Quilp eventually " closes down " and sells up the shop. Nell and her grandfather leave secretly to escape the dwarf, and in their long and wearisome journey meet many people and experience strange adventures. They are being searched for by the brother of Nell's grandfather, but, as they are being hunted by Quilp, and the fear of him is constantly before them, they are always moving on and endeavouring to cover their traces. They are ultimately discovered in a little village where they have been befriended by the schoolmaster they had met on their travels, who had then become the parish clerk. When they are found Nell has just died broken in health, but not in spirit. Her death shatters what remains of her grandfather, and shortly after he, too, is found lying dead on her grave. Running parallel with this, the central theme of the story, is another thread of less importance. Kit Nubbles was shop boy at the Old Curiosity Shop, and when that is disposed of he enters the service of the Garlands. A false charge is proffered against him by Sampson Brass, but he is liberated from prison through the instrumentality of the Marchioness, the maid-of-all-work at the Brass's, and Dick Swiveller, who was the friend of Nell's brother and had been employed by Sampson at the instance of Quilp. Dick Swiveller marries the Marchioness. Kit marries Barbara. Quilp is found dead on the river bank and his wife marries again on the strength of his money. Sampson and Sally Brass become outcasts.

Pic Nic Papers. (By various writers. Edited by Dickens) (Published **1841.**)

Sketches of Young Couples. (Published **1840.**)

The Young Couple—The Formal Couple—The Loving Couple—The Contradictory Couple—The Couple who dote on their Children—The Cool Couple—The Plausible Couple—The Nice little Couple—The Egotistical Couple—The Couple who coddle themselves—The Old Couple.

Barnaby Rudge. (Published in volume form **1841.**)

This also appeared first in *Master Humphrey's Clock.* The story opens some five years before the Gordon Riots in 1788, at the *Maypole* Inn. The circumstance embracing the murder of Reuben Haredale and the missing gardener and steward, leading up to the main theme of the story are here related. Mrs. Rudge and Barnaby leave the neighbourhood of Chigwell to escape a mysterious stranger. Geoffrey Haredale, brother of Reuben, who succeeds to the estates, is suspected of the murder. His daughter Emma falls in love with Edward Chester, the Son of Sir John Chester, the villain of the story. The respective fathers, although enemies, unite in an attempt to prevent the lovers marrying. Joe Willet, son of the landlord of the *Maypole,* is in love with Dolly Varden, daughter of Gabriel Varden, the locksmith, but the machinations of Sir John Chester ruin this love affair also. Joe "takes the shilling" and leaves the country. Just before the riots Barnaby and his mother enter London in the hope of being lost sight of, but the stranger discovers them. Barnaby, a half-witted but harmless boy, is drawn into the excitement without any clear understanding of what it is all about. The effects of the riots are disastrous for some of the characters of the story. Mr. Haredale's home, the "Warren," is burnt down. And eventually Sir John Chester is killed in a duel by Geoffrey Haredale, who then enters a monastry. The mysterious visitor to Mrs. Rudge is discovered to be her husband, who had murdered not only Reuben Haredale but also the gardener. He is afterwards executed. Maypole Hugh the illegitimate son of Sir J. Chester; Simon Tappertit, Gabriel Varden's apprentice; Dennis the hangman and others all take a part in the riots. Hugh and Dennis are hanged. Barnaby is released by the efforts of his friends. Simon loses his legs, becomes a shoeblack and marries. Miggs, who had been an undesired admirer of Simon, leaves the service of Mrs. Varden and becomes a wardress. Mrs. Varden herself becomes somewhat more of a model wife when she is no longer under the domination of Miggs. Joe Willet returns from the American Revolution with the loss of an arm in time to assist in the discovery of Emma Haredale and

Dolly Varden. Emma and Edward are married, and Joe and Dolly make another couple. Joe succeeds his father in the *Maypole* Inn near by where Barnaby and his mother spend the rest of their lives on the farm with the animals Barnaby loves so much.

American Notes. (Published in volume form **1842.**)

A discursive account of the author's first visit to the United States.

A Christmas Carol in Prose. (Published **1843.** Now included in Christmas Books.)

Depicts the change wrought in the nature of Ebenezer Scrooge, a hard-hearted miser, by the revelations of the spirits in a dream.

Life and Adventures of Martin Chuzzlewit. (Published in volume form **1844.**)

Mr. Pecksniff was an architect living near Salisbury. He makes his living by taking pupils at a premium of £500. To him comes Martin Chuzzlewit Junior, who has quarelled with his grandfather of the same name. The immediate cause of the rupture is Mary Graham, a sweet girl companion and attendant to Old Martin, with whom young Martin, has fallen in love. Pecksniff is a canting hypocrite believing that by sheltering the young man he will advance his own ends. Old Martin, however, causes his grandson to be turned out, and in turn becomes an inmate of Pecksniff's house; the architect, thinking in this way to do still better for himself with regard to the old man's money. Pecksniff has two daughters, Mercy and Charity, and a devoted attendant, Tom Pinch. When young Martin leaves the house he goes to London in company with Mark Tapley; from there they go to America, where they meet with all sorts of adventures and nearly die of fever at Eden, where they have bought a plot of land. During their absence Jonas Chuzzlewit, son of Anthony Chuzzlewit, a brother of old Martin marries Mercy Pecksniff. Desiring his father's death he attempts to poison him. His design is frustrated, however, though Anthony dies and Jonas believes his scheme has been successful. Jonas invests his money in the Anglo-Bengalee Life Insurance Company and becomes a director. The company is a fraudulent one, and the promoter, Montague Tigg, in the interest of his own pocket, obtains a hold upon Jonas by discovering,through the instrumentality of a spy, the suspicious circumstances of Anthony's death. Pecksniff is persuaded by Jonas to put his money into the concern. Jonas murders Montague Tigg and hopes to bury all knowledge of his former attempted crime. While these events have been going on in London, affairs have been rapidly nearing a head in Pecksniff's home. Pecksniff proposes to marry Mary Graham. Tom Pinch at last discovers his employers' baseness and is dismissed. He also goes to London, where he visits John Westlock, who had been one of Pecksniff's pupils immediately before young Martin went to his kinsman. Tom and his sister, who had been a governess, set up housekeeping; and Tom obtains the appointment of librarian to some one whose identity is hidden from him. The threads of the story are unravelled as follows: Martin (the Grandfather) reveals himself as the benefactor of Tom Pinch, and denounces Pecksniff as a scoundrel. The revelation takes place in the room where Tom has been at work on his books, and the result is a general reconciliation. Martin is taken back to favour and marries Mary Graham; John Westlock marries Ruth Pinch; Mark Tapley marries the landlady of the *Blue Dragon.* Tom Pinch is attached to Old Martin. Mercy, whose husband (Jonas) poisoned himself on the way to prison after the exposure of his villanies, is watched over by old Martin who becomes the *deus ex machina.* Charity is deserted at the foot of the alter and returns to her father. Pecksniff, after the loss of his money, becomes an outcast and lives as much as possible on the money he can squeeze from Tom Pinch. Throughout the story Bailey, Poll Sweedlepipe, Mrs. Gamp, and Betsey Prig, with Mould the undertaker, make frequent spasmodic appearances, but they are not essential to the plot.

The Chimes. (Published **1844.** Now included in Christmas Books.)

The Chimes has a somewhat similar moral to that of the Christmas Carol. Toby Veck takes the place of Scrooge, and in a dream is taken up to the belfry, where the bells take facial expression, and the goblin of the great Bell appoints the Spirit of the Chimes to show him pictures of the future. These are, however, only pictures, although Toby profits by their lessons.

Cricket on the Hearth. (Published **1845.** Now included in Christmas Books.)

Edward Plummer is engaged to May Fielding, but goes to South America. In his absence May is to marry old Tackleton, but with the assistance of Mrs. Peerybingle matters are rearranged and May and Edward are married. Bertha Plummer, a blind girl, is in love with old Tackleton and is terribly disappointed when she learns he is about to marry May, but her father confesses to having deceived her, and everything ends happily more or less.

Pictures from Italy. (Published **1846.**)

Letters of travel first appearing in *The Daily News.*

Battle of Life. (Published **1846.** Now included in Christmas Books.)

The central figures are Alfred Heathfield, Marion Jeddler, and her sister Grace. Heathfield is a ward of Dr. Jeddler. He is engaged to Marion On his return from a Continental tour Marion disappears—it is supposed she elopes. Eventually Alfred marries Grace, when it transpires that Marion had not eloped, but had taken refuge with an aunt, as she had discovered that her sister loved Alfred, until the time when Grace's happiness should be complete. She afterwards marries Michael Warden, with whom she is supposed to have eloped earlier in the story.

Dealings with the Firm of Dombey and Son. (Published in volume form **1848.**)

Paul Dombey is the head of the firm Dombey and Son. He has a daughter whose existence he practically ignored because she was not a boy. At length a son is born. But when little Paul sees the light his mother dies. The boy, of a sweet and lovable, but old-fashioned disposition, is not strong. He is placed in charge of Mrs. Pipchin, but although he grows older he grows no stronger. In spite of this, however, he must be fitted for his place as " son " in the business, and is placed in Dr. Blimber's school. The natural consequence follows and little Paul dies. His sister Florence is now more distasteful than ever before to her father. She is lost in London, robbed by Good Mrs. Brown and brought home by Walter Gay. She makes the acquaintance of Walter's uncle, Solomon Gills, and his friend Captain Cuttle. Walter is engaged in the office, but is sent by James Carker to the Indies, ostensibly as a promotion. On the voyage the ship is wrecked. Edith Granger, a proud, high-spirited woman, is married to Mr. Dombey. There is no love between them, but Dombey wants her " presence," whilst she marries him for his money and position. Misfortunes then begin. Affection springs up between the second Mrs. Dombey and Florence : this displeases Mr. Dombey, and he annoys her by conveying messages of displeasure by his manager, Carker. She elopes with

Carker to revenge herself on her husband, and immediately leaves him, both as a punishment for his presumption and because she has no love for him. Carker follows her, however, and on his return is killed on the railway. Walter, who had been supposed lost with the ship, returns home, as also does his uncle Solomon Gills. Florence leaves home after being still further ill-treated by her father. Walter and Florence are married. After Carker's defection it is found that the business requires the utmost care. This the head of the firm does not give, and bankruptcy follows. When the smash comes Florence returns to her father and persuades him to make his home with them. He is broken in health. His wealth has vanished, and he instinctively turns to the daughter he had spurned. Toots, the friend of little Paul at Dr. Blimber's, marries Susan Nipper. Harriet Carker, sister of John and James Carker, marries Mr. Morfin. Miss Tox remains Miss Tox and undertakes the reformation of Robin Toodle.

The Haunted Man. (Published **1848.** Now included in Christmas Books.)

The burden of the story is " Lord keep my memory green," Redlaw is visited by an evil spirit which wipes out his recollections of the sufferings he had experienced. He finds, however, that he is in an unfortunate state and communicates the evil to others. He is restored by the influence of Milly Swidger.

The Personal History of David Copperfield. (Published in volume form in **1850.**)

David is a posthumous child born at the Rookery, Blunderstone. He is brought up by his mother and Peggotty for several years. Then Mr. Murdstone lays siege to his mother. He is sent to Yarmouth with Pegotty, where he meets Daniel and Ham Peggotty and Little Emily. On his return he finds that his mother is married to Mr. Murdstone. Then begins a period of repression and persecution by Murdstone and his sister that results in David being sent away to school. His mother's spirit is broken and she dies, when David is called home again from Salem House, where he has experienced a great deal of ill-treatment, but has made friends with Steerforth and Traddles, who become important characters in the book. Peggotty marries Barkis, and David is sent into the Murdstone and Grinby factory, where he cleans bottles for a few shillings weekly. His lodgings are with the Micawbers, who now first appear in the story and reveal a new phase of life to the small boy. This does not continue very long, however, as David runs away and takes refuge with his aunt, Betsey Trotwood, at Dover. He is placed at Dr. Strong's School at Canterbury, and lodges with the Wickfields in the same town, where he meets Uriah Heep, then Mr. Wickfield's clerk. After leaving school David looks about him, and while doing so spends a short time at Yarmouth with the Peggottys. He met Steerforth in London, who accompanied him. Steerforth betrays little Emily and they elope, leaving England for the continent. David is articled to Spenlow and Jorkins and falls in love with Dora Spenlow. Uriah Heep has gained a complete ascendency over his employer, and is largely feathering his own nest. Betsey Trotwood loses her money, which is in the care of Mr. Wickfield; she comes up to London and surprises David by announcing her loss in her characteristically abrupt way. Peggotty's husband dies leaving her provided for. Daniel Peggotty sets out on foot in search of Little Emily. David obtains a post as secretary to Dr. Strong, assisting him on the Dictionary, and studies shorthand with a view to reporting. He eventually masters the mystery of the art and turns it to good account. Mr. Spenlow dies leaving Dora almost unprovided for, and she and David are married. Dora knows nothing of household duties and they have many unpleasant experiences. Daniel Peggotty succeeds in tracing Emily through the instrumentality of Martha Endell, and they all emigrate to Australia. Micawber has been employed by Uriah Heep, who designs to make a tool of him by advancing small sums of money. But Micawber has been able to collect evidence of Heep's malpractice, which he reveals to Traddles, with the result that Uriah is unmasked. His designs to marry Agnes Wickfield are frustrated and he is compelled to refund the money he has appropriated, part of it being Betsey Trotwood's five thousand pounds. The Micawbers also emigrate to Australia, where something " turns up " and they prosper. David's child-wife dies and he travels for some time, during which he continues his literary work and becomes famous. He afterwards marries Agnes. Steerforth is drowned off Yarmouth ; and Ham is drowned while attempting to rescue him. Peggotty and Betsey Trotwood live together. Tommy Traddles marries the " dearest girl in the world " and rises to the top of his profession. Steerforth's man, Littimer, finds himself next cell neighbour to Uriah Heep in prison. And Mr. Dick attaches himself to David's children.

The Child's History of England. (Published in volume form in **1853.**)

For obvious reasons this work is not included in the present Dickens Dictionary.

Bleak House. (Published in volume form **1853.**)

Bleak House is the story of a long-drawn-out suit in Chancery, or rather, the Chancery suit is the peg on which the very human story is hung. John Jarndyce refuses to take any part in the fight for the Jarndyce money, but he has as his wards Ada Clare and Richard Carstone, both interested in the settlement of the suit. To them comes Esther Summerson, who has been brought up by her aunt Miss Barbary, and afterwards at Greenleaf, a school at Windsor kept by Miss Donny. Esther is companion to Ada, but she soon becomes housekeeper, and confidant of them all. The two wards fall in love one with the other. Richard finds one path in life would suit him just as well as another, and so tries several, with the like result each time of finding something that would suit him better. The suit brings them all into touch with people many and curious, among them Miss Flite, Krook, Snagsby and Jo. Caddy Jellyby is the daughter of a woman with a " mission." Caddy has no liking for the " mission," or the work it entails. She becomes the friend of Esther Summerson. Lawrence Boythorn is a friend of John Jarndyce, and his neighbours are Sir Leicester and Lady Dedlock. Tulkinghorn is the family lawyer of the Dedlocks, and he discovers a " past " of Lady Dedlock, using the information to terrorise his victim. Lady Dedlock is interested in the death of Captain Hawdon, who, as Nemo, had executed law copying for Snagsby. George Rouncewell, Mr. George had been his orderly. The secret, which is not revealed in the book till much later, is that Esther Summerson was the illegitimate daughter of Captain Hawdon and Lady Dedlock before she married. Lady Dedlock only became aware of Esther's relationship by the revelation of Guppy, who had secured some papers from Krook's shop. Harold Skimpole is a weak but cunning man who preys on John Jarndyce. At one time a broker, Coavinses, as Skimpole calls him, is in possession. Later the man dies, and Esther has Charlotte as her maid, John Jarndyce befriending the other children, who are left. Jo, the street sweeper, is " moved on " so effectively that he is hounded out of London. He is found at Bleak House, ill and half-starved and is taken in. He moves on again, but has communicated smallpox to Charlotte. Esther nurses Charlotte and in turn catches the disease. Richard follows his usual practice and throws up the Army. Returning home he settles down to watch the progress of the suit in Chancery in company with Vholes. Ada thinks she can better assist Richard as his wife, so she marries him. Esther receives a proposal from John Jarndyce, and from a sense of duty, as well as for other reasons, attempts to stifle her affection for Allan Woodcourt. Tulkinghorn threatens to reveal Lady Dedlock's secret on the morrow, but he is found dead. Suspicion falls on George Rouncewell, who had visited him earlier, and those who know something of Lady Dedlock's circumstances suspect her. But the crime is traced by Inspector Bucket to Mademoiselle, Lady Dedlock's maid. Lady Dedlock has left home, however, and Inspector Bucket, accompanied by Esther, endeavour to trace her; they find her—dead at the gate of the cemetery where Captain Hawdon lies buried. John Jarndyce finds that although Esther will marry him her heart has been given to Allan. Secretly he prepares a home for them and they are married. Richard Carstone dies leaving Ada with a little son. The suit has consumed the estate in costs and the case was never settled, but the shock was more than Richard could stand, broken as his health was. Caddy Jellyby marries Prince Turveydrop. Phil Squod and Mr. George are installed at Chesney Wold in the service of Sir Leicester Dedlock.

Hard Times for these Times. (Published in volume form **1854.**)

Hard Times draws a picture showing the futility of eliminating love and kindness from human life and intercourse. Thomas Gradgrind professes to rule his life and those dependent upon him according to fact and logical calculation. He has a friend, Josiah Bounderby, millowner and banker. Cissy Jupe is left by her father friendless in Coketown and is taken into the home of the Gradgrinds. Gradgrind's son of the same name, is a selfish and cunning rascal; when he is old enough he has a stool in Bounderby's Bank. Louisa, his sister, marries Bounderby, but without affection. Tom uses his sister both before and after her marriage without scruple to further his own ends. Even this is not sufficient, however, to cover his needs, and he appropriates the Bank money, arranging matters so that it appears a robbery has been committed. Suspicion is directed against Stephen Blackpool. Louisa arranges to elope with Harthouse, who has come to Coke town on political business; instead of doing so she flies to her father. But the arrangements have been overheard by Bounderby's housekeeper, Mrs. Sparsit, who eagerly embraces the opportunity of doing some mischief to Louisa by carrying the tale to her husband. Bounderby hurries in turn to tell the tale to Gradgrind, but finds not only that Louisa has been before him, but that she is sheltered there. He refuses to listen to any one and offers Louisa a choice; the result is that she remains with her father. A reward is offered for the arrest of Blackpool, who has left the town in search of work. His friend Rachael endeavours to clear his name, and ultimately she and Cissy find him injured at the bottom of a disused shaft. He dies. Tom leaves Coketown. His father follows him, and is in turn followed by Bitzer, who secures Tom; but with the assistance of Sleary and his company Gradgrind is able to effect his son's escape. Bounderby dies in a fit. Cissy Jupe marries; and Gradgrind sorts his ideas afresh.

Little Dorrit. (Published in volume form **1857.**)

William Dorrit, a prisoner in the Marshalsea. He has been there for so many years that he has become the "Father of the Marshalsea." Little

Dorrit, his daughter Amy, is engaged casually by Mrs. Clennam. While there she is seen by Arthur Clennam, who has just returned to this country. Clennam attempts to assist the family, but the circumlocution of the Circumlocution Office renders it impossible. He enters into partnership with Daniel Doyce and almost falls in love with "Pet" Meagles. She however marries Henry Gowan, an artist without much steadiness of character. Flora Finching, a widow, and daughter of Mr. Casby, was a former sweetheart of Clennam's, but he has lost whatever love he may have had for her, although she is still arch and coy in an elephantine way. Little Dorrit's father inherits a large fortune. He leaves the prison and travels on the Continent. His wealth makes him proud and condescending; it has a similar effect on Fanny and Edward, his son and elder daughter, only Amy and his brother Frederick are unaffected by the sudden accession of wealth. Fanny marries Edmund Sparkler, the son of Mrs. Merdle by a former husband. Mr. Merdle is a financial magnate of the first water, with whom Clennam and Dorrit, as well as many others, are persuaded to invest their money. The inevitable crash follows. The Dorrits are ruined; Clennam is ruined. Fortunately Mr. Dorrit himself died before the disclosure. Clennam relinquishes everything to the creditors and becomes an inmate of the Marshalsea. Little Dorrit finds him and nurses him through an illness. His partner Doyce returns and reinstates him in the firm, and he and Little Dorrit are married. This is the warp of the story. Crossing it at intervals is the dark shadow of Rigaud, the villain adventurer, who blackmails Mrs. Clennam on the strength of his know- of her secret. He is buried in the ruins of Mrs. Clennam's house.

Reprinted Pieces. (Published in volume form **1858.**)

1850. Begging-Letter Writer.
Child's Dream of a Star.
Christmas Tree.
Detective Police.
Ghost of Art.
Poor Man's Tale of a Patent.
Three Detective Anecdotes.
Walk in a Workhouse.

1851. Bill Sticking.
Births. Mrs. Meek, of a Son.
Flight.
Monument of French Folly.
On Duty with Inspector Field.
Our English Watering-Place.
Our School.

1852. Child's Story.
Lying Awake.
Our Bore.
Our Honourable Friend.
Our Vestry.
Plated Article.
Poor Relation's Story.

1853. Down with the Tide.
Long Voyage.
Noble Savage.
Nobody's Story.
Schoolboy's Story

1854. Our French Watering-Place.
1855. Prince Bull: a Fairy Tale.
1856. Out of the Season.
Out of Town.

A Tale of Two Cities. (Published in volume form **1859.**)

Dr. Manette has been incarcerated in the Bastille for many years. His daughter Lucie and Mr. Lorry from Tellson's Bank repair to Paris to bring the released prisoner to London. His reason has suffered, but under the fostering care of his daughter his mind and body both improve. Charles Darnay, who has relinguished his title and all claim on the French estates of the family, is tried at the Old Bailey on a charge of treason— a serious one at this period of the French Revolution: he is acquitted largely through a resemblance he bears to Sydney Carton, a lawyer in the court, Carton, a dissolute genius, Stryver, and Darnay all aspire to the hand of Lucie Manette. Darnay is accepted and marries Lucie: Carton has too good a knowledge of his own shortcomings, but he is ready to do anything for Lucie's happiness. Darnay goes to Paris to secure the liberation of Gabelle, and is himself imprisoned as an aristocrat. Lucie and Dr. Manette go to Paris to his relief and secure his release; but he is rearrested at once on another charge and sentenced by the Tribunal. Sydney Carton undertakes the work at this point. By his knowledge of the antecedents of the spy, who has become a turnkey, he obtains admission to the prison, where he impersonates Darnay. Darnay and his friends all succeed in escaping from France—Miss Pross with the greatest difficulty, leaving Madame Defarge dead behind her. Jerry Cruncher relinquishes his trade of body-snatcher. And Sydney Carton dies beneath the blade of the guillotine.

Lazy Tour of Two Idle Apprentices. (With Wilkie Collins.) (Published **1857.**)

A series of articles written by Dickens and Wilkie Collins, describing a holiday tour.

Hunted Down. (Published **1860.**)

The story of the pursuit of Mr. Julius Slinkton by Mr. Meltham, and his ultimate detection. Slinkton poisons his niece, who was married to Meltham, and attempts to poison Meltham, who had assumed another name.

The Uncommercial Traveller. (Published in volume form **1861.**)

Travel papers from home and abroad dealing with many subjects grave and gay.

Great Expectations. (Published in volume form **1861.**)

Pip is introduced as a very small orphan boy, being "brought up, by hand" by his sister, wife of Joe Gargery, blacksmith in a village in the Kentish marshes. He falls in with a convict escaped from the marshes, who terrifies him into purloining food and a file. Pip sees his convict captured with another by the soldiers, and his petty theft is not discovered. Things go on in their quiet way, Pip meantime being educated at the village dame-school, until he is taken by Uncle Pumblechook to play with Miss Havisham. Miss Havisham is a demented lady who was deserted on the eve of her wedding. Miss Havisham's only companion is Estella, whom she is bringing up to break men's hearts. The girl begins early and practises on Pip. His visits to Miss Havisham cease, however, and he is is apprenticed to Joe Gargery, Miss Havisham paying for his indentures. Joe's "man," Orlick, entertains a deadly hatred for Pip, and almost murders

Mrs. Joe, although the perpetrator of the crime is not discovered until long afterwards. The Great Expectations enter into the story when Mr. Jaggers takes Pip to London to make a gentleman of him. The secret benefactor is believed to be Miss Havisham. Pip quickly adapts himself to his new circumstances, spending money at a great rate. He shares chambers with Herbert Pocket, and is tutored by his friend's father. This continues for some years until the return of Provis reveals to Pip that he does not owe his rise to Miss Havisham, but to the convict whom he had assisted whilst a little boy in the marshes. The great business then is to secure the safety of Provis, who is in instant danger of capture. Their plans are all laid, and the boat from which they are to board the steamer far down the river. But on the very brink of success Provis is recaptured through the instrumentality of Compeyson, a fellow convict, and the man who had so cruelly wrecked Miss Havisham's life. Provis is sentenced to death, but the injuries he received in his endeavour to escape prove fatal, and he dies before his execution takes place. Pip now finds himself penniless, and soon after he passes through a serious illness. He recovers to find that Joe has nursed him and has paid his debts. He goes down home, intending to propose to Biddy, the homely friend of his childhood, but learns that she has married Joe, whose wife died as a result of the injuries inflicted by Orlick. Miss Havisham dies, and Estella marries Bently Drummle, who leads her an unhappy life until his death. Pip becomes a clerk in Herbert's firm and ultimately becomes a partner. He pays a visit to England, and accidently meets Estella, whom he marries.

Our Mutual Friend. (Published in volume form in **1865.**)

Old Harmon has made an enormous fortune as a dust contractor, which he leaves to his son on condition that he marries Bella Wilfer. The son on his return to England is supposed to be drowned and the money is inherited by Mr. Boffin. Young John Harmon is not drowned, however, but adopts the names first of Julius Handford and then of John Rokesmith, and becomes the private secretary of Mr. Boffin. The Boffins take a large mansion and adopt Bella. John falls in love with Bella, but she repulses him as only the secretary. Mrs. Boffin discovers Rokesmith's identity, and they all concoct a plot by which Bella's interest and love are to be aroused. Boffin feigns to be a miser and abuses his secretary in season and out of season until the end is attained and John and Bella are married. The simple deception is continued, however, for some time, until Rokesmith is arrested by the police for his own murder. The revelation is then made. Side by side with this are at least two other stories : Gaffer Hexam is a questionable riverside character who is accused by his former accomplice, Rogue Riderhood, of the murder of Harmon, but on the evening of his arrest he is found drowned. His son and daughter, Lizzie and Charley, separate. Charley has been secretly educated and becomes a pupil-teacher and, later on, a full-fledged schoolmaster. Lizzie supports herself and meets Eugene Wrayburn, the friend of Mortimer Lightwood, the lawyer entrusted with Mr. Boffin's affairs. Eugene does not know whether he is serious or not in his intentions, but he arouses the intense jealousy of Bradley Headstone, the superior of Charley Hexam. Headstone attempts to murder Eugene up the river, where he has pursued Lizzie. Rogue Riderhood has become a deputy lock keeper, and discovers Headstone's dark secret. He uses it to obtain hush-money from his victim, but Headstone is driven mad by his thoughts and his jealousy, and commits suicide, drowning Rogue at the same time. Eugene recovers and marries Lizzie. A friend of Lizzie's is the girl Cleaver, Jenny Wren. She is a dolls' dressmaker and obtains her pieces from Riah the Jew who is ostensibly Pubsey and Co., In reality Pubsey and Co. are Fascination Fledgeby. Fascination enters into an agreement with Alfred Lammle to pay him a sum of money on Lammle bringing about his (Fledgeby's) marriage with Georgina Podsnap. Lammle is a fortune hunter who has married Miss Akersham, only to discover that she also is a fortune hunter. Having no fortune between them they are obliged to live by their wits. The marriage scheme falls through, and Fledgeby ruins Lammle by buying up bills against him. Lammle discovers his duplicity and administers a sound thrashing before leaving England. When Boffin comes into his fortune he employs Silas Wegg, a man "*with* a wooden leg" to read to him. Wegg is a precious rascal who thinks he has discovered a will that will dispossess his employer, and threatens him with absolute ruin. He takes a man named Venus into his confidence, but Venus has no liking for the part, and informs Mr. Boffin of the plot. The will turns out to be valueless, having been invalidated by one of a later date. The grand climax is reached when Wegg is unmasked and turned out, and the real state of affairs is revealed to Bella. Venus marries Pleasant Riderhood.

Christmas Stories. (Published **1854-1867.**)

Seven Poor Travellers. (1845.)
Holly Tree. (1855.)
Wreck of the *Golden Mary*. (1856.)
Perils of Certain English Prisoners. (1857.)
Going into Society. (A House to Let.) (1858.)
Haunted House. (1859.)
Message from the Sea. (1860.)
Tom Tiddler's ground. (1861.)
Somebody's Luggage. (1862.)
Mrs. Lirriper's Lodgings. (1862.)
Mrs. Lirriper's Legacy. (1864.)
Dr. Marigold. (1865.)
Two Ghost Stories. (Dr. Marigold's Prescriptions.) (1865-6.)
Mugby Junction. (1866.)
No Thoroughfare. (1867.)

George Silverman's Explanation. (Published **1868.**)

The story of an orphan who is befriended and educated, By his exertions he secures a scholarship at Cambridge, and is eventually presented with a "living" by Lady Fareway. Lady Fareway's daughter studies under his direction, and an affection grows up between them. He perceives the disparity between them, however, and endeavours to transfer her affection to Granville Wharton. He succeeds, and the two young people are married. George Silverman is dismissed from his living by Lady Fareway, but he secures a college living through the assistance of the young couple.

Holiday Romance. (Published **1868.**)

King Watkins the First has many children, but his eldest child is Alicia, who is mother to her brothers and sisters and housewife as well. Her godmother gives her a magic fishbone, which for one occasion only will bring her what she wishes for. She keeps the fishbone until the King's money is all gone and he is unable to get any more anywhere, when she wishes for Quarter Day. It is Quarter Day and the King's salary falls down the chimney. The Princess Alicia is married by her godmother to Prince Certainpersonio.

Mystery of Edwin Drood. (Published in volume form **1870.**)

This, the last novel, was never completed, and various guesses have been made from time to time as to the conclusion. The scene is laid in Cloisterham. John Jasper is the choirmaster of Cloisterham Cathedral and uncle and guardian of Edwin Drood, but secretly he is addicted to the opium habit. Edwin Drood is a young engineer who has been betrothed by his late father to Rosa Bud. Edwin and Rosa do not feel that they love one another sufficiently to marry. Neville and Helena Landless come to Cloisterham, the latter to the Nun's House, the former to study under the Rev, Crisparkle. They make the acquaintance of Edwin and Rosa. A quarrel arises between the two young men, and this John Jasper fans and magnifies. Jasper is in love with Rosa, although ignorant that she and Edwin have proposed to be brother and sister only in their affections. Crisparkle intervenes and the young men become reconciled. They both visit Jasper on Christmas Eve. After the event Edwin disappears and Neville is arrested on the charge of having murdered him. He is released, however, but leaves Cloisterham and takes up his residence in London. Rosa flies to London to her guardian on account of Jasper's unwelcome attentions; and Helena joins her brother. Two new characters enter the story at this point, Lieutenant Tarter, and Datchery. The latter is a mysterious old man generally believed to be one of the other characters disguised. What place he had to fill can only be guessed And the murderer of Edwin cannot be singled out with any certainty.

Miscellaneous Papers, Plays and Poems. (Published in volume form **1908**).

These miscellaneous essays and tracts are gathered from several periodicals and spread over a period from 1838 to 1869. They do not warrant a minute analysis here, but a list of the contents will be found under the abbreviations.

" A." *M.P., F.N.P.*

" A." Colonel. " Nobody." *R.P., N.S.*

A. Miss = Miss Havisham. (*Which see.*) *G.E.* xxvii.

A. Mr. = Mr. Arndt. *A.N.* xvii

AARON. Mr. Mr. Riah. (*Which see.*)

ABADEEN = The Addled. Lord Aberdeen. *M.T., P.O.H.*

ABBAYE. Prison of the. Paris. *T.T.C.* b. ii., ch. xxiv.

Note.—The prison in which Gabelle was incarcerated.

ABBAYE. The. *R.P., O.o.S.*

ABBEVILLE. *R.P., A.F.*

ABBEY. " Short for Abigail." *See* Potterson (Miss). *O.M.F.*, vi.

ABBEY TOWN. Scene of Gabriel Grub's adventures. *P.P.* xxix.

ABEL. One of Kit's children. *O.C.S.* Chap. The last

ABEL COTTAGE. Finchley. *O.C.S.* xxi.

It was a beautiful little cottage with a thatched roof and little spires at the gable ends, and pieces of stained-glass in some of the windows.

ABERDEEN. Lord. *See also* Abadeen. *M.P., I.*

ABERDEEN. *U.T.* xxii.

ABOH. *M.P., N.E.*

ABOU SIMBEL. Temple of. *M.P., E.T.*

ABRAHAM. Deceased brother of Philip Pirrip. *G.E.* i.

ABSENT. City of the. *U.T.* xxi.

ABSOLON. Mr. *M.P., C.f.B.*

ABSTINENCE SOCIETY. Grand Amalgamated Total. *U.T.* xxxi.

ABYSSINIA. *R.P., M.O.F.F.*, and *T.L.V.*; *U.T.*, xv.

ACADEMY. The Royal. *B.H.* xiv.; and *R.P., O.B.*

ACADEMY. Mr. Cripples' Evening. *L.D.* ix.

Combining day and Evening Tuition. . . . She (Little Dorrit) had herself received her education, such as it was, in Mr. Cripples' Evening Academy.

ACADEMY. Mr. Turvedrop's. *B.H.* xiv.

ACADEMY. Signor Billsmithi's Dancing. *S.B.B., Char.* ix.

Not a dear dancing academy—four-and-sixpence a quarter is decidedly cheap on the whole.

ACCOUNTANT - GENERAL. The. *B.H.* ix.

ACHILLES. The, Iron armoured plated ship. *U.T.* xxiv.

ACQUAPENDENTE. *P.F.I., R.P.S.*

ACTON. *U.T.* xx.

ACTOR. An. *M.P., G.F.*

ADA'S MOTHER. Deceased. *B.H.* vi.

ADAM. *M.P., L.A.V.* i.

ADAM AND EVE COURT. *S.B.B.*, Scenes xx.

ADAMS. Head boy at School. *D.C.* xvi.

ADAMS. Captain. Friend of Sir Mulberry Hawk. *N.N.L.*

ADAMS. Jane. *S.Y.C.*

ADAMS. Mr., Confidential Clerk of Mr. Sampson. *H.D.* ii.

ADAMS. W. P. Jack Adams. *D. and S.* xxxvi.

A man with a cast in his eye, and slight impediment in his speech—sat for somebody's borough. We used to call him W. P. Adams, in consequence of his being Warming Pan for a young fellow who was in his minority.

ADELAIDE. Queen Dowager. *M.P., C.C.*

ADELINA. Only daughter of Lady Fareway. *G.S.E.* vii.

ADLEPHI. The. *D.C.* xi. and *L.D.* xlv.; *M.C.* xiii.; *M.P., O.S.*; *P.P.* lvii.; *S.B.B.*, Tales iii.; *U.T.* xiv.

ADELPHI HOTEL. *A.N.I.*; and *C.S., M.L.L.* i.

ADELPHI THEATRE. *P.P.* xxxi.

ADMIRAL BENBOW. The. An Inn. *R.P., O.O.S.*

ADMIRAL NAPIER. An Omnibus. *S.B.B.*, Tales xi.

ADMIRAL NELSON. A Dining House. *C.S., S.L.* i.

ADMIRAL. Aboard the Argonaut. *U.T.* xv.

ADMIRAL. Presiding. *M.P., N.Y.D.*

ADMIRALTY. *L.D.* xxi. ; *M.P., T.O.H.* ; and *M.P., L.A.V.*

ADMIRALTY PIER.. Dover. *U.T.* xvii.

ADRIATIC. *C.S., N.T., Act* i.

ADVERTISER. *N.N.* iv.

ADVOCATE. In High Court of Chancery. *B.H.* i.

Large, with great whiskers, a little voice, and an interminable brief, and outwardly directing his contemplation to the lantern in the roof, where he can see nothing but fog.

ADVOCATE. Italian. *U.T.* xxviii.

AFFERY. *See* Flintwinch, Affery.

AFRICA. *L.D.* xxi. ; and *M.C.* vi. ; *M.P., A.P.* ; *M.P., B.A.* ; *M.P., N.E.* ; *R.P., A.P.A.* ; *U.T.* xix.

AFRICAN KNIFE SWALLOWER. *N.N.* xlviii.

AFRICAN STATION. *B.H.* xiii.

AGED. The. Wemmick's Father. *G.E.* xxv.

A very old man in a flannel coat : clean, cheerful, comfortable and well cared for, but intensely deaf.

AGENT. Parliamentary. *M.P., H.H.*

AGENTS. Maid and Courier. *L.D.* li.

Sent to Paris for purchase of an outfit for a bride.

AGGS. Mr. *O.M.F.* viii.

AGNES. *See* Wickfield, Agnes.

AGNES. Mrs. Bloss' servant. *S.B.B.*, Tales i.

In a cherry-coloured merino dress, openwork stockings and shoes with sandals like a disguised Columbine.

AGNES. Little. David Copperfield's eldest child. *D.C.* xxxiv.

AGNEW. Sir Andrew. *S.U.T.H.* i.ii.

AIREY ! Sir Richard. *M.P., S.F.A.*

AIX ROADS. *M.P., L.A.V.* ii.

AKERMAN. Mr. Head jailer at Newgate. *B.R.* lxiv.

AKERSHEM. Horatio. The late. *O.M.F.* x.

AKERSHEM. Sophronia. The mature young lady, who marries Mr. Lammle. *O.M.F.* x.

ALABAMA. *M.C.* xvi.

ALBANO. *L.D.* l. ; and *P.F.I., R.*

ALBANY. A large and busy town. *A.N.* xv.

ALBANY. The. *U.T.* x. ; and *O.M.F.* xxii.

ALBARO. *P.F.I., A.G.*

ALBEMARLE. St., *M.P., N.J.B.*

ALBERT. H. R. H. Prince. *M.P., E.S., M.P., N.E.*

"**ALBERT.**" Ship. *M.P., N.E.*

ALBINA. Lady, One of Magsman's troupe. *C.S., G.i.S.*

Showing her white hair to the army and navy in correct uniform.

"**ALCOHOL.**" Steamboat. *A.N.* xi.

ALDBOROUGH. Lord. *M.P., I.*

ALDERMAN. *B.R.*, lxi. ; and *M.H.C.* i.

ALDERMAN. An ex-M.P. *S.B.B.*, Scenes xviii.

Small gentleman with a sharp nose—a sort of amateur fireman.

ALDERMANBURY. *M.C.* xxxvii.

ALDERMEN. Of the City of London. *M.P., M.B.V.*

ALDERSGATE STREET. *E.D.* xxiii., and *L.D.* xiii. ; *M.P., L.T., U.T.*

ALDERSHOT. *M.P., S.F.A.*

ALDGATE. *P.P.*i. and *S.B.B.* xlii.

ALDGATE PUMP. *D. and S.* lvi. ; and *N.N.* xli. ; *U.T.* iii.

ALDRICH. Mr. *M.P., I.W.M.*

ALDRICH. Mrs. *M.P., I.W.M.*

ALDRIDGE. Mr., as a monk. *M.P., N.Y.*

ALE HOUSE. Blunderstone. *D.C.*

ALESSANDRIA. *P.F.I.*, *P.M.B.*

ALEXANDER. Deceased brother of Philip Pirrip. *G.E.* i.

ALEXANDER. Mr. Grazinglands. *U.T.* vi.

ALFRED.. Alfred Heathfield. *C.B.*, *B.O.L.* i.

ALFRED. Alfred Lammle. (*Which see*).

ALFRED. Alfred Raybrock. *C.S.*, *M.f.T.S.* ii.

ALFRED. Alfred Starling. *C.S.*, *H.H.*

ALFRED. Fifth and youngest son of Mrs. Pardiggle. *B.H.* viii.

ALGERIA. *U.T.* xxv.

ALICE. *R.P.*, *A.C.T.*

ALICE. Alice Rainbird. *H.R.* i.

ALICE. Daughter of "Good Mrs. Brown." *See* Brown Alice.

ALICE. The youngest of the Five Sisters of York. *N.N.* vi.
The blushing tints in the soft bloom on the fruit, or the delicate painting on the flower, are not more exquisite than was the blending of the rose and lily in her gentle face, or the deep blue of her eye.

ALICE. Mistress, Only daughter of Bowyer. *M.H.C.* i.

ALICIA. Princess, Eldest child of King Watkins the First. *H.R.* ii.

ALICK. Son of Mr. and Mrs. Octavius Budden. *S.B.B.*, Tales ii.

ALICK. Child on board Gravesend Packet. *S.B.B.*, Scenes x.
A damp earthy child in red worsted socks.

ALICUMPAINE. Mrs. *H.R.* iv.

"ALL IN A MIND." *M.P.*, *O.S.*

ALLAH. *M.P.*, *W.S.*

ALLEGHANY MOUNTAINS. *A.N.* x.

ALLEN. Arabella, Sister of Benjamin Allen. *P.P.* xxviii.
Black-eyed young lady, in a very nice little pair of boots with fur round the top.
Note.—Designed by her brother to marry Bob Sawyer, she ran away and married Winkle, largely with the assistance of Sam Weller and Mr. Pickwick.

ALLEN. Benjamin, Brother of Arabella Allen. *P.P.* xxx.
A coarse, stout, thick-set young man, with black hair cut rather short, and a white face cut rather long—embellished with spectacles.
Note.—A friend of Bob Sawyer, both rollicking medical students rather disreputable in appearance, and introduced in an atmosphere of beer and oysters. Reconciled to his sister after her marriage and went to Bengal with Bob Sawyer.

ALLEN. Benjamin, Mr., Aunt of. *P.P.* xlviii.

ALLEN. Capt. William. *M.P.*, *N.E.*

ALLEN. Mr. *M.P.*, *E.T.*

ALLEY. Mr. *O.M.F.* viii.

ALLIGWY. *U.T.* ii.

ALLISON. Major. *A.N.* xvii.

ALLISON. Miss, as Mrs. Lovetown. *M.P.*, *I.S.*, *H.W.*

ALLISON AND CO. T. G., Mercantile Merchants. *A.N.* xvii.

ALL MUGGLETONIAN CLUB. The Muggleton Cricket Club which played the Dingley Dellers. *P.P.* vii.

ALLONBY. *L.T.* iii.

ALMACK'S. Assembly-room of the Five Point fashionables. *A.N.* vi.

ALMACK'S. Landlady of, A buxom fat mulatto woman. *A.N.* vi.

ALMSHOUSE. Workhouse of New York. *A.N.* vi.

ALMSHOUSES. Of the Cork Cutter's Company. *C.S.*, *S.L.* i.

ALMSHOUSES. Titbull's. *See* Titbull's Almshouses.

ALPHONSE. Mrs. Wititterley's page. *N.N.* xxi.

ALPS. The. *L.D.* xxxvii.; *P.F.I.*, *L.R.G.A.*; and *R.P.*, *O.o.T.*

ALREDAH. Character in Nursery Story. *U.T.* xv.

ALTHORP. Lord. *M.P., R.T.*

AMATEUR GALLERY. 121, Pall Mall. *M.P., C.*

AMAZON. The. An Emigrant Ship. *U.T.* xx.

AMAZON. Captain of the. *U.T.* xx.

AMBASSADOR. *M.P., I.*

AMBIGU. Paris. *M.P., W.*

AMBIGUOUSLY COMIC THEATRE. *M.P., N.Y.D.*

AMBLER. *M.P., S.B.*

AMBOISES. Bay of. *M.P., N.E.*

AMELIA. Another daughter of stout lady visitor at Ramsgate library. *S.B.B.*, Tales iv.

AMELIA. *M.P., S.R.*

AMELIA COTTAGE. Stamford Hill. *S.B.B.*, Tales ii.

AMERICA.. *See* United States.

AMERICA JUNIOR. *M.C.* xxii.

AMERICA. South. *C.B., C.H.* i.; *C.S., H.H.*; *C.S.M.f.T.S.* ii.

AMERICA. South, Waters. *C.S., P.o.C.E.P.*

AMERICA SQUARE. *C.S., M.f.T.S.* v.

AMERICAN. *M.P., N.J.B.*

AMERICAN COURT OF LAW. *A.N.* iii.

AMERICAN FALL. The. *A.N.* xiv.

AMERICAN MINISTER. (1834). *M.P., N. G.K.*

AMETER. Mr. X. *M.P., T.B.*

AMETER. Mr., X., brother of *M.P., T.B.*

AMETER. Mr. X., great uncle of. *M.P., T.B.*

AMETER. Mr. X., second son of. *M.P., T.B.*

AMIENS. *C.S., M.J.* v.; *R.P., A.F., M.T.* xvii.

AMPHITHEATRE. Old, of Rome. *L.D.* li.

AMPHITHEATRE. Roman. *P.F.I., V.M.M.S.S.*

AMSTERDAM. *B.R.* lxxxii.; and *L.D.* lxvii.

AMY. "Little Dorrit" (*which see.*)

AMY. Old woman in Workhouse, nursing dying inmate. *O.T.* xxiv.

ANALYTICAL. The, Veneering's Butler. *O.M.F.* ii.

ANCESTOR. Veneering's Crusading. *O.M.F.* ii.

ANCIENT BRITONS. *M.P., H.H.*

ANDERSON. John. A Tramp. *U.T.* xi.

ANDERSON. Mr., Actor. *M.P. M.B.*; *M.P., R.S.L.*

ANDERSON. Mrs., Wife of John Anderson. *U.T.* xi.

ANDREWS. Jack. *M.P., N.E.*

ANDREWS. Little. *M.P., V.D.*

ANGEL. *P.P.* xxix.
Looking down upon, and blessing.

"**ANGEL.** The," in Bury St. Edmunds. *P.P.*, xvi.
In a wide open street, nearly facing the old abbey.

"**ANGEL,** The," Islington. *O.T.* xlii.
Where—London began in earnest.

"**ANGEL.** The," Public House. *C.S., N.T.*

ANGEL COURT. *L.D.* Pref.

ANGELA. Emmeline's cousin and sweetheart of Charley. *C.S., H.T.*

ANGELICA. A sometime sweetheart of the Uncommercial Traveller. *U.T.*, ix.

ANGLAIS, L'. Monsieur—the Englishman Mr. Langley. *C.S., S.L.* ii.

ANGLER'S INN. *O.M.F.* li.

ANGLESEY. *U.T.* ii.

ANGLO - BENGALEE DISINTERESTED LOAN AND LIFE ASSURANCE COMPANY. Offices of the. *M.C.* xxvii.
In a new street in the City, comprising the upper part of a spacious house, resplendent in stucco, and plate glass, with wire blinds in all the windows, and "Anglo-Bengalee" worked into the pattern of every one of them.

ANIMALS. Society for the Prevention of Cruelty to. *U.T.* xxxv.

ANIO. The River. *P.F.I., R.*

ANNE. *S.Y.C.*

ANNE. Queen, Late Queen Dowager. *M.P., T.D.*

ANNE. Dombey's housemaid. *D. and S.* xviii.

Note.—Towlinson and Anne "make it up" and agree to set up together in the general greengrocery line.

ANNE. Mrs. Chickenstalker. *C.B., C.C.* iv.

ANNIE. Dr. Strong's Wife's cousin. *D.C.* xvi.

ANNUNCIATA. The Church of the. *P.F.I., G.A.N.*

ANNY. *O.T.* xxiv.

"**ANOTHER**." Husband of Dust Contractor's daughter. *O.M.F.* ii.

Was so cut up by the loss of his young wife that if he outlived her a year it was as much as he did.

ANTHONY. Doctor Jeddler. *C.B., B.o.L.* iii.

ANTHONY. Runaway Slave. *A.N.* xvii.

ANTHONY. William S. *M.P., I.W.M.*

ANTIPODES. The. *U.T.* v.

ANTOINE. A son of Madame Doche. *R.P., M.O.F.F.*

ANTONIO. *P.F.I., G.A.N.*

ANTONIO. A lodger at Meggisson's. *U.T.* v.

A swarthy youth with a guitar. A young foreign sailor—a Spaniard.

ANTWERP. *H.T., R.* vii. ; and *L.D.* lxvi. *G.E.*

ANYSHIRE. *D. and S.* xxxvi.

APARTMENT. French. *D. and S.* liv.

Comprising some half dozen rooms —a dull cold hall or corridor, a dining-room, a drawing-room, a bed chamber, and an inner drawing-room or boudoir, smaller and more retired than the rest.

APENNINES. The. *P.F.I., R.*

APOTHECARY. *O.T.* xxiv.

APOTHECARY. A certain calm *D. and S.* xiv.

Who attended at the establishment when any of the young gentlemen were ill.

APOTHECARY. Attending death-bed of Nicholas Nickleby, senior. *N.N.* I.

"Cheer up" said the Apothecary.

APPARITOR. The. The officer of the Court. *S.B.B.*, Scenes viii.

APPIAN WAY. *P.F.I., R.*

APPIUS CLAUDIUS. *M.P., V.* and *B.S.*

APPLICANT. Next, for lodgings. *S.B.B., O.P.* vii.

A tall thin gentleman with a profusion of brown hair, reddish whiskers and very slightly developed moustaches and had altogether a military appearance.

APPRENTICE. *S.B.B., O.P.*, viii.

Pauses every other minute from his task.

APPRENTICE. Apothecary's, the parish. *O.T.* xxiv.

APPRENTICE. Engravers', who painted Miss Bravassa's likeness. *N.N.* xxiii.

APPRENTICE. Lobbs'. *P.P.* xvii.

Bony apprentice with the thin legs.

APPRENTICES. At Greenwich fair. *S.B.B.*, Scenes xii.

APPRENTICES. Four London. *S.B.B.*, Characters i.

They are only bound, now, by indentures. Four all arm in arm, with white kid gloves like so many bridegrooms, light trousers of unprecedented patterns ; and coats for which the English language has yet no name—a kind of cross between a great-coat and a surtout, with the collar of the one, the skirts of the other, and pockets peculiar to themselves. Each of the gentlemen carried a thick stick with a large tassel at the top, the whole four walking with a paralytic swagger. . . . They are a peculiar class and not the less pleasant for being inoffensive.

APPRENTICES. Milliners'. *S.B.B.*, Scenes i.

The hardest worked—the worst paid—poor girls.

APPRENTICES. Staymakers'. *S.B.B.*, Scenes I.

Poor girls !—the hardest worked —the worst paid.

APPRENTICES. Two, of Peffer and Snagsby. *B.H.* x.

ARA COELI. Church of. *P.F.I.*, *R.*

ARABELLA. Mrs. Grazinglands. *U.T.* vi.

ARABELLA. *See* Allen, Arabella.

ARABS. *L.D.* lxx.

ARAGO. M. *M.P.*, *M.M.*

ARAMINTA. *M.P.*, *G.D.*

ARCADE. The. *U.T.* x.

ARCADE. Beadles of the. *U.T.*, xvi.

ARCHBISHOP. *M.P.*, *C.C.*

ARCHBISHOP OF GREENWICH. *O.M.F.* liv.

Head waiter in Hotel.

ARCHES. Adelphi. *See* Adelphi.

ARCHES. Commemorative of Rome. *L.D.* li.

ARCHES COURT. The, In Doctors' Commons. *S.B.B.*, Scenes viii.

AREZZO. *P.F.I.*, *R.D.*

ARGONAUT. The, A ship. *U.T.* xv.

ARIEL. *M.P.*, *R.T.*

ARIOSTO'S HOUSE. *P.F.I.*, *T.B.F.*

ARISTOTLE. *M.P.*, *P.L.U.*

ARKANSAS. *A.N.* xvii. ; and *M.C.* xvi.

ARMES. Place d'—of High Town *R.P.*, *O.F.W.*

A little decayed market is held.

ARMY. The, Characters in Play. *S.B.B.*, Scenes xiii.

Two dirty men with corked countenances in very old green tunics, and dirty drab boots.

ARMY. British. *M.P.*, *T.I.P.*

ARMY. Nephews in the, Character in play given by Mr. V. Crummles' Company. *N.N.* xxiii.

ARNDT. The Hon. Charles C. P. *A.N.* xvii.

Member for the Council of Brown County.

ARNO. River. *P.F.I.*, *R.D.* ; and *R.P.*, *D.W.T.T.*

ARNO. Valley of the. *P.F.I.*, *R.D.*

ARNOTT. Dr. *M.P.*, *A.J.B.* ; and *M.P.*, *S.S.U.*

ARPIN. Mr. P. *A.N.* xvii.

ARRAS. *C.S.*, *M.J.* v. ; and *U.T.* xvii.

ARROW. An Indian Chief. *A.N.* ix.

ARSENAL. The, at Woolwich. *B.R.* lxvii.

ARTFUL DODGER. *See also* Dawkins, Jack. *M.P.*, *T.T.C.D.*

ARTHUR. Half-brother to Miss Havisham. *G.E.* xlii.

ARTHUR. Negro Slave. *A.N.* xvii.

ARTHUR'S SEAT. Edinburgh. *P.P.* xlix.

ARTICLE. Plated. *R.P.*, *P.A.*

ARTIST. A Street. *C.S.*, *S.L.* iii.

A shabby person of modest appearance who shivered dreadfully (though it wasn't at all cold) was engaged in blowing the chalk-dust off the moon.

ARTISTS. *M.P.*, *T.B.*

Individual artists will be found under their names both in real life and the artistic characters of the books.

ARUNDEL. *C.S.*, *M.L.Lo.* i.

ASCENSION. Island of. *M.P.*, *L.T.* ; and *M.P.*, *N.E.*

ASHBURTON. Lord. *A.N.* xiv.

ASHES. Name of a Bird. *B.H.* xiv.

ASHFORD. *D.C.* xviii. ; and *R.P.*, *A.F.*

ASHFORD. Nettie, A schoolgirl. *H.R.* i.
Aged half-past six.

ASHLEY, Lord. *M.P.S.S.*

ASHLEY. Hon. William. *M.P.*, *C.C.*

ASIA. *M.P.*, *B.A.* ; and *M.P.*, *N.S.E.*

ASPATRIA. *L.T.* iii.

ASSEMBLY ROOMS. The. *P.P.* xxxv.

ASSEMBLY ROOMS. At English Watering Place. *R.P.*, *O.E.W.*
A bleak chamber—understood to be available on hire for balls or concerts.

ASSEMBLY ROOMS. Library attached to. *R.P.*, *O.E.W.*
This is the library for the Minerva Press.

ASSEMBLY. Two Houses of. Washington. *A.N.* viii.

ASSOCIATED BORES. My Club. *M.P.*, *I.M.*

ASSOCIATION. A certain Brandy-wine. *M.C.*, Preface

ASSURANCE COMPANY. The Anglo-Bengalee Disinterested Loan and Life. *M.C.* xxvii.

ASTERISK. *M.P.W.*

ASTLEY'S. A Circus. *O.C.S.*, xxxix. ; and *S.B.B.* Scenes xi.
It was not a Royal Amphitheatre in those days . . . with all the paint, gilding, and looking-glass ; the vague smell of horses suggestive of coming wonders.

ASTLEY'S THEATRE. *B.H* xxi. ; *M.P.*, *M.B.V.* ; and *M.P.*, *R.H.F.*

ASTLEY'S VISITORS. (Audience in Circus). *S.B.B.*, Scenes xi.
Three little boys and a little girl occupied the front row (of box), then two more little girls, ushered in by a young lady, evidently the governess. Then came three more little boys, dressed like the first, in blue jackets and lay down shirt collars : then a child in a braided frock.—Then came ma and pa, and then the eldest, a boy of fourteen years old.

ASYLUMS. *A.N.* iii.
The various asylums mentioned in the works will be found under their names.

ATHENAEUM CLUB. The. *M.P.*, *B.A.* ; *M.P.*, *I.M.T.* ; and *N.N.* i.

ATHERFIELD. Mrs. Passenger on board the *Golden Mary*. *C.S.*, *W.o.G.M.*
A blooming young wife, who was going out to join her husband in California.

ATKINS. Will. Personage in Nursery Tale. *U.T.* xv.

ATKINSON'S. Mr., The perfumers. *U.T.* xvi.

ATLANTIC. The. *A.N.*, ii. ; *H.T.R* i. ; *M.C.*, xiii. ; *R.P.*, *T.D.P.*, and *U.T.* xx.

ATTAH OF IDDAH. *M.P.*, *N.E.*

ATTENDANT. At Bachelor's Inns at Temple Bar. *M.C.* xlv.
A Fiery-faced matron attired in a crunched bonnet with particularly long strings to it hanging down her back.

ATTENDANT. Female, at Ralph Nickleby's. *N.N.* xxix.

ATTENDANT. Of Lady Client of General Agency Office. *N.N.* xvi.
A red-faced, round-eyed, slovenly girl.

ATTENDANT. Upon the stranger. *M.H.C.* i.

ATTORNEY. A Small. *S.B.B.*, *O.P.* vii.

ATTORNEY. An. *M.P.*, *H.H.*

ATTORNEY. London. *P.P.* xxi.
A man of of no great nicety in his professional dealings.

ATTORNEY'S CLERK. Making a search in Vestry. *D. and S.* v.
Over-aged, and over-worked, and underpaid.

ATTORNEY-GENERAL. The. *M.P., S.F.A.*; *R.P., P.M.T.P. T.T.C., bk.* ii., *ch.* ii., and *U.T.* xi.

ATTORNEY-GENERAL'S CHAMBERS. *R.P., P.M.T.P.*

ATTORNEY-GENERAL. For Ireland. *M.P., Ag. Int.*

ATTORNEYS. *P.P.* xl.

AUBER. M. *M.P., M.M.*

AUBURN. Mount, Suburb of Cincinnati. *A.N.* xi.

AUBURN. Prison. *A.N.* vi.

AUGUSTA. *B.H.* x.
A lean young woman from a workhouse has fits which the parish can't account for; aged three or four and twenty, but looking a round ten years older.

AUGUSTUS. Son of Mr. and Mrs. Borum. *N.N.* xxiv.
A young gentlemen who was pinching the phenomenon apparently with a view of ascertaining if she were real.

AUNT. Allen's. *P.P.* xlviii.

AUNT. Grey-haired, of Kate. *D. and S.* xxiv.

AUNT. Miss Pankey's at Rottingdean. *D. and S.* viii.

AUNT. Mr. F's, Flora's Legacy. *L.D.* xiii.
An amazing little old woman, with a face like a staring wooden doll too cheap for expression, and a stiff yellow wig, perched unevenly on the top of her head . . . seemed to have damaged her face in two or three places with some blunt instrument in the nature of a spoon; particularly the tip of her nose—several dints—answering to the bowl of that article. The major characteristics were extreme severity and grim taciturnity; sometimes interrupted by a propensity to offer remarks in a deep warning voice traceable to no association of ideas.

Note.—Flora had inherited the aunt from her late husband. The "staring wooden doll" took a great dislike to Arthur Clenman and let off her remarks, of which "There's milestones on the Dover Road" is perhaps the best known, at him with the deadliest marksmanship.

AUNT. Mr. Home's. *M.P., M.M.*

AUNT. My. *See* Trotwood, Betsy.

AUSTERLITZ. *R.P., O.F.W.*

AUSTIN. John. *M.P., P.F.*

AUSTIN. Mrs. *M.P., R.H.F.*

AUSTIN FRIARS. *M.C.* xxxviii.; *M.P., G.A.*

AUSTRALIA. *C.S., S.L.* i.; *D.C.* xxii; *D. and S.* xxv.; *M.P., C.*; *M.P., E.T.*; *M.P., P.P.*; *M.P., S.R.*; *M.P., W.*; *U.T.* ii.

AUSTRIA. *C.S.*, ii.; *M.P., W.H.*; *R.P., O.B.*; *U.T.* xxviii.

AVALLON. *P.F.I., G.T.F.*

AVENGER. The. *See* Pepper.

AVIGNON. *B.H.* xii.; *C.S.* ii.; *L.D.* xi.; *P.F.I., L.R.G.A.*; *P.F.I., P.M.B.*

AVVOCATE. *P.F.I.*

AWKWARD SQUAD. Full Private Number One in The. *See* Sloppy.

AYLESBURY. *M.P., C.P.*

AYNHO. *M.P.. E.S.*

AYRESLEIGH. Mr., under arrest. *P.P.*, xl.
A middle-aged man in a very old suit of black, who looked pale and haggard.

AZORES. *M.P., L.A.V.* ii.

B

"**B.**" C. of. The Countess. *N.N.* xxviii.

B. Count de. *M.P., M.M.*

"**B.**" D. of. The Duchess. *N.N.* xxviii.

B. M. *M.P., F,S.*

B. Madame. *M.P., A.A.P.*

B. Major. "Nobody." *R.P., N.S.*

B. Master, Ghost of. *C.S., H.H.*
Dressed in an obsolete fashion, or rather was not so much dressed as put into a case of inferior pepper-and-salt cloth, made horrible by means of shining buttons.

B. Miss L., of Bungay, Suffolk. *M.P., W.R.*

B. Mr. *M.P., W.R.*

B. Mr. Mr. Bridgman. *A.N.* xvii.

B. Mr. John. *M.P., R.T.*

B. Mrs. Mrs. Benjamin Britain. *C.B., B.o. L.* iii.

B. Mrs. *M.P., S.F.A.*

B. Mrs. *M.P., W.R.*

B. Young. *M.P., W.R.*

BABBY. The Young Peerybingle. *C.B., C.o.H.* iii.

BABER. *M.P., C.* Pat.

BABIES. (In arms) at Tea Gardens. *S.B.B.* Scenes ix.

BABLEY. Mr. Richard. *See* Dick, Mr.

BABY. Great. The Public. *M.P., G.B.*

BABY. Kitterbell's baby. *See* Kitterbell, Master Frederick Charles William.

BABY. *See* Meagles, Minnie.

BABY. Dying, of Brickmaker's wife. *B.H.* viii.

BABY. New. of the Kenwigs. *N.N.* xxvi.

BABY. The Old, Lillyvick Kenwigs. *N.N.* xxxvi.

BACHELOR. The. *O.C.S.* lii.
The little old gentleman was the active spirit of the place, the adjuster of all the differences, the promoter of all the merry-makings, the dispenser of his friend's bounty, and of no small charity of his own besides.

Note.—The extract admirably illustrates the Bachelor's character. Nell and her grand-father made acquaintance with him at the village where the schoolmaster procured them the appointment of care-takers of the old church. The little old gentleman had lived at the Parsonage House for fifteen years.

BACHELOR'S HALL. The name given to Quilp's riverside place, first named in chapter I of Old Curiosity Shop. This was the Counting House which the dwarf converted into a temporary dwelling place during his "displeasure" with his wife. *See* also Quilp.

"**BACHELORS.** The Three Jolly." *D. and S.* xxvii.

BACK. *M.P., L.A.V.* i.

BACK YARD. Of Mrs. Chivery's Establishment. *L.D.* xxii.
In this yard a wash of sheets and table cloths tried (in vain for want of air) to get dried on a line or two.

BACON. Friar. *M.P., P.M.B.*

Note.—The originator and supporter of the men's village club.

BACON. Lawyer. *M.P., C.P.*

BADAJOS. *C.S., S.P.T.* ii.

BADEN-BADEN. *D.C.* xxxi.; and *M.P., P.M.B.*

BADGER. Black. *D. and S.* xxii.

BADGER. Mr. Bayham, Physician. Mr. Kenge's Cousin. *B.H.* xiii.
A pink, fresh-faced, crisp-looking gentleman, with a weak voice, white teeth, light hair and surprised eyes.

Note.—This Chelsea practitioner was the one to whom Richard Carstone was articled in his first choice of a profession. Besides his Chelsea practice he attended a large public institution. His most prominent trait was a habit of praising the two former husbands of his wife.

BADGER. Mrs. Laura, wife of Mr. Bayham Badger. *B.H.* xiii.
A lady of about fifty, youthfully dressed, and of a very fine complexion.

Note.—Her "first" was Captain Swosser of the Royal Navy, her "second" Professor Dingo: Mr. Badger was her "third."

BAGDAD. *U.T.* xv.

BAGDAD. The Bazaar at. *M.P., G.A.*

BAGGS. Mr. *O.M.F.* viii.

BAGGS. Lilburn W., late Governor of State, at Independence. *A.N.* xvii.

BAGMAN. The, Traveller at the "Peacock." *P.P.* xiv.

A stout hale personage of about forty, with only one eye—a very bright black eye, which twinkled with a roguish expression of fun and good humour.

Note.—The Bagman was the narrator of the now famous "Bagman's Story" and the "Story of the Bagman's Uncle." The latter contains incidentally a lively account of the old coaching days. Pickwick meets the Bagman on two occasions, first at Eatanswill and afterwards at Bristol.

BAGMAN'S UNCLE. Employee of Tiggin and Welps, and friend of Tom Smart. *P.P.* xlix.

One of the merriest, pleasantest, cleverest fellows that ever lived. In appearance, my uncle was a trifle shorter than the middle size—a trifle stouter, too—his face might be a trifle redder.

BAGNERELLO. Signor. *P.F.I., G.A.N.*

BAGNERELLO. Villa. *P.F.I., G.A.N.*

BAGNET. Matthew, an ex-artilleryman and proprietor of musician's shop. *B.H.* xxvii.

Tall and upright, with shaggy eyebrows, and whiskers like the fibres of a cocoanut, not a hair upon his head, and a torrid complexion. Voice, short, deep and resonant, not at all unlike the tones of the instrument (bassoon) to which he is devoted.

Note.—Friend of George Rouncewell. Formerly an artilleryman, but when he enters the story he is in "the musical business." His wife is the head of the family, but to maintain "discipline" he never admits it to her. The story leaves him and his family as occasional visitors at "Chesney Wold."

BAGNET. Mrs., Wife of Matthew Bagnet. *B.H.* xxvii.

Not an ill-looking woman. Rather large-boned, a little coarse in the grain, and freckled by the sun and wind which have tanned her hair upon her forehead; but healthy, wholesome and bright-eyed. Clean, hardy, and economically dressed. A strong, busy, active honest-faced woman of from forty-five to fifty.

Note.—When she says a thing she'll do it. She sets out with a few shillings for Lincolnshire to bring Mrs. Rouncewell to George. And, as Lignum said, she made her way home once, from another quarter of the world."

BAGNET. Malta, Elder daughter of the Bagnets. *B.H.* xxvii.

Note.—Named "Malta" from the name of the place of her birth.

BAGNET. Quebec, Younger daughter of the Bagnets. *B.H.* xxvii.

Note.—Named from the place of her birth in the same way as the other children of the family.

BAGNET. Woolwich, Son of the Bagnets. *B.H.* xxvii.

Note.—Named from the place of his birth.

BAGNET. Mrs., Old Father of. ... *B.H.* xxvii.

BAGNET. Old Mother of, in Scotland. *B.H.* xxvii.

BAGSTOCK. Major, Lodger in house in Princess' Place. *D. and S.* vii.

A wooden-featured, blue-faced Major, with his eyes starting out of his head. Something so truly military—had arrived at what is called, in polite literature, the grand meridian of life, and was proceeding on his journey down-hill with hardly any throat, and a very rigid pair of jawbones, and long-flapped elephantine ears.

Note.—The major lives near Miss Tox, whom he watches from his window. He exchanges little courtesies with her. Makes the acquaintance of Mr. Dombey, and introduces him to Edith Grainger his second wife. The friendship between the Major and Miss Tox comes to nothing.

BAIAE. *P.F.I., R.D.*

" **BAIL.**" A. Trader in bailing prisoners out. *P.P.* xl.

" What, am I to understand that these men earn a livelihood by walking about here to perjure themselves before the judges of the land at the rate of half-a-crown a crime ? "

BAILEY. Benjamin. Belonging to Commercial Boarding House. *M.C.*, viii.

With a large red head, and no nose to speak of, and a very dirty Wellington boot on his left arm—" I thought you was the Paper," replied the boy, " and wondered why you didn't shove yourself through the grating as usual."

Note.—The boy at Mrs. Todger's boarding-house. He has a variety of names bestowed upon him by the boarders. He is a friend of Mr. Sweedlepipe, with whom he afterwards enters the hair-dressing business. In the meantime he has been " tiger " to Tigg Montague.

BAILEY. Captain. *D.C.* xviii.

BAILEY. Old, Courts at. *C.S., T.C.S.* i. ; *N.N.* xx. ; and *S.B.B.*, Scenes xxiv.

Nothing so strikes the person who enters them for the first time, as the calm indifference with which the proceedings are conducted.

BALIM. Mr. *S.Y.G.*

BAILLIE. A. *P.P.* xlix.

Mac something and four syllables after it, who lived in the old town of Edinburgh.

BAILLIE'S GROWN-UP SON. *P.P.* xlix.

BAILLIE'S THREE DAUGHTERS. *P.P.* xlix.

Very pretty and agreeable.

BAILLIE'S WIFE. *P.P.* xlix.

" One of the best creatures that ever lived."

BAINES. Mr., An Actor. *R.P., O.O.S.*

BAKER. Mr *S., Y.G., Y.L.*

BAKER. Mr., A Coroner. *U.T.* iii.

BAKER. Mr. E. S., Nominated Member of Grant County. *A.N.* xvii.

BAKER. A. *M.P., G.A.*

BAKER. A (in Somerstown). *B.H.* xliii.

A sort of human hedgehog rolled up said Mr. Skimpole—from whom he borrowed a couple of armchairs. When they were worn out, he wanted them back. He objected to their being worn.

BAKER. The. *G.E.* viii.

BAKERS' TRAP. A Thames Dock, famous for Suicide Scenes. *U.T.* iii.

BAKERS. *S.B.B.*, Scenes i.

BALAKLAVA. *M.P., G.D.* ; *M.P. N.S.E.* ; and *M.P., S.F.A.*

BALDERDASH. Great Parochial Joint Stock Bank of. *R.P., O.V.*

BALDERSTONE. Thomas, Mrs. Gauleton's brother. *S.B.B.* ; Tales ix.

" **BALD-FACED STAG.**" *M.C.* xxxvi.

Away with four fresh horses from the Bald-faced Stag, where topers congregate about the door admiring.

BÁLE. *P.F.I., V.M.M.S.S.*

BALFE. Mr. *M.P., M.M.*

BALLANTYNE FAMILY. Scott's Publishers. *M.P., S.P.*

BALLANTYNE. Alexander. *M.P., S.P.*

BALLANTYNE. James. *M.P., S.P.*

BALLANTYNE. John. *M.P., S.P.*

BALLAST-HEAVERS. At Ratcliff. *U.T.* xxx.

Occupants of one room.

BALLEY. Mr. *O.M.F.*viii.

BALLON. Rev. Adin. *M.P., S.B.* ; *M.P., R.S.D*

BALLS. Golden, in connection with uncle. *M.C.* i.

Certain entertainments, so splendid and costly in their nature, that he calls them " Golden Balls."

BALL'S POND. *D.S.* xviii.; and *S.B.B.*, Tales iii.

BALSAMO. Mr. *M.P.*, *M.M.*

BALTIC SEA. *D. and S.* iv.

BALTIMORE, U.S.A. *A.N.* viii.; and *M.P.*, *I.W.M.*

BAMBER. *M.H.C.* iv.

He is a strange secluded visionary.

BAMBER. Residence of. *M.H.C.* iv.

One of these dull lonely old places—often shut up close for several weeks together.

BAMBER. Jack, An attorney's clerk. *P.P.* xx.

Never heard to talk of anything else but the inns, and he has lived alone in them till he's half crazy. . . .

A little yellow high-shouldered man . . . a fixed grim smile perpetually on his countenance . . . a long skinny hand with nails of extraordinary length.

Note.—The old man knew more about the "Inns" (of Court), than anyone. Mr. Pickwick succeeded in "drawing" him when he joined Mr. Lowten's convivial company at the "Magpie and Stump" on the occasion of his search after Mr. Perker's clerk regarding the Bardell case.

BAMBINO. *P.F.I.*

BAND. A brass. *D. and S.* xxxi.

In the person of an artful trombone, lurks and dodges round the corner, waiting for some traitor tradesman to reveal the place and hour of the wedding-breakfast for a bribe.

BAND. The, taking part in election. *P.P.* xvi.

BAND OF MUSIC. In pasteboard caps. *P.P.* xv.

BAND OF PENSIONERS. Captain and Lieutenant of. *M.P.*, *M.B.V.*

BANDOLINING ROOM. At Mugby Junction. *C.S.*, *M.J.* v.

It's led to by the door behind the counter, which you''ll notice usually stands ajar, and it's the room where our missis and our young ladies Bandolines their hair.

BANDS OF HOPE. Juvenile. *M.P.*, *F.F.*

BANGER. CAPTAIN, A vestryman. *R.P.*, *O.V.*

BANGHAM. Mrs., Charwoman and messenger. *L.D.* vi.

Who was not a prisoner (though she had been once) but was the popular medium of communication with the outer world.

BANGOR. *M.P.*, *E.S.*; and *U.T.* ii.

BANJO BONES. Mr., A professional at the Snug. *U.T.* v.

Comic favourite—looking very hideous with his blackened face and limp Sugar-loaf hat.

BANJO BONES. Mrs., Wife of Mr. Banjo Bones. *U.T.* v.

In her natural colours—a little heightened.

BANK. The. Coketown. *H.T.*, *R.* i.

Red brick house, with black outside shutters, green blinds inside, a black street door up two white steps, a brazen door plate, and a brazen door handle full stop.

BANK IN SALISBURY. *M.C.* v.

BANK. In Venice. *L.D.* xlii.

BANK. Mill Pond. *G.E.* xlvi.

BANK OF ENGLAND. *B.R.* lxvii.; *C.S.*, *G.S.*; *D.S.* xiii.; *L.D.* xxvi.; *M.C.* xxxvii.; *M.P.*, *E.T.*; *M.P.*, *I.M.*; *N.N.* xxxv.; *P.P.* lv.; *U.T.* ix.

BANK. The, and National Credit Office. *M.C.* xxiii.

BANK CLERK. Tim Linkinwater's friend. The Superannuated. *N.N.* xxxvii.

BANKER. Banker at *Rouge-et-noir* table. *N.N.* I

A plump, paunchy, sturdy-looking fellow, with his under-lip a little pursed from a habit of counting money inwardly as he paid it.

BANKS. Major. An old East India Director. *H.D.* iv.

BANKS. *U.T.* xxi.

BANQUO. Character in Play. *S.B.B.*, Scenes xiii.

Snuff-shop looking figure.

BANTAM. Angelo Cyrus. *P.P.* xxxv.

Dressed in a very bright blue coat with resplendent buttons, black trousers, and the thinnest possible pair of highly polished boots. A gold eye-glass was suspended from his neck by a short broad black ribbon; a gold snuff-box was lightly clasped in his left hand; gold rings innumerable glittered on his fingers; and a large diamond pin, set in gold, glistened in his shirt frill. He had a gold watch, and a gold curb chain with large gold seals; and he carried a pliant ebony cane with a heavy gold top. His linen was of the very whitest, finest, and stiffest; his wig of the glossiest, blackest, and curliest. His snuff was prince's mixture; his scent *bouquet du roi*. His features were contracted into a perpetual smile; and his teeth were in such perfect order that it was difficult at a small distance to tell the real from the false.

Note.—The Grand Master at Ba-ath is of secondary importance, but is an example of Dickens' faculty of introducing a character "full grown." Bantam is Bantam and could be nobody else, and no other could be Bantam. The above description is of interest, as it contains one of Dickens' errors, which occurs in stating Bantam's cane to have been pliant ebony.

BANVARD. Mr. *M.P.*, *A.P.*; and *M.P.*, *E.T.*

BAPS. Mr., Dancing master at Dr. Blimbers. *D. and S.* xiv.

BAPS. Mrs., Wife of dancing master. *D. and S.*, xiv.

BAPTISTE. Billeted on the poor water-carrier. *C.S.*, *S.L.* ii.

Sitting on the pavement, in the sunlight—his martial legs asunder, one of the water-carrier's spare pails between them, which he was painting bright-green outside and bright-red within.

BAPTISTERY. Parma. *P.F.I.*, *P.M.B.*

BAPTISTERY. The, Pisa. *P.F.I.*, *R.P.S.*

"**BAR.**" Guest of Mr. Merdle. *L.D.* xxi.

With the jury droop, and persuasive eye-glass.

BARBADOES. *D.S.* xiii.; and *M.P.*, *L.A.V.* v.

BARBARA. One of Kit's children. *O.C.S.* Chap. The last

BARBARA. The Garland's maid. *O.C.S.* xxii.

A little servant girl, very tidy, modest and demure, but very pretty too.

Note.—The servant at Mr. Garland's where she first enters the story. She makes friends with Kit and his mother and the other members of the family and eventually marries Kit.

BARBARA'S MOTHER. *O.C.S.* xxxix.

BARBARY. Miss, Godmother and aunt of Esther Summerson. *B.H.* iii.

She was a good, good woman. She went to Church three times every Sunday, and to morning prayers on Wednesdays and Fridays. She was handsome; and if she had ever smiled would have been like an angel—but she never smiled.

Note.—Miss Barbary resided at Windsor where Esther stayed with her until her death. Presumably she was the sister of Lady Dedlock, to which entry reference may be made.

BARBARY.. Mrs. Captain. *L.D.* xii.

BARBARY CORSAIRS. *P.F.I.*, *G.A.N.*

BARBER. *C.S.*, *H.H.*

BARBER. *C.S.*, *M.H.C.*

BARBER. *C.S.*, *S.L.*

BARBER. The talkative = Praymiah. *M.P.*, *T.O.H.*

BARBICAN. *B.R.* viii.; *L.D.* xiii.; *M.C.* xxxvii.; and *O.T.* xxi.

One of the narrow streets which

diverged from that centre, from the main street, itself little better than an alley, a low-browed door-way led into a blind court or yard, profoundly dark, unpaved, and reeking with stagnant odours.

BARBOX BROTHERS. The firm of. *C.S., M.J.* ii.

Had been some off-shoot or irregular branch of the Public Notary, and bill-broking tree.

BARBOX BROTHERS. Mr. Jackson. *C.S., M.J.*, i.

A man within five years of fifty either way, who had turned grey too soon, like a neglected fire; a man of pondering habit, brooding carriage of the head, and suppressed internal voice.

Note.—Mr. Jackson is the last member of the firm. He has been disappointed and resolves to travel. He alights on the impulse of the moment at Mugby Junction. The experiences and adventures he goes through from that time have a beneficial effect on his character, and so compensate him for his earlier disappointment.

BARCLAY AND PERKINS. Brewers. *D.C.* xxviii.

BARDELL. Master Tommy, The son of Mr. Pickwick's landlady. *P.P.* xii.

Note.—Master Tommy appears on several occasions, but does not occupy a very important place in the story. His most noticeable appearance is probably that in the "trial" scene.

BARDELL. Mrs. Martha, Mr. Pickwick's landlady; and the plaintiff in Bardell v. Pickwick. *P.P.* xii.

The relict and sole executrix of a deceased custom-house officer.

Note.—Mrs. Bardell was Mr. Pickwick's landlady. Possibly because the wish was father to the thought, she jumped to the conclusion that, when Mr. P. was gently breaking the news to her that he proposed engaging a manservant (Sam Weller), he was proposing to her. This led to the famous trial Bardell v. Pickwick in chap. xxxiv. Mrs. Bardell is imprisoned by Dodson and Fogg for costs, but is released on Mr. Pickwick's paying them.

BARGE. A lime. *N.T.* xxiv.

A white horse on a barge's sail, that barge is a lime barge.

BARGEMAN. A, Bradley Headstone *O.M.F.* li.

BARING. Mr. *M.P., T.B.*

BARING BROTHERS. *M.P., G.A.*; and *M.P., F.L.*

BARK. Lodging - house keeper and receiver of stolen goods. *R.P., D.W.I.F.*

BARK'S. Deputy. *R.P., D.W.I.F.*

BARKER. Owner of an assumed name *S.B.B.*, Scenes xiii.

BARKER. Phil. *O.T.* xxvi.

BARKER. R. B. *M.P., S.B.*

BARKER. William. *S.B.B.*, Scenes xvii.

Assistant waterman to the Hackney Coach Stand, and later 'Bus Conductor. A distant relative of a waterman of our aquaintance—weakness in his early years—a love of ladies, liquids, and pocket-handkerchiefs.

BARKING CREEK. *R.P., D.W.T.T.*

BARKIS. Clara Peggotty. *See* Peggotty.

BARKIS. Mr., Carrier. *D.C.* ii.

Of a phlegmatic temperament, and not at all conversational.

Note.—The carrier who sent his message "Barkis is willin'," to Peggotty by little David. He married Peggotty, and when he died left his money to her.

BARKLEMYS. *M.C.* xlix.

BARKS. Light screw, At Chatham. *U.T.* xxiv.

BARKSHIRE. *D. and S.* xxxvi.

BARLEY. Miss Clara. Clara. *G.E.* xlvi.

Pretty, gentle, dark-eyed girl.

BARLEY. Old Mr., Clara's father. *G.E.* xlvi.

BARLOW. Mr., A tutor. *U.T.* xxxiii.

Irrepressible, instructive monomaniac.

"**BARLOW.**" Mr. Gifts on Christmas tree. *R.P., A.C.T.*

BARMAID. Of the "George and Vulture." *P.P.* xxxi.

BARMAID. At "Town Arms." *P.P.* xiii.

"Bribed to hocus the brandy and water of fourteen unpolled electors as was a stoppin' in the house."

BARMAIDS. In gin palace. *S.B.B.* xxii.

Two showily - dressed damsels with large necklaces.

BARMECIDE. *M.P., T.O.H.*

BARNACLE. Clarence, Tite Barnacle's son. *L.D.* xvii.

The born idiot of the family—most agreeable and most endearing blockhead!—with a kind of cleverness in him too.

BARNACLE. Ferdinand, Private Secretary to Lord Decimus. *L.D.* xlviii.

The sprightly young Barnacle.

BARNACLE. John. *L.D.* xxvi.

BARNACLE. Junior, Son of Mr. Tite-Barnacle. In Circumlocution Office. *L.D.* x.

Had a youthful aspect, and the fluffiest little whisker, perhaps, that ever was seen.

BARNACLE. Lord Decimus Tite, Pilot of the ship-circumlocution office. *L.D.* xiii.

In the odour of circumlocution—with the very smell of despatch-boxes upon him.

BARNACLE. Mr. Tite, High in the Circumlocution Office. *L.D.* x.

He wound and wound folds of white cravat round his neck, as he wound and wound folds of tape and paper round the neck of the country. His wristbands and collar were oppressive, his voice and manner were oppressive.

BARNACLE. Tom, Dick, or Harry. *L.D.* xxvi.

BARNACLE. William. *L.D.* xxvi.

BARNACLE FAMILY. The Tite, *L.D.* ix.

The Barnacle family had for some time helped to administer the Circumlocution Office. The Tite-Barnacle Branch, indeed, considered themselves in a general way as having vested rights in that direction, and took it ill if any other family had much to say to it.

BARNACLES. Less distinguished Parliamentary. *L.D.* xxxiv.

BARNACLES. Three other young. *L.D.* xxxiv.

Insipid to all the senses, and terribly in want of seasoning.

BARNARD. Sir Andrew. *M.P., C.C.*

BARNARD CASTLE. *N.N.* vii.

BARNARD'S INN. Young Mr. Pocket's rooms. *G.E.* xx.

The dingiest collection of shabby buildings ever squeezed together in a rank corner as a club for tomcats.

BARNET. *B.H.* vi.; *O.T.* vii.; *U.T.* xiv.

BARNEY. One of Fagin's confederates. *O.T.* xv.

Waiter in a low public house in Saffron Hill.

Note.—Barney is one of those casual elusive characters for which Dickens was so famous. He appears to have neither beginning nor end in the story. As his name implies, he was a Jew. He was engaged at the Three Cripples, and always spoke through his nose.

BARNSTAPLE. *C.S., M.f.T.S.* v.

BARNUM. Mr. *M.P., Th. Let.*

BARNUM'S HOTEL. Baltimore. *A.N.* ix.

BARNWELL. George. *R.P., A.C.T. P.P.* x.; *G.E.* xv.; *M.C.* ix.; *S.B.T.* v.

BARNWELL. Benjamin Bailey. *M.C.* ix.

BARON. A. *M.P., S.D.C.*

BARON. A lusty young, Son of Baron von Koëldwethout. *N.N.* vi.

In whose honour a great many fireworks were let off, and a great many dozens of wine drunk.

BARONESS. Young, Daughter of Baron von Koëldwethout. *N.N.* vi.

BARRACK CABARET. *P.F.I., L.R.G.A.*

BARRACKS. The, Room in. *B.R.* lviii.

A stone-floored room, where there was a very powerful smell of tobacco, a strong thorough draught of air, and a great wooden bedstead.

BARRIERS. *M.P., N.Y.D.*

BARRISTERS. *S.B.B.*, Scenes xxiv.

BARRONEAU. Monsieur Henri (Publican of the Cross of Gold) *L.D.* i.

Sixty-five at least, and in a failing state of health, had the misfortune to die.

BARRONEAU. Madame, widow of M. Henri Barroneau *L.D.* i.

She was two-and-twenty, had gained a reputation for beauty, and was beautiful. Unfortunately the property of Madame Barronneau was settled on herself.

BARROW. Sir John. *M.P., L.A.V.* ii.

BARRY. *M.P., R.S.L.*

BARRY'S PALACE. Sir Charles. *M.P., M.P.*

BARSAD. John. The assumed name of Solomon Pross, *which see.*

BART. *See* Smallweed, Bartholomew.

BARTHÈLEMY. *M.P., M.E.*

BARTHOLOMEW. Deceased brother of Philip Pirrip. *G.E.* i.

BARTHOLOMEW CLOSE. *G.E.* xx.

BARTHOLOMEW FAIR. *M.P., J.G.*

BARTHOLOMEW'S. Nursing Institution. *M.C.* xxv.

BARTLEY. Mr. *M.P., R.S.L.*

BARTON. Mr. Jacob, brother of Mrs. Malderton *S.B.B.*, Tales v.

A large grocer—never scrupled to avow that he wasn't above his business.

BARTON. Mr. *S.B.B.*, Tales v.

BASINGSTOKE. *C.S. H.T.* i.

BASLE. *C.S., N.T.*, Act iii.

BASS. Thin-faced man in black. *S.B.B.*, Scenes ii.

He can go down lower than any man. So low sometimes that you can't hear him.

BASTILLE. *M.P., C.S.; M.P., W.H.; M.P., W.S.G.; T.T.C.*, bk. ii., ch. xxi.

So resistless was the force of the [human] ocean bearing him on . . . he was landed in the outer courtyard of the Bastille. (*T.T.C.*)

BATES. Belinda. *C.S., H.H.*

A most intellectual, amiable and delightful girl, has a fine genius for poetry, goes in for woman's mission, woman's rights, woman's wrongs.

BATES. Charles. *O.T.*, ix.

Note.—Bates was one of Fagin's "pupils." In spite of his trade and surroundings he was a jolly boy always laughing. After Sikes' crime and Fagin's execution he relinquished his former life, and, "from being a farmer's drudge, and a carrier's lad, he is now the merriest young grazier in all Northamptonshire."

BATH. *B.H.* xxviii.; *M.P., L.L.*; and *P.P.* xxxv.

BATTENS. Mr., a Titbull Pensioner. *U.T.* xxvii.

This old man wore a long coat, such as we see Hogarth's chairmen represented with—of that peculiar green-pea hue without the green, which seems to come of poverty.

BATTERSEA. *C.B., H.M.* i.; and *R.P., D.W.T.T.*

BATTERY GARDENS. New York. *A.N.* vi.

BATTERY. Old, on the Marshes. *G.E.* i.

BATTLE BRIDGE. *D. and S.* xxxi.; *M.P., R.H.F.*; *O.M.F.* iv.; *O.T.* xxxi.; and *S.B.B.*, Scenes xx.

BATTLE MONUMENT. Baltimore. *A.N.* ix.

BATTY. *M.P., M.B.V.*

BAUDI. Countess Cornelia de. *B.H.*, Pref. and xxxiii.

BAVARIAN COUNTESS. A Pilgrim to Rome. *P.F.I.*, *R.*

BAY OF BISCAY. *D. and S.* xxxix.

BAY OF FUNDY. *A.N.* ii.

BAY o' NAPLES. *R.P.*, *G.o.A.*

BAYSWATER. *U.T.* x.

BAYTON. Mrs. To be buried parochially. *O.T.* v

BAZAAR. In Soho Square, London *M.P.*, *N.Y.D*

BAZANCOURT. M. de. *M.P.*, *S.F.A.*

BAZZARD. Mr. Mr. Grewgious's Clerk. *E.D.* xi.

BEADLE. *L.D.* ii.

If there is anything that is not to be tolerated on any terms—a type of Jack-in-office insolence and absurdity—that represents in coats, waistcoats, and big sticks, our English holding-on by nonsense, after every one has found it out, it is a beadle.

BEADLE. *B.H.* xi.; and *P.P.* xvii.

BEADLE. A. *B.H.* iv.

BEADLE. A portentous in the Church where Paul Dombey was christened. *D. and S.* v.

BEADLE. Of Church where Walter and Florence are married. *D. and S.* lvii.

BEADLE. Of some deceased old Company. *U.T.* ix.

BEADLE. Of the Tallow Chandlers' Company. *M.P.*, *M.B.V.*

BEADLE. Coroner's. *U.T.* xviii.

BEADLE. Under of the Worshipful Company of Tallow Chandlers. *M.P.*, *M.B.V.*

BEADLE. Harriet. *See* Tattycoram.

BEADLE'S SON-IN-LAW. *M.C.* xxv.

BEAK. A Magistrate. *O.T.* viii.

BEAN. Mrs. *M.P.*, *S.R.*

"**BEAR YE ONE ANOTHER'S BURTHENS.**" *M.P.*, *O.S.*

BEAR. Prince, At war with Prince Bull. *R.P.*, *P.B.*

BEARER. A *M.C.* xix.

BEARER. Nat., Captain of a Merchantman. *C.S.*, *H.H.*

A thick-set wooden face, and figure—an intelligent man, with a world of watery experiences in him.

BEARERS. Of sedan chair, Two. *B.R.* xxiii.; also *P.P.* xxxvi.

BEAST MARKET. A. *R.P.M.O.F.F.*

BEATRICE. Polly's mother. *C.S.*, *M.J.* iv.

A careworn woman, with her hair turned grey.

BEAUFORD PRINTING House. *C.S.*, *S.L.* iv.

BEAUTY. Famous. *M.P.*, *C.P.*

BEAUVAIS. *T.T.C.*, Book iii., Chap. i.

But when they came to the town of Beauvais he could not conceal from himself that the aspect of affairs was very alarming.

BEAVERTON, BOONE CO. Ill., U.S. *M.P.*, *S.F.A.*

BEBELLE. Playful name for Gabrielle. *Which see.*

BECKWITH. Alfred. *H.D.* iii.

BEDFORD. *D. and S.* lx.

BEDFORD. The. *D. and S.* xli.

BEDFORD ROW. *S.B.B.*, Scenes xvi.; and *U.T.* xiv.

BEDFORD SQUARE. *M.P.*, *A.P.*; *S.B.B.*, Tales v.

BEDFORD STATION. *M.P.*, *R.S.*

BEDFORD STREET. *M.P.*, *W.S.G.*

BEDLAM. *B.H.* xlvii.; *B.R.* lxvii.; *C.B.*, *C.C.*, *S.* i.; *C.B.*, *C.H.* ii.; *L.D.* lxvii.; *M.P.*, *K.C.*; and *MP.* *W.H.*

BEDLAMITE. *D. and S.* xxvii.

BEDWIN. Mrs., Mr. Brownlow's housekeeper. *O.T.* xii.

A motherly old lady, very neatly and precisely dressed.

Note.—Mrs. Bedwin was a kindly old soul, who had great difficulty in believing any evil of Oliver, and welcomed him back on his restoration.

BEECHER. Rev. Charles. *M.P., R.S.D.*

BEECHER. Rev. Henry Ward. *M.P., R.S.D.*

BEECROFT. Mr., Pilot. *M.P., N.E.*

BEEF HOUSE. A LA MODE. *D.C.* xi.

" **BEER.**" The nine o'clock. *S.B.B.*, Scenes ii.

Comes round with a lantern in front of his tray.

BEETHOVEN. *M.P., O.L.N.O.*

BEFILLAIRE. Colonel, Character in a novel read by Kate Nickleby to Mrs. Wititterly. *N.N.* xxviii.

BEGGING-LETTER WRITER. *R.P., T.B.W.*

BEGGING - LETTER WRITER. Brother of. *R.P., T.B.W.*

BEGGING LETTER WRITER. Wife of. *R.P., T.B.W.*

BEGS. Mrs. Ridger, late Miss Micawber. *D.C.* xxxiv.

BEINGS. Such. *S.B.B.*, Scenes iii.

Who can walk from Covent Garden to St. Paul's Churchyard and back into the bargain without deriving some amusement—instruction—from his perambulation—and yet there are such. Large stocks and light waistcoats, jet canes and discontented countenances, are the characteristics of the race.

BELGIAN VILLAGES. *R.P., N.S.*

BELGIUM. *M.P., C.P.* ; and *U.T.* xxv.

BELGRAVE SQUARE. *N.N.* xxi ; *P.F.I., G.T.F.* ; and *R.P., O.T.*

BELGRAVIA. *M.P., F.C.* ; and *M.P., S.D.C.*

BELGRAVIAN BORDERS. *O.M.F.* xx.

BELINDA. A correspondent of Master Humphrey's. *M.H.C.* ii.

BELINDA. Mrs. Matthew Pocket —*which see.*

BELINDA. Mrs. Walter Waters. *S.B.B.*, Tales iv.

BELIZE. *C.S., P.o.C.E.P.*

BELL & CO. Oxford Street. *M.P., W.R.*

BELL YARD. A narrow alley. *B.H.* xiv.

BELLA. Refer to Wilfer, Bella.

BELLA. Housemaid of Miss Pupford. *C.S., T.T.G.* vi.

BELLA. The younger prisoner about to enter prison van. *S.B.B.*, Char. xii.

BELLA. Baby, Daughter of John and Bella Rokesmith. *O.M.F.* lxii.

BELLA. Isola. *P.F.I., V.M.M.S.S.*

BELLAMY'S. *S.B.B.*, Scenes xviii.

BELLE. Spirit of. *C.B., C.C.* s. ii.

BELLE. Spirit of husband of. *C.B., C.C.* s. ii.

BELLE SAVAGE. *P.P.*x.

" Parish ? " says the lawyer. " Bell Savage," says my father ; for he stopped there wen he drove up, and he know'd nothing about parishes, *he* didn't."

BELLER. Henry, Convert to temperance. *P.P.* xxxiii.

For many years toast-master at various Corporation dinners ; during which time he drank a great deal of foreign wine ; is out of employ now ; and never touches a drop of foreign wine by any chance.

BELLEVILLE. *A.N.* xiii.

A small collection of wooden houses, huddled together in the very heart of the bush and swamp.

BELLING. Master, A Taunton boy, pupil of Mr. Squeers. *N.N.* iv.

On the trunk was perched—his lace-up half-boots and corduroy trousers dangling in the air—a diminutive boy, with his shoulders drawn up to his ears, and his hands planted on his knees.

Note.—Belling was a natural child confided to the tender mercies of the Yorkshire schoolmaster:

BELLOWS. Fictitious name of correspondent leaving gift for the father of the Marshalsea. *L.D.* vi.

" **BELLOWS,**" Brother. Guest of Mr. Merdle. *L.D.* xxi.

BELLOWS. Mrs. *M.P., S.Pigs.*

BELLS. The. *Chimes, 3rd quarter.*

BELLS. The men who play. *D. and S.* xxxi.

Have got scent of the marriage, —are practising in a back settlement near Battle Bridge.

BELL TOTT. Miss Bell Tott. *C.S.*; *P.o.C.E.P.*

BELL TOTT. Mrs. Bell Tott. *C.S., P.o.C.E.P.*

BELMORE. Mr. G., as Mr. Bintry. *M.P., N.Y.*

BELVAWNEY. Miss, Member of Mr. Crummles' Company. *N.N.* xxiii.

Seldom aspired to speaking parts, and usually went on as a page, in white silk hose, to stand with one leg bent, and contemplate the audience, or twisting up the ringlets of the beautiful Miss Bravassa.

Note.—A member of Crummles' company. Looked with some favour on Nicholas, and when he hinted at his departure, " actually shed tears."

BELVILLE. Assumed name. *S.B.B.*, Scenes xiii.

BEN. *Laz. Tour.*

BEN. Guard of mail from London. *O.T.* xlviii.

BEN. Negro-slave. *A.N.* xvii.

BEN. Waiter at inn in Rochester. *C.S., S.P.T.* i.

BENBOW. Admiral. *R.P., O. of the S.*

" **BENCH.**" Guest of Mr. Merdle. *L.D.* xxi.

BENCHERS. Old. *B.H.* i.

Blue-nosed, bulbous-shoed.

BENEDICT. Mr. *M.P., M.M.*

BENGAL. *D.S.* viii.; *P.P.* lvii.; and *R.P., T.B W.*

BENJAMIN. *B.R.* viii

BENJAMIN. Thomas, Suitor in a divorce suit. *D.C.* iv.

Under an ingenious little statute (repealed now, I believe, but in virtue of which I have seen several marriages annulled) The husband had taken out his marriage licence as Thomas only. *Not* finding himself as comfortable as he expected, he now came forward, by a friend, after being married a year or two, and declared that his name was Thomas Benjamin, and therefore he was not married at all. Which the court confirmed.

BENNETT. Mr. George. *S.Y.G., Theat.*

BENNETT. Dr. Sterndale. *M.P., M.M.*

BENNETT. Mr. W. Actor. *M.P., M.B.*

BENNETT. As George Edmunds. *M.P., V.C.*

BENSON. Lucy. *M.P., V.C.*

BENSON. Old. *M.P., V.C.*

BENSON. Young. *M.P., V.C.*

BENTING. *M.P., S.R.*

BENTON. Miss, Housekeeper to Master Humphrey. *M.H.C.* i.

BERBERNI. *P.F.I., R.*

BERINTHIA. Mrs. Pipchin's middle-aged niece. *D. and S.* viii.

Possessing a gaunt and iron-bound aspect, and much afflicted with boils on her nose.

BERKELEY. Assumed name. *S.B.B.*, Scenes xiii.

BERKELEY. Mr. = Bob Tample. *M.P., G.D.*

BERKELEY HEATH. *P.P.* l.

BERKELEY SQUARE. London. *M.P., N.Y.D.*

BERMONDSEY. *L.D.*, Pref.; and *R.P., a.F.*

BERNERS STREET. *M.P., W.S.P.*; and *S.B.B.*, Char. ix.

BERRY. *See* Berinthia.

BERTHA. Dolls' dressmaker. *C.B., C.o.H.* ii.

Blind daughter of Caleb Plummer.

BERWICK. Miss Mary. *M.P., A.A.P.*

BERWICK. *R.P., O.H.F.*; and *S.B.B.*, Tales viii.

BEST AUTHORITY. *M.P., B.A.*

BETHEL CHAPEL. *S.B.B.*, Char. ix.

BETHEL. Little. *O.C.S.* lxi.

BETHLEHEM HOSPITAL. *U.T.* xiii.

BETHNAL GREEN. *O.M.F.* xliii.; and *U.T.* x.

BETHNAL GREEN ROAD. *O.T.* xxi.

BET. BETSY. Fagin's accomplice. *O.T.* ix.

Wore a good deal of hair, not very neatly turned up behind.

Note.—One of Fagin's female thieves and on rather friendly terms with Tom Chitling.

BETLEY. Mr. *C.S., Mrs. L.Lo.*

BETSEY. *M.P., N.G.K.*

BETSEY. Maid of Britain (Mr. and Mrs.). *C.B., B.o.L.* iii.

BETSEY JANE. Mrs. Wickham's uncle's child. *D. and S.* viii.

As sweet a child as I could wish to see. Everything that a child could have in the way of illness, Betsey Jane had come through. The cramps was as common to her, said Mrs. Wickham, " as biles is to yourself, Miss Berry."

BETSEY. Miss. *See* Trotwood Miss Betsey.

BETSY. Betsy White. *U.T.* v.

BETSY. A black woman (slave). *A.N.* xvii.

BETSY. Mrs. Cluppins. *P.P.* xvli.

BETSY. Bob Sawyer's maid. *P.P.* xxxii.

A dirty slipshod girl in black cotton stockings, who might have passed for the neglected daughter of a superannuated dustman in very reduced circumstances.

BETSY. *See* Quilp, Mrs.

BETTERTON. *M.P., R.S.L.*

BEULAH SPA. *S.B., S.v., T.x.*

BEVAN. Boarder at Pawkins'. *M.C.* xvi.

A middle-aged man, with a dark eye, and a sunburnt face . . . something very engaging and honest in the expression of his features.

Note.—A contrast to most of those Martin meets in America; a good friend who provides the necessary money for the return of Martin and Mark Tapley to England.

BEVERLEY. Mr. *M.P., G.F.*

BEVERLEY. Mr., Otherwise Loggins. *S.B.B.*, Scenes xiii.

BEVIS MARKS. In the city of London. *O.C.S.* xi.

Note.—The locality of the office of Sampson Brass and his sister Sally.

BIANCHINI. Prebendary of Verona. *B.H.* Pref.; and *B.H.* xxxiv.

BIB. Mr. Julius Washington Merryweather. *M.C.* xxxiv.

A gentleman in the lumber line.

" **BIBLES.** The Three." A Publisher's place on London Bridge. *M.H.C.* iii.

BIBO. *B.H.* xxxii.; and *M.P. L.E.J.*

BICKLE, BUSH AND BODGER. *U.T.* xiv.

BIDDY. Mr. Wopsle's Great-Aunt's Grand-daughter. *G.E.* vii.

Her hair always wanted brushing, her hands always wanted washing, and her shoes always wanted mending and pulling up at heel. On Sundays she went to Church elaborated.

Note.—She is introduced in her grandmother's little general shop and school. When the old lady conquered a " confirmed habit of living," Biddy came to the forge to nurse Pip's sister, Mrs. Gargery. Pip is much taken with Biddy, but when his fortunes improve he overlooks her. In the meantime she has become a schoolmistress. When later he would make amends he finds she has become Joe's second wife on the death of the first.

BIFFINS. Miss. *N.N.* xxxvii; and *M.C.* xxviii.

BIG BIRD. Indian brave. *M.P., E.T.*

BIG CANOE. An Indian Chief. *A.N.* ix.

BIG GRAVE CREEK. *A.N.* xi.

BIGBY. Mrs., Mrs. Meek's mother. *R.P., B.M.S.*

BIGWIG FAMILY. *R.P., N.S.*
Composed of the stateliest people thereabout.

BILBERRY. Lady Jemima. *L.D.* xvii.

BILER. Toodles, Robin—*which see.*

BILKINS. *M.P., W.*

BILKINS. An Authority on Taste. *R.P., O.F.W.*

BILL. Driver of Omnibus. *S.B.B.*, Scenes xvi.

BILL. A Turnkey. *P.P.* xli.
Very old, of No. 20, Coffee Room Flight.

BILL. Aggerawatin, Bill Borker. *S.B.B.*, Scenes xvii.

BILL. Black, Prisoner in Newgate. *G.E.* xxxii.

BILL. My. Melia's husband. *G.E.* xx.

BILL. Plain, Alphonse. *N.N.* xxi.

BILL. Uncle, At Tea Gardens. *S.B.B.*, Scenes ix.

BILL. Uncle, Niece of in Tea Gardens. *S.B.B.*, Scenes ix.

BILLICKIN. Mrs., Lodging-house keeper. *E.D.* xxii.
Personal faintness and overpowering personal candour were the distinguishing features of Mrs. Billickin's organization.
Note.—A casual character. Rosa Bud's landlady and widowed cousin of Mr. Bazzard, clerk to Mr. Grewgious.

BILLINGS. Ann, A spirit. *M.P., S.B.*

BILLINGSGATE. *G.E.* liv. ; *L.D.* vii. : and *M.P., N.J.B.*

BILLINGTON. Mr., as Mrs. Walter Wilding. *M.P., N.T.*

BILLINGTON. Mrs., as the Veiled Lady. *M.P., N.T.*

BILLSMETHI. Signor, Of the King's Theatre, Teacher of dancing. *S.B.B.*, Char. ix.

BILLSMETHI. Master. *S.B.B.* Char. ix.

BILLSMETHI. Miss, Daughter of Billsmethi. *S.B.B.*, Char. ix.

BILLSMETHI. Fourteen pupils of *S.B.B.*, Char. ix.
Who danced a grand Sicilian shawl-dance. The most exciting thing that ever was beheld—such a whisking, rustling and fanning, and getting ladies into a tangle with artificial flowers and then disentangling them again.

BILLSMETHI. Pupil of Signor. *S.B.B.*, Char. ix.
In brown gauze over white calico.

BILLSTICKERS. King of the. *R.P., B.S.*
A good-looking little man of about fifty, with a shining face, a tight head, a bright eye, a moist wink, a quick speech, and a ready air. The oldest and most respected member of the " old school of bill sticking."

BILLSTICKERS. Father of the King of the. *R.P.B.S.*
Was Engineer, Beadle, and Billsticker to the Parish of St. Andrew's, Holborn. Employed women to post bills for him.

BILSON AND SLUM. Commercial House. *P.P.* xiv.

BILSTON. *M.P., F. and S.*

BINKLE. Lady Fitz. *S.B.B.*, Scenes xiv.

BINTRY. Mr., Solicitor. *C.S., N.T.*, Act i.
A cautious man with twinkling beads of eyes in a large overhanging bald head.

BINTRY. Mr. *M.P., N.T.*

BIRD FANCIERS. *S.B.B.*, Scenes v.

BIRDS. The Prisoners in Marseilles prison. *L.D.* i.

BIRMINGHAM. A Drysalter. George Silverman's Guardian. *G.S.E.* iii.

BIRMINGHAM. Mr. and Mrs. *U.T.* xxii.
Host and Hostess of the Lord Warden Hotel.

BIRMINGHAM. *B.R.* lxxxii.; *D. and S.* xx.; *M.H.C.* iii.; *M.P., Ag. Int.*; *M.P., E.S.*; *M.P., F. and S.*; *M.P., M.E.R.*; *N.N.* xxvii.; *O.T.* xlviii.; *P.P.* l.; *R.P., P.M.T.P.*; *R.P., T.D.P.*

BIRMINGHAM. Intelligent workmen of. *M.P., E.T.*

BIRMINGHAM. Member for. *M.P., S.S.*

BIRMINGHAM. Town Hall. *M.P., Ag. Int.*

BIRMINGHAM TUNNEL. *M.P., F. and S.*

BIRTHDAY CELEBRATION. Heroine of. *U.T.* xix.

Peach-faced creature in a blue sash, and shoes to correspond.

BISCUIT BAKER'S DAUGHTERS. Fourteen, from Oxford Street. *N.N.* xlix.

"**BISHOP.**" Guest of Mr. Merdle. *L.D.* xxi.

BISHOP. A. *P.P.* xvii.

Once, and only once in his life Nathaniel Pipkin had seen a bishop—a real bishop with his arms in lawn sleeves, and his head in a wig.

"**BISHOP MAGNATE.**" Guest of Mr. Merdle. *L.D.* xxi.

BISHOP OF LONDON. *M.P., G.B.*

BISHOPS. An Extra Waiter. *C.S., S.L.* i.

By calling a plate-washer.

BISHOP'S STORTFORD. *M.P., E.S.*

BISHOPSGATE STREET. *B.R.* lxxvii.; ans *M.P., W.*

BISHOPSGATE STREET WITHIN. *N.N.* ii.

BISHOPSGATE STREET WITHOUT *D. and S.* ix.

BITHERSTONE. Pupil at Dr. Blimber's. *D. and S.* viii.

No longer Master Bitherstone of Mrs. Pipchin's—in collars and a neckcloth, and wears a watch.

BITHERSTONE. Bill, Father of Master Bitherstone *D. and S.* x.

His friend (Major Bagstock's) who had written to ask him, if he ever went that way (Brighton) to bestow a call upon his only son.

BITZER. A Pupil at Coketown. *H.T.* ii.

Light-eyed, and light-haired, after wards Light Porter, and then clerk at Bounderby's Bank in Coketown.

Note.—Introduced early in the book as a special example of the pupils in Gradgrind's school, from which all fancy is eliminated, and in which fact, fact, fact is taught. After leaving school he is employed in Bounderby's Bank where Tom Gradgrind occupies a higher position. Tom robs the bank, and Bitzer discovers it. In the hope of being given Tom's post he captures the culprit and almost succeeds in securing him. It is only due to Sleary that he fails. Nevertheless Bitzer becomes the "show young man" of Josiah Bounderby.

BISCAY. Bay of. *S.B.B.*, Scenes x.

BIZAGNO. The river. *P.F.I., G.A.N.*

BLACK. A Constable. *R.P., D.W.I.F.*

"**BLACK BADGER.**" The. *D. and S.* xxii.

"**BLACK BOY.**" At Chelmsford. *P.P.* xx.

BLACK COUNTRY. Round about Birmingham. *U.T.* xxiii.

BLACK HOLE. Regimental Prison. *C.S., S.P.T.* ii.

"**BLACK LION.**" Inn. *B.R.* xiii.

Instructed the artist who painted his sign to convey into the features of the lordly brute, whose effigy it bore, as near a counterpart of his own face (the landlord's), as his skill could compass, and devise—supposed to be the veritable portrait of the host as he appeared on the occasion of some great funeral ceremony or public mourning.

"**BLACK LION.**" Landlord of the. *B.R.* xxxi.

Note.—Landlord of the inn of the same name. He could only see things from one point of view, that of his pocket, and had no regard for glory as represented by the army.

BLACK. Mrs., One of Mrs. Lemon's pupils. *H.R.* iv.

" **BLACK** " or " Blue Boar " or " Bull." *U.T.* iii.

BLACK SEA. *M.P., S.F.A.*

BLACKBIRD. Joseph. *M.P., P.M.B.*

BLACKBOY AND STOMACHACHE. *Mudfog papers 2nd meet.*

BLACKBOY. Mr., A Fictitious name. *D.C.* ii.

Elaborately written on lid of a box carried by Mr. Barkis, containing his hoards and labelled, " Mr. Blackboy, to be left with Barkis till called for."

BLACKBURN. *G.S.E.* v .; *M.P.O.S.*

BLACKDASH. *M.P., W.*

BLACKEY. A Beggar. *R.P., D.W.I.F.*

Who stood near London Bridge these five and twenty years, with a painted skin to represent disease.

BLACK-EYED SUSAN. *M.P., N.Y.D.*

BLACKFRIARS. *B.R.* xlix. ; *D.C.* xi. ; *R.P., D.W.T.T.*

BLACKFRIARS BRIDGE. *B.H.* xix. ; *D.C.* xvii. ; *G.E.* xlvi. ; *L.D.* xii. ; *S.B.B.*, Scenes xv.

BLACKFRIARS BRIDGE. Toll Houses on. *B.R.* lxvii.

BLACKFRIARS ROAD. *B.H.* xxvii.

BLACKHEATH. Home of Mr. and Mrs. Rokesmith. *O.M.F.* liv.

A modest little cottage, but a bright and fresh, and on the snowy tablecloth the prettiest of little breakfasts.

Also *C.S., S.P.T.* ; *D.C.* xiii. ; *U.T.* vii. *See also* Salem House.

BLACK-MAN. A Greyhaired. *M.C.* xvii.

BLACKMORE. Mr., Entertainer in Vauxhall Gardens. *S.B.B.*, Scenes xiv.

BLACKPOOL. Stephen. A Mill Hand. *H.T.* x.

A rather stooping man, with a knitted brow, a pondering expression of face, and a hardlooking head, sufficiently capacious, on which his iron-grey hair lay long and thin. Forty years of age—looked older.

Note.—He is married to a woman who proves a drunkard and ruins his home. He turns to Rachael for comfort, but cannot marry her. He is a hand in Mr. Bounderby's factory, but when the others unite he will not join them, but because he does not agree with Mr. Bounderby in running them down he is discharged. Every man's hand is against him in Coketown and he leaves to look for work elsewhere. He is accused of robbing the bank, and on his way back to refute the charge he falls down a disused shaft. After some days he is rescued, but he has suffered such injuries that he dies. His name is cleared by the discovery that the theft was committed by young Gradgrind.

BLACKPOOL. Wife of Stephen. *H.T.* x.

Such a woman ! a disabled drunken woman—a creature so foul to look at, in her tatters, stains and splashes . . . dangling in one hand, by the string, a dunghill fragment of a bonnet.

BLACKPOT. =Blackpool. *H.T., R.* viii.

BLACKSMITH. *M.P., B.*

BLACKSTONE. Lawyer. *M.P., C.P.*

BLACKWALL. *M.P., C.J.* ; *R.P., T.D.P.* ; *S.B.B.*, Scenes x.

BLACKWALL RAILWAY. *R.P., T.D.P.* ; *U.T.* ix.

BLACKWOOD. Messrs., Mercers. *M.P., S.P.*

BLADUD. Prince, Founder of the public baths in Bath. *P.P.* xxxvi.

The illustrious Prince being afflicted with leprosy—shunned the Court of his royal father, and consorted moodily with husbandmen and pigs—Among the herd was a pig of solemn countenance. This sagacious pig was fond of bathing in rich moist mud. The prince resolved to try the purifying qualities. He washed and was cured. Hastening to his father's court, he paid his best respects, and returning founded the city and its famous baths.

BLAIZE. Madame. *M.P., C.P.*

BLAKE. Jim, Runaway Negro Slave. *A.N.* xvii.

BLAKE. Mr. Warmint. *S.Y.G.*

BLANDOIS. M. *See* Rigaud, Monsieur.

BLANK. Mr. *Mudfog Papers.*

BLANK BLANK. The Reverend. *O.M.F.* x.

BLANK. Mount. Mont Blanc. *C.S., H.T.*
So-called by Americans.

BLANKSHIRE. *M.P., W.*

BLANQUO. Pierre, A Guide. *R.P., O.B.*

BLATHERS. Bow Street Officer. *O.T.* xxxi.

A portly man in a great-coat—a stout personage of middle height, aged about fifty: with shiny black hair, cropped pretty close; half whiskers, a round face, and sharp eyes.

Note.—Bow Street officers engaged on the attempted burglary at Mrs. Maylie's house. Blathers and Duff have wonderful theories, but they do not meet with much success.

BLAZE AND SPARKLE. Jewellers. *B.H.* ii.

BLAZES. M. Tuckle *P.P.* xxxvii.

BLAZO. Sir Thomas, Jingle's opponent in a cricket match in the West Indies. *P.P.* vii.

BLEAK HOUSE. Near to St. Alban's. *B.H.* i.

What seemed to be an old-fashioned house, with three peaks in the roof in front, and a circular sweep leading to the porch.

One of those delightfully irregular houses where you go up and down steps out of one room into another, and where you come upon more rooms when you think you have seen all there are—a bountiful provision of little halls and passages—where you find still older cottage-rooms in unexpected places, with lattice windows and green growth pressing through them.

BLEEDING HEART YARD. *L.D.* ix.

No inappropriate destination for a man who had been in official correspondence with my lords and the Barnacles—and perhaps had a misgiving also that Britannia herself might come to look for lodgings in Bleeding Heart Yard.

Note.—The yard in which Casby's property lay, and where Doyce and Clennam had their office in the neighbourhood of Hatton Gardens.

BLESSINGTON. LADY. *M.P., L.L.*

BLIGH. *M.P., L.A.V.* ii.

BLIGH. Captain, Of the "Bounty." *R.P., T.L.V.*

BLIGHT. Mortimer Lightwood's Clerk. *O.M.F.* viii.
Dismal boy.

BLIMBER. Doctor. *D. and S.* xi.

A portly gentleman in a suit of black, with strings at his knees, and stockings below them. He had a bald head, highly polished; a deep voice; and a chin so very double, that it was a wonder how he ever managed to shave into the creases. He had likewise a pair of little eyes that were always half shut up, and a mouth that was always half expanded into a grin.

Note.—The proprietor of the school to which Paul Dombey was sent was an educational gardener of the forcing variety. He produced mental fruit at all seasons of the year. This he did from a sense of duty, as he was always sufficiently kind to the ten pupils he took. Curiously enough there are seventeen boys shown in the illustration of the pupils enjoying themselves. The Dr. is last seen at Mrs. Feeder's wedding.

BLIMBER'S HOUSE. Doctor. *D. and S.* xi.

A mighty fine house, fronting the sea. Not a joyful style of house within, but quite the contrary. Sad-coloured curtains, whose proportions were spare and lean, hid themselves despondently behind the windows. The tables and chairs were put away in rows, like figures in a sum: fires were so rarely lighted in the rooms of ceremony, that they felt like wells, and a visitor represented the bucket.

BLIMBER'S SCHOOL. Dr. *D. and S.* xi.

Was a great hot house, in which there was a forcing apparatus incessantly at work. Mental green peas were produced at Christmas, and intellectual asparagus all the year round. Mathematical gooseberries (very sour ones too) were common at untimely seasons, and from mere sprouts of bushes, under Doctor Blimber's cultivation. Every description of Greek and Latin vegetable was got off the driest twigs of boys under the frostiest circumstances. No matter what a young gentleman was intended to bear, Doctor Blimber made him bear to pattern somehow or other.

BLIMBER. Mrs., Doctor Blimber's wife. *D, and S.* xi.

Was not learned herself, but she pretended to be, and that did quite as well. She said at evening parties that if she could have known Cicero, she thought she could have died contented.

BLIMBER. Miss Cornelia, Doctor Blimber's daughter. *D. and S.* xi.

A slim and graceful maid. She kept her hair short and crisp, and wore spectacles. She was dry and sandy with working in the graves of deceased languages. None of your live languages for Miss Blimber. They must be dead—stone dead—and then Miss Blimber dug them up like a ghoul.

BLINDER. Chandler's shop, name of. *B.H.* xiv.

BLINDER. Bill (deceased), An hostler. *M.H.C.* iv.

Had charge of them two well-known piebald leaders.

BLINDER. Mrs. *B.H.* xv.

A good-natured-looking old woman, with a dropsy or an asthma, or perhaps both.

BLINKINS. Mr., Latin Master at Our School *R.P., O.S.*

BLOCKADE MAN. At Ramsgate. *S.B.B.*, Tales iv.

BLOCKITT. Mrs., Mrs. Dombey's nurse. *D. and S.* i.

A simpering piece of faded gentility, who did not presume to state her name as a fact, but merely offered it as a mild suggestion.

BLOCKSON. Mrs., Charwoman employed by Knags. *N.N.* xviii.

Employed in the absence of the sick servant and remunerated with certain eighteenpences to be deducted from her wages due.

BLOGG. Mr., The Beadle of Poorhouse. *O.M.F.* xvi.

BLOODY ISLAND. *A.N.* xiii.

The dwelling-ground of St. Louis.

BLOOMER. Mrs. Colonel. *M.P., F.F.*; *M.P., S.Pigs.*

BLOOMSBURY SQUARE. *E.D.* xv .; *M.H.C.* i.

BLOOMSBURY SQUARE. Lord Mansfield's House in. *B.R.* lxvi.

BLORES. Mrs., Wooden Leg Walk, Tobacco Stopper Row, Wapping. *M.P., G.A.*

BLOSS. Mr., Deceased husband of Mrs. Bloss. *S.B.B.*, Tales i.

BLOSS. Mrs., Relict of the departed Bloss. *S.B.B.*, Tales i.

A boarder at Mrs. Tibbs.

In a pelisse the colour of the interior of a damson pie; a bonnet of the same, with a regular conservatory of artificial flowers; a white veil, and a green parasol with a cobweb border. Mrs. Bloss was very fat and red-faced, an odd mixture of shrewdness and simplicity, liberality and meanness.

BLOSSOM. Little, Dora. *D.C.* xii.

BLOTTON. Mr., Member of the Pickwick Club. *P.P.*, i.

With a mean desire to tarnish the lustre of the immortal name of Pickwick, actually undertook a journey to Cobham, in person, to disprove the antiquity of the inscription on the famous stone found at Cobham.

Note.—Mr. Blotton of Aldgate is one of the earliest characters in the *Pickwick Papers*, but he drops out of the narrative

BLOWERS. Mr., " Eminent Silk gown." *B.H.* i.

Said " Such a thing might happen when the sky rained potatoes."

BLUBB. Mr. *Mudfog Papers, 2nd meet.*

BLUE ANCHOR ROAD. *C.S., S.L.* i.

" **BLUE BOAR.** The," An Inn. *G.E.* xiii.

" **BLUE BOAR.**" Leadenhall Market. *P.P.* xxxiii.

BLUE CANDIDATE. The Hon. Mr. Slumkey. *P.P.*, li.

BLUE DRAGON. Sign before Village Ale-house door. *M.C.* ii. and iii.

A faded, and an ancient dragon he was ; and many a wintry storm of rain, snow, sleet, and hail, had changed his colour from a gaudy blue to a faint lack-lustre shade of grey. But there he hung ; rearing, in a state of monstrous imbecility, on his hind legs.

BLUE FISH. Indian brave. *M.P., E.T.*

BLUE LION AND STOMACH WARMER. *S.B.B.*, Tales viii.

" The Lion " Inn at Great Winglebury.

BLUE LION AND STOMACH WARMER. Upper Boots of the. *S.B.B.*, Tales viii.

A man thrust in a red head with one eye in it, and being asked " to come in " brought in the body and the legs to which the head belonged, and a fur cap which belonged to the head.

BLUE LION INN. Muggleton. *P.P.* vii.

BLUE LION STREET. *M.P., G.H.*

BLUEBOTTLE. Mrs. *S.Y.C.*

BLUES. Parliamentary Candidates. *P.P.* xiii.

BLUFFY. Mr. George. *B.H.* xxvii.

BLUMB. Of the Royal Academy. *R.P., O.B.*

BLUNDER-BRITON. A Vestry, man. *R.P., O.V.*

BLUNDER-SNOZZLE. A Vestry-man. *R.P., O.V.*

BLUNDERBORE. A legendary being. *P.P.* xxii.

The ferocious giant Blunderbore was in the habit of expressing his opinion that it was time to lay the cloth, Ha Hum !

BLUNDERBORE. Capt. *Mudf. Papers 2nd meet.*

BLUNDEREM. Mr. *Muf. Papers. 1st meet.*

BLUNDERSTONE. In Suffolk. *D.C.* i.

Note.—The village in Suffolk where David Copperfield was born.

BLUNDERSTONE CHURCH. *D.C.* ii.

What a high-backed pew ! With a window near it.

BOAR. Squires of The. *G.E.* lviii.

Landlord of the Blue Boar.

" **BOAR'S HEAD.**" *M.C.* xxxviii.

BOARD. The, Administrators of Parish relief. *S.B.B., O.P.* i.

All sit behind great books, with their hats on.

BOARD. Of the Workhouse. *O.T.* ii.

Eight or ten fat gentlemen . . . very sage, deep, philosophical men.

BOARD. The Treasury. *D. and S.* lxi.

BOARD OF HEALTH. *M.P., P.T.*

" **BOARD OF HONOUR.** The." *A.N.* xvii.

BOARDING-HOUSE. The. *S.B.B.*, Tales i.

There were meat-safe looking blinds in the parlour windows, blue and gold curtains in the drawing room, and spring roller blinds all the way up.

BOAT. Releasing passengers from Quarantine. *L.D.* ii.

Was filled with the cocked hats to which Mr. Meagles entertained a natural objection.

BOATMAN. At Broadstairs. *R.P.*; *O.W.P.*

BOATMEN. *O.C.S.* iii.

BOB. *S.B.B.*, Tales ix.

BOB. Bob Redforth. *H.R.* i.

BOB. Guard of Early Coach. *S.B.B.*, Scenes xv.

BOB. The Marshalsea Turnkey. *L.D.* vii.

Note.—Turnkey at the Marshalsea. A favourite of Mr. Dorrit's and god-father to little Dorrit. It is for Bob Mr. Dorrit calls when in his last illness he thinks himself back in the Marshalsea.

BOB. Runaway Slave of J. Surgette. *A.N.* xvii.

BOB. Tom, Servant of English Prime Minister. *M.P.*, *W.*

BOBADIL. Captain. *M.P.*, *R.S.D.*

Note.—Dickens' acting part.

BOBBO. In love with Seraphina's Sister. *C.S.*, *M.L.Lo.* ii.

BOBBS AND CHOLBERRY. *M.C.* xliv.

BOBSTER. Mr., Father of Miss Cecilia. *N.N.* xl.

Note.—The father of the young lady whom Newman Noggs mistook for Madeline Bray. Nicholas was desirous of discovering the identity of the beautiful visitor of the Cheeryble Brothers, and Newman watched for the servant, but he followed the wrong person.

BOBSTER. Miss Cecilia. *N.N.* xl.

An only child, her mother was dead; she resided with her father.

Note.—Miss Cecilia was persuaded by Newman to see his friend and let him plead his cause. Newman had made the unfortunate mistake of following the wrong person and thought that Miss Bobster was Madeline Bray. Nicholas and Newman were admitted into a back kitchen or cellar, and just as the mistake had been discovered Bobster knocked thunderously at the front door.

BOCCACCIO'S HOUSE. *P.F.I.*, *R.D.*

BOCKER. Tom. *O.M.F.* ix.

BODDLEBOY. *M.P.*, *T.B.*

BODGER. *M.P.*, *I.*

BODLEIAN LIBRARY. *M.P.*, *T.O.H.*

BOFFER. Expelled the Exchange. *P.C.* lv.

BOFFIN. Henrietty, Wife of N. Boffin. *O.M.F.* v.

A stout lady of a rubicund and cheerful aspect, dressed in a low evening dress of sable satin, and a large velvet hat and feathers. A Highflyer at Fashion.

Note.—The wife of the Golden Dustman. A motherly old soul, who, when they inherit the Harmon money, flies high at fashion. She befriends Bella Wilfer, and when she recognises John Harmon in Rokesmith enters heartily into the scheme to bring him and Bella into closer touch. After the marriage and the settling down of the young couple Mr. and Mrs. Boffin are left staying with them indefinitely.

BOFFIN. Father of Mrs., named Henery. In the Canine Provision Trade. *O.M.F.* v.

BOFFIN. Mother of Mrs., named Hetty. *O.M.F.* v.

BOFFIN. Nicodemus. *O.M.F.* v.

A broad, round-shouldered, one-sided old fellow in mourning, dressed in a pea overcoat and carrying a large stick. He wore thick shoes, and thick leather gaiters and thick gloves like a hedger's—with folds in his cheeks, and his fore-head, and his eyelids, and his lips, and his ears; but with bright, eager, childishly-enquiring grey eyes, under his ragged eyebrows, and broad-brimmed hat.

Note.—The illiterate but good-hearted servant of John Harmon. Harmon leaves his property to his son on condition that he marries Miss Bella Wilfer; in the event of his not doing so the property falls to Noddy Boffin. Young John Harmon returns from Africa, to fulfil the conditions of the will, but disappears immediately on his arrival, and a drowned body in the Thames is identified as his. As a result of this Boffin inherits the great wealth of his old master. One of his first acts is to offer a large reward, through Mortimer Lightwood, for the identification of the murderer of John Harmon. The supposed murdered man is not dead, however, and enters Boffin's employment as private secretary. Bella Wilfer is adopted by the Boffins and they are thrown together. Rokesmith (the name assumed by John Harmon) falls in love with her.

BOFFIN'S BOWER. *O.M.F.* v.

A charming spot, is the Bower. It is a spot to find out the merits of, little by little, and a new 'un every day. There's a serpentining walk up each of the mounds, that gives you the yard and neighbourhood changing every moment. When you get to the top, there's a view of the neighbouring premises, not to be surpassed. And the top of the High Mound is crowned with a lattice-work arbour.

BOFFIN'S EQUIPAGE. The driver of. *O.M.F.* ix.

A long hammer-headed young man—had been formerly used in the business, but was now entombed by an honest jobbing tailor of the district in a perfect sepulchre of coat and gaiters sealed with ponderous buttons.

BOGSBY. Mr. James George. *B.H.* xxxiii.

Landlord of the "Sol's Arms."

BOGUEY. Old. Mr. Krooks. *B.H.* xxxii.

BOGUS. Mr. and Mrs. *U.T.* vi.

BOHEME. *M.P., R.S.L.*

BOILED BEEF OF NEW ENGLAND. *U.T.* xxiii.

BOILER. "Boanerges." *U.T.* ix.

BOILER MAKER. *U.T.* xxx.

Wife of out-of-work. She did slop-work; made pea-jackets—she got for making a pea-jacket, tenpence-halfpenny, and she could make one in something less than two days.

BOKUM. Widow of Mr., dearest friend of Mrs. Macstinger. *D. and S.* lx.

BOLBY. A Policeman. *U.T.* iii.

BOLDER. Little. Pupil at Dotheboy's Hall. *N.N.* vii.

An unhealthy-looking boy, with warts all over his hands.

BOLDER'S FATHER. Father of one of Squeers' pupils. *N.N.* viii.

"Two pound ten short."

BOLDHEART. Capt. *H.R.* iii.

BOLDWIG. Captain, Sir Geoffrey Manning's neighbour. *P.P.* xix

A little fierce man, in a stiff black neckerchief, and blue surtout, who when he did condescend to walk about his property, did it in company with a thick rattan stick with a brass ferule, and a gardener, and sub-gardener, with meek faces, to whom (the gardeners, not the stick) Captain Boldwig gave his orders with all due grandeur and ferocity.

Note.—Captain Boldwig is an imperious gentleman with high ideals regarding the sacred nature of land and game. Mr. Pickwick, who was temporarily lame, had been left in a barrow by his friends, while they continued their sport. It appeared they were trespassing, however, and Mr. Pickwick was discovered by the captain and his keepers asleep after too much cold punch. As the keeper was unable to wheel the somnolent Pickwick to the "devil"—the first destination proposed by Boldwig—he took him to the pound, where the redoubtable founder of the Pickwick Club was found by his friends. (*See* Muggleton, etc.)

BOLES. Miss. *M.P., N.Y.D.*

BOLES. Mr. *M.P., N.Y.D.*

BOLES. Mrs., Wife of Mr. Boles. *U.T.* xii.

BOLES'S. A School of Boles. *U.T.* xii.

BOLO. Miss, One of Whist Party at Assembly Rooms, Bath. *P.P.* xxxv.

Of an ancient and whist-like appearance.

BOLOGNA. *P.F.I., P.M.B.*

BOLOGNA CEMETERY. *P.F.I.*

BOLSENA. Lake of. *P.F.I., R.P.S.*

BOLTER. Morris, Mr. and Mrs. The names assumed by Noah Claypole and Charlotte in their dealings with Fagin. *See* Claypole, Noah and Charlotte.

BOLTON. Mr. Robert, *S.B.B.*, *R.B.*

BOMBAY. *M.P.*, *O.P.* ; *P.F.I.* *V.M.M.S.S.* ; *R.P.*, *A.C.T.*

BONAPARTE. Napoleon. *C.S.*, *M.J.* ; *C.S.*, *S.P.T.*, *U.T.* xii.

BOND STREET. *D. and S.*, xxxi. ; *M.P.*, *I.M.* ; *N.N.* xxxii. ; *O.M.F.* lviii. ; *S.B.B.*, Tales v. ; *U.T.* xvi.

BONDSMAN. An Hereditary. *S.B.B.*, Scenes xviii.

An Irish Correspondent of an Irish Newspaper.

BONDY. Forest of. *M.P.*, *A.P.*

BONES. Mr., Banjo. *See* Banjo Bones, Mr.

" **BONNET**." A friend of the Dwarf at a gaming-booth. *C.S.*, *G.i.S.*

BONNET. Father of. *C.S.*, *G.i.S.* In the livery-stable line.

BONNEY. Mr. Promoter of United Metropolitan Improved Hot Muffin and Crumpet Baking and Punctual Delivery Company. *N.N.* ii.

A pale gentleman with his hair standing up in great disorder all over his head, and a very narrow cravat tied loosely round his throat. Taking off a white hat which was so full of papers that it would scarcely stick upon his head.

BONNY. African Town. *M.P.*, *N.E.*

BONOMI. Mr. *M.P.*, *E.T.*

BOOBY. The.. The last of the Patriarchs. *L.D.* xiii.

Drifting Booby, much as an unwieldy ship on the Thames river may sometimes be seen heavily driving with the tide—making a great show of navigation.

BOODLE. *M.P.*, *W.*

BOODLE. Lord. *B.H.* xii.

BOOKING OFFICE CLERK. At " White-horse Cellar." *P.P.* xxxv.

BOOKSTALL KEEPER. *O.T.* xi. An elderly man of decent but poor appearance, clad in an old suit of black.

BOOLEY. Mr., Extraordinary traveller. *M.P.*, *C.M.B.* ; *M.P.*, *E.I.* *M.P.*, *M.B.V.*

BOON ISLAND. *M.P.*, *L.A.V.* ii.

BOONE CO. Ill., U.S. *M.P.*, *S.F.A.*

BOORKER. Bill, William Barker. *S.B.B.*, Scenes xvii.

" **BOOT.** The." A tavern. *B.R.* xxxvii.

A lone house of public entertainment situated in a field at the back of the Foundling Hospital—a very solitary spot and quite deserted after dark.

BOOTH. *M.P.*, *R.S.L.*

BOOTH. An immense, At Greenwich Fair. *S.B.B.*, Scenes xii. With the large stage in front, so brightly illuminated with variegated lamps.

BOOTH. The Circus. *H.Ts.*, *S.* vi.

BOOTJACK. The, and Countenance. *Mud. Pap.* ii.

BOOTLE. *M.P.*, *E.S.*

BOOTS. *S.B.B.*, Tales viii.

BOOTS. At Inn. *M.C.* xlii.

BOOTS. Guest of Veneerings. *O.M.F.* ii.

" **BOOTS.**" The, of " Holly Tree Inn." *C.S.*, *H.T.*

BOOZEY BILL. A mutinous sailor. *H.R.* iii.

BOOZLE. *S.Y.G.*

BOOZLE. Earl of. *M.P.*, *N.G.K.*

BOOZLE. Castle. *M.P.*, *N.G.K.*

BO-PEEP POLICE OFFICE. *M.P.*, *G.B.*

BORDEAUX. *M.P.*, *H.J.B.* *U.T.* xxiii.

BORE. Our. *R.P., O.B.*
He may put fifty people out of temper, but he keeps his own.

BOROUGH.
B.R. lxxxii.; *L.D.* lxx.; *M.S., E.S.*; *R.P., D.W.I.F.*; *U.T.* xiii.

BOROUGH. Sequestered pot-shop in. *P.P* lii.

" **BOROUGH.**" King's Bench Prison *D.C.* xi.

BOROUGH CLINK. *B.R.* lxvii.

BOROUGH HIGH STREET. *L.D.* xxxvi., *P.P.* xxi.

BOROUGH MARKET. *P.P.* xxxiii.

BOROUGHBRIDGE. *N.N.* xiii.

BORRIOBOOLA-GHA. *B.H.* iv.

BORRIOBOOLA. King of. *B.H.* lxvii.
Wanting to sell everybody.

BORUM. Mr., Patron of Mr. V. Crummles' Company. *N.N.* xxiv.

BORUM. Mrs., Wife of Mr. Borum. *N.N.* xxiv.

BOSTON U.S.A. *A.N.* i.; *M.P., I.C.*; *M.P., R.S.D.*; *M.P., S.B.*; *R.P., T.D.P.*; *U.T.* iii.; *U.T.* xxiii.

BOSTON. South. *A.N.* iii.

BOSTON BANTAM = James Ripley Osgood. *M.P., I.W.M.*

BOSTON MELODEON. *M.P., S.B.*

BOSWELL COURT. *S.B.B.*, Tales vii.

BOSWORTH FIELD. *G.E.* xv.

BOTANY BAY. *N.N.* xli.

BOTELER. ... *M.P., R.S.L.*

BOTTLE-OF-BEER. *M.P., N.E.*

BOTTLES. Stable-man. *C.S., H.H.*
Deaf tenant of haunted house. A phenomenon of moroseness not to be matched in England.

BOUCLET. Madame, Concierge. *C.S., S.L.* ii
A compact little woman of thirty-five or so.

BOUCLET. Monsieur, Husband of Madame. *C.S., S.L.* ii.
Great at billiards.

BOUCLET. Husband, and two children of married sister of madame. *C.S., S.L.* ii.

BOUCLET. Nephew and book-keeper of. *C.S., S.L.* ii.
Who held the pen of an angel.

BOULEVARD. The. *M.P., N.Y.D.*; and *R.P., A.F.*

BOULEVARDE THEATRES. . *M.P., W.*

BOULOGNE. *S.B.B.*, Tales i.

BOUNDERBY. Mr., a Banker. *H.T.* iv.
A big loud man, with a stare, and a metallic laugh. A man made out of coarse material—with great puffed head and forehead, swelled veins in his temples, and such a strained skin to his face, that it seemed to hold his eyes open. Seven or eight and forty
Note.—Close *friend* of Gradgrind. Successful man in Coketown. He is interested in many concerns of magnitude and appeared to have all the faults without any of the redeeming features of the rich man. After he attains to riches he pays his mother to keep away, but she comes on occasion just to " take a proud peep " at him. He marries Louisa Gradgrind, but the union is an unhappy one. His wife is assailed by an accomplished man and flies to her father. Her husband insists on her return, but she does not comply, and he casts her off. He dies and leaves a will providing for " five and twenty humbugs."

BOUNDERBY. Father of. *H.T.* v.
Died when he (Bounderby) was eight years old.

BOUNDERBY. Mother of = Pegler, Mrs. *H.T.* s. iv.

BOUNDERBY. Grandmother of, kept a chandler's shop. *H.T.* s. iv.

BOUNDERBY. Loo, Née Louisa Gradgrind, *which see.*

BOURNE. Old. *E.D.* xi.

BOURSE. The. *M.P., R.D.*; and *O.M.F.* xxi.

BOUSEFIELD. William. *M.P., D.M.*

BOW. Little house at. *N.N.* xxxv.

BOW BELLS. *D. and S.* iv.

BOW STREET. Police Court. *O.T.* xliii.

The room smelt close and unwholesome, the walls were dirt-discoloured . . . a dusty clock above the dock. The only thing present which seemed to go on as it ought; for depravity, or poverty, or an habitual acquaintance with both, had left a taint, on all the animate matter.

Also *B.R.* lviii.; *M.P.*, *W.M.*; *S.B.B.*, Scenes xiv.; *S.B.B.*, Char. xi.; *U.T.* iv.

BOW STREET MEN. *G.E.* xvi.

BOWER. The. *O.M.F.* xv.

A gloomy house, with sordid signs on it of having been, through its long existence—in miserly holding—bare of paint, bare of paper on the walls, bare of furniture, bare of experience of human life.

BOWERY. The, Street in New York. *A.N.* vi.

BOWERY THEATRE. The, New York. *A.N.* vi.

BOWES. *See* Dotheboy's Hall.

BOWLEY. Sir Joseph. *C.B.*, *C.G.* ii.

I am the poor man's friend and father.

BOWLEY. My Lady, Wife of Sir Joseph Bowley. *C.B.*, *C.G.* ii.

A stately lady in a bonnet.

BOWLEY. Master, The heir of Bowley. *C.B.*, *C.G.* iii.

Son of Sir Joseph Bowley.

BOWLEY. Porter of Sir Joseph. *C.B.*, *C.G.* ii.

Underwent some hard panting before he could speak, his voice—a long way off, and hidden under a load of meat.

"**BOWLEY HALL,**" Residence of Sir Joseph Bowley. *C.B.*, *C.G.* iii.

BOWYER. Honest, a money-lender. *M.H.C.* i.

Was in the habit of lending money on interest to the gallants of the Court.

BOWYER. Sam'l, Workhouse inmate. *R.P.*, *W.I.A.N.*

BOXALL. *M.P.*, *L.L.*

BOY. King. *O.M.F.*; *M.P.*, *N.E.*

BOY. *Haunted Man*, i.

BOY. *L.D.*, Pref.

The smallest I ever conversed with, carrying the largest baby I ever saw, offered a supernaturally intelligent explanation of the locality in its old uses, and very nearly correct.

BOY. A rioter. *B.R.* lxxvii.

Hanged in Bow Street.

BOY. At George and Vulture. *P.P.* xxxiii.

A young boy of about three feet high, or thereabouts; in a hairy cap, and fustian overalls, whose garb bespoke a laudable ambition to attain, in time, the elevation of an hostler.

BOY. Carrying Tim Linkinwater's sister's cap. *N.N.* xxxvii.

BOY. Emerging from Fort at Chatham. *U.T.* xxiv.

A young boy, with an intelligent face burnt to dust colour by the summer sun, and with crisp hair of the same hue.

BOY. Errand, of Mr. Pickles. *H.R.* ii.

BOY. Ginger-beer, of the audience, in theatre. *N.N.* xxiv.

BOY. In common lodging-house in Liverpool. *U.T.* v.

Carefully writing a copy in a copying-book in the middle of the night.

BOY. In grey livery—of Sawyer's late Nockemorf. *P.P.* l.

Busily employed in putting up the shutters.

BOY. Inattentive, from inn in Rochester, with hot plates. *C.S.*; *S.P.T.*, i.

BOY. Little, In tea gardens *S.B.B.*, Scenes ix.

Diminutive specimen of mortality in the three-cornered pink satin hat with black feathers.

BOY. Little, Son of lady in distress. *S.B.B., O.P.* v.

BOY. Little, Walter and Florence Gay's. *D. and S.* lxii.

BOY. Living in back attic of No. 6, The Court. *N.N.* xl.

Hyacinths, blossoming in old blacking-bottles belong to a sickly bed-ridden hump-backed boy. There he lies, looking now at the sky, and now at his flowers, which he still makes shift to trim and water, with his own thin hands.

BOY. Monotonous, Theatre employé. *L.D.* xx.

BOY. Negro, Slave. *A.N.* xvii.

Had round his neck a chain dog-collar with De Lampert on it,

BOY. Of young medical practitioner. *S.B.B.*, Tales vi.

A corpulent round-headed boy, who in consideration of the sum of one shilling per week and his food, was let out by the parish to carry medicine and messages.

BOY. Patient in hospital. *P.P.* xxxii.

Said he wouldn't lie there to be made game of.

BOY. The prowling. *See* Pirip, Philip. *G.E.* xxi.

BOY. Queer small. *U.T.* vii.

BOY. Saved from the wreck. *M.P., S.W.*

BOY. Sharp. *M.P., S.S.U.*

BOY. Sharpest small. *M.P., B.S.*

BOY. Sir Jeoffrey Manning's. *P.P.* xix.

There's the boy with the basket as punctual as clockwork . . . taking from his shoulder a couple of large stone bottles fastened together by a leathern strap. Cold punch in t'other!

BOY. Small, In the fleet. *P.P.* xlv.

BOY. Small, Passenger in stage coach. *S.B.B.*, Scenes xvi

Of a pale aspect, with light hair, and no perceptible neck, coming up to town under the protection of the guard.

BOY. Son of brother of Lieutenant. *M.H.C.* ii.

Confided to care of lieutenant's wife.

BOY. Son of George and Mary. *P.P.* xxi.

The hard realities of the world, with many of its worst privations—hunger and thirst, and cold and want—had come home to him from the first dawnings of reason. "The child's young heart was breaking." The child was dead.

BOYLSTON SCHOOL. South Boston *A.N.* ii.

Asylum for neglected and indigent boys who have committed no crime.

BOYS. At tea gardens. *S.B.B.* xvi.

With great silk hats just balanced on the top of their heads, smoking cigars, and trying to look as if they liked them.

BOYS. Foundlings. *M.P., N.Y.*

BOYS. Gay old. *S.B.B.*, Char. vii.

Paunchy old men in the disguise of young ones—who assume all the foppishness and levity of boys, without the excuse of youth or inexperience.

BOYS. Interviewing Martin. *M.C.* xxii.

BOYS. New York paper. *M.C.* xvi.

BOYS. Seeing Mark Tapley off. *M.C.* vii.

BOYS. Steady old. *S.B.B.*, Char. vii.

Certain stout old gentlemen of clean appearance, who are always to be seen in the same taverns, at the same hours every evening, smoking and drinking in the same company.

BOYS. Two, Demanded money for the rioters. *B.R.* lxvii.

Armed with bars taken from the railings of Lord Mansfield's House.

BOYS. Two other, Pupils of Mr. Squeers. *N.N.* v.

BOYTHORN. Lawrence, School fellow of Mr. Jarndyce's. *B.H.* ix.

His head thrown back like an old soldier, his stalwart chest squared, his hands like a clean blacksmith's, and his lungs !—talking, laughing or snoring, they make the beams of the house shake . . . a very handsome old gentleman—with a massive grey head.

Note.—Friend of Mr. Jarndyce, residing in Lincolnshire. His land adjoined the estate of Sir Leicester Dedlock, with whom he had a standing feud as to a right of way. After Sir Leicester's misfortunes, Mr. Boythorn would have sunk his differences, but the baronet took this as pity, and so the feud had to be revived and continued.

" **BOZ.**" Pseudonym of Charles Dickens, *A.N.* xiv. ; *M.P.*, *E.C.* ; *S.B.B.O.P.* i.

BOZZOLO. *P.F.I.*, *V.M.M.S.S.*

BRA. Piazza di. *P.F.I.*, *V.M.M.S.S.*

BRACCO. Pass of. *P.F.I.*, *R.P.S.*

BRADBURY AND EVANS. Printing house of. *M.P.*, *M.E.R.*

BRAHAM. Mr., as Squire Norton. *M.P.*, *V.C.*

BRANDLEY. Mrs., A widow. *G.E.* xxxviii.

Complexion was pink . . . set up for frivolity.

BRANDLEY. Miss, Daughter of Mrs. Brandley. *G.E.* xxxviii.

Complexion was yellow . . . set up for theology.

BRANSCOMBE. Mr., as Jean Paul. *M.P.*, *N.Y.*

BRASS. Foxey, The father of Sampson and Sally. Dead. *O.C.S.* xxxvi.

BRASS. Sally, Sister to Sampson Brass. *O.C.S.* xxxiii.

A kind of amazon at common law . . . . a lady of about thirty-five or thereabouts, of a gaunt and bony figure . . . Miss Brass wore no collar or kerchief except upon her head, which was invariably ornamented with a brown gauze scarf.

Note.—The sister of Sampson Brass and, if that were possible, more villanous than he. She was his able partner in their business of attorney, and when he was ruined she too was seen " in the obscene hiding-places in London, in archways, dark vaults and cellars."

BRASS. Sampson, Mr. Quilp's lawyer. *O.C.S.* xi.

An attorney of no very good repute . . . he was a tall, meagre man, with a nose like a wen, a protruding forehead, retreating eyes, and hair of a deep red.

Note.—Brass, although himself a rogue, was the catspaw of Quilp, the dwarf. He was a disreputable attorney living in Bevis Marks, with his sister. At Quilp's command he engages Dick Swiveller as clerk. Ultimately his villanies and illegalities lead to his imprisonment with hard labour, after that he became a bird of evil omen haunting the byways of the city.

BRASS AND COPPER FOUNDER. *M.C.* ix.

Middle-aged gentleman with a pompous voice and manner.

BRASS PEOPLE. African tribe. *M.P.*, *N.E.*

BRATS. Two, " Farmed " out to branch workhouse. *O.T.* ii.

BRAVASSA. The beautiful Miss, Member of Mr. V. Crummles' Company. *N.N.* xxiii.

Had once had her likeness taken in character—whereof impressions were hung up for sale in the pastrycook's window, and the greengrocer's, and the circulating library, and the box office, whenever the announce bills came out for her annual night.

Note.—Usually went " on " in white silk hose as a page boy. Actually shed tears when Nicholas expressed the fear that he must leave the company.

BRAVE. The, The Courier. *P.F.I.*, *P.M.B.*

BRAY. Miss Madeline. *N.N.* xvi.

The beautiful girl who had so engrossed his (Nicholas Nickleby's) thoughts—seemed now a thousand times more beautiful Not nineteen

—dark eyes, long eyelashes, ripe and ruddy lips.

Note.—Nicholas first meets Madeline in the registry office, where he was immediately struck with her appearance. Later he recognises her at the Cheeryble brothers. Although not related to them, she was the daughter of a friend of theirs. Her mother had died early. Her father was one of those selfish, debased characters which Dickens could draw so well. He endeavoured to force her into a repulsive marriage with Gride. While Nicholas is preventing this as far as he is able, Bray dies in the floor above. Nicholas removes Madeline, in spite of all opposition, to his mother's and Kate's care. He afterwards marries her.

BRAY. Mr. Walter, Madeline Bray's father. *N.N.* xlvi.

He was scarce fifty, perhaps, but so emaciated as to appear much older. His features presented the remains of a handsome countenance.

Note.—The miserable and selfish debauchee, father of Madeline. He had so far forgotten his duty as a father that he endeavoured to force his daughter into a marriage with Gride. He dies suddenly just as his plan appears to be on the point of completion.

BRAY'S WIFE. Walter, Madeline's deceased mother. *N.N.* xlvii.

BRAZEN HEAD. The, of the Circumlocution Office. *L.D.* x.

BRAZIL. *M.P., L.A.V.* ii.

BREAK NECK STAIRS. Main approach to business of Wilding and Co. *C.S, N.T.*, Act i.

" **BREAK OF DAY.**" The. *L.D.* xi.

Curtained windows clouded the " Break of Day," but it seemed light and warm. There one could find meat, drink, and lodgings, whether one came on horseback, or came on foot.

" **BREAK OF DAY.**" Landlord of the. *L.D.* xi.

Who acted as cook.

" **BREAK OF DAY.**" Landlady of the. *L.D.* xi.

A smart, neat, bright little woman with a good deal of cap, and a good deal of stocking.

BREES. Mr. *M.P., E.T.*

BRENTFORD. *G.E.* xlii.; *M.P., M.M.*; *O.M.F.* xvi.; *O.T.* xxi.; *U.T.* x.

BRENTFORD. King of. *M.P., I.*

BREWER. Guest of Veneerings. *O.M.F.* ii.

BREWSTER. *M.P., R.S.D.*

BRICK. Mr. Jefferson, War Correspondent of Rowdy Journal. *M.C.* xvi.

A small young gentleman of very juvenile appearance, and unwholesomely pale in the face. He wore his shirt collar turned down over a black ribbon; and his lank hair, a fragile crop, was not only smoothed and parted back from his brow—but had, here and there, been grubbed up by the roots. He had that order of nose, on which the envy of mankind has bestowed the appellation " snub."

BRICK. Mrs. Jefferson. *M.C.* xvi. The matron in blue.

BRICK. Two young children of Mrs. Jefferson Brick. *M.C.* xvi.

BRICK. The, Fictitious name of correspondent leaving gift for Father of Marshalsea. *L.D.* vi.

BRICK LANE BRANCH. Of the united Grand Junction Ebenezer Temperance Association. *P.P.* xxxiii.

BRICKLAYER AND HIS FAMILY. *M.P., G.D.*

BRICKLAYER'S LABOURER. *S.B.B.*, Scenes v.

There they are in their fustian dresses, spotted with brick-dust and whitewash leaning against posts. We never saw a regular bricklayer's labourer take any other recreation, fighting excepted.

BRICKMAKER. *B.H.* viii.

All stained with clay and mud, lying at full length on the ground, smoking a pipe.

BRICKMAKER. Wife of.
B.H. viii.
A woman with a black eye, nursing a poor little gasping baby by the fire.

BRIDE. Lucretia. *D. and S.* v.

BRIDE. The, in a thin white dress.
S.B.B., Scenes vii.

BRIDE'S AUNT. Aunt of Sophronia Akershem. *O.M.F.* x.
A widowed female of a medusa sort, in a stony cap, glaring petrefaction at her fellow-creatures.

BRIDE'S TRUSTEE. *O.M.F.* x.
An oilcake-fed style of business-gentleman with mooney spectacles.

BRIDEGROOM. At wedding.
D. and S. v.

BRIDEGROOM. In hackney coach.
S.B.B., Scenes vii.
In blue coat, yellow waistcoat, white trousers, and Berlin gloves to match.

BRIDEGROOM. Chosen friend of, in hackney coach.
S.B.B., Scenes iii.

BRIDESMAID. *D. and S.* xxxi.
Distantly connected with the family . . . who so narrowly escaped being given away by mistake.

BRIDESMAID. In hackney coach.
S.B.B., Scenes vii.

BRIDESMAIDS. Of Cornelia Blimber. *D. and S.* lx.
Gauzy little bridesmaids.

BRIDESMAIDS. *O.M.F.* x.

BRIDEWELL.
B.R. lxvii. ; *R.P.*, *L.A.*

BRIDGE. *G.E.* xlvi.

BRIDGE. Canal. *U.T.* xviii.
See also Baker's Trap.

BRIDGE. The Iron. *L.D.* ix.

BRIDGE OF SIGHS.
P.F.I., *A.I.D.*

BRIDGE OF THE GANTHER.
C.S., *N.T.*, Act iii.

BRIDGE ROAD. *B.R.* xlviii.

BRIDGEMAN. Laura, Inmate of Blind Asylum. *A.N.* iii.
Blind, deaf and dumb girl.

BRIDGMAN. Mr. *A.N.* xvii.

BRIEG. Town. *C.S.*, *N.T.*, Actiii.

BRIG PLACE. *D. and S.* ix.

BRIGAND. Mr. Tupman in costume of. *P.P.* x.
A very tight jacket ; sitting like a pincushion over his back and shoulders : the upper portion of his legs encased in the velvet shorts, and the lower part thereof swathed in the complicated bandages to which all brigands are peculiarly attached.

BRIGGS. Pupil of Dr. Blimber.
D. and S. xii.
The stony pupil—sat looking at his task in stony stupefaction and despair . . . he would wish himself dead, if it weren't for his mother and a blackbird he had at home.

BRIGGS. Mr. Alexander, Brother of Samuel Briggs.
S.B.B., Tales vii.
Under articles to Mr. Samuel Briggs.

BRIGGS. Mr. Samuel, An attorney.
S.B.B., Tales vii.

BRIGGS. Mrs., A widow.
S.B.B., Tales vii.

BRIGGS. Mr. and Mrs.
S.Y.C. Egotistical

BRIGGS SENIOR. Father of pupil. at Dr. Blimber's. *D. and S.* xii.

BRIGGSES. The, family of.
S.B.B., Tales vii.

BRIGHT. Mr. John. *M.P.*, *T.B.*

BRIGHT CHANTICLEER = Boston Bantam. *M.P.*, *I.W.M.*

BRIGHTON. *B.H.* xiv. ; *D. and S.* viii. ; *M.P.*, *G.D.* ; *M.P.*, *N.S.* ; *N.N.*, l. ; *S.B.B.*, Tales iv. ; *U.T.* xi.
All the coaches had been upset. in turn, within the last three weeks ; each coach had averaged two passengers killed, and six wounded ; and in every case—no blame what-

ever was attributable to the coachman.

BRIMER. Mr., Fifth mate of the Halsewell. *R.P., T.L.V.*

BRINKLE. Lord Fitz, Chairman of Indigent Orphans' Friend's Benevolent Institution. *S.B.B.*, Scenes xix.

A little man, with a long and rather inflamed face, and grey hair brushed bolt upright in front. He wears a wisp of black silk round his neck, without any stiffener, as an apology for a neckerchief.

BRISTOL. *B.R.* lxxxi. ; *M.P., L.W.O.Y.* ; *P.P.* xxxviii. ; *U.T.* xx.

BRISTOL. Dean of in 1850. *M.P., L.W.O.Y.*

BRITAIN. Mrs., née Clemency Newcome. *C.B., B.O.L.* iii.

BRITAIN. Manservant of Doctor Jeddler. *C.B., B.O.L.* i.

A small man, with an uncommonly sour and discontented face.

Note.—The landlord of the "Nutmeg Grater," as Britain became, was known as "Little Britain."

BRITAIN. Great. *C.S., H.T.*

BRITAIN. Little, Benjamin Britain. *C.B., B.O.L.* i.

BRITAINS. Two Masters, Sons of Britain. *C.B., B.O.L.* iii.

BRITANNIA. The Captain of the. *A.N.* i.

A well-made, tight-built dapper little fellow, with a ruddy face.

BRITANNIA AT HOXTON. *U.T.* iv.

A gallery at threepence, another gallery at fourpence, a pit at sixpence, boxes and pit-stalls at a shilling, and a few private boxes at half-a-crown.

BRITISH LION. *M.P., B.L.*

BRITISH MUSEUM. *A.N.* xii. ; *L.D.* iii. ; *M.P., N.J.B.* ; *M.P., O.C.* ; *M.P., S.F.A.* ; *R.P., D.W.I.F.* ; *S.B.B.*, Scenes xxiii. ; *U.T.* xxiii.

BRITON. Old. A Juryman. *G.E.* xxv.

BRITTANY. *M.P., L.A.V.* ii.

BRITTEEN. = Britain. *M.P., T.O.H.*

BRITTLES. Lad of all work to Mrs. Maylie. *O.T.* xxviii.

Note.—One of Mrs. Maylie's servants. A rather weak-minded boy, who had been a "slow boy" for upwards of thirty years. Brittles "assisted" in the capture of Oliver after the burglary.

BRIXTON. *M.C.* xxvii. ; P.P. i. ; *S.B.B.*, Tales v. ; *U.T.* vi.

BROAD COURT. Bow Street. *N.N.* xxx.

BROAD STREET. Cross in. *N.N.* xxxi.

BROADWAY. The. *M.C.* xvi.

BROADWAY. The, New York. *A.N.* vi.

BROBINGNAY. *U.T.* xv.

BROBITY. Miss, Proprietress of a School. *E.D.* iv.

BROGLEY. Broker and appraiser. *D. and S.* ix.

Who kept a shop where every description of second-hand furniture was exhibited in the most uncomfortable aspect, and under circumstances and in combinations the most completely foreign to its purpose.

Mr. Brogley was a moist-eyed, pink-complexioned, crisp-haired man of a bulky figure and an easy temper.

BROGSON. Guest of Budden. *S.B.B.*, Tales iii.

An elderly gentleman in a black coat; drab knee-breeches, and long gaiters.

BROKER. A bill. *S.B.B., O.P.* vii.

BROKER. Neighbouring, of the Kenwigs. *N.N.* xvi.

BROKER. Stout, Visitor in Bar parlour. *S.B.B.*, Char. iii.

In a large waistcoat.

BROKER'S MAN. Mr. Bung. *S.B.B., O.P.* v.

BROKER'S MEN. In Fancy Stationer's. *S.B.B.*, Scenes iii.

Removing the little furniture there was in the house.

BROKERS' SHOPS. *S.B.B.*, Scenes xxi.

Strange places — would furnish many a page of amusement, and many a melancholy tale. The goods here are adapted to the taste, or rather the means, of cheap purchasers—a turn-up bedstead is a blunt, honest piece of furniture—ornament it as you will—seems to defy disguise—how different—a sofa-bedstead—it has neither the respectability of a sofa—nor the virtues of a bed. A small dirty shop exposing for sale the most extraordinary and confused jumble of old, worn out, wretched articles. Our wonder at their ever having been bought, is only to be equalled by our astonishment at the idea of their ever being sold again. Some half dozen high-backed chairs, with spinal complaints and wasted legs—pickle-jars, and surgeon's ditto—miscellanies of every description.

BROKERS' SHOPS. In Seven Dials. *S.B.B.*, Scenes v.

Which would seem to have been established by humane individuals, as refuges for destitute bugs.

BROMPTON. New, *Refer* to New Brompton.

BROMPTON. *N.N.* xxi.

BROOK STREET. Grosvenor Square. *D.and S.* xxx.; *U.T.* xvi.

BROOKE. Rajah. *M.P., P.F.*

BROOKER. Mr. *N.N.* xliv.

A spare dark withered man, with a stooping body and a very sinister face rendered more ill favoured by hollow and hungry cheeks deeply sunburnt; and thick black eyebrows, blacker in contrast with the perfect whiteness of his hair. Roughly clothed in shabby garments of a strange and uncouth make, and having about him an indefinable manner of depression and degradation.

Note.—The hand of Brooker is observable throughout the book, but it is only in the later chapters that he appears. He had been in Ralph Nickleby's employ, with, possibly a natural result, that he hated his master. Taking the opportunity when offered, he persuaded Ralph that his boy was dead. In reality it is in poor Smike, left at Squeers' school, that we find Ralph's boy; only to see his father hunt him and persecute him.

BROOKS'S. *D. and.S.* xli.

BROOKS. Pupil at Dotheboys' Hall. *N.N.* vii.

BROOKS. Hon. Preston S., Kansas *M.P., M.E.*

BROOKS. Mr., A Pieman; fellow-lodger of Wellers'. *P.P.* xix.

BROOKS. Of Sheffield. The name by which Murdstone referred to David Copperfield before he married Mrs. Copperfield, when in the company of his friends. *D.C.* ii.

BROOKS DINGWALLS. The. *S.B.B.*, Tales iii.

BROTHARTOON. Chamber candlestick. *M.P., T.O.H.*

BROTHER. A Lonely, of Josephine's. *H.T., G.* ix.

Died in hospital of fever—died in penitence and of love of you.

BROTHER. (Deceased) of Joey B. (Major Bagstock). *D. and S.* x.

BROTHER. Plymouth. *C.S., M.L. Leg.* i.

BROTHER of Passenger on Coach. *N.N.* v.

BROTHER SOLDIER. Who had served with Lieutenant. *M.H.C.* ii.

BROTHERS TWIN. The, Charles and Edwin Cheeryble—*which see.*

BROUGHAM. Lord. *M.P., F.C.*; *M.P., M.M.*, and *M.P., S.S.*

BROWDIE. John, Son of corn-factor. Miss Price's fiancé. *N.N.* ix.

His hair very damp from recent washing, and a clean shirt, whereof the collar might have belonged to some giant ancestor . . . together with a waistcoat of similar dimensions—something over six feet high.

Note.—A Yorkshire farmer, big and strong, but kindly and jolly. 'Tilda Price is a friend of Fanny Squeers, and John Browdie is betrothed to, and ultimately marries Miss Price; on his first meeting Nicholas, at a tea party with Miss Squeers—he is jealous, but Nicholas afterwards owes much to honest John, who becomes his good friend. Browdie assists at the break up of Dotheboy's Hall, and aids the boys with food and sundry sixpences and shillings.

BROWDIE. Mrs., née Price—*which see.*

BROWN. *P.P.* xxxix.

BROWN. Alice. *D. and S.* xxxiii.

A solitary woman of some thirty years of age; tall; well formed; handsome; miserably dressed; the soil of many country roads in varied weather—dust, chalk, clay, gravel, clotted on her grey cloak by the streaming wet; no bonnet on her head, nothing to defend her rich black hair from the rain, but a torn handkerchief.

Note.—Known as Alice Marwood, Alice Brown was first cousin to Mrs. Edith Dombey, and daughter of "Good" Mrs. Brown. She enters the story on her return from transportation, and is befriended by Harriet Carker. She leaves the tale on her death, still befriended by the same good woman.

BROWN. Conversation, at the Treasury Board. *D. and S.* lxi.

Four-bottle man—with whom the father of my friend Gay was probably acquainted.

BROWN. Of Muggleton. Maker of Miss Rachael Wardle's shoes. *P.P.* x.

BROWN. One of Mrs. Lemon's pupils. *H.R.* iv.

BROWN. Passenger on Gravesend Packet. *S.B.B.*, Scenes x.

BROWN. Captain John, of the Polyphemus. *D. and S.* iv.

BROWN. Emily. *S.B.B.*, Tales viii.

Married at Gretna Green to Horace Hunter.

BROWN. Fanny. *M.P.L.*

BROWN. Miss. *M.P.*, *S.P.*

BROWN. Mr. *M.P.*, *F.S.*

BROWN. Mr. *O.C.S.*, xxi.

Who was supposed to be then a corporal in the East Indies.

BROWN. Mr. *Mud. Pap.* ii.

BROWN. Mr. *S.B.B.*, Tales ix.

Plays the Violoncello.

BROWN. Mr. Henry. *S.B.B.*, *O.P.* vi.

BROWN. Mrs., Rag and bone vendor. *D. and S.* vi.

A very ugly old woman, with red rims round her eyes, and a mouth which mumbled and chattered of itself when she was not speaking. She was miserably dressed, and carried some skins over her arm.

Note.—The mother of Alice Marwood. She kidnaps Florence Dombey and steals her clothes. She leaves the story on the death of her daughter.

BROWN. Room—dark and ugly—of good Mrs. *D. and S.* xxxiv.

There was no light in the room save that which the fire afforded—a heap of rags, a heap of bones, a wretched bed, two or three mutilated chairs or stools, the black walls and blacker ceiling, were all its winking brightness shone upon.

BROWN. Tom. *M.P.*, *N.Y.B.*

BROWN AND CO. Misses. *S.B.B.*, *O.P.* vi.

BROWNDOCK. Miss, Kate Nickleby's father's cousin's sister-in-law. *N.N.* xvii.

Was taken into partnership by a lady that kept a school at Hammersmith—and made her fortune in no time at all. Was the same lady that got the ten thousand pounds prize in the lottery.

BROWNLOW. Mr. *O.T.* x.

A very respectable-looking personage, with powdered head and gold spectacles. He was dressed in a bottle-green coat, with a black velvet collar; wore white trousers; and carried a smart bamboo cane under his arm.

Note.—Mr. Brownlow was a benevolent old gentleman, who ultimately adopted Oliver Twist as his son. The introduction was effected by the Artful Dodger stealing Mr. Brownlow's pocket-handkerchief: Oliver is captured as the thief and taken to the magistrate's office, and doubtless would have been conveyed to prison but for the opportune arrival of a witness in the person of the bookseller. Mr. Brownlow takes Oliver home with him and tends him during his weakness, but he is recaptured by Nancy's aid. Mr. B. is greatly distressed by Oliver's non-return, and is forced to the conclusion that he must have decamped. Future events, however, reinstate Oliver in Mr. Brownlow's opinion, with the result already mentioned.

BROWNS. Three Miss. *S.B.B.*, *O.P.*, ii.

BRUCE. Traveller. *M.P.*, *E.T.*; *M.P.*, *L.A.V.* ii.

"**BRUIN.**" Hugh of the Maypole. *B.R.* xl.

BRUNEL. *M.P.*, *S.*

BRUSSELS. *C.S.*; *S.P.T.*, ii.; *M.P.*, *S.F.A.*; *N.N.* l.; *O.M.F.* ii.; *U.T.* xvii.

BRUSSELS. School at. *O.M.F.* xxx.

BRYANSTONE SQUARE. *D and S.* iii.

BUCKET. Mr., a detective officer. *B.H.* xxii.

A stoutly-built, steady-looking, sharp-eyed man in black, of about the middle age, with a face as unchanging as the great mourning ring on his little finger, or the brooch, composed of not much diamond and a good deal of setting, which he wears in his shirt.

Note.—Detective officer whose industry and penetration make him appear more than mortal to the poor wretches he hunts down. He is good-hearted, however, and does what he can. He is closely connected with the main threads of the story, and it is he who in company with Esther Summerson tracks Lady Dedlock, although he is too late to be of any service. He is the means of obtaining possession of the later will from Smallweed, but that, too, is of no value, as the case has eaten up the estate. He leaves the story unceremoniously and unostentatiously seeing to the chairing-home of Grandfather Smallweed.

BUCKET. Mr., Aunt of. *B.H.* liii.

BUCKET. Mr., Brother-in-law of. *B.H.* liii.

BUCKET. Mr., Brother of. *B.H.* liii.

BUCKET. Mr., Father of. *B.H.* liii.

BUCKET. Mrs., Wife of Mr. Bucket. *B.H.* xlix.

A lady of natural detective genius—dependent on her lodger for companionship and conversation."

Note.—Leads on Mademoiselle Hortense to incriminate herself.

BUCKINGHAM. Duke of. *S.B.B.*, Scenes xiii.

BUCKINGHAM. Duke of, and tenants. *M.P.*, *Ag. Int.*

BUCKINGHAM PALACE. *M.P.*; *Th. Let.*, *M.P.*, *N.G.K.*

BUCKLERSBURY. *S.B.B.*, Char. i.

BUD. Miss Rosa, A pupil at Mrs. Twinkleton's. *E.D.* iii.

Wonderfully pretty, wonderfully childish, wonderfully whimsical. A husband has been chosen for her by will and bequest.

Note.—One of the principal characters of the story. She is introduced as the pet pupil of the Nuns' House. She and Edwin Drood are betrothed while children by their parents, and they have grown up accepting that condition of affairs. They discover, however, that they cannot be made to love by order, and agree to become "brother and sister." Rosa is loved by John Jasper, but does not reciprocate, and to some extent fears him.

BUDDEN. Mr. Octavius, Cousin of Minns. *S.B.B.*, Tales ii.

BUDDEN. Master Alexander Augustus. *S.B.B.*, Tales ii.
Habited in a sky-blue suit with silver buttons—possessing hair of nearly same colour as metal.

BUDDEN. Son of Octavius. *S.B.B.*, Tales ii.
Mr. Augustus Minns—consented to become godfather by proxy.

BUDDEN. Mrs., Amelia, Wife of Octavius Budden. *S.B.B.*, Tales ii.

BUDDEN. "Boy" of Mr. *S.B.B.*, Tales ii.
"In drab livery, cotton stockings and high lows."

BUDDEN. House of Mr. *S.B.B.*, Tales ii.
"Yellow brick house with a green door, brass knocker and door-plate, green window frames—a garden—a small bit of gravelled ground with one or two triangular beds—a Cupid on each side of the door, perched upon a heap of chalk flints, variegated with pink conch shells.

BUDGER. Mrs. *P.P.* ii.
A little old widow, whose rich dress and profusion of ornament bespoke her a most desirable addition to a limited income. The "little old widow" was the cause of the threatened duel between Dr. Slammer of the 97th, and Mr. Winkle.

BUFF CANDIDATE. Fiskin, Horatio. Esq. *P.P.* li.

BUFF PARTY. The. *P.P.* xiii.

BUFFALO. An Indian Chief. *A.N.* ix.

BUFFALO. *A.N.* xiv.

BUFFER. Dr., *Mud. Pap. 2nd meet.*

BUFFERS. Two other stuffed. *O.M.F.* ii.
Guests of Veneerings.

BUFFLE. Mr., Collector of Taxes. *C.S., M.L.Leg.* i.
His manners, when engaged in his business, were not agreeable.

BUFFLE. Mr., Articled Young gentleman of. *C.S., M.L.Leg.* i.

BUFFLE. Mrs., Wife of Tax Collector. *C.S., M.L.Leg.* i.

BUFFLE. Miss. *C.S., M.L.Leg.* i.

BUFFON. G. L. L. *M.P., R.F.H.*

BUFFS. Colours of, Parliamentary candidates. *P.P.* xiii.

BUFFUM. Oscar. *M.C.* xxxiv.

BUFFY. *M.P., W.*

BUFFY. The Right Honourable William. *B.H.* xii.

BUILDING. The, that had succeeded Stagg's Gardens. *D. and S.* xxii.

BUILDINGS. The, Jerusalem Buildings. *C.B., H.M.* i.

BUILDINGS. The Company's own. *D. and S.* xv.

BULDER. Colonel. Head of the garrison. *P.P.* ii.
Present at the charity ball, Rochester.

BULDER. Mrs., Colonel. *P.P.* ii.
Present at the charity ball, Rochester.

BULDER. Miss. *P.P.* ii.
Present at the charity ball, Rochester.

BULE. Miss, Pupil of Miss Griffin. *C.S., H.H.*

BULL. Mr. John Bull. *M.P. A.J.B.*; *M.P., B.S.*; *M.P., H.H.*; *M.P., M.E.*; *M.P., N.J.B.*; *M.P., O.C.*

BULL. Mrs. *M.P., A.J.B.*; *M.P., N.J.B.*

BULL. Prince, A Powerful Prince. *R.P., P.B.*

BULL'S FAMILY. Mr., members of. *M.P., H.H.*

"**BULL.**" The Black, At Holburn. *M.C.* xxv.

"**BULL.**" Chambermaid of the. *M.C.* xxv.

"**BULL.**" Head-chambermaid of the. *M.C.* xxv.

"**BULL.**" Landlady of the. *M.C.* xxv.

"**BULL.**" Landlord of the. *M.C.* xxv.

"**BULL INN.**" High Street, Rochester. *P.P.* ii.

Good house—nice beds.

Note.—The real name of the "Bull" since Queen Victoria passed a night there has been "The Royal Victoria and Bull Hotel." Mr. Pickwick's room has been identified as No. 17, Mr. Tupman's as No. 13, and Mr. Winkle's as No. 19.

"**BULL" INN.** Whitechapel. *P.P.* xxii.

"**BULL'S HEAD.**" The Old Hotel. *U.T.* vi.

With its old-established knife boxes on its old-established sideboards, its old established flue under its old established four-post bedsteads, in its old established airless rooms, its old established frowziness upstairs and downstairs, its old-established cookery and its old-established principles of plunder.

BULLAMY. Porter in the service of the Anglo Bengalee Disinterested Loan and Life Assurance Company *M.C.* xxvii.

A wonderful creature, in a vast red waistcoat, and a short-tailed pepper-and-salt coat.

Note.—His evident respectability was one of the company's assets.

BULLDOG. *M.P., F.L.*

BULLDOGS. The United. *B.R.* viii.

BULLFINCH. *U.T.* xxxii.

BULLMAN. At law against Ramsey. *P.P.* xx.

BULLOCK. Churchwarden. *D.C.* xxix.

Excommunication case in court. Tipkins against Bullock, of a scuffle between two churchwardens.

BULLS OF ROME. *M.P., A.J.B.*

"**BULLUM.**" Boulogne. *R.P., A.F.*

BULPH. A pilot. *N.N.* xxiii.

Who sported a boat green door, with window-frames of the same colour, and had the little finger of a drowned man on his parlour mantelshelf, with other maritime and natural curiosities.

BUMBLE. Mr., Workhouse beadle. *O.T.* ii.

A fat man, and a choleric.

Note.—The Beadle, who ever since the publication of "Oliver Twist" has stood for the symbol of the office. It was he who "invented" Oliver's name. When the poor orphan was nine years old he is removed by the Beadle from the "farm" to the workhouse. Later on he "sells" himself as a husband to Mrs. Corney, matron of the workhouse "for six teaspoons, a pair of sugar-tongs, and a milk-pot, with a small quantity of second-hand furniture, and twenty pound in money." Mrs. Corney, when she becomes Mrs. Bumble, subjugates the Beadle, who is now master of the workhouse. Together they sell the locket and ring left by Oliver's mother, when she died in the workhouse, to Monks. Misfortune overtakes them: they are deprived of their situation, and eventually become inmates of the same workhouse.

BUMBLE. Mrs., *See* Corney, Mrs.

BUMPLE. Defendant in brawling case. *S.B.B.*, Scenes viii.

BUN HOUSE. The old original. *B.H.* liii.

"**BUNCH.**" Mother." Gift on Xmas tree. *R.P., A.C.T.*

BUNG. Spruggins' opponent. *S.B.B., O.P.* iv.

In a cast-off coat of the captain's, a blue coat with bright buttons, white trousers, and a description of shoes familiarly known by the appellation of "high lows."

BUNGAY. Suffolk. *M.P., W.R.*

BUNKER HILL STREET. *M.C.* xxii.

BUNKIN. Mrs. *P.C.* xxxiv.

Which clear-starched.

BUNSBY. Captain, *D. and S.* xv.

With one stationary eye in the mahogany face, and one revolving one, on the principle of some lighthouses. This head was decorated with shaggy hair like oakum, which had no governing inclination towards the north, east, west, or south, but inclined to all four quarters of the compass, and to every point upon it. The head was followed by a dreadnought pilot-coat and by a pair of dreadnought pilot-trousers, whereof the waistband was so very broad and high, that it became a succedaneum for a waistcoat : being ornamented nearer the wearer's breastbone with some massive wooden buttons, like backgammon men. Would deliver such an opinion on this subject, or any other that could be named, as would give Parliament six and beat 'em. . . Been knocked overboard twice, and none the worse for it. Was beat in his apprenticeship, for three weeks (off and on) about the head with a ringbolt. And yet a clearer-minded man don't walk.

Note.—The eccentric captain of the "Cautious Clara." He is regarded by Captain Cuttle as infallible. He is vastly afraid of his landlady, Mrs. MacStinger, and is eventually captured by her and married.

BUNSBY. Mrs., late Mrs. MacStinger. *D. and S.* lx.

BURFORD. Mr. *M.P., E.T.*

BURGESS AND CO. Toots' tailor. *D. and S.* xii.

BURIAL GROUND. *N.N.* lxii.

A dismal place, raised a few feet above the level of the street, and parted from it by a low parapet-wall, and an iron railing; a rank, unwholesome, rotten spot, where the very grass and weeds seemed, in their frowsy growth, to tell that they had sprung from paupers' bodies, and had struck their roots in the graves of men, sodden while alive, in steaming courts and drunken hungry dens.

BURLINGTON. Iowa. *A.N.* xvii.

BURLINGTON ARCADE. London. *M.P., I.* ; *U.T.* xvi.

BURLINGTON GARDENS. *U.T.* xvi.

BURLINGTON HOUSE GARDENS. *U.T.* x.

BURNETT. Henry. *M.P., I.G.*

BURNINGSHAME. Borough of. *M.P., H.H.*

BURNLEY. Workman from. *M.P., O.S.*

BURNS. Spirit of Robert. *M.P., S.F.A.*

BURTON. Mr., of the General Furnishing Ironmongery Warehouse. *M.P., S.S.*

BURTON. Thomas, Convert to Temperance. *P.C.* xxxiii.

Purveyor of cat's meat to the Lord Mayor and sheriffs and several members of the Common Council—has a wooden leg; finds a wooden leg expensive, going over the stones ; used to wear second-hand wooden legs,—wears new wooden legs now, and drinks nothing but water and weak tea. The new legs last twice as long as the others.

BURY. A man named. *A.N.* xvii.

BURY. George, Brother of John's wife. *R.P., P.M.T.P.*

BURY. *M.P., O.S.*

BURY St. Edmunds. *D.C.* xxx. ; *P.P.* xv. *S.B.B.*liv. ; *U.T.* xxiii.

A handsome little town, of thriving and cleanly appearance.

"**BUSH.**" The, Inn. *P.P.* xxxviii.

BUSHMEN. The. *R.P., T.N.S.*

BUSINESS. A Man of, Trustee for Miss Wade. *L.D.* lvii.

BUSTS. Waxen. *O.M.F.* 2. iii.

BUSTS. Waxen, In hairdressers. *N.N.* lii.

Of a light lady, and a dark gentleman.

BUTCHER. William, A moderate Chartist. *R.P., P.M.T.P.*

BUTCHERS. A syndicate or guild of. *R.P., M.O.F.F.*

BUTLER. Mrs. Lavinia. *S.B.B.*, Tales iii.

BUTLER. Cheeryble Brothers'. *N.N.* lxiii.

BUTLER. Dr. BLIMBER'S. *D. and S.* xii.

In a blue coat and light buttons, who gave quite a winey flavour to the table beer; he poured it out so superbly.

BUTLER. Mr. Merdle's chief. *L.D.* xxi.

Stateliest man in the company. He did nothing, but he looked on as few other men could have done.

BUTLER. Of Great Sibthorp. *M.P., S.P.*

BUTLER. Silver-headed, hired by Mrs. Skewton. *D. and S.* xxx.

BUTLER. Theodosius, Miss Crumpton's Cousin. *S.B.B.*, Tales iii.

One of those geniuses to be met with in almost every circle. They usually have very deep monotonous voices.

BUTTON. Mr. William, Signor Jupe. *H.T., S.* iii.

BUXTON. Sir Thomas Fowell. *M.P., N.E.*

BUZFUZ. Serjeant, Barrister for Bardell. *P.P.* xxxiv.

With a fat body and a red face.

Note.—Buzfuz was counsel for the plaintiff in the trial. Although drawn from nature, the introduction of the character is supposed to have had as its object the lessening of the bullying of witnesses.

BWISTOL. Bristol. *P.P.* xxxv.

BYRON. Honourable Lord. *M.C.* xxii.; *M.P., L.A.V.* ii.; *S.B.B.*, Scenes xiii.

C

C.D. Captains, "Nobodies." *R.P., N.S.*

CAB. Fare of red. *S.B.B.*, Scenes xvii.

A tall weazen-faced man, with an impediment in his speech.

CAB. Another fare of red. *S.B.B.*, Scenes xvii.

A loquacious little gentleman in a green coat—had paid more than he ought and avowed his determination to 'pull up' the cabman in the morning.

"**CABBAGE AND SHEARS.**" Inn. *C.S., D.M.*

CABBERY. Another suitor of Mrs. Nickleby. *N.N.* xli.

CABBURN. *R.P., B.S.*

CAB-DRIVER. The last. *S.B.B.*, Scenes xvii.

A brown-whiskered white-hatted, no-coated cabman, his nose was generally red, and his bright blue eye not unfrequently stood out in bold relief against a black border of artificial workmanship. His boots were of the Wellington form, pulled up to meet his corduroy knee smalls—his neck was usually garnished with a bright yellow handkerchief. In summer he carried in his mouth a flower; in winter a straw.

CAB-DRIVERS. *S.B.B.*, Scenes i.

Wondering how people can prefer them wild beast cariwans of homnibuses, to a regular cab with a fast trotter.

CABINET. A. *B.H.* xii.

CABINET MAKER. *P.P.* xlv.

CACHOTS. The. *P.F.I., L.R.G.A.*

CACKLES. My Cousin. *M.P., B.A.*

CAD. Conductor of Omnibus. *S.B.B.*, Scenes xvi.

CADDO GAZETTE. A newspaper. *A.N.* xvii.

CADELL. *M.P., S.P.*

CADI. Chief. *M.P., T.O.H*

CADOGAN PLACE. Sloane Street *N.N.* xxi.

CAEN WOOD. Lord Mansfield's Country Seat. *B.R.* lxvi. *O.T.* xlviii.

CAESARS. The Palace of the. *P.F.I., R.*

CAFÉ DE LA LUNE. *M.P., R.D.*

CAFFRARIA. *R.P., T.L.V.*

CAGGS. Mr. *O.M.F.* viii.

CAGLIOSTRO. Spirit of. *M.P., M.M.*

" **CAIN, A MYSTERY.**" *M.C.* xxii.

CAIRAWAN. The Caravan. *C.S., G.i.S.*

CAIRO. *M.P., E.T.*

CAIRO. On the Mississippi. *A.N.* xii.
Detestable morass.

CAIUS CESTIUS. Burial place of. *P.F.I., R.*

CALAIS. *L.D.* xxiv. ; *M.P., W.* ; *O.M.F.* lxvii. ; *R.P., B.S.* ; and *U.T.* xvii. *and L.T.* v.

CALAIS. A native of *L.D.* lvi.
In a suit of grease, and a cap of the same material.

CALAIS. Hotel de, Calais. *U.T.* xvii.

CALAIS HARBOUR. *U.T.* xvii.

CALCRAFT. Mr. *M.P., F.S.* ; *M.P., I.M.* ; *M.P., M.P.* ; *M.P., T.B.*

CALCUTTA. *M.P., E.T.* ; and *U.T.* viii.

CALEB. Caleb Plummer. *C.B., C.O.H.* i.

CALIFORNIA. *C.S., H.N.* ; *C.S., W.O.G.M.* ; *M.P., R.H.F.* ; and *R.P., O.S.*

CALLEY. Mr. *O.M.F.* viii.

CALLOW. An eminent physician. *R.P., O.B.*

CALOMEL. *C.S., H.H.*, ii.

CALTON. Mr., A boarder at Mrs. Tibbs'. *S.B.B.*, Tales i.
He used to say of himself that although his features were not regularly handsome, they were striking . . . It was impossible to look at his face without being reminded of a chubby street-door knocker, half-lion, half-monkey. He was exceeding vain, and inordinately selfish.

CALTON HILL. *P.P.* xlix.

CAMBERLING TOWN. *D. and S.* vi.

CAMBERWELL. *L.D.* viii. ; *M.C.* ix. ; *N.N.* xxxvii. ; *P.P.* xx. ; *P.P.* xxxiii.; *G.E.* xv.; *S.B.B.*, Tales v.

CAMBERWELL GREEN. *G.E.* lv.

CAMBERWELL GROVE. *S.B.B.*, Tales v.

CAMBRIDGE. *C.S., M.L.Leg.* i. ; *G.E.* xxiii. ; *G.S. E.* vi. ; *M.P., C.H.T.* ; *R.P., T.B.W.* ; *T.T.C.*, bk. ii., ch. x.

CAMBRIDGE. University of. *A.N.* iii.

CAMBRIDGE. Young Duke of. *M.P., G.H.*

CAMDEN TOWN. *C.B., C.C., S.* i.; *C.S., H.H., D.C.* xxvii. ; *D. and S.* vi. ; *M.P., R.S.* ; *O.T.* xlii. ; *P.P.* xxi. ; *S.B.B.*, Scenes i ; *S.B.B.*, Scenes xx.

CAMDEN TOWN. Post Office. *D.C.* xxviii.

CAMEL. In Zoological Gardens. *M.P., R.H.F.*

CAMEL - CUM - NEEDLE'S - EYE. Extensive parish. *M.P., G.B.*

CAMILLA. Mr., Husband of Mrs. Camilla. *G.E.* xi.

CAMILLA. Mrs., Mr. Pocket's sister. *G.E.* xi.
Note.—One of the most prominent of Miss Havisham's fawning relatives.

CAMOGLIA. *P.F.I., R.P.S.*

CAMPAGNA. The solitary. *L.D.* lv.

CAMPANILE. Parma. *P.F.I., P.M.B.*

CAMPBELL. Dr. John. *M.P., R.S.D.*

CAMPBELL. Lord. *M.P., M.E.*

CAMPBELL. Mr., Mr. Provis (alias Abel. Magwich.) *G.E.* xlvi.

CAMPBELL. Sir John. *M.P., S.F.A.*

CAMPO SANTO. *P.F.I., R.D.*

CAMPO SANTO. The Church of, Pisa. *P.F.I., R.P.S.*

CANADA. *A.N.* ix. ; *L.D.* vii.

CANAL BRIDGE. *U.T.* xviii.
See also Baker's Trap.

CANE. Grotto del. *P.F.I.*, *R.D.*

CANNANA. Mr. Hamet Safi, Secretary to H[is] R[olling] H[ulk] the Hippopotamus. *M.P.*, *R.G.H.*

CANNING. Mr. *M.P.*, *W.*

CANNON STREET. *M.C.* ix.

CANONGATE. Edinburgh. *M.P.*, *S.P.* ; and *P.P.* xlix. ; and *H.T.* xxxiv.

There shot up against a dark sky, tall, gaunt straggling houses, with time-stained fronts, and windows that seemed to have shared the lot of eyes in mortals, and to have grown dim and sunken with age. Six, seven, eight stories high were the houses ; story piled above story, as children build with cards.

CANTERBURY. *A.N.* xviii. ; *B.R.* li. ; *D.C.* xvi. ; *L.D.* liv. ; *U.T.* vii

CANTERBURY. Archbishop of. *B.R.* lxxxii. ; *M.H.C.* iii.

CANTERBURY POST OFFICE. *D.C.* xx.

CANTERBURY PRECINCT. *M.P.*, *N.Y.D.*

CANTON DE VAUD. *L.D.* i. ; *M.P.*, *C.H.T.*

CAPE COAST CASTLE. *M.P.*, *N.E.*

CAPE. Mr. *S.B.B.*, Tales ix.

Practised the violin.

CAPITOL. The. *L.D.* li.

CAPITOL. The, Washington. *A.N.* viii.

A fine building of the Corinthian order.

CAPPER. Mr. *S.Y.G.*

CAPPER. Mrs. *S.Y.G.*

CAPPUCCHINO. *P.F.I.*

CAPRI. *P.F.I.*, *R.D.*

CAPTAIN. Of the Screw. *M.C.* xvi.

CAPTAIN. The, a very old frequenter of Bellamy's. *S.B.B.*, Scenes xviii.

Spare, squeaking old man—a cracked bantam sort of voice—much addicted to stopping " after the House is up "—a complete walking reservoir of spirits and water.

CAPTING. Of " The Esau Slodge." *M.C.* xxxiii.

CAPUANA. Porta. *P.F.I.*, *R.D.*

CAPULETS. The House of the. *P.F.I.*, *V.M.M.S.S.*

CARAVAN. Sombre, A hearse. *S.B.B.* Scenes xvi.

In which we must one day make our last earthly journey.

CARBOY. Of Kenge and Carboy. *B.H.* iii.

CARDINALS. *P.F.I.*, *R.*

CAREW. Bamfylde Moore, the reigning successor of. *M.P.*, *G.A.*

CARIBBEAN SEAS. *C.S.*, *P.O.C.E.P.*

CARKER. Harriet, Sister of John and James Carker. *D. and S.* xxxiii.

This slight, small, patient figure, neatly dressed in homely stuffs—leaning on the man still young, but worn and grey—his sister, who of all the world, went over to him in his shame, and put her hand in his, and with a sweet composure and determination, led him hopefully upon his barren way.

Note.—She befriends Alice Brown. She lives quietly with her brother John, who is under a cloud, and eventually marries Mr. Morfin.

CARKER. Mr. James, Manager in Dombey and Son's office. *D. and S.* iv.

A gentleman thirty-eight or forty years old, of a florid complexion, and with two unbroken rows of glistening teeth, whose regularity and whiteness were quite distressing—bore so wide a smile upon his countenance—that there was something in it like the snarl of a cat.

Note.—Brother of John and Harriet Carker. Manager of the house of Dombey and Son. He is entirely in Mr. Dombey's confidence, and possesses a great amount of influence over him. He is employed by his master to carry messages to his wife with the object of humiliating her. In return she elopes with Carker, and then leaves Carker when he thinks he has obtained his desire. Dombey's manager uses his position in the firm to further his own ends, and by doing so amasses a fortune. Although he does not lay hands on any of the firm's money, he has so involved it in rash and extensive speculation that it fails. In an endeavour to escape Mr. Dombey, Carker is killed on the railway. Paddock Wood Station in Kent, has been suggested as the scene of his death.

CARKER JUNIOR. Mr. John, in Dombey and Son's. *D. and S.* vi.

He was not old, but his hair was white; his body was bent, or bowed as if by the weight of some great trouble: and there were deep lines in his worn and melancholy face. The fire of his eyes, the expression of his features, the very voice in which he spoke were all subdued and quenched, as if the spirit within him lay in ashes. He was respectably though very plainly, dressed in black, but his clothes, moulded to the general character of his figure, seemed to shrink—and seemed to join in the sorrowful solicitation which the whole man from head to foot expressed, to be left unnoticed, and alone in his humility. Brother of Carker the manager. Two or three years older than he, but widely removed in station.

Note.—Brother of James and Harriet Carker. When he is introduced in the story he occupies a very junior position which he discharges with patient industry. It transpires that in his youth he robbed the firm, but that, instead of being dismissed, he was put into the post in which he is found, while his brother occupies the position of manager. After his brother elopes with Mrs. Dombey, he is discharged. But when his brother meets with his accidental death he inherits the wealth accumulated by his brother. As however, he looks upon his brother's fortune as in some measure due to his abuse of his position in the firm., John secretly makes over the interest year by year to old Mr. Dombey, after his bankruptcy.

CARLAVERO. Giovanni, Wine shopkeeper. *U.T.* xxviii.

His striking face is pale, and his action is evidently that of an enfeebled man — was a galley-slave in the north of Italy—a political offender.

CARLAVERO. Wife of Giovanni. *U.T.* xxiii.

CARLISLE *C.S., D.M. and L.T.* i.

CARLISLE HOUSE. *B.R.* iv.

CARLO FELICE. The. *P.F.I., G.A.N.*

CARLTON CLUB HOUSE. *M.P., B.A.*

CARLTON HOUSE HOTEL. New York. *A.N.* vi.

CARLTON NEPHEWS. *M.P., S. for P*

CARLTON TERRACE. *S.B.B.*, Scenes xx.

CARLYLE. Mr. Thomas, Author. *A.N.* iii.; *M.P., P.F.*; *M.P., W.H.*; *M.P., W.S.G.*

CARNABY MARKET. *R.P., D.P.*

CARNAK. Temple of. *M.P., E.T.*

CAROLINA. North. *A.N.* xvii.

CAROLINA. South. *A.N.* xvii.

CAROLINE. *C.B., C.C.*, s. iv.

A mild and patient creature.

CAROLINE. A Negress slave. *A.N.* xvii.

CAROLINE. Queen. *M.P., L.A.V.* i

CARONDELET. Nicknamed Vide Poche. *A.N.* xiv.

CARPET-BEATER. A. *S.B.B.*, Scenes v.

CARR. Mr. Alfred, A West Indian gentleman of colour. *M.P., N.E.*

CARRARA. *P.F.I., R.P.S.*

CARROCK FELL. *C.S., L.T.i.*

CARROT. Matthew. *M.P., P.M.B.*

CARSTONE. Ada, née Clare. *B.H.* li.

CARSTONE. Richard, ward in chancery and distant cousin of Ada Clare. *B.H.* iii.

A handsome youth, with an ingenious face, and a most engaging laugh—he was very young; not more than nineteen then.

Note.—Ward of Mr. Jarndyce, and a party to the great case Jarndyce *v.* Jarndyce. His want of fixity of purpose and his slackness in his expenditure, based on the prospect of the termination of the chancery suit, spoil a character otherwise charming. He first tries law, from that he studies medicine under Mr. Bayham Badger, and then turns his attention to the Army. But he is unable to concentrate his attention on either, and returns to the chancery suit, which he resolves to watch in person. The anxiety undermines his health and breeds distrust of his guardian. He marries Ada Clare the other ward of John Jarndyce. The chancery suit terminates with the absorption of the estate in costs, and this accelerates Richard's death.

CARSTONE. Richard, Son of Ada and Richard. *B.H.* lxvii.

CARTER. Mr. *Mud Pap.* I.

CARTER. A. *B.R.* xxxi.

In a smock frock.

CARTHAGE. *A.N.* xvii.

CARTON. Captain (Admiral Sir George). *C.S., P.O.C.E.P.*

With bright eyes, brown face, and easy figure.

CARTON. Lady, Née Marion Maryon. *C.S., P.O.C.E.P*:

CARTON. Sydney, Stryver's Jackal. *T.T.C.*, Book ii., Chap. iii.

"I am a disappointed drudge, sir. I care for no man on earth, and no man on earth cares for me."

Note.—One of the most dramatic figures in the story. A debauched lawyer, and jackal to Mr. Stryver. He is instrumental in obtaining the discharge of Darnay on the count of treason by the close resemblance existing between them. He falls in love with Lucy Manette although, to others, he affects indifference to her. But he declares his love for her and leaves her. After she is married to Darney her husband is obliged to go to Paris. He is arrested by the Revolutionists and sentenced to death. Carton follows, takes his place in prison and suffers execution by the guillotine.

CASBY. Mr. Christopher, Landlord of Bleeding Heart Yard, formerly town agent to Lord Decimus Tite-Barnacle. *L.D.* xii.

A man advanced in life, whose smooth grey eyebrows seemed to move—as the firelight flickered on them, sat in an armchair, with his list-shoes on the rug, and his thumbs slowly revolving over one another. His shining bald head, which looked so large, because it shone so much; long grey hair at its sides and back, like floss silk, or spun glass, which looked so benevolent because it was never cut.—Various old ladies in the neighbourhood spoke of him as the "Last of the Patriarchs." His smooth face had a bloom upon it like ripe wall-fruit.—He had a long wide-skirted bottle-green coat on, and a bottle-green pair of trousers, and a bottle-green waistcoat.

Note.—The Patriarch was the landlord of Bleeding Heart Yard, which he bled by means of Mr. Pancks. He was the father of Mrs. Flora Finching. He is shown up eventually by Pancks, to the whole yard.

CASGAR. Great plain at the feet of the mountains of. *M.P., T.O.H.*

CASHIM TAPA. *M.P., T.O.H.*

Rich elder brother of Scarli Tapa.

CASHIM TAPA. Wife of. *M.P., T.O.H.*

CASSIM. Barrister's clerk. *O.M.F.* iii.

CASSINO. Monte. *P.F.I., R.D.*

CASTEL-A-MARE. *P.F.I., R.D.*

CASTIGLIONE. *P.F.I., R.D.*

CASTLE. Abode of Mrs. Pipchin. *D. and S.* viii.

The castle was in a steep by-street at Brighton—where the front-gardens had the unaccountable property of producing nothing but marigold, whatever was sown in them. In winter time the air couldn't be got out of the castle, and in the summer-time it couldn't be got in.

CASTLE. Coavinse's, In Cursitor Street. *B.H.* xiv.
A house with barred windows.

CASTLE. The, Mr. Wemmick's house. *G.E.* xxv.

CASTLE DUNGEON. Room in Mrs. Pipchin's. *D. and S.* viii.
An empty apartment at the back, devoted to correctional purposes . . . looking out upon a chalk wall and a water-butt, and made ghastly by a ragged fireplace without any stove in it.

CASTLES. German. *R.P., A.C.T.*
Where we sit up alone to wait for the spectre.

CASTRO. *M.P., L.L.*

CASUALTY WARD. In hospital. *S.B.B.*, Char. vi.

CASWELL. Oliver, Inmate of Asylum for the Blind at Boston. Blind, deaf and dumb. *A.N.* iii.

CAT. In " Happy Family." *M.P., R.H.F.*

CAT. Le. Historian. *B.H.*, Pref.
One of the most renowned surgeons produced by France.

CATACOMBS. *P.F.I.*

CATESBY. *S.B.B.*, Scenes xiii.

CATHEDRAL. In Florence. *P.F.I., R.D.*

CATHEDRAL. Old. *E.D.* i.
The massive gray square tower of an old cathedral rises before the sight of a jaded traveller. The Virginia creeper on the cathedral wall has showered half its deep red leaves on the pavement.
Other Cathedrals will be found under their various names.

CATHERINE STREET. Strand. *S.B.B.*, Scenes xiii. ; *U.T.* iv.

CATLIN. Mr. *R.P., T.N.S.*

" **CATTIVO SOGGETTO MIO.**" *L.D.* xlii.

CAUKABY. Lady, Mrs. Dombey. *D. and S.* i.

CAULON. Brother of Walker. *U.T.* v.

CAVALIER. A masked. *M.H.C.* iii.
A man pretty far advanced in life, but of a firm and stately carriage. His dress was of a rich and costly kind—but soiled and disordered.

CAVALLETTO. Signor John Baptist. *L.D.* i.
A sunburnt, quick, lithe, little man, though rather thick-set. Earrings in his brown ears, white teeth lighting up his grotesque brown face, intensely black hair clustering about his brown throat, a ragged red shirt open at his brown breast. Loose seamanlike trousers, decent shoes, a long red cap, a red sash round his waist, and a knife in it. The little man was an Italian.
Note.—Intoduced as a prisoner in the same cell with Rigaud, who dominates him and abuses him, and of whom he is always somewhat afraid. He finds his way to England, and is eventually employed by Arthur Clennam in the works. He is instrumental in finding Rigaud and, having lost his fear, he accompanies his former prison companion, as servant.

CAVENDISH SQUARE. *L.D.* xx. ; *N.N.* x. ; *O.M.F.* v.

CAVETON. *S.Y.G.*

CAWBERRY. *M.P., F.C.*

CAY. Mr. Sheriff. *M.P., S.P.*

CECIL STREET. Strand. *S.B.B.*, Tales x.

CECILIA METELLA. Tomb of. *P.F.I., R.*

CELIA. Charity child. *U.T.* xxi.
Shaking mats in City churchyard.

CELLAR. In house near Barbican. *B.R.* viii.
Where there was a small copper fixed in one corner, a chair or two, a form and a table, a glimmering

fire, and a truckle bed, covered with a ragged patchwork rug.—The floors were of sodden earth, the walls and roof of damp, bare brick, tapestried with the tracks of snails and slugs.

CEMETERY. The *C.S., S.L.* ii.

In all Britain you would have found nothing like it.—There were so many little gardens and grottos made upon graves in so many tastes, with plants and shells and plaster figures and porcelain pitchers, and so many odds and ends . . . nothing of the solemnity of death here.

CENCI. Palace of the. *P.F.I., R.*

CENTRAL CRIMINAL COURT. *C.S., T.G.S.* i.; and *M.P., I.*

CENTRAL DISTRICT. London. *M.P., F.F.*

CERTAINPERSONIO. Prince. *H.R.* ii.

CEYLON. *M.P., E.T.*

CHADBAND. Mr., In the Ministry. *B.H.* xix.

A large yellow man, with a fat smile, and a general appearance of having a good deal of train-oil in his system.

Note.—Friend of Mrs. Snagsby. A canting hypocrite of no defined denomination. He is engaged in an attempt by Smallweed to blackmail Sir Leicester Dedlock.

CHADBAND. Mrs., Formerly Mrs. Rachael. *B.H.* xix.

A stern, severe-looking, silent woman.

Note.—Introduced as the austere and self-seeking servant of Esther Summerson's aunt. Becomes the wife of Chadband and is concerned with him in the blackmail of Sir Leicester Dedlock.

CHADWICK. Mr. *M.P., S.S.U.*

CHADWICK. Mr. *U.T.* xxix.

CHADWICK'S ORCHARD. Preston. *M.P., O.S.*

CHAFFWAX. Deputy. *R.P., P.M.T.P.*

CHAIRMAKER. Cornish. *C.S., H.T.*

The chairs assigned were mere frames, altogether without bottoms of any sort, so that we passed the evening on perches.

CHAIRMAN. A Preston weaver. *M.P., O.S.*

CHAIRMAN. At a harmonic meeting. *S.B.B.*, Scenes ii.

Little pompous man, with the bald head, just emerging from the collar of his green coat.

CHAIRMAN. The. *O.M.F.* lxvii.

CHAIRMEN. Guests at Dombey's housewarming. *D. and S.* xxxvi.

CHAIRMEN. One short and fat and one long and thin. *P.P.* xxxvi.

CHALK FARM. *U.T.* xviii. *S.U.T.H.*, l.

CHALONS. *L.D.* xi.; *P.F.I., G.T.F.*

The flat expanse of country about Chalons lay a long, heavy streak, occasionally made a little ragged by a row of poplar trees, against the wrathful sunset.

CHALONS. The Café. *L.D.* xi.

With its bright windows and its rattling of dominoes.

CHALONS. Dyers in. *L.D.* xi.

With its strips of red cloth on the doorposts.

CHALONS. Hotel in. *L.D.* xi.

With its gateway, and its savoury smell of cooking.

CHALONS. Its silversmiths. *L.D.* xi.

With its earrings, and its offerings for altars.

CHALONS. Tobacco dealers. *L.D.* xi.

With its lively group of soldier customers coming out pipe in mouth.

CHAMBERMAID. Head, at Furnival's Inn. *E.D.* xx.

CHAMBERMAID. Head. *C.S., S.L.* i.

CHAMBERS. *P.P.* xxi.
What is there in Chambers in particular ?

CHAMOUNI. *R.P., O.B.*

CHAMPEAUX. Café, near the Bourse. *M.P., N.Y.D.*
CHAMPLAIN. Lake. *A.N.* xv.

CHAMPS ELYSÉES. *M.P., R.D.*

CHANCELLOR. Lord. *R.P., P.M.T.P.*
CHANCELLOR. Lord, in 1813. *M.P., C.P.*
CHANCELLOR. The Lord High. *B.H.* i.
With a foggy glory round his head, softly fenced in with crimson cloth and curtains.

CHANCELLOR OF THE EXCHEQUER. The. *S.B.B.*, Scenes xviii. ; *U.T.* xxii.
CHANCELLOR OF THE EXCHEQUER. Office of. *M.P., R.T.*
CHANCERY. *P.P.* xliv. ; *S.B.B.*, Scenes iii.
CHANCERY. Court of. *B.H.* i. ; *M.P., L.W.O.Y.* ; *P.P.* xliv. ; *S.B.B.*, Scenes iii.
Which has its decaying houses and its blighted lands in every shire, its worn-out lunatics in every madhouse.

CHANCERY. Master in. *R.P., P.M.T.P.*
CHANCERY. Masters in. *U.T.* xxvi.
Holding up their black petticoats.

CHANCERY BAR. *M.P., L.E.J.*

CHANCERY LANE. *B.H.* i. ; *O.M.F.* viii. ; *P.P.* xl. ; *R.P., B.S.* ; *S.B.B.* viii.
CHANCERY PRISONER. In the Fleet. *P.P.* xlii.
A tall, gaunt, cadaverous man, in an old great-coat and slippers ; with sunken cheeks, and a restless, eager eye. His lips were bloodless and his bones sharp and thin. God help him ! The iron teeth of confinement and privation had been grinding him down for twenty years.

CHANDLER. The little, Shop of. *S.B.B.*, Scenes ii.
The crowds which have been passing to and fro during the whole day are rapidly dwindling away.

CHANEY. (China). *D. and S.* iii.

'CHANGE. *See* Exchange, Royal.

CHANNEL. The. *C.S., M.f.T.S.* v. ; *L.D.* lvi. ; *O.M.F.* xxi. ; *R.P., O.F.M.*
CHANNEL ISLANDS. *M.P., G.D. and L.T.* iii.
CHANNING. Dr., A preacher. *A.N.* iii.
CHAPEL. Newgate prison. *S.B.B.*, Scenes xxv.
The meanness of its appointments—the bare and scanty pulpit—the women's gallery with its heavy curtain—the tottering little table at the altar—so unlike the velvet and gilding, marble and wood of a modern church, are strange and striking.

CHAPEL. Newgate prison, Condemned pew in. *S.B.B.*, Scenes xxv.
Immediately below the reading-desk, on the floor of the chapel, and forming the most conspicuous object in its little area—black pen, in which the wretched people, who are singled out for death, are placed on the Sunday preceding their execution—to hear prayers for their own souls, and join in responses of their own burial service.—At one time—the coffins of the men about to be executed were placed—upon the seat by their side.

CHAPEL. Of the Holy Office. *P.F.I., L.R.G.A.*
CHAPEL WALKS. Preston. *M.P., O.S.*
CHAPLIN. Miss Ellen, as, Rosina. *M.P., M.N.D.*

CHARACTER. A well-known. An M.P. *S.B.B.*, Scenes xviii.

The quiet gentlemanly-looking man in the blue surtout, grey trousers, white neckerchief and gloves, whose closely-buttoned coat displays his manly figure and broad chest. He has fought a good many battles in his time.

CHARACTERS. *S.B.B.*, Char. i.

CHARING CROSS. *C.S.*, *M.L.Lo.* i.; *M.P.*, *T.D.*; *N.N.* ii.; *O.M.F.* xliii.; *S.B.B.*, Scenes vii. *and D.C.* xix.

CHARING CROSS. The golden cross. *D.C.* xix.

CHARING CROSS. The statue at. *N.N.* xli.

CHARIOTEER. At Ramsgate pier. *S.B.B.*, Tales iv.

Offering services to the Tuggs.

CHARITABLE GRINDERS. A Worshipful Company. *D. and S.* v.

An ancient establishment; where not only is a wholesome education bestowed upon the scholars, but where a dress and badge is likewise provided for them. The dress—is a nice warm, blue baize tailed coat and cap, turned up with orange-coloured binding; red worsted stockings; and very strong leather small clothes.

CHARKER. Harry, Corporal of marines in chase of pirates. *C.S.*, *P.O.C.E.P.*

CHARLES. *S.Y.C.*

CHARLES. Old, Waiter at west country hotel. *C.S.*, *S.L.* i.

Considered Father of the waitering

CHARLES. Old, Widow of. *C.S.*, *S.L.* i.

An inmate of the Almshouses of the Cork Cutters' Company.

CHARLES STREET. Drury Lane. *U.T.* xxxvi.

CHARLESTON. *A.N.* viii.

CHARLEY. *See* Hexam, Charley.

CHARLEY. *See* Neckett, Charlotte. *B.H.* xv.

CHARLEY. The bashful man. A barrister. *C.S.*, *H.T.*

CHARLEY. Little, Son of Mrs. Blockson. *N.N.* xviii.

Fell down an airy and put his elber out.

"**CHARLEY.**" Marine store shop-keeper. *D.C.* xiii.

An ugly old man, with the lower part of his face all covered with a stubbly grey beard.

Note.—The marine store's man to whom David sells his jacket.

CHARLEY, Potboy of "Magpie and Stump." *P.P.* xx.

A shambling potboy, with a red head.

CHARLEY AND ANGELA. Eight children of. *C.S.*, *H.T.*

CHARLOTTA. Charlotte Tuggs. *S.B.B.*, Tales iv.

CHARLOTTE. *O.T.* iv.

CHARLOTTE. *S.Y.C.*

CHARLOTTE. An old lady of ninety-nine. *R.P.*, *A.C.T.*

CHARLOTTE. Daughter of John. *R.P.*, *P.M.T.P.*

CHARLOTTE. Daughter of Mr. and Mrs. Borum. *N.N.* xxiv.

CHARLOTTE. Deceased daughter of Mr. Pocket. *G.E.* xxx.

CHARLOTTE. One of the children brought up with Miss Wade. *L.D.* lvii.

Stupid mite—my chosen friend—one time I went home with her for the holidays—my false young friend.

CHARLOTTE. Mrs. Sowerberry's maid. *O.T.* iv.

A slatternly girl in shoes down at heel, and blue worsted stockings very much out of repair.

Note.—Servant of Mrs. Sowerby, wife of the undertaker to whom Oliver was apprenticed. She robs the till and travels to London with Noah Claypole. There they fall in with Fagin and become thieves.

Afterwards with Noah she becomes an informer.

CHARLOTTE. *See* Neckett, Charlotte.

CHARLOTTE STREET. *S.B.B.*, Char. ix.

CHARLOTTE'S AUNT. *L.D.* lvii.

CHARLOTTE'S CROWD. Of cousins and acquaintances. *L.D.* lvii.

CHARTERHOUSE. The *B.R.* iv.

CHARTRES STREET. *A.N.* xvii.

CHARWOMAN. Phantom. *C.B.*, *C.C.S.* iv.

I wish it was a little heavier judgment, and it should have been—if I could have laid my hands on anything else.

CHÂTEAU. Of the Old Guard. *R.P.*, *O.F.W.*

CHATHAM. *B.R.* xxxi ; *C.S.*, *P.O.C.E.P.* ; *C.S.*, *S.P.T.* ; *D.C.* xiii. ; *P.P.* ii. ; *R.P.*, *D.W.T.* ; *R.P.*, *T.D.P.* ; *U.T.* v.

CHATHAM. Dockyard *U.T.* xxiv.

Made no display, but kept itself snug under hillsides of cornfields, hopping gardens, and orchards ; its great chimneys smoking with a quiet —almost a lazy air, like giants smoking tobacco. It resounded with the noise of hammers beating upon iron.

CHATHAM DOCKYARD. Workshop in. *U.T.* xxiv.

Where they make all the oars used in the British Navy.

" **CHAUNTER.**" A. *L.D.* xii.

Not a singer of anthems, but a seller of horses.

CHAYMAID. Chambermaid at coffee-house. *L.D.* iii.

CHEAP. The ward of. *M.C.* xxxv.

CHEAP JACK. *U.T.* xi.

CHEAPSIDE. *B.R.*, xxxvii ; *D. and S.* xiii. ; *G.E.* xx. ; *L.D.* iii. ; *M.C.* xxv. ; *M.P.*, *M.B.V.* ; *N.N.* xxvi. ; *O.M.F.* iv. ; *P.P.* xx. ; *R.P.*, *T.D.A.* ; *U.T.* xii.

CHEERFUL. Mr. *M.P.*, *B.S.*

CHEERYBLE. Mr. Charles, Younger twin-brother of Mr. Ned. *N.N.* xxxv.

A sturdy old fellow in a broad skirted blue coat, made pretty large to fit easily, with no particular waist ; his bulky legs clothed in drab breeches, and high gaiters, and his head protected by a low-crowned, broad-brimmed white hat, such as a wealthy grazier might wear. He wore his coat buttoned, his dimpled double-chin rested in the folds of a white neckerchief—not one of your stiff starched, apoplectic cravats, but a good easy, old-fashioned white neck-cloth. — What principally attracted the attention—was the old gentleman's eye—never was such a clear, twinkling, honest, merry happy eye as that.

Note.—The Cheeryble Brothers were merchants in a prosperous business. They were exceedingly charitable and good, so much so that it has been urged that their character is an impossible one. They befriended Nicholas and employed him in their office. And Nicholas' whole fortunes are due in a large measure to them ; as was also the happiness and prosperity of other characters of the book. The brothers retire from the business, which is carried on by Frank Cheeryble and Nicholas.

CHEERYBLE. Frank, Nephew of Cheeryble brothers. *N.N.* xliii.

A sprightly, good - humoured, pleasant fellow, with much both in his countenance and disposition that reminded Nicholas very strongly of the kind-hearted brothers. His manner was as unaffected as theirs.

Note.—Nephew of the brothers Cheeryble. He eventually succeeds to the business with Nicholas and marries Kate Nickleby.

CHEERYBLE. Kate, Mrs. Frank. Kate Nickleby. *N.N.* lxv.

CHEERYBLE. Ned (Edwin), Twin brother of Mr. Charles Cheeryble. *N.N.* xxxv.

Another old gentleman, the very type and model of himself (Mr.

Charles Cheeryble). The same face, the same figure, the same coat, waistcoat, and neckcloth, the same breeches and gaiters, nay there was the very same white hat hanging against the wall.

CHEESEMAN. Mrs., Née Jane Pitt. *R.P., T.S.S.*

CHEESEMAN. Old. The schoolboy. *R.P., T.S.S.*

Wasn't Latin master then; he was a fellow—very small—never went home for his holidays. At last made second Latin master.

CHEESEMONGER'S. A. *S.B.B.*, Scenes ii.

CHEGGS. Mr. Alick, Dick Swiveller's successful rival for the fair Sophia Wackles. *O.C.S.* viii.

Mr. Cheggs was a market-gardener and shy in the presence of ladies.

CHEGGS. Miss. *O.C.S.* viii.

Mr. Cheggs came not alone or unsupported, for he prudently brought along with him his sister, Miss Cheggs.

CHELSEA. *B.H.* xiii.; *B.R.* xvi.; *N.N.* xxi.; *O.C.S.* viii.; *R.P., T.D.P.*; *R.P., P.M.T.P.*

CHELSEA. Bun-house. *B.R.* xlii.

CHELSEA FERRY. *O.M.F.* xv.

CHELSEA PENSIONER. *U.T.* xxvii.

CHELSEA WATERWORKS. *P.P.* xxiii.

CHELTENHAM. *L.D.* xii.; *M.P., E.S.*; *R.P., T.D.P.*

CHEMIST. Gloomy analytical. Fifth retainer of Veneering's. *O.M.F.* ii.

CHERRY. "Fond" for Charity Pecksniff—*which see.*

CHERTSEY. *O.M.F.* xli.; *O.T.* xix.

CHERUB. Amiable. *See* Wilfer, Mr.

CHESAPEAKE BAY. *A.N.* ix.

CHESELBOURNE. *O.C.S.* lxvi.

Rebecca Swiveller . . . of Cheselbourne in Dorsetshire.

CHESHIRE COAST. *U.T.* xxxi.

CHESHIREMAN FAMILY. Mr. Cheeseman's. *R.P., T.S.S.*

CHESNEY WOLD. Sir Leicester and Lady Dedlock's home in Lincolnshire. *B.H.* vii.

CHESNEY WOLD. Little church in the park in. *B.H.* ii.

Is mouldy—and there is a general smell and taste as of the ancient Dedlocks in their graves.

CHESNEY WOLD. Ghost's Walk in Lady Dedlock's place in. *B.H.* ii.

Broad-flagged pavement, called from old time the Ghosts' Walk.

CHESNEY WOLD VILLAGE. *B.H.* vii.

CHESTER. Mr. *M.H.C.* vi.

CHESTER. Edward. *B.R.* i.

A young man of about eight-and-twenty, rather above the middle height — gracefully and strongly made. He wore his own dark hair, and was accoutred in a riding-dress —together with his large boots (resembling those of our lifeguardsmen of the present day).—Lying upon the table beside him—were a heavy riding-whip and a slouched hat—a pair of pistols in a holster-case, and a short riding-cloak.

Note.—Edward is in love with Emma Haredale. Both her father and his endeavour to prevent the marriage, but eventually the former relents. The wedding takes place and Edward and his wife go abroad, although they return to England when "the riots are many years old."

CHESTER. Edward, Great-grandfather of. *B.R.* xv.

CHESTER. Edward, Maternal grandfather of. *B.R.* xv.

CHESTER. Edward, Mother of. *B.R.* xv.

CHESTER. Edward and Emma, Children of. *B.R.* lxxxii.

CHESTER. Edward, Wife of, née Emma Haredale—*which see.*

CHESTER. Old Mr. (Sir John). *B.R.* v.

A staid, grave, placid gentleman, something past the prime of life, yet upright in his carriage for all that. He wore a riding-coat of a somewhat brighter green than might have been expected of a gentleman of his years, with a short black velvet cape, and laced pocket-holes and cuffs,—his linen, too, was of the finest kind, worked in a rich pattern at the wrists and throat, and scrupulously white.

Note.—Father of Edward Chester; becomes Sir John in chap. xl. He endeavours, by all the means in his power, to prevent the marriage of his son and Miss Emma Haredale. He obtains control of Hugh and uses him for his own ends. Utterly without honour in the real sense he discards his tools when they are of no further use to him. He is eventually killed by Mr. Haredale in a duel.

CHESTER. Son of Mr. *M.H.C.* vi.

CHESTERTON. Mr., Prison Governor. *M.P., C. and E.*

CHESTLE. Mr. *D.C.* xviii.

Note.—The hop-grower who supplants David and marries the eldest Miss Larkins.

CHEVALIER. The. *P.F.I., L.R.G.A.*

CHEYPE. The ward of. *M.H.C.* i.

CHIAJA. The, Or public gardens. *P.F.I., R.D.*

CHIB. Mr., A vestry-man. *R.P., O.V.*

Father of the vestry.

CHICK. Young Smallweed—*which see.*

CHICK. Frederick. *D. and S.* i.

CHICK. John, Husband of Dombey's sister. *D. and S.* i.

A stout old gentleman, with a very large face, and his hands continually in his pockets, and who had a tendency to whistle and hum tunes. In their matrimonial bickerings they were, upon the whole, a well-matched, fairly balanced, give-and-take couple.

CHICK. Louisa, Sister of Dombey. *D. and S.* i.

A lady rather past the middle age than otherwise, but dressed in a very juvenile manner, particularly as to the tightness of her bodice.

Note.—Mr. Dombey's sister and friend of Miss Tox. She entreats everybody, from the first Mrs. Dombey, at the birth of little Paul, to her brother, on the ruin of the house, to " make an effort." The latter is the last occasion on which she emerges from her obscurity.

CHICKABIDDY LICK. Plains of. *M.C.* xxi.

CHICKENSTALKER. Mrs., Shopkeeper. *C.B., C.G.* ii.

In the general line.

CHICKENSTALKER. Shop of Mrs. *C.B., C.G.* iv.

Crammed and choked with the abundance of its stock—everything was fish that came to the net of this greedy little shop, and all articles were in its net.

CHICKETT. The girl from the workhouse. *D.C.* xi.

CHICKSEY AND STOBBLES. *O.M.F.* iv.

Former masters of Veneering.

CHICKSEY, VENEERING, AND STOBBLES. *O.M.F.* iv.

Drug house.

CHICKWEED. Conkey, A burglar. *O.T.* xxxi.

Kept a public-house, and he had a cellar, where a good many young lords went to see cock-fighting, and badger-drawing, and that.

CHICK-WEED. Young Smallweed—*which see.*

CHIEF. Of the gravediggers. *M.P., L.W.O.Y.*

CHIEF. The, Mr. Dorrit—*which see.*

CHIGGLE. Sculptor. *M.C.* xxxiv.

CHIGWELL. Essex. *B.R.* i.

CHIGWELL CHURCH. *B.R.* xxxi.

CHIGWELL ROW. *B.R.* i.

CHILD. *R.P., C.D.S.*

CHILD. *M.P., C.H.*

CHILD. A washerwoman's. *S.B.B., O.P.* ii.

CHILD. In common lodging-house in Liverpool. *U.T.* v.

She drags out a skinny little arm from a brown dust-heap on the ground.

CHILD. Of Betsy Martin's. Convert to temperance. *P.P.* xxxiii.

CHILD. Of prisoner in the Fleet. *P.P.* xli.

CHILD-BED-LINEN SOCIETY. *S.B.B., O.P.* vi.

CHILDERS. E. W. B., One of Sleary's Troupe. *H.T., S.* vi.

His face close-shaven, thin and sallow, was shaded by a quantity of dark hair, brushed into a roll all round his head, and parted in the centre. He was dressed in a Newmarket coat, and tight-fitting trousers, wore a shawl round his neck.

CHILDERS. Mrs. E. W. B., Josephine. *H.T., G.* vii.

CHILDREN. *S.B.B.*, Scenes i.

CHILDREN. Four of five, in house in George's Yard. *S.B.B., O.P.* v.

Grovelling about among the sand on the floor, naked.

CHILDREN. Groups of (singing carols). *P.P.* xxix.

Curly-headed little rascals.

CHILDREN. In chaises, at tea-gardens. *S.B.B.*, Scenes i.

CHILDREN. Of fancy stationer. *S.B.B.*, Scenes iii.

In mourning — in the little parlour behind the shop—clean, but their clothes were threadbare.

CHILDREN. Of Mr. and Mrs. Britain. *C.B., B.o.L.* iii.

CHILDREN. Our. *M.P., W.L.*

CHILDREN. Rosy, living opposite to Mr. Dombey's house. *D. and S.* xviii.

CHILDREN. Seeing Mark Tapley off. *M.C.* vii.

CHILDREN. Six, of brother of passenger on coach. *N.N.* v.

CHILDREN. Six small, of widow. *S.B.B., O.P.* i.

CHILDREN. Some ragged, of Corpse. *O.T.* v.

CHILDREN. Three or four, of lady in distress. *S.B.B., O.P.* v.

Fine-looking little children.

CHILDREN. Two little. *M.P., L.W.O.Y.*

CHILDREN-IN-ARMS. Taking part in election. *P.P.* xiii.

"To pat on the head and inquire the age of" . . . "if you *could* manage to kiss one of 'em."

CHILDREN'S HOSPITAL. The. *O.M.F.* xxvi.

CHILL. Uncle, Relation of Mr. Michael. *R.P., P.R.S.*

CHILLIP. Dr. *D.C.* i.

He walked as softly as the ghost in Hamlet, and more slowly. He carried his head on one side, partly in modest depreciation of himself, partly in modest propitiation of everybody else.

Note.—He ushers little David into the world. Some years later he left Blunderstone and vanishes until David meets him in a coffee-house. He has bought a little practice within a few miles of Bury St. Edmunds where he is doing well.

CHILLIP'S BABY. *D.C.* xxii.

A weazen little baby, with a heavy head that it couldn't hold up, and two weak staring eyes, with which it seemed to be always wondering why it had ever been born.

CHILLIP'S. Mr., Second wife. *D.C.* xxii.

Tall, raw-boned, high-nosed.

CHIMES. The, Church bells. *C.B., C.* i.

Centuries ago, these bells had been baptized by bishops.

CHIMNEY SWEEPER. Master. *D. and S.* xv.

A man who had once resided in that vanished land (Stagg's Gardens), who now lived in a stuccoed house three stories high, and gave himself out, with golden flourishes upon a varnished board, as contractor for the cleaning of railway chimneys by machinery.

CHIN TEE. Chinese idol. *M.P., C.J.*

CHINA. (Country.) *B.H.* xi. ; *C.S.*, *D.M.* ; *H.T.*, *S.* xv. ; *L.D.* v. ; *M.P.*, *S.R.* ; *M.P.*, *T.O.H.* ; *R.P.*, *B.S.* ; *R.P.*, *W.D.T.*

CHINA. In London. *M.P., C.J.*

CHINAMAN. *E.D.* i.

CHINAMAN. Jack. *E.D.* i.

CHINAMAN. Sailor. *U.T.* xx.

CHINK'S BASIN. *G.E.* xlvi.

CHIPPING NORTON. *R.P., O.S.*

CHIPS. Character in one of Nurse's Stories. *U.T.* xv.

Had sold himself to the devil for an iron pot, and a bushel of tenpenny nails, and half a ton of copper and a rat that could speak.

CHIRRUP. Mr. *S.Y.C.*

CHIRRUP. Mrs. *S.Y.C.*

CHISWELL STREET. *O.T.* xxi.

CHISWICK. *O.M.F.* vi. ; *O.T.* xxi.

CHITLING. Tom, Recently released prisoner. *O.T.* xviii.

He had small twinkling eyes, and a pock-marked face ; wore a fur cap, a dark corduroy jacket, greasy fustian trousers, and an apron.

Note.—Another of Fagin's pupils. Rather more than friendly with Bet. Is first met with when he comes out of prison and last seen in the house by the Folly Ditch.

CHIVERY AND CO. Tobacconists. *L.D.* xxii.

Importers of pure Havannah cigars, Bengal cheroots, and fine-flavoured Cubas, dealers in fancy snuffs, etc., etc.

It was a very small establishment, wherein a decent woman sat behind the counter working at her needle. Little jars of tobacco, little boxes of cigars, a little assortment of pipes, a little jar or two of snuff, and a little instrument like a shoeing horn for serving it out, composed the retail stock in trade.

CHIVERY. Mrs., Mother of young John. *L.D.* xviii.

Kept "a snug tobacco business round the corner of Horsemonger Lane."

CHIVERY. Senior, A non-resident turnkey at the Marshalsea. *L.D.* xviii.

CHIVERY. Young John, Sentimental son of the turnkey. *L.D.* xviii.

Was small of stature, with rather weak legs and very weak light hair. One of his eyes was also weak, and looked larger than the other, as if it couldn't collect itself. Young John was gentle likewise ; but he was of great soul. Poetical, expansive, faithful. Was neatly attired in a plum-coloured coat, with as large a collar of black velvet as his figure could carry ; a silken waistcoat bedecked with golden sprigs ; a chaste neckerchief much in vogue in that day—pantaloons so highly decorated with side stripes—and a hat of state very high and hard—a pair of white kid gloves, and a cane like a little finger post.

Note.—Son of John Chivery. Lover of Little Dorrit at first in secret. Eventually he tells her of his love, but she refuses him. The blow upsets him very much but he continues to love her. He is last seen at Little Dorrit's wedding.

CHIZZLE. Mr. *B.H.* i.

CHOBBS AND BOLBERRY. *M.C.* xliv.

CHOCTAW TRIBE. Of Indians. *A.N.* xii. ; *M.P., E.T.*

CHOKE. General. *M.C.* xxi.

Very lank gentleman, in a loose limp white cravat, a long white waistcoat and a black great-coat.

CHOKESMITH. *See* Rokesmith.

CHOLLOP. Hannibal *M.C.* xxxiii.

A lean person in a blue frock and a straw hat, with a short black pipe in his mouth; and a great hickory stick, studded all over with knots, in his hand, smoking and chewing as he came along.

CHOPPER. Great-uncle of William Tinkling. *H.R.* i.

CHOPPER. Mrs. *S.Y.C.*

CHOPS. The dwarf. *C.S., G.i.S.*

CHOPSKI. The dwarf. *C.S., G.i.S.*

CHORLEY. Mr. *M.P., A.P.*

CHOWLEY. *See* Mac Stinger, Charles.

CHOWSER. Colonel, Guest of Ralph Nickleby. *N.N.* xix.

CHRIST. *M.P., M.M.*

CHRISTCHURCH, Oxford. Library of. *M.P., T.O.H.*

CHRISTIAN. Fletcher. *R.P., L.P.V.*

One of the officers of the "Bounty."

CHRISTIAN. Thursday October. *R.P., T.L.V.*

Son of Fletcher Christian by a savage mother.

CHRISTIANA. One - time sweetheart of Mr. Michael. *R.P., P.R.S.*

CHRISTIANA. Widowed mother of. *R.P., P.R.S.*

CHRISTINA. Donna, Only daughter of Don Bolaro Fizzgig. *P.P.* ii.

Note.—One of Jingle's imaginary conquests.

CHRISTMAS FAMILY - PARTY. Grandmama at. *S.B.B.*, Char. vii.

CHRISTMAS. Rev. Henry. *M.P., I.M.*

"**CHRISTMAS PAST.**" First spirit. *C.B., C.C., S.* ii.

"**CHRISTMAS PRESENT.**" Second spirit. *C.B., C.C.S.* iii.

"**CHRISTMAS YET TO COME.**" Third spirit. *C.B., C.C.S.* iv.

CHRISTOPHER. A waiter. *C.S., S.L.* i.

"**CHRISTOPHER HARDMAN'S MEN.**" *M.P., O.S.*

CHRISTOPHER-WREN CHURCH. *C.S., N.T.*, Act i.

"**CHRONICLE.**" *N.N.* iv.

CHRONICLE. The gentlemanly, writer of a letter to Master Humphrey. *M.H.C.* i.

CHRONOLOGY. Precincts of. *M.P., L.W.O.Y.*

CHUCKSTER. Mr., Clerk to Mr. Witherden. *O.C.S.* xiv.

Note.—Mr. Chuckster was Mr. Witherden's clerk, a friend of Dick Swiveller, and, in his own way, Kit's enemy. When Kit's name was cleared, Mr. Chuckster thought him rather worse than before because his guilt would have shown his spirit. Chuckster leaves the story as the occasional visitor of Dick and the Marchioness.

CHUFFEY. Anthony Chuzzlewit & Son's clerk. *M.C.* xi.

A little blear-eyed, weazen-faced, ancient man. He was of a remote fashion, and dusty like the rest of the furniture; he was dressed in a decayed suit of black; with breeches garnished at the knees with rusty wisps of ribbon, the very paupers of shoe-strings; on the lower portion of his spindle legs were dingy worsted stockings of the same colour.

Note.—The old clerk of Anthony Chuzzlewit is so wrapped up in his master that he seems dead to the rest of the world.

CHUMBLEDON SQUARE. *R.P., O.V.*

CHURCH. *R.P., C.D. of S.*

CHURCH. An old city. *U.T.* ix.

Christening would seem to have faded out of this church long ago, for the font has the dust of desuetude thick upon it, and its wooden cover (shaped like an old-fashioned tureen cover) looks as if it wouldn't come off, upon requirement. The altar—rickety and the Commandments damp.

CHURCH. Anglo-Norman style. *D. and S.* xli.

They've spoilt it with whitewash.

CHURCH. Belonging to Foundling Hospital. *L.D.* ii.

I saw all those children ranged tier above tier, and appealing from the Father none of them had known on earth, to the Father of us all in heaven.

CHURCH. Down in Devonshire. *D.C.* xxvii.

CHURCH IN THE MARSHES. Pip's village. *G.E.* i.

CHURCH. In which Paul Dombey was christened. *M.C.* v.

CHURCH. In which Wemmick and Miss Skiffins were married. *G.E.* lv.

CHURCH. Little, In the park. *B.H.* xviii.

CHURCH. Near Rood Lane. *U.T.* ix.

There was often a subtle flavour of wine.

CHURCH. New, In Coketown. *H.T.*, s. v.

A stuccoed edifice with a square steeple over the door, terminating in four short pinnacles like florid wooden legs.

CHURCH. New, Saint Pancras. *S.B.B.*, Tales i.

CHURCH OF ENGLAND MISSIONARY SOCIETY. *M.P., N.E.*

CHURCH. One obscure, In the heart of City. *U.T.* ix.

Which had broken out in the melodramatic style, and was got up with various tawdry decorations, much after the manner of the extinct London maypoles.

CHURCH STREET. *O.M.F.* xviii.

CHURCH. The. *B.R.* i.

CHURCH. Where Bella Wilfer and Rokesmith were married. *O.M.F.* liv.

CHURCH. Where Little Nell was buried. *O.C.S.* lxxii.

CHURCH. Where Walter and Florence were married. *D. and S.* lvi.

A mouldy old church in a yard, hemmed in by a labyrinth of back streets and courts, with a little burying-ground round it, and itself buried in a kind of vault, formed by the neighbouring houses, and paved with echoing stones. It was a great, dim, shabby pile, with high old oaken pews, among which about a score of people lost themselves every Sunday.

CHURCHES. City of London. *U.T.* x.

CHURCHWARDEN. The Senior *S.B.B., O.P.* i.

CHURCHWARDENS. The. *S.B.B., O.P.* i.

CHURCHYARD. *P.P.* xxi.

Beneath a plain gravestone, in one of the most peaceful and secluded churchyards in Kent, where wild-flowers mingle with the grass, and the soft landscape around forms the fairest spot in the garden of England.

CHURCHYARD. *G.E.* i.

Bleak place, overgrown with nettles.

CHURCHYARD. A., *O.M.F.* xxxii.

A paved square court, with a raised bank of earth about breast-high in the middle, enclosed by iron rails.

CHURCHYARD. A hemmed-in. *B.H.* xi.

Whence malignant diseases are communicated to the bodies of our dear brothers and sisters who have not departed.

CHURCHYARD. Approach to a City. *U.T.* xxi.

A dairy exhibiting in its modest

window one very little milk-can and three eggs, would suggest to me the certainty of finding the poultry, hard by, pecking at my forefathers.

CHURCHYARD. In Bedfordshire. *L.D.* xxv.

CHURCHYARD. Of a City church. *U.T.* ix.

Like the great, shabby, old mignonette box, with two trees in it and one tomb.

CHURCHYARD. Phantom. *C.B., C.C.,* s. iv.

CHURCHYARDS. City. *U.T.* xxi.

Sometimes so entirely detached from churches, always so pressed upon houses; so small, so rank, so silent, so forgotten, except by the few people who ever look down on them from their smoky windows.

CHURCHYARDS. City, Visitors to. *U.T.* xxi.

Blinking old men, let out of workhouses—have a tendency to sit on bits of coping stone—with both hands on their sticks, and asthmatically gasping. The more depressed class of beggars, too, bring hither broken meats, and munch.

CHUZZLEWIT. *M.P., T.O.P.*

CHUZZLEWIT. A certain male Chuzzlewit. *M.C.* i.

Whose birth must be admitted to be involved in some obscurity, was of very mean and low descent.

CHUZZLEWIT. A, In the Gunpowder Plot. *M.C.* i.

CHUZZLEWIT. Anthony, *M.C.* iv.

The face of the old man was so sharpened by the wariness and cunning of his life, that it seemed to cut him a passage through the crowded room, as he edged away behind the remotest chairs.

Note.—Old Anthony was brother to the elder Martin, and father of Jonas Chuzzlewit. He was cunning, and to some extent unscrupulous. This is reflected in his son, who makes an unsuccessful attempt to poison his father. Old Anthony, however, soon dies.

CHUZZLEWIT. Diggory. *M.C.* i.

Making constant reference to an uncle, in respect of whom he would seem to have entertained great expectations, as he was in the habit of seeking to propitiate his favour by presents of plate, jewels, books, watches, and other valuable articles.

CHUZZLEWIT FAMILY. *M.C.* i.

Undoubtedly descended in a direct line from Adam and Eve.

CHUZZLEWIT. George, A gay bachelor cousin of Mr. Martin Chuzzlewit. *M.C.* iv.

Who claimed to be young, but had been younger, and was inclined to corpulency, and rather overfed himself: to that extent, indeed, that his eyes were strained in their sockets, as if with constant surprise; and he had such an obvious disposition to pimples, that the bright spots on his cravat, the rich pattern on his waistcoat, and even his glittering trinkets, seemed to have broken out upon him.

CHUZZLEWIT. Jonas, Son of Anthony Chuzzlewit. *M.C.* iv.

Had so profited by the precept and example of his father, that he looked a year or two the elder of the twain, as they stood winking their red eyes, side by side.

Note.—Young Jonas has inherited his father's cunning without his knowledge. He is cruel and miserly. He makes an attempt to poison his father, old Anthony, and as his intended victim soon dies, he believes he has succeeded. With the object of removing traces of the crime he takes precautions. But the secret is known to old Chuffey. He marries "Merry" Pecksniff, and carrying out his intention, he breaks her spirit with harshness and cruelty. Still under the impression that his plot to murder his father succeeded, he believes himself in the power of Montague of the Anglo-Bengalee. Acting under this influence, he pays a good amount of his inheritance to his knavish friend. One thing leads to another, and he commits another crime by murdering Tigg. This is found out, and on his way to the prison he poisons himself.

CHUZZLEWIT. Jonas, Mrs., *See* Pecksniff, Mercy.

CHUZZLEWIT. Martin. *M.C.* iii.

An old gentleman, travelling unattended in a rusty old chariot with post-horses.

Note.—Cousin to Pecksniff, grandfather to Martin the younger, and brother to Old Anthony Chuzzlewit. Old Martin is first seen ill and suspicious alike of his true friends and his covetous and hypocritical relatives. He goes to live with Pecksniff, who has endeavoured to persuade him of his disinterestedness. While there he pretends to be convinced of the other's good motives, and places himself entirely under Pecksniff's control. He is largely responsible for Martin's journey to London, and for many of the misfortunes attending the good characters of the story. Secretly, however, he does what he can to relieve Tom Pinch. When the day of retribution arrives he denounces and discards Pecksniff and reinstates Martin in his affections.

CHUZZLEWIT. Young Martin, grandson of Martin Chuzzlewit, a new pupil at Pecksniff's. *M.C.* iii.

He was young—one-and-twenty perhaps—and handsome, with a keen, dark eye. " I'm a sort of a relation of Pecksniff's—My grandfather is his cousin."

Note.—The title-character of the story is somewhat of a snob in the earlier chapters, and the author carries him through the narrative until he emerges considerate, kind, and with a more moderate idea of himself. He is brought up to rely on his expectations from his grandfather of the same name. He falls in love with Mary Graham. This displeases his grandfather, who turns him out. After this he goes to another relation, Pecksniff, to learn drawing and designing. Owing to the influence of his grandfather, however, Pecksniff turns him out. He then emigrates to America with Mark Tapley. Their ideas regarding the new continent are scarcely realized Their money is invested in land in the City of Eden, which is described in glowing terms by the agent. They discover it to be a dismal swamp, fever infected; without drainage, clearings, or houses. Martin is attacked by the prevalent fever, and is only saved by the attentions of Mark Tapley, who, in turn, is stricken down. They leave Eden, and with the assistance of Mr. Beavan return to England. Martin goes back to Pecksniff's to acknowledge his error to his grandfather, but is turned from the door. He returns to London, and eventually finds that his grandfather has been proving Pecksniff's intentions. After the denunciation of the hypocritical architect, Martin finds himself reinstated in his uncle's affections, and marries Mary Graham.

CHUZZLEWIT. Mrs. Ned, Widow of a deceased brother of Mr. Martin Chuzzlewit. *M.C.* iv.

Having a dreary face, and a bony figure and a masculine voice, was, in right of these qualities, what is commonly called a strongminded woman.

CHUZZLEWIT. One. *M.C.* i.

Came over with William the Conqueror.

CHUZZLEWIT. Toby, Son of a certain Male Chuzzlewit *M.C.* i.

Upon his deathbed this question was put to him, in a distinct, solemn, and formal way : " Toby Chuzzlewit, who was your grandfather? " to which he replied—and his words were taken down—the Lord No. Zoo.

CHUZZLEWIT AND CO. Martin Chuzzlewit and Mark Tapley. *M.C.* xxiii.

CHUZZLEWIT AND SON. The firm of Anthony. *M.C.* xi.

Manchester Warehousemen.

CHUZZLEWIT AND SON. Place of business of Anthony, *M.C.* xi.

In a very narrow street behind the Post Office. A dim, dirty, smoky, tumbledown, rotten old house it was, as any one would desire to see, but there the firm—transacted all their business and their pleasure too, such as it was; for neither the young man nor the old had any other residence, or any care or thought beyond its narrow limits.

CHUZZLEWITS. Many. *M.C.* i.

Being unsuccessful in other pursuits, have, without the smallest rational hope of enriching themselves, or any conceivable reason, set up as coal merchants.

CICERO. Negro Emancipated Slave. *M.C.* xvii

Bought his freedom, which he got pretty cheap at last, on account of his strength being nearly gone, and he being ill.

CICERONE. *P.F.I.*, *P.M.B.*

CIGAR SHOP. A West End. *S.B.B.*, Scenes iii.

CINCINNATI. *A.N.* x. ; *M.P.*, *E.T.* ; *M.P.*, *S.B.*

CINDERELLA. *M.P.*, *F.F.*

CIRCUMLOCUTION OFFICE. *L.D.* ix. ; *M.P.*, *M. in E.R.*

The Most Important Department under Government . . . no public business of any kind could possibly be done at any time without the acquiescence of the Circumlocution Office.—Whatever was required to be done, the Circumlocution Office was beforehand with all the public departments in the art of perceiving —*How Not to Do It.*

CIRCUMLOCUTION OFFICE. Pagoda Department of. *U.T.* viii.

CIRCUMLOCUTION SAGES. *L.D.* x.

CIRCUS OF ROMULUS. *P.F.I.*, *R.*

CIRENCESTER. *M.P.*, *E.S.*

CITIZEN. A substantial *M.H.C.*, i.

CITY. (London). *C.S.*, *M.L.L.* i. ; *C.S.*, *S.L.* iv. ; *G.E.* xxiv. ; *M.C.* viii. ; *M.H.C.* . ; *N.N.* xi. ; *O.M.F.* xxxiv. ; *P.P.* xxxii. ; *R.P.*, *A.F.* ; *R.P.*, *B.S.* ; *S.B.B.*, Scenes i. ; *S.B.B.*, Scenes xvii.

CITY CHURCHYARD. Another. *U.T.* xxi.

In another City Churchyard of —cramped dimensions, I saw—two comfortable Charity children.

CITY CLERK. Occupant of house next door, without the knocker. *S.B.B.*, *O.P.* vii.

CITY COUNTING HOUSES. Youths from, *S.B.B.*, Scenes xiii.

CITY OF THE ABSENT. *U.T.* xxi.

CITY SQUARE. *N.N.* xxxvii.

CIVITA VECCHIA. *L.D.* liv. ; *R.P.*, *P.M.T.P.*

CLAPHAM. *M.P.*, *N.Y.D.*, *M.P.I.*

CLAPHAM GREEN. *P.P.* xxxv.

CLAPHAM ROAD. *R.P.*, *P.R.S.*

CLAPPERTON. *M.P.*, *N.E.*

CLAPTON. *S.B.B.*, Scenes ix.

CLARA. Secretly engaged to Herbert Pocket. *G.E.* xxx.

CLARE. *R.P.*, *T.D.P.*

CLARE. Miss Ada, Ward in Chancery. *B.H.* iii.

A beautiful girl with such rich golden hair, such soft blue eyes, and such a bright innocent, trusting face —about seventeen.

Note.—A ward of Mr. Jarndyce. She is troubled about her cousin Richard Carstone on account of his shiftlessness and his absorption in the chancery suit. But in spite of her entreaties he is unable to alter what is really his nature, and in spite of her knowledge of his temperament, Ada marries him, but is early left a widow. Unlike Richard, she continues her trust in their guardian, and is a close friend of Esther Summerson.

CLARE MARKET. *B.R.* lvi ; *P.P.* xx. ; *R.P.*, *L.A.* ; *R.P.*, *M.F.F.* ; *S.B.B.*, Scenes xxii.

CLARENCE DOCK. *R.P.*, *B.*

CLARENDON HOTEL. *M.P.*, *L.T.*

CLARIONET. The, One of the Waits. *C.S.* ; *S.P.T.* iii.

CLARISSA. The other Miss Spenow. *D.C.* xli.

CLARK. Betsy. Servant next door. *S.B.B* Scenes i.

CLARK. Mr., Employed by Dombey and Son. *D. and S.* vi.

Looking at the neighbouring masts and boats, a stout man stood whistling, with his pen behind his ear, and his hands in his pockets, as if his day's work were nearly done.

CLARK. Mrs. *N.N.* xvi.

CLARK'S CIRCUS. *M.P., J.G.*
The illegitimate drama.

CLARKE. Maria. *M.P., F.S.*

CLARKE. Mr., Mrs. Weller's first husband. *P.P.* xxvii.
Relict and sole executrix of the dead and gone Mr. Clarke. *See* Weller, Mrs.

CLARKE. Mr. Samuel, of Beaverton, Boone Co., U.S. *M.P., S.F.A.*

CLARKE COUNTY. (Mo). *A.N.* xvii.

CLARKINS. Mr., "Old." *M.P., W.R.*

CLARKINS. Mrs. *M.P., W.R.*

CLARKINS. Mrs. "Young." *M.P., W.R.*

CLARKSON. Mr. *M.P., V.D.*

CLARKSON. Mr., A Solicitor. *R.P., T.D.P.*

CLARRIKER AND CO. House of. *G.E.* xxxvii.
I must not leave it to be supposed that we were ever a great house. We were not in a grand way of business, but we had a good name.

CLATTER. A physician. *R.P., O.B.*

CLAXTON. Mr. Marshall. *M.P., C.*

CLAY. Mr. *M.P., I.C.*

CLAYPOLE. Noah, A Charity boy. *O.T.* v.
A large-headed, small-eyed youth, of lumbering make, and heavy countenance—a red nose, and yellow smalls.—Mother a washerwoman and father a drunken soldier.
Note.—Noah Claypole is the elder apprentice at Sowerby's the undertaker, who relieves the workhouse of Oliver Twist. He robs his master and makes for London. Here he becomes one of Fagin's dupes. He is set to watch Nancy, and it is through him that her friendship for Oliver is discovered, and she suffers death at the hands of Sikes. On the break-up of the thieves' school he turns Queen's evidence, and from that he becomes an informer.

CLEAR. Cape. *A.N.* xvi.

CLEAVER. Fanny, Dolls' Dressmaker. *O.M.F.* xviii.
A child—a dwarf—a girl—a something sitting on a little low old-fashioned armchair, which had a kind of little working bench before it. . . .
"I can't get up" "because my back's bad, and my legs are queer." A queer, but not ugly face,—bright grey eyes.
Note.—"Jenny Wren" was Lizzie Hexam's "landlady" after the death of the latter's father. The deformed dolls' dressmaker was greatly exercised by her "bad child."—her drunken, dissolute father. She is a friend to Lizzie Hexham. Her bad child dies in the street. She is called to Eugene Wrayburn's bedside, where she guesses the magic word. The last seen of her is where she is receiving a visit from Sloppy, and the inference is that Sloppy is "he" who was expected.

CLEAVER. Mr. *O.M.F.* xviii.
Note.—Mr. Dolls was Jenny Wren's "bad child," but her father. He was in a chronic state of drunkenness through multitudinous threepennyworth's o' rum. He betrays his trust for the same fiery liquor and meets his death through his debauchery. Jenny finds him on a police stretcher in the street, but when he is conveyed to the nearest "doctor's shop" it is found that he is dead.

CLEEFEWAY. Ratcliffe Highway. *R.P., O.F.W.*

CLEM. Little, Daughter of Mr. and Mrs. Britain. *C.B., B.O.L.* iii.

CLEM. *G.E.* xii.
Note.—Pip's song is from the song of the blacksmiths of Chatham which was sung on St. Clement's Day.

CLEM. Poor. *See* Clemency.

CLEMENCY. Maidservant of Dr. Jeddler. *C.B., B.o.L.* i.
About thirty years old, had a plump and cheerful face—twisted up into an odd expression of tight-

ness that made it comical. Her dress was a prodigious pair of self-willed shoes—blue stockings; a printed gown of many colours, and the most hideous pattern procurable for money, and a white apron—She always wore short sleeves. — In general a little cap placed somewhere on her head.

CLEMENT'S DANES. *C.S., M.L., Leg.* i.

CLEMENTS INN. *U.T.* xiv.

CLEMMY. *See* Clemency.

CLENNAM. Arthur. *L.D.* ii.

A grave, dark man of forty. The brown, grave gentleman who smiled so pleasantly, who was so frank and considerate in his manner.

Note.—One of the chief characters of the story. He is first seen on his return from China, where he has been assisting his father in business. His supposed mother, however, shows no great love for him. At his mother's house, he meets Little Dorrit, whom he befriends and assists. He enters into partnership with Doyce, but he is unfortunate and is thrown into the Marshalsea for debt. While there Little Dorrit tends him, and she having lost her money, they are married. Doyce sets the business on its legs again, and Clennam takes up his old position. It transpires that Arthur was the son of Mr. Clennam, but by another woman before he married: thus explaining Mrs. Clennam's coldness to him and want of interest.

CLENNAM. Arthur's father's Uncle Gilbert. *L.D.* xv.

CLENNAM. Mr., Arthur's father. *L.D.* iii.

Your ascendency over him was the cause of his going to China to take care of the business there.

CLENNAM. Mrs., Widowed stepmother of Arthur. *L.D.* iii.

On a black bier-like sofa—propped up behind with one great angular black bolster, like the block at a state execution in the good old times, sat his mother in a widow's dress—cold grey eyes, and her cold grey hair, and her immovable face, as stiff as the folds of her stony head-dress.—On her little table lay two or three books, her handkerchief, a pair of steel spectacles—and an old-fashioned watch in a heavy double case.

Note.—When she is introduced to the reader she is a crippled invalid, although her business capacity is unimpaired and she continues to manage the English affairs of the firm. She is supposed to be the mother of Arthur Clennam, but it transpires that she is only the wife of his father. She has suppressed a will by which Little Dorrit would have benefited. Rigaud or Blandois discovers it and endeavours to blackmail her. But she appeals to Little Dorrit, who not only forgives her, but accedes to her request to keep the information from Arthur until she shall be dead.

CLENNAM'S HOUSE. Mrs. *L.D.* iii.

An old brick house so dingy as to be all but black, standing by itself within a gateway. Before it, a square courtyard where a shrub or two or a patch of grass were as rank (which is saying much) as the iron railings enclosing them were rusty; behind it, a jumble of roots. It was a double house, with long, narrow, heavily-framed windows.—It had been propped up, and was leaning on some half-dozen gigantic crutches.

CLENNAMS. Parents of Mr. *L.D.* ii.

I am the only son of a hard father and mother—parents who weighed, measured, and priced everything; for whom what could not be weighed measured, and priced, had no existence.

CLENNAMS. Of Cornwall. *L.D.* xiii.

CLEOPATRA. Mrs. Skewton. *D. and S.* xxi.

CLERGYMAN. *C.B., C.C.*, s.i.

CLERGYMAN. Attending death-bed of Nicholas Nickleby, Sr. *N.N.* i.

" It is very sinful to rebel."

CLERGYMAN. Benevolent old. *P.P.* xxviii.

Guest at wedding of Bella and Trundle.

Note.—As the "Ivy Green" was not originally written for "Pickwick," it is possible that the Clergyman was not intended as a character; this would no doubt account for the very small place he occupies in the story.

CLERGYMAN. Officiating. *S.B.B., O.P.* i.

CLERGYMAN. Who christened Paul Dombey. *D. and S.* v.

An amiable and mild-looking young curate, but obviously afraid of the baby—like the principal character in a ghost story "a tall figure all in white"—at sight of whom Paul rent the air with his cries.

CLERICAL GENTLEMAN. Chaplain. Prisoner in the Fleet. *P.P.* xlii.

Who fastened his coat all the way up to his chin by means of a pin and a button alternately, had a very course red face, and looked like a drunken chaplain: which, indeed, he was.

CLERK. *C.B., C.C.,* s. i.

CLERK. A. *P.P.* xl.

In spectacles, standing on a box behind a wooden bar at another end of the room, who was "taking the affidavits," large batches of which were, from time to time, carried into the private room, for the judge's signature.

CLERK. Angular, Mr. Grewgious. *E.D.* ix.

CLERK. Attorney's, In Doctors' Commons. *S.B.B.,* Scenes viii.

CLERK. Common law. *P.P.* xl. With a bass voice.

CLERK. Copying, in "Six Clerks' Office." *B.H.* i.

CLERK. Early. *S.B.B.,* Scenes i.

CLERK. In a Government Office. *P.P.* xliv.

A very pleasant gen'l'm'n too—one o' the precise and tidy sort, as puts their feet in little india-rubber fire-buckets wen it's wet weather—he saved up his money on principle, wore a clean shirt every day on principle; never spoke to none of his relations on principle, "fear they shou'd want to borrow money of him"—dined every day at the same place.

CLERK. In church where Paul was christened. *D. and S.* v.

The only cheerful-looking object there, and *he* was an undertaker.

CLERK. Of church where Walter and Florence are married. *D. and S.* lvii.

A dusty old clerk, who keeps a sort of evaporated news-shop underneath an archway opposite.

CLERK. Of hotel in Brook Street. *L.D.* lii.

CLERK. Of Mr. Jaggers'. *G.E.* xxiv.

A high-shouldered man with a face-ache tied up in dirty flannel, who was dressed in old black clothes that bore the appearance of having been waxed.

CLERK. Of Mr. Jaggers'. *G.E.* xxiv.

A little flabby terrier of a clerk with dangling hair.

CLERK. Of Mr. Jaggers'. *G.E.* xxiv.

Looked something between a publican and a rat-catcher.

CLERK. Of the Patents. *R.P., P.M.T.P.*

CLERK. Office of the Judges. *P.P.* xl.

A room of specially dirty appearance, with a very low ceiling and old panelled walls.

CLERK. Parish. *M.H.C.* i.

CLERK. Postal, On Railway Train. *U.T.* xiii.

CLERK. Superannuated Bank, friend of Tim Linkinwater. *N.N.* xxxvii.

CLERKENWELL. *B.H.* xxvi.; *B.R.* iv.; *M.P., M,P.*; *O.M.F.* vii; *O.T.* x.; *T.T.C.* bk. ii., ch. vi.

Although there were busy trades—and working jewellers by scores, it was a purer place, with farm-houses nearer to it than many modern Londoners would readily believe, and lovers' walks at no great distance, which turned into squalid courts.

CLERKENWELL. House in a street in. *B.R.* iv

A modest building, not over-newly fashioned, not very straight not large, not tall; not boldfaced with great staring windows, but a shy, blinking house, with a conical roof going up into a peak over its garret window of four small panes of glass.

CLERKENWELL. New jail at. *B.R.* lxvi.

CLERKENWELL GREEN. *U.T.* x.

CLERKENWELL SESSIONS. *O.T.* xvii.

CLERKS. Articled. *B.H.* i.

CLERKS. At Gray's Inn Square. *P.P.* liii.

CLERKS. In Mr. Dombey's Office. *D. and S.* xiii.

Not a whit behindhand in their demonstrations of respect. The wit of the counting-house became in a moment as mute as the row of leather fire-buckets hanging up behind.

CLERKS. Managing. *P.P.* xl.

CLERKS. Two spare, in a Bank in Venice. *L.D.* xlii.

Like dried dragoons, in green velvet caps adorned with golden tassels.

CLEVELAND. *A.N.* xiv.

CLEVERLY. Susannah, Emigrant. *U.T.* xx.

CLEVERLY. William, Emigrant. *U.T.* xx.

CLICK. Mr., A Lodger. *C.S., S.L.* iii.

The rest of the house generally give him his name, as being first ront, carpeted all over, his own furniture, and if not mahogany, an out-and-out imitation.

CLICK. Mister, A Pickpocket. *R.P., D.W.I.F.*

CLICKITS. *S.Y.C.*

CLICKITT. The youngest Miss, but one. *M.P., N.Y.D.*

CLIFFORD STREET. *U.T.* xvi.

CLIFFORD'S INN. *B.H.* xxxiv.; *L.D.* vii.; *O.M.F.* viii.; *P.P.* xxi.

CLIFFORD'S INN. Plantation in. *O.M.F.* viii.

Mouldy little plantation, or cat preserve—sparrows were there, cats were there, dry rot and wet rot were there.

CLIFTON. *P.P.* xxxviii.

CLIP. Mr. *Mr. R.B.*

CLISSOLD. Lawrence, A Clerk. *C.S., M.f.T.S.* v.

CLIVE. Mr., Clerk in another Department of Circumlocution Office. *L.D.* x.

CLOCK ROOM. In haunted house. *C.S., H.H.*

CLOCK TOWER. Of Royal Exchange. *C.S., W.O.G.M.*

CLOCKER. Mr., A Grocer. *R.P., O.O.S.*

CLOISTERHAM. *E.D.* iii.

An ancient city,—and no meet dwelling-place for any one with hankerings after the noisy world, deriving an earthy flavour throughout from its cathedral crypt. The streets are little more than one narrow street.

CLOISTERHAM. Mayor of. *See* Sapsea, Mr. *E.D.* xii.

CLOISTERHAM JAIL. *E.D.* v.

CLOISTERHAM WEIR. *E.D.* vi.

CLOSE. The. *E.D.* ii.

CLOWN. At Astley's. *S.B.B.*, Scenes xi.

CLOWN. On stage in Britannia. *U.T.* iv.

CLOWNS. Four, in Booth at Greenwich Fair. *S.B.B.*, Scenes xii.
In Roman dresses, with their yellow legs and arms, long black curly heads, bushy eyebrows, and scowl expressive of assassination, and vengeance, and everything else that is grand and solemn.

CLOWNS. Two, May Day dancers. *S.B.B.*, Scenes xx.
Walked on their hands in the mud.

CLUB. Allotment. *M.P.*, *P.M.B.*

CLUB HOUSE. The Strangers'. *N.N.* l.

CLUBBER. Sir Thomas, Head of the Dockyard. *P.P.* ii.
Tall gentleman in blue coat and bright buttons.
Note. — Present at Charity Ball, Rochester.

CLUBBER. Lady, Wife of Sir Thomas Clubber. *P.P.* ii.
Large lady in blue satin.
Note. — Present at Charity Ball, Rochester.

CLUBBERS. The Miss, Daughters of Sir Thomas Clubber. *P.P.* ii.
Two large young ladies in fashionably made dresses of blue satin.
Note. — Present at Charity Ball, Rochester.

CLUBMEN. *M.P.*, *P.M.B.*

CLUBMEN. Of St. James's Street. *M.P.*, *P.M.B.*

CLUPPINS. Mrs., Particular acquaintance of Mrs. Bardell. *P.P.* xxvi.
A little brisk, busy-looking woman.

CLY. Roger, Servant to Charles Darnay. *T.T.C.*, Book ii. ; Chap. iii.
Police spy and witness against Darnay at the Old Bailey.
Note.—Spy. Partner with " Barsad " in the accusation against Darnay and other evil plots. Occupies the position of servant to Darnay. According to the " prophetic vision " he suffered death by the guillotine.

CLYDE. The Banks of the. *L.D.* xvi.

COACH AND HORSES. The. *O.T.* xxi.

COACH OFFICE. *D.C.* xvii.

COACH-OFFICE. All alive. *S.B.B.*, Scenes i.
Surrounded by the usual crowd of Jews and Nondescripts.

COACH OFFICE. Booking clerks of. *S.B.B.*, Scenes xv.
One with a pen behind his ears, and his hands behind him, is standing in front of the fire, like a full-length portrait of Napoleon.

COACH OFFICE. Booking office of. *S.B.B.*, Scenes xv.

COACH OFFICE. Porters of. *S.B.B.*, Scenes xv.
Stowing the luggage away, and running up the steps of the booking-office, and down the steps of the booking-office, with breathless rapidity.

COACH STANDS. *S.B.B.*, Scenes i.

COACHING HOUSE. *U.T.* xxii.

COACHMAKER. A. *U.T.* xxii.
A dry man, grizzled, and far advanced in years, but tall and upright who—pushed up his spectacles against his brown paper cap.

COACHMAKER. Gallant. *B.R.* xxxi.
Vowed that Mrs. Varden held him bound in adamantine chains.

COACHMAKER. Mother of gallant. *B.R.* xxxi

COACHMAKER. The *G.E.* vi i.

COACHMAN. *D.C.* xix.

COACHMAN. *P.P.* xxxvii.
In an embroidered coat reaching down to his heels, and a waistcoat of the same.

COACHMAN. First. *P.P.* lv.
Mottle-faced man.

COACHMAN. Of coach. *N.N.* v.

COACHMAN. Of coach to Yorkshire. *C.S., H.T.*

COACHMAN. Of doctor attending on Jinkinson. *M.H.C.* v.

COACHMAN. Of hackney-coach. *M.C.* xxviii.

COACHMAN. Of hackney-coach. *S.B.B.*, Scenes vii.

In his wooden-soled shoes.

COACHMAN. Of stage-coach. *S.B.B.*, Scenes xvi.

COACHMAN. On box of coach. *M.C.* xi.

COACHMAN. Requested to find Stagg's Gardens. *D. and S.* xv.

COACHMAN. Second. *P.P.* lv.

COACHMAN. Third. *P.P.* lv.

A hoarse gentleman.

COALHEAVER. Visiting hair-dresser's. *N.N.* lii.

Big, burly, good-humoured, with a pipe in his mouth,—requested to know when a shaver would be disengaged.

COAL PORTER. Out of work. *U.T.* xxx.

COAL PORTERS. At Ratcliff. *U.T.* xxx.

Occupants of one room.

COAN. Mrs., Medium. *M.P., S.F.A.*

COASTGUARD. *U.T.* ii.

COAVINSES. *See* Neckett, Mr.

COAVINSES' A 'ouse. *B.H.* vi.

COAVINSES' OFFICE. Boy in. *B.H.* xiv.

A very hideous boy.

COBB TOM. General Chandler and Post Office Keeper. *B.R.* i.

Beyond all question—the dullest dog of the party.

COBBEY. Pupil at Dotheboys' Hall. *N.N.* viii.

Cobbey's grandmother is dead, and his Uncle John has took to drinking, which is all the news his sister sends, except eighteenpence, which will just pay for that broken square of glass.

COBBLER. *M.P., T.O.H.*

COBBLER. Prisoner in the Fleet. *P.P.* xliv.

Who rented a small slip-room in one of the upper galleries—bald-headed. He was a sallow man—all cobblers are—and had a strong bristly beard—all cobblers have. His face was a queer, good-tempered piece of workmanship.

"COBBLER DICK." *M.P., O.S.*

COBBLER'S WIFE. Deceased. *P.P.* xliv.

COBBS. *M.P.T.T.*

COBBS. The Boots at the "Holly Tree Inn." *C.S., H.T.* v.

Formerly under-gardener to Mr. Walmer. A mowing and sweeping, and weeding and pruning and this and that.

COBBY. The Giant. *U.T.* xi.

COBDEN. Richard. *M.P., Ag. Int.*

COBHAM CHURCHYARD. *P.P.* xi.

COBHAM HALL. *P.P.* xi., *C.S., S.P.T.* iii.

An ancient hall, displaying the quaint and picturesque architecture of Elizabeth's time.

COBHAM VILLAGE. *P.P.* xi.

Really, for a misanthrope's choice, this is one of the prettiest and most desirable places of residence I ever met with.

COBHAM WOODS. *C.S.*; *S.P.T.* iii.

COBURG. *A.N.* xv.

"COBURG, THE." *N.N.* xxx.

COBURG DOCK. At Liverpool. *A.N.* i.

COBWEB. Esther Summerson. *B.H.* viii.

COCKER. Mr. Indignation, guest at Temeraire. *U.T.* xxxii.

COCKSPUR STREET. Charing Cross. *M.P., T.D.*

COCKSWAIN. The, of boating party. *S.B.B.*, Scenes x.

COE. Mrs., As Susan. *M.P., M.N.D.*

CODGER. Miss, Literary lady. *M.C.* xxxiv.

Sticking on the forehead—by invisible means, was a massive cameo, in size and shape like the raspberry tart which is ordinarily sold for a penny, representing on its front the Capitol at Washington.

CODGERS. *M.P., N.G.K.*

CODGERS. Mr. *L.T.*

CODLIN. Thomas, "Punch" showman. *O.C.S.* xvi.

Had a surly, grumbling manner, and an air of always counting up what money they hadn't made.

Note.—One of the two men with the Punch, Little Nell and her grandfather meet with early in their travels. The showmen had the idea that there was something to be made out of the two wanderers, and the one endeavoured to influence Nell at the other's expense. Hence arose the saying "Codlin's the friend, not Short."

COFFEE-HOUSE. In Covent Garden *B.R.* xxviii.

COFFEE-HOUSE. Serjeant's Inn. *P.P.* xliii.

COFFEE-ROOM FLIGHT. Stairs in the Fleet. *P.P.* xli.

These staircases received light from sundry windows placed at some distance above the floor, and looking into a gravelled area bounded by a high brick wall, with iron *chevaux-de-fris* at the top.

COFFEE-SHOP. Theatrical. *S.B.B.*, Scenes xiii.

COFFIN. The, The Argonaut. *U.T.* xv.

COFFIN LANE. Which led to the churchyard. *P.P.* xxix.

Into which the townspeople did not much care to go, except in broad daylight.

COGSFORD. Of Cogsford Brothers and Cogsford. *M.P., S.R.*

COGSHALL. *M.P., S.B.*

COILER. Mrs., A widow. *G.E.* xxiii.

Of that highly sympathetic nature that she agreed with everybody, blessed everybody, and shed tears on everybody, according to circumstances.

COINER. A, Prisoner in Newgate. *G.E.* xxxii.

In a well-worn olive-coloured frock coat, with a peculiar pallor overspreading the red in his complexion—his hat, which had a greasy and fatty surface like cold broth.

COKE. Caleb, of Wolverhampton. *M.P., R.S.*

COKETOWN. *H.T.*, s. iv.

A town of red brick, or of brick that would have been red if the smoke and ashes had allowed it. A town of machinery and tall chimneys. It had a black canal in it, and a river that ran purple with ill-smelling dye. It contained several large streets. all very like one another

COLDVEAL. Lady. *M.P., T.T.*

COLE. King. "The venerable" illustrious potentate. *P.P.* xxxvi.

COLEMAN STREET. *P.P.* xl.; and *S.B.B.*, Char. v.

COLERIDGE. Mr. Justice. *M.P., C.P.*

COLES. Mrs., Wife of Mr. Coles. *U.T.* xii.

COLES. Rev. T. S. *M.P., E.C.*

COLES'S. Coles's School. *U.T.* xii.

COLESHAW. Miss, Passenger on board "Golden Mary." *C.S.W.o.G.M.*

A sedate young woman in black, about thirty I should say, who was going out to join a brother.

COLISEUM. At Rome. *P.F.I., R.*; *R.P., L.A.*

COLLAN. *See* Bailey, Benjamin. *M.C.* ix.

COLLEGE. The. *M.C.* xxvii.

COLLEGE. The. *P.P.* xliv.

COLLEGE. Lilliputian (Miss Pupford's). *C.S., T.T.G.* vi.

COLLEGE. Of Upper Canada, Toronto. *A.N.* xv.

COLLEGE GREEN. *S.B.B.*, Tales i.

COLLEGE HILL. Mark Lane. *U.T.* xxi.

COLLEGE YARD. The aristocratic or pump side. *L.D.* xix.

COLLEGE YARD. The poor side. *L.D.* xix.

COLLEGIAN. The. *L.D.* xix.

In the seaside slippers, who had no shoes.

COLLEGIAN. The. *L.D.* xix.

In the dressing-gown, who had no coat.

COLLEGIAN. The poor lean clerk. *L.D.* xix.

In buttonless black, who had no hopes.

COLLEGIAN. The stout greengrocer. *L.D.* xix.

In the corduroy knee-breeches, who had no cares.

COLLIERS. Heavy old, at Chatham. *U.T.* xxiv.

COLLINGSWORTH. John, a spirit. *M.P., S.B.*

COLLINS. *M.P., O.L.N.O.*

COLLINS. Police-officer. *S.B.B.*, Scenes xviii.

COLLINS. Mr. Wilkie. *M.P., E.C.*; *M.P., N.T.*

COLLINS. Mr. Wilkie, as Lithers. *M.P., M.N.D.*

COLMAN Mr. *M.P., A.in E.*

COLONIAL OFFICE. *M.P., R.T.*

COLOSSEUM. *U.T.* xxi.

COLUMBIA. *A.N.* xvii.

COLUMBINE. A stage, in Britannia. *U.T.* iv.

COLUMBINE. In Booth at Greenwich Fair. *S.B.B.* xix.

COLUMBUS. *A.N.* xiv.

COMEDIAN. The low, Of the establishment. *S.B.B.*, Scenes xii.

Whose face is so deeply seared with the small-pox, and whose dirty shirt-front is inlaid with openwork and embossed with coral studs like ladybirds.

COMEDIAN. Principal, At Astley's. *S.B.B.*, Scenes xi.

COMIC ACTOR. *M P, G.A.*

COMIC SINGER. The, At Vauxhall Gardens. *S.B.B.*, Scenes xiv.

A marvellously facetious gentleman.

COMMERCIAL ROAD. London. *D.S.* ix.; *R.P.*, *T.D.P.*; and *U.T.* iii.

COMMERCIAL STREET. Whitechapel. *U.T.* xxiii.

COMMISSIONER. *M.P., S.R.*

COMMISSIONER. A, School Inspector. *H.T.*, s. ii.

A Government officer—in his way a professed pugilist—always in training with a system to force down the general throat like a bolus.

COMMISSIONER. Chief of Police. *U.T.* xxxiv.

COMMISSIONER. Mrs., Mrs. Pordage. *C.S., P.o.C.E.P.*

COMMISSIONER. Mrs. *M.P., S.R.*

COMMISSIONER. Of bankrupts. *P.P.* xlvii.

COMMISSIONERS. *M.P., N.E.*

COMMISSIONERS. Lottery. *R.P., B.S.*

COMMITTEE. Ladies' sick visitation. *S.B.B., O.P.* vi.

COMMITTEE. Of the Methodistical Order. *P.P.* xxii.

Fourteen women a passin "resolutions, and wotin" supplies, and all sort o' games.

COMMITTEE. Slumkey's, One of. *P.P.* xiii.

Addressing six small boys . . . as men of Eatanswill.

COMMON. A. *M.P., U.N.*

COMMON. The. *D.C.* xiv.

COMMON COUNCIL. *M.P., P.F.*

COMMON COUNCIL. Court of. *N.N.* xli.

COMMON COUNCILMAN. *M.H.C.* i.

COMMON HARD. Portsmouth. *N.N.* xxiii.

COMMON PLEAS. Court of. *U.T.* xxvi.

COMMON SENSE. An ill-conditioned friend of mine. *M.P., T.T.C.D.*

COMMONS. House of. *D. and S.* xxxi.; *M.C.* xxix; *M.H.C.* i; *M.P., H.H.* xli.; *N.N.*; *S.B.B.*, Scenes xiv.

COMMONS. A member of the House of. *S.B.B.*, Scenes xviii.
Singularly awkward and ungainly.

COMMONS. Messenger of the House of. *S.B.B.*, Scenes xviii.
With the gilt order round his neck.

COMMONS. An officer of the House of. *B.R.* xlix.

COMO. Lake of. *P.F.I., R.D.*

COMPAGNIA DELLA MISERICORDIA. Member of. *P.F.I., R.D.*

COMPANION. A. *M.P., N.S.L.*

COMPANION. My old, Master Humphrey's clock. *M.H.C.* i.

COMPANY. St. Katherine's Dock. *S.B.B.*, Scenes x.

COMPEYSON. Miss Havisham's false lover. *G.E.* xlii.

Note.—The second convict Pip sees on the marshes. He is recaptured with Magwitch. After his return from penal servitude he sees Magwitch, and gives information. He is killed at the recapture of Magwitch. He proves to have been the villianous lover of Miss Havisham

COMPEYSON. Wife of. *G.E.* xlii.

COMPORT. Jane, Sweetheart of young Dowgate. *U.T.* ix.

COMPTON. Mr., Actor. *M.P., M.B.*

CONCIERGERIE. *T.T.C.*, bk. iii., ch. xiii.

In the black prison of the Conciergerie, the doomed of the day awaited their fate.

CONCORD. A room in the Royal George Hotel, Dover. *T.T.C.* iv.

CONCORDE. Place de la. *R.P., O.o.S.*; *U.T.* xxiii.

CONDEMNED CELLS. In Newgate prison. *S.B.B.*, Scenes xxv.
The entrance is by a narrow and obscure passage leading to a dark passage, in which a charcoal stove casts a lurid tint over the objects in its vicinity. There are three of these passages, and three of these ranges of cells. Prior to the recorder's report being made, all the prisoners under sentence of death are removed from the day-room at five o'clock in the afternoon, and locked up in these cells, where they are allowed a candle until ten o'clock; and here they remain till seven next morning. When the warrant for a prisoner's execution arrives, he is removed to the cells, and confined in one of them until he leaves it for the scaffold.

CONDUCTOR. Gold-laced, The beadle. *S.B.B., O.P.* i.

CONDUCTOR. Of omnibus, Cad. *S.B.B.*, Scenes xvi.

His great boast is that he can chuck an old gen'lm'n into the buss, shut him in, and rattle off, before he knows where it's a going to.

CONDUCTOR. Of this Journal (*Household Words*). *M.P., B.A.*

CONDUCTOR. To one of the omnibuses. *N.N.* xlv.
Wears a glazed hat.—He has a wart on his nose.

CONFRATÉRNITA. *P.F.I., G.A.N.*

CONFRATÉRNITA. Blue. *P.F.I., G.A.N.*

CONGRESS. *M.P., Y.M.C.*

CONNECTICUT. *A.N.* iii.

CONNECTICUT RIVER. *A.N.* v.

CONOLLY. Dr. *M.P., S.B.*

CONSCRIPTS. French-Flemish. *U.T.* xxv.

Who had drawn unlucky numbers in the last conscripton and were on their way to a famous French garrison town.

CONSORT. Prince. *M.P., N.E.*

CONSTABLE. *O.T.* xxx.
Had a large staff, a large head, large features, and large half-boots.

CONSTABLE. A. *G.E.* iv.

CONSTABLE. The. *B.H.* xix.

CONSTABLES. *S.B.B.*, Scenes xvii.

CONSTABLES. The. *G.E.* xvi.
The extinct red waiscoated police.

CONSTABLES. With blue staves. *P.P.* xiii.

CONSTANT COMPANION. *R.P., C.D.O.S.*

CONSUL. The British. *L.D.* li.

CONSUL'S. A gentleman from the. *C.S., M.L.Leg.* ii.
Dark, with his hair cropped what I should consider too close.

CONTADINI. *P.F.I., R.*

CONTRACTOR. Railway. *M.P.T.B.*

CONTRACTOR. The. *O.M.F.* lxvii.

CONVENT. In St. Louis. *A.N.* xii.
For the ladies of the Sacred Heart.

CONVICT HULKS. *G.E.* i.

CONWAY. General, A soldier. *B.R.* xlix.
I am a soldier—and I will protect the freedom of this place with my sword.

COODLE. Lord. *B.H.* xii.

COOK. At number 25. *S.B.B., O.P.* iii.

COOK. Captain. *M.P., E.T., and S.B., T.* v.

COOK. Capt., Captain of steamship " Russia." *U.T.* xxxi.

COOK. In the house with the green gate. *P.P.* xxiii.

COOK. In Weller's service. *P.P.* lii.
A very buxom-looking cook, dressed in mourning, who had been bustling about in the bar, glided into the room—and bestowed many smirks of recognition on Sam, silently stationed herself at the back of his father's chair, and announced her presence by a slight cough.

COOK. Mrs. Jellyby's. *B.H.* iv.
In pattens—frequently came and skirmished with the housemaid at the door. There appeared to be ill-will between them.

COOK. Of Cheeryble Brothers. *N.N.* xxxv.

COOK. Of Mrs. Maylie. *O.T.* xxviii.

COOK'S COURT. *B.H.* x.

COOK'S STRAITS. *M.P., E.T.*

COOKING DEPÔT. For the working classes. *U.T.* xxiii.
Where accommodation is provided for dining comfortably 300 persons at a time.
Note.—This was one of the earliest experiments of " Cheap food." The building has been converted to other uses.

COOPER. Augustus. In the oil and colour line. *S.B.B.*, Char. ix.
Just of age, with a little money, a little business, and a little mother.

COOPER. Apprentice of Augustus. *S.B.B.*, Char. ix.

COOPER. Mr. Artist. *A.N.* xii.

COOPER. Mr. *M.P., F.C.*

COOPER. Mother of Mr. Augustus. *S.B.B.*, Char. ix
Managed her husband and his business in his lifetime, took to managing her son and his business after his decease.

COPE. *M.P., O.L.N.O.*

COPELAND. *R.P., A.P.A.*

COPENHAGEN HOUSE. *S.B.B.*, Scenes xx.

COPPERFIELD. Agnes, David's eldest child. *D.C.* xxxiv.

COPPERFIELD. Clara, David's mother. *D.C.* i.
My mother was, no doubt, unusually youthful in appearance, even for her years.

Note.—David's mother. Some years after the death of her husband she marries Mr. Murdstone. Her life after this is an unhappy one; so unhappy, in fact, that she dies under the treatment of her husband and his sister, her baby being buried with her.

COPPERFIELD. David, The elder. *D.C.* i.

My father's eyes had closed upon the light of this world six months, when mine opened on it.

COPPERFIELD. David. *D.C.* i.

Born at Blunderstone, in Suffolk, or "thereby" as they say in Scotland, I was a posthumous child. My father's eyes had closed upon the light of this world six months, when mine opened on it.

Note.—The title-character of the book is usually considered to have many of the characteristics of and similar experiences to those of Dickens himself. Little David was born at Blunderstone in Suffolk, with a caul, some six months after his father's death. The child lived with his mother, attended by old Peggotty, for some years until the appearance of Mr. Murdstone. During David's visit to Peggotty's brother at Yarmouth, his mother and Mr. Murdstone are married. Then commences a period of misery for him: a misery accentuated by the loss of a great deal of his mother's kindness. Murdstone and his sister inaugurate a system to train up the mother and to break down the child, which culminates in a dramatic outburst. David is sent to Creakle's school, where he meets Steerforth and Traddles, two characters who occupy important places in the narrative. David's mother and her child die and are buried together: David is first neglected and then put to the lowest kind of work at the counting-house of Murdstone and Grinby, in the wine trade. Lodgings are taken for him by his stepfather with Mr. Micawber. The life is more than the sensitive boy can bear and he leaves it, tramping on foot to Dover, where he succeeds in finding his aunt. His aunt, Betsey Trotwood, puts him to a good school in Canterbury. Later on he is articled to Messrs. Spenlow and Jorkins, proctors. His aunt loses her money and he takes to reporting and literary work, in which he succeeds. He marries Dora, Spenlow's daughter. Spenlow himself having died, leaving her only a comparatively small sum. Dora dies and he marries Agnes, the daughter of Mr. Wickfield, his aunt's solicitor in Canterbury. The story leaves him and his wife in happiness.

COPPERFIELD. Mrs. David. *See* Spenlow, Dora.

COPPERFIELD. Mrs. David. *See* Copperfield, Mrs. Clara.

COPPERFULL. Mr., Name given to David by Mrs. Crupp.

COPPERNOZE. Mr. *Mud. Pap.*ii.

COPPICE ROW. *O.T.* viii.

COPYING-CLERKS. Low. *S.B.B.*, Scenes xiii.

CORAM. "Originator of the Institute for these poor Foundlings." *L.D.* ii.

CORINTHIAN PILLARS. *P.P.* xxxvi.

CORK. *R.P.*, *N.S.*

CORNEY. Mr., Deceased husband of matron of workhouse. *O.T.* xxiii.

Who had not been dead more than five-and-twenty years.

CORNEY. Mrs., The matron of the workhouse. *O.T.* xxiii.

A poor desolate creature . . . a discreet matron.

Note.—Mrs. Corney was matron of the workhouse at which Oliver was born. In that capacity she obtains possession of a locket and ring stolen from the dead body of Oliver's mother, and disposes of them to Monks. She marries Bumble the beadle. They lose their situations and both become inmates of the workhouse over which they had formerly reigned as master and matron.

CORNHILL. *B.R.* i.; *C.B.*, *C.C.*, *S.* i.; *C.S.*, *S.L.* iv.; *C.S.*, *W.o.G.* *M.*; *M.C.* xxxviii.; *M.P.*, *L.H.*; *P.P.* xx.; *R.P.*, *B.S.*; *U.T.* ix.

CORNICE ROAD. *F.P.I.*, *G.A.N.*

CORNISH GENTLEMAN. A, An Athlete. *D. and S.* xxii.

CORNWALL. *D. and S.*, iv.; *L.D.* xiii.; *N.N.* x.; *S.B.B.*, Char. iii.; *U.T.* xxvii.

CORNWALL. Mining districts of. *M.C.* xxi.

CORONER. *B.H.* xi.

CORONER'S JURY. *U.T.* xviii.

CORPORALS. Certain, Of Royal East London Volunteers. *B.R.*, xliii.

CORPORATION. Eden Land- *M.C.* xxi.

CORRECTION. House of. *O.T.*, xiii. ; *S.B.B.*, Scenes xvi.

CORRECTION. Middlesex house of. *R.P.*, *W.I.A.W.*

CORRESPONDING SOCIETY. Of the Pickwick Club. A branch of the United Pickwickians, or the Pickwick Club. *P.P.* i.

Note.—The members of the branch were Pickwick, Tupman, Snodgrass, and Winkle. They were requested to forward from time to time, authenticated accounts of their journeys and investigations . . . to the Pickwick Club stationed in London.

" **CORRESPONDING SOCIETY.** Of Begging-Letter Writers." *R.P.*, *B.L.W.*

CORSO. The. *L.D.* xliii ; *P.F.I.*, *V.M.M.S.S.*

COSTA. Signor. *M.P.*, *M.M.*

COSTELLO. Mr. Dudley, As Mr. Nightingale. *M.P.*, *M.N.D.*

COSTERMONGERS. *S.B.B.*, Scenes v.

COSY. Room in Six Jolly Fellowship Porters. *O.M.F.* vi.

COTTAGE. Miss Trotwood's. *D.C.* xiii.

A very neat little cottage with cheerful bow-windows ; in front of it. a small square gravelled court, or garden full of flowers, carefully tended, and smelling deliciously.

COTTAGE. Next door to that of Mrs. Nickleby. *N.N.* xli.

Which, like their own, was a detached building.

COTTAGERS. *O.C.S.* xv.

COTTINGHAM. James. *A.N.* xvii.

COULSON. Mr., as Will, a waiter at the St. James's Arms. *M.P.*, *S.G.*

COUNCIL CHAMBER. The. *A.N.* xvii.

COUNSEL. *M.P.*, *P.L.U.*

COUNSEL. *M.P.*, *L.E.J.*

COUNSEL, *B.H.* i.

A very little Counsel, with a terrific bass voice.

COUNSEL. In the cause. *B.H.* i.

COUNSEL. The, in the Arches Court. *S.B.B.*, Scenes viii.

Wore red gowns.

COUNSEL. Two or three, never in any cause. *B.H* i.

COUNSEL'S OFFICE. *P.P.* lv.

COUNT. The usual French. *L.D.* lv.

Guest of Mrs. Merdle.

COUNTESS. Eliza Grimwood. *R.P.*, *T.D.A.* i.

COUNTESS. Guest of Mr. Merdle. *L.D.* xxi.

Secluded somewhere in the core of an immense dress, to which she was in the proportion of the heart to the overgrown cabbage.

COUNTING HOUSE. At the works of Doyce and Clennam. *L.D* lxii.

COUNTING HOUSE. *See* Cheeryble Brothers.

COUNTRY. French-Flemish. *U.T.* xxv.

Three-quarters Flemish, and a quarter French.

COUNTRYMAN. *M.P.*, *S.D.C.*

COUNTRYMAN. Comic, Member of Mr. V. Crummles' Company. *N.N.* xxiii.

" With a turned-up nose, a large mouth, broad face, and staring eyes."

COUNTRYMAN. Prisoner in " the poor side " of the Fleet. *P.P.* xlii.

Flicking with a worn-out hunting-whip, the top boot that adorned his right foot ; his left being (for he had dressed by easy stages) thrust into an old slipper. Horses, dogs, and drink had brought him there.—There was a rusty spur on the solitary boot.

COUNTY. English. *M.P.*, *P.M.B.*

COUNTY GAOL. Reading.
M.P., P.P.

COUNTY INN. Canterbury.
D.C. xvii.

COUNTY INSTITUTIONS. For idiots.
B.R. xlvii.

COUNTY JUSTICE. The.
B.R. xlvii.

COUNTY MEMBER. Of Parliament.
S.B.B., Scenes xviii.

The old, hard-featured man—a good specimen of a class of men, now nearly extinct.—Look at his loose, wide, brown coat, with capacious pockets on each side; the knee-breeches and boots, the immensely long waistcoat, and silver watch-chain dangling below it, the wide-brimmed brown hat, and the white handkerchief tied in a great bow, with straggling ends sticking out beyond his shirt frill.

COUPLE. Some three or four. At Greenwich Fair.
S.B.B., Scenes xii.

COURIER. A, of Dorrit's party.
L.D. xxxvii.

COURIER. French.
P.F.I., G.T.F.

COURT. The, No. 6 in. *N.N.* xl.

COURT-HOUSE. *C.S., T.G.S.* li.

COURT-KEEPER. The, in Doctor's Commons.
S.B.B., Scenes viii.

A respectable-looking man in black of about twenty stone weight or thereabout.

COURTIER. A spruce young.
M.H.C. i.

COURTIER. A better—still.
M.H.C. i.

COURTIERS. Of the goblins.
P.P., xxix.

Who kick whom royalty kicks, and hug whom royalty hugs.

COURTS OF LAW. *B.R.* lxvii.; and *U.T.* xiii.

COURVOISIER. *M.P., C.P.*

COUSIN. A, of Sir Leicester Dedlock. *B.H.* xl.

A languid cousin with a moustache.

COUSIN. Debilitated, Of Sir Leicester Dedlock. *B.H.* liii.

COUSIN. Solitary female, Of Mr. Martin Chuzzlewit. *M.C.* iv.

Who was remarkable for nothing but being very deaf, and living by herself, and always having the toothache.

COUSIN. Young scapegrace of a.
S.B.B., Char. ii.

Guest at Christmas family party.

COUSIN JOHN. Mr. Jarndyce.
B.H. vi.

COUSIN TOM. Captain Boldheart's cousin. *H.R.* iii.

COUSINS. Rest of the, Of Sir Leicester Dedlock. *B.H.* xxviii.

Ladies and gentlemen of various ages and capacities.

"**COVE.**" A, A thief.
R.P., D.W.T.T.

COVENT GARDEN. *G.E.* xlv.; *L.D.* xiii.; *M.P., W.M.*; *M.P.,W.S.G.*; *S.B.B.*, Scenes i.; *S.B.B.*, Scenes vi.; *U.T.* i.

COVENT GARDEN MARKET.
D.C. xxiv.; *G.E.* xxi.; *M.C.* xl.; *O.C.S.* i.; *O.M.F.* lix.; *P.P.* xlvii.; *U.T.* xiii.

Of dozing women—drunkards especially, you—come upon such specimens there, in the morning sunlight—such stale, vapid rejected cabbage-leaf, and cabbage-stalk dress, such damaged-orange countenance, such squashed pulp of humanity.

COVENT GARDEN THEATRE. *C.S., M.L. Leg.* i.; *D.C.* xix.; *M.P., A.G.L.*; *M.P., S.Q.F.*; *M.P., T. Let.*

COVENTRY. *P.P.* li.

Note.—Said also to be the town where Mrs. Jarley gave the performance on the night after meeting Nell and her grandfather.

COWER'S. Clerk from, The solicitors. *S.B.B.*, Tales iv.

Habited in black cloth, and bore with him a green umbrella, and a blue bag.

COWER'S. Solicitors. *S.B.B.*, Tales iv.

CRACKIT. Mr. Toby, Confederate of Fagin. *O.T.* xxii.

He was dressed in a smartly-cut snuff-coloured coat, with large brass buttons ; an orange neckerchief ; a coarse staring shawl-pattern waistcoat ; and drab breeches —Had no very great quantity of hair, either upon his head, or face ; but what he had, was of a reddish dye, and tortured into long corkscrew curls —He was a trifle above the middle size, and apparently rather weak in the legs.

Note.—A housebreaker belonging to Fagin's gang. He and Sikes were the principal operators in the attempt on Mrs. Maylie's house. After the failure, he repairs to the house on Jacob's Island, where he is last seen.

CRADDOCK. Mrs. Landlady, of a house in Royal Crescent, Bath, where Pickwick took lodgings for self and friends. *P.P.* xxxvi.

CRAGGS. Mr. A lawyer. *C.B.*, *B.O.L.*, i.

A cold, hard, dry man, dressed in grey, and white, like a flint ; with small twinkles in his eyes, as if something struck sparks out of them.

CRAGGS. Mrs. Wife of Mr. Craggs. *C.B.*, *B.O.L.*, ii.

CRATCHIT. Belinda. Second daughter of Bob Cratchit.

CRATCHIT. Bob, Scrooge's clerk. *C.B.*, *C.C.*, *S.* i.

CRATCHIT. Master Peter, Son of Bob Cratchit. *C.B.*, *C.C.*, *S.* iii.

CRATCHIT. Mrs., Wife of Bob Cratchit. *C.B.*, *C.C.*, *S.* iii.

Dressed out but poorly, in a twice-turned gown, but brave in ribbons, which are cheap, and make a goodly show for sixpence.

CRATCHIT. Mrs. *M.P.*, *I.W.M.* *C.B.*, *C.C.*, *S.* iii.

CRATCHITS. Two smaller. *C.B.*, *C.C.*, *S.* iii.

Boy and girl.

CRAVEN STREET, STRAND. *O.T.* xli.

CRAWLEY. Mr. (the youngest), Visitor at the Assembly Rooms, Bath. *P.P.* xxxv.

His father has eight hundred a year, which dies with him.

CREAKLE. Mr., Schoolmaster of Salem House. *D.C.* v.

Mr. Creakle's face was fiery, and his eyes were small, and deep in his head ; he had thick veins in his forehead, a little nose, and a large chin. . . . I'll tell you what I am. . . . . I'm a Tartar.

Note.—The master and proprietor of Salem House. His son left home and he terrorises over his wife and daughter. After David leaves the school Creakle drops out of the story until he is disposed of finally by being exhibited as a Middlesex magistrate tenderly considerate of the prisoners.

CREAKLE. Miss. *D.C.* v.

I heard that Miss Creakle was regarded by the school in general as being in love with Steerforth.

CREAKLE. Mrs. *D.C.* v.

CREDITORS. Unlucky. *M.P.*, *L.E.J.*

CREEBLE. Miss, Of the Misses Creeble's Boarding and Day Establishment for Young Ladies. *M.P.*, *E.T.*

CREEVY. Miss La. *See* La Creevy, Miss. *N.N.* lxiii.

CREMONA. *P.F.I.*, *V.M.M.S.S.*

CREMORNE GARDENS. *M.P.*, *R.H.F.*

CREWLER. Mrs., Sophy's mama. *D.C.* xli.

CREWLER. Reverend Horace. Sophy's papa. *D.C.* xli.

An excellent man, most exemplary in every way.

CREWLER. Sophy, Dearest girl in the world. *D.C.* xxxiv.

Note.—Daughter of the Rev. Horace Crewler. She is the moral mainstay of the family. After waiting some years she and Traddles are married—on the

Britannia metal footing, though the silver plate arrives in course of time.

CRIEL. *R.P.*, *A.F.*

CRIMEA. *M.P.*, *S.F.A.*

CRIMINAL COURTS. *S.B.B.*, Scenes xxiv.

CRIMP. David, Tapster at "Lombards' Arms." *M.C.* xxvii.

CRIMPLE. David, Esquire (Secretary and resident Director of the Anglo-Bengalee Disinterested Loan and Life Assurance Company. *M.C.* xxvii.

This gentleman's name, by the way, was originally Crimp, but as the word was susceptible of an awkward construction and might be misrepresented, he had altered it to Crimple.

CRINKLES. *Mud. Pap.* ii.

CRIPP. Mrs., Bob Sawyer's boy's mother. *P.P.* l.

CRIPPLE CORNER. Belonged to Wilding and Co. *C.S.*, *N.T.*, Act i.

There was a pump in Cripple Corner. There was a tree in Cripple Corner. All Cripple Corner belonged to Wilding and Co. Their cellars burrowed under it, their mansion towered over it.

CRIPPLES. Master, *L.D.* ix.

Behind the blind was a little white-faced boy, with a slice of bread and butter, and a battledore.

CRIPPLES. Mr., Of Mr. Cripples' Academy. *L.D.* ix.

CRIPPLES. Pupils of Mr. *L.D.* ix.

CRIPPLES. Two, Both mere boys. *B.R.* lxxvii.

One with a leg of wood, one who dragged his twisted limbs along by the help of a crutch, were hanged in the same Bloomsbury Square.

"**CRIPPLES.** The Three," Inn in Saffron Hill frequented by Fagin. *O.T.* xxvi.

CRISPARKLE. Mrs., Mother of the Rev. Septimus. *E.D.* vi.

Pretty old lady. "What is prettier than an old lady—when her eyes are bright, when her figure is trim and compact, when her face is cheerful and calm, when her dress is as the dress of a china shepherdess, so dainty in its colours."

CRISPARKLE. Sister of Mrs., A childless widow. *E.D.* vi.

Another piece of Dresden china.

CRISPARKLE. The Reverend Septimus, Minor Canon. *E.D.* ii.

Fair and rosy—early riser, musical, cheerful, classical, kind, good-natured, social, contented, and boy-like; feinting and dodging with the utmost artfulness, while his radiant features teemed with innocence, and soft-hearted benevolence beamed from his boxing-gloves.

Note.—A minor canon of Cloisterham, living with his mother in minor Canon Corner. He takes Neville Landless as pupil, and it is while with him that Neville is suspected of the murder of Edwin Drood.

CRISPARKLES. Six little, Deceased brothers of the Reverend Septimus Crisparkle. *E.D.* vi.

Went out, one by one, as they were born, like six weak little rush-lights, as they were lighted.

CRISPIN & CRISPANUS INN. Strood. *U.T.* xi

CROCKFORD'S CLUB. *N.N.* ii.

CROCUS. Doctor, A phrenologist. *A.N.* xiii.

A tall, fine-looking Scotchman, but rather fierce and warlike in appearance.

CROFTS. *S.Y.C.*

CROOKED BILLET. *B.R.* xxxi.

CROOKEY. Attendant. *P.P.* xl.

Who might have passed for a neglected twin brother of Mr. Smouch . . . looked something between a bankrupt grazier, and a drover in a state of insolvency.

CROPLEY. Miss, A friend of Mrs. Nickleby's. *N.N.* xxxiii.

"CROSS KEYS." The, Wood Street. *G.E.* xx. ; *L.D.* i. ; *N.N.* : xxxiii. *S.B.B.*, Scenes xvi. ; *U.T.* xii.

CROWL. Mr., Fellow-lodger of Newman Noggs. *N.N.* xiv.

A hard-featured, square-faced man, elderly and shabby. Wore a wig of short, red hair, which he took off with his hat, and hung upon a nail.

Note.—The grumbling individual who is introduced making himself comfortable in Newman Noggs' room. It is he who receives Nicholas and Smike on their first arrival. He occupies a secondary place amongst the characters of the book and does not continue for long.

CROWN. *See* Muggleton. *P.P.* vii.

"CROWN." In Silver Street. *N.N.* vii.

"CROWN." The, A public house. *S.B.B.*, Char. iv.

"CROWN AND ANCHOR." A temporary ballroom at Greenwich Fair. *S.B.B.*, Scenes xii.

The price of admission to which is one shilling. . . . There is a raised orchestra, and the place is boarded all the way down, in patches, just wide enough for a country dance.

CROWN STREET. *O.T.* xxi.

CROXFORD'S. *M.P.*, *B.A.*

CROYDON. *R.P.*, *A.F.* ; *U.T.* xi.

CROZIER. Hotel in Cloisterham. *E.D.* xviii.

CRUIKSHANK. Mr. George. *M.P.*, *D.C.* ; *M.P.*, *F.F.* ; *M.P.*, *J.G.*

CRUMLINWALLINER. A bard whose name sounded like. *B.H.* xvii.

CRUMMLES. Master, Elder son of Mr. Vincent Crummles. *N.N.* xxii.

CRUMMLES. Master Percy, Younger son of Mr. Vincent Crummles. *N.N.* xxii.

CRUMMLES. Mr. Vincent, Manager of travelling theatre. *N.N.* xxii.

He had a very full under-lip, a hoarse voice, as though he were in the habit of shouting very much, and very short black hair, shaved off nearly to the crown of his head—to admit of his more easily wearing character wigs of any shape or pattern.

Note.—Crummles is manager-proprietor of a travelling theatre and company. He met Nicholas and Smike, and persuaded them to enter the company. After Nicholas left the company he lost sight of the Crummleses until he accidentally saw a bill advertising positively the last appearance of Mr. Crummles outside a Minor Theatre. It turned out that the family was on the point of their departure for America. Crummles was nicknamed old " bricks and mortar " by subordinate members of his company.

CRUMMLES. Miss Ninetta, daughter of Mrs. Vincent Crummles. *N.N.* xxiii.

A little girl in a dirty white frock, with tucks up to the knees, short trousers, sandalled shoes, white spencer, pink gauze bonnet, green veil and curl-papers.

Note.—" The Infant Phenomenon," who had been ten years old for the past five years. Daughter of Mr. and Mrs. Crummles. She was always given good parts in the plays at the theatre, much to the disgust of some of the other members of the company.

CRUMMLES. Mrs., Wife of Mr. Vincent Crummles. *N.N.* xxiii.

A stout, portly female, apparently between forty and fifty, in a tarnished silk cloak, with her bonnet dangling by the strings in her hand, and her hair (of which she had a great quantity) braided in a large festoon over each temple.

Note.—A wonderful woman : mother of the Phenomenon.

CRUMPTON. Miss Amelia. *S.B.B.*, Tales iii.

Owned to thirty-eight.

CRUMPTON. Miss Maria. *S.B.B.*, Tales iii.

Admitted she was forty.

CRUMPTON. The Misses, Proprietresses of boarding-school. *S.B.B.*, Tales iii.

They dressed in the most interesting manner—like twins! and looked as happy as a couple of marigolds run to seed. They were very precise—wore false hair—always smelt strongly of lavender.

CRUNCHER. Jeremiah, General messenger, and in particular for Tellson and Co's Bank during the day, and Resurrectionist at night. *T.T.C.* ii.

He had eyes . . . of a surface black, with no depth in the colour or form, and much too near together.

Note.—He is present at the trial of Darnay, and crops up repeatedly in the story. The scenes of the French Revolution so affect him, however, that he renounces his nightly trade and resolves not to ill-treat his wife for " flopping."

CRUNCHER. Mrs., Wife of Jerry Cruncher. *T.T.C.*, bk. ii., ch. i.

You're a nice woman! What do you mean by flopping yourself down and praying agin me?

CRUNCHER. Young Jerry. *T.T.C.*, bk. ii., ch. i.

He (Jerry's father) was never absent during business hours, unless upon an errand, and then he was represented by his son, a grisly urchin of twelve.

Note.—Son of Jerry Cruncher, and general assistant to his father when he is away from his post outside Tellson's. Young Jerry is very curious to discover the trade his father practises by night. He is supposed to succeed his father as outside messenger.

CRUPP. Mrs., David's landlady in chambers in the Adelphi. *D.C.* xxiii.

Note.—After Miss Trotwood's loss of fortune she comes up to David, and there is war between her and Mrs. Crupp, in which the latter is worsted.

CRUSHTON. The Honourable Mr., Lord Mutanhed's bosom friend. *P.P.* xxxv.

The other gentleman, in the red under-waistcoat, and dark moustache.

CRUSOE. Robinson. *M.C.* v.

CRUSOE'S ISLAND. *M.C.* xxi.

CRYPT. The. *E.D.* xii.

CRYSTAL PALACE. *U.T.* xxxi.

CUFFY. *B.H.* xii.

CUMBERLAND. *L.T.* i, ii, iii.

CUMMINS. Tom. *P.P.* xx.

CUNARD. The, Steam packet. *A.N.* xvi.

CUNARD LINE. Shipowners. *U.T.* xxxi.

CUNNING. Name of bird. *B.H.* xiv.

" **CUPID.**" Clipper, schooner. *M.C.* xliv.

CUPID. Kidderminster. *H.T.*, *S.* vi.

CURATE. Our. *S.B.B.*, *O.P.* ii.

A young gentleman of prepossessing appearance, and fascinating manners. He parted his hair on the centre of his forehead in the form of a Norman arch, wore a brilliant of the first water on the fourth finger of his left hand, which he always applied to his left cheek when he read prayers.

CURDLE. Mr., Literary man. *N.N.* xxiv.

Had written a pamphlet of sixty-four pages, post octavo, on the character of the nurse's deceased husband in Romeo and Juliet.

He wore a loose robe on his back, and his right fore-finger on his forehead, after the portraits of Sterne. . . . to whom somebody or other had once said he bore a striking resemblance.

CURDLE. Mrs., Patroness of Mr. V. Crummles' Company. *N.N.* xxiv.

Dressed in a morning wrapper, with a little cap stuck upon the top of her head.

CURÉ. Monsieur, The. *U.T.* vii.

CURIOSITY DEALER'S WAREHOUSE. *See* Old Curiosity Shop.

CURSITOR STREET. *B.H.* x.; *R.P., B.S.*; *S.B.B.*, Tales x.

CURSITOR STREET. Little dairy in. *B.H.* xxv.

CURZON. Daughter of Thomas. *B.R.* viii.

CURZON. Thomas, Hosier. *B.R.* viii.

Mark Gilbert's master.

CUSTOM-HOUSE. *D. and S.* lx.; *G.E.* xlvii.; *L.D.* xxix.; *O.M.F.* iv.; *P.F.I., G.A.N.*; *U.T.* vii.

CUSTOM-HOUSE OFFICERS. Calais. *U.T.* xvii.

In green and grey.

CUSTOMER. Of Kidney Pie Merchant. *S.B.B.*, Scenes ii.

CUT. New, London. *S.B.B.*, Scenes xi.

"**CUTAWAY.**" Fictitious name. *L.D.* vi.

CUTE. Alderman, A justice. *C.B., C.* i.

Coming—at that light heavy pace—that peculiar compromise between a walk and a jog-trot—which a gentleman upon the smooth downhill of life, wearing creaking boots, a watch-chain, and clean linen, *may* come out of his house.

CUTE. Alderman, Mrs. *C.B., C.* i.

CUTLER. Mr. and Mrs. *N.N.* xiv.

Newly married couple, who had visited Mr. and Mrs. Kenwigs in their courtship.

CUTTLE. Captain Ned, Late pilot, privateer's man or skipper. *D. and S.* iv.

A gentleman in a wide suit of blue, with a hook instead of a hand attached to his right wrist; very bushy black eyebrows; and a thick stick in his left hand, covered all over (like his nose) with knobs. He wore a loose silk handkerchief round his neck, and such a very large coarse shirt-collar, that it looked like a "small sail." When you see Ned Cuttle bite his nails, Wal'r, then you may know that Ned Cuttle's aground.

Note.—Captain Cuttle, who is best known for his now famous saying, "when found, make a note of," was the friend of Sol Gills. He is a fairly constant figure throughout the story, and befriends Florence Dombey. He leaves the story the partner of Sol Gills, proud of the fact that he is now a man of science.

CYMON. Simon Tuggs. *S.B.B.*, Tales iv.

D

D. A. J., *M.P., S.B.*

DABBER. Sir Dingleby. *N.N.* xxvii.

DADSON. Mr., Writing-master at Minerva House. *S.B.B.*, Tales iii.

In a white waistcoat, black knee-shorts, and ditto stockings, displaying a leg large enough for two writing-masters.

DADSON. Wife of Mr. *S.B.B.*, Tales iii.

In green silk, with shoes and cap-trimmings to correspond.

DAGGS. Mr. *O.M.F.* viii.

DIARY. Late ladies' school. *S.B.B.*, Scenes iii.

DAISY. Solomon, Parish clerk and bell-ringer. *B.R.* i.

A little man—had round black shiny eyes like beads—wore at the knees of his rusty black breeches, and on his rusty black coat, and all down his long-flapped waistcoat, queer little buttons like nothing except his eyes. He seemed all eyes from head to foot.

DALLEY. Mr. *O.M.F.* viii.

DAMASCUS. *U.T.* xv.

DAME DURDEN. *See* Summerson, Esther.

DAMIENS. *T.T.C.*, bk. ii., ch. xv.

DAMON AND PYTHIAS. *S.B.B.*, char. xi.

DAMSEL. A wiry-faced old, Guest at Pawkins. *M.C.* xvi.

Who held strong sentiments

touching the rights of women, and had diffused the same in lectures.

DANBY. *M.P., O.L.N.O.*

DANCER. A May day. *S.B.B.*, Scenes xx.

The "green" animated by no less a personage than our friend in the tarpauling suit.

DANCING-MASTER. A, Inmate of the Marshalsea. *L.D.* vii.

"**DANDO.**" Head man at Searle's boating establishment. *S.B.B.*, Scenes x.

Magnificent, though reddish whiskers.

DANTE. *L.D.* xlii.

DANTE. The spirit of. *M.P., S.F.A.*

DANTON. Mr., Guest at Christening party of the Kitterbells . *S.B.B.*, Tales xi.

DAPH. Pointer belonging to Sir Jeoffrey Manning. *P.P.* xix.

DARBEE. Derby. *M.P., T.O.H.*

DARBY. A constable. *B.H.* xxii.

DARBY'S. A lodging-house. *U.T.* v.

DARBY'S. A weekly lodger at. *U.T.* v.

A deserter.

DARDANELLES. *M.P., L.A.V.*

DARK JACK. Landlord of little public house in Liverpool. *U.T.* v.

A negro—in a Greek cap, and a dress half-Greek and half-English.

DARLING. Grace. *M.P., S. Pigs.*

DARNAY. Charles. *T.T.C.*, bk. ii., ch. ii.

A young man of about five-and-twenty, well-grown and well-looking with a sunburnt cheek and a dark eye.

Note.—Son of Marquis St. Evrèmond. A French Emigré, who renounces his fortune in France in favour of his poor tenants. He becomes a teacher, etc., in London. Tried for treason in England and discharged. He marries Lucy Manette. In Paris he is arrested and sentenced. By the sacrifice of Sydney Carton, who dies in his stead, he is saved.

DARNAY, Mrs. *See* Manette, Miss Lucie.

DARTFORD. *L.D.* liv.

DARTLE. Miss Rosa, Mrs. Steerforth's companion. *D.C.* xx.

She had black hair and eager black eyes, and was thin and had a scar upon her lip. She was a little dilapidated—like a house—with having been so long to let.

Note.—Companion to Mrs. Steerforth. She loves Steerforth in her own fierce way, and despises the Peggottys—particularly Little Emily. She is left alternately caressing and quarrelling with Mrs. Steerforth.

DARWEN. River. *G.S.E.* v.

DASH. Dash, The Reverend. *O.M.F.* x.

DASH BLANK. Lord. *M.P., T.T.*

DATCHERY. Dick, A mysterious personage. *E.D.* xviii.

Buttoned up in a tightish blue surtout, with a buff waistcoat and grey trousers. He had something of a military air. This gentleman's white head was unusually large, and his shock of white hair was unusually thick and ample. A single buffer.

Note.—The identity of Datchery is one of the secondary mysteries of the book upon which probably the principal mystery depends. He enters the story rather late, after Edwin Drood's disappearance, with the object of watching John Jasper. In this work he keeps a tally of the points he makes by a score of uncouth chalk marks on his cupboard wall. He has been identified with Edwin Drood, Helena Landless, Bazzard, and Tartar by different writers.

DAUGHTER. Eldest, Of the widow. *M.C.* iv.

Expressed a general hope that some people *would* appear in their own characters.

DAUGHTER. Of Baron von Swillenhausen. *N.N.* vi.

DAUGHTER. Of elderly lady—poultry-dealer in Leadenhall Market. *D. and S.* xlix.

Engaged by Captain Cuttle to come and put Florence Dombey's room in order and render her any little services she required.

DAUGHTER. Of Mrs. Wugsley. *P.P.* xxxv.

Much older than her sister. Lord Mutanhed has been introduced to me. I said I thought I was *not* engaged.

DAUGHTER. Of old lady, married. *S.B.B.*, Scenes vii.

DAUGHTER. Of Prison-keeper. *L.D.* i.

Three or four years old—fair little face, touched with divine compassion—was like an angel's in the prison.

DAUGHTER. Of the deaf old gentleman. *M.H.C.* vi.

Who fled from her father's house.

DAUGHTERS. Growing up, of Majestic English Mama and Papa. *L.D.* ii.

Who were keeping a journal for the confusion of their fellow-creatures

DAUGHTERS. Of Matchmaking Mamas — visitors in Assembly Rooms, Bath. *P.P.* xxxv.

Remembering the maternal injunction to make the best use of their youth, had already commenced incipient flirtations in the mislaying of scarfs, putting on gloves, setting down cups, and so forth.

DAUGHTERS. Three, Of widow of deceased brother of Mr. Martin Chuzzlewit. *M.C.* iv.

Three in number, and of gentlemanly deportment, who had so mortified themselves with tight stays that their tempers were reduced to something less than their waists, and sharp lacing was expressed in their very noses.

D'AULNAIS. The name of Charles Darnay's mother, from which he forms the name he adopts in England. *See* Darnay.

DAVENPORT. Mr., Actor. *M.P.*, *V. and B.S.*

DAVENTRY. *P.P.* li.

DAVID. Ancient Butler of Cheeryble Brothers. *N.N.* xxxvii.

Of apoplectic appearance, with very short legs.

DAVID. Gravedigger. *O.C.S.* liv.

You're getting very deaf, Davy, very deaf to be sure.

DAVID. Shopman in pawnbroker's. *M.C.* xiii.

DAVIES. Mr., English tourist. *P.F.I.*, *R.*

DAVIES. Mrs., English tourist. *P.F.I.*, *R.*

DAVIES. Sir D. *M.P.*, *C.C.*

DAVIS. Andrew Jackson. *M.P.*, *R.S.D.*; *M.P.*, *S.B.*

DAVIS. Father of Gill. *C.S.*, *P.o.C.E.P.*

A shepherd.

DAVIS. Gill, Private in the Royal Marines. *C.S.*, *P.o.C.E.P.*

"**DAVY.**" Or safety-lamp. *N.N.* vi.

DAWES. Nurse in the poor nobleman's family. *L.D.* lvii.

DAWKINS. Jack, A thief. *O.T.* viii.

He was a snub-nosed, flat-browed, common-faced boy enough; and as dirty a juvenile as one would wish to see; but he had about him all the airs of a man. He was short of his age; with rather bow legs, and little sharp ugly eyes. His hat was stuck on the top of his head so lightly that it threatened to fall off every moment. He wore a man's coat, which reached nearly to his heels. He had turned the cuffs back, half way up his arm, to get his hands out of his sleeves: apparently with the ultimate view of thrusting them into the pockets of his corduroy trousers; for there he kept them.!

Note.—The most interesting and successful of Fagin's young thieves. The Dodger finds Oliver weak and tired and hungry on his way to London. He shares his "only one bob and a magpie" with Oliver and carries him off to London. In spite of his adroitness in thieving he is captured while attempting to pick a pocket. In court he maintains a game sang-froid, and carries it off with a commendable boldness, from his own point of view. While in the "jug" before his transportation he is maintained by Fagin "like a gentleman," to compensate for the possibility of his not finding a place in the Newgate Calendar.

DAWLISH. *N.N.* xxxvii.

DAWS. Mary, Young kitchenmaid. *D. and S.* lix.

Of inferior rank—in black stockings who, having sat with her mouth open for a long time, unexpectedly discharges from it words to this effect: "Suppose the wages shouldn't be paid"—"If *that* is your religious feelings,"—says cook warmly, "I don't know where you mean to go."

DAWSON. Mr., Surgeon. *S.B.B., O.P.* iii.

DAYVLE. The devil. *B.H.* xl.

DEAD SEA. *M.P., T.O.H.*

DEAF AND DUMB ESTABLISHMENT. *C.S., D.M.P.*

DEAL. *B.H.*, xlv.; *M.P., F.S.*

DEALER. In Marine Stores. *S.B.B.*, Scenes xxi.

DEALER. Marine Store. *S.B.B.*, Scenes iii.

At corner of the street.

DEALER. Principal slipper and dog's-collar man. *D. and S.* xiii.

Who considered himself a public character—threw up his forefinger to the brim of his hat as Mr. Dombey went by.

DEAN. Miss. *E.D.* ii.

DEAN. Mr. *E.D.* ii.

DEAN. Mrs. Abigail. The Earl of Aberdeen. *M.P., B.S.*

DEAN. The. *E.D.* ii.

DEATH. *M.P., D.V.*

DEATH. Name of bird. *B.H.* xiv.

DEBT. A payer off of the National. *O.M.F.* ii.

Guest of Veneerings.

DEBTOR. A, A Plasterer. *L.D.* vi.

Who had been taken in execution for a small sum the week before, had "settled" in the course of that afternoon, and was going out.

DEDLOCK. Favourite brother of wife of Sir Morbury. *B.H.* vii.

Killed in the civil wars.

DEDLOCK. Lady, Wife of Sir Morbury. *B.H.* vii.

She was a lady of haughty temper, lamed—never spoke of being crippled—or in pain—said "I will die here where I have walked, and I will walk here, though I am in my grave.

DEDLOCK. My Lady, Wife of Sir Leicester Dedlock. *B.H.* ii.

For years now, my Lady Dedlock had been at the centre of the fashionable intelligence, and at the top of the fashionable tree.—An exhausted composure, a wornout placidity, an equanimity of fatigue not to be ruffled by interest or satisfaction, are the trophies of her victory.—She has a fine face. Her figure is elegant, and has the effect of being tall.

Note.—Wife of Sir Leicester Dedlock. Before she is married she has a child, the Esther Summerson of the story, by Captain Hawdon. She is a true wife to Sir Leicester, and although she has no "family" to match his own, successfully supports the dignity of the position. She always retains the knowledge of her early secret, which is hidden from her husband. The family lawyer, Tulkinghorn becomes acquainted with it, however, and threatens to disclose. She leaves home, and with the assistance of some brickmakers succeeds in putting off pursuit. She is found dead at the gate of the cemetery in which Captain Hawdon lies buried, by her illegitimate daughter Esther and Inspector Bucket, who carries her husband's full forgiveness.

DEDLOCK. Sir Leicester, Bart.
B.H. ii.

There is no mightier baronet than he. His family is as old as the hills, and infinitely more respectable.—The world might get on without hills, but would be done up without Dedlocks. He is honourable, obstinate, truthful, high-spirited, intensely prejudiced, a perfectly unreasonable man. He will never see sixty-five again, nor perhaps sixty-six, or sixty-seven—has a twist of the gout now and then.—He is of a worthy presence, with light grey hair and whiskers, his fine shirt-frill, his pure white waistcoat, and his blue coat with bright buttons always buttoned.

Note.—Owner of Chesney Wold, and the head of a great county family, Conservative and reserved, not to say haughty, he becomes the husband of a woman, beautiful and witty, but without "family." She has had a child by Captain Hawdon, before her marriage. Sir Leicester Dedlock is ignorant of the secret. But Tulkington becomes acquainted with it and threatens to expose her She leaves home on the eve of the threatened disclosure and dies. Sir Leicester forgives his wife and instructs Mr. Bucket to find her and bring her home. He only succeeds in finding her dead at the gate of the cemetery in which Captain Hawdon was buried. Sir Leicester never recovers from his illness and the shock, but lives a broken man in the quiet of his place in Lincolnshire.

DEDLOCK. Sir Leicester.
M.P., L.L.

DEDLOCK. Sir Morbury. Ancestor of Sir Leicester. *B.H.* vii.

DEDLOCK. Volumnia, cousin of Sir Leicester Dedlock.
B.H. xxviii.

A young lady (of sixty) who is doubly highly related; having the honour to be a poor relation, by the mother's side, to another great family—lives slenderly on an annual present from Sir Leicester—and makes occasional resurrections in the country houses of her cousins.

Note.—Cousin of Sir Leicester Dedlock. She is one of his annuitants, and after Lady Dedlock's death she takes up her residence at Chesney Wold, where she reads to the invalid Sir Leicester; cheered in the dull surroundings by a glimpse she has obtained of a paper providing for the contingency of "something happening" to her kinsman.

DEDLOCK'S. Lady, woman.
B.H. xii.

DEDLOCK'S. Sir Leicester, man.
B.H. xii.

"**DEDLOCK ARMS.**" The, Clean little tavern. *B.H.* xxxvi.

A long sanded passage to his best parlour; a neat carpeted room with more plants in it than were quite convenient, a coloured print of Queen Caroline, several shells, a good many tea-trays, two stuffed and dried fish in glass cases, and either a curious egg, or pumpkin—hanging from his ceiling.

DEEDLES. The banker.
C.B., C. iii.

DEEDLES BROTHERS. Bankers.
C.B., C. iii.

DEFARGE. Ernest, Keeper of a wineshop. *T.T.C.* v.

A bull-necked, martial-looking man of thirty.

Note.—Husband of Madame Defarge. He is a leader of men of the Revolution as she is of the women. Together they keep a wineshop in St. Antoine. He is concerned with the release of Dr. Manette, whose servant he had been in his youth, and discovers a document which the old man had hidden. This is produced against Darnay when he is imprisoned in Paris.

DEFARGE. Madame Thérèse, wife of the wine-shop keeper.
T.T.C. v.

A stout woman with a watchful eye, a large hand heavily ringed, a steady face, strong features, and great composure of manner.

Note.—One of the knitting women. Wife of M. Defarge. A notable character and leader of the women of the Revolution. She shows herself dispassionate, and, to modern ideas, utterly unwomanly. She is killed in a struggle with Miss Pross in Paris.

DEFRESINER. Of Defresiner et Cie. *C.S.N.T.* Act iii.

DEFRESINER ET CIE. Champagne Merchants. *C.S., N.T.* Act i.

DELAFONTAINE. Mr. *S.B.B.*, Tales v.

DELAWARE. *A.N.* xiii.

DELEGATES. *M.P., O.S.*

DEMERARA. *D. and S.* lvi.; *P.P.* liii.

DEMON OF UNREST. Sloppy. *Which see.* *O.M.F.* lxiii.

DEMPLE. George, Boy at Salem House. *D.C.* v.

Father was a doctor.

DENBIGH. Lord. *M.P., C.C.*

DENHAM. Mr., A student. *C.B., H.M.* ii.

DENNIS. Joe, Negro slave. *A.N.* xvii.

DENNIS. Mr. *B.R.* Pref.

DENNIS. Ned, The hangman. *B.R.* xxxvi.

A squat, thick-set personage, with a low, retreating forehead, a coarse shock of red hair, and eyes so small and near together that his broken nose alone seemed to prevent their meeting and fusing into one of the usual size. A dingy handkerchief, twisted like a cord about his neck—his dress was of threadbare velveteen—a faded, rusty, whitened black, like the ashes of a pipe—in lieu of buckles at his knees, he wore unequal lengths of pack-thread.

Note.—The common hangman who with a certain amount of secrecy is a ringleader in the Gordon Riots. By virtue of his trade he wants to "work off" all the opponents, but when he is arrested and condemned to the death he has seen so many suffer, he becomes a coward and cries continuously for a reprieve.

DENTIST'S SERVANT. *U.T.* xvi.

He knows what goes on in the little room where something is always being washed or filed.

DEPTFORD. *B.H.* xx.; *C.S., G.i.S*; *D. and S.* iv.; *R.P., P.M.T.P.*; *U.T.* vi.

DEPUTY. *E.D.* v.

I'm man-servant up at the Travellers' Twopenny in Gasworks Garding.

Note.—"Deputy" or "Winks" or both combined was employed at "The Traveller's Twopenny" in Cloisterham. He is first seen as the guardian angel, or Devil, of Durdles, whom he is pelting with stones to make him go home. The doggerel rhyme he chants was at one time and in one form well known as entering into a boy's street game:

Widdy, widdy wen!
I-ket-ches-Im-out-ar-ter-ten,
Widdy Widdy wy!
Then-E-don't-go-then-I-shy—
Widdy Widdy Wake-cock warning.

So far as the book goes he is seen as the enemy of Jasper, obtaining information for Datchery.

DEPUTY. The carriers. *C.B., C.O.H.* iii.

DEPUTY. In charge of lodging-house. *R.P., D.W.I.F.*

DERBY. Late Lord. *M.P., O.S.*

DERBY. Lord. *M.P., T.B., M.P., T.O.H.*

DERRICK. John. *C.S., T.G.S.* i.

DESDEMONA. *P.F.I., A.I.D.*

DESERT. The, The plains. *U.T.* xx.

DESOLATION. Great desert of. *M.P., T.O.H.*

DESPAIR. Name of bird. *B.H.* xiv.

DESPARD. *M.P., S. for P.*

DESSIN. Hôtel, Calais. *U.T.* xvii.

D'ESTE. Mrs., As the second wife. *M.P., N.T.*

D'ESTE. Villa. *P.F.I., R.*

DESTRUCTIVES. M.P's. *S.B.B.*, Scenes xviii.

DETAINERS. *S.B.B.*, Tales x.

DETECTIVE SERGEANT. Of Police. *R.P., D.W.I.F.*

DETECTIVES. *R.P., T.D.P.*

DEVASSEUR. Loyal. *R.P., O.F.W.*

In that part of France a husband always adds to his own name the family name of his wife.

Note.—Landlord of house in French watering-place, and town councillor.

DEVIL'S PUNCH BOWL. *N.N.* xxv.

DEVON. *D. and S.* xxi; *M.P., P.F.D.*; *N.N.* i.; *R.P., A.P.A.*; *S.B.B.*, Tales x.; *T.T.C.*, bk. ii., ch. xiii.

DEVONSHIRE. North. *C.S., M.f.T.S.* i.; *G.S.E.* vii.

DEVONSHIRE FLOWER. Kitty. *C.S., M.f.T.S.* ii.

DEVONSHIRE HOUSE. *M.P., G.L.A., M.P., M.N.D.*

DEVONSHIRE TERRACE. *M.P., I.C.*

DIALS. The. Seven Dials. *S.B.B.*, Scenes v.

DIAVOLO. Piazza del, (Mantua). *P.F.I., V.M.M.S.S.*

DIBABS. Jane. *N.N.* lv.

Married a man who was a great deal older than herself, and she *would* marry him.

DIBABSES. The. *N.N.* lv.

Lived in a beautiful little thatched white house one story high, covered all over with ivy and creeping plants—where the earwigs fell into one's tea on a summer evening.

DIBBLE. Dorothy, Emigrant. Wife of Sampson. *U.T.* xx.

DIBBLE. Sampson, Emigrant. *U.T.* xx.

DIBBS. *M.P., F.S.*

DIBDIN. Mr., The late, Poet. *P.P.* xxxiii.

Seeing the error of his ways, had written "Who hasn't heard of the Jolly Young Waterman," a temperance song.

DICK. *See* Wilkins, Dick.

DICK. *L.T.*

DICK. An orphan playmate of Oliver's. *O.T.* vii.

Good-bye, dear, God bless you—The blessing was the first Oliver had ever heard invoked upon his head.

Note.—The little friend of Oliver at the branch workhouse where Oliver was farmed for sevenpence-halfpenny a week. Oliver says good-bye to him when running away from Sowerby. He is a delicate child not rendered any stronger by "farming" and, as the doctor said, dying.

DICK. Guard of coach. *N.N.* v.

A stout old Yorkshireman.

DICK. Hostler at tavern in Salisbury. *M.C.* v.

DICK. Joram's younger apprentice. *D.C.* xxii.

DICK. Mr., Miss Trotwood's guest or lodger. *D.C.* xiii.

A florid, pleasant-looking gentleman with a grey head.

DICK. One of Kit's children. *O.C.S.* Chap. The last.

DICK. Sally's sweetheart. *C.S., N.T.*

DICKENS. Charles. *A.N.* i.; *M.P., A. in H.H.*; *M.P., A.T.V., M.P., C.H.T.*; *M.P., I.W.M.*; *M.P., L.S.*; *M.P., M.E.R.*; *M.P., M.N.D.*; *M.P., N.S.L.*; *M.P., S.F.A.*; *M.P., V.C.*

DICKENSON'S LANDING. St. Lawrence. *A.N.* xv.

DIDCOT. *M.P., E.S.*

DIGBY. Mr., Smike acting as a tailor. *N.N.* xxx.

With one tail to his coat, and a little pocket-handkerchief with a hole in it, and a woollen nightcap, and a red nose, and other distinctive marks peculiar to tailors on the stage.

DIJON. *D. and S.* lii.

DILBER. Mrs., Phantom laundress. *C.B., C.C.S.* iv.

Produced sheets and towels, a little wearing apparel, old fashioned silver teaspoons, sugar tongs and a few boots.

DINGLEY DELL. *P.P.* v.
Dingley Dell, gentlemen—fifteen miles, gentlemen—cross road [from Rochester]. *See also* Muggleton.

DINGLEY DELL CLUB. The cricket club which played the All-Muggleton Club. *P.P.* vii.

DINGO. Professor, Of European reputation. *B.H.* xiii.
Second husband of Mrs. Badger.

DINGWALL. Esq., M.P., Cornelius Brook. *S.B.B.*, Tales iii.
He had, naturally, a somewhat spasmodic expression of countenance, which was not rendered the less remarkable by his wearing an extremely stiff cravat.

DINGWALL. Master Brook, Son of M.P. *S.B.B.*, Tales iii.
One of those public nuisances, a spoilt child—in a blue tunic, with a black belt, a quarter of a yard wide, fastened with an immense buckle, looking like a robber in melodrama seen through a diminishing glass.

DINGWALL. Miss Brook (Lavinia). *S.B.B.*, Tales iii.
Daughter of M.P.

DINGWALL. Mrs. Brook, Wife of M.P. *S.B.B.*, Tales iii.

DIOGENES. Dr. Blimber's dog. *D. and S.* xiv.
Had never in his life received a friend into his confidence, before Paul . . . a blundering, ill-favoured, clumsy, bullet-headed dog.
Note.—Florence Dombey's dog, given her by Mr. Toots.

DIRECTOR. A bank, Guest at Dombey's housewarming. *D. and S.* xxxvi.
Reputed to be able to buy up anything, but who was a wonderfully modest-spoken man.

DIRECTOR. East India, Guest at Dombey's housewarming. *D. and S.* xxxvi.
Of immense wealth, in a waistcoat apparently constructed in serviceable deal by some plain carpenter, but really engendered in the tailor's art, and comprised of the material called nankeen.

DIRECTORS. *M.P.*, *R.S.*

DIRECTORS. More, Guests at Dombey's housewarming. *D. and S.* xxxvi.

DIRTY DICK. *See* Dorrit, Mr. Frederick. *L.D.* ix.

DISMAL JEMMY. The teller of "The Stroller's tale." *P.P.* iii.
His eyes were almost unnaturally bright and piercing; his cheekbones were high and prominent; and his jaws were long and lank.
Note.—A member of the theatrical profession and a friend of Jingle.

DISPENSARY. Ladies'. *S.B.B.*, *O.P.* vi.

DISRAELI. Mr. Benjamin. *See also* Dizzee. *M.P.*, *T.B.*

D'ISRAELI. Isaac. *M.P.*, *L.L.*; *M.P.*, *T.O.H.*

DISSENTERS' MISSIONARY SOCIETY. *S.B.B.*, *O.P.* vi.

DIVER. Colonel, Editor of New York Rowdy Journal. *M.C.* xvi.
A sallow gentleman, with sunken cheeks, black hair, small twinkling eyes, and a singular expression.

DIURNO. The Teatro. *P.F.I.*, *G.A.N.*

DIXON. Mr., Mr. Dick. *D.C.* xxiii.

DIXON. Mr. Hepworth, *M.P.*, *P.P.*

DIXONS. The. *S.B.B.*, Tales ix.

DIZZEE = Disraeli. *M.P.*, *T.O.H.*

"**DOADY.**" Corruption of David. *See* Copperfield, David.

DOBBLE. Daughters of Mr. *S.B.B.*, Char. iii.

DOBBLE. Mr., Junior, Son of Mr. Dobble. *S.B.B.*, Char. iii.

DOBBLE. Mrs., Wife of Mr. Dobble. *S.B.B.*, Char. iii.

DOBBS. *M.P.*, *T.T.*

DOBBS. Julia. *M.P.*, *S.G.*

DOCHE. Madame, Selling calves. *R.P.*, *M.O.F.F.*

DOCK-LABOURERS. At Ratcliff. *U.T.* xxx.

DOCK SLIP. In Government yard. *U.T.* xv.

DOCKHEAD. *U.T.* x.

DOCKHEAD. *O.T.* l.

DOCKS. *C.S.*, *M.L.L.* i.; *D.C.* xxii; *E.D.* i.; *O.M.F.* iii.; *S.B.B.*, Scenes ii.; *S.B.B.*, Tales vii.

DOCKS. East India. *U.T.* xxxiv.

DOCTOR. *P.P.* xliv.

In a green fly, with a kind o' Robinson Crusoe set o' steps, as he could let down when he got out, and pull up arter him wen he got in, to perwent the necessity o' the coachman's gettin' down, and thereby undeceivin' the public by lettin' em see that it wos only a livery coat as he'd got on, and not the trousers to match.

DOCTOR. Astonishing. *M.P.*, *Q.D.P.*

DOCTOR. Attending Anthony Chuzzlewit. *M.C.* xix.

Looked as distant and unconscious as if he had heard and read of undertakers, and had passed their shops, but had never before been brought into communication with one.

DOCTOR. Attending birth of Marigold, accepting no fee but a tea-tray. *C.S.*, *D.M.*

DOCTOR. Attending Jinkinson. *M.H.C.* v.

DOCTOR. Attending patient at the "Bull." *M.C.* xxv.

DOCTOR. Attending Sam Weller's mother-in-law at time of her demise. *P.P.* lii.

DOCTOR. Examining emigrants on board the Amazon. *U.T.* xx.

DOCTOR. Of Civil Law. *S.B.B.*, Scenes viii.

His wig was put on all awry, with the tail straggling about his neck, his scanty grey trousers and short black gaiters, made in the worst possible style, imparted an inelegant appearance to his uncouth person, and his limp, badly-starched shirt-collar almost obscured his eyes.

DOCTOR'S SERVANT. *U.T.* xvi.

A confidential man—he lets us into the waiting-room, like a man who knows minutely what is the matter with us, but from whom the rack would not wring the secret.

DOCTOR'S COMMONS.

D.C. xxiii.; *M.H.C.* iv.; *O.M.F.* viii.; *P.P.* x.; *S.B.B.*, Scenes viii.

A quiet and shady court-yard, paved with stone, and frowned upon by old red-brick houses. . . . A lazy old nook near St. Paul's Churchyard. . . . A little out-of-the-way place, where they administered what is called ecclesiastical law, and play all kind of tricks with obsolete old monster Acts of Parliament, which three-fourths of the world know nothing about. . . . The place where they grant marriage-licences to love-sick couples, and divorces to unfaithful ones; register the wills of people who have any property to leave.

DOCTORS. Some. *B.H.* xi.

DODD. Dr. *M.P.*, *P.P.*

DODDLES. Blinkiter. *L.D.* xlviii.

DODGER. The artful *See* Dawkins, Jack *O T* viii.

"**DODO.**" The, An inn. *R.P.*, *A.P.A.*

DODSON. Mr., Of Dodson and Fogg. *P.P.* xx.

A plump, portly, stern-looking man.

DODSON AND FOGG. His Majesty's attorneys. *P.P.* xx.

At the Court of King's Bench, and Common Pleas at Westminster.

Note.—The plaintiff's attorney (Mrs. Bardell's) in the "Case." Typical specimens of shady lawyers. They take up the case as a speculation, trusting to get costs from Mr. Pickwick. Failing to do so, however, they incarcerate Mrs. Bardell in the Debtors' Prison, where she is discovered by Sam Weller. In this way she is the indirect means of enabling Messrs. Dodson and Fogg to obtain their costs, as Pickwick's obstinacy is not proof against Perker's pleading for Mrs. Bardell.

DOE. John. *B.H.* xx.; *M.P.*, *L.E.J.*

DOFFIN. *O.M.F.* xxv.

DOG. In "Happy Family." *M.P., R.H.F.*

DOGE. The. *C.S., N.T.*, Act i.

DOGGINSON. A vestryman. *R.P.O.V.*

DOGS. The. *M.P., G.D.*

DOGS. The, Seeing Mark Tapley off. *M.C.* vii.

DOGS' MEAT MAN. Fictitious name. *L.D.* vi.

DOKE. Mr. *M.P., R.S.D.*

DOLBY. George, "The man of Ross." *M.P., I.W.M.*

DOLLOBY. Mr. *D.C.* xiii.

Who kept a shop, where it was written up that ladies' and gentlemen's wardrobes were bought.

DOLLS. Mr., *See* Cleaver, Mr.

DOLLY. Dear faithful. *B.H.* iii.

DOLLY'S CHOP HOUSE. *R.P., L.A.*

DOLLYS. Small children of Joe and Dolly Willet. *B.R.* lxxxii.

DOLPH. Adolphus Tetterby. *C.B., H.M.* ii.

DOLPHIN. The. *D.C.* xxi.

DOLPHIN'S HEAD. Ex-stage coach-house. *U.T.* xxii.

DOLPHIN'S HEAD. Waitress at. *U.T.* xxii.

A mournful young woman, with one eye susceptible of guidance, and one uncontrollable eye.

'DOLPHUS. *See* Tetterby, Adolphus.

DOMBEY. Mr. Paul. *D. and S.* i.

About eight-and-forty years of age—was rather bald, rather red, and though a handsome, well-made man, too stern and pompous in appearance to be prepossessing. On the brow of Dombey, Time and his brother Care had set some marks, as on a tree that was to come down in good time—remorseless twins they are for striding through their human forests, notching as they go.

Note.—The existing head of the firm. The "house" of Dombey and Son fills his horizon. His daughter Florence is obnoxious to him because she was not born a boy, and his son Paul is weak and dies a child. After this he marries again, but the marriage is rendered an unhappy one because there is no love, and an infinity of pride, in both husband and wife. This culminates in the elopement of the second Mrs. Dombey with Carker, the manager for the firm. But having punished her husband in this way, she immediately leaves Carker as revenge on him. Carker leaves the firm in an embarrassed position, and Dombey now proves himself incapable of nursing it over the crisis, and the crash comes. His bankruptcy has the effect of breaking his pride, and when his despised daughter comes to him, he is persuaded to go with her to her home with Walter Gay, where he ends his days in the receipt of a mysterious income.

DOMBEY. Florence. *D. and S.* i.

Deep dark eyes, the child in her grief and neglect was so gentle, so quiet and uncomplaining; was possessed of so much affection that no one seemed to care to have; and so much sorrowful intelligence that no one seemed to mind, or think about the wounding of.

Note.—Florence was the neglected sister of little Paul. Paul loves her, and she tends and nurses him. Ultimately she marries Walter Gay, and her father eventually relies upon his despised daughter in his adversity.

DOMBEY. Mrs. Fanny, Wife of Dombey and mother of Florence and Paul. *D. and S.* i.

Clinging fast to that slight spar (her little daughter) within her arms, the mother drifted out upon the dark and unknown sea that rolls round all the world. . . . Had always sat at the head of his table, and done the honours of his table, in a remarkably ladylike and becoming manner.

Note.—Dombey's first wife and mother of Florence and Paul. Apparently a gentle, patient woman, she dies at Paul's birth for want of "an effort."

DOMBEY. Paul, Son of Mr. *D. and S.* i.

He was a pretty little fellow; though there was something wan and wistful in his small face. His temper gave abundant promise of being imperious in after life. He had a strange, old-fashioned, thoughtful way—of sitting brooding in his miniature armchair; when he looked (and talked) like one of those terrible little beings in the fairy tales, who at a hundred and fifty, or two hundred years of age, fantastically represent the children for whom they have been substituted.

Note.—The long-hoped-for heir of the house of Dombey and Son. His mother dies at his birth, leaving him a frail child, to the care of strangers. As he grows his health does not improve. His father sends him to Brighton to the care of Mrs. Pipchin. From there he goes to Dr. Blimber's school. But this educational hothouse does not improve his strength and he returns home. Here he takes to bed, and gradually sinks, until he leaves the "house" without a successor, tended to the last by his sister.

DOMBEY. Second Mrs. *D. and S.* xxi.

Very handsome, very haughty, very wilful, who tossed her head and drooped her eyelids, as though, if there were anything in all the world worth looking into, save a mirror, it certainly was not the earth or sky. Married at eighteen.

Note.—The second Mrs. Dombey was the widow of Colonel Granger and the daughter of Mrs. Skewton. She makes an unhappy marriage with Dombey. She marries him as a business proposition: her beauty in return for his wealth and position. The two proud spirits clash, and the aversion which takes the place of mere indifference is fostered by Carker, Dombey's manager, with an object in view. He believes he has attained this object when Edith elopes with him. She deliberately takes this course to punish her husband, and having done so she immediately leaves Carker, in this way revenging herself on him for his unwelcome attentions. The story leaves her seeking oblivion—a changed woman to some extent.

"**DOMBEY AND SON.**" The house of. (The Firm). *D. and S.* i.

The earth was made for Dombey and Son to trade in, and the sun and moon were made to give them light. Rivers and seas were formed to float their ships; rainbows gave them promise of fair weather. Stars and planets circled in their orbits—to preserve inviolate a system of which they were the centre.

DOMBEY'S HOUSE. Mr. *D. and S.* iii.

It was a corner house, with great wide areas containing cellars frowned upon by barred windows, and leered at by crooked-eyed doors leading to dustbins. It was a house of dismal state, with a circular back to it, containing a whole suit of drawing-rooms looking upon a gravelled yard, where two gaunt trees with blackened trunks and branches rattled, rather than rustled, their leaves were so smoke-dried.

DOMESTIC. Female, At Dr. Blimber's. *D. and S.* xli.

DOMESTICS. Two female, Of six Jolly Fellowship Porters. *O.M.F.* vi.

Two robust sisters with staring black eyes, shining flat red faces, blunt noses, and strong black curls, like dolls.

DON DIEGO. Inventor of flying machines. *R.P.*, *A.F.*

DON QUIXOTE. Character in Nursery Story. *U.T.* xv.

DONCASTER. *U.T.* xvi. *and L.T.* ii, iii, v.

DONKEY. *M.P.*, *R.H.F.*

"**DONKEY DRIVER.**" *M.P.*, *O.S.*

DONNY. Miss, Proprietress of boarding-school. *B.H.* iii.

Note.—Meets Esther Summerson and takes her to "Greenleaf," her own boarding-school, where Esther spends six years at Mr. Jarndyce's expense. She occupies no other position in the narrative beyond that short notice.

DONNY'S. Miss, A very neat maid. *B.H.* iii.

DONNYS. Miss, Two—twin sisters. *B.H.* iii.

DOODLE. Cocker, Esq. *M.P.*, *N.G.K.*

DOODLE. Sir Thomas. *B.H.* vii.

DORA. *See* Spenlow, Dora.

DORR. Madame, Marguerite's companion. *C.S.*, *N.T.*, Act i.

A true Swiss impersonation—

from the breadth of her cushionlike back, and the ponderosity of her respectable legs, to the black velvet band tied tightly round her throat for the repressing of a rising tendency to goître; or higher still, to her great copper-coloured gold ear-rings, or higher still, to her head-dress of black gauze stretched on wire.

DORKER. A former pupil of Mr. Squeers. *N.N.* iv.

Who unfortunately died at Dotheboys' Hall. . . . Dry toast and warm tea offered him every night and morning when he could not swallow anything—a candle in his room on the very night he died.

DORKING. *U.T.* x.; *P.P.* xxvii.

DORKING CHURCHYARD. *P.P.* lii.

DORNTON. Sergeant, A detective. *R.P., T.D.P.*

About fifty years of age, with a ruddy face, and a high sunburnt forehead.

DORRIT. Amy. *L.D.* iii.

Her diminutive figure, small features, and slight spare dress, gave her the appearance of being much younger than she was.—A woman of probably not less than two-and-twenty, she might have been passed in the street for little more than half that age. At so much—or at so little—from eight to eight, Little Dorrit was to be hired. It was not easy to make out Little Dorrit's face; she was so retiring.—Born in the Marshalsea. She was christened one Sunday afternoon, when the turnkey, being relieved, was off the lock—went up to the font of Saint George's Church, and promised, and vowed, and renounced on her behalf.

Note.—Amy Dorrit is the title-character of the book. She is the daughter of William Dorrit, born in the Marshalsea. She is the mainstay of her father. Being at liberty to leave the prison, she goes to Mrs. Clennam's to do needlework, where she meets Arthur, through whose assistance her father is released from the Marshalsea. She accompanies her father on his travels. And when he dies and their money is lost she nurses Arthur Clennam in the same old Marshalsea, and after his recovery marries him.

DORRIT. Edward. Tip. *L.D.* vi.

Tip tired of everything . . . his small second mother got him into a warehouse, into the hop trade, into the law again, into an auctioneer's, into a brewery, into a stockbroker's, into the law again, into a coach-office, etc., etc. . . . but whatever Tip went into, he came out of tired, announcing that he had cut it.

Note.—Tip was the brother of Little Dorrit. His sister obtained numerous situations for him, but he is too deeply imbued with the spirit of the Marshalsea to remain long in any employment. He is in his majesty when the family inherit their wealth, but is returned to his natural element by their loss of it.

DORRIT. Fanny. *L.D.* vii.

Became a dancer. A pretty girl of far better figure and much more developed than Little Dorrit, though looking younger in the face when the two were observed together.

Note.—Fanny is the spoilt elder sister of Little Dorrit. When the story opens she is a dancer where her uncle is in the orchestra. Mr. Sparkler is infatuated with her, but Fanny is bought off by Mrs. Merdle. Later on when the Dorrits acquire wealth, Fanny again meets the Sparkler and they are married.

DORRIT. Frederick, Brother of William Dorrit. *L.D.* vii.

He was dirtily and meanly dressed, in a threadbare coat, once blue, reaching to his ankles and buttoned to his chin, where it vanished in the pale ghost of a velvet collar—a confusion of grey hair and rusty stock and buckle which altogether nearly poked his hat off. A greasy hat it was, and a napless. His trousers were so long and loose, and his shoes so clumsy and large, that he shuffled like an elephant.

Note.—Brother of Mr. William Dorrit. He is a clarionet player in a small theatre orchestra. When his brother enters on his inheritance Frederick accompanies the family on its travels, when he is the principal companion of Little Dorrit.

DORRIT. Mrs., Wife of debtor. *L.D.* vi.

Came—with a little boy of three years old, and a little girl of two . . . . When his youngest child (Little Dorrit) was eight years old, his wife who had long been languishing away of her own inherent weakness—not that she retained any greater sensitiveness as to her place of abode than he did—went upon a visit to a poor friend and old nurse in the country, and died there.

DORRIT. William, A debtor in the Marshalsea. *L.D.* vi.

A very amiable and very helpless middle-aged gentleman—shy retiring man; well-looking, though in an effeminate style; with a mild voice, curling hair, and irresolute hands—rings upon the fingers in those days—which nervously wandered to his trembling lips a hundred times in the first half-hour of his acquaintance with the jail. The Father of the Marshalsea. . . . Brought up as a gentleman . . . with the soft manner and white hair.

Note.—First introduced as the Father of the Marshalsea, a prisoner for debt for some twenty-five years. He was dependent upon his daughter, Little Dorrit, to a very large extent, but he was looked up to by all the other prisoners, largely on account of "his family." Later on he inherits a very large estate which has lain unclaimed and has accumulated. He immediately travels in a style fitting his new rank, engaging Mrs. General as a companion for his daughters. He makes himself rather ridiculous. His long imprisonment has had its effect on him. Not only are his ideas somewhat old, but his mind has become a little impaired. Through it all Little Dorrit comforts him. He is taken ill at a dinner party given by the Merdles, calling on Bob the Marshalsea turnkey to assist him. A few days later he dies under the impression that he is still in the prison, giving instructions to pawn his jewellery to purchase delicacies. His vast wealth has been handed over to Mr. Merdle, and when the great financier breaks, the Dorrits' money is gone.

DORRIT'S ROOM. In Marshalsea, Mr. *L.D.* viii.

The bare walls had been coloured green, evidently by an unskilled hand, and were poorly decorated with a few prints. The window was curtained, and the floor carpeted; and there were shelves and pegs, and other such conveniences, that had accumulated in the course of years. It was a close, confined room, poorly furnished; and the chimney smoked to boot, but constant care had made it neat, and—comfortable.

D'ORSAY. Count. *M.P., L.L.*

DORSETSHIRE. *O.C.S.* vii.; *R.P., A.P.A.*

See also Cheselbourne.

D'OSSOLA. Domo. *P.F.I., V.M.M.S.S.*

DOT. *See* Peerybingle, Mrs. *C.B., C.O.H.* i.

DOTHEBOYS' HALL. *N.N.* iii.

A long, cold-looking house, one story high, with a few straggling outbuildings behind, and a barn and stable adjoining.

DOT'S FATHER. *C.B., C.O.H.* iii.

DOT'S MOTHER. *C.B., C.O.H.* iii.

DOUAI. *U.T.* xvii.

DOUBLEDICK. Richard, Enlisting as a soldier. *C.S., S.P.T.* ii.

Age, twenty-two, height five foot ten, had gone wrong, and run wild. His heart was in the right place, but it was sealed up. . . . This made him Private Richard Doubledick, with a determination to be shot.

Note.—Private Richard turns over a new leaf—with the aid of his officer, and becomes Corporal, Sergeant, Lieutenant, Captain, and Major.

DOUBLEDICK. Son of Major Richard. *C.S., S.P.T.* ii.

DOUGLAS. Rev. Dr., Bishop of Salisbury. *M.P., R.S.D.*

DOUGLAS. *M.P., E.S.*

DOUNCE. Mr. John, A widower.. *S.B.B.*, Char. vii.

He was a short, round, large-faced, tubbish sort of man, with a broad-brimmed hat, and a square coat, and had that grave, but confident kind of roll, peculiar to old boys in general—a retired glove-and-braces maker—a widower with three daughters—all unmarried. Married his cook, and lives, a hen-pecked husband.

DOUNCES. Miss. Three. *S.B.B.*, Char. vii.

Went off on small pensions.

DOVE DELEGATE. From America. *M.P., W.H.*

DOVE. In "Happy Family." *M.P., R.H.F.*

DOVE. Mr. *M.P., M.P.*

DOVE. Mrs. *M.P., M.P.*

DOVER. *D.C.* xiii. ; *G.E.* xlv. ; *L.D.* iii. ; *M.P., W.* ; *P.F.I., V.M.M.S.S.* ; *R.P., B.S.* ; *R.P., O.F.W.* ; *T.T.C.* iv. ; *U.T.* v.

DOVER. *See also* Royal George Hotel.

DOVER CASTLE. *B.H.* lii.

DOVER HARBOUR. *U.T.* xvii.

DOVER ROAD. *D.C.* xii. ; *L.D.* liv. ; *P.P.* xliii. ; *T,T.C.* ii.

The Dover road lay beyond the Dovermail as it lumbered up Shooters' Hill.

DOW. Lorenzo, A spirit. *M.P., S.B.*

DOWGATE. Young, Courting Jane Comport. *U.T.* ix.

DOWGATE FAMILY. *U.T.* ix.

DOWLER. Mr., An officer in His Majesty's Service, traveller on coach to Bath. *P.P.* xxxv.

A stern-eyed man of about five-and-forty, who had a bald and glossy forehead, with a good deal of black hair at the sides and back of his head, and large black whiskers. He was buttoned up to the chin in a brown coat ; and had a large seal-skin travelling cap, and a great coat and cloak.

Note.—A would-be redoubtable ex-army officer. First makes the acquaintance of Mr. Pickwick and his friends at the White Horse Cellar, where they are all waiting for the Bath coach. Captain and Mrs. Dowler relieve the Pickwickians of a bedroom and sitting-room at the house in the Royal Crescent, Bath. Captain Dowler fell asleep while waiting up for his wife ; this led to Mr. Winkle's amusing adventure of the sedan chair. Captain Dowler threatens to cut Winkle's throat from ear to ear ; but in the morning both endeavour to avoid each other from a feeling of cowardice.

DOWLER. Mrs., Mr. Dowler's wife. *P.P.* xxxv.

A rather pretty face in a bright blue bonnet.

DOWN EASTERS. *A.N.* x.

DOWNING STREET. *M.P., O.C.* ; *M.P., R.T.* ; *M.P., T.T.* ; *M.P., T.W.M.*

DOWNS. The. *B.H.* xlv. ; *M.P., L.A.V.* ii. ; *P.P.* xxxix.

DOYCE. Daniel, A smith and engineer. *L.D.* x.

A short, square, practical looking man, whose hair had turned grey, and in whose face and forehead there were deep lines of cogitation, which looked as though they were carved in hard wood. He was dressed in decent black, a little rusty, and had the appearance of a sagacious master in some handicraft—a certain free use of the thumb that is never seen, but in a hand accustomed to tools.

Note.—An inventor who is driven from pillar to post in his endeavour to get an invention adopted by Government. In the end he takes it abroad, where it is at once adopted and Doyce made much of. Arthur Clennam becomes his partner in the home firm, but meets with financial reverses. Doyce, however, clears him and reinstates him.

DOYCE. Daniel, Partner of. *L.D.* xvi.

A good man he was. But he has been dead some years.

DOZE. Prof. *Mud. Pap.* i.

DRAGON. The. *See* Blue Dragon. *M.C.* ii.

DRAGOONS. Piedmontese. *P.F.I., R.*

DRAGOONS. Pope's. *P.F.I., R.*

DRAWER. In cotton works. *M.P., O.S.*

DRAWLEY. Mr. *Mud. Pap.* ii.

DRAYTON. *M.P., T.D.*

DREARY ONE. I, the. *M.P., P.M.B.*

DREDGERMEN. Water thieves. *R.P., D W.T.T.*

Who under pretence of dredging up coals—from the bottom of the river, hung about barges and other undecked craft, and when they saw an opportunity, threw any property they could lay their hands on overboard.

DRESSMAKER. Lodger in two-pair back. *N.N.* xiv.

Young lady who made Mrs. Kenwigs' dress.

DRINGWORTH BROTHERS. *C.S., M.f.T.S.* v.

DRIVER. New, of fresh coach. *N.N.* vi.

DRIVER. Of coach. *L.D.* liii.

DRIVER. Of coach. *M.C.* xx.

DRIVER. Omnibus, Of rival. *S.B.B.*, Scenes xvi.

Taunts our people with his having "regularly done" 'em out of that old swell"—an old gentleman.

DRIZZLE. *B.H.* i.

DROOCE. Sergeant of Marines. *C.S., P.o.C.E.P.*

Most tyrannical non-commissioned officer in His Majesty's service.

DROOD. Father of Edwin. *E.D.* ix.

Left a widower in his youth.

DROOD. Young, Edwin Drood. *E.D.* ii.

Note.—The title-character of the story. He is an orphan and betrothed by his father to Rosa Bud. He studies in London, but in the opening of the story he is visiting his uncle, John Jasper, at Cloisterham, at the same time he is to see Rosa who is at the Nun's House in the same town. Possibly as a result of this early arrangement of their destinies they rebel against it and agree to abandon it. The appearance of Helen and Neville Landless completely alter the relations. Rosa takes a great interest in Neville, while Edwin is drawn to Helen. The two young men, on the other hand, dislike one another. This dislike is fostered by Jasper for his own ends, and after a bitter quarrel at Jasper's house, they are induced to make it up. For this purpose they again repair to Jasper's room, but after that Edwin is missed, and his watch found in the river. Neville has set off on a walking tour and is suspected.

DROUET. *M.P., H.H.W.*; *M.P. P.P.*; *M.P., P.T.*

DROUET'S. Mr., Brother. *M.P., P.T.*

DROUET'S. Mr., Farming establishment. *M.P., P.T.*

DROWSYSHIRE. Member for. *M.P., F.C.*

DROWVEY AND GRIMMER. School mistresses. *H.R.* i.

DROWVY. Miss, A teacher. *H.R.* i.

DRUID. A. *U.T.* i.

DRUM. The, A private friend of Trotty's. *C.B., C.G.* iv.

DRUMMLE. Bentley. *G.E.* xxiii.

An old-looking young man, of a heavy order of architecture . . . next heir but one to a Baronetcy . . . A sulky kind of fellow—idle, proud, niggardly, reserved, and suspicious.

Note.—Boards at Mr. Pocket's, where Pip stays. Although not a friend of Pip's he is what Wemmick calls one of the gang." He marries Estella; ill-treats her in all possible ways, and is himself killed "consequent on his ill-treatment of a horse." He is known as "The Spider."

DRUMMLE. Mrs. Bentley. *See* Estella.

DRUMMOND STREET. *S.B.B.*, Char. viii.

DRUNKARD. The. *S.B.B.*, Tales xii.

His dress was slovenly and disordered, his face inflamed, his eyes bloodshot and heavy . . . poorer, shabbier, but the same irreclaimable drunkard.

DRUNKARD. Mother-in-law of the. *S.B.B.*, Tales xii.

With her face bathed in tears, supporting the head of the dying woman—her daughter.

DRUNKARD. Wife of the, Dying. *S.B.B.*, Tales xii.

Grief, want, and anxious care, had been busy at the heart for many a weary year.

DRURY LANE. *M.P., C.P.*; *M.P., G.F.*; *M.P., W.M.*; *O.C.S.* vii.; *S.B.B.*, Scenes xi.; *M.P.*, Scenes xxi.; *U.T.* x. *S.U.T.H.* i.

DRURY LANE THEATRE. *M.P., B.S.*; *M.P., M.B.*; *M.P., S.Q.F.*; *N.N.* xxv.; *P.P.* xliv.; *R.P., D.W.T.T.*; *R.P., L.A.*; *U.T.* iv.

DUBBLEY. Officer of justice. *P.P.* xxiv.

A dirty-faced man, something over six feet high, and stout in proportion.

DUBLIN. *M.P., E.S.*; *S.B.B.*, Tales i.; *R.P., D.W.T.T.*

DUCROW. A rider at Astley's. *S.B.B.*, Scenes xi.

DUCROW. Mr. *M.P., C.C.*

DUFF. Bow Street officer. *O.T.* xxxi.

A red-headed, bony man, in top boots; with a rather ill-favoured countenance, and a turned up sinister-looking nose.

Note.—Bow Street officer engaged, in company with Blathers, on the attempted burglary at Mrs. Maylie's house.

DUFFY. *B.H.* xii.

DUKE. *M.C.* xxviii.

DUKE OF YORK. *M.P., N.E.*

DUKE STREET. *B.R.* l.; *O.M.F.* ii.

DUKE'S PLACE. Aldgate. *O.C.S.* xxxiii.

DULL. Mr. *Mud. Pap.* ii.

DULL LITTLE TOWN. Rochester. *M.P., J.G.*

DULLBOROUGH. *U.T.* xii.

DULLBOROUGH. Fishmongers in. *U.T.* xii.

A compact show of stock in his window, consisting of a sole and a quart of shrimps.

DULLBOROUGH. High Street. *U.T.* xii.

DULLBOROUGH. Mechanics' Institution. *U.T.* xii.

"It led a modest and retired existence up a stable-yard—no mechanics belonged to it, and it was steeped in debt to the chimney-pots."

DULLBOROUGH. Serious Booksellers in. *U.T.* xii.

DULLBOROUGH. Theatre. *U.T.* xii.

DULLBOROUGH. Town Hall of. *U.T.* xii.

DULLBOROUGH TOWN. Playing-field. *U.T.* xii.

The station had swallowed up the playing-field.

DULWICH CHURCH. *P.P.* lvii.

DULWICH GALLERY. *P.P.* lvii.

DULWICH. House of Pickwick. *P.P.* lvii.

The house I have taken—is at Dulwich. It has a large garden, and is situated in one of the most pleasant spots near London.

DUMBLEDON. A parlour-boarder at our school *R.P., O.S.*

DUMBLEDON. Mrs., Mother of Dumbledon. *R.P., O.S.*

DUMKINS. Mr., A most renowned member of the All-Muggletonian. *P.P.* vii.

DUMMINS. Mr. *S.Y.G.*

DUMMY. Mr. *Mud. Pap.* ii.

DUMPS. Mr., Nicodemus, Bank clerk. *.P.* vii.; *S.B.B.* Tales xi.

A bachelor, six feet high, and fifty years old: cross, cadaverous, odd, and ill-natured. He was afflicted with a situation in the Bank worth five hundred a year.

DUNCAN. *P.F.I., R.*

DUNCAN. King of Scotland, Character in play. *S.B.B.*, Scenes xiii.

Boy of fourteen, who is having his eyebrows smeared with soap and whitening.

DUNCHURCH. *P.P.* li.

DUNDAY. Dr. *R.P., D.P.*

DUNDEE. *M.P., E.S., P.P.* xlix.

DUNDEY. Doctor, A Robber. *R.P., T.D.P.*

DUNKLE. Doctor Ginery, a shrill boy. *M.C.* xxxiv.

A gentleman of great poetical elements.

DUNN. Judge. *A.N.* xvii.

DUNSTABLE. Butcher. *G.E.* iv.

DURDLES. A stonemason. *E.D.* iv.

Chiefly in the gravestone, tomb, and monumental way, and wholly of that colour from head to foot. In a suit of coarse flannel with horn buttons, a yellow neckerchief with draggled ends, an old hat more russet-coloured than black, and laced boots of his stony calling.

Note.—Stonemason in Cloisterham. He appears to spend most of his time in and about the cathedral finding, by tapping with his ever ready hammer, where long-buried celebrities have been built in. He is the foil for Jasper's evil intentions. Jasper obtains possession of Durdles' keys and thoroughly examines the locked portion of the cathedral. There is little doubt that Durdles would have entered the story again, but for some chapters he is lost sight of.

DURHAM. A clerk at. *L.D.* xxv.

DUST. Name of bird. *B.H.* xiv.

DUST-BIN. The, Royal old Dust-bin. *C.S.*, *S.L.* i.

DUSTMAN. The Golden. *See* Boffin, Mr.

DUSTMEN. The National, Members of Parliament. *H.T.*, *R.* xii.

DUSTWOMAN. My lady. *See* Boffin, Mrs.

DUTCHMAN. Cheeseman. *R.P.*, *T.S.S.*

DWARF. *M.P.*, *T.O.P.*

DWARF. A, One of Magsman's Showmen. *C.S.*, *G.i.S.*

A most uncommon small man, with a most uncommon large Ed; and what he had inside that Ed, nobody ever knowed but himself. It was always his opinion that he was entitled to property.

DWARF CHILD. An unlucky, A nursemaid. *D. and S.* xxxi.

With a giant baby, who peeps in at the porch.

DWARFS. The, At Greenwich Fair. *S.B.B.*, Scenes xii.

The best thing about a dwarf is, he always has a little box, about two feet six inches high, into which, by long practice, he can just manage to get, by doubling himself up like a bootjack.

DWELLINGS. Pirate. *C.S.*, *P.o.C.E.P.*

DYERS. In Chalons. *L.D.* xi.

DYCE. Artist. *M.P.*, *O.L.N.O.*

E

EAGLE. *M.P.*, *R.H.F.*

EAGLE. *S.B.B.*, Char. iv.

Gentleman with large whiskers.

" **EAGLE.**" The, Gardens of Amusement. *S.B.B.*, Char. iv.

There were walks, beautifully gravelled and planted, and the variegated lamps shedding their rich light upon the company's heads—and the place for dancing ready chalked for the company's feet.

" **EAGLE.**" Visitors to the. *S.B.B.*, Char. vi.

Gentleman in a plaid waistcoat.

" **EAGLE SALOON.**" City Road. *M.P.*, *A.P.*

EAST. The. *L.D.* ii.; *M.P.*, *W.S.*

EAST INDIA COMPANY. *N.N.*, xli.; *P.P.* lvii.; *R.P.B.L.W.*

EAST INDIA DOCKS. *N.N.* xxxv.

EAST LONDON Branch Aid Ramification. *B.H.* xiii.

EAST SMITHFIELD. *B.R.* liii.

EASTERN KINGS. A toy. *R.P.*, *A.C.T.*

EASTERN PASSAGE. *A.N.* ii.

EASTERN PENITENTIARY. Prison in Philadelphia. *A.N.* vii.

The system here is rigid, strict, and hopeless solitary confinement—cruel and wrong.

EASTERN POLICE MAGISTRATE. *U.T.* iii.

Said, through the morning papers, that there was no classification at the Wapping Workhouse for women.

EASTLAKE. *M.P.*, *O.L.N.O.*

EASTLAKE. Mr., Sec. to Fine Arts Commission. *M.P.*, *S. of C.*

EATANSWILL. Pocket borough returning member. *P.P.* xi.

We have traced every name in Schedules A and B without meeting with that of Eatanswill . . . we are therefore led to believe that Mr. Pickwick, with that anxious desire to abstain from giving offence to any, and with those delicate feelings for which all who knew him well know he was so eminently remarkable, purposely substituted a fictitious designation.

EATON SQUARE. *S.B.B., O.P.* vii.

EBENEZER JUNCTION. *P.P.* xxxiii.

ECCLES. Late, of Blackburn. *M.P., O.S.*

ECCLESIASTICAL COURT. The. *B.R.* lxxxii.

"**EDDARD.**" Coster's donkey. *O.M.F.* v.

EDDY. *See* Drood, Edwin.

EDDYSTONE LIGHTHOUSE. *M.P., L.*

EDEN. *M.C.* xxi.

A flourishing city! an architectural city. There were banks, churches, cathedrals, market-places, factories, hotels, stores, mansions, wharves; an exchange, a theatre; public buildings of all kinds. . . . So choked with slime and matted growth was the hideous swamp which bore that name.

EDEN. The valley of. *M.C.* xxi.

EDEN SETTLEMENT. The office of the. *M.C.* xxi.

It was a small place; something like a turnpike. But a great deal of land may be got into a dice-box, and why not a whole territory be bargained for in a shed.

EDEN STINGER. The office of. *M.C.* xxi.

EDGE-ER. (Edgware) Road. *S.B.B.,* lv.

EDGWARE ROAD. *N.N.* xl.

EDINBURGH. *M.P., E.S.*; *M.P., S.S.*; *P.P.* xlix.; *R.P., O.H.T.*; *U.T.* xxiii.

EDINBURGH AND LONDON MAIL. *P.P.* xlix.

EDINBURGH APPRENTICE SCHOOL ASSOCIATION. *M.P., E.A.S.*

EDITH. Mrs. Granger. *D. and S.* xxi.

EDKINS. Mr., A member of the Honourable Society of the Inner Temple. *S.B.B.,* Tales vii.

A pale young gentleman in a green stock, and spectacles of the same colour. Member of a debating society.

EDMONDS. George, *M.P., V.C.*

EDMONTON. *O.T.* xxxi.

EDMUND. Mr., Mr. Longford, alias Denham. *C.B., H.M.* iii.

EDMUNDS. John, the subject of "The Convict's return" told at the Manor Farm. *P.P.* vi.

Note.—The hero or villain of the clergyman's story of "The Convicts' Return." If Gravesend is Muggleton, the churchyard of the story is probably that of Shorne—a favourite place with Dickens.

EDMUNDS. The father of John Edmunds, the returned convict. *P.P.* vi.

EDMUNDS. Mrs., The mother of John Edmunds the returned convict. *P.P.* vi.

EDSON. Mr., A lodger of Mrs. Lirriper's. *C.S., M.L. Lo.* i.

EDSON. Mrs., supposed wife of Mr. Edson. *C.S., M.L.Lo.* i.

A pretty young thing and delicate.

EDWARD. Bertha's brother. *C.B., C.O.H.* iii.

EDWARD. The Deaf man in the cart. *C.B., C.O.H.* iii.

EDWARD. Lord. *M.P., T.T.*

EDWARD. Negro slave, branded E on arm. *A.N.* xvii.

EDWARD. Prince of Saxe-Weimar. *M.P., C.C.*

EDWARD. Theodosius Butler. *S.B.B.* Tales iii.

EDWARDS. Miss, Boarder at Miss Monflatheres' establishment. *O.C.S.* xxxi.

This young lady being motherless and poor, was apprenticed at the school.

Note.—It was Miss Edwards who picked up Little Nell's handkerchief and was rebuked by Miss M. for doing so.

EDWARDS'. Miss, sister. *O.C.S.* xxxii.

This was her sister, her little sister, much younger than Nell, whom she had not seen for five years, and to bring whom to that place on a short visit, she had been saving her poor means all that time.

EDWIN. Schoolfellow of Charley's. *C.S., H.T.*

EDWIN AND EMMELINE. Seven children of. *C.S., H.T.*

EEL PIE ISLAND. *N.N.* lii.

" **E.F.G. LIEUTENANTS.** Nobodies. *R.P., N.S.*

EGBERT. Eldest son of Mrs. Pardiggle. *B.H.* viii.

EGG. Mr. Augustus. *M.P., M.N.D.*

EGHAM RACES. *C.S., G.i.S.*

EGYPT. *C.S.* ; *S.P.T.* ii. ; *E.D.* iv.

EGYPT. Old. *R.P., D.W.T.T.*

EGYPTIAN HALL. *M.P., A.P.* ; *M.P., L.A.P.*

EGYPTIANS. *M.P., S.*

ELDON. Lord. *M.P., C.P.*

ELEPHANT & CASTLE. *B.H.* xxvii.

ELFIN. The, Smallweed. *B.H.* xxi.

ELGIN MARBLES. *R.P., P.A.*

ELIZABETH. Miss. *O.M.F.* v. Inhabitant of Corner House.

ELLENBOROUGH. Lord. *M.P., C.P.*

ELLIE. " Negro boy " slave. *A.N.* xvii.

ELLIS. Mr., Visitor to Bar Parlour. *S.B.B.*, Char. iii.

Sharp-nosed, light-haired man in a brown surtout reaching nearly to his heels.

" **ELMESES.**" The. *C.S., H.T.*

ELMS. The city of, New Haven. *A.N.* v.

ELTON. Mr. *M.P., R.S.L.*

ELTON DISTRICT. *M.P., O.S.*

ELY PLACE. *D.C.* xxiv.

ELYSIAN FIELDS. *B.H.* xii. ; *M.P., N.Y.D.*

EMANUEL. Stiggins' chapel. *P.P.* lii.

EMERSON. Mr. Ralph Waldo, author. *A.N.* iii.

EMIGRANTS. On board the " Amazon." *U.T.* xx.

Some with cabbages, some with loaves of bread, some with cheese and butter, some with milk and beer, some with boxes, beds, and bundles, some with babies—nearly all with children—nearly all with bran new tins for their daily allowance of water.

EMILE. Billeted at the clockmaker's *C.S., S.L.* ii.

EMILIA. Mrs. Orange's baby. *H.R.* iv.

EMILY. *M.P., A.A.P.*

EMILY. Little. *D.C.* iii.

Note.—Mr. Peggotty's niece. David meets her, while they are both children, on his visit to her uncle at Yarmouth, and falls in love with her. She is afterwards affianced to Ham Peggotty. David takes Steerforth on a visit with him to Yarmouth and eventually Emily elopes with Steerforth. After some time he tires of her and proposes to hand her over to Littimer. Thereupon she leaves him, but is ultimately discovered by her uncle, and they emigrate together. They do well in Australia.

EMILY. A suicide. *U.T.* iii.

EMILY. The elder prisoner. *S.B.B.*, Tales i.

About to enter prison van.

EM'LY. *See* Emily, Little.

EMMA. Little. *D.C.* xii. The girl twin.

EMMA. Maid at Manor Farm. *P.P.* xxviii.

EMMA. Servant at the Manor Farm, Dingley Dell. *P.P.* v.

EMMA. Waitress at an Anglers' Inn. *C.S., H.T.*

EMMELINE. Angela's cousin, and Edwin's sweetheart. *C.S., H.T.*

EMMY. *M.P., S.R.*

EMPEROR. *M.P., S.F.A.*

ENCHANTRESS. Compact, Passenger in train. *R.P., A.F.*

"**ENDEAVOUR.**" Steward of the *S.B.B.*, Tales vii.

"**ENDEAVOUR.**" Steward's wife of the. *S.B.B.*, Tales vii.

ENDEAVOUR STRAITS. *M.P., L.A.V.* ii.

ENDELL. Martha, Schoolfellow of Em'ly's and used to work for Mr. Omer. *D.C.* xxii.

Note. The "unfortunate" who discovers Little Em'ly for her uncle. She was at one time at Omer's working side by side with little Em'ly.

ENGINE DRIVER. American Railway train. *M.C.* xxi.

He leaned with folded arms and crossed legs against the side of the carriage smoking.

ENGINE DRIVER. On G.W.R. *M.P., R.S.*

ENGINEER. An. Guest of Veneerings. *O.M.F.* ii.

ENGINEERS. Officer of, At Chatham. *U.T.* xxiv.

ENGINEMEN AND FIREMEN. On the Bedford Station. *M.P., R.S.*

ENGLAND. Sir Richard. *M.P., S.F.A.*

ENGLAND. *A.N.* ii.; *C.B., B.o.L.* i.; *C.S., N.T.* iv.; *C.S., S.P.T.* i.; *C.S., T.G.S.*; *H.R.* iii.; *H.T., S.* ii.; *L.D.* xi.; *M.P., A in* E.; *M.P., A.P.*; *M.P., B.*; *M.P.E.S.*; *M.P., I.C.*; *M.P., I.M.*; *M.P., J.T., M.P., L.A.V.*; *M.P., L.L.*; *M.P., L.W.I.Y.*; *M.P., N.E.*; *M.P., N.G.K.*; *M.P., N.J.B.*; *M.P., O.F.A.*; *M.P., P.A.P.*; *M.P., P.M.B.*; *M.P.; P.P.*; *M.P. R.D.*; *M.P., R.S.*; *M.P., R.T.*; *M.P.S.*; *M.P., S.D.C.*; *M.P., S.S.*; *M.P., T.T.*; *N.N.* vi.; *R.P., T.H.S.*; *U.T.* iii.

ENGLAND. West of. *M.P., L.W.O.Y.*; *O.M.F.* xvii.

ENGLISH COURT. *M.P., C.C.*

ENGLISH PUBLIC. *M.P., R.S.*

ENGLISH WATERING-PLACE. *R.P., O.E.W.*

ENGLISH WATERING-PLACE. Boatmen of our. *R.P., O.E.W.*

Looking at them, you would say that surely these must be the laziest boatmen in the world—let them hear—the signal guns of a ship in distress, and these men spring into activity, so dauntless, so valiant, and heroic, that the world cannot surpass it.

ENGLISH WATERING-PLACE. Church in our. *R.P., O.E.W.*

A hideous temple of flint, like a great petrified haystack.

ENGLISH WATERING-PLACE. Main street of our. *R.P., O.E.W.*

Always stopped up with donkey chaises.

ENGLISH WATERING-PLACE. Pier at. *R.P., O.E.W.*

A queer old wooden pier, fortunately without the slightest pretensions to architecture, and very picturesque in consequence.

ENGLISH WATERING-PLACE. Preventive station at our. *R.P., O.E.W.*

ENGLISH WATERING-PLACE. The sands at our. *R.P., O.E.W.*

The children's great resort. They cluster there, like ants.

ENGLISHMAN. Daughter of Mr. The. *C.S., S.L.* ii.

His erring and disobedient and disowned daughter.

ENGLISHMAN. Monsieur The. *See* Langley, Mr.

ENGLISHMEN. *M.P., N.J.B.*

ENGLISHMEN. A few shadowy. *U.T.* xvii.

Passengers on Dover-Calais Packet

ENGROSSING CLERK. Of Patent Office. *R.P., P.M.T.P.*

"**ENOUGH,**" **HOUSE.** "Satis." *G.E.* viii.

ENTERPRISE. Fort. *M.P., L.A.V.* i.

ENTRIES. Blind Alleys in Liverpool. *U.T.* v.

Kept in wonderful order by the police.

EPPING FOREST. *B.R.* i. ; *U.T.* xxvii.

EPPS. Dr. *M.P., C.*

EPSOM. *R.P., T.D.A.* ii.

EQUITY. Court of. *B.H.* xv. ; *M.P., L.E.J.*

ERIE. Lake. *A.N.* xiv.

ERIE. The town of. *A.N.* xiv.

ERINGOBRAGH. Miss = Ireland. *M.P., A.J.B.*

ESQUIMAUX. *M.P., L.A.V.* i.

ESSEX. *G.E.* liv. ; *M.P., N.S.L.* ; *D. and S.*, i. ; *O.M.F.* xii.

ESSEX MARSHES. *B.H.* i.

ESSEX STREET. *G.E.* xl.

ESTABLISHMENT. Normal. *R.P., T.D.P.*

ESTELLA. Daughter of Magwich. Adopted by Miss Havisham. *G.E.* viii.

Who was very pretty and seemed very proud—pretty brown hair.

Note.—She is first seen by Pip at Miss Havisham's, who has adopted her. She is being trained by her deranged foster-mother to break men's hearts, as the only possible revenge on the sex for the injury done to her by Compeyson. She marries Bentley Drummle, the Spider, a man with much money, a family pedigree, but no intelligence. Pip loves her, and even after the marriage cannot quite forget her. Drummle illtreats her, and she separates from him. Later on he is killed by an accident " consequent on his ill-treatment of a horse." Estella and Pip accidentally meet on the site of the old Satis House some two years after Drummle's death, and when Pip leaves with her, it is with " no shadow of another parting from her." She proves to be the daughter of Magwich and Molly, Mr. Jaggers' housekeeper.

ESTELLA. Mother of. *G.E.* xlviii.

ETERNAL CITY. The. *P.F.I., R.P.S.*

ETERNAL HEAVENS. *M.P., D.V.*

ETHELINDA. Reverential wife of Thomas Sapsea. *E.D.* iv.

ETON. *M.P., I.M.T., S.U.T.H.* i.

ETON SLOCOMB. *N.N.* v.

ETTY. *M.P., O.L.N.O.*

EUGENE. Billeted at the Tinman's. *C.S., S.L.* ii.

Cultivating, pipe in mouth, a garden four foot square, for the Tinman, behind the shop.

EUGÈNE. A solicitor, Friend of Mortimer, guest of Veneerings. *O.M.F.* ii.

Buried alive in the back of his chair, behind a shoulder—and gloomily resorting to the champagne chalice whenever proffered.

EUPHEMIA. Miss Pupford's assistant. *C.S., T.T.G.* vi.

EUROPE. *A.N.* xviii. ; *M.P., B.A.*; *M.P., C.C.* ; *M.P., E.C.* ; *M.P., G.H.* ; *M.P., I.* ; *M.P., I.C.* ; *M.P., N.S.E.* ; *M.P., S.B.* ; *M.P., S.F.A.* ; *R.P., O.H.T.*

EUROPE. The capital of. *M.H.C.* i.

EUSTACE. The celebrated Mr. *L.D.* xli.

The classical tourist.

EUSTON HOTEL. *M.P., E.S.*

EUSTON SQUARE. *A.N.* i. ; *M.P., E.S.* ; *N.N.* xxxvii. ; *S.B.B.* Char. viii.

EVANS. Miss Jemima, a shoe binder and straw-bonnet maker. *S.B.B.*, Char. iv.

In a white muslin gown—a little red shawl—a white straw bonnet trimmed with red ribbons, a small necklace, a large pair of bracelets, Denmark satin shoes, and open-work stockings, white cotton gloves—and a cambric pocket handkerchief.

EVANS. Mr., Friend of the Gattletons. *S.B.B.*, Tales ix.

A tall, thin pale young gentleman, with extensive whiskers, talent for writing verses in albums and playing the flute.

EVANS. Richard, schoolboy. *O.C.S.* lii.

An amazing boy to learn, blessed with a good memory and a ready understanding.

EVANS. Superintendent, Thames Police Officer. *R.P., D.W.T.T.*

EVANS AND RUFFY. Messrs., Bill Printers. *R.P., B.S.*

EVENSON. Mr. John, Boarder at Mrs. Tibbs. *S.B.B.*, Tales i.

Very morose and discontented, a thorough Radical, and used to attend a great variety of public meetings, for the express purpose of finding fault with everything that was proposed; was in receipt of an independent income—from various houses he owned in the different suburbs.

EXCAVATORS' HOUSE OF CALL. The. *D. and S.* vi.

"**EXCHANGE OR BARTER.**" Boy at Salem House. *D.C.* vi.

One boy, who was a coal-merchant's son, came as a set-off against the coal bill, and was called, on that account, "Exchange or Barter."

EXCHANGE. Royal. *M.P., G.A. N.N.* xli.; *U.T.* iv.

EXCHEQUER. *M.P., R.T.*

EXCHEQUER COFFEE-HOUSE. *O.M.F.* iii.

EX-CHURCHWARDEN. The. *S.B.B., O.P.* iv.

Supporter of Spruggins.

EXCISE OFFICE. The. *O.M.F.* iv.

EXETER. *C.S., D.M.*; *N.N.* xxi.; *U.T.* xxiii.

EXETER. Bishop of. *M.P., Ag. Int.*; *M.P., L.W.O.Y.*; *M.P., P.F.*

EXETER 'CHANGE. *S.B.B.*, Char. i.

EXETER HALL. *M.P., G.B.*; *M.P., N.E.*; *M.P., S.S.*; *N.N.* v.; *S.B.B., O.P.* vi.

EXETER STREET. *R.P., T.D.A.* i.

EXHIBITION. Miss Linwood's. *D.C.* iv.

Mausoleum of needlework.

EXMOUTH. *C.S., S.P.T.* ii.

EXMOUTH STREET. *O.T.* viii.

EXTERNAL PAPER-HANGING STATION. The. *R.P., B.S.*

EYE. A little town in Suffolk. *M.P., E.C.*

EZEKIEL. The boy at Mugby Junction. *C.S., M.J.* v.

F

FACCIO. Monte. *P.F.I., G.A.N.*

FACE-MAKER. The. *U.T.* xxv.

A corpulent little man in a large white waistcoat, with a comic countenance, and with a wig in his hand.

FACTORY. The. *H.T., S.* xii.

FAGGS. Mr. *O.M.F.* viii.

FAGIN. A thief. *O.T.* viii.

A very old, shrivelled Jew, whose villainous and repulsive face was obscured by a quantity of matted red hair. He was dressed in a greasy flannel gown, with his throat bare.

Note.—The crafty old Jew who kept a thieves' school near Field Lane in Saffron Hill, and acted as receiver to the older members of his gang of burglars. Oliver falls into his hands and he is paid by Monks to make the boy as bad a thief as the companions he is forced to associate with. His dupes are detected, but the Jew himself escapes until the murder of Nancy breaks up the whole gang. Fagin is charged with complicity in the murder, and after being sentenced to death becomes mad in his cell and beseeches Oliver to assist him to escape. He suffers the extreme penalty of the law.

FAHEY. Mr. *M.P., E.T.*

FAIDO. A Swiss village. *P.F.I., R.D.*

FAIR. The, In the Fleet. *P.P.* xli.

"You don't really mean that any human beings live down in those wretched dungeons?" "Don't I," said Mr. Roker.

FAIR GUVAWNMENT. Fair Government. *M.P., T.O.H.*

FAIRFAX. Mr. *S.Y.G.*

FAIRIES. *M.P., F.F.*; *M.P., G.F.*

FAIRY. John Kemble. *M.P., G.F.*

FAIRY. Master Edmund. *M.P., G.F.*

FAIRY. Miss. *M.P., G.F.*

FAIRY. Miss Angelica. *M.P., G.F.*

FAIRY. Miss Rosina. *M.P., G.F.*

FAIRY. Mr. *M.P., G.F.*

FAIRY. Mrs. *M.P., G.F.*

FALKLAND ISLANDS. *B.R.* Pref.

FALKNER AND CO. *M.P., S.P.*

FALL. Mr., Editor of the *Vicksburg Sentinel.* *A.N.* xvii.

FALLEY. Mr. *O.M.F.* viii.

FALMOUTH. *C.S., M.f.T.S.* v.

FAMILY. An Irish. *P.P.* l.

Keeping up with the chaise and begging all the time.

FAMILY MANSION. Of Uncommercial traveller. *U.T.* xviii.

In a certain distinguished metropolitan parish.

FAMILY PARTY. Christmas. *S.B.B.*, Char. ii.

Not a mere assemblage of relations. It is an annual gathering of all the accessible members of the family, young or old, rich or poor; and all the children look forward to it, for two months beforehand, in a fever of anticipation.

FAMILY PARTY. Grandpapa at Christmas. *S.B.B.*, Char. ii.

Produces sprig of mistletoe from his pocket, and tempts the little boys to kiss their little cousins under it—says, that when he was just thirteen and three months old, *he* kissed grandmama under a mistletoe, too.

FAMILY SPY. New York. *M.C.* xvi.

FAN. Scrooge's sister. *C.B., C.C.* s. ii.

FANCHETTE. *R.P., O.B.*

FANE. General. *M.P., S.F.A.*

FANG. Mr., Police Magistrate. *O.T.* xi.

A lean, long-backed, stiff-necked middle-sized man, with no great quantity of hair, and what he had, growing on the back and sides of his head. His face was stern, and much flushed.

Note.—The police-magistrate before whom Oliver was taken when charged with stealing Mr. Brownlow's handkerchief. He is overbearing in manner, violent in language, and without any regard for justice. He had summarily sentenced Oliver to three months' hard labour on the flimsiest evidence, when the keeper of the bookshop breathlessly arrived with testimony which could not be ignored.

FANG'S. Mr., Office. *O.T.* xi.

FANNY. Father and mother of. *S.B.B.*, Tales x.

FANNY. Guest at Christmas party. *R.P., T.C.S.*

FANNY. Mrs. Parsons. *S.B.B.*, Tales x.

FARADAY. *M.P., M.M.*; *M.P., R.S.D.*

FAREWAY. Lady, Widow of Sir Gaston Fareway. *G.S.E.* vii.

FAREWAY. Mr., Second son of Lady Fareway. *G.S.E.* vii.

FAREWAY PARK. Home of Lady Fareway. *G.S.E.* ix.

FARM HOUSE. Deputy of landlady of. *R.P., D.W.I.F.*

FARM HOUSE. Landlady of. *R.P.,D.W.I.F.*

FARM HOUSE. The old, Common lodging house. *R.P., D.W.I.F.*

FARMER. *M.P., A.A.P.*

FARMER'S SON. *M.P., A.A.P.*

FARMERS. Young and old, In Salisbury Market Place. *M.C.* v.

With smock-frocks, brown great-coats, drab great-coats, red worsted comforters, leather leggings, wonderful-shaped hats, hunting whips, and rough sticks.

FARMERS' WIVES. In Salisbury Market Place. *M.C.* v.

In beaver bonnets and red cloaks.

FARRIER. A tall. *M.H.C.* iii.

Who having been engaged all his life in the manufacture of horse-shoes must be invulnerable to the power of witches.

FARRINGDON STREET. *B.R.* lx.; *C.S., S.L.* iv.; *M.P., S.S.U.*; *P.P.* xli.; *S.B.B.*, Scenes xvi.

FAT BOY. Joe. *P.P.* xxviii.

FATHER. Aged, Of Mr. Vholes. *B.H.* xxxvii.

FATHER. A stout, Of a stout family. *S.B.B.*, Scenes x.

On board the "Gravesend Packet."

FATHER. Briggs'. *D. and S.* xiv.

Never would leave him alone.

FATHER. Husband of mother illustrated by Goblin. *P.P.* xxix.

Wet and weary. . . . the children crowded round him, and seizing his cloak, stick, and gloves—with busy zeal, ran with them from the room.

FATHER. Monsieur Rigaud's. *L.D.* i.

My father was Swiss.

FATHER. Of George, Prisoner at Marshalsea. *P.P.* xxi.

Who *would* have let him die in gaol, and who *had* let those who were far dearer to him than his own existence, die of want, and sickness of heart that medicine cannot cure—had been found dead on his bed of down.

FATHERS. One of the young, At Great St. Bernard. *L.D.* xxxvii.

The host, a slender, bright-eyed, young man of polite manners, whose garment was a black gown with strips of white crossed over it like braces, who no more resembled the conventional breed of the Saint Bernard Monks, than he resembled the conventional breed of the Saint Bernard dogs.

FATHERS. Two young, On the Great St. Bernard. *L.D.* xxxvii.

FAUNTLEROY. Criminal. *M.P., C.P.*

FAWKES. Guy. *N.N.* xxviii.; *L. D.* 2. xvi.; *O.M.F.* 1. xiii., 2. iii.; *M.C.* i; *D. & S.* xxxvi.; *U.T.* xxi.

FECHTER. Mr., Actor. *M.P., O.F.A.*; *M.P., M.M.*

FECHTER. Mr., As Jules Obenreizer. *M.P., N.T.*

FEE. Dr. *Mud. Pap*, i.

FEEDER, B.A. Mr., Dr. Blimber's Assistant. *D. and S.* xi.

He was a kind of human barrel-organ, with a little list of tunes at which he was continually working, over and over again, without any variation.

Note.—He afterwards marries Miss Blimber and succeeds the doctor in the school.

FEEDER, M. A. The Reverend Alfred, Brother of Mr. Feeder. *D. and S.* lx.

FEEDER. Mrs., née Cornelia Blimber. *D. and S.* lx.

FEENIX. Mrs. Granger's cousin. *D. and S.* xxi.

A man about town forty years ago.

Note.—Cousin of the second Mrs. Dombey, and therefore nephew to Mrs. Skewton. Although he is a rather ancient nobleman, he endeavours to appear youthful. Albeit he is good at heart, and he is last seen on an errand of mercy, taking Florence to bid farewell to her stepmother.

FEENIX. Old cousin. *M.P., P.M.B.*

FEENIX. The late Lord, Brother of the Honourable Mrs. Skewton. *D. and S.* xxi.

The family are not wealthy—they're poor, indeed—but if you come to blood, sir.

FELIX. Fourth son of Mrs. Pardiggle. *B.H.* viii.

FELLOW. A tall, Fresh from a slaughter-house, a rioter. *B.R.* lxiv.

Whose dress and great thigh-boots smoked hot with grease and blood.

FELLOW. Passenger by coach. *P.P.* xlix.

An uncommonly ill-looking fellow in a close brown wig and a plum-coloured suit, wearing a very large sword, and boots up to his hips.

FELLOW. That young, Hanging outside stage-door at Astley's. *S.B.B.*, Scenes xi.

In the faded brown coat, and very full light green trousers, pulls down the wrist-bands of his check shirt, as ostentatiously as if it were of the finest linen, and cocks the white hat of the summer before last as knowingly over his right eye, as if it were a purchase of yesterday.

FELLOWS IN THE WEST INDIES. Some of our. *L.D.* lx.

FEMALE. A, Guest at Dombey's housewarming. *D. and S.* xxvi.

A bony and speechless female with a fan.

FEMALE. From Inn in Rochester. *C.S.*; *S.P.T.* i.

FENCHURCH STREET. *O.M.F.* xxv.

FENDALL. Sergeant, A detective. *R.T.*, *T.D.P.*

A light-haired, well-spoken, polite person.

FENNING. Eliza. *M.P.*, *C.P.*

FERDINAND. Miss, Pupil at the Nun's house. *E.D.* ix.

FERGUSON. *M.P.*, *F.C.*

FERGUSON. *N.N.* ii.

FERN. William, Will Fern. *C.B.*, *C.G.* ii.

A sun-browned, sinewy, country-looking man, with grizzled hair, and a rough chin—in worn shoes—rough leather leggings, common frock, and broad slouched hat.

FERNANDO PO. *M.P.*, *N.E.*

FEROCE. M., Bathing machine proprietor. *R.P.*, *O.F.W.*

Gentle and polite, immensely stout—of a beaming aspect, decorated with so many medals (for saving people from drowning) that his stoutness seems a special dispensation of Providence to enable him to wear them.

FERRARA. *P.F.I.*, *T.B.F.*

FETTER LANE. *S.B.B.*, Char. ix.

FEZZIWIG. Mrs. *C.B.*, *C.C.* s. ii.

FEZZIWIG. Old. *C.B.*, *C.C.* s. ii.

An old gentleman in a Welsh wig.

FEZZIWIG. Two 'prentices of old. *C.B.*, *C.C.* s. ii.

Their beds—under a counter in the back shop.

FEZZIWIGS. Three Miss. *C.B.*, *C.C.* s. ii.

Daughters of old Fezziwig.

FIBBITSON. Mrs., An inmate of the almshouses. *D.C.* v.

Another old woman in a large chair by the fire.

FIDDLER. At Uncle Tom's Cabin blowing room. *M.P.*, *O.S.*

FIELD. Rev. Mr. *M.P.*, *P.P.*

FIELD. Sacred. *P.F.I.*, *R.*

FIELD AND CO. Inspector, policemen. *R.P.*, *D.W.I.F.*

FIELD LANE. *M.P.*, *C. and E.*; *M.P.*, *S.S.U.*; *O.T.* viii.

FIELDING. Emma. *S.Y.C.*

FIELDING. May, Tackleton's fiancée. *C.B.*, *C. o. H.* ii.

Her hair is dark . . . her shape—there's not a doll's in all the room to equal it . . . and her eyes.

FIELDING. Mrs., Mother of May. *C.B.*, *C. o. H.* ii.

A little querulous chip of an old lady with a peevish face, who in right of having preserved a waist like a bedpost, was supposed to be a most transcendant figure.

FIELDING. Sir John, A magistrate. *B.R.* lviii.

FIELDS. James T. *M.P.*, *I.W.M.*

FIELDS. Mistress Annie. *M.P.*, *I.W.M.*

FIERY FACED MATRON. *M.C.* xii.

FIESOLE. *M.P.*, *L.L.*

FIESOLE. The Convent at. *P.F.I.*, *R.D.*

FIGURE. Ghost in wooden press. *P.P.* xxi.

A pale and emaciated figure in soiled and worn apparel. The figure was tall and thin, and the countenance expressive of care and anxiety.

FIKEY. A forger. *R.P.*, *T.D.P.*

FILER. Mr. *C.B.*, *C.G.* i.

A low-spirited gentleman of middle age, of a meagre habit, and a dissonsolate face; who kept his hands continuously in the pockets of his scanty pepper-and-salt trousers, very large and dog-eared from that custom; and was not particularly well brushed or washed.

FILEY. *H.D.* iv.

FILLETOVILLE. Marquess of, Only son of. *P.P.* xlix.

The young gentleman in sky blue.

FINCHBURY. Lady Jane. *D. and S.* xli.

FINCHES. A club. *G.E.* xxxiv.
The members should dine expensively once a fortnight.

FINCHING. Flora. *L.D.* xiii.
Always tall, had grown to be very broad, too, and short of breath—a lily, had become a peony—Flora, who had seemed enchanting in all she said and thought, was diffuse and silly.

Note.—The relict of Mr. Finching and daughter of Casby. Formerly a sweetheart of Arthur Clennam, she is introduced desiring to practice all those endearing, artless wiles of twenty years before. She is last seen at Little Dorrit's wedding with Arthur Clennam.

FINCHING'S. Aunt, *See* Aunt, Mr. F's.

FINCHLEY. *See* Abel Cottage.

FINCHLEY. *D. and S.* xxxii.; *B.R.* lxviii.

FINE ARTS COMMISSIONERS. *M.P., S. of C.*

FINLAYSON. Mr., The Government actuary. *M.P., Th. Let.*

FINSBURY SQUARE. *O.T.* xxi.; *S.B.B.*, Char. v.

FIPS. Mr. *M.C.* xxxviii.
Grave, business-like, sedate-looking . . . small and spare, and looked peaceable, and wore black shorts, and powder.

Note.—The mysterious lawyer who is in old Martin's confidence to some extent, and who acts as his agent in doing good while old Martin himself is acting the part he has chosen.

FIRE ENGINE. The parish. *S.B.B., O.P.* i.

FIREMAN. The, Of American railway train. *M.C.* xxi.
Who beguiled his leisure by throwing logs of wood from the tender, at the numerous stray cattle on the line.

FIREMAN. Waterman, An old. *S.B.B.*, Tales vii.
Dressed in a faded red suit, just the colour of the cover of a very old Court-Guide.

FIREWORKS. Rev. Jabez. *M.P., W.H.*

"**FIRST AND LAST.** The," A beer shop. *U.T.* xxii.

FISH. An Indian chief. *A.N.* ix.

FISH. Mr., Confidential Secretary to Sir Joseph Bowley. *C.B., C.G.* ii.
A not very stately gentleman in black, who wrote from dictation.

FISH. Mrs. *M.P., S.B.*

FISH STREET HILL. *D.C.* xxx.; *O.M.F.* xx.

FISHER. Fanny, Married daughter of Mrs. Venning. *C.S., P.o.C.E.P.*
Quite a child she looked, with a little copy of herself holding to her dress.

FISHMONGERS' HALL. *M.P., N.G.K.*

FITZ. Lord Fitz-Brinkle. *S.B.B.*, Scenes xix.

FITZBALL. *S.Y.G.*

FITZ-JARNDYCE. Miss Flite's name for Esther Summerson. *Which see.*

FITZ-LEGIONITE. Percival. *M.P., C.Pat.*

FITZ-MARSHALL. Mr. Charles. *See* Jingle, Mr. Alfred.

FITZROY SQUARE. *S.B.B.* Scenes vii.

FITZ-SORDUST. Col. *S.Y.G.*

FITZ-WARREN. Mr. *M.P., G.A.*

FIVE POINTS. New York. *A.N.* vi.

FIXEM. Old, A bailiff, The broker's man's master. *S.B.B., O.P.* v.

FIZKIN. Horatio, Esq. of Fizkin Hall. *P.P.* xiii.
A tall, thin gentleman, in a stiff white neckerchief . . . desired by the crowd . . . to send a boy home, to ask whether he hadn't left his voice under the pillow.

Note.—The defeated candidate for Parliamentary honours at the Eatanswill election.

FIZKIN'S COMMITTEE. *P.P.* xiii.

FIZMAILE. Mr. *M.P., T.T.*

FIZZGIG. Don Bolaro, Jingle's Spanish grandee. *P.P.* ii.

FIZZGIG. Donna Christina, Jingle's imaginary conquest. *P.P.* ii.

Splendid creature — high-souled daughter . . . never recovered the [effects of] stomach pump.

FLABELLA. Lady, Character in a novel read by Kate to Mrs. Wititterly. *N.N.* xxviii.

FLADDOCK. General, A passenger in the " Screw." *M.C.* xvii.

FLAIR. The Honourable Augustus. *S.B.B.*, Tales viii.

FLAM. Hon. Sparkins. *M.P., V.C.*

FLAM. Mr., Of the Minories. *M.P., N.G.K.*

FLAM. The real doctor. *M.P.*, *Q. D.P.*

FLAMWELL. Mr. *S.B.B.*, Tales v.

A little spoffish man, with green spectacles—one of those gentlemen —who pretend to know everybody, but in reality know nobody.

FLANDERS. *U.T.* xxvi.

FLANDERS' NEPHEW. *U.T.* xxvi.

To whom, Flanders, it was rumoured, had left nineteen guineas.

FLANDERS. Sally, A married servant. Once nurse of Uncommercial Traveller. *U.T.* xxvi.

After a year or two of matrimony, became the relict of Flanders . . . an excellent creature, and had been a good wife.

FLANDERS' UNCLE. *U.T.* xxvi.

A weak little old retail grocer, had only one idea, which was that we all wanted tea.

FLANDERS' WIFE'S BROTHER. *U.T.* xxvi.

Guest at funeral of Flanders.

FLASHER. Wilkins, Esq., Stockbroker. *P.P.* lv.

FLASHER. Wilkins, Clerk of. *P.P.* lv.

FLASHER. Wilkins, Esq., Groom of. *P.P.* lv.

On his way to the West End to deliver some game.

FLASHER. Wilkins, Esq., House of. *P.P.* lv.

The house of Wilkins Flasher, Esq., was in Surrey. The horse and " Stanhope " of—were at an adjacent stable.

FLAY. George. *M.P., E.S.*

FLEANCE. Character in Play. *S.B.B.*, Scenes xiii.

Young lady with the liberal display of legs.

FLEDGEBY. Mr., Father of (deceased). *O.M.F.* xxii.

Had been a money-lender.

FLEDGEBY. Mr., Mother of (deceased). *O.M.F.* xxii.

FLEDGEBY. Young. *O.M.F.* xxi.

Had a peachy cheek, or a cheek compounded of the peach, and the red, red wall on which it grows, and was an awkward, sandy-haired, small-eyed youth, exceedingly slim—and prone to self-examination in the articles of whiskers and moustache.

Note.—Fledgeby has a dual personality in the story ; one, his own ; the other as Pubsey and Co., money-lenders and bill-brokers. He wishes to be married and agrees to pay Mr. Lammle a thousand pounds when he is united to Miss Georgina Podsnap. The marriage does not take place, however, and Lammle does not receive his money. Pubsey and Co. are hard dealers, and Fledgeby carries out the deceit in detail by pleading for some mercy for the creditors. Retribution overtakes him in the form of Mr. Alfred Lammle and in the shape of a " stout lithe cane."

FLEECE. Golden, Shop of Thomas Curzon. *B.R.* xxxviii.

FLEET. The. *B.H.* xxiv. ; *B.R.* vii. ; *M.P., S.S.U.* ; *N.N.* lv. *P.P.* xl.

FLEET MARKET. *B.R.* viii. ; *M.P., S.S.U.*

At that time, a long irregular row of wooden sheds and pent-houses, occupying the centre of what is now called Farringdon Street.

FLEET PRISON. The poor side. *P.P.* xlii.

In which the most miserable and abject class of debtors are confined. A prisoner having declared upon the poor side pays neither rent nor chummage. His fees, upon entering and leaving the gaol, are reduced in amount, and he becomes entitled to a share of some small quantities of food: to provide which, a few charitable persons have, from time to time, left trifling legacies in their wills.

FLEET STREET. *B.R.*, xv. ; *C.S. H.T.* i. ; *D.C.* xxiii. ; *G.E.* xlv. ; *M.P.*, *T.D.* ; *O.M.F.* viii. ; *P.P.* xl. ; *S.B.B.*, Scenes xviii. ; *S.B.B.* Tales xii.

FLEETWOODS. The, Mr. Fleetwood. *S.B.B.*, Tales vii.

Mrs. Fleetwood, and Master Fleetwood, of the steam excursion party.

FLEMING. Agnes, Oliver Twist's mother. *O.T.* li.

Note.—The mother of Oliver Twist and sister of Rose Maylie. Betrayed by the father of Monks she makes her way to the workhouse where she dies in giving birth to Oliver.

FLEMING. Rose, Miss Maylie. *O.T.* liii.

FLESTRIN. Junior, Quinbus, or, The Young Man Mountain, Edmund Sparkler. *L.D.* lx.

FLETCHER. Christian. *R.P.*, *L.V.*

FLIMKINS. Mr. *S.Y.G.*

FLIMKINS. Mrs. *S.Y.G.*

FLINTWINCH. Ephraim. *L.D.* lxvi.

Twin brother of Jeremiah's. The Lunatic keeper.

Note.—Jeremiah's brother. A keeper of a lunatic asylum who is obliged to leave the country. When he does so he is entrusted, by his brother, with a box of papers stolen from Mrs. Clennam. This box gets into the hands of Rigaud, who endeavours to make money by the contents.

FLINTWINCH. Jeremiah. *L.D.* iii.

An old man, bent and dried, but with keen eyes. He was a short, bald old man, in a high-shouldered black coat, and waistcoat, drab breeches, and long drab gaiters. He might, from his dress, have been either clerk, or servant, and in fact had long been both. His neck was so twisted, that the knotted ends of his white cravat usually dangled under one ear.—he had a weird appearance of having hanged himself at one time—and having gone about ever since halter and all—as some timely hand had cut him down.

Note.—Mrs. Clennam's manager-partner. He discovers and abstracts papers relating to private matters of the family which give him a hold over Mrs. Clennam. He sends the papers for safe keeping to his brother. They get into the possession of Rigaud and lose their value to Flintwinch. He, however, fraudulently obtains a large sum from the firm and decamps.

FLINTWINCH. Mrs. Affery. *L.D.* iii.

Though a tall, hard-favoured sinewy old woman, who in her youth might have enlisted in the Foot Guards without much fear of discovery, she collapsed before the little keen-eyed, crab-like old man.

Note.—Wife of Clennam's confidential servant. She hears noises and sees sights, but is in a constant state of terror of her husband.

FLIPFIELD. Friend of the Uncommercial Traveller. *U.T.* xix.

FLIPFIELD. Long lost brother of. *U.T.* xix.

FLIPFIELD. Miss, Sister of Flipfield. *U.T.* xix.

FLIPFIELD. Mrs., Senior, Mother of Flipfield. *U.T.* xix.

With a blue-veined miniature of the late Mr. Flipfield round her neck.

FLITE. Miss, "An Ancient Ward" in Chancery. *B.H.* i.

A little mad old woman in a squeezed bonnet always in Court (Chancery) expecting some incomprehensible judgment to be given in her favour—was a party to a suit; but no one knows for certain; and no one cares. She carries some small litter in a reticule—which she calls her documents; principally consisting of paper, matches, and dry lavender.

Note.—A suitor in chancery. a regular attendant who had become rather mad through the never-ending proceedings. She was a good little soul. She appointed Richard her executor, in the event of her death, to watch over her interests, as he, too, was such a regular attendant; but on the result of the Jarndyce case being known she liberates a number of birds she had caged and named oddly.

FLITE'S. Miss, Brother (deceased). *B.H.* xxxv.
Had a builder's business.

FLITE'S. Miss, Father (deceased) *B.H.* xxxv
Had a builder's business.

FLITE'S. Miss, Sister (deceased). A tambour worker. *B.H.* xxxv.

FLOPSON. One of the young Pocket's nurses. *G.E.* xxii.

FLORENCE. *L.D.*, li.; *M.P.*, *L.L.*; *N.N.* i.; *P.F.I.*, *T.B.F.*

FLORENCE STREET. 30. *U.T.* xx. Latter-Day Saints. Book Depôt.

FLOUNCEBY. *M.P.*, *B.A.*

FLOUNCEBY. Mrs. *M.P.*, *B.A.*

FLOWER. The, Of ours. *See* Bagstock.

"**FLOWER-POT.** The," Bishopsgate Street. *S.B.B.*, xlvi.
A public house.

FLOWERS. Mrs. Skewton's maid. *D. and S.* xl.

FLOWERS. Tom. *M.P.*, *G.D.*

FLUGGERS. Old, Member of Mr. V. Crummles' Company. *N.N.* xxx.
Does the heavy business.

FLUMMERY. Mr. *Mud. Pap.* ii.

FLY. A, A werry large—reg'lar bluebottle. *S.B.B.*, Tales iv.

FLYNTERYNGE. Mynheer von Jeremiah. *See* Flintwinch.

FOGG. Mr., Of Dodson and Fogg. *P.P.* xx.
An elderly, pimply-faced, vegetable diet sort of man, in a black coat, dark mixture trousers, and small black gaiters: a kind of being who seemed to be an essential part of the desk at which he was writing, and to have as much thought and sentiment.

FOGLE. Jackson. *U.T.* v.

FOLEY. Acquaintance of Cousin Feenix; on a blood mare. *D. and S.* xli.

FOLAIR. Mr., Pantomimist in Mr. Vincent Crummles' Company. *N.N.* xxiii.
Note.—A somewhat mischievous member of Crummles' company, acting the savage on his first introduction. It was he who carried the cartel of defiance from Mr. Lenville, and in the capacity of mutual friend acted as tale-bearer.

FOLKESTONE. *M.P.*, *S.R.*; *R.P.*, *A.F.*

FOLLY. Name of one of Miss Flite's birds. *B.H.* xiv.

FOLLY. Lady James's. (Severndroog Castle, Shooter's Hill. *S.U.T.H.* i.

FOLLY DITCH. *O.T.* l.

FONDI. *P.F.I.*, *R.D.*

FONDLING. The. *N.N.* xxxvi.

FOODLE. Duke of. *B.H.* xii.

FOOTBOY. Of Mrs. Gowan. *L.D.* xxvi.
Microscopically small . . . who waited on the malevolent man who hadn't got into the post office.

FOOTMAN. *M.C.* ix.
With such great tags upon his liveried shoulder, that he was perpetually entangling and hooking himself among the chairs and tables, and led such a life of torment, which could scarcely have been surpassed if he had been a bluebottle in a world of cobwebs.

FOOTMAN. *P.P.* xxxvii.
Gentleman in a yellow waistcoat with coach trimming border.

FOOTMAN. *P.P.* xxxvii.
Selection in purple cloth.

FOOTMAN. *P.P.* xxxvii.
Gentleman in light blue suit.

FOOTMAN. Dr. Blimber's footman. *D. and S.* xi.
A weak-eyed young man, with the first faint streaks or early dawn of a grin on his countenance.

FOOTMAN. Liveried, of Madam Mantalini. *N.N.* x.

FOOTMAN. Mr. Bantam's. *P.P.* xxxv.
Powder-headed, tall footman.

FOOTMAN. Mr. Tite-Barnacle's. *L.D.* x.

The footman was to the Grosvenor Square footmen, what the house was to the Grosvenor Square houses. Admirable in his way, his way was a back and a bye way. His gorgeousness was not unmixed with dirt; and both in complexion and consistency he had suffered from the closeness of his pantry—had as many large buttons with the Barnacle crest upon them, on the flaps of his pockets, as if he were the family strong box, and carried the family plate and jewels about with him buttoned up.

FOOTMAN. Mr. Wititterley's. *N.N.* xxi.

FOOTMAN. Of doctor attending on Jinkinson. *M.H.C.* v.

FOOTMEN. Two. *M.P., M.M.*

FOOTMEN. Two, Of Dorrit's party. *L.D.* xxxvii.

FOREIGN MILITIA. *R.P.O.o.S.*

FOREIGN POWERS. *N.N.* xli.

FOREIGNER. A. *PF.I., T.R.P.*

FORELAND. South. *D.C.* xiii.; *U.T.* xvii.

FORESTER. Mr., as Charles Tomkins. *M.P., S.G.*

FORESTER. Mr., as the Hon. Sparkins Flam. *M.P., V.C.*

FORESTER. Mr., as Alfred Lovetown. *M.P., I.S.H.W.*

FORGE. Joe's, Adjoining our house *See* Gargery. Joe. *G.E.* ii.

FORGOTTEN. The Tower of the. *P.F.I., L.R.G.A.*

FORMIVILLE. Mr. *M.P., M.N.D.*

FORSTER. Mr. John. *M.P., L.L.*

FORSTER COLLECTION. *M.P.,L.*

FORT. The, The Mine. *C.S., P.o.C.E.P.*

FORT PITT. Chatham. *P.P.* ii.

It was beyond this, at a secluded place, that Mr. Winkle's affair of honour with Dr. Slammer was to take place.

FORUM. The Roman. *P.F.I., R.*

FOSCARI. *P.F.I., R.D.*

FORTESCUE. Miss, Actress. *M.P., M.B.*

FOULON. Old. *T.T.C.*, bk. ii., ch. xxii.

Who told the famished people they might eat grass.

FOUNDLING. The. *S.B.B.*, Tales i.

FOUNDLING CHILDREN. Hospital for. *B.R.* xxxviii.; *C.S., N.T.o.*; *L.D.* ii.

Time was, when the foundlings were received without question in a cradle at the gate. Time is, when enquiries are made respecting them. and they are taken as by favour from the mothers, who relinquish all natural knowledge of them and claim to them for evermore.

FOUNDLING HOSPITAL. Governors of the. *C.S., N.T.o.*

FOUNDLING HOSPITAL. Matron of. *C.S., N.T.o.*

An elderly female attendant.

FOUNDLING HOSPITAL. Neat attendants of. *C.S., N.T.o.*

Silently glide about the orderly and silent tables.

FOUNDLING HOSPITAL. Treasurer of. *C.S., N.T.*, Act i.

FOUNTAIN. Runaway man-slave. *A.N.* xvii.

FOUNTAIN. The, In Vauxhall Gardens. *S.B.B.*, Scenes xiv.

That had sparkled so showily by lamp-light, presented very much the appearance of a water-pipe that had burst: all the ornaments were dingy.

FOUNTAIN COURT. Temple. *B.R.* xv.; *M.C.* xlv.

FOUR ASHES. *M.P., E.S.*

FOX. George. *M.P., R.S.D.*

FOX. The Misses. *M.P., S.B.*

FOX. Mr. *M.P., T.O.H.*

FOX. Mr., of Oldham. *M.P., P.F.*

FOXEY. Dr. *Mud. Pap.* ii.

FRA DIAVOLO. Fort of. *P.F.I., R.D.*

FRANCE. *B.H.* iii.; *B.R.* lxxxii.; *C.S., M.L.Lo.* i.; *D.C.* xxii.; *D. and S.*, Pref.; *L.D.* i.; *M.H.C.* i.;

M.P., A. in E.; *M.P., C.P.*; *M.P., E.S.*; *M.P., L.A.V.* ii.; *M.P., N.G.K.*; *M.P., N.J.B.*; *M.P., R.D.*; *M.P., T.O.H.*; *N.N.* vi.; *P.F.I., G.T.F.*; *R.P., O.B.*; *T.T.C.* i.; *U.T.* vii.

FRANCE. The inns of. *C.S., H.T.*

With the great church-tower rising above the courtyard—and clocks of all descriptions in all the rooms, which are never right.

FRANCE. King of. *M.P., L.W.O.Y.*

FRANCE. Mouse, delegate from. *M.P., W.H.*

FRANCE. Queen of. *B.R.* lxxxii.

FRANCIS. Father. *M.P., N.T.*

FRANCO. Porto. *P.F.I., G.A.N.*

FRANÇOIS. From restaurant. *D. and S.* liv.

A dark bilious subject in a jacket, close shaved, and with a black head of cropped hair.

FRANÇOISE. Monsieur, A butcher. *R.P., M.O.F.F.*

FRANK. Little, Child of first cousin of poor relation. *R.P., P.R.S.*

A diffident boy by nature.

FRANK. Mother of little. *R.P., P.R.S.*

FRANKFORT. *U.T.* xxiii.

FRANKLIN. *M.P., P.F.D.* *M.P., R.S.D.*

FRANKLIN. Benjamin, the spirit of. *M.P., S.B.*

FRANKLIN. Sir John. *M.P., L.A.V.* i.

FRASCATI. *P.F.I., R.*

" **FRATERNITY.**" *M.P., O.S.*

FRED. Mrs. *C.B., C.C.* s. iii.

A dimpled, surprised-looking, capital face; a ripe little mouth, that seemed made to be kissed—as no doubt it was.

FRED. Scrooge's nephew. *C.B., C.C.* s. iii.

FREDERICKSBURG. *A.N.* ix.

FREE TRADE HALL. Manchester. *M.P., Ag. Int.*

FREEDOM. Fair, A lovely princess. *R.P., P.B.*

FREEMAN'S COURT. Cornhill. *P.P.* xviii.

House of Dodson and Fogg.

FREEMASONS' TAVERN. The. *S.B.B.*, Scenes xix.

FRENCH. Emperor of the. *M.P., R.S.D.*

FRENCH. The. *C.S., S.P.T.* ii.

FRENCH-FLEMISH COTTAGES. *U.T.* xxv.

In the wayside cottages the loom goes wearily—rattle and click, rattle and click—a poor weaving peasant—man or woman, bending at the work, while the child, working too, turns a hand-wheel upon the ground to suit its height.

FRENCH-FLEMISH COUNTRY CHAPELS. *U.T.* xxv.

Little whitewashed black holes—with barred doors and Flemish inscriptions, abound at roadside corners, and often they are garnished with a sheaf of wooden crosses, like children's swords.

FRENCH-FLEMISH WINDMILLS. *U.T.* xxv.

Are so damp and rickety, that they nearly knock themselves off their legs at every turn of their sails, and creak in loud complaint.

FRENCH-FLEMISH YOUTH. *U.T.* xxv.

FRENCH OFFICER. *C.S., S.P.T.* ii.

FRENCH OFFICER. Baby-boy of. *C.S., S.P.T.* ii.

FRENCH OFFICER. Château of. *C.S., S.P.T.* ii.

A large château of the genuine old ghostly kind, with round towers, and extinguishers.—There were immense out-buildings fallen into partial decay, masses of dark trees, terrace gardens, balustrades, tanks of water—statues, weeds and thickets of iron railings.

FRENCH OFFICER. Child of. *C.S., S.P.T.* ii.

A girl with a most compassionate heart.

FRENCH OFFICER. Son of. *C.S. S.P.T.* ii.

FRENCH OFFICER. Wife of. *C.S.*, *S.P.T.* ii.
An engaging and beautiful woman.

FRENCH RAILWAY. Passengers on. *U.T.* xvii.
One a compatriot (of the Uncommercial Traveller) in an obsolete cravat—the other, a young priest, with a very small bird in a very small cage.

FRENCH WATERING-PLACE. *R.P.*, *O.F.W*
Once solely known to us as a town with a very long street, beginning with an abbattoir and ending with a steam-boat—wholly changed since those days.

FRENCH WATERING-PLACE. French visitors to. *R.P.*, *O.F.W.*
Bathe all day long, and seldom appear to think of remaining less than an hour at a time in the water.

FRENCH WATERING-PLACE. Fish market in. *R.P.*, *O.F.W.*

FRENCHMAN. *S.B.B.*, Scenes v.

FRENCHMAN. A, Passenger in train. *R.P.*, *A.F.*
In Algerine wrapper, with peaked-hood behind, who might be Abdel-Kader dyed rifle-green.

FRENCHMAN. Melancholy, Passenger in train. *R.P.*, *A.F.*
With black vandyke beard, and hair close-cropped, with expansive chest to waistcoat, saturnine as to his pantaloons, calm as to his feminine boots, precious as to his jewellery, smooth and white as to his linen.

FRENCHMEN. *M.P.*, *N.J.B.*

FRENCHMEN. Shadowy. *U.T.* xvii.
Passengers on Dover-Calais Packet.

FRIAR. Carthusian. *P.F.I.*, *G.A.N.*

FRIAR. Of Saint Benedict. *N.N* vi.

FRIARS. *P.F.I.*, *T.R.P.*

FRIARS. Dominican. *P.F.I.*, *V.M.M.S.S.*

FRIBOURG. *P.F.I.*, *V.M.M.S.S.*

FRIDAY. Character in Nursery Tale. *U.T.* xv.

FRIDAY STREET. *R.P.*, *T.D.P.*

FRIEND. Giving bride away at wedding. *D. and S.* v.
A superannuated beau, with one eye, and an eyeglass stuck in its blank companion.

FRIEND. Landor's. *M.P.*, *L.L.*

FRIEND. Our Honourable, M.P. *R.P.*, *O.H.F.*

FRIEND. To Em'ly abroad. *D.C.* xxii.
In a little cottage she found room for Em'ly (her husband was away at sea).

FRIENDS. Two or three of Toots. *D. and S.* xxii.

FRITHERS. Mr. *S.Y.C.*

FROME. *C.S.*, *S.P.T.*, ii.

FROST. Miss. *R.P.*, *O.S.*
A pupil in our school.

FROST AND CO. *M.P.*, *S. for P.*

FRRWENCH CONSUL'S. *C.S.*, *M.L. Leg.* i.

FRY. Mrs. *M.P.*, *S. Pigs.*

FRY. Mrs. *S.B.B.*, Scenes xxiv.

FRYING-PAN. The. *A.N.* v.

FUFFY. *B.H.* xii.

FULHAM. *D. and S.* xxiii. ; *L.D.* xvi. ; *R.P.*, *O.F.W.*

FUNAMBULES. *M.P.*, *W.*

FURNIVAL'S INN. *E.D.* xi. ; *S.B.B.*, Tales vii.

G

G. Mr. J. *M.P.*, *S.F.A.*

G. Mrs. *M.P.*, *S.F.A.*

G. P., A widow lady. *L.D.* xlviii.

"**G.**" Supposed ex-lover of Miss Pupford. *C.S.*, *T.T.G.* vi.
A short chubby old gentleman, with little black sealing-wax boots up to his knees.

GABELLE. Monsieur Théophile, Postmaster and tax functionary. *T.T.C.*, bk. ii. ch. viii.
Note.—Local functionary in the village by the estate of the St. Evremonds. He

is imprisoned by the Republicans and liberated to appear as a witness against Charles Darnay in Paris.

GABLEWIG. Mr., of the Inner Temple. *M.P., M.N.D.*

GABRIELLE. Child at the barber's shop. *C.S., S.L.* ii.

GAD'S HILL. *U.T.* vii.

GAD'S HILL GASPER = Charles Dickens. *M.P., I.W.M.*

GAFF. Tom. *M.P., N.G.K.*

GAG. Tom. *M.C.* xxviii.

GAGARINES QUAY. St. Petersburg. *M.P., M.M.*

GAGGS. Mr. *O.M.F.* viii.

GAIETY. Theatre of. *M.P., N.Y.D.*

GAL. The, Jonas Chuzzlewit's maid. *M.C.* xxvi.

GALILEO. The Tower of. *R.F.I., R.D.*

GALLANBILE. Mr. M. P., Family of. *N.N.* xvi.

Applicant of General AgencyOffice. for cook.

GALLAND. Mr. *M.P., T.O.H.*

GALLERY. Mr. Catlin's. *A.N.* xii.

GALLERY OF PRACTICAL SCIENCE *S.U.T.H.* iii.

(Now Gattis' Adelaide Gallery).

GALLERY. Reporters'. *S.B.B.*, Scenes xviii.

GALLERY. The Strangers'. *B.R.* xlix.

GALLEY. Mr. *O.M.F.* viii.

GALLEY-SLAVES' PRISON. *P.F.I., G.A.N.*

GALLY. Major C. *A.N.* xvii.

GALT HOUSE. Hotel in Louisville. *A.N.* xii.

GAMBAROON. Lord. *M.P., T.T.*

GAME CHICKEN. The. *D. and S.* xxii.

Was always to be heard of at the bar of the "Black Badger," wore a shaggy white great-coat in the warmest weather, and knocked Mr. Toots about the head three times a week, for the small consideration of ten and six per visit.

Note.—The pugilistic attendant of Mr. Toots.

GAMFIELD. Mr., Chimney-sweep. *O.T.* iii.

Whose villanous countenance was a regular stamped receipt for cruelty.

GAMMON. Name of a bird. *B.H.* xiv.

GAMMONRIFE. Member for. *M.P., F.C.*

GAMP. Husband deceased of Mrs. Gamp. *M.C.* xix.

When Gamp was summoned to his long home, and I see him a-lying in Guy's Hospital with a pennypiece on each eye, and his wooden leg under his left arm, I thought I should have fainted away.

GAMP. Mr. *M.P., G.B.*

GAMP. Mrs. *M.P., S.F.A.*

GAMP. Mrs., midwife. *M.C.* xix.

A fat old woman with a husky voice, and a moist eye, which she had a remarkable power of turning up and only showing the white of it. Having very little neck, it cost her some trouble to look over herself, if one may say so, at those to whom she talked. She wore a very rusty black gown, rather the worse for snuff, and a shawl and bonnet to correspond. The face—the nose in particular—somewhat red and swollen.

Note.—The story of Mrs. Gamp shows a picture of the very unprofessional nurse, now happily seldom met with. Her care for herself and her creature comforts is the sole end she has in view. She appears on the scene on several occasions in the capacity of monthly nurse, sick nurse, and "layer out" of the dead. She is dismissed, and, if exposure were necessary in such a case, exposed at the general family meeting when Pecksniff is awarded his just dues. It is Mrs. Gamp's friend, Mrs. Harris, who has become a household word.

GANDER. Mr., Boarder at Todger's establishment. *M.C.* ix.

Of a witty turn, who had originated the sally about "collars."

GANGES. River. *M.P., T.O.H.*; *U.T.* xv.

GARDEN COURT. Temple. *G.E.* xli.; *M.C.* xlv.

GARDEN ON THE ROOF. The. *O.M.F.* xxii.

A blackened chimney-stack over which some humble creeper had been trained—a few boxes of humble flowers and evergreens completed the garden.

GARDENER. A market. *S.B.B.*, Scenes vi.

GARDENER. Miss Donny's. *B.H.* iii.

Ugly, lame, old gardener.

GARDENS. Tea. *S.B.B.*, Scenes ix.

GARDINER. Captain. *M.P.*, *L.A.V.* ii.

GARDNER. Dr. *M.P.*, *R.T.*

GARDNER. Mr., as Mr. Lanbury. *M.P.*, *I.S.H.W.*

GARDNER. Mr., as John Maddox. *M.P.*, *V.C.*

GARDNER. Mr., as Tom Sparks. *M.P.*, *S.G.*

GARGERY. Joe, The blacksmith. *G.E.* i.

A fair man with curls of flaxen hair on each side of his smooth face, and with eyes of such a very undecided blue that they seemed to have somehow got mixed with their own whites. Mild, good-natured, sweet-tempered, easy-going, foolish, dear fellow.

Note.—The blacksmith of the story; and one of its chief characters. He is the husband of Pip's sister, and both he and Pip are badly treated by her. Joe makes up to Pip for this by taking him as something of a friend and companion. In the course of the story it transpires that Joe was the son of a drunken father. He went to work and kept his father until that individual went off in a "purple leptic" fit. He then had to keep his mother until she died. After that he got acquainted with Pip's sister and married her, when his "hammering" was still continued. His wife is savagely attacked by Orlick and subsequently dies. Joe comes up to London when Pip is ill and nurses him and pays his debts. When Pip goes down to see Joe again, he finds he has married Biddy. In later years Joe and Biddy are seen living happily with a little Pip of their own.

GARGERY. Little girl, daughter of Joe and Biddy. *G.E.* lix.

GRAGERY. Mrs. Biddy (second wife). *G.E.* lix.

GARGERY. Mrs. Joe, Sister of Philip Pirrip. *G.E.* i.

She was not a good-looking woman, with black hair and eyes, and such a prevailing redness of skin. She was tall and bony, and almost always wore a coarse apron, fastened over her figure behind with two loops, and having a square, impregnable bib in front, that was stuck full of pins and needles.

Note.—Wife of Joe Gargery, and sister of Pip. She is killed by the results of a murderous attack made on her by Orlick.

GARGERY. Pip., Son of Joe. *G.E.* lix.

"We giv' him the name of Pip for your sake, dear old chap."

GARLAND. Mr. Abel. *O.C.S.* xiv.

Mr. Abel had a quaint old-fashioned air about him, looked nearly of the same age as his father, and bore a wonderful resemblance to him in face and figure . . . in the neatness of the dress and even in the club-foot, he and the old gentleman were precisely alike.

Note.—The son of Mr. Garland, articled to Witherden. Mr. Abel enters, in due time, into partnership with Witherden and marries a bashful young lady.

GARLAND. Mr. *O.C.S.* xiv.

A little, fat, placid-faced old gentleman.

Note.—Mr. Garland is introduced driving a fat pony. Kit Nubbles holds the pony while the old gentleman visits Witherden. Mr. Garland has no small change to give Kit and tells him to return on another occasion to work out the remainder. Much to the general surprise Kit does this. When Kit leaves Little Nell's service he is engaged by Mr. Garland who befriends him.

GARLAND. Mrs. *O.C.S.* xiv.

Beside the little old gentleman sat a little old lady, plump and placid like himself.

GARRAWAY'S COFFEE - HOUSE. *L.D.* xxix.; *M.C.* xxvii.; *P.P.* xxxiv., *R.P.*, *P.R.S.*, *U.T.* xxi.

GARRICK. *M.P.*, *R.S.L.*

GASHFORD. Mr., Lord George Gordon's Secretary. *B.R.* xxxv.

Angularly made, high-shouldered, bony, and ungraceful. His dress, in imitation of his superior, was demure and staid in the extreme; his manner formal and constrained. This gentleman had an overhanging brow, great hands and feet and ears, and a pair of eyes that seemed to have made an unnatural retreat into his head . . . the man that blows the fire, a servile, false, and truckling knave.

Note.—Lord George Gordon's secretary is an unscrupulous villain who urges his master on his disastrous career, taking great care to keep himself free from complicity. After the failure of the riots he makes a precarious living by selling Lord Gordon's secrets, and then becomes a Government spy. Finally he commits suicide by taking poison in an obscure inn.

GASPARD. *T.T..C.*, bk. ii., ch. xvi.

Note.—The father of the child who was killed by the coach of Monsieur the Marquis. He in turn kills the Marquis St. Evrémonde. And he is hanged on a gallows forty feet high.

GASPER = Charles Dickens. *M.P., I.W.M.*

GASWORKS GARDING. *E.D.* v.

GATE OF ST. MARTIN. Theatre of the. *M.P., N.Y.D.*

GATE OF SAN GIOVANNI LATERANO. (Rome). *P.F.I., R.D.*

GATE OF THE STAR. The. *B.H.* xii.

GATE. The Traitor's. *M.H.C.* i.; *G.E.*, liv.

GATEHOUSE. The old stone (crossing the Close). *E.D.* ii.

Pendent masses of ivy and creeper covering the building's front.

GATEWAY. Old, In which Little Nell saw Quilp. *O.C.S.* xxvii.

GATTLETON. Lucinia. *S.B.B.*, Tales ix.

GATTLETON. Mr. A stock-broker in especially comfortable circumstances. *S.B.B.*, Tales ix.

GATTLETON.. Mr. Sempronius. *S.B.B.*, Tales ix.

Son of Mr. Gattleton.

GATTLETON. Mrs., Wife of Mr. Gattleton. *S.B.B.*, Tales ix.

A kind, good-tempered, vulgar soul, exceedingly fond of her husband and children.

GAY. Walter. *D. and S.* iv.

Note.—Sol Gills' nephew. He is employed in the house of Dombey and Son. He is able to render some service to Florence Dombey when she is lost. Mr. Dombey is displeased with him. and to get him out of the way sends him to the Barbadoes branch of the firm. The ship in which he sails is lost, it is believed, with all on board. But some time after Walter returns and marries Florence. Later on old Mr. Dombey comes to live with them.

GAZINGI. Miss, Member of Mr. V. Crummles' Company. *N.N.* xxiii.

With an imitation ermine boa tied in a loose knot round her neck, flogging Mr. Crummles Junior for fun

GENERAL ASSEMBLY. *A.N.* ii.

GENERAL BOARD OF HEALTH. *M.P., F.F.*; *R.P., O.o.T.*

GENERAL COVE. A gentleman. *U.T.* iii.

GENERAL. The King of Bill-stickers. *R.P., B.S.*

GENERAL. Mrs., Matron or Chaperon of Mr. Dorrit's daughters. *L.D.* xxxvii.

The daughter of a clerical dignitary in a cathedral town. A lady, well-bred, accomplished, well-connected. . . . In person, Mrs. General, including her skirts, was of a dignified and imposing appearance; ample rustling, gravely voluminous. Her countenance and hair had rather a floury appearance. If her eyes had no expression, it was probably because they had nothing to express.

Note.—An aristocratic widow engaged by Mr. Dorrit after his accession to wealth to be a companion to his daughters and to improve their minds and manners. It is presumed that she has designs of becoming Mrs. Dorrit, and almost gets this length. But after Mr. Dorrit's attack at the Merdles he does not know her and thinks she wishes to take the place of a woman at the Marshalsea.

GENERAL. Old. *B.H.* liii.

GENERAL AGENCY OFFICE. *N.N.* xvi.

For places and situations of all kinds enquire within . . . a little floor-clothed room, with a high desk railed off in one corner.

GENERAL AGENCY OFFICE. Proprietress of. *N.N.* xvi.

A very fat old lady in a mob cap—who was airing herself at the fire.

GENERAL POST OFFICE. London. *O.T.* xxxvi. ; *N.N.* xxxiv.

GENERIC FRENCH OLD LADY. *M.P.*, *W.*

GENEVA. *L.D.*, xxiii. ; *C.S.*, *N.T.* Act iii.

GENEVA. The Lake of. *L.D.* xxxvii.

GENIE. *M.P.*, *T.O.H.*

GENII. *M.P.*, *S.*

GENII. The Guardians of the City. Gog and Magog. *M.H.C.* i.

GENIUS. Aspiring, of Harmonic Meeting. *S.B.B.*, Scenes ii.

GENIUS. Of Despair and Suicide. *N.N.* vi.

A wrinkled, hideous figure, with deeply sunk and bloodshot eyes, and an immensely long cadaverous face, shadowed by jagged and matted locks of coarse black hair. He wore a kind of tunic, of a dull bluish colour, which—was clasped or ornamented down the front with coffin-handles. His legs, too, were encased in coffin-plates, as though in armour, and over his left shoulder he wore a short dusky cloak, which seemed made of a remnant of some pall.

GENOA. *P.F.I.*, *T.R.P.* ; *R.P.*, *P.M.T.P.* ; *U.T.* xxviii.

GENTLEMAN. Accomplice of three thimbles' man. *S.B.B.*, Scenes xii.

In top boots, standing by, regrets his inability to bet—left his purse at home.

GENTLEMAN. American, passenger in the Screw. *M.C.* xvi.

Wrapped up in fur and oil-skin, ... appeared in a very shiny, tall, black hat, and constantly overhauled a very little valise of pale leather.

GENTLEMAN. (Another clerk) in Secretarial Department of Circumlocution Office. *L.D.* x.

GENTLEMAN. Another elderly, Member of Mr. V. Crummles' Company. *N.N.* xxiii.

Paying especial court to Mrs. Crummles, a shade more respectable, who played the irascible old man.

GENTLEMAN. Another masked. *M.H.C.* iii.

GENTLEMAN. At dining-room of house which shall be nameless. *C.S.*, *S.L.* iv.

He had one of the new-fangled uncollapsible bags in his hand. His hair was long and lightish.

GENTLEMAN. Boarder at Pawkins's. *M.C.* xvi.

Started that afternoon for the Far West on a six months' business tour ; his equipment—just such another shiny hat—and just such another little pale valise, as had composed the luggage of the gentleman who came from England in the Screw.

GENTLEMAN. Boarder at Todger's *M.C.* ix.

Of a theatrical turn, recites.

GENTLEMAN. Boarder at Todger's *M.C.* ix.

Of a literary turn, repeated (by desire) some sarcastic stanzas he had recently produced.

GENTLEMAN. Boarder at Todger's *M.C.* ix.

Of a debating turn, rises and suddenly lets loose a tide of eloquence which bears down everything before it.

GENTLEMAN. Brother of Jewish. *U.T.* ii.

One of the drowned at the wreck of the " Royal Charter."

GENTLEMAN. Brother of Smike's mother. *N.N.* lx.

A rough, fox-hunting, hard-drinking gentleman, who had run

through his own fortune, and wanted to squander away that of his sister.

GENTLEMAN. Catholic, of small means. *B.R.* lxi.

Having hired a waggon to remove his furniture by midnight, had had it all brought down into the street to save time in the packing. The poor gentleman, with his wife and servant and their little children, were sitting trembling among their goods in the open street.

GENTLEMAN. Children of Catholic. *B.R.* lxi.

GENTLEMAN. Corpulent, with one eye. *M.P., T.B.*

GENTLEMAN. Deaf old, Friend of Master Humphrey. *M.H.C.* i.

His hair was nearly white—I never saw so patient and kind a face.

GENTLEMAN. Elderly inebriated. Member of Mr. V. Crummles' Company. *N.N.* xxiii.

In the last depths of shabbiness, who played the calm and virtuous old men.

GENTLEMAN. Fat old, In the pit of theatre. *N.N.* xxiv.

GENTLEMAN. Fine old English. *M.P., F.O.E.G.*

GENTLEMAN. Foreign. *O.M.F.*, xi.

GENTLEMAN. French. *C.S., Mrs. L. L.*

GENTLEMAN. Frequenter of the "Magpie and Stump." *P.P.* xx.

In a checked shirt and mosaic studs, with a cigar in his mouth.

GENTLEMAN. Friend of Alderman Cute's. *C.B., C.G.* i.

Had a very red face, as if undue proportion of the blood in his body were squeezed up into his head, which perhaps accounted for his having also the appearance of being rather cold about the heart. . . . A full-sized, sleek, well-conditioned gentleman, in a blue coat with bright buttons, and a white cravat.

GENTLEMAN. Guest at Pawkins'. *M.C.* xvi.

From neighbouring states; on monetary affairs.

GENTLEMAN. Guest at Pawkins'. *M.C.* xvi.

From neighbouring states; on political affairs.

GENTLEMAN. Guest at Pawkins'. *M.C.* xvi.

From neighbouring states; on sectarian affairs.

GENTLEMAN. Guest in a great Hotel at Marseilles. *L.D.* ii.

A tall French gentleman, with raven hair and beard, of a swart and terrible, not to say genteely diabolical aspect, but who had shown himself the mildest of men.

GENTLEMAN. In a flannel jacket and a yellow neck-kerchief. *M.P., G.A.*

GENTLEMAN. In office of Dombey and Son. *D. and S.* li.

Who has been in the office three years, under continual notice to quit on account of lapses in his arithmetic.

GENTLEMAN. Harpist of Gravesend Packet. *S.B.B.*, Scenes xi.

"In the forage cap."

GENTLEMAN. Hoarse. *O.M.F.* v.

Driving his donkey in a truck, with a carrot for a whip.

GENTLEMAN. In next house to Mr. Nickleby. *N.N.* xxxvii.

He is a gentleman, and has the manners of a gentleman, although he does wear smalls, and grey worsted stockings.

GENTLEMAN. Legal. *O.M.F.* xx.

At Pocket Breaches Branch Station, with an open carriage, with a printed bill "Veneering for ever."

GENTLEMAN. Mature young(guest of Veneerings). *O.M.F.* ii.

With too much nose on his face, too much ginger in his whiskers, too much torso in his waistcoat, too much sparkle in his studs, his eyes, his buttons, his talk, and his teeth.

GENTLEMAN. Member of Mr. V. Crummles' Company. *N.N.* xxiii.

Who played the low-spirited lovers and sang tenor songs.

GENTLEMAN. A neighbour. *S.B.B., O.P.* vii.
Red-faced in a white hat.

GENTLEMAN. Number four, A, Barnacle. *L.D.* x.
Clerk in Circumlocution office.

GENTLEMAN. Of a Mosaic Arabian cast of countenance. *D. and S.* lix.
With a massive watch-guard, whistles in the drawing-room, and while he is waiting for the other gentleman, who always has pen and ink in his pocket, asks Mr. Towlinson (by the easy name of Old Cock) if he happens to know what the figure of them crimson and gold hangings might have been, when new bought.

GENTLEMAN. Of the Palace. *M.P., F.L.*

GENTLEMAN. Old. *C.B., C.o.H.* i.

GENTLEMAN. Old, for whom Cobbler in the Fleet used to work. *P.P.* xliv.

GENTLEMAN. Old, one of the Board. *O.T.* iii.
In tortoise-shell spectacles.

GENTLEMAN. Old, who lives in our row. *S.B.B., O.P.* iv.
A tall thin, bony man, with an interrogative nose, and little restless perking eyes.

GENTLEMAN. One of the Board. In white waistcoat. *O.T.* iii.
Most positively and decidedly affirmed that not only would Oliver be hung, but that he would be drawn and quartered into the bargain.

GENTLEMAN. One of the visitors to Vauxhall Gardens. *S.B.B.*, Scenes xiv.
With his dinner in a pocket-handkerchief.

GENTLEMAN. One, boarder at Todger's. *M.C.* ix.
Who travelled in the perfumery line, exhibited an interesting nicknack in the way of a remarkable cake of shaving-soap which he had lately met with in Germany.

GENTLEMAN. "Ordered six" at Searle's Boating Establishment. *S.B.B.*, Scenes x.

GENTLEMAN. Pale young. *See* Pocket, Herbert.

GENTLEMAN. Particularly small. *S.B.B.*, Scenes xiv.
Entertainer at Vauxhall Gardens in a dress coat.

GENTLEMAN. "Pink-faced." *P.P.* xiii.
Who delivered a written speech of half-an-hour's length.

GENTLEMAN. Powder-headed, of No. 3. *S.B.B., O.P.* vii.

GENTLEMAN. Red-faced. *M.H.C.* iii.
With a gruff voice.

GENTLEMAN. Retired from business and owner of a garden. *S.B.B.* Scenes ix.
Always something to do there—digging—sweeping and cutting and planting with manifest delight.

GENTLEMAN. Since deceased. *M.C.* i.
Credible and unimpeachable member of the Chuzzlewit family.

GENTLEMAN. Solitary, Inside passenger in coach. *N.N.* v.
Of very genteel appearance, dressed in mourning, his hair was grey.

GENTLEMAN. Son of, died about five years old. *S.B.B.*, Scenes i.

GENTLEMAN. Straightforward, who trains the birds and mice. *M.P., G.H.*

GENTLEMAN. Successor to officer in our Chapel of Ease. *S.B.B., O.P.* ii.
A pale, thin, cadaverous man, with large black eyes, and long straggling black hair—dress slovenly in the extreme, manner ungainly, doctrines startling.

GENTLEMAN. Traveller by coach. *P.P.* xlix.
In a powdered wig, and a sky-blue coat trimmed with silver, made very

full and broad in the skirts, which were lined with buckram.

GENTLEMAN. Venerable, 1850. *M.P., L.W.O.Y.*

GENTLEMAN. Very fine. *M.P., F.L.*

GENTLEMAN. Very old. *S.B.B.*, Scenes vi.

With a silver-headed stick.

GENTLEMAN. Very quiet, respectable, dozing, old. *S.B.B., O.P.* ii.

Who had officiated in our Chapel-of-ease for twelve years.

GENTLEMAN. Vocal, Boarder at Todger's. *M.C.* ix.

Regales them with a song.

GENTLEMAN. Walking. *S.B.B.*, Scenes xi.

The dirty swell.

GENTLEMAN. Wife of Catholic. *B.R.* lxi.

GENTLEMAN. Wife of—retired from business. *S.B.B.*, Scenes ix.

Takes great pride in the garden, too, on a summer's evening—you will see them sitting happily together in the little summer-house.

GENTLEMAN. With one eye. The Bagman. *P.P.* xlviii.

Smoking a large Dutch pipe; with his eye intently fixed on the round face of the Landlord.

GENTLEMAN. Young, Attached to the stable department of "The Angel." *P.P.* xvi.

GENTLEMAN. Young, Clerk in Kenge and Carboy's. *B.H.* iii.

GENTLEMAN. Young, May Day dancer. *S.B.B.*, Scenes xx.

In girl's clothes and a widow's cap.

GENTLEMAN. Young, under articles to a civil engineer. *M.P., O.L.N.O.*

GENTLEMAN. Youngest, At Todger's Establishment. *M.C.* ix.

GENTLEMAN'S WHIST CLUB. *S.B.B.*, Tales viii.

Winglebury Buffs at "The Lion Inn."

GENTLEMAN'S WHIST CLUB.

Winglebury Blues at the "Winglebury Arms." *S.B.B.*, Tales viii.

GENTLEMANLY INTEREST. The member for. *M.C.* xxxv.

GEN'L'M'N. The next, in restaurant *P P.* xliv.

GENTLEMEN. A stream of, interviewing Martin. *M.C.* xxii.

Every one with a lady on his arm—came gliding in; every new group fresher than the last.

GENTLEMEN. Country. *S.B.B.*, Scenes i.

GENTLEMEN. In Tea Gardens. *S.B.B.*, Scenes ix.

In alarming waistcoats, and steel watch-guards, promenading about, three abreast, with surprising dignity.

GENTLEMEN. In Tea Gardens. *S.B.B.*, Scenes ix.

In pink shirts and blue waistcoats, occasionally upsetting either themselves or somebody else, with their own canes.

GENTLEMEN. Old decrepit, visitors in Assembly Rooms, Bath. *P.P.* xxxv.

GENTLEMEN. Three, In another department of Circumlocution Office. *L.D.* x.

Number one doing nothing particular; number two doing nothing particular; number three doing nothing particular.

GENTLEMEN. Two. *B.H.* xxiii.

GENTLEMEN. Two. *M.P., P.M.B.*

GENTLEMEN. Two portly. *C.B., C.C.*, s. i.

Desiring some slight provision for the poor and destitute from Scrooge.

GENTLEWOMAN. The, Character in play. *S.B.B.*, Scenes xiii.

Black-eyed female.

GEORGE. Mrs. Jarley's servant. *O.C.S.* xxvi.

Appeared in a sitting attitude, supporting on his legs a baking-dish and a half-gallon stone-bottle, and bearing in his right hand a knife, and in his left a fork.

Note.—George ultimately marries Mrs. Jarley, whose caravan he has driven so long.

GEORGE. *N.N.* xii.
A young man, who had known Mr. Kenwigs when he was a bachelor, and was much esteemed by the ladies.

Note.—The bachelor friend of the Kenwigses, who attempted to joke about the rate collector.

GEORGE. Articled clerk of Mr. Buffle. *C.S., M.L.Leg* i.

GEORGE. Aunt. *S.B.B.*, Char. ii.
On Christmas morning at home dusting decanters and filling castors.

GEORGE. Eldest son of visitors to Astley's. *S.B.B.*, Scenes xi.
Who was evidently trying to look as if he did not belong to the family.

GEORGE. Friend of Mr. Weller Senior, insolvent. *P.P.* xliii.
Had contracted a speculative but imprudent passion for horsing long stages, which led to his present embarassments . . . soothing the excitement of his feelings with shrimps and porter.

GEORGE. Guard of coach. *C.S., H.T.*

GEORGE. King. *M.P., N.E.*

GEORGE. Master. *O.M.F.* v.
Inhabitant of Corner House.

GEORGE. Master. *See* Vendale, George.

GEORGE. Mrs., One of Mrs. Quilp's visitors. *O.C.S.* iv.
Before I'd let a man order me about as Quilp orders her . . . I'd kill myself and write a letter just to say he did it.

GEORGE. One of boating-crew training for race. *S.B.B.*, Scenes x.

"**GEORGE.**" Porter at Railway Station. *U.T.* xxi.

GEORGE. Queer client—prisoner in Marshalsea. *P.P.* xxi.
Deepest despair and passion scarcely human had made such fierce ravages on his face and form . . . that his companions in misfortune shrunk affrighted from him as he passed by.

GEORGE. Second lieutenant at bar of dining-rooms of house which shall be nameless. *C.S., S.L.* iv.

GEORGE. Son of Mrs. Chick. *D. and S.* i.

"**GEORGE.**" The Inn. *O.T.* xxxiii.

"**GEORGE.**" The Boro. *L D.I.* xxii.

GEORGE. Uncle, Host at Christmas family party. *S.B.B.*, Char. ii.
On Christmas Eve—coming down into the kitchen, taking off his coat, and stirring the pudding for half an hour or so—to the vociferous delight of the children and servants. On Christmas day Uncle George tells stories, carves poultry, takes wine, and jokes with the children at the side table.

GEORGE. Visitor at Greenwich Fair. *S.B.B.*, Scenes xii.

GEORGE AND FREDERICK. Sons of Mrs. Chick. *D. and S.* viii.
Both ordered sea air.

"**GEORGE AND NEW INN.**" *N.N.* vi.

"**GEORGE AND THE GRIDIRON.**" Dining Rooms. *C.S.S.L.* i.

"**GEORGE AND VULTURE.**" Tavern and Hotel, George Yard, Lombard Street. *P.P.* xxvi.

GEORGE'S ST. *U.T.* iii.; *S.B.B.* T. xi.

GEORGE STREET. *S.B.B.*, Char. viii.

'**GEORGE THE SECOND.**" The. *D. and S.* iv.

GEORGE THE THIRD. His Majesty King. *O.M.F.* x.

"**GEORGE THE THIRD.**" Kept by a Watkins. *N.N.* xviii.

GEORGE TOWN. Suburb of Washington. *A.N.* viii.

GEORGE TOWN. Jesuit College in. *A.N.* viii.

GEORGE TOWN. President of Jesuits' College (Mansion of the). *A.N.* viii.

More like an English club-house. both within and without, than any other kind of establishment.

GEORGE YARD. *P.P.* xxxiii.

GEORGE'S YARD. *S.B.B., O.P.* v.

That little dirty court at the back of the gas works.

GEORGIANA. A cousin of Mr. Pocket. *G.E.* xxv.

An indigestive single woman who called her rigidity her religion and her liver love.

Note.—One of Miss Havisham's fawning relatives who is left " twenty pound down.'

GEORGIANA. Deceased mother of Philip Pirrip. *G.E.* i.

GEORGIANA M'RIA. Pip's sister. *G.E.* lviii.

GERMAN. *M.P., N.J.B.*

GERMANS. *M.P., W.M.*

GERMANS. Shadowy, Passengers on Dover-Calais Packet. *U.T.* xvii.

In immense fur coats and boots.

GERMANY. *C.S., S.P.T.* ii. ; *L.D.* xvi. ; *M.C.* ix. ; *M.P., W.H.* ; *R.P., O.B.* ; *U.T.* xxv.

GERRARD STREET. Soho. *G.E.* xxvi.

GHASTLY GRIM. Saint. *U.T.* xxi.

A City churchyard.

It is a small churchyard with a ferocious strong spiked iron gate, like a jail. This gate is ornamented with skulls and cross-bones, larger than the life wrought in stone. The skulls grin aloft horribly, thrust through and through with iron spears. . . . It lies in the City, and the Blackwall railway shrieks at it daily

GHOST. Marley's. *C.B., C.C.S.* i.

Marley in his pigtail, usual waistcoat, tights and boots ; the tassels on the latter bristling, like his pigtail, and his coat-skirts, and the hair upon his head. The chain he drew was clasped about his middle. It was long, and wound about him like a tail ; and it was made of cash-boxes, keys, padlocks, ledgers, and heavy purses wrought in steel.

GHOST. Of Art, Artist's model. *R.P., G.o.A.*

GHOST. Of Christmas past. *C.B., C.C.* s. ii.

GHOST. Of Christmas present. *C.B., C.C.* s. iii.

The second spirit of the three.

GHOST. Of Christmas yet to come. Third spirit. *C.B., C.C.* s. iv.

GHOST. One old. *C.B., C.C.* s. i.

In a white waistcoat with a monstrous iron safe attached to its ankle.

GHOST. The. *C.B., H.M.* i.

GHOST WALK. Chesney. *B.H.* ii.

GIANT. A, Rinaldo di Velasco. *C.S., D.M.P.*

A languid young man, he had a little head, and less in it—weak eyes, and weak knees—amiable though timid—his mother let him out and spent the money.

GIANT. *See* Sloppy.

GIANT. The, Of Show Tramp Troupe. *U.T.* xi.

GIANT. The, Magsman's. *C.S., G.i.S.*

In Spanish trunks and a ruff.

GIANTESS. A, Exhibited at Greenwich Fair. *S.B.B.*, Scenes xii.

GIANTS. In Guildhall. *M.P., G.A.*

GIBBS. Villain, A young hairdresser. *M.H.C.* v.

GIBRALTAR. *M.P., E.T.*

GIBRALTAR OF AMERICA. Quebec. *A.N.* xv.

GIGGLES. Miss, Pupil at the Nun's House. *E.D.* ix

GIL BLAS. Character in Nursery Story. *U.T.* xv.

GILBERT. Gill. *C.S., P.o.C.E.P.*

GILBERT. Mark, Apprentice of a hosier. *B.R.* viii.

Age nineteen, loves Curzon's daughter, cannot say that Curzon' daughter loves him—an ill-looking, one-sided, shambling lad, with sunken eyes set close together in his head.

GILDED HOUSE. *M.P., N.Y.D.*

GILES. Jeremie, and Messrs., Bankers. *C.S., N.T.* Act i.

GILES. Mr., Butler and steward to Mrs. Maylie. *O.T.* xxviii.

Note.—The would-be valiant butler of Mrs. Maylie. A kind-hearted man with the failings of his exalted situation. Accompanied by two other servants he pursues Sikes and Toby Crackit after the attempted burglary—for a short distance. Giles is parted with in the last chapter, when he is quite bald, although he still remains in his old post.

GILL. Mr. and Mrs. *M.C.* xxix.

GILLESPIE. Mr. James, of Allison and Co. *A.N.* xvii.

GILLS. Gill. *C.S., P.o.C.E.P.*

GILLS. Solomon, Instrument maker and proprietor of a ship's chandler's shop. *D. and S.* iv.

An elderly gentleman, in a Welsh wig, which was as plain and stubborn a Welsh wig as ever was worn, and in which he looked anything but a Rover. He was a slow, quiet-spoken, thoughtful old fellow, with eyes as red as if they had been small suns looking at you through a fog—and a newly awakened manner. The only change ever known in his outward man was from a complete suit of coffee-colour, cut very square, and ornamented with glaring buttons, to the same suit of coffee-colour minus the inexpressibles, which were then of a pale nankeen.—He wore a very precise shirt frill, and carried a pair of first-rate spectacles on his forehead, and a tremendous chronometer in his fob.

Note.—Walter Gay's uncle. He keeps a nautical instrument maker's shop without many customers or doing much business. When Walter's ship is lost, he refuses to believe that the boy has gone down with her, and starts out in search of him. Afterwards his investments prove a success, and he takes Captain Cuttle into partnership, although he no longer troubles about the absence of custom.

GILTSPUR STREET. *G.E.* li.

GIMBLET. Brother, A drysalter. *G.S.E.* vi.

An elderly man with a crabbed face, a large dog's-eared shirt-collar, and a spotted blue neckerchief reaching up behind to the crown of his head.

GIN SHOP. Customers. *S.B.B.*, Scenes xxii.

Two old washerwomen—rather overcome by the head dresses and haughty demeanour of the young ladies who officiate.

Young fellow in a brown coat and bright buttons ushering in two companions. . . . Female in faded feathers. Two old men come in just to have a drain—finished their third quartern, have made themselves crying drunk . . . fat comfortable-looking elderly women . . . throngs of men, women and children . . . knot of Irish labourers.

GIN SHOP. Ostensible proprietor of. *S.B.B.*, Scenes xxii.

A stout coarse fellow in a fur cap, put on very much on one side to give him a knowing air, and display his sandy whiskers to the best advantage.

GINGERBREAD AND TOYS. Vendors of, at Greenwich Fair. *S.B.B.*, Scenes xii.

GIPSY. At Greenwich Fair. *S.B.B.*, Scenes xii.

A sunburnt woman in a red cloak.

GIPSY. Sentenced to die. *B.R.* lxxv.

A sunburnt, swarthy fellow, almost a wild man.

GIPSY-TRAMP. *U.T.* xi.

GIPSY WOMAN. Good Mrs. Brown. *D. and S.* xxvii.

A withered and very ugly old woman, dressed not so much like a gipsy as like any of that medley race of vagabonds who tramp about the country, begging and stealing, and tinkering and weaving rushes, by turns, or all together—munching with her jaws, as if the death's head beneath her yellow skin were impatient to get out.

GIRARD COLLEGE. The, Philadelphia. *A.N.* vii.

A most splendid unfinished marble structure.

GIRL. A bold, In brickmaker's. *B.H.* viii.

Doing some kind of washing in very dirty water.

GIRL. Case No. 13. *M.P., H.H.W.*

GIRL. Case No. 14. *M.P., H.H.W.*

GIRL. Case No. 19. *M.P., H.H.W.*

GIRL. Case No. 27. *M.P., H.H.W.*

GIRL. Case No. 50. *M.P., H.H.W.*

GIRL. Case No. 51. *M.P., H.H.W.*

GIRL. Case No. 54. *M.P., N.H.W.*

GIRL. Case No. 58. *M.P., H.H.W.*

GIRL. Irish, Domestic at Pawkins'. *M.C.* xvi.

GIRL. Little, Daughter of the Robinsons. *S.B.B., O.P.* iii.

GIRL. Little, in Ohio. *M.P., S.B.*

GIRL. Little, Watching baby Kenwigs. *N.N.* xv.

Might be thirteen years old.

GIRL. Odd. *C.S., H.H.*

GIRL. Servant at Inn in Marlborough Downs. *P.P.* xiv.

Smartly dressed, with a bright eye, and a neat ankle.

GIRL. Spirit of a fair young, in mourning dress. *C.B., C.C.* s. ii.

GIRL. Walter and Florence Gay's. *D. and S.* lxii.

GIRL. Young, Belonging to Mrs. Bayton . . . of thirteen or fourteen. *O.T.* v.

GIRLS. At Tea Gardens. *S.B.B.*, Scenes ix.

GIRLS. Little, Neighbours of the old lady. *S.B.B.* ii.

GIRLS. On board Gravesend Packet. *S.B.B.*, Scenes x.

Brought the first volume of some new novel in their reticule, become extremely plaintive.

GIRLS. Two. *M.P., N.T.*

GLAMOUR. Bob. *O.M.F.* vi.

GLASGOW. *M.P., C.P.* ; *M.P., G.S.* ; *M.P., S.S.* ; *P.P.*, xlix. ; *R.P., T.D.P.* ; *U.T.* xxiii.

GLASTONBURY. *G.S.* xv.

GLAVORMELLY. Mr., Actor at the Coburg. *N.N.* xxx.

GLIB. Mr. *M.P., W.H.*

GLIBBERY. Bob, Potboy of Six Jolly Fellowship Porters. *O.M.F.* vi.

GLIBBERY. Late mother of Bob. *O.M.F.* vi.

Systematically accelerated his retirement to bed with a poker.

"**GLIMPSE OF GREEN.**" Common public house. *M.P., G.B.*

GLOBSON. Bully. *U.T.* xix.

Schoolfellow of Uncommercial Traveller.

GLOGWOOD. Sir Chipkins. *S.Y.C.*

GLORIOUS APOLLERS. *O.C.S.* xiii.

A convivial circle, of which Mr. Dick Swiveller had the honour to be "Perpetual Grand."

"**GLORY.**" Monsieur the Landlord of the. *R.P., M.O.F.F.*

"**GLORY.**" The, An Inn. *R.P., M.O.F.F.*

GLOSS. Mr. *M.P., W.H.*

GLO'STER. Duke of. *S.B.B.*, Scenes xiii.

GLO'STERMAN. Double, Cheeseman. *R.P., T.S.S.*

GLOUCESTER GATE. *U.T.* xviii.

GLOUCESTERSHIRE. *A.N.* xv.

GLUBB. Drawer of Paul's little carriage. *D. and S.* viii.

Grandfather of ruddy-faced lad—a weazen, old, crab-faced man, in a suit of battered oilskin, who had got tough and stringy from long pickling in salt water, and who smelt like a weedy sea-beach when the tide is out.

GLUMPER. Sir Thomas. *S.B.B.*, Tales ix.

Knighted in the last reign for carrying up an address on somebody's escaping from nothing.

GLYN AND CO. *U.T.* xxi.

GLYN AND HALIFAX. *M.P., G.A.*

GLYN. Mr. *M.P., R.S.*

"**GOAT AND BOOTS.**" The, An inn. *S.B.B., O.P.* ii.

GOAVUS. Mr. *M.P.*, *G.D.*

GOBLER. Mr., Boarder at Mrs. Tibbs'. *S.B.B.*, Tales i.

In a very delicate state of health—a lazy, selfish, hypochondriac—tall, thin, and pale—his face invariably wore a pinched, screwed-up expression . . . he looked as if he had got his feet in a tub of exceedingly hot water against his will.

GOBLER. Mrs., Late Mrs. Bloss. *S.B.B.*, Tales i.

GOBLIN. Of the Bells. *C.B.*, *C.G.* iii.

GOBLIN. Seated on an upright tombstone. *P.P.* xxix.

A strange unearthly figure. His long fantastic legs, which might have reached the ground, were cocked up, and crossed after a quaint, fantastic fashion : his sinewy arms were bare ; and his hands rested on his knees . . . he was grinning at Gabriel Grub with such a grin as only a goblin could call up.

GOBLINS. King of the. *P.P.* xxix.

GOBLINS. Troups of. *P.P.* xxix.

GODALMING. *N.N.* xxii.

" **GODMOTHER.**" *See* Riah, Mr.

GOFF. George. *A.N.* xvii.

GOG. The elder giant. *M.H.C.* i.

Had a flowing grey beard. The giant warder of this ancient city, [London].

GOG AND MAGOG. *D. and S.* iv. ; *M.H.C.* i. ; *N.N.* xli.

GOLDEN APE. The. *B.H.* xii.

GOLDEN CROSS. *D.C.* xxx. ; *P.P.* ii. ; *S.B.B.*, Scenes vii., xvi.

GOLDEN DUSTMAN. *See* Boffin, Nicodemus.

GOLDEN HEAD. A French restaurant. *D. and S.* liv.

" **GOLDEN LION.**" Hotel of the, Mantua. *P.F.I.*, *V.M.M.S.S.*

GOLDEN LION COURT. *B.R.* ix.

" **GOLDEN MARY.**" Sailing vessel. *C.S.*, *W.O.G.M.*

" **GOLDEN MARY.**" Armourer, or smith of. *C.S.*, *W.O.G.M.*

" **GOLDEN MARY.**" Carpenter aboard of. *C.S.*, *W.O.G.M.*

" **GOLDEN MARY.**" Second mate of. *C.S.*, *W.O.G.M.*

" **GOLDEN MARY.**" Two apprentices aboard. *C.S.*, *W.O.G.M.*

One a Scotch boy.

GOLDEN SQUARE. *B.R.* l. ; *D.C.* xxi ; *N.N.* ii.

Although a few members of the graver professions live about Golden Square, it is not exactly in anybody's way to or from anywhere. It is one of the Squares that have been. A quarter of the town that has gone down in the world, and taken to letting lodgings. Many of its first and second floors are let, furnished, to single gentlemen ; and it takes boarders besides. It is a great resort of foreigners—street bands are on their mettle in Golden Square.

GOLDING. Mary, Bathing at Ramsgate. *S.B.B.*, Tales iv.

In her bathing costume, looked as if she were enveloped in a patent macintosh.

GOLDSMITHS. The. *S.B.B.*, Scenes xix.

GOLDSMITHS' COMPANY. The *C.B.*, *C.g.* iii.

GOLDSTRAW. Mrs., Mr. Wilding's housekeeper. *C.S.*, *N.T.* Act i.

Perhaps fifty, but looking younger with a face remarkable for placid cheerfulness, and a manner no less remarkable for its quiet expression of equability of temper.

GOLDSTRAW. Sarah, Mrs. Goldstraw. *C.S.*, *N.T.* Act i.

GOOD HOPE. Cape of. *M.P.*, *S.* ; *R.P.*, *T.L.V.*

GONOPH. A street arab. *R.P.*, *D.W.I.F.*

GOOD REPUBLICAN. Brutus of antiquity. Wineshop. *T.T.C.* bk. iii. ; chap. viii.

Not far from the National Palace.

Note.—It was here Miss Pross recognized her brother, Solomon Pross alias John Barsad, who was thought to be dead.

GOODCHILD. Francis. *L.T.*

GOODLE. *B.H.* xii.

GOODMAN'S FIELDS. *M.P., G.A.*

GOODWIN. Mrs. Potts' "Bodyguard." *P.P.*xviii.

A young lady, whose ostensible employment was to preside over her toilet, but who rendered herself useful in a variety of ways, and none more so than in the particular department of constantly aiding and abetting her mistress in every wish and inclination opposed to the desires of the unhappy Pott.

GOODWINS. The. *D. and S.* xxiii. *R.P., O.E., W.P.*

GOODY. Old Mrs., Grandchild of *O.M.F.* ix.

GORDON. Colonel, near relation of Lord George Gordon. *B.R.* xlix.

GORDON. Emma, Tight-rope Lady . . . one of Sleary's Troupe. *H.T., S.* vi.

GORDON. Lord George. *B.R.* xxxv.

About the middle height, of a slender make, and sallow complexion, with an aquiline nose, and long hair of a reddish-brown, combed perfectly straight and smooth about his ears, and slightly powdered, but without the faintest vestige of a curl. He was attired, under his great-coat, in a full suit of black, quite free from any ornament, and of the most precise and sober cut.

President of the great Protestant Association.

Note.—The Lord George Gordon of the book is very faithful to the real Lord George Gordon of the historic "No Popery" riots. Lord George was the third son of the third Duke of Gordon, and was born on September 19, 1750. He was the chief actor in the dramatic scenes of the Gordon riots, 1780, he was not convicted on the charge. Later on, however, he was convicted of writing a libellous pamphlet on the queen of France. He escaped to Holland, but was refused sanctuary and returned to England, where he died on November 1, 1793, a professed member of the Jewish religion.

GORDON. Mr. Sheriff. *M.P., E.A.S.*

GORDON PLACE. No. 25, Residence of the Miss Willises. *S.B.B., O.P.* iii.

It was fresh painted and papered from top to bottom; the paint inside was all wainscoted, the marble all cleaned, the old grates taken down, and register stoves, you could see to dress by, put up.

GORE HOUSE. *M.P., L.L.*

GORHAM. *M.P., R.H.F.*

GORHAMBURY. *U.T.* xiv.

GORHAMBURY. Brother-in-law of the Bishop of. *M.P., T.T.*

GORTON DISTRICT. *M.P., O.S.*

GOSWELL STREET. *P.P.* ii.

Mr. Samuel Pickwick . . . threw open his chamber window. . . Goswell Street was at his feet, Goswell Street was on his right hand—as far as the eye could reach, Goswell Street extended on his left; and the opposite side of Goswell Street was over the way.

GOTHARD. Great Saint. *P.F.I., R.D.*

GOUDO. The Gorge of. *P.F.I., V.M.M.S.S.*

GOUNOD. M. *M.P., M.M.*

GOVERNESS. Of visitors to Astley's. *S.B.B.*, Scenes xi.

Peeped out from behind the pillar, and timidly tried to catch ma's eye, with a look expressive of her high admiration of the whole family.

GOVERNOR. Jack, A sailor. *C.S., H.H.*

The finest-looking sailor that ever sailed—gray now, but as handsome as he was a quarter a century ago. A portly, cheery, well-built figure of a broadshouldered man, with a frank smile, a brilliant dark eye, and a rich dark eyebrow. . . A man of wonderful resources.

GOVERNOR. Our, *See* Tackleton, Mr.

GOVERNOR. The Landlord of "Holly Tree" Inn. *C.S., H.T.*

GOWAN. Harry. *L.D.* xvii.

This gentleman looked barely thirty. He was well dressed—" An artist, I infer from what he says ? " " A sort of one," said Daniel Doyce —" What sort of one ? " asked Clennam. " Why he has sauntered into the arts at a leisurely Pall-Mall pace."

Note.—A young artist, marries Minnie Meagles. He lives to a large extent on his wife's generosity. Eventually he discovers that it would be better for him not to know the Meagles, but the money still continues to come to Minnie.

GOWAN. Mrs., Family servant of. *L.D.* xxvi.

Who had his own crow to pluck with the public, concerning a situation in the Post Office which he had for some time been expecting, and to which he was not yet appointed.

GOWAN. Mrs. *See* Meagles, Minnie.

GOWAN. Mrs., Mother of Henry Gowan. *L.D.* xvi.

A courtly old lady, formerly a beauty, and still sufficiently well favoured to have dispensed with the powder on her nose, and a certain impossible bloom under each eye.

Note.—Henry Gowan's mother. Living on a pension in apartments at Hampton Court Palace.

GOWAN FAMILY. *L.D.* xvii.

A very distant ramification of the Barnacles ; . . . the paternal Gowan, originally attached to a legation abroad, had been pensioned off as a commissioner of nothing particular somewhere or other, and had died at his post with his drawn salary in his hand, nobly defending it to the last extremity.

GOWER. Tomb of old—in St. Saviour's, Southwark. *U.T.* ix.

He lies in effigy with his head upon his book.

GOWER STREET.
P.P. xxxi. ; *S.B.B.*, Char. ix.

GRACECHURCH STREET.
R.P., *B.S.* ; *U.T.* xxi.

GRADGRIND. Jane. *H.T.*, s. iv.

GRADGRIND. Louisa. *H.T.*, s. iii.

A child . . . of fifteen or sixteen ; but at no distant date would seem to become a woman all at once. . . . She was pretty.

Note. — Louisa eventually marries Bounderby without having any love for him. She is persecuted by another man and takes refuge with her father. Her husband insists on her immediate return ; failing this he casts her off and she remains with her father.

GRADGRIND. Mr. Thomas, A mill-owner. *H.T.*, s. iii.

The speaker's square forefinger emphasized his observations by underscoring every sentence with a line on the schoolmaster's sleeve. The speaker's voice—inflexible, dry and dictatorial—hair, which bristled on the skirts of his bald head—all covered with knobs, like the crust of a plum pie.

Note.—A wealthy man retired from busines living at Stone Lodge near Coketown. He is obsessed with figures and facts, and their importance ; and rules his life by them, as well as a school he controls. On the same principle he arranges the marriage of his daughter with Mr. Bounderby. The marriage turns out an unhappy one. His son Tom is placed in Bounderby's bank, but he becomes wild as a result of the earlier repression, and robs the bank. These two failures result in changing Gradgrind's point of view, particularly as the only friendship and assistance he meets with is from Sleary and the members of his circus troupe, and he realizes that his facts and figures must be leavened by love and forbearance.

GRADGRIND. Mrs., Wife of Thomas Gradgrind. *H.T.*, s. iv.

A little, thin, white, pink-eyed bundle of shawls, of surpassing feebleness, mental and bodily, who was always taking physic.

GRADGRIND. Thomas. Clerk in Bounderby's Bank. *H.T.*, s. iii.

Note.—A sullen, selfish cub. He enters Bounderby's Bank. Before long he robs the safe. The blame falls on Blackpool. But he is cleared. Tom eventually manages to escape from the country by the aid of Sleary and his troupe.

GRADGRINDS. Five young, Children of Mr. Gradgrind.
H.T., s. iii.

GRAHAM. Hugh, Apprentice of Bowyer. *M.H.C.* i.

GRAHAM. Mary. *M.C.* iii.

She is very young; apparently no more than seventeen. She was short in stature; and her figure was slight. Her face was very pale. Her dark brown hair—had fallen negligently from its bonds, and hung upon her neck.—Her attire was that of a lady, but extremely plain.

Note.—Mary Graham is first introduced tending to old Martin Chuzzlewit. It was because of his love for her that young Martin displeased his grandfather. The young people remain true to one another, however, and after Martin's return from America they are finally married.

GRAINGER, Dr. *M.P., P.T.*

GRAINGER. Steerforth's friend. *D.C.* xxiv.

GRAND CAIRO. *M.P., E.T.*

GRAND CANAL. The, Venice. *L.D.* xli.

GRAND DUKE. At Baden-Baden. *D. and S.* xxxi.

GRAND VIZIER. *C.S., H.H.*

GRANDFATHER. Doctor Marigold. *C.S., D.M.P.*

GRANDFATHER. Little Nell's. *See* Trent, Little Nell's Grandfather.

GRANDMAMA. Kate Nickleby's. *N.N.* xxxv.

When she was a young lady, before she was married—ran against her own hairdresser, as she was turning the corner of Oxford Street,—the encounter made her faint away.

GRANDMARINA. Fairy. *H.R.* ii.

Dressed in shot-silk of the richest quality, smelling of dried lavender.

GRANDMOTHER. Cinderella's. *M.P., F.F.*

GRANDMOTHER. Of Tom Pinch. *M.C.* ii.

A gentleman's housekeeper—died happy to think she had put me with such an excellent man.

GRANDMOTHER. Of unimpeachable member of the Chuzzlewit family. *M.C.* i.

Contemplating venerable relic—a dark lantern of undoubted antiquity; rendered still more interesting by being, in shape and pattern, extremely like such as are in use at the present day. "Aye, Aye! This was carried by my fourth son on the fifth of November, when he was a Guy Fawkes."

GRANDMOTHER. Of (Mr.) Vholes. *B.H.* xxxvii.

Who died in her hundred-and-second year.

GRANDMOTHER. Of (Miss) Wade. *L.D.* lvii.

A lady who represented that relative to me, and who took that title on herself. She had some children of her own family in her house, and some children of other people.

GRANDMOTHER. Old, In tea gardens. *S.B.B.*, Scenes ix.

GRAND-NEPHEW. Of Mr. Martin Chuzzlewit. *M.C.* iv.

Very dark, and very hairy, and apparently born for no particular purpose but to save looking-glasses the trouble of reflecting more than just the first idea and sketchy notion of a face, which had never been carried out.

GRANDPAPA. With a beautifully plaited shirt-frill and white neckerchief. *S.B.B.*, Char. ii.

GRANGER. Edith. *See* Dombey, Mrs.

GRANGER. Colonel, of Ours (deceased). *D, and S.* xxi.

A de-vilish handsome fellow, sir, of forty-one.

GRANNETT. Mr., Overseer at workhouse. *O.T.* xxiii.

Who relieved an outdoor dying pauper with offer of a pound of potatoes, and half a pint of oatmeal.

GRANT COUNTY. Sheriff of. *A.N.* xvii.

GRANTHAM. *N.N.* v.

GRANVILLE. Mr. *See* Wharton, Mr. Granville. *G.S.E.* ix.

GRAVE-DIGGER. The. *B.R.* i.
Ill in bed from long working in a damp soil and sitting down to take his dinner on cold tombstones.

GRAVE. Family, Of the Chuzzlewits. *M.C.* i.

GRAVES. Phantom. *C.B., C.C., S.* iv.

GRAVESEND. *B.R.* xxxi.; *D.C.* xiii.; *D. and S.* xviii.; *G.E.* lii.; *L.D.* liv.; *S.B.B.*, Scenes x.; *S.B.B.*, Tales iv.; *U,T.* vii.

GRAY. Dr., the residence of. *M.P., S.B.*

GRAYMARSH. Pupil at Dotheboys' Hall. *N.N.* vii.
Graymarsh's maternal aunt—is very glad to hear he's so well and happy and sends her respectful compliments to Mrs. Squeers, and thinks she must be an angel.

GRAYPER. Mrs., Neighbour of the Copperfields. *D.C.* ii.
She's going to stay with Mrs. Grayper.

GRAYPER. Mr. and Mrs. *D.C.* xxii.

GRAY'S INN. *P.P.* xx.
Curious little nooks in a great place like London, these old inns are.

GRAY'S INN. Chambers in. *U.T.* xiv.
An upper set in a rotten staircase with a mysterious bunk or bulkhead on the landing outside them, of a rather nautical and screw collier-like appearance, than otherwise, and painted an intense black.

GRAY'S INN. The Honourable Society of. *U.T.* xiv.; *D.C.* xxx.

GRAY'S INN. Traddles' Chambers. *D.C.*

GRAY'S INN COFFEE HOUSE. *D.C.* liv.

GRAY'S INN GARDENS. *L.D.* xiii.

GRAY'S INN LANE. *O.T.* xlii.; *P.P.* xlvii.; *R.P., D.W.I.F.*; *S.B.B.*, Scenes xiii.
Intricate and dirty ways—lying between Gray's Inn Lane and Smithfield—render that part of the town, one of the lowest and worst that improvement has left in the midst of London.

GRAY'S INN ROAD. *M.P., V.D.*

GRAY'S INN ROAD. Lodgings which Mr. Micawber occupied as Mr. Mortimer prior to coach journey to Canterbury. *D.C.* vii.

GRAY'S INN ROAD. A street in. *L.D.* xiii.
Which had set off from that thoroughfare with the intention of running at one heat down into the valley, and up again to the top of Pentonville Hill; but which had run itself out of breath in twenty yards, and had stood still ever since. —It remained there for many years, looking with a baulked countenance at the wilderness patched with unfruitful gardens, and pimpled with eruptive summerhouses, that it meant to run over in no time.

GRAY'S INN SQUARE. Set of chambers in, of Mr. Percy Noakes. *S.B.B.*, Tales vii.
His sitting-room presented a strange chaos of dress-gloves, boxing-gloves, caricatures, albums, invitation cards, foils, cricket-bats—in the strangest confusion.

GRAZINGLANDS. Mr., Of the Midland Counties. *U.T.* vi.
A gentleman of a comfortable property.

GRAZINGLANDS. Mrs., Wife of Mr. Grazinglands. *U.T.* vi.
Amiable and fascinating.

GREAT BRITAIN. *A.N.* xiv.; *H.T., R.* ii.; *L.D.* xi.; *M.P., E.T*; *M.P., L.A.V.* ii.; *M.P., N.E.*; *M.P., R.S.*; *M.P., R.T.*; *U.T.* x.

GREAT CORAM STREET. *S.B.B.*, Tales i.

GREAT DESERT. The. *R.P., D.W.T.T.*

GREAT FATHERS. Of the Revolution. *M.P., Y.M.C.*

GREAT HORSESHOE FALL. The. *A.N.* xiv.

GREAT MARLBOROUGH STREET. *C.S., S.L.* iv.; *S.B.B.*, Tales vii.

GREAT NATIONAL SMITHERS' TESTIMONIAL. *B.H.* viii.

GREAT NORTH ROAD. *C.S., H.T.*; *O.T.* xlii.

GREAT ORMOND STREET. Lord Chancellor's in. *B.R.* lxvii.

GREAT PAVILIONSTONE HOTEL. *R.P., O.O.T.*

GREAT PORTLAND STREET. *R.P., O.B.*

GREAT PYRAMID. *M.P., T.B.*

GREAT QUEEN STREET. *O.C.S.* viii.; *S.B.B.*, Scenes xix.

GREAT RUSSELL STREET. *U.T.* iv.

GREAT SAINT BERNARD. The pass of the. *L.D.* xxxvii.; *R.P., L.A.*

GREAT SALT LAKE. The. *U.T.* xx.

GREAT SPHINX. *M.P., E.T.*

GREAT SQUARE. *P.F.I., R.*

GREAT TWIG STREET. *M.P., U.N.*

"**GREAT WHITE HORSE.**" Chambermaid of the. *P.P.* xxii.

"**GREAT WHITE HORSE.**" Chambermaids at the. *P.P.* xxiv.

"**GREAT WHITE HORSE.**" Ipswich. *P.P.* xxii.

Famous in the same degree as a prize ox, or unwieldy pig, for its enormous size.

"**GREAT WHITE HORSE.**" Landlord of the. *P.P.* xxii.

A corpulent man, with a fortnight's napkin under his arm, and coeval stockings on his legs.

GREAT YARMOUTH. *M.P., E.S.* *See also* Yarmouth.

GREECE. *L.T.* iii.

GREEK WARRIOR. *P.F.I., R.*

GREEN. A constable. *R.P., D.W.I.F.*

GREEN. Miss. Child sweetheart of Uncommercial Traveller. *U.T.* xii.

GREEN. Miss. *N.N.* xiv.

Elderly lady from back parlour.

GREEN. Mr. *M.P., R.H.F.*

GREEN. Mr. An Aeronaut. *S.B.B.*, Scenes xiv.

GREEN. Mr., Jun. *S.B.B.*, Scenes xiv.

GREEN. Mrs. *O.C.S.* xxi.

Lodger at the cheesemonger's round the corner.

GREEN. Mrs., Son of, a law writer. *B.H.* xi.

Aboard a vessel bound for China.

GREEN. The. *O.T.* x.

GREEN. The, Richmond. *G.E.* xxxiii.

GREEN. Tom. A gonoph. *R.P., D.W.I.F.*

GREEN. Tom, A soldier. *B.R.* lviii.

A gallant, manly, handsome fellow, but he had lost his left arm—his empty coat-sleeve hung across his breast—he wore a jaunty cap and jacket.

GREEN GATE. The very, belonging to Mr. Nupkin's residence. *P.P.* xxv.

GREEN LANES. *B.R.* xliv.

GREEN PARK. *C.S., S.L.* iii.

GREEN YARD. Of Dockhead district. *U.T.* x.

GREENACRE. Mr. *M.P., T.F.*

GREENGROCER. *U.T.* xii.

GREENGROCER. Hired to wait by the Kitterbells at christening party. *S.B.B.*, Tales xi.

Hired to wait for seven-and-sixpence, and whose calves alone were worth double the money.

GREENGROCER'S SHOP, BATH. *P.P.* xxxvii.

GREENHITHE. *E.D.* xxiii.

GREENHORNS. Some, At Greenwich Fair. *S.B.B.*, Scenes xii.

GREENLAND. *O.T.* viii.; *U.T.* xix.

"**GREENLEAF.**" Miss Donny's house. *B.H.* iii.

GREENOUGH. Mr., A sculptor. *A.N.* viii.

GREENWICH. *G.E.* xlv.; *O.M.F.* xxv.; *S.B.B.*, Scenes xii.; *S.U.T.H.* i.

GREENWICH FAIR. *S.B.B.*, Scenes xii.

A periodical breaking out—a sort of Spring rash: a three days' fever.

GREENWICH HOSPITAL. *M.P., I.M.*

GREENWICH PARK. *C.S., S.P.T.*, iii.; *M.P., R.H.F.*; *O.M.F.* liv.; *S.U.T.H.* i.

GREENWICH PENSIONERS. *U.T.* xxvii.

GREENWOOD. Joby. *C.S., H.H.*

GREENWOOD. Miss. *S.Y.G.*

GREGOIRE. A son of Madame Doche. *R.P., M.O.F.F.*

GREGORY. Foreman packer in Murdstone and Grinby's. *D.C.* xi.

GREGSBURY. Mr., M.P. *N.N.* xvi

The great member of Parliament, wanted a young man to keep his papers and correspondence in order. A tough, burly, thick-headed gentleman, with a loud voice, a pompous manner, a tolerable command of sentences with no meaning in them.

Note.—The preposterous member of Parliament who required a secretary and to whom Nicholas applied.

GRENELLE. The Abattoir of. *R.P., M.O.F.F.*

GRETA BRIDGE. In Yorkshire. *N.N.* iii.

GRETNA GREEN. *C.S., H.T.*; *M.P., S.G.*

GREWGIOUS. Mr., Rosa's guardian (an official receiver of rents). *E.D.* ix.

An arid, sandy man. He had a scanty flat crop of hair, in colour and consistency like some very mangy yellow fur tippet. Certain notches in his forehead, as though nature had been about to touch them into sensibility or refinement, when she had thrown away the chisel.

Note.—Rosa Bud's guardian with chambers in Staple Inn. He pays flying visits to his ward in Cloisterham, and when, after Edwin Drood's disappearance, she leaves Cloisterham, it is to her guardian she travels. He is very much upset by her recital of John Jasper's persecutions, and takes apartments for her with Billickin. He then decides to investigate Edwin's disappearance, with his suspicions very much pronounced against John Jasper.

GREWGIOUS. Angular Clerk of Mr. *E.D.* ix.

GREWGIOUS. Clerk of Mr. *E.D.* xi.

A pale, puffy-faced, dark-haired man of thirty, with big dark eyes that wholly wanted lustre, and a dissatisfied doughy complexion that seemed to ask to be sent to the baker's. A gloomy person, with tangled locks.

GREY. Lord. *M.P., P.P.*

GREY. Misses. *S.Y.G.*

GREY. Sir George. *M.P., S.*

GRIDE. Arthur, A money-lender. *N.N.* xlvii.

A little old man of about seventy or seventy-five years of age, of a very lean figure, much bent, and slightly twisted. He wore a grey coat with a very narrow collar, an old-fashioned waistcoat of ribbed black silk, and such scanty trousers as displayed his shrunken spindle-shanks.

Note.—A miserly old money-lender. He arranges with Ralph Nickleby's assistance to compel Mr. Bray to persuade Madeline to marry him. Mr. Bray is heavily in debt to both Gride and Ralph, and the scheme prospers. The interposition of Nicholas and the timely death of her father save Madeline from her threatened fate. Some years later his house was broken into and he himself murdered.

GRIDLEY. Mr., The man from Shropshire. *B.H.* xv.

"A tall, sallow man, with a care-worn head, on which but little hair remained, a deeply-lined face and prominent eyes. He had a pen in his hand, and in the glimpse I caught of his room in passing, I saw that it was covered with a litter of papers."

Note.—A suitor in chancery. One of two brothers. By his father's death he inherited the farm with a legacy of £300 to pay his brother. The question was whether his brother had not received part of this in board, lodging, etc. The brother took this question to chancery, and there it became a problem of infinite ramification. He and his brother were ruined. He attends the court, unable to understand that he can do nothing, and always hoping for something. He is committed for contempt, but offends again. He ends his days, utterly worn out, in George Rouncewell's shooting-gallery, hiding from the officers of the law.

GRIDLEY. Mr., Brother of. *B.H.* xv.

Claimed his legacy of three hundred pounds—I, and some of my relations, said he had had a part of it already in board and lodgings, and some other things. That was the question and nothing else—I was obliged to go into this accursed chancery.

GRIDLEY. Mr., Father of, A farmer. *B.H.* xv.

Left his farm and stock and so forth to my mother for her life.

GRIEVANCE. A, Guest of Veneerings. *O.M.F.* ii.

GRIEVE. Mr. *M.P., E.T.*

GRIFFIN. Miss, School teacher. *C.S., H.H.*

GRIG. Tom. *M.P., L.*

GRIGGINS. Mr. *S.Y.G.*

GRIGGS. *M.P., I.*

GRIGGS'S. Friends of the Nupkins. *P.P.* xxv.

GRIMBLE. Sir Thomas, Of Grimbly Hall. *N.N.* xxxv.

A very proud man, with six grown-up daughters, and the finest park in the county.

GRIMBLES. The, Of Grimbly Hall. *N.N.* xxxv.

GRIMBLY HALL. Somewhere in the West Riding. *N.N.* xxxv.

GRIME. Prof. *Mud. Pap.* ii.

GRIMMER. Miss, A teacher. *H.R.* i.

GRIMWIG. Mr., A lawyer—A friend of Mr. Brownlow. *O.T.* xiv.

A stout old gentleman rather lame in one leg, who was dressed in a blue coat, striped waistcoat, nankeen breeches and gaiters, and a broad-brimmed white hat, with the sides turned up with green. A very small plaited shirt-frill stuck out from his waistcoat, and a very long steel watch-chain, with nothing but a key at the end, dangled loosely below it.

Note.—A friend of Mr. Brownlow. Somewhat short-tempered, but good-hearted. He is quite sure Oliver will not return when he is trusted with books and money by Mr. Brownlow, and as Oliver does not return he maintains he was correct. His characteristic phrase is " Or, I'll eat my head." At the end of the book he is a frequent visitor of Mr. Losberne, on which occasions he " plants, fishes, and carpenters with great ardour."

GRIMWOOD. Eliza, A young woman. *R.P., T.D.A.* i.

GRINDER. A, A coach, or tutor. *G.E.* xxiii.

GRINDER. Mr., Travelling showman. *O.C.S.* xvii.

GRINDER. Toodles junior. *D. and S.* xxii.

GRINDER'S LOT. A travelling show. *O.C.S.* xvii.

Consisted of a young gentleman and a young lady on stilts. . . the public costume of the young people was of the Highland kind.

GRINDOFF. The miller. *R.P., A.P.A.*

"**GRIP.**" Barnaby's raven. *B.R.* vi.

Balancing himself on tiptoe, as it were, and moving his body up and down in a sort of grave dance, rejoined, " I'm a devil, I'm a devil, I'm a devil."

Note.—Barnaby's raven, Grip, was his constant companion, even in Newgate when his master was imprisoned for complicity in the riots. He recovered his good looks " and became as glossy as ever." He had lost his gift of speech, however, in prison. At the end of a year he again speaks " and from that period . . . he constantly practised and improved himself in the vulgar tongue.

GRISE. Wife of Hown, Negro slave. *A.N.* xvii.

GRISSELL AND PETO. Messrs. *R.P., B.S.*

GRITTS. Right Hon. Mr. *M.P., C. Pat.*

GROBUS. Right Hon. Sir Gilpin Grobus. *M.P., C. Pat.*

GROCER. The. *G.E.* viii.

GROFFIN. Thomas, Juryman-Chemist. *P.P.* xxxiv.

A tall, thin, yellow-visaged man. I am to be sworn, my lord, am I.

Very well, my lord, then there'll be murder before this trial's over. . . . I've left nobody but an errand boy in my shop. . . . The prevailing impression on his mind is, that Epsom salts means oxalic acid; and syrup of senna, laudanum.

GROGGLES. Mr., Member of the Common Council. *M.P., L T.*

GROGGLES. Mrs. *M.P., L.T.*

GROGINHOLE. Hon. member for. *M.P., F.C.*

GROGUS. The great ironmonger. *S.B.B.*, Tales ii.

GROGZWIG. In Germany. *N.N.* vi.

GROMPUS. Mr., Guest of Mr. Podsnap. *O.M.F.* xi.

GROOM. A, At Astley's. *S.B.B.*, Scenes xi.

GROOMBRIDGE WELLS. *C.S., N.T.* Act i.

GROPER. Colonel. *M.C.* xxxiv.

"**GROSVENOR.**" East Indiaman. *R.P., T.L.V.*

"**GROSVENOR.**" Carpenter of the. *R.P., T.L.V.*

"**GROSVENOR.**" Cooper of the. *R.P., T.L.V.*

"**GROSVENOR.**" Little child of seven on board the. A passenger. *R.P., T.L.V.*

"**GROSVENOR.**" Steward of the. *R.P., T.L.V.*

GROSVENOR PLACE. *C.S., S.L.* iii.; *N.N.* xxi.

GROSVENOR SQUARE. *L.D.* ix.; *S.B.B.*, Scenes xx.

GROSVENOR SQUARE. Lord Rockingham's in. *B.R.* lxvii.

GROSVENOR REGION. By-streets in. *L.D.* xxvii.

Parasite little tenements, with the cramp in their whole frame, from the dwarf hall-door on the giant model of His Grace's in the square to the squeezed window of the boudoir. Rickety dwellings of undoubted fashion, but of a capacity to hold nothing comfortably except a dismal smell, looked like the last result of the great mansions' breeding in-and-in, and where their little supplementary bows and balconies were supported on thin iron columns, seemed to be scrofulously resting upon crutches.

GROUND. Tom Tiddler's. *C.S., T.T.G.* i.

A nook in a rustic by-road.

GROVE. The. *G.E.* xxxiv.; *U.T.* xi.

GROVE HOUSE ACADEMY. *M.C.* v.

GROVES. James. Public house keeper and gambler. *O.C.S.* xxix.

Jem Groves—honest Jem Groves, as is a man of unblemished moral character, and has a good dry skittle-ground.

Note.—The unimpeachable landlord of the "Valiant soldier," who assisted the gamblers in their trade. He is exposed by the detection of Frederick Trent, his young confederate.

GROWLERY. The, In Bleak House. *B.H.* viii. and lxvii.

A small room, in part a little library of books and papers. . . When I am out of humour I come and growl here said Mr. Jarndyce.

GRUB. Gabriel, Old, A sexton. *P.P.* xxviii.

An ill-conditioned, cross-grained, surly fellow—a morose and lonely man, who consorted with nobody but himself, and an old wicker bottle which fitted into his large and deep waistcoat pocket—and who eyed each merry face, as it passed him by, with such a deep scowl of malice and ill-humour, as it was difficult to meet without feeling something the worse for.

Note.—The central figure of the "Story of the Goblins." The goblins steal him, and so treat him that he is completely changed on his return to earth.

GRUB. Mr. *Mud. Pap.* ii.

GRUBBLE. W., Landlord of the "Dedlock Arms." *B.H.* xxxvii.

A pleasant looking, stoutish, middle-aged man, who never seemed to consider himself cosily dressed for his own fireside, without his hat, and top boots, but who never wore a coat except at church.

Note.—Landlord of the "Dedlock Arms."

GRUDDEN. Mrs., Member of Mr. V. Crummles' company. *N.N.* xxiii.

In a brown cloth pelisse and a beaver bonnet, who assisted Mrs. Crummles in her domestic affairs, and took money at the doors, and dressed the ladies, and swept the house, and held the prompt book when everybody else was on for the last scene.

GRUEBY. John, Servant of Lord George Gordon. *B.R.* xxxv.

A square-built, strong-made, bull-necked fellow of the true English breed—was to all appearance five-and-forty—Had a great blue cockade in his hat, which he appeared to despise mightily.

Note.—Grueby, as personal servant to Lord George Gordon, did all in his power to preserve his master, and attended him with a touching devotion. When Lord George was eventually imprisoned, John Grueby continued to serve him to the last.

GRUFF AND GLUM. An old pensioner. *O.M.F.* liv.

Two wooden legs had this gruff and glum old pensioner.

GRUFF AND GRIM. Mr. Barley. *G.E.* xlvi.

GRUFF AND TACKLETON. Toymakers. *C.B., C.o.H.*

GRUFFSHAW. Professional speaker. *M.P., O.S.*

GRUMMER. *P.P.* xxiv.

Elderly gentleman in top-boots, who was chiefly remarkable for a bottle nose; a hoarse voice, a snuff coloured surtout and a wandering eye. A somewhat forbidding countenance.

GRUMMIDGE. Dr. *Mud. Pap.* ii.

GRUNDY. Madam. *M.P., I.*

GRUNDY. Mr., At number twenty. *M.P., R.H.F.*

GRUNDY. Mr., Frequenter of "Magpie and Stump." *P.P.* xx.

Note.—An example of a type of London clerk. Met with at the "Magpie and Stump," where each of Mr. Lowten's friends is more an illustration of a class, than a study of an individual.

GRUNDY. Mrs. *M.P., R.H.F.*

GUARD. At Mugby Junction. *C.S., M.J.* i.

GUARD. Collected, of train. *R.P., a.F.*

GUARD. Of coach. *P.P.* xxviii.

GUARD. Of coach. *P.P.* xlix.

With a wig on his head, and most enormous cuffs to his coat, had a lantern in one hand, and a huge blunderbuss in the other.

GUARD. Of coach to Yorkshire. *C.S., H.T.*

GUARD. Of stage-coach. *S.B.B.*, Scenes xvi.

GUARD. On railway train.

In a red coat. *U.T.* xiii.

GUARDIAN. *M.P., P.T.*

"**GUARDIAN.**" Mr. Jarndyce. *B.H.* viii.

GUARDIANS. Stepney Board of. *U.T.* xxix.

GUBBINS. Mr. *S.B.B., O.P.* ii.

GUBBINSES. The, Guests of the Gattletons. *S.B.B.*, Tales ix.

GUBBLETON. Lord *S.B.B.*, Tales v.

GUDGEON. Mr. J. *M.P., E.C.*

GUEST. At Mr. Podsnap's. *O.M.F.* xi.

With one eye screwed up into extinction and the other framed and glazed.

GUESTS. At Pawkins' boarding house. *M.C.* xvi.

All the knives and forks were working away at a rate which was quite alarming,—everybody seemed to eat his utmost in self defence, as if a famine were expected to set in before breakfast-time to-morrow morning.

GUEST. At Wedding of Caroline Jellyby. *B.H.* xxx.

An extremely dirty lady, with her bonnet all awry, and the ticketed price of her dress still sticking on it, whose neglected home—was like a filthy wilderness, but whose church was like a fancy fair.

GUEST. Gentleman at Caroline Jellyby's wedding. *B.H.* xxx.

Who said it was his mission to be

everybody's brother, but who appeared to be on terms of coolness with the whole of his large family.

GUFFY. *B.H.* xii.

GUILD. Of literature and art. *M.P., G.L.A.*

GUILDFORD. *N.N.* xxv.; *R.P., T.D.A.* ii.

GUILDFORD. Picnic held near. *D.C.* iv.

GUILDHALL. *B.R.* lxvii; *M.H.C.*i.; *M.P., R.L.M.*; *P.P.* xxxv. *S.B.B.*, Scenes xix.

GUILDHALL. The. Canterbury. *D.C.* xxiii.

GUILLOTINE. *L.D.* ii.; *T.T.C.* ii.

GUINEA-PIG. In happy family. *M.P., P.F.*

GULD PUBLEEK = Gulled Public. *M.P., T.O.H.*

GULPIDGE. Mr., Something to do at secondhand with the law business of the Bank. *D.C.* xxv.

GULPIDGE. Mrs., Wife of Mr. Gulpidge. *D.C.* xxv.

GUMMIDGE. Mrs., Widow of Mr. Peggotty's partner. *D.C.* iii.

Note.—Mrs. Gummidge is introduced as an inmate of Mr. Peggotty's house. She is the widow of his former partner. and her perpetual grievance is that she is a "lone, lorn creetur." She accompanies Dan'l Peggotty and Little Em'ly to Australia, however, and becomes a bright and cheerful helper.

GUMPTON HOUSE. *R.P., O.V.*

GUNPOWDER. Great, A Creek. *A.N.* viii.

GUNPOWDER. Little, A Creek. *A.N.* viii.

GUNTER. Mr., Visitor to Bob Sawyer. *P.P.* xxxii.

In a shirt emblazoned with pink anchors, expressed his decided unwillingness to accept of any sauce on gratuitous terms from the irascible young gentleman with the scorbutic countenance, or any other person who was ornamented with a head.

GUNTER. Signor, Berkeley Square, London. *M.P., N.Y.D.*

GUPPY. Mrs., Mother of Mr. Guppy. *B.H.* ix.

An old lady in a large cap, with rather a red nose, and rather an unsteady eye, but smiling all over. In danger of cracking herself like a nut in the front parlour-door, by peeping out before she was asked for.

Note.—She lives in Old Street Road, but when her son takes a 'ouse she is to go and live with him. She is seen at the end of the book being removed by her son and Mr. Jobling, with some difficulty, from Mr. Jarndyce's house.

GUPPY. Mr. William, Clerk to Kenge and Carboy. *B.H.* iv.

He had an entirely new suit of clothes on, a shining hat, lilac kid gloves, a neckerchief of a variety of colours, a large hot-house flower in his buttonhole, and a thick gold ring on his little finger.

Note.—A burlesqued character employed as a clerk by Kenge and Carboy. Sometimes engaged on private matters for the firm, he obtains a good deal of information. On these occasions he is sometimes brought in contact with Esther Summerson, with whom he falls in love. She is only amused at his subsequent offer and refuses him. After her illness when her face is disfigured, she again meets Mr. Guppy, who is afraid she has come to claim fulfilment of his promise, and is only re-assured. with much difficulty and quasilegal formality that she has no desire to marry him. Guppy, with the meannes of an unauthorised amateur detective, also obtains information of the secret of Lady Dedlock. He again offers marriage to Esther, having re-considered it.

GUSHER. Mr., A Missionary. *B.H.* viii.

A flabby gentleman with a moist surface, and eyes much too small for his moon of a face.

Note.—Friend of Mrs. Pardigle.

GUSTER. Augusta. *B.H.* x.

Note.—Servant to the Snagsbys. She has fits and falls into anything handy, convenient, or inconvenient. She is useful in clearing up the mystery of Lady Dedlock's flight.

GWYNN. Miss, Writing and ciphering governess at "Westgate House." *P.P.* xvi.

GYE AND BALNE. Messrs., Bill Printers. *R.P., B.S.*

GYMNASE. Paris. *M.P., W.*

H

HACKNEY. *S.B.B.*, Scenes ix.

HACKNEY COACH STANDS. *S.B.B.*, Scenes vii.

HACKNEY-COACHMEN. *S.B.B.*, Scenes i.

Admiring how people can trust their necks into one of them crazy cabs, when they can have a 'spectable 'ackney cotche with a pair of 'orses as von't run away with no vun.

HACKNEY ROAD. *U.T.* x.

HAGGAGE. Doctor. In Marshalsea. *L.D.* vi.

Amazingly shabby, in a torn and darned rough-weather sea jacket, out at elbows, and eminently short of buttons (he had been in his time the experienced surgeon carried by a passenger ship) the dirtiest white trousers conceivable by mortal man, carpet slippers, and no visible linen.

HAGUE. The. *L.D.* lxvii.

HAIRDRESSER. Journeyman. *N.N.* lii.

Who was not very popular among the ladies, by reason of his obesity and middle age.

"HALF MOON AND SEVEN STARS." The, An obscure alehouse. *M.C.* iv.

HALFPAY CAPTAIN. *S.B.B.*, *O.P.* ii.

Near neighbour, a retired officer. Ordnance Terrace.

HALFWAY HOUSE. *B.R.* ii.

HALFWAY HOUSE. *D. and S.* xxiii.

HALFWAY HOUSE. *G.E.* xxviii.

HALFWAY HOUSE. *N.N.* xlix.

HALIFAX. *A.N.* i.

HALIFAX HARBOUR. *A.N.* ii.

HALL. Mr. *M.P.*, *W.M.*

HALL. The. *M.C.* xxvii.

HALL. The, In Budden's house. *S.B.B.*, Tales ii.

Passage, denominated by courtesy "The Hall."

HALL FLIGHT. In the Fleet. *P.P.* xli.

A dark and filthy staircase, which appeared to lead to a range of damp and gloomy stone vaults, beneath the ground and those I suppose are the little cellars where the prisoners keep their small quantities of coals.

HALL OF EXAMINATION. In the Hôtel de Ville. *T.T.C.* bk. ii.; ch. xxii.

HALLEY. Mr. *O.M.F.* viii.

HALLIDAY. Brother, A Mormon agent. *U.T.* xx.

HALLIFORD. *O.T.* xxi.

HALLIFORD. Lower. *O.T.* xxi.

HALLOCK. Dr., the residence of. *M.P.*, *S.B.*

"**HALSEWELL.**" Crew of the. *R.P.*, *T.L.V.*

"**HALSEWELL.**" Petty officers of the. *R.P.*, *T.L.V.*

"**HALSEWELL.**" Soldiers on the. *R.P.*, *T.L.V.*

HAMMERSMITH. *G.E.* xxi.; *M.P.*, *G.D.*; *N.N.* xvii.; *O.T.* xxi.; *S.B.B.*, Tales iii.; *U.T.* x.

HAMMERSMITH SUSPENSION BRIDGE. *S.B.B.*, Scenes vi.

HAMMOND. Rev. Charles. *M.P.*, *S.B.*

HAMPSTEAD. *B.R.* xvi., *D.C.* vi. *M.P.*, *G.B.*, *R.P.*, *L.A.*, *S.U.T.H.* i.

HAMPSTEAD. Village of. *O.T.* xlviii.

HAMPSTEAD HEATH. *M.P.*, *N.S.E.*, *O.T.* xlviii.

HAMPSTEAD PONDS. *P.P.* i.; *U.T.* x.

This Association has heard read . . . the paper communicated by Samuel Pickwick, Esq., . . . entitled, Speculations on the Source of the Hampstead Ponds.

Note.—There is no doubt that the ponds here referred to are those close to Hampstead Heath Station. Although the reference to them is facetious, their source was at one time a matter of some small interest. They are fed by a small stream having its rise in Caen Wood.

HAMPSTEAD PONDS. Miss Griffin's establishment in. *C.S.*, *H.H.*

HAMPSTEAD ROAD. *S.B.B.*, Scenes ix.

HAMPTON. *N.N.* l.; *O.T.* xxi; *O.M.F.* xii.
HAMPTON CHURCH. *O.M.F.*, viii.
HAMPTON CLUB HOUSE. *N.N.* l.
HAMPTON COURT. *L.D.* xii.; *S.B.B.* Scenes v., *M.P.*, *G.B.*
HAMPTON COURT PALACE. *M.P.*, *P.L.U.*
HANAPER. The clerk of the. *R.P.*, *P.M.T.P.*
HANAPER. Deputy clerk of the. *R.P.*, *P.M.T.P.*
HANCOCK. Mr. *M.P.*, *F.M.*
HANCOCK AND FLOBBY. *M.C.* xxii.
HANDEL. Herbert Pocket's name for Pip. *G.E.* xxii.
HANDEL. *M.P.*, *O.L.N.O.*
HANDFORD. Mr. Julius, *See* Harmon, John.
HANDS. The, Mill-workers. *H.T.* s. x.
HANGING-SWORD ALLEY. Whitefriars. *B.H.* xxvii.; *T.T.C.* bk. ii. ch. i.

Jerry Cruncher's lodgings were in Hanging-sword-alley, and they "were not in a savoury neighbourhood."

HANNAH. Servant girl to Miss La Creevy. *N N.* iii.

With an uncommonly dirty face.

HANOVER. *A.N.* iii.
HANOVER SQUARE. *N.N.* xxxvii.; *U.T.* iii.
HANSARDADE. Daughter of the Grand Vizier Parmarstoon. *M.P.*, *T.O.H.*

Note.—Hansard's Parliamentary Debates, etc.

HANSARD'S. Luke, pages. *M.P.*, *Q.D.P.*
HANWELL. Middlesex. *M.P.*, *S.B.*
HAPPY CHARLES. Street of. *M.P.*, *N.Y.D.*
HAPPY COTTAGE. *L.D.* xlix.
HAPPY FAMILY. Austin's Animals in one cage. *M.P.*, *P.F.*
HARDINGE. Miss Emma. *M.P.*, *R.S.D.*
HARDY. Mr., "The funny gentleman." *S.B.B.*, Tales vii.

A stout gentleman of about forty, a practical joker—always engaged in some pleasure excursion or other—could sing comic songs, imitate hackney-coachmen and fowls, play airs on his chin and execute concertos on the Jew's harp.

HAREDALE. Miss Emma, Niece of Mr. Geoffrey Haredale. *B.R.* i.

An orphan, foster sister of Dolly Varden—a lovely girl.

Note.—Emma was the neice of Mr. Geoffrey Haredale, and daughter of Reuben. After many vicissitudes she is married to Edward Chester.

HAREDALE. Mr. Geoffrey. *B.R.* i.

A burly, square-built man, negligently dressed, rough and abrupt in manner, stern, and, in his present mood, forbidding both in look and speech.

Note.—Roman Catholic. Somewhat disliked, but on account of his religion, specially obnoxious to the Gordon Rioters. The Warren, his residence, is burned, and beside the ruins he fights a duel with Sir John Chester, and kills him. He leaves the country and spends the rest of his days under the severe discipline of a monastry.

HAREDALE. Reuben, Father of Miss Haredale and elder brother of Mr. Geoffrey Haredale. *B.R.* i.

He is not alive, and he is not dead—not dead in a common sort of way . . . found murdered in his bed-chamber; and in his hand was a piece of the cord attached to an alarm-bell outside the roof.

HAREDALE. Reuben, Gardener of. *B.R.* i.
HAREDALE. Reuben, Steward of. *B.R.* i.
HAREDALE. Reuben, Two women servants of. *B.R.* i.
HAR'FORDSHIRE. *M.C.* xxix.
HARKER. Mr., Police officer. *C.S.*, *T.G.S.* i.

Sworn to hold us (The Jury) in safekeeping. He had an agreeable presence, good eyes, enviable black whiskers, and a fine sonorous voice.

HARLEIGH. Mr. *S.B.B.*, Tales ix.
HARLEQUIN. In booth in Greenwich fair. *S.B.B.*, Tales xii.

HARLEQUIN. On stage in Britannia. *U.T.* iv.

HARLEY. J. P. *M.P., V.C.*

HARLEY. Mr., As Felix Tapkins. Esq. *M.P., T.S.H.W.*

HARLEY. Mr., As Mr. Martin. Stokes. *M.P., V.C.*

HARLEY. Mr., As the strange gentleman. *M.P., S.G.*

HARLEY STREET. *L.D.* xx.; *U.T.* xvi.

HARMON. Daughter of dust contractor. *O.M.F.* ii.

He (the dust contractor) chose a husband for her, entirely to his own satisfaction, and not in the least to hers.—The poor girl respectfully intimated that she was secretly engaged to that popular character whom the novelists and versifiers call "another."—Immediately the venerable parent anathematised, and turned her out.

HARMON. John, Son of dust contractor. (Alias Julius Handford, alias John Rokesmith.) *O.M.F.* ii.

Only son of a tremendous old rascal who made his money by dust. A boy of spirit and resource pleads his sister's cause—venerable parent turns him out—gets aboard ship. A boy of fourteen, cheaply educating at Brussels, when his sister's expulsion befell.

Note.—The son of the Harmon of the Harmon estate. He returns from the Cape on the death of his father to take over his inheritance and to fulfil the condition of his father's will by marrying Bella Wilfer. On his return he is attacked, robbed and seriously injured. He is thrown into the Thames as dead, but he revives and swims ashore. In the meantime the man Radfoot, who robs him, quarrels over the spoil and is killed and thrown into the river. When his body is found it is identified as that of John Harmon on account of the property and clothes found on him. Harmon then changes his name to Julius Handford, so that he may make personal investigations without being recognised. He does not retain this alias long, however, but engages himself as private secretary to Mr. Boffin as John Rokesmith. Here he meets Bella Wilfer, and with the assistance of the Boffins, who have recognised him, he succeeds in winning the girl's love. He marries her, and when he is about to reveal his identity to her, he is arrested for his own murder. His identity is discovered by Mrs. Boffin, and she and her husband enter into a scheme to assist him. Noddy Boffin pretends to be miserly, and subjects his secretary to continual insults; this excites Bella's sympathy, and then her love follows and they are married. Boffin discovers a later will giving everything to him unconditionally. This he ignores, and makes over the greater portion of the property to Rokesmith. His connections with Silas Wegg and Mr. Venus are scarcely essential, but serve to illustrate and illuminate the story.

HARMON. Mrs., Wife of dust contractor—dead. *O.M.F.* ii.

HARMON. Mrs., *See* Wilfer Bella.

HARMON. Old Mr., Deceased dust contractor. *O.M.F.* iii.

HARMON'S. Old. Boffin's Bower. *O.M.F.* v.

HARMONIC MEETING. Waiter at. *S.B.B*, Scenes ii.

Pale-faced man with the red head.

HARMONIC MEETING. Guests of. *S.B.B*, Scenes ii.

Some eighty or a hundred.

HARMONIC MEETINGS. Chairman of. *B.H.* xi.

HARMONY JAIL. Boffin's Bower. *O.M.F.* v.

"Not a proper jail, wot you and me would get committed to—they give it the name, on account of old Harmon living solitary there."

HARRIET. *See* Carker, Harriet.

HARRIS. Greengrocer. *P.P.* xxxvii.

Waiting on members and guests of Select Company at Footmen's friendly swarry.

HARRIS. Mary, Nurse at Holborn Union. *M.P., V.D.*

HARRIS. Mr., "Punch showman." *O.C.S.* xvi.

A little merry-faced man, with a twinkling eye and a red nose.

Note.—Harris was Short, Trotters, or Short Trotters indiscriminately to his friends.

HARRIS. Mr. *M.C.* xlix. *M.P., S.F.A.*

HARRIS. Mr. Law stationer. *S.B.B.*, Char. vii.

HARRIS. Mrs. *M.P., L.E.J.*

HARRIS. Mrs., Friend of Mrs. Gamp. *M.C.* xix.

Whom no one in the circle of Mrs. Gamp's acquaintance had ever seen : neither did any human being know her place of residence. The prevalent opinion was that she was a phantom of Mrs. Gamp's brain.

HARRIS. Thomas L. *M.P., R.S.D.*

HARRIS. Tommy, Little. *M.C.* xlix.

HARRISBURG. *A.N.* ix.

HARRISON. General. *A.N.* iv.

HARRISON. Little. *O.M.F.* ix.

HARROW. *G.E.* xxiii. ; *U.T.* x.

HARROWGATE. *D. and S.* xxi.

HARRY. Coachman of early coach. *S.B.B.*, Scenes xv.

In a rough blue coat, of which the buttons behind are so far apart that you can't see them both at the same time.

HARRY. Cousin. *R.P., A.C.T.*

HARRY. Master, Son of Mr. Walmer. *C.S., H.T.*

HARRY. Our eighth royal. *M.P., T.B.*

HARRY. A pedlar. *O.T.* xlviii.

This was an antic fellow, half pedlar, half mountebank, who travelled about the country on foot, to vend hones, strops, razors, washballs, harness-paste, medicine for dogs and horses, cheap perfumery, cosmetics, and such-like wares, which he carried in a case slung to his back.

HARRY. The grandson of Dame West, and the schoolmaster's favourite scholar. *O.C.S.* xxv.

He was a very young boy ; quite a little child. His hair still clung in curls about his face, and his eyes were very bright ; but their light was of heaven, not earth.

HART. Mr., Assistant master of Asylum for the Blind at Bolton. *A.N.* iii.

HARTFORD. *A.N.* v.

HARTHOUSE. Mr. James, Political agent. *H.T., R.* ii.

Five-and-thirty, good-looking, good figure, good teeth, good voice, good breeding, well dressed, dark hair, bold eyes.

HARVEYS. *S.Y.C.*

HARWICH. *B.R.* lxxxii.

HASTINGS. *M.P., T.B.*

HATCH. Mrs., Cora. *M.P., R.S.D.*

HATCHWAY. *M.P., G.F.*

HATFIELD. *C.S., M.L.Lo.* i.

HATFIELD. Small public house at. *O.T.* xlviii.

There was a fire in the taproom, and some country labourers were drinking before it.

HATFIELD CHURCHYARD. *C.S., M.L.Leg.* i.

HATTER. The. *U.T.* xvi.

HATTER. Of New York. *M.P., T.O.P.*

HATTON GARDEN. *B.H.* xxvi. ; *R.P., B.S.* ; *S.B.B.*, Tales xi.

HAUNTED HOUSE = House of Parliament. *M.P., H.H.*

HAUNTED HOUSE. Cook at the. *C.S., H.H.*

HAUNTED HOUSE. Odd girl at the. *C.S., H.H.*

One of the Saint Lawrence's Union Female orphans.

HAUNTED HOUSE. Room of Master B in. *C.S., H.H.*

A triangular cabin under the cock-loft, with a corner fireplace —and a corner chimney-piece like a pyramidal staircase to the ceiling.

HAUNTED MAN. The. *C.B., H.M.* i.

His hollow cheeks, sunken brilliant eye ; his black figure, indefinably grim, although well knit, and well proportioned, his grizzled hair hanging, like tangled seaweed, about his face

HAUNTED MAN. Dwelling of. *C.B., H.M.* i.

Solitary and vault-like—an old retired part of an ancient endowment for students—once a brave edifice planted in an open space, but now the obsolete whim of forgotten architects; smoke-aged, and weather-darkened, squeezed on every side by the overgrowing of the great city, and choked, like an old well, with stones and bricks.

HAVELOCK'S MEN. *U.T.* viii.
Discharged soldiers who had recently returned from India.

HAVEN. Head. *E.D.* vi.

HAVEN OF PHILANTHROPY. *E.D.* vi, xvii.

HAVISHAM. Junr., Son of Mr. Havisham and half-brother to Miss Havisham. *G.E.* xxii.
Riotous, extravagant, undutiful, altogether bad.

HAVISHAM. Mr., Deceased father of Miss Havisham. *G.E.* xxii.
A brewer, very rich and very proud.

HAVISHAM. Miss, Pip's benefactress. *G.E.* vii.
An immensely rich and grim old lady who lived in a large and dismal house barricaded against robbers, and who led a life of seclusion. She was dressed in rich materials, satins and lace and silks—all of white. Her shoes were white—a long white veil depended from her hair, and she had bridal flowers in her hair, but her hair was white. Some bright jewels sparkled on her neck and on her hands.

Note.—First seen in the story, a mentally deranged woman living in Satis House with all daylight excluded. Pip goes there to play, and meets Estella, Miss Havisham's adopted daughter, and sees many strange things. Miss Havisham is training Estella to break men's hearts. When Pip goes no more to Satis House, Miss Havisham pays Joe a premium of twenty-five guineas for his indentures. When she dies she has left most of her wealth to Estella, "a cool" four thousand to Matthew Pocket, and insignificant sums to other relatives. It transpires through the story that Miss Havisham had been a beautiful heiress basely deserted on the wedding-day by Compeyson, the intended husband. The shock had unhinged her mind. She then adopted Estella to wreak her vengeance on the whole of mankind she came in contact with.

HAVISHAM. Mother of Miss, deceased. *G.E.* xxii.
Died when she (Miss Havisham) was a baby.

HAWDON. A law-writer. *B.H.* x.
His hair is ragged, mingling with his whiskers and his beard—dressed in shirt and trousers, with bare feet.

Note.—Captain Hawdon's identity is hidden for a long time. He is introduced as an unknown law-writer, living over Krook's rag-and-bone shop, and going under the name of Nemo. It transpires that he was a military officer, formerly a lover of Lady Dedlock to be, and father of Esther Summerson. He befriends Jo, and dies in his garret. Jo is called up at the "Inkwhich" with unfortunate results to himself. Nemo is buried in the strangers' ground in the neighbouring churchyard, and it is there that Lady Dedlock is found dead clinging to the railings of the closed gate.

HAWDON. Esther. *See* Summerson, Esther.

HAWK. Sir Mulberry, Guest and client of Ralph Nickleby. *N.N.* xix.
Another superlative gentleman, something older, something stouter, something redder in the face.

Note.—A man about town: maintains himself largely by fleecing young men of wealth less versed in the way of the world than himself. One of these, a character in the book, is Lord Verisopht. Hawk fought a duel with him and killed him. This obliged Sir Mulberry to leave the country. He resided abroad for some years, but on returning to this country he was thrown into prison, where he died. Hawk was a connection of Ralph Nickleby's from whom he learns about Kate. Nicholas heard him insult his sister by name in a public place, and in spite of his refusal to disclose his identity Nicholas managed to inflict punishment upon him.

HAWKINS. A middle-aged baker. *L.D.* xxv.
Defendant in Miss Rigg's action for breach of promise.

HAWKINSES. The landed gentry. *N.N.* xxxv.
They are much richer than the Grimbles, and connected with them by marriage.

HAWKINSON. Aunt. *O.M.F.* lii.

HAWKYARD. Mr. Verity. *G.S.E.* iv.

A yellow-faced, peak-nosed gentleman, clad all in iron grey to his gaiters.

HAYDEN. Mrs., M. B. *M.P., C.*

HAYMARKET. The. *B.H.* xxi.; *U.T.* x.; *S.B.B.*, Scenes xvii.

HAYNES. Inspector, Of Police Force. *R.P., D.W.I.F.*

HAYWARD. Mr. *M.P., S.F.A.*

HAZEBRONCKE. *U.T.* xvii.

HAZEBRONCKE. *C.S., M.J.* v.

HEAD REGISTRAR. Of births. *M.P., L.W.O.Y.*

HEADSTONE. Mr. Bradley, Schoolmaster. *O.M.F.* xviii.

In his decent black coat and waistcoat, and decent white shirt, and decent formal black tie, and decent pantaloons of pepper and salt, with his decent silver watch in his pocket, and its decent hair-guard round his neck, looked a thoroughly decent young man of six-and-twenty.

Note.—Pauper lad trained as a teacher, and at the opening of the story is master of the boys' department of a school on the borders of Kent and Surrey. Charley Hexam becomes a pupil of his and Bradley falls passionately and unreasoningly in love with Lizzie Hexam. She, however, desires to have nothing to do with him; in fact goes rather in fear of him. Bradley broods so much on his unrequited love and is so intensely jealous of Eugene Wrayburn, that his mind becomes distorted. He attempts to murder Wrayburn, and believes he has succeeded. He is dogged by Rogue Riderhood, who has discovered the attempted murder and has traceed him to school. Rogue blackmails him heavily and renders his life unbearable by his persecution and insistence. Bradley, while at the Lock, which the Rogue attends, suddenly forces his enemy into the water locked in his own embrace, and both are drowned.

HEALTH. Officer of. and **HUMBUGS.** Variety of, in cocked hats *L.D.* ii.

HEATHFIELD. Daughter of Mr. and Mrs. *C.B., B.o.L.* iii.

HEATHFIELD. Doctor, Alfred. *C.B., B.o.L.* iii.

HEATHFIELD. Mr., Alfred, Ward of Dr. Jeddler. *C.B., B.o.L.* i.

A handsome young man.

HEATHFIELD. Mrs., Neé Grace Jeddler. *C.B., B.o.L.* iii.

"**HEDGERS.** The Three Jolly," An Inn. *U.T.* xi.

HEENAN. Mr. John, Picture of. *U.T.* x.

HEEP. Mr., Uriah's father. *D.C.* xxxix.

Brought up at a foundation school for boys.

HEEP. Mrs., Uriah Heep's mother. *D.C.* xxxix.

Brought up at a public sort of charitable establishment, "Taught us a deal of umbleness."

HEEP. Uriah, Mr. Wickfield's clerk. *D.C.* xv.

A youth of fifteen, but looking much older—whose hair was cropped as close as the closest stubble, who had hardly any eyebrows, and no eyelashes, and eyes of a red-brown.

Note.—Uriah is first clerk to Mr. Wickfield, but he is humble and hypocritical, and, behind his back, schemes successfully for years. Part of his plan is to make himself indispensable to his employer, and so Uriah's influence becomes stronger, until he is taken into partnership. By sharp practice, deception, and dishonest manipulation, he obtains control of the property at the intended expense of Wickfield's ruin. This, however, is prevented by Mr. Micawber, who was taken as Uriah's clerk and factotum. But instead of being the tool, willing or unwilling, but compelled by necessity, he is the means of producing Uriah's downfall. And Mr. Wickfield's name is saved.

HEIDELBERG. Student beerhouses at. *C.S., H.T.*

HEIRESSES. Characters in play. *N.N.* xxiii.

Given by Mr. V. Crummles' Company.

HELENA. Miss Mell, fourth daughter of Doctor Mell. *D.C.* xxxiv.

HELL GATE. *A.N.* v.

HELMSMAN. Spirit. *C.B., C.C.* s. iii.

HELVES. Captain, One of Steam Excursion party. *S.B.B.*, Tales vii.

HENDERSON. *M.P.*, *R.S.L.*

HENDERSON. Mrs. *M.P.*, *R.S.D.*

HENDON. *O.T.* xlviii.

HENLEY. *L.D.* xiii.

HENRI. A young man who had belonged to the Inn in Switzerland ... who had disappeared. *C.S.*, *H.T.*

HENRIETTA. Mr. Click's sweetheart. *C.S.*, *S.L.* iii.
In the bonnet-trimming.

HENRIETTA. Miss Nupkins. *P.P.* xxv.
Possessed all her mamma's haughtiness without the turban, and all her ill-nature without the wig.

HENRY. A Negro man-slave. *A.N.* xvii.

HENRY. Brother of Kate. *P.P.* xvii. Cousin of Maria Lobbs.

HENRY. Mr., Gentleman behind counter in pawnbroker's shop. *S.B.B.*, Scenes xxiii.
With curly black hair, diamond ring, and double silver watch-guard.

HENRY. Son of the drunkard. *S.B.B.*, Tales xii.
Dead. Shot like a dog by a gamekeeper.

HENRY V. *M.P.*, *W.H.*

HEPBURN. English seaman. *M.P.*, *L.A.V.* i.

HER MAJESTY'S THEATRE. *U.T.* iv.

HERALD. *N.N.* iv.

HERALDS' COLLEGE. *O.M.F.* ii.

HERBERT. *See* Pocket, Herbert.

HERBERT. Mr., *M.P.*, *O.L.N.O.*

HERBERT. Mr., M.P. *B.R.* lxxiii.
Rose, and called upon the House to observe that Lord George Gordon was then sitting under the gallery with the blue cockade, the signal of rebellion in his hat.

HERCULANEUM. *P.F.I.*, *R.D.*

HERMIT. A. *C.S.*, *T.T.G.* i.
A slothful, unsavoury, nasty reversal of the laws of human nature.

HERMITAGE. *P.F.I.*

" **HERO OF WATERLOO.**" A public house. *R.P.*, *D.W.T.T.*

HEROD. *M.P.*, *R.D.*

HEROES. Roman, clowns in Booth in Greenwich Fair. *S.B.B.*, Scenes xii.

HERRING. Mr. *M.P.*, *T.C.f.B.*

HERSCHEL. John, John's first cousin. *C.S.*, *H.H.*

HERSCHEL. Mrs., Wife of John Herschel. *C.S.*, *H.H.*

HERTFORDSHIRE. *B.H.* iii.; *C.S.*, *M.L.Lo.* i.; *M.P.*, *C.P.*; *M.P.*, *S.R.*; *O.M.F.* xliii.; *U.T.* xi.; *R.P.T.D.P.*

HERTFORDSHIRE FRIEND. *M.P.*, *P.M.B.*

HESKETH. Newmarket. *L.T.* i.

HE SING. Mandarin passenger. *M.P.*, *C.J.*

HEWITT. Bro. *M.P.*, *S.B.*

HEXAM. Charlie. *O.M.F.* i.
Note.—Son of Gaffer Hexam and brother of Lizzie. His great aim is to become "respectable." His sister assists him to study while he is a boy. He becomes a pupil of Bradley Headstone, and endeavours to persuade Lizzie to accept the schoolmaster's offer of marriage. When she rejects Bradley he renounces her. And later he connects Bradley with the attack on Eugene Wrayburn and casts him off—because any acquaintance with a suspected murderer would interfere with his respectability. The story leaves him an under-master at another school, looking forward to filling the shoes of the headmaster and planning if he desires it, to marry the schoolmistress.

HEXAM. Dwelling of. *O.M.F.* iii.
The low building had the look of having once been a mill. There was a rotten wart of wood upon its forehead that seemed to indicate where the sails had been. The boy lifted the latch of the door. They passed at once into a low, circular room. The fire was in a rusty brazier, not fitted to the hearth, and a common lamp, shaped like a hyacinth root, smoked and flared in the neck of a stone bottle on the table. There was a wooden bunk or berth

in a corner, and in another corner a wooden stair leading above.

HEXAM. "Jesse, Gaffer." A waterman. *O.M.F.* i.

A strong man with ragged, grizzled hair, and a sun-browned face—no covering on his matted head—brown arms bare to between elbow and shoulder—loose knot of a loose kerchief lying low on his bare breast, in a wilderness of beard and whisker—a hooknosed man, and with that and his bright eyes and his ruffled head bore a certain likeness to a roused bird of prey.

Note.—Gaffer Hexam was one of the "night birds" of the river robbing dead bodies floating on the tide. He finds the body believed to be that of John Harmon and, chiefly owing to the insinuations of Rogue Riderhood, is accused of his murder. When preparations are made to arrest him on the charge, he is found trailing in the wake of his own boat.

HEXAM. Lizzie, Daughter of Hexam. *O.M.F.* i.

A dark girl of nineteen or twenty, pulling a pair of sculls very easily.

Note.—Daughter of Gaffer Hexam, and sister of Charley. She is very much opposed to her father's method of making a living, although she assists him, to the extent of rowing the boat. When her father is drowned, she leaves home. Eugene Wrayburn becomes greatly interested in her and assists her; Bradley Headstone falls in love with her, but she refuses his offer of marriage. Headstone becomes intensely, even madly, jealous of Eugene, and annoying to Lizzie. To avoid his distasteful attentions and to lessen the risk of meeting Eugene, Lizzie leaves London secretly, and with the assistance of Riah obtains employment in a mill up the river. Wrayburn succeeds in tracing her by bribing "Mr. Dolls." He follows her, and is in turn followed by Bradley Headstone. After Eugene has seen Lizzie, Bradley makes a murderous attack upon him. He is rescued by Lizzie, although his life is despaired of. He (Wrayburn) marries her, and recovers.

HEXAM. Lizzie, Temporary lodging of. *O.M.F.* xviii.

Some little quiet houses in a row—one of these. The boy knocked at a door, and the door promptly opened with a spring and a click—a parlour door within a small entry stood open.

HEYLING. George's surname. *P.P.* xxi.

Although evidently not past the prime of life, his face was pale and haggard. Disease or suffering had done more to work a change in his appearance than the mere hand of time could have accomplished in twice the period of his whole life.

Note.—Heyling's wife's father casts him into prison for debt. Heyling's father dies leaving him a wealthy man. He at once obtains his release from the Marshalsea. During his imprisonment his wife and child die from property and its privation. He devotes himself to revenge. First he sees his wife's brother drown without making an effort to save him, despite the entreaties of the father. He then reduces the father to a state he himself had occupied. The churchyard in which the young mother and child lie buried is that of Shorne.

HICKS. Septimus, A boarder at Mrs. Tibbs. *S.B.B.*, Tales i.

A tallish, white-faced man, with spectacles, and a black ribbon round his neck instead of a neckerchief—a most interesting person: a poetical walker of the hospitals, and a very talented man . . . fond of lugging into conversations all sorts of quotations from Don Juan.

HICKS. Septimus, Father of. *S.B.B.*, Tales i.

HICKSON. Mr., *S.B.B.*, Scenes xix.

HICKSONS. The, Guests of the Gattletons. *S.B.B.*, Tales ix.

HIGDEN. Betty, Home of. *O.M.F.* xvi.

A small home with a very large mangle in it, at the handle of which machine stood a very long boy.—In a corner below the mangle, on a couple of stools, sat two very little children. The room was clean and neat. It had a brick floor and a window of diamond panes, and a flounce hanging below the chimney-piece and strings nailed from bottom to top outside the window, on which scarlet beans were to grow.

HIGDEN. Mrs. Betty. *O.M.F.* xvi.

An active old woman, with a bright dark eye, and a resolute face, yet quite a tender creature too; nigher fourscore year than three-score and ten.

Note.—Poor old Betty kept a "minding school" and a mangle, at Brentford. By the aid of both she had kept out of the poor house, and she hoped to do so through out. She refuses much assistance from the Boffins, and starts out on a tramp with little goods for sale; but the "deadness" steals over her more frequently and more completely, until at last she dies in Lizzie Hexam's arms.

HIGHBURY BARN. *M.P., E.T.*

HIGH 'CHANGE. *L.D.* lxi.

HIGHGATE. *B.H.* lvii.; *B.R.* iv.; *D.C.* xx.; *P.P.* i.; *S.U.T.H.* i.

HIGHGATE. Dr. Strong's house in. *D.C.* vii.

Not in that part of Highgate where Mrs. Steerforth lived, but quite on the opposite side of the little town.

HIGHGATE. Village of. *O.T.* xlviii.

HIGHGATE ARCHWAY. *O.T.* xlii.; *C.S.H.T.*

HIGHGATE HILL. *O.T.* xlviii.

HIGH HOLBORN. *L.D.* xii.; *M.C.* xlix.

HIGHLANDS. Of the North River. *A.N.* xv.

HIGHLANDS. Scottish. *C.S., H.T.*; *R.P., A.C.T.*

HIGH SCHOOL. Edinburgh. *M.P., S.P.*

HIGH SHERIFF. Of Suffolk. *M.P., F.S.*

HIGH STREET. *M.P., G.H.*; *N.N.* xxiii; *O.M.F.* xli; *O.T.* iii.

HIGH STREET. Borough. *P.P.* xxx. *See also* "White Hart Inn."

HIGH STREET. Cloisterham. *E.D.* xii.

The natural channel in which the Cloisterham Channel flows.

HIGH STREET. Mr. Sapsea's premises in. *E.D.* iv.

(Over and against the Nuns' House) irregularly modernised here and there—more and more, that they preferred air and light to Fever and Plague.

HIGH STREET. Of market town. *G.E.* viii.

HIGH STREET. Rochester. *E.D.* iii.; *P.P.* ii. *See also* "Bull Inn."

HIGH STREET. The, Where the prison stood. *L.D.* ix.

HIGHWAYS. Old trodden, Of Rome. *L.D.* li.

H. I. J. Ensigns. Nobodies. *R.P., N.S.*

HILL. Mr. Rowland. *M.P., M.E.R.*; *M.P., S.S.*; *M.P., R.H.F.*

HILTON. Mr., Guest at Minerva House. *S.B.B.,* Tales iii.

Undertaken the office of Master of the Ceremonies on occasion of half-yearly ball, given by the Misses Crumpton.

HILTON. Young. *S.B.B.,* Tales iii.

HIMALAYA MOUNTAINS. *M.P., R.T.*; *M.P., S.R.*

HIMSELF. Somebody. *C.S., S.L.* iv.

HINE. William, A young duellist, aged thirteen. *A.N.* xvii.

HIPPOPOTAMUS. The Good. *M.P., G.H.*

HIS WIFE. And two sisters-in-law." *U.T.* ii.

Came in among the bodies of ten of the shipwrecked.

HOBBS. *M.P., T.T.*

HOBLER. Mr., The Lord Mayor's Clerk. *S.B.B.,* xvii.

HOCKER. Thomas, Murderer. *M.P., C.P.*

HOCKLEY-IN-THE-HOLE. *O.T.* viii.

HOGARTH. *M.P., C.P.*; *M.P., O.L.N.O.*; *M.P.S.*; *M.P., S.F.A.*

HOGARTH. James, Mrs. J. Ballantyne's brother. *M.P., S.P.*

HOG'S BACK. The. *A.N.* v.

HOGG. Sir James. *M.P., G.A.*

HOGHTON TOWERS. A farmhouse. *G.S.E.* iv.

A house, centuries old, deserted and falling to pieces.

HOLBEIN. *M.P., R.D.*

HOLBORN. *B.H.* iv. ; *E.D.* xi. ; *L.D.* xiii. ; *M.C.* xiii. ; *P.P.* xlvii. ; *O.T.* xxi. ; *S.B.B.*, Scenes vii. *S.U.T.H.* i.

HOLBORN COURT. Now South Square. *D.C.* xxx. ; *P.P.* xxxii.

HOLBORN HILL. *B.H.* i. ; *O.T.* xxvi. ; *G.E.* xxi. ; *B.R.* lxi.

HOLBORN UNION. *M.P., P.T.* ; *U.T.* xiv.

HOLLAND. *B.R.* lxxxii.

HOLLAND. King of. *M.P., R.S.D.*

HOLLAND STREET. *R.P., D.W.T.T.*

HOLLIDAY. Arthur. *L.T.*

HOLLIN'S SOVEREIGN MILL. Mr. *M.P., O.S.*

HOLLINSWORTH. Mr., As Mr. Owen Overton. *M.P., S.G.*

HOLLOWAY. *O.M.F.* iv. ; *S.B.B.*, Scenes xvii.

HOLLOWAY. Professor, Of Holloway's ointment. *M.P., F.F.* ; *M.P.M.P.* ; *R.P., B.S.*

HOLLOWAY ROAD. *N.N.* xxxvi.

"**HOLLY TREE.**" The, An Inn. *C.S., H.T.*

Place of good entertainment for man and beast.

"**HOLLY TREE INN.**" Bedrooms in. *C.S., H.T.*

"**HOLLY TREE INN.**" Landlady of. *C.S., H.T.*

"**HOLLY TREE INN.**" Landlord of. *C.S., H.T.*

"**HOLLY TREE INN.**" The ostler, potboy, and stable authorities of. *C.S., H.T.*

HOLMES. Dr. Oliver Wendell. *M.P., I.W.M.*

HOLMES. Mrs. *M.P., I.W.M.*

HOLYHEAD. *A.N.* xvi. ; *B.H.* xxiv.; *M.P., E.S.* ; *S.B.B.* Scenes xv.

HOLYROOD. Palace, and chapel. *P.P.* xlix. ; *U.T.* xxxiv.

HOLYWELL STREET. *S.B.B* Scenes vi.

HOME. Daniel Dunglas. *M.P., M.M.* ; *M.P., R.S.D.*

HOME. Mrs. *M.P., M.M.*

HOME. For homeless women. *M.P., H.H.W.*

HOME. Of James Carker, Manager of Dombeys'. *D. and S.* xxxiii.

Situated in the green and wooded country near Norwood. It is not a mansion ; it is of no pretensions as to size ; but it is beautifully arranged and tastefully kept.

HOME. Of John Carker, "the junior" in Dombey's. *D. and S.* xxxiii.

It is a poor, small house, barely and sparely furnished, but very clean ; and there is even an attempt to decorate it, shown in the homely flowers trained about the porch and in the narrow garden. The neighbourhood in which it stands has as little of the country to recommend it, as it has of the town.

HOME DEPARTMENT. Secretary of State for. *M.P., F.C.* ; *O.T.* xi.

HOME OFFICE. *R.P., P.M.T.P.*

HOME SECRETARY. *R.P., P.M. T.P.* ; *M.P., M.P.* ; *M.P., S.D.C.* ; *R.P., O.o.T.*

HOMINY. Major. *M.C.* xxii.

One of our choicest spirits ; and belongs to one of the most aristocratic families.

HOMINY. Miss. *M.C.* xxii.

HOMINY. Mrs. Wife of Mr. Hominy. *M.C.* xxii.

Very straight, very tall, and not at all flexible in face or figure. On her head she wore a great straw bonnet, with trimmings of the same colour—in her hand she held a most enormous fan.

HONDURAS. *C.S., P.o.C.E.P.*

HONDURAS SWAMPS. *U.T.* xxiv.

HONEST TOM. Colleague of—M.P. *S.B.B.*, Scenes xviii.

The large man in the cloak with the white lining, with the light hair hanging over his coat collar.

HONEYTHUNDER. Old Mr. (Luke). Chairman of Committee of Philanthropists. *E.D.* vi.

Note.—One of those canting hypocrites without which a novel by Dickens would be scarcely complete. He is guardian to Helen and Neville Landless, and is first seen when he brings his wards to Cloisterham. After Neville is suspected of the murder of Edwin Drood, Mr. Honeythunder gladly washes his hands of his guardianship in favour of the Rev. Crisparkle, who tells him a few truths about himself.

HONG KONG. *B. H.* lv.

HONORIA. Lady Dedlock. *B.H.* liv.

HOOD. Mr. Tom. *M.P., Ag. Int.*; *M.P., L.A.V.* i.; *M.P., L.S.*; *M.P., Th. Let.*

HOODLE. *B.H.* xii.

HOOKEM. Sir Snivey. *Mud. Pap.* ii.

HOPE. Miss Flite's bird. *B.H.* xiv.

HOPKINS. *O.M.F.* xlviii.

HOPKINS. Candidate for beadle's post, with seven small children. *S.B.B., O.P.* iv.

HOPKINS. Captain, Debtor in King's Bench prison. *D.C.* xi. Shared the room with Mr. Micawber.

HOPKIN'S. Captain, daughters. *D.C.* xi.

Two were girls with shock heads of hair.

HOPKINS. Jack, Hospital Student. *P.P.* xxxii.

He wore a black velvet waistcoat, with thunder-and-lightning buttons; and a blue-striped shirt, with a white false collar.

Note.—A medical student at Bartholomews, the friend of Bob Sawyer, and somewhat of the same kidney.

HOPKINS. Mr. *S.Y.G.*

HOPKINS. Mrs., Captain Hopkins' wife. *D.C.* xi.

A very dirty lady.

HOPKINS. The Heaven-born. *M.H.C.* iii.

The great witch-finder of the age.

HOPWOOD. *M.P., O.S.*

HORN. Cape. *C.S., M.f.T.S.* ii.

"**HORN COFFEE-HOUSE.**" In Doctors' Commons. *P.P.* xliv.

HORNBY. Henry, Of Blackburn. *M.P., O.S.*

HORNER. L. *M.P., O.C.*

HORNER. Mr. *S.B.B.*, Scenes xii.

The man of Colosseum notoriety.

HORNSEY. Churchyard at. *D.C.* xxv.

HORSE GUARDS. The. *B.R.* lxxxii.; *D.C.*, vi.; *M.C.* xiv.; *M.P., Th. Let.*; *M.P., T.O.H.*; *N.N.* xli.

"**HORSE GUARDS.**" Guest of Mr. Merdle. *L.D.* xxi.

HORSEMAN. A. *B.R.* lvi.; *M.H.C.* iii.

HORSEMONGER LANE. *L.D.* xviii.; *M.P., F.S.*

HORSEMONGER LANE JAIL. *R.P., L.A.*

HORTENSE. Mlle., Lady Dedlock's maid. *B.H.* xii.

A Frenchwoman of two-and-thirty—a large-eyed brown woman with black hair; who would be handsome but for a certain feline mouth, and general uncomfortable tightness of face, rendering the jaws too eager, and the skull too prominent. Like a very neat she-wolf imperfectly tamed.

Note.—Maid to Lady Dedlock. When she is introduced to the story she has been in the service five years, and becomes jealous of Rosa. She learns something of Lady Dedlock's secret, and shoots Mr. Tulkinghorn. The crime is carefully traced to her by Mr. Bucket, and she leaves the story in custody, still defiant.

HORTON. Miss, P., Actress. *M.P., R.S.L.*

HOSIER LANE. *O.T.* xxi.

HOSPICE. The. *C.S., N.T.* Act iii.

HOSPICE. The, founded by Napoleon. *P.F.I., V.M.M.S.S.*

HOSPITAL. A patient in casualty ward. *S.B.B.*, Char. vi.

Her recovery was extremely doubtful.... A fine young woman of about two or three and twenty. Her face bore marks of the ill-usage she had received. She was evidently dying.... It was an accident. "He didn't hurt me, he wouldn't for the world. Jack, they shall not persuade me to swear your life away. He never hurt me. Some kind gentleman, take my love to my poor old father. He said he wished I had died a child—oh, I wish I had."

HOSPITAL. Dressers at. *S.B.B.*, Char. vi.
A couple of young men who smelt strongly of tobacco.

HOSPITAL. East London Children's. *U.T.* xxx.
Established in an old-sail-loft or storehouse, of the roughest nature, and on the simplest means. I found it airy, sweet and clean.

HOSPITAL. House Surgeon of. *S.B.B.*, Char. vi.

HOSPITAL. Medical officers and directors of East London Children's. *U.T.* xxx.
A young husband and wife, both have had considerable practical experience of medicine and surgery.

HOSPITAL. Some public. *S.B.B.*, Char. vi.
A refuge and resting place for hundreds, who but for such institutions must die in the streets and doorways.

HOSPITAL. The Royal. *P.F.I.*, *R.D.*

HOSPITALS. One of the large, In London. *D.C.* xxv.
You understand it now, "Trot," said my aunt. "He is gone." "Did he die in Hospital?" "Yes."

HOSTLER. *P.P.* li.
Expected the first gold medal from the Humane Society—for taking the postboy's hat off; the water descending from the brim of which—must inevitably have drowned him (the postboy) but for his great presence of mind.

HOSTLER. From Inn in Rochester. *C.S.*, *S.P.T.* i.

HOSTLERS. At the Great White Horse. *P.P.* xxiv.

HOTEL. At Leamington, where Dombey stayed. *D. and S.* xx.

HOTEL. Coketown. *H.T.*, *R.* ii.

HOTEL. Handsome, Where Nicholas overheard Sir Mulberry Hawk. *N.N.* xxxii.

HOTEL. In Brook Street. *L.D.* lii.

HOTEL. In Brook Street. Landlord of. *L.D.* lii.

HOTEL. At which Mr. Dick stopped in Canterbury. *D.C.* xvii.

HOTEL. In Canterbury. *D.C.* lii.
Thro' various close passages; which smelt as if they had been steeped, for ages, in a solution of soup and stables.

HOTEL. In Yarmouth. *D. C.* v.

HOTEL. National. *M.C.* xxi
An immense white edifice, like an ugly hospital.

HOTEL. Near Charing Cross. *B.R.* lxvi.

HOTEL. Pegwell Bay. *S.B.B.*, Tales iv.

HOTEL. Two waiters of Pegwell Bay. *S.B.B.*, Tales iv.

HOTEL CAPULET. Padrona of the. *P.F.I.*, *V.M.M.S.S*

HÔTEL DE FRANCE. Calais. *U.T.* xvii.

HÔTEL DE VILLE. *T.T.C.*, bk. ii. ch. xxii.

HÔTEL DE VILLE. Premises of Monsieur Salcy. *U.T.* xxv.
Had established his theatre in the whitewashed Hotel de Ville.

HOTEL, GREENWICH. Lovely woman. *O.M.F.* xxv.

HOUNSDITCH. *B.R.* lxiii.; *P.P.* xliii.; *R.P.*, *B.S.*

HOUNDSDITCH CHURCH. *U.T.* xxxiv.

HOUNSLOW. *M.C.* xiii.; *O.T.* xxi.; *U.T.* xiv.

HOUNSLOW HEATH. *G.E.* xlviii.; *M.P.*, *R.T.*

HOUSE. A large wooden, in Putney. *M.H.C.* iii.

HOUSE. In Thames Street. *N.N.* xi.
Old and gloomy and black, in truth it was, and sullen and dark were the rooms, once so bustling with life and enterprise.

HOUSE. In George's Yard. *S.B.B.*, *O.P.* v.
There was a little piece of enclosed dust in front of the house, with a cinder path leading up to the door, and an open rain-water butt on one

side. A dirty striped curtain, on a very slack string, hung in the window, and a little triangular bit of broken looking-glass rested on the sill inside.

HOUSE. In St. Mary Axe. *O.M.F.* xxii.

A yellow-overhanging plaster-fronted house.

HOUSE. On the Common Hard, Portsmouth, where Nicholas and Smike lodged. *N.N.* xxiii.

HOUSE. Lodging in Ramsgate. *S.B.B.*, Tales iv.

With a bay window from which you could obtain a beautiful glimpse of the sea—if you thrust half your body out of it, at the imminent peril of falling into the area.

HOUSE. Near Barbican. *B.R.* viii.

From whose defaced and rotten front the rude effigy of a bottle swung to and fro like some gibbeted malefactor.

HOUSE. Occupied by city clerk. *S.B.B.*, *O.P.* vii.

A neat, dull little house, on the shady side of the way, with new narrow floorcloth in the passage, and new narrow stair-carpets up to the first floor. The paper was new, the paint was new, and all three bespoke the limited means of the tenant.

HOUSE. Our, Corner House—not far from Cavendish Square. *O.M.F.* v.

It was a great dingy house, with a quantity of dim side window and blank back premises.

HOUSE. Our. Joe Gargery's. *G.E.* ii.

A wooden house, as many of the dwellings in our country were.

HOUSE. Private, Tenant of. *S.B.B.*, Scenes iii.

HOUSE. Senate. *P.F.I.*, *G.A.N.*

HOUSE. Silver, The Fort, the Mine. *C.S.*, *P. o. C.E.P.*

HOUSE. The. *B.H.* xii.

HOUSE. The, Workhouse. *O.M.F.* xvi. ; *S.B.B.*, *O.P.*

"**HOUSE.** The Early Purl," Inscription on the doorpost of The Six Jolly Fellowship Porters. *O.M.F.* vi.

HOUSE. The Haunted. *C.S.*, *H.H.*

HOUSE. The Nuns'. *E.D.* ii.

In the midst of Cloisterham—a venerable brick edifice. The house front is old and worn, and the brass plate is so shining and staring, that the general result has reminded imaginative strangers of a battered old beau with a large modern eyeglass in his blind eye.

HOUSE. Which shall be nameless, where somebody's luggage was left. *C.S.*, *S.L.* i.

HOUSE. With the green blinds. *S.B.B.*, Char. iii.

HOUSE AT BATH. *P.P.* xxxvi.

HOUSE GOVERNMENT. *P.F.I.*, *G.A.N.*

HOUSE OF ASSEMBLY. Members of the. *A.N.* ii.

HOUSE OF COMMONS. *M.P.*, *B.S*; *M.P.*, *C.P.* ; *M.P.*, *F.C.* ; *M.P.*, *G.B.*, ; *M.P.*, *I.M.* ; *M.P.*, *O.C.* ; *M.P.*, *P.L.U.* ; *M.P.*, *R.T.* ; *M.P.*, *S.S.* ; *M.P.*, *Th. Let.* ; *S.B.B.* s. iv., xiv.

HOUSE OF CORRECTION. *M.P.*, *L.W.O.Y.* ; *M.P.*, *S.*

HOUSE OF CORRECTION. Middlesex. *M. P.*, *C. and. E.*

HOUSE OF CORRECTION FOR THE STATE. S. Boston. *A.N.* iii.

HOUSE OF DETENTION. Clerkenwell. *M.P.*, *M.P.*

HOUSE OF INDUSTRY. South Boston. *A.N.* iii.

Worthy of notice. Self Government, quietude and peace.

HOUSE OF LORDS. *M.P.*, *C.P.* ; *M.P.*, *P.P.* ; *P.P.* lv. ; *S.B.B.* Scenes xviii.

HOUSE OF REFORMATION. For Juvenile Offenders. South Boston. *A.N.* iii.

HOUSE OF REPESENTATIVES. Washington. *M.P.*, *Y.M.C.*

HOUSEBREAKER. Keeper of a country Inn. *C.S., H.T.*
Had had his right ear chopped off.

HOUSEBREAKER. Wife of. *C.S., H.T.*

Who heated the poker and terminated his career, for which—she received the compliments of royalty on her great discretion and valour.

" HOUSEHOLD WORDS " OFFICE. *R.P., T.D.P.*

HOUSEKEEPER. John Podger's. *M.H.C.* iii.

Afflicted with rheumatism— burnt as an undoubted witch.

HOUSEKEEPER. Of Cheeryble Brothers. *N.N.* xxxvii.

HOUSEMAID. At Number 23. *S.B.B., O.P.* iii

HOUSEMAID. Dombey's. *D. and S.* xviii.

HOUSEMAID. Mrs. Tibbs'. *S.B.B.*, Tales i.

HOUSEMAID. Of Cheeryble Brothers. *N.N.* xxxvii.

HOUSEMAID. Of Mrs. Maylie. *O.T.* xxviii.

HOUSES. The night. *S.B.B.*, Scenes i.

HOVELLERS. *R.P., O.o.S.*

Kentish name for longshore boatmen.

HOWARD. Mr. *M.P., S. Pigs.*

HOWE. Dr. Head of Asylum for the Blind at Boston. *A.N.* iii.

HOWE. Lord. *M.P., C.C.*

HOWE. Lord Chamberlain. *M.P., S. for P.*

HOWITT. Mr. William. *M.P., M.M.* ; *M.P., R.S.D.*

HOWLER. Reverend Melchisedech Minister of the Ranting Persuasion *D. and S.* xv.

Having been one day discharged from the West India Docks on a false suspicion (got up expressly against him by the general enemy) of screwing gimlets into puncheons and applying his lips to the orifice, had announced the destruction of the world for that day two years, at ten in the morning, and opened a front palour for the reception of ladies and gentlemen of the Ranting persuasion.

HOWN. A runaway negro slave. *A.N.* xvii.

HOWSA KUMMAUNS. Peerless Chatterer. Official name of wife of Taxedtaurus. *M.P., T.O.H.*

Note.—House of Commons.

HUBBLE. Mr. The Wheelwright. *G.E. iv.*

A tough, high-shouldered, stooping old man, of a saw-dusty fragrance, with his legs extraordinarily wide apart.

Note.—Friend of Joe Gargery's wife. Last seen in the funeral procession of Mrs. Gargery.

HUBBLE. Mrs., Wife of wheelwright. *G.E.* iv.

A little curly, sharp-eyed person in sky blue.

HUDDART. Miss. *M.P., R.S.L.*

HUDIBRAS. Lud, King of Great Britain. *P.P.* xxxvi.

He was a mighty monarch. The earth shook when he walked: he was so very stout. His people basked in the light of his countenance: it was so red and glowing. He was indeed every inch a king. And there were a good many inches of him too, for although he was not very tall —the inches he wanted in height he made up for in circumference.

HUDSON. *A.N.* xv.

HUDSON. Mr. *M.P., G.A.*

HUDSON'S BAY COMPANY. *M.P., L.A.V.* i.

HUFFY. *B.H.* xii.

HUGGIN LANE. A City church in. *U.T.* ix.

HUGH. Father of, Sir John Chester. *B.R.*, lxxv.

HUGH. Mother of. *B.R.* xi.

Hung when he was a little boy, with six others, for passing bad notes.

HUGH. Ostler at the " Maypole." *B.R.* x.

He sleeps so desperate hard— that if you were to fire off cannon-balls into his ears, it would not wake him, said the distracted host. " Brisk enough when he is awake," said the guest. . . . Loosely attired in the coarsest and roughest garb, with scraps of straw and hay—his usual bed—clinging here and there, and mingling with his uncombed locks.

Note.—Hugh enters the story as hostler and general man at the " Maypole Inn." He is *au fait* with everything connected with horses, but he is entangled with the rioters and becomes a prominent figure amongst them. His extreme strength and wild devil-may-care athleticism render him particularly suitable for the part he plays. He gets into the power, the seductive power, of the superior gentleman Sir John Chester, and becomes a tool in his hand. It transpires that he is the illegitimate son of Sir John, but when he is threatened with the gallows, his father refuses to intervene on his behalf. And Hugh, the friend of Barnaby, suffers the extreme penalty with the utmost composure, or, rather, indifference.

HUGHES. Ladies of the family of the Reverend Stephen Roose. *U.T.* ii.

HUGHES. R., Gimaldi's executor. *M.P., J.G.*

HUGHES. Reverend Hugh Robert, of Penrhos. Brother of Stephen Roose Hughes. *U.T.* ii.

HUGHES. Reverend Stephen Roose. Clergyman of Llanallgo. *U.T.* ii.

I read more of the New Testament in the fresh, frank face (going up the village beside me) in five minutes, than I have read in anathematising discourses in all my life.

HUGO. M. Victor. *M.P., L.L.*

HULKS. *G.E.* ii., v., xv., xvi., liii.

"Hulks are prison-ships right 'cross th' meshes."

Note.—The hulk was the prison-ship from which the convict Magwitch escaped; and to which he was taken back when re-captured. Lying out a little way from the mud of the shore, the prison-ship, cribbed and barred, and moored by massive rusty chains, seemed, in Pip's young eyes, to be ironed like the prisoners.

HULL. *M.H.C.* i.

HULLAH. John. *M.P., F.C.*; *M.P., S.F.A.*; *M.P., V.C.*

HUMAN INTEREST. Brothers. *U.T.* i.

HUMBUG. Wan. *M.P.B.L.*

HUME. Joseph. *M.P., S. for P.* *M.P., T.D.*

HUMM. Mr. Anthony, President of the Ebenezer Temperance Association. *P.P.* xxxiii.

Straight-walking, a converted fireman, now a schoolmaster, and occasionally an itinerant preacher. A sleek, white faced man in a perpetual perspiration.

HUMMUMS. An Inn. In Covent Garden. *G.E.* xlv.; *S.B.B.*, Scenes i.

HUMPHREY. Duke, His Grace. *M.C.* i.

HUMPHREY. Master. *M.H.C.* i.

A misshapen, deformed old man.

HUMPHEY. Master. Such a very old man. *O.C.S.* i.

Note.—The " I " of the earlier chapters is supposed to be Master Humphrey, who is narrating the story. The " Old Curiosity Shop," first commenced in the fourth number of " Master Humphrey's Clock," a serial publication edited by Dickens, but which " became one of the lost books of the earth."

HUMPHREY. Master, House of. *M.H.C.* i.

A silent, shady place, with a paved courtyard. Its wormeaten doors, and low ceilings crossed by clumsy beams; its walls of wainscot, dark stairs, and gaping closets; its small chambers, communicating with each other by winding passages or narrow steps; its many nooks scarce larger than its corner cupboards; its very dust and dullness are all dear to me.

" **HUNGERFORD STAIRS**." Public-house. *D.C.* lvii.

The Micawber family were lodged in a little, dirty, tumble-down public-house, which in those days was close to the stairs, and whose protruding wooden rooms overhung the river.

HUNT. Captain Boldwig's head gardener. *P.P.* xix.

HUNT. Leigh. *M.P., L.H.*

HUNT. Leigh, Eldest son of. *M.P., L.H.*

HUNT. Robert. *M.P., P.S.*

HUNT AND ROSKELL. Messrs., Jewellers in New Bond Street. *M.P., I.M.*; *U.T.* xvi.

HUNTER. Horace. *S.B.B.*, Tales viii.

Note.—Party to a duel which never came off—who married Miss Emily Brown at Gretna Green.

HUNTER. Mr., Husband of Mrs. Leo Hunter. *P.P.* xv.

"Is it a gentleman?" said Mr. Pickwick. "A wery good imitation o' one, if it ain't," replied Mr. Weller. A grave man, with an air of profound respect.

Note.—Mr. Hunter lived in the reflected light of his wife.

HUNTER. Mrs. Fogle. *Mud. Pap.* ii.

HUNTER. Mrs. Leo, Poetess of "The Den," Eatanswill. *P.P.* xv.

"To-morrow morning, sir, we give a public breakfast . . . feasts of reason, sir, and flow of souls." . . . Mrs. Leo Hunter, writer of some delightful pieces .Ode . . to an Expiring Frog. It commenced:

Can I view thee panting, lying
On thy stomach, without sighing?
Can I unmoved see thee dying
On a log,
Expiring frog?

HUSBAND. First. *M.P., N.T.*

HUSBAND. Of friend to Little Em'ly. *D.C.* xxii.

The husband was come home then; and the two together put her aboard a small trader.

HUSBAND. Of other lady at wedding of Bunsby. *D. and S.* lx.

The short gentleman with the tall hat.

HUSBAND. Of the daughter of the deaf gentleman. *M.H.C.* vi.

HUSBAND. Of the married Miss Hominy. *M.C.* xxiii.

HUSBAND. Second. *M.P., N.T.*

HUSBANDS IN PERSPECTIVE. At tea gardens. *S.B.B.*, Scenes ix.

Ordering bottles of ginger-beer for the objects of their affections with a lavish disregard of expense.

HUTCHING. Mr. Thomas. *M.P., S.B.*

HUTLEY. James. *See* Dismal Jemmy.

HYDE PARK. *D.C.* xxviii,; *O.T.* xxxix.; *M.P., R.H.F.*

HYDE PARK CORNER. *G.E.* xxx.; *M.P., T.T.*; *O.M.F.* xliv.; *O.T.* xxi.; *R. P.,T.N.S.*

HYGEIAN COUNCIL of the British College of Health. Members of the. *M.P., M.P.*

HYGEIAN ESTABLISHMENT. King's Cross. *M.P., Ag. Int.*

HYPOLITE. Private, Billeted at the Perfumer's. *C.S., S.L.* ii.

Volunteered to keep shop, while the fair perfumeress stepped out to speak to a neighbour or so.

HYTHE. *D.C.* xii.

I

ICELAND. *O.M.F.* xxviii.

IDDÀH. On the Niger. *M.P., N.E.*

IDLE. Thomas. *L.T.*

IDLERS. Seeing Mark Tapley off. *M.C.* vii.

IDOL. The presiding, Of the Circumlocution Office. *L.D.* x.

IKEY. Sheriff officer's mercury. *S.B.B.*, Tales x.

A man in a coarse Petersham great-coat, whity-brown neckerchief, faded black suit. Gamboge-coloured top-boots, and one of those large crowned hats—now very generally patronised by gentlemen and costermongers.

IKEY. Stable man of Inn. *C.S., H.H.*

A high-shouldered young fellow, with a round face, a short crop of sandy hair, a very broad, humorous mouth, a turned-up nose, and a great sleeved waistcoat of purple bars, with mother-of-pearl buttons.

IMPERIAL. *M.P., W.*

IMPUDENCE. Little Miss. *E.D.* ii.

IMYANGER. An, A Witch doctor. *R.P., T.N.S.*

Sent for to Nooker the Umtargartie, or smell out the witch.

INCHBALD. Mrs. *M.P., L.S.*

INDEPENDENCE. *A.N.* xvii.

INDIA. *C.S., S.P.T.*; *C.S., T.T.G.* vi.; *D. and S.* viii.; *H.T. S.* xv.; *L.D.* lvii.; *M.C.*, xxvii.; *M.P., E.T.*; *M.P., L.L.*; *M.P., M.E.R.*; *M.P., N.G.K.*; *M.P., S.F.A.*; *R.P., A.C.T.*; *R.P., O.E.W.*; *R.P., P.M.T.P.*; *R.P., T.B W.*; *R.P., T.C.S.*; *U.T.* iv.

INDIA DOCKS. *D. and S.* ix.

INDIA HOUSE. *M.P., E.T.*; *M.P.*; *G.A.*; *M.P., I.S.H.W.*; *M.P. L.T.*; *U.T.* iii.

INDIAN. *C.S., G. into Soc.*

INDIAN. A wild, Exhibited at Greenwich Fair. *S.B.B.*, Scenes xii.

A young lady of singular beauty, with perfectly white hair and pink eyes.

INDIAN OCEAN. *H.R.* iii.

INDIAN PROPERTY. Mr. Bull's fine. *M.P., H.H.*

INDIANS. Chiefs of. *A.N.* ix.

INDIANS. North American. *U.T.* xxvi.

INDIANS. Ojibbeway. *R.P., T.N.S.*

INDIANS. Wyandot. *A.N.* xiv.

INDIES. East. *E.D.* iv.

INDIES. The. *U.T.* xv.

INDIES. West *S.B.B., O.P.* i.

INDIGENT ORPHANS' FRIENDS' BENEVOLENT INSTITUTION. A member of. *S.B.B.*, Scenes xix.

A large-headed man, with black hair and bushy whiskers.

INDIGENT ORPHANS' FRIENDS'. BENEVOLENT INSTITUTION. A member of. *S.B.B.*, Scenes xix.

A stout man in a white neckerchief and buff waistcoat, with shining dark hair, cut very short in front, and a great round, healthy face.

INDIGENT ORPHANS' FRIENDS' BENEVOLENT INSTITUTION. A member of. *S.B.B.*, Scenes xix

A round-faced person, in a dress-stock, and blue under-waistcoat.

INDIGENT ORPHANS' FRIENDS' BENEVOLENT INSTITUTION. Secretary of. *S.B.B.*, Scenes xix.

INDIGENT ORPHANS' FRIENDS' BENEVOLENT INSTITUTION. Titled visitors at dinner of. *S.B.B.*, Scenes xix.

INESTIMABLE. The, Life Assurance Office. *H.D.* ii.

INFANT BONDS OF JOY. *B.H.* viii.

INFANTS. *M.P., L.E.J.*

INGLIS. Sir Robert, Member for the University of Oxford. *M.P., C.J.*

INGOLDSBY. Thomas. *M.P., A.P.*

INN. *G.E.* lii.

Once been a part of an ancient ecclesiastical house.

INN. About half a quarter of a mile from the end of the Downs. *P.P.* xiv.

A strange old place, built of a kind of shingle, inlaid, as it were, with cross-beams, with gable-topped windows projecting completely over the pathway, and a low door with a dark porch.

INN. A famous, in Salisbury. *M.C.* xii.

The hall a very grove of dead game, and dangling joints of mutton; and in one corner an illustrious larder, with glass doors, developing cold fowls and noble joints, and tarts wherein the raspberry jam coyly withdrew itself—behind a lattice-work of pastry.

INN. A spacious. *B.H.* lvii.

Solitary, but a comfortable, substantial building "

INN. At Mugby. *C.S., M.J.* i.

INN. At which Wrayburn was nursed. *O.M.F.* lvi.

INN. Cornish. *C.S., H.T.*

INN. In Rochester. *C.S., S.P.T.* i.

INN. In the North of England. *C.S., H.T.*
Haunted by the ghost of a tremendous pie—a Yorkshire pie, like a fort, an abandoned fort, with nothing in it. The waiter had a fixed idea that it was a point of ceremony at every meal to put the pie on the table.

INN. In the remotest part of Cornwall. *C.S., H.T.*

INN. Landlord of an. *C.S., H.T.*
By the roadside, whose visitors unaccountably disappeared for many years, until it was discovered that the pursuit of his life had been to convert them into pies.

INN. Little, At which Micawber stopped in Canterbury. *D.C.* xvii.

INN. On the Welsh border *C.S., H.T.*
In a picturesque old town.

INN. Roadside, Where Nicholas met Crummles. *N.N.* xxii.

INN. Swiss. *M.P., N.T.*

INNER TEMPLE. *M.P., M.N.D.*

INNKEEPER. *L.T.*

INNS. English posting. *C.S., H.T.*
Which we are all so sorry to have lost.

INNS. German. *C.S., H.T.*
Where all the eatables are soddened down to the same flavour.

INNS. Highland. *C.S., H.T.*
With the oatmeal bannocks, the honey—the trout from the loch, the whiskey and—perhaps the Athol Brose.

INNS. The Anglers. *C.S., H.T.*

INNS. Welsh. *C.S., H.T.*
With the women in their round hats, and the harpers with their white beards (venerable, but humbugs, I am afraid) playing outside the door.

INNS OF COURT. B.R. lxvii. *M.H.C.* iv.; *S.B.B.*, Scenes i.

INSOLVENT COURT. *P.P.* xlii.

INSOLVENT COURT. Commissioners of the. *P.P.* xliii.
One, two, three, or four gentlemen in wigs, as the case may be, with little writing-desks before them, constructed after the fashion of those used by the judges of the land, barring the French polish. There is a box of barristers on their right hand; there is an enclosure of insolvent debtors on their left; and there is an inclined plane of most especically dirty faces in their front.

INSOLVENT DEBTORS COURT. *S.B.B.* xlii.

INSPECTOR. Connected with Circumlocution Office. *U.T.* viii.

INSPECTOR. Night. *O.M.F.* iii.
With a pen and ink and ruler posting up his books in a whitewashed office.

INSTITUTION. Indigent Orphans' Friends' Benevolent *S.B.B.*, Scenes xix.

INSTITUTIONS. Ladies' charitable. *S.B.B., O.P.* vi.

INSTITUTION FOR THE FOUND CHILDREN. In Paris. *L.D.* ii.

INTEREST. Monied, Passenger in train. *R.P., A.F.*

IOWA. *A.N.* xvii.; *D.C.* xxvi.; *M.P., F.S.*; *P.P.* xx.

IPSWICH. Market Place. *C.S., D.M.*

IPSWICH GAOL. Governor of. *M.P., F.S.*

IRELAND. *A.N.* xv.; *B.H.* xxiv. *H.T., R.* ii.; *M.P., E S*; *M.P, E.T.*; *M.P., F.O.E.G.*; *M.P., H.H.*; *M.P., L.W.O.Y.*; *M.P., Q.D.P.*; *M.P., R.S.*; *S.B.B.*, Tales i.; *U.T.* xxxi.

IRISH PEDLAR. *S.B.B., O.P.* vi.

IRISHWOMAN. An, at Mr. Skimpole's. *B.H.* lxi.
Breaking up the lid of a water-butt with a poker, to light the fire with.

IRON BRIDGE. *L.D.* xxii.

IRONWORKER. *O.C.S.* xliv.

IRVING. Washington. *M.P., I.C.*

IRVING. Washington. Appointed Minister at the Court of Spain. *A.N.* viii.

ISAAC. Coach driver. *P.P.* xlvi.
A shabby man in black leggings . . . with a thick ash stick in his hand . . . seated on the box (of the coach) smoking a cigar. The bashful gentleman.

ISAAC. Man slave. *A.N.* xvii.

ISLE OF MAN. *M.P., E.S., C.S., M.L.Lo.* i. ; *U.T.* xvii.

ISLE OF THANET. *R.P., A.P.A.*

ISLE OF WIGHT. *O.M.F.* x.

ISLEWORTH. *O.T.* xxi.

ISLINGTON. *B.H.* lix. ; *B.R.* xxxi.; *C.S., H.T.* iv. ; *C.S , M.L.Lo.* i ; *D. and S.* xiii. ; *M.C.* xxxvi. ; *M.H.C.* vi. ; *M.P., E.T., M.P., P.P.* ; *N.N.* xxxix. ; *O.T.* viii. ; *S.B.B.*, Scenes i. ; *S.B.B.*, Char. i.

ISLINGTON ROAD. *S.B.B.*, Char. i.

ITALIAN BOULEVARD. *U.T.* xii.

ITALIAN BOYS. *M.P., G.H.*

ITALIAN CAVALIERE. *M.P., N.Y.D.*

ITALIAN CITY. Protestant Cemetery near. *U.T.* xxvi.

ITALIAN PALACE. *C.S., H.H.*

ITALIAN PRISONER. *U.T.* xxviii.

ITALIANS. *P.P.* xxxiii. ; *P.F.I., T.R.P.*

ITALY. *C.S., H.T.* ; *C.S., S.P.T.* ; *D.C.* xi. ; *M.P., C.P.* ; *M.P., M.M.* ; *P.F.I.* ; *R.P., D.W.T.T.* ; *R.P., L.A.* ; *R.P., O.B.* ; *U.T.* vii.

ITALY, Inns in old monastry. *C.S., H.T.*
With their massive quadrangular staircases, whence you may look from among clustering pillars into the blue vault of heaven.

ITALY. Roadside Inns of. *C.S., H.T.*
When the mosquitoes make a raisin pudding of your face in summer, and the cold bites it blue in winter. Where you get what you can, and forget what you can't.

ITALY. The old palace inns. *C.S., H.T.*

ITRI. *P.F.I., R.D.*

IVINS. Friend of Miss Jemima. *S.B.B.*, Char. iv.

IVINS. Miss, Miss Jemima Evans. *S.B.B.*, Char. iv.
The pronounciation most in vogue with the circle of her acquaintance.

IVINS. Mrs. Mother of Jemima. *S.B.B.*, Char. iv.

IVINS. One of the younger Misses. *S.B.B.*, Char. iv.

IVINS. The youngest Miss. *S.B.B.*, Char. iv.

IVINS. The youngest Miss—but one *S.B.B.*, Char. iv.

IVINS. Young man of friend of Jemima. *S.B.B.*, Char. iv.

IVORY. A runaway negro man-slave. *A.N.* xvii.

IZZARD. Mr. *M.C.* xxxix.

J

JACK. A British, in the "Snug." *U.T.* v.
A little maudlin and sleepy, lolling over his empty glass as if he were trying to read his fortune at the bottom.

JACK. Cheap. *U.T.* xxii.

JACK. Engaged at Searle's boating establishment. *S.B.B.*, Scenes x.

JACK. Frying pan. *M.P., N.E.*

JACK. The Lord Mayor. *M.H.C.* i.

JACK. Mrs. Lupin's man. *M.C.* xxxvi.

JACK. Of the Little Causeway. *G.E.* liv.
Had a bloated pair of boots on, which he exhibited—as interesting relics—taken a few days ago from the feet of a drowned seaman washed ashore. . . . Probably it took about a dozen drowned men to fit him out completely.
Note.—The odd-job man at the Ship. (The "Ship and Lobster" near Gravesend.)

JACK. Prisoner under arrest. *S.B.B.*, Char. vi.
A powerful, ill-looking young fellow at the bar, undergoing an examination, on the very common charge of having, on the previous night, ill-treated a woman, with

whom he lived in some court hard by.

JACK. Runaway "negro boy" slave. *A.N* xvii.

JACK. Sailor. *U.T.* xx.

JACK. Secretary of Master Humphrey's Club. *M.H.C.* iv.

JACK. Suicide. *R.P., D.W.T.T.*

JACK OF SWEDEN. Visitor at the "Snug." *U.T.* v.

JACK SMOKE. *M.P., N.E.*

JACK SPRAT. *M.P., N.E.*

JACK THE FINN. Visitor at the "Snug." *U.T.* v.

JACKMAN. Major, Mrs. Lirriper's lodger. *C.S., M.L.L.o.*

Though he is far from tall, he seems almost so when he has his shirt-frill out, and his frock-coat on and his hat with the curly brim. His mustachios as black and shining as his boots, his head of hair being a lovely white.

JACKS. Cheap, *C.S., D.M.*

We tell 'em the truth about themselves to their faces, and scorn to court 'em.

JACKS. Dear, *C.S., D.M.*

Members of Parliament, platforms, pulpits, counsel learned in the law. These Dear Jacks soap the people shameful.

JACKSON. A certain, A turnkey. *L.D.* xix.

JACKSON. A crimp. *U.T.* v.

JACKSON. Andrew Davis. *M.P., R.S.D.*

JACKSON. General. *A.N.* iv.

JACKSON. Joe, A sailor. *U.T.* xx.

JACKSON. Michael. *B.H.* lvii.

With a blue velveteen waistcoat, with a double row of mother-of-pearl buttons.

JACKSON. Mr. *M.P., F.C.*

JACKSON. Mr. *S.Y.C.*

JACKSON. Mr., Clerk of Dobson and Fogg. *P.P* xx.

JACKSON. Mrs. *S.Y. C.*

JACKSON. Trainer for the ring. *D. and S.* lxi.

Kept the boxing-rooms in Bond Street—man of very superior qualifications—used to mention that in training for the ring they substituted rum for sherry.

JACKSON. Young, Of the firm of Barbox Brothers. *C.S., M.J.* ii.

JACOB'S ISLAND. *O.T.* l.; *U.T.* x.

JACOBS. Establishment of Mr. Solomon, Lock-up House. *S.B.B.*, Tales x.

JACOBS. Mr. Solomon. *S.B.B.*, Tales x

JACQUES. One to Four. *T.T.C.* v.

Note.—Principals in the Revolution, with Defarge.

JACQUES. Five. *T.T.C.* v.

Note.—The road-mender of the earlier part of the story. He becomes a woodsawyer, and ignorant but faithful watcher. A member of Defarge's revolutionary party.

JAGGERS. A lawyer. *G.E.* xviii.

A burly man of exceedingly dark complexion, with an exceedingly large head, and a correspondingly large hand—prematurely bald on the top of his head—had bushy black eyebrows that stood up bristling. His eyes were set very deep in his head, and were disagreeably sharp and suspicious.

Note.—Miss Havisham's legal advisor. He is first met with at Satis House, but he is frequently seen throughout the story in his characteristic attitude of biting his fore-finger. He is the only person Pip knows in connection with his great good fortune for a long time, as everything done for him is through Jaggers. He has a large criminal clientèle and conducted the case for Magwitch when he was recaptured. This is the last time he appears.

JAIL. *B.H.* vi.

JAIL. Kingston. *G.E.* xlii.

JAIL. The County. *G.E.* xii.

JAIL. The Pink. *P.F.I., G.A.N.*

JAILER. Of Marseilles prison. *L.D.* i.

Carrying his little daughter.—"My little one you see, going round with me to have a peep at her father's birds."

JAILS. Her Majesty's. *S.B.B.*, Char. xii.

JAIRING'S. First waiter at. *U.T.* vi.

Denuded of his white tie, making up his cruets.

JAIRING'S. Hotel for families and gentlemen. *U.T* vi.

JAIRING'S. Second waiter at. *U.T.* vi.

In a flabby undress, cleaning the windows of the empty coffee-room.

JAMAICA. *C.S., P. o.C.E.P.*; *D. and S.* xxxii.; *O.M.F.* ii.

JAMAICA HARBOUR. *D. and S.* iv.

JAMANNE. Miss. *M.P., U.N.*

JAMES. *S.Y.C.*

JAMES. Henry, Commander of barque "Defiance." *D. and S.* xxxi.

JAMES. Mr. Bayham Badger's butler. *B.H.* xiii.

JAMES. Mr. William Robert, Solicitor and clerk to the Holborn Union. *M.P., P.T.*

JAMES. Mrs. Tibbs' boy. *S.B.B.*, Tales i.

In a revived black coat of his master's.

JAMES. Negro boy-slave. *A.N.* xvii.

JAMES. Son of John. *R.P., P.M.T.P.*

JAMES RIVER. *A.N.* ix.

JAMES STREET. *N.N* vii.; *U.T.* xiv.

JAMES THE FIRST. King. *M.H.C.* iii.

JANE. Aunt, Baby of. *S.B.B.*, Char. ii.

Guest at Christmas family party.

JANE. Aunt, Inhabitant of corner house. *O.M.F.* v.

JANE. Daughter of a stout lady visitor at Ramsgate library. *S.B.B.*, Tales iv..

JANE. Hebe of Bellamy's. *S.B.B.*, Scenes xviii.

Female in Black—a character in her way. Her leading features are a thorough contempt for the great majority of her visitors: her predominant quality, love of admiration—no bad hand at repartees.

JANE. Mr. Orange's maid. *H.R.* iv.

JANE. Mr. Pecksniff's "Serving-maid." *M.C.* xxxi.

JANE. Servant at the Manor Farm Dingley Dell. *P.P.* v.

JANE. Servant girl in obscure public-house. *M.C.* xiii.

JANE. Servant of Mr. and Mrs. Kitterbell. *S.B.B.*, Tales xi.

JANE. Servant to Mr. and Mrs. Pott. *P.P.* xiii.

JANE. Sister of young lady, fiancee of great lord. *N.N.* xviii.

JANE. Suicide. *U.T.* iii.

JANE. Wardrobe woman at school. *R.P., T.S.S.*

JANE. Wife of Uncle Robert. *S.B.B.*, Char. ii.

Guest at Christmas family party.

JANET. Miss Trotwood's maid. *D.C.* xiii.

A pretty, blooming girl of about nineteen or twenty, and a perfect picture of neatness.

JANUS. Sir Jasper. *M.P., C. Pat.*

JAPAN. *E.D.* iv.

JARBER. *C.S., G. i. S.*

JARGON. Name of a bird. *B.H.* xiv.

JARLEY. Mrs., Of Jarley's wax-works. *O.C.S.* xxvi.

At the open door of the caravan sat a Christian lady, stout and comfortable to look upon, who wore a large bonnet trembling with bows.

Note.—The proprietor of the travelling wax-works. She falls in love with Little Nell and engages her to display the wax-works to visitors. Eventually she married her driver George. *See also* Coventry.

JARNDYCE. John. *B.H.* ii.

A handsome, lively, quick face, full of change and motion; and his hair was silvered iron-g ey—nearer sixty than fifty, but he was upright, hearty, and robust.

Note.—One of the parties in Jarndyce and Jarndyce, the interminable Chancery case that has become a household word. He was the guardian of Richard Carstone and Ada Clare. He engages Esther Summerson as companion and friend to Ada, but is so pleased with her kindly ways and modest thoughtfulness that he asks her to marry him. She consents. After preparing everything for the wedding he releases her in favour of Allen Woodcourt, as he has seen that there is a greater affection between them. He is a visitor at their house, however, and they erect a "growlery" for him. He detests the great case, and endeavours to keep Richard out of it, but without success. Ultimately it is found that all the estate has been eaten up in costs, without any decision having been arrived at. He is a kindly, generous man, who when he is displeased explains that the "wind is in the East" to account for his ill-humour.

JARNDYCE. Old Tom, of Jarndyce and Jarndyce. *B.H.* i.

Blew his brains out in a coffee-house in Chancery Lane.

JARNDYCE AND JARNDYCE. The famous chancery suit on which the story hangs. *B.H.*

JARVIS. A clerk in Wilding and Co. *C.S.N.T.*, Act i.

JASPER. Mr. Jack. *E.D.* ii.

A dark man of some six-and-twenty, with thick, lustrous, well-arranged black hair and whiskers. His voice is deep and good, his face and figure are good, his manner is a little sombre.

Note.—Uncle of Edwin Drood and secret suitor for the hand of Rosa Bud. He is introduced in an East End opium den. He is addicted to the habit, and it would appear from the story that some discovery of importance hinges upon his infirmity. He foments the ill-feeling between his nephew and Neville Landless, although he appears to be desirous of making them friendly. So far as the book is completed he is suspected of the murder of Edwin by several people, and is being constantly watched by Datchery.

JASPER'S GATEHOUSE. *E.D.* ii.

JAVELIN-MAN. *B.R.* lxi.

JEAN. A son of Madame Doche. *R.P., M.O.F.F.*

JEDDLER. Doctor, A great philosopher. *C.B., B.o.L.*

The heart and mystery of his philosophy was to look upon the world as a gigantic practical joke. Had a streaked face like a winter pippin, with here and there a dimple, and a very little bit of pigtail behind that stood for the stalk.

JEDDLER. Doctor, Wife of. *C.B., B.o.L.* i.

The Doctor's wife was dead.

JEDDLER. Grace. *C.B., B.o.L.* i.

So gentle and retiring.

JEDDLER. House of Doctor. *C.B., B.o.L.* i.

JEDDLER. Marion. *C.B.B.o.L.* i.

JEDDLER. Martha, Spinster sister of Doctor Jeddler. *C.B., B.o.L.* i.

JEFFERSON. Judge. *A.N.* xiv.

JEFFERY. *M.P., M.E.R.*

JEFFREYS. [Judge]. *M.P., A. in E.*

JELLYBY. Caddy, Eldest daughter of Mrs. Jellyby. *B.H.* iv.

From her tumbled hair to her pretty feet, which were disfigured with frayed and broken satin slippers trodden down at heel, she really seemed to have no article of dress upon her, from a pin upwards, that was in its proper condition, or in its right place.

Note.—Eldest daughter of Mrs. Jellyby. She is introduced working as unpaid secretary to her mother. She has been negletcted in many ways, but in spite of this she is a pleasing character. She marries Prince Turveydrop and escapes the uncongenial surroundings of her home. She has now to work hard in her new sphere, however, and prospers so much that she keeps her own little carriage. She has a deaf and dumb little girl to whom she devotes her spare time and energies.

JELLYBY. Mr., Husband of Mrs. Jellyby. *B.H.* iv.

He may be a very superior man; but he is, so to speak, merged in the more shining qualities of his wife. A mild, bald gentleman in spectacles.

Note.—Mrs. Jellyby's husband. A quiet, unobtrusive man. He is neglected by his wife and becomes bankrupt. In the end Mr. Jellyby is seen spending his evenings at Caddy's new house, still with his head against the wall.

JELLYBY. Mrs. *B.H.* iv.

A lady of very remarkable strength of character, who devotes herself entirely to the public—has devoted herself to an extensive variety of public subjects— is at present devoted to the subject of Africa—

cultivation of the coffee-berry—and the natives. Pretty, very diminutive, plump woman, of from forty to fifty, with handsome eyes.

Note.—Mrs. Jellyby is a caricature of the woman with a mission; she is first seen promoting a scheme for the natives of Borrioboola-Gha on the Niger. She is so absorbed in this work that she neglects her home, her husband, and her children. Eventually her husband becomes a bankrupt. After the failure of the Niger scheme she takes up the rights of women to sit in Parliament, " a mission involving more correspondence than the old one."

JELLYBY'S House in Thavies Inn. *B.H.* iv.

A narrow street of high houses like an oblong cistern to hold the fog. The house at which we stopped had a tarnished brass plate on the door, with the inscription Jellyby.

JELLYBYS. One of the young. Peepy. *B.H.* iv.

One of the dirtiest little unfortunates I ever saw—fixed by the neck between two iron railings.

Note.—Son of the Jellybys and rather more neglected than the others. He is befriended by Esther Summerson, and is last seen in the Custom House, " and doing extremely well."

"**JEM.**" A carol singer. *P.P.* xxviii.

JEM. Boy of Mr. Soloman Jacobs. *S.B.B.*, Tales x.

A sallow faced, red-haired, sulky boy.

JEMIMA. Sister of Mrs. Toodle. *D. and S.* ii.

JEMMY. Dismal, Job's brother. *See* Dismal Jemmy.

JEMMY. Son of Mrs. Edson. *C.S.*, *M.L.Lo.* i.

JENKINS. Miss. *S.B.B.*, Tales ix.

Whose talent for the piano was too well known to be doubted for an instant.

JENKINS. Mr. *S.Y.C.*

JENKINS. Owner of an assumed name. *S.B.B.*, Scenes xiii.

JENKINS. Sir Mulberry Hawk's man. *N.N.* i.

JENKINSON. Messenger in Circumlocution Office. *L.D.* x.

Who was eating mashed potatoes and gravy behind a partition by the hall fire.

JENNER. Dr. *M.P.*, *N.J.B.*; *M.P.*, *S.C.*

JENNINGS. Miss, Pupil at the Nuns' House. *E.D.* ix.

JENNINGS. Mr. *Mud. Pap.*

JENNINGS. Mr., Robe-maker. *S.B.B.*, Char. vii.

JENNINGS. Pupil at Dotheboys' Hall. *N.N.* vii.

JENNY. Brickmaker's wife. *B.H.* viii.

Note.—Wife of one of the brick-makers. She is not a bad woman, but is dominated by her drunken husband. She changes her outer garment with Lady Dedlock to enable the latter to elude those in search of her.

JERROLD. Mr. Douglas. *M.P.*, *I.M.T.*; *M.P.*, *V. and B.S.*

JERRY. A travelling showman with performing dogs. *O.C.S.* xviii.

A tall, black-whiskered man in a velveteen coat.

JERUSALEM BUILDINGS. Row of shops. *C.B.*, *H.M.* i.

Tetterby's was the corner shop in Jerusalem Buildings.

JERUSALEM COFFEE-HOUSE. *L.D.* xxix.

JESUITS. The. *P.F.I.*, *G.A.N.*

JEW AND CHRISTIAN VAMPIRES. Attending sale of Dombey's furniture. *D and S.* lix.

Herds of shabby vampires, Jew and Christian, overrun the house, sounding the plate glass mirrors with their knuckles, striking discordant octaves on the grand piano, drawing wet forefingers over the pictures, breathing on the blades of the best dinner-knives, punching the squabs of chairs and sofas with their dirty fists, touzling the feather beds, opening and shutting all the drawers, balancing all the silver spoons and forks, looking into the very threads of the drapery and linen, and disparaging everything.

JEWBY. Clients of Snagsby. *B.H.* x.

JEWELLER'S SHOP. In Paris. Attendant in. *L.D.* liv.

A sprightly little woman, dressed in perfect taste.

JEWESS. *P.P.* xli.

A magnificent Jewess of surpassing beauty.

JEWESS. The stout. *S.B.B.*, Scenes xiii.

Mother of the pale, bony little girl, with the necklace of blue glass beads sitting by her. She is being brought up to the profession.

JEWISH GIRL. A beautiful. *B.R.* lxxxii.

Who attached herself to him (Lord George Gordon while in Newgate) from feelings half-religious, half-romantic, but whose virtuous and disinterested character appears to have been beyond the censure even of the most censorious.

JEWISH PASSENGERS. On board "Royal Charter." *U.T.* ii.

JEWS. Hawkers. *P.P.* xxxv.

With the fifty-bladed knives.

JEWS. In Holywell Street. *S.B.B.*, Scenes vi.

Red-headed, and red-whiskered, who forcibly haul you into their squalid houses, and thrust you into a suit of clothes, whether you will or not.

JEWS. Lenders of fancy dresses. *S.B.B.*, Scenes xiii.

A sure passport to the amateur stage.

JIBBS. *M.P.*, *F.S.*

JIDDA. In the Dead Sea. *M.P.*, *L.A.V.* ii.

J. J. Mr., of Peckham. *M.P.*, *S.F.A.*

JILKINS. A physician. *R.P.*, *O.B.*

JIM. Negro man-slave. Ran away. *A.N.* xvii.

JINGLE. Alfred, Strolling p ayer. *P.P.* ii.

He was about the middle height but the thinness of his body, and the length of his legs, gave him the appearance of being much taller. The green coat had been a smart dress garment . . . the soiled and faded sleeves scarcely reached to his wrists. . . .His scanty black trousers displayed here and there those shiny patches which bespeak long service. . . . His long black hair escaped in negligent waves beneath each side of his old, pinched-up hat. . . . His face was thin and haggard ; but an indescribable air of jaunty impudence and perfect self-possession pervaded the whole man.

Note.—Jingle enters the story at an early chapter as a rollicking, entertaining eccentric ; and leaves it, the recipient of Mr. Pickwick's generosity, for the West Indies, having passed through real adventures surely as wonderful as those fables he narrated with such profusion. He masquerades as Charles Fitz-Marshall and occasions the Pickwickians a vast amount of trouble, but is discovered by Mr. Pickwick in a most deplorable condition in the debters' prison.

JINIWIN. Miss Betsy. *See* Quilp, Mrs.

JINIWIN. Mrs., Mrs. Quilp's mother. *O.C.S.* iv.

Mrs. Quilp's parent was known to be laudably shrewish in her disposition and inclined to resist male authority.

Note.—Quilp s mother-in-law, Mrs. Jiniwin, is in mortal dread of the dwarf, but she endeavours to make some show of opposing and defying him. On Mrs. Quilp's second marriage it was made a condition that her mother should be an out-pensioner.

JINKINS. Customer come to redeem some tools. *S.B.B.*, Scenes xxx.

Was enjoying a little relaxation from his sedentary pursuits, a quarter of an hour ago, in kicking his wife.

JINKINS. Mr. Gentleman boarding at Todger's. *M.C.* viii.

Was of a fashionable turn ; being a regular frequenter of the Park on Sundays, and knowing a great many carriages by sight—was much the oldest of the party, being a fish saleman's book-keeper, aged forty—was the oldest boarder also ; and in right of his double seniority, took the lead in the house.

" JINKINS." Resident at inn in Marlborough Downs. *P.P.* xiv.

A very tall man in a brown coat and bright basket buttons, and black whiskers, and wavy black hair who was seated at tea with the widow, and who it required no great penetration to discover was in a fair way of persuading her to be a widow no longer.

Note.—Introduced in the Bagman's story. Attempts to marry the widowed landlady, but is frustrated by Tom.

JINKINS. Wife of, Takes in mangling. *S.B.B.*, Scenes xxiii.

A wretched, worn-out woman, apparently in the last stage of consumption, whose face bears evident marks of ill-usage, and whose strength seems hardly equal to the burden—light enough, God knows! of the thin, sickly child she carries in her arms.

JINKINSON. A barber. *M.H.C.* v.

JINKINSON'S. Children of. *M.H.C.* v.

JINKINSON'S. A barber's shop. *M.H.C.* v.

JINKS. Mr., Magistrate's clerk. *P.P.* xxiv.

A pale, sharp-nosed, half-fed, shabbily-clad clerk, of middle age, . . . had a legal education of three years in a country attorney's office.

JO. Crossing-sweeper. *B.H* xi.

Very muddy, very hoarse, very ragged, knows a broom's a broom, and knows it's wicked to tell a lie.

Note.—The boy is befriended by Captain Hawdon, then an unknown law-writer. He knew nothing—who he was or his name. Questioned before the coroner's jury, he is a pathetic figure. Accidentally he is involved in Lady Dedlock's secret without knowing the meaning of his knowledge. But Mr. Tulkinghorn has him hounded on from one place to another. He falls ill, and communicates the smallpox to "Charley," and "Charley" gives it to Esther. He is found in London by Allan Woodcourt, and taken to George's Shooting Gallery, where he is cared for, but dies and, it is presumable, buried in the strangers' ground beside Captain Hawdon.

JOBBA. Mr. *Mud. Pap.* i.

JOBBER. A grimly satirical. *U.T.* xxii.

Who announced himself as having to let "A neat one-horse fly, and a one horse cart."

JOBBIANA. A discreet slave. *M.P.*, *T.O.H.*

JOBBING MAN. A. *S.B.B.*, Scenes v.

JOBLING. John, Esquire, M.R.C.S., Medical Officer to the Anglo-Bengalee Disinterested Loan and Life Assurance Company. *M.C.* xxvii.

The same medical officer who had followed poor old Anthony Chuzzlewit to the grave, and who had attended Mrs. Gamp's patient at the "Bull." His neckerchief and shirt-frill were ever of the whitest, his clothes of the blackest and sleekest, his gold watchchain of the heaviest, and his seals of the largest. His boots, which were always of the brightest, creaked as he walked.

JOBLING. Tony. *B.H.* xx.

His hat presents at the rim a peculiar appearance of a glistening nature, as if it had been a favourite snail-promenade. He has the faded appearance of a gentleman in embarrassed circumstances.

Note.—Law-writer to Snagsby. He passes under the name of "Weevle." He is a friend of Mr. Guppy and accompanies that gentleman on his visit to Esther Summerson, when he renews his offer of marriage. It appears then that Jobling will occupy the position of clerk to Mr. Guppy when he sets up his own legal establishment.

JOB-MASTER. A, Who taught riding. *D. and S.* xxii.

JOBSON FAMILY. Emigrants. *U.T.* xx.

JOBY. *C.S.*, *H.H.*

"A hold chap, a sort of one-eyed tramp."

JOCK. *L.T.*

JOCK. Rev. Jared. *M.P.*, *F.F.*

JOCKEY CLUB. A member of. *M.C.* xxvi.

JODD. Mr. *M.C.* xxxiv.

JODDLEBY. A. *L.D.* xvii.

JOE. Driver of 'bus plying to Cloisterham. *E.D.* vi.

JOE. Fat boy. *P.P.* iv.

"Damn that boy, he's gone to sleep again."

Note.—Joe was the celebrated fat boy who was servant to Mr. Wardle. Athough he wakened up to do a duty, immediately the task was accomplished he went to sleep. Curiously enough he is one of the few characters in Pickwick which do not undergo some development. He is the same fat boy in chapter lvi.as in chapter iv.

JOE. Guard of the Dover mail. *T.T.C.* ii.

JOE. Jack Adams' brother. *D. and S.* xxxvi.

JOE. Labourer. *D. and S.* vi.

JOE. Man-cook in a family hotel. *O.T.* xxxix.

In a quiet but handsome street near Hyde Park.

JOE. Mrs., Mrs. Joe Gargery. *G.E.* ix.

JOE. Old, Dealer in rags and bones. *C.B., C.C.* iv.

A grey-haired rascal, nearly seventy years of age.

JOES. Small, Children of Joe and Dolly Willet. *B.R.*lxxxii.

JOEY. Captain. *O.M.F.* vi.

The bottle-nosed regular customer (at the "Six Jolly Porters") in the glazed hat.

JOEY. Mr., Joey Ladle. *C.S., N.T.* Act iii

JOHN. *C.S., H.H.*

JOHN. *M.P., S.B.*

JOHN. *M.P., S.G.*

JOHN. *M.P., S.R.*

JOHN. *R.P., A.C.T.*

JOHN [Bull]. *M.P., T.O.P.*

JOHN. Boiler maker out of work in Ratcliff. *U.T.* xxx.

JOHN. Boy of the Parsons. *S.B.B.*, Tales x.

JOHN. Host at Christmas party. *R.P., P.R.S.*

JOHN. Miss La Creevy's brother. *N.N.* xxxi.

JOHN. Mr. *S.Y.C.*

JOHN. Mr. Malderton's man. *S.B.B.*, Tales v.

A man who, on ordinary occasions, acted as half-groom, half-gardener—touched up to look like a second footman.

JOHN. Negro slave. *A.N.* xvii.

Committed to jail.

JOHN. Of Sunderland. *G.E.* liv.

JOHN. Old Charles. *C.S., S.* li.

JOHN. Servant in livery. *S.B.B., O.P.* v.

JOHN. Servant to Lovetown. *M.P., I.S.H.W.*

JOHN. Son of the drunkard. *S.B.B.*, Tales xii.

JOHN. Subject of "The Stroller's Tale." *P.P.* iii.

A low pantomime actor. . . an habitual drunkard.

JOHN. Tenant of Haunted House. *C.S., H.H.*

JOHN. Very poor man, out of work. *D. and S.* xxiv.

Went roaming about the banks of the river when the tide was low, looking out for bits and scraps in the mud.

JOHN. Waiter in "Saracen's Head." *P.P.* li.

JOHN EDWARD. Youngest grandson of Nandy. *L.D.* xxxi.

Son of Mr. and Mrs. Plornish.

"**JOHN, OLD.**" *R.P., P.M.T.P.*

"I have been called 'Old John' ever since I was nineteen years of age, on account of not having much hair."

JOHNNEE. *M.P., T.O.H.*

JOHNNY. *O.M.F.* xvi.

A pretty boy—blue eyes—fat dimpled hand.

Note.—In their hunt for a child to adopt, the Boffins light on Betty Higden's grandson, but before the project can be carried out Johnny dies.

JOHNNY =Lord John Russell. *M.P., B.S.*

JOHNNY CAKES. *A.N.* x.

JOHNSON. Dr. *M.P., R.S.D.*

JOHNSON. John. *M.P., S.G.*

JOHNSON. Mr.
The name which Newman Noggs had bestowed upon Nicholas Nickleby in his conversation with Mrs. Kenwigs. *See* Nickleby, Nicholas.

JOHNSON. Parkers. *S.B.B., O.P.* vi.

JOHNSON. Pupil of Dr. Blimber. *D. and S.* xii.
"Said Doctor Blimber, 'Johnson will repeat to me to-morrow morning before breakfast, without book, and from the Greek Testament, the first chapter of the Epistle of Saint Paul to the Ephesians'."

JOHNSON. Tom, Acquaintance of cousin Feenix. *D. and S.* xli.
Man with cork leg, from White's.

JOHNSON. Traveller to Paris. *R.P., O.F.W.*

JOHNSON'S. *S.B.B., O.P.* v.

JOHNSON'S. Nursery ground. *S.B.B.*, Scenes ix.

JOLLIE. Miss. *M.P., S.P.*

JOLLSON. Mrs. Former occupant of 9, Brig Place. *D. and S.* xxxix.

JOLLY BARGEMEN. *See* Three Jolly Bargemen.

JOLLY BOATMEN. *Mud. Pap.*

"JOLLY SANDBOYS." *O.C.S.* xvii.
A small roadside inn of pretty ancient date.

JOLLY TAPLEY. The "Blue Dragon." *M.C.* xlii.

JOLTERHEAD. Sir W. *Mud. Pap.* ii.

JOMILLAH. *M.P., T.O.H.*

JONATHAN. *M.P., T.O.P.*

JONATHAN. *O.M.F.* vi.

JONATHAN. Young. *M.P., A.J.B.*

JONES. Barrister's clerk. *S.B.B.*, Char. vii.
Capital company—full of anecdote.

JONES. Blackberry. *O.M.F.* xlviii.

JONES. Boy. *M.P., B.A.* *M.P., Th. Let.*
Reference to "General" Tom Thumb.

JONES. George. *O.M.F.* vi.
In a faded scarlet jacket.

JONES. George, Wife of. *O.M.F.* vi.

JONES. Husband of Mary. *B.R.* Pref.
It was a time when press warrants were issued. The woman's husband was pressed, their goods seized for some debts of his, and she, with two small children, turned into the streets a-begging.

JONES. Mary, hanged at Tyburn. *B.R.* xxxvii.
"Who came up to Tyburn with an infant at her breast, and was worked off for taking a piece of cloth off the counter of a shop—and putting it down again when the shopman see her; and who had never done any harm before, and only tried to do that in consequence of her husband being pressed three weeks previous, and she being left with two young children."

JONES. Mary, Two small children of. *B.R.* Pref.
The younger suckling at her breast when she (Mary Jones) set out for Tyburn.

JONES. Master. *D.C.* xviii.
A boy of no merit whatever.

JONES. Mr. *B.H.* lviii.
The rawest hand behind the Counter.

JONES. Mr., Friend of the Budden family. *S.B.B.*, Tales ii.
A little smirking man with red whiskers.

JONES, SPRUGGINS AND SMITH. Messrs. *S.B.B.*, Tales v.

JONES. Tom. *M.P., P.P.*

JOODLE. *B.H.* xii.

JOPER. Billy. *D. and S.* xli.
"A man at Brook's—you know him no doubt—man with a glass in his eye."

JORAM. Mrs. *See* Omer, Minnie.

JORAM. Undertaker's assistant to Mr. Omer. *D.C.* ix.
Note.—Marries Omer's daughter

JORGAN. Captain, A new Englander. *C.S., M.f.F.S.* i.
An American-born—a citizen of the world, and a combination of most of the best qualities of most of its best countries. In long-skirted blue coat, and blue trousers.

JORKINS. Mr., Mr. Spenlow's partner. *D.C.* xxiii.

A mild man of a heavy temperament, whose place in the business was to keep himself in the back ground, and be constantly exhibited by name as the most obdurate, and ruthless of men.

JOSEPH. Charity child. *U.T.* xxi.

Shaking mats in City churchyard.

JOSEPH. Head waiter at Slamjam Coffee-House, London, E.C. *C.S., S.L.* i.

JOSEPHINE. Again a wife. *H.T., G.* ix.

JOSEPHINE. Children of. *H.T., G.* ix.

JOSEPHINE. Son of. *H.T., G.* vii.

" The Little Wonder of Scholastic Equitation. Tho' only three years old, he sticks on to any pony you can bring against him."

JOSIAH. A negro man. *A.N.* xvii.

Branded I.M. on hip.

JOVE. *M.P., G.F.*

JOWL. Mat. Fellow gambler with Isaac List. *O.C.S.* xxix.

A bulky fellow of middle age, with large black whiskers, broad cheeks, a coarse wide mouth, and bull-neck.

Note.—One of the two gamblers who, with the assistance of Groves, tempt Little Nell's grandfather. The gang is broken up by the unintentional intervention of Frederick Trent.

JOY. Name of bird. *B.H.* xiv.

JOY. Thomas, A carpenter. *R.P., P.M.T.P.*

J. U. *M.P., S.B.*

JUDGE. *M.P., P.L.U.*

JUDGE. *T.T.C.* bk. ii, ch. ii.

JUDGE. A certain constitutional. *M.C.* xxi.

Who laid down from the Bench, the noble principle, that it was lawful for any white mob to murder any black man.

JUDGE. In Doctors' Commons. *S.B.B.*, Scenes viii.

A very fat and red-faced gentleman, in tortoiseshell spectacles.

JUDGE. The, In Court of Chancery. *B.H.* i.

JUDGE'S CHAMBERS. *B.H.* x.

JUDGES. The. *C.S., T.G.S.* i.

JUDGES. The. *U.T.* xi.

JUDGES. The wery best-two o' them. *P.P.* lv

The wery best judges of a horse you ever knowed, added Mr. Weller.

JUDY. Mulatto woman, Runaway slave. *A.N.* xvii.

JUFFY. *B.H.* xii.

JUGGLER. The. *D. and S.* xviii.

Sky-blue fillet round his head, and salmon-coloured worsted drawers.

JUGGLER'S BABY. *D. and S.* xviii.

JUGGLER'S WIFE. *D. and S.* xviii.

A child's burial has set her thinking that perhaps the baby underneath her shawl may not grow up to be a man.

JULIA. *R.P., G.o.A.*

JULIUS CAESAR. *B.H.* liv.

JULIUS CAESAR. Mr. Slinkton. *H.D.V.*

JULLIEN. M. *R.P., B S.*

JUMBLE. The. *O.M.F.* xviii.

The school at which young Charley Hexam had first learned from a book—a miserable loft in an unsavoury yard. Its atmosphere was oppressive and disagreeable——half the pupils dropped asleep, or fell into a state of waking stupefaction.

JUPE. Cecilia, A stroller's daughter. *H.T., S.* ii.

So dark-eyed, and dark-haired, that she seemed to receive a deeper and more lustrous colour from the sun.

Note.—Cissy is introduced as a shy girl in Gradgrind's school frightened and browbeaten by Bounderby. She is the daughter of a member of Sleary's troupe, and Bounderby thinks the influence an evil one in the school: so it is decided that Cissy must go. It is found however, the Signor Jupe has vanished, and Mr. Gradgrind takes her home with him. Although Cissy has not too happy a life with the Gradgrinds, it is due to her that Mr. Gradgrind does not suffer much more than he does. Cissy clears Mr. Harthouse out of the way, and by doing so saves Louisa's reputation, and it is also through her and her influence with Sleary that Tom is enabled to escape.

JUPE. Cissy. Her children. *H.T.* bk. iii., ch. ix.

JUPE. Signor, A Clown in Sleary's Circus. *H.T., S.* iii.

JURA MOUNTAINS. *P.F.I., V.M.M.S.S.*

JURY. *M.P., L.E.J.*

JURY. *P.P.* xxxiv.

JURY. A member of the. (A vestry. man). *C.S., T.G.S.* i.

"The greatest idiot I have ever seen at large."

JURY. At Inquest. *B.H.* xi.

JURY. Coroner's *U.T.* viii.

JURY. Foreman of the. *C.S., T.G.S.* i.

JUSTICE. Blind, *M.P., T.T.C.D.*

JUSTICE. Courts of. *R.P., T.D.P.*

"**JUSTICE.**" Russian officer of, Mr. Potts as. *P.P.* xv.

With a tremendous knout in his hand. Tastefully typical of the stern and mighty powers of the "Eatanswill Gazette."

JUSTICE OF PEACE. *B.R.* xlvii.

A stout gentleman with a long whip in his hand, and a flushed face —called by some a genuine John Bull.

JUSTICIES. The. *G.E.* xiii.

JUVENILE DELINQUENT SOCIETY. *O.T.* xix.

K

KAFFIRLAND. *R.P., T.N.S.*

KAFFIRS. Zulu. *R.P., T.N.S.*

KAGS. A returned transport. *O.T.* l.

A robber of fifty years, whose nose had been almost beaten in, in some old scuffle, and whose face bore a frightful scar, which might probably be traced to the same occasion.

Note.—A member of Fagin's gang who has returned from transportation. He is present in the house on Folly Ditch when Sikes takes refuge in it.

KARS. *M.P., N.S.E.*

KATE. An orphan child. *D. and S.* xxiv.

Note.—She visits at Lady Skettles' while Florence Dombey is there.

KATE. Maria Lobbs' cousin. *P.P.* xvii.

An arch, impudent-looking, bewitching little person.

KATSKILL MOUNTAINS. *A.N.* xv.

KEAN. *M.P., D.M.*; *and M.P., R.S.L.*

KEATS. Grave of the bones of. *P.F.I., R.*

KEDGICK. Captain, Landlord of National Hotel. *M.C.* xxii,

Note.—Captain Kedgick, in his capacity of landlord, arranged a levee for Martin Chuzzlewit, and his mysterious behaviour led mark Tapley to hope they had discovered the most remarkable man in the United States and so used up the "breed."

KEELEY. *M.P., M.B.*

KEEPER. Of Mrs. Nickleby's neighbour. *N.N.* xli.

A coarse, squat man.

KELEY. Patrick, of Kildare. Ireland. *M.P., F.S.*

KELSO. *M.P., S.P.*

KEMBLE. *M.P., R.S.L.*

KENGE. Mr., Of Kenge and Carboy. Solicitors. *B.H.* iii.

A portly, important-looking gentleman, dressed all in black, with a white cravat, large gold watch-seals, a pair of gold eyeglasses, and a large seal-ring upon his little finger.

Note.—Kenge is ushered into the story unostentatiously, and although he is present in some of the most dramatic scenes, it is rather as stage property than as a principal actor, and he disappears with the termination of the famous chancery suit, Jarndyce and Jarndyce, in the same way that he enters the book.

KENILWORTH. *D. and S.* xxvi.

KENNINGTON. *B.H.* xxxix.; and *R.P.*; *T.D.A.* i.

KENNINGTON OVAL. *M.P., E.T.*

KENNINGTON STATION HOUSE. *C.S., M.L.Lo.* i.

KENSAL GREEN CEMETERY. *M.P., I.M.T.* and *M.P., T.D.*

KENSINGTON. *B.R.* xvi.; *M.P.*, *P.T.*; *M.P.*, *T.B.*; *O.T.* xxi.; *P.P.* xliv.

KENSINGTON GARDENS. *S.B.B.*, Tales x.

KENSINGTON GRAVEL. *N.N.* xxviii.

KENSINGTON TURNPIKE. *P.P.* xxxv.

KENSINGTON UNION. *M.P.*, *P.T.*

KENT. *B.H.* xxvii.; *C.S.*, *S.P.T.*; *D.S.* lvi.; *O.M.F.* xii.; *P.P.* ii.; *R.P.*, *A.C.T.*, *O.o.T.*; *T.B.W.*; *U.T.* xii.

Everybody knows Kent—apples, cherries, hops, and women.

Note.—Kent enters largely into the "Pickwick Papers," and in fact into many of Dickens' works. It was his favourite county. Reference should be made to the various places mentioned.

KENT. The hop grounds of. *M.P.*, *G.A.*

KENT ROAD. *D.C.* xiii.

KENT STREET. *U.T.* xiii.

KENTISH HEIGHTS. *B.H.* i.

KENTISH TOWN. *B.R.* xvi.

KENTUCKY. *M.P.*, *A.P.*

KENTUCKY GIANT. *A.N.* xii.

KENWIGS. Lillyvick, Son of Mr. and Mrs. Kenwigs. *N.N.* xv.

Christened after the collector.

KENWIGS. Mr., Turner in ivory. *N.N.* xiv.

Who was looked upon as a person of some consideration on the premises, inasmuch as he occupied the whole of the first floor, comprising a suit of two rooms.

Note.—Kenwigs occupied a floor in the house in which Newman Noggs had a room. Their outlook on life was limited by their expectations from Mr. Lillyvick, the water-rate collector. As is natural, the collector married and disappointed them, until his wife ran away. There is a subtle resemblance in the "atmosphere" of the Kenwigs' home to that of Micawber.

KENWIGS. Mrs., Wife of Mr. Kenwigs. *N.N.* xiv.

Quite a lady in her manners, and of a very genteel family . . . was considered a very desirable person to know.

Note.—Wife of Mr. Kenwigs; and mother of the wonderful children. She was very much upset by the marriage of the collector; and when the collector's wife ran away with a half-pay captain and Lillyvick returned to them—to the room in which he had met Miss Petowker—to cast her off for ever, Mrs. Kenwigs was again upset, but speedily recovered.

KENWIGS. Morleena. *N.N.* xiv.

Had flaxen hair, tied with blue ribands, hanging in luxuriant pigtails. . . and wore little white trousers with frills round the ankles.

Note.—The eldest daughter of the Kenwigses. She had acquired, or inherited, her parent's artless hypocrisy in dealing with Mr. Lillyvick.

KENWIGSES. Little. *N.N.* xiv.

KENWIGSES. The two eldest. *N.N* xiv.

Went twice a week to a dancing school in the neighbourhood, and, had flaxen hair, tied with blue ribands, hanging in luxuriant pigtails down their backs; and wore little white trousers with frills round the ankles.

KESWICK VALE. *M.P.*, *A.P.*

KETCH. Mr. John, The great state schoolmaster. *M.P.*, *F.S.*; *Mud. Pap.* 2nd Meeting, and *O.T.* xxvi.

KETTLE. Mr. *M.P.*, *N.G.K.*

KETTLE. Mr. La Fayette. *M.C.* xxi.

Languid and listless in his looks, his cheeks were so hollow that he seemed to be always sucking them in; and the sun had burnt him not a wholesome red or brown, but dirty yellow. He had bright dark eyes, which he kept half closed—in the palm of his left hand, as English rustics have their slice of cheese, he had a cake of tobacco: in his right a penknife.

Note.—Kettle is one of the most typical of Dickens' caricatures of American personalities. He was secretary of the Watertoast Association of United Sympathisers, and Martin Chuzzlewit met him on his travels.

KEW. *G.E.* xxx.

KEW BRIDGE. *O.T.* xxi.

KEYHOLE REPORTER. New York. *M.C.* xvi.

KIBBLE. Mr. Jacob, Fellow-passenger of Mr. John Harmon. *O.M.F.* iii.

KIDDERMINSTER. One of Sleary's troupe. *H.T.*, *S.* vi.

A diminutive boy with an old face—made up with curls, wreaths, wings, white bismuth, and carmine. This hopeful young person soared into so pleasing a cupid.

KIDGERBURY. Mrs., A charwoman. *D.C.* xliv.

The oldest inhabitant of Kentish Town, I believe, who went out charing, but was too feeble to execute her conceptions of that art.

KILBURN ROAD. *S.B.B.*, Scenes ix.

KILDARE. Ireland. *M.P.*, *F.S.*

KILNS. In Pottery. *R.P.*, *A.P.A.*

KIMMEENS. Miss, A pupil of Miss Pupford. *C.S.*, *T.T.G.* vi.

A little girl with beautiful bright hair. She wore a plain straw hat, and had a doorkey in her hand.

KIMMEENS. Papa of Kitty. A widower in India. *C.S.*, *T.T.G.* vi.

KINDHEART. Mr., Friend of Uncommercial Traveller. *U.T.* xxvi.

An Englishman of amiable nature, great enthusiasm, and no discretion.

KING. The. *B.R.* lxxviii.

KING, In Cinderella. *M.D. F.F.*

KING. Of Little Dorrit's tale to Maggy. *L.D.* xxiv.

KING. Christian George. A Sambo. *C.S.*, *P.o.C.E.P.*

No more a Christian than he was a King or a George.

KING ARTHUR'S ARMS." Inn. *C.S.*, *M.f.T.S.* v.

KING CHARLES 1st. *D.C.* xiv.

KING CHARLES 1st. Statue at Charing Cross. *D.C.* xx.

KING GEORGE THE FOURTH. *B.H.* xii.

KING OF BILL-STICKERS. *R.P.*, *B.S.*

KING STREET. Covent Garden. *M.P.*, *W.S.G.*

KING. Tom. *S.B.B.*, Scenes v.

"**KING'S ARMS.**" The. *D. and S.* liii.

KING'S ARMS AND ROYAL HOTEL. Lancaster. *C.S.*, *D.M.P.*

KING'S BATH. *P.P.* xxxv.

KING'S BENCH. *B.R.* lxvii.

KING'S BENCH OFFICE. *B.H.* x.

KING'S BENCH PRISON. *U.T.* xiii.

KING'S BENCH PRISON. Debtor's prison in the Borough. *D.C.* xi.; *N.N.* xlvi.; *S.B.B.*, Scenes xxi.

KING'S BENCH WALK. *See* Temple.

"**KING'S HEAD.**" Barnard Castle. *N.N.* vii.

KING'S SON. In Cinderella. *M.P.*, *F.F.*

KINGSGATE STREET. Holborn. *M.C.* xix.

KINGSMILL. Rev. Mr. *M.P.*, *P.P.*

KINGSTON. *A.N.* xv.; *D.S.* xxxvi.; *M.H.C.* iii.; *M.P.*, *E.S.*; *O.M.F.* xli.; *N.N.* xxii.

KITCHEN. Bellamy's, A refreshment room. *S.B.B.*, Scenes xviii.

Common to both Houses of Parliament . . . large fire and roasting jack at one end of the room—the little table for washing glasses and draining jugs at the other—the deal tables and wax candles. The damask tablecloths, and bare floor—the plate and china on the tables, and the gridiron on the fire.

KITCHEN SERVANTS. A select staff of, Hired by Mrs. Skewton. *D. and S.* xxx.

KITT. Miss, One of picnic party near Guildford. *D.C.* xxxiii.

Daughter of Mrs. Kitt, dressed in pink . . . with little eyes.

Note.—David Copperfield went and sat with the "creature in pink and inwardly raged at Red Whisker who was monopolising Dora.

KITT. Mrs., Mother of Miss Kitt. *D.C.* xxxiii.

Lady dressed in green.

KITTEN. Mr., Vice-Commissioner and Deputy Consul of Silver Store Island. *C.S.*, *P.o.C.E.P.*

KITTERBELL. Charles, Nephew of Dumps. *S.B.B.*, Tales xi.

A small, sharp, spare man, with a very large head, and a broad, good-humoured countenance. He looked like a faded giant, with the head and face partially restored, and he had a cast in his eye which rendered it quite impossible for any one to know where he was looking.

KITTERBELL. Family of Mr. *S.B.B.*, Tales xi.

Two sons and a daughter.

KITTERBELL. Frederick Charles William. *S.B.B.*, Tales xi.

Infant son of Mr. and Mrs. Charles Kitterbell.

KITTERBELL. Mama of Mrs. *S.B.B.*, Tales xi.

KITTERBELL. Mrs., Wife of Mr. Charles Kitterbell. *S.B.B.*, Tales xi.

A tall, thin young lady, with very light hair, and a particularly white face . . . one of those women who almost invariably . . . recall to ones mind the idea of a cold fillet of veal.

KITTERBELL. Papa of Mrs. *S.B.B.*, Tales xi.

KITTERBELL. Sisters of Mrs. *S.B.B.*, Tales xi.

KITTERBELL. Son of Mrs. and Charles. *S.B.B.*, Tales xi.

KITTERBELLS. Guest at Christening party of. *S.B.B.*, Tales xi.

An old lady in a large toque, and an old gentleman in a blue coat, and three female copies of the old lady in pink dresses, and shoes to match.

KITTY. Alfred Raybrock's sweetheart. *C.S., M.f.T.S.* i.

A very pretty girl . . . very simply dressed, with no other ornament than an autumnal flower in her bosom. She wore neither hat nor bonnet, but merely a scarf or kerchief, folded squarely back over the head, to keep the sun off.

KLEM. Miss, Daughter of Mr. and Mrs. Klem. *U.T.* xvi.

Apparently ten years older than either of them.

KLEM. Mr., Husband of Mrs. Klem. *U.T.* xvi.

A meagre and mouldy old man.

KLEM. Mrs., A caretaker. *U.T.* xvi.

An elderly woman labouring under a chronic sniff.

KNAG. Miss, Madame Mantalini's forewoman. *N.N.* x.

A short, bustling, over-dressed female . . . who still aimed at youth, although she had shot beyond it years ago.

Note.—Miss Knag was a typical time-server. From professing a liking for Kate Nickleby she conceived an intense jealousy. Although manageress, she ultimately acquired Madame Mantalini's business.

KNAG. Mr. Mortimer, Miss Knag's brother. *N.N.* xviii.

An ornamental stationer and small circulating library keeper—who let out, by the day, week, month, or year, the newest old novels . . . a tall, lank gentleman of solemn features, wearing spectacles, and garnished with much less hair than a gentleman bordering on forty or thereabouts usually boasts.

KNAG. Uncle of Miss Knag. *N.N.* xviii.

Had a most excellent business as a tobacconist. . . had such small feet that they were no bigger than those which are usually joined to wooden legs.

KNIFE-SWALLOWER. African, Actor. Member of Mr. V. Crummles' company. *N.N.* xlviii.

Spoke remarkably like an Irishman.

KNIGHT BELL. Dr. *Mud. Papers, 1st meeting.*

KNIGHTSBRIDGE. *S.B.B.*, Scenes i.

KNOWLES Mr. *M.P., V. and B.S.*

KNOWSWHOM. Lord. *M.P., I.*

KOËLDWETHOUT. The Baron von. *N.N.* vi.

A fine swarthy fellow, with dark hair and large moustachios, who rode a-hunting in clothes of Lincoln green, with russet boots on his feet, and a bugle slung over his shoulder, like the guard of a long stage.

KOËLDWETHOUT. Baroness, Daughter of Baron von Swillenhaussen. *N.N.* vi.

Note.—Characters in a story introduced into the book as being told in an inn on the breakdown of the stage-coach.

KONG. Ty. *M.P., C.J.*

KOODLE. *B.H.* xii.

KROOK. Mr., Dealer in rags and bones, etc. *B.H.* v.

An old man in spectacles and a hairy cap . . . short, cadaverous and withered; with his head sideways between his shoulders, and the breath issuing in visible smoke from his mouth, as if he were on fire within. His throat, chin and eyebrows were so frosted with white hairs, and so gnarled with veins and puckered skin, that he looked, from his breast upward, like some root in a fall of snow.

Note.—Krook was the only brother of Mrs. Smallweed. He was the landlord of Miss Flite and Captain Hawdon. Old and eccentric, he was usually accompanied by a large and savage gray cat. He appeared to accumulate "stock" without any idea of disposing of it, and seemed to have no idea of what his place really contained. He was so saturated with spirits that his ultimate end was spontaneous combustion, leaving what seemed to be the "cinder of a small charred and broken log of wood sprinkled with white ashes."

KUFFY. *B.H.* xii.

KUTANKUMAGEN. Dr. *Mud. Papers, 1st meeting.*

KWAKLEY. Mr. *Mud. Papers, 1st meeting.*

L

LA COUR. Monsieur Le Capitaine de. *C.S., S.L.* ii.

LA CREEVY. Miss, Miniature painter. *N.N.* iii.

A mincing young lady of fifty, wearer of yellow head-dress, who had a gown to correspond, and was of much the same colour herself.

Note.—The bright little miniature painter with whom the Nickleby's first lodge on their coming to London. In spite of Ralph Nickleby's attempt to influence her against them, she becomes one of the best of friends to Kate and her mother and brother, and assists them in many ways with her kindness. In spite of their ages, she and Tim Linkinwater eventually marry.

LA CROIX. *R.P., O.B.*

LA FORCE. Prison. *T.T.C.* bk. iii. ch. ix.

Note.—It was in La Force that Charles Darney was first confined. After his condemnation he was imprisoned in the Conciergerie, from which he was rescued by Sydney Carton.

LA SCALA. Theatre in Milan. *P.F.I., V.M.M.S.S.*

LA TRANQUILLITÉ. A wineshop. *U.T.* xxv.

Opposite the prison in the prison alley.

LABOURER. A bricklayer's. *S.B.B.*, Scenes i.

With the day's dinner tied up in a handkerchief, walks briskly to his work.

LABOURER. An Irish. *S.B.B.*, Scenes v.

LABOURERS. At Ratcliff. *U.T.* xxx.

LABOURING MEN. Two. *M.P., S.D.C.*

LACHINE. The village of. *A.N.* xv.

LAD. Office. *P.P.* xl.

Fourteen, with a tenor voice.

LAD. Proposed as drawer of carriage. *D. and S.* viii.

A ruddy-faced lad, set aside by Paul, who selected, instead, his grandfather.

LAD LANE. *L.D.* xiii.

LADELLE. Monsieur Zhoe. *See* Ladle, Joey.

LADIES. All the, In the Prison—Marshalsea. *L.D.* vi.

LADIES. Artistes of Mr. V. Crummles' company. *N.N.* xxiii.

LADIES. At tea gardens. *S.B.B.*, Scenes ix.

With great, long, white pocket-handkerchiefs like small tablecloths, in their hands, chasing one another on the grass in the most playful and interesting manner.

LADIES. Elderly, Guests at Dombey's housewarming. *D. and S.* xxxvi.

Carrying burdens on their heads for full dress.

LADIES. Of distinction and liveliness, three or four. *L.D.* xviii.

Used to say to one another, "Let us dine at our dear Merdle's next Thursday."

LADIES. Of Friar Bacon's family. *M.P., P.M.B.*

LADIES. Of the Bedchamber. *M.P., M.E.R.*

LADIES. Of the booth at Greenwich Fair. *S.B.B.*, Scenes xii.

Were there ever such innocent and awful-looking beings?

LADIES. Of the court martial. *M.P., N.Y.D.*

LADIES. Old, Visitors in Assembly Rooms, Bath. *P.P.* xxxv.

LADIES. Two, In Seven Dials. *S.B.B.*, Scenes v.

On the eve of settling the quarrel satisfactorily by an appeal to blows.

LADIES. Two old maiden, At Peckham. *D. and S.* xiv.

LADIES. Two smart young, Clients (and friends) of General Agency Office. *N.N.* xvi.

LADIES. Unmarried (diverse). Visitors at Assembly Rooms, Bath. *P.P.* xxxv.

Seated on some of the back benches, where they had already taken up their positions for the evening, were diverse unmarried ladies, past their grand climacteric, who, not dancing—and not playing—were in the favourable position of being able to abuse everybody without reflecting on themselves.

LADIES' BIBLE AND PRAYER-BOOK CIRCULATION SOCIETY. *S.B.B., O.P.* vi.

LADIES' BLANKET DISTRIBUTION SOCIETY. *S.B.B., O.P.* vi.

LADIES' CHILD'S EXAMINATION SOCIETY. *S.B.B., O.P.* vi.

LADIES' COAL DISTRIBUTION SOCIETY. *S.B.B., O.P.* vi.

LADIES' SCHOOL. *M.P., U.N.*

LADIES' SCHOOL. Mrs. Wilfer's. *O.M.F.* iv.

LADIES' SOUP DISTRIBUTION SOCIETY. *S.B.B., O.P.* vi.

LADLE. Joey. *M.P., N.T.*

LADLE. Joey, Head cellarman of Wilding and Co., *C.S., N.T.* Act i.

A slow and ponderous man, of the drayman order of human architecture, dressed in a corrugated suit and bibbed apron, apparently a composite of doormat and rhinocerous hide.

LADS. Small office, In large hats. *S.B.B.*, Scenes i.

Who are men before they are boys.

LADY. Bulky, in charge of shop *S.B.B.*, Scenes vi.

Of elderly appearance, who was seated in a chair at the head of the cellar steps.

LADY. Elderly, Selling poultry in Leadenhall Market. *D. and S.* xlix.

Who usually sat under a blue umbrella.

LADY. Fastidious, Inside passenger on coach to Yorkshire. *N.N.* v.

With an infinate variety of cloaks and small parcels.

LADY. Fat. *C.S., H.W.L.*

LADY. Foreign, beloved by Prince Bladud. *P.P.* xxxvi.

Married to a foreign noble of her own country.

LADY. Husband of old. *S.B.B., O.P.* ii.

LADY. In amber. A Barmaid. *S.B.B.*, Scenes iii.

With large earrings, who, as she sits behind the counter in a blaze of adoration and gaslight, is the admiration of all the servants in the neighbourhood.

LADY. In cloth boots. *S.B.B.*, Scenes vi.

LADY. Mature young, Guest of Veneerings. *O.M.F.*ii.

Raven locks, and complexion that lights up well when powdered.

LADY. Middle-aged, In yellow curl-papers—in "The Great White Horse" inn. *P.P.* xxii.

LADY. Munificent. *M.P., C.*

'**LADY.** My," *S.B.B.*, Scenes xxi.

Taking part in May Day dances. To preside over the exchequer.

LADY. Of the counter. *M.P., R.D.*

LADY. Of the establishment where Miss Pinch was governess. *M.C.* ix.

Curious in the natural history and habits of the animal called Governess, and encouraged her daughters to report thereon whenever occasion served. . . . With what may be termed an excisable face, or one in which starch and vinegar were decidedly employed.

LADY. Of the house. *M.P., M.M.*

LADY OF THE HOUSE. Landlady in a house in the Rules. *N.N.* xlvi.

Busily engaged in turpentining the disjointed fragments of a tent bedstead at the door of the back parlour.

LADY. Old, Grandchildren of. *S.B.B.*, Scenes vii.

LADY. Old, Guest at Dombey's housewarming. *D. and S.* xxxvi.

Like a crimson velvet pin-cushion stuffed with banknotes, who might have been the identical Old Lady of Threadneedle Street, she was so rich, and looked so unaccommodating.

LADY. Old, Next door but one to shop. *S.B.B.*, Scenes iii.

LADY. Old, Of a censorious countenance. *B.H.* xiv.

Whose two nieces were in the class.

LADY. Old, Of our parish. *S.B.B., O.P.* ii.

Her name always heads the list of any benevolent subscription subscribed towards the erection of an organ in our church. Her entrance into church on Sunday is always the signal for a little bustle in the side aisle.

LADY. Old, Of ten years. *M.P., G.F.*

LADY. Old, Passenger for Hackney coach. *S.B.B.*, Scenes vii.

LADY. Old, Pensioners of. *S.B.B., O.P.* ii.

A regular levee of old men and women in the passage, waiting for their weekly gratuity.

LADY. Old, Residence of. *S.B.B., O.P.* ii.

The little front parlour is a perfect picture of quiet neatness, the carpet is covered with brown holland, the glass and picture frames are carefully enveloped in yellow muslin; the table-covers are never taken off except when the leaves are bees-waxed.

LADY. Particularly tall. Entertainer at Vauxhall Gardens. *S.B.B.*, Scenes xiv.

In a blue sarcenet pelisse, and bonnet of the same, ornamented with large white feathers.

LADY. Reverend old. *S.B.B.*, Scenes xi.

Who instilled into our mind the first principles of education for ninepence per week.

LADY. Son of old, In India. *S.B.B., O.P.* ii.

A fine handsome fellow.

LADY. The other, At wedding of Bunsby. *D. and S.* lx.

LADY. Traveller by coach. *P.P.* xlix.

Attired in an old-fashioned, green velvet dress, with a long waist and stomacher.

LADY. Under distraint. *S.B.B., O.P.* v.

"As white as ever I see anyone in my days, except about the eyes, which were red with crying."

LADY. Veiled. *M.P., N.T.*

LADY. Veiled. *C.S.*, *N.T.*, *O.*

Who flutters up and down near the postern-gate of the Hospital for Foundling Children.

LADY. Young. *M.P., T.T.C.D.*

LADY. Young, At No. 17. *S.B.B.*, *O.P.* iii.

LADY. Young, At No. 18. *S.B.B.*, *O.P.* iii.

LADY. Young, At No. 19. *S.B.B.*, *O.P.* iii.

LADY. Young, Behind the counter. *M.P.*, *W.R.*

LADY. Young, Client of General Agency Office. *N.N.* xvi.

Who could be scarcely eighteen, of very slight and delicate figure, exquisitely shaped . . . a countenance of most uncommon beauty, though shaded by a cloud of sadness. . . . She was neatly, but very quietly, attired. *See* Bray: Madeline.

LADY. Young. Daughter of lady in whose house the brokers were. *S.B.B.*, *O.P.* v.

LADY. Young, Fiancée of great lord. *N.N.* xviii.

Of no family in particular.

LADY. Young, Guest at Dombey's housewarming. *D. and S.* xxxvi.

Of sixty-five, remarkably coolly dressed, as to her back and shoulders, who spoke with an engaging lisp, and whose eyelids wouldn't keep up well, without a great deal of trouble on her part, and whose manners had that indefinable charm which so frequently attaches to the giddiness of youth.

LADY. Young, In blue. *S.B.B.*, Char. vii.

LADY. Young, In the Fleet. *P.P.* xlv.

LADY. Young, Of five times that age (10 years). *M.P.*, *G.F.*

LADY JANE. Krook's large grey cat. *B.H.* vi.

LADY VISITOR. Of medical practitioner. *S.B.B.*, Tales vi.

A singularly tall woman, dressed in deep mourning—the upper part of her figure was carefully muffled in a black shawl, as if for the purpose of concealment, and her face was shrouded by a thick black veil.

LADYBIRD. *See* Mannette, Miss Lucie.

LADYSHIP. Her, Partner of " My Lord." *S.B.B.*, Scenes xx.

Attired in pink crape over bed-furniture, with low body and short sleeves. The symmetry of her ankles was partially concealed by a very perceptible pair of frilled trousers—her white satin shoes—a few sizes too large—firmly attached to her legs with strong tape sandals . . . . Her head was ornamented with a profusion of artificial flowers; and in her hand she bore a large brass ladle, to receive, what she figuratively denominated, "The Tin."

LAGNIER. *See* Rigaud, Monsieur.

LAKE OF GENEVA. *D. and S.*, Pref.; *U.T.* vii.

LALLEY. Mr. *O.M.F.* viii.

LAMBERT. Daniel. *N.N.* xxxvii.

LAMBERT. Mr. *S.Y.G.*

LAMBETH. *M.P.*, *A.P.*,; *M.P.*, *M.B.V.*; *N.N.* lvii. *R.P.*, *O.B.*

LAMBETH LODGING. *N.N.* lix.

LAMBKIN FAMILY. *M.P.*, *F.F.*

LAMMLE. Alfred. *O.M.F.* x.

The mature young gentleman.

Note.—An unscrupulous adventurer. Friend of the Veneerings. He marries Sophronia Akershem. Each believes the other to have money—being led on in that belief by Veneering—and when, after their marriage, they discover their error, they decide to prey upon society in every way they are able. They endeavour to entangle Miss Podsnap in an alliance with young Fledgeby, but fail. They also attempt to obtain a footing in the household of Nicodemus Boffin, but fail also in this. They then leave the country.

LAMMLE. Mrs. *O.M.F.* x.

Note.—Miss Akershem married Mr. Lammle in the belief that he had a large income, while Mr. Lammle had entertained the same belief with regard to her. When they discover one another, they agree to join forces and prey generally upon their friends. This does not prove very successful, and they are last seen dismissed from the Boffin's with a hundred pounds on their way to France.

LAMPERT, DE. Owner of slaves. *A.N.* xvii.

LAMPLIGHTER. *L.D.* iii.

LAMPLIGHTER. In Coketown. *H.T., R.* vi.

LAMPS. A porter at Mugby Junction. *C.S., M.J.* i.

A spare man—with his features whimsically drawn upwards as if they were attracted by the roots of his hair. He had a peculiarly shining, transparent complexion, probably occasioned by constant oleaginous application; and his attractive hair, being cut short, and being grizzled—was not very unlike a lamp-wick.

LANCASHIRE. *M.P., O.S.*

LANCASTER. *C.S., D.M., L.T.* iii., iv.

LANDING-PLACE. At New Thermopylae. *M.C.* xxiii.

A steep bank with an hotel, like a barn, on the top of it; a wooden store or two, and a few scattered sheds.

LANDLADY. Mr. Nicodemus Dumps'. *S.B.B.*, Tales xi.

LANDLADY. Of "Magpie and Stump." *P.P.* xx.

An elderly female.

LANDLADY. Of spacious inn. *B.H.* lvii.

LANDLADY. Of spacious inn, Daughters of. *B.H.* lvii.

Three fair girls. The youngest a blooming girl of nineteen.

LANDLESS. Miss Helena. *E.D.* vi.

An unusally handsome lithe girl, very dark, and very rich in colour—of almost the gypsy type. (Twin sister to Neville.)

Note.—Ward of Mr. Honeythunder and sister of Neville Landless. She was born of English parents in Ceylon. Mr. Honeythunder sends her to Cloisterham to school, where she meets Rosa Bud and Edwin Drood. Afterwards, when Neville is suspected of the murder of Edwin and is obliged to leave Cloisterham, she goes to his rooms in Staple Inn to take him "into the sunlight."

LANDLESS. Neville. *E.D.* vi.

An unusually handsome, lithe young fellow—very dark, slender, supple, quick of eye and limb; half-shy, half-defiant; fierce of look.

"I have been always tyranically held down by the strong hand. This has made me secret and revengeful—false and mean."

Note.—Brother of Helena Landless, and ward of Mr. Honeythunder. He goes to study with the Rev. Septimus Crisparkle. He meets Rosa Bud and Edwin Drood. He has the beginnings of a warm attachment for Rosa, but dislikes Edwin: a dislike fostered by John Jasper. After Edwin's disappearance Neville is suspected of his murder, and although there is not sufficient evidence to warrant his detention in custody, public opinion is so strong against him that he is obliged to leave Cloisterham. He then resides in Staple Inn, where the Rev. Septimus visits him occasionally, and where his sister goes to keep him company. His guardian disowns him, but he lives in the hope of being cleared.

LANDLORD. *M.P., N.T.*

LANDLORD. Mrs. Raddles'. *P.P.* xxxii.

LANDLORD. Of house in George's Yard. *S.B.B., O.P.* v.

LANDLORD. Of inn. *C.S., H.H.*

LANDLORD. Of lonely inn. *N.N.* vi.

LANDLORD. Of private house. *S.B.B.*, Scenes iii.

Got into difficulties.

LANDLORD. Of "The George." *O.T.* xxxiii.

A tall gentleman in a blue neckcloth, a white hat, drab breeches, and boots with tops to match.

LANDLORD. Of "The Bush."

A jolly-looking old party. *P.P.* xlviii.

LANDOR. Robert. *M.P., L.L.*

LANDOR. Walter Savage. *M.P., L.L.*

LANDORA. La Signora. *M.P., L.L.*

LANDSEER. E., Sir E. Landseer. *M.P., O.L.N.O.*; *M.P., S. for P.*

LANE. Miss, Governess to young Borums. *N.N.* xxiv.

LANE. Mr. *M.P., S.*

LANGDALE. Vintner and distiller. *B.R.* lxi.

A portly old man, with a very red, or rather purple face.

Note.—The vintner of Holborn. A rubicund, choleric, but good-hearted gentleman. He takes the part of the *deus ex machina*, and his premises suffer in the riots.

LANGHAM PLACE. London. *P.P* xxxiii.

LANGLEY. Monsieur the Englishman. *C.S., S.L.* ii.

LANREAN. *C.S., M.F.S.* ii.

LANSDOWNE. Marquis of. *M.P., T.B.*

LANT STREET. In the Borough. *P.P.* xxx.

There is a sort of repose in Lant Street, which sheds a gentle melancholy upon the soul. There are always a good many houses to let in Lant Street; it is a by-street, too, and its dullness is soothing. . . . If a man wished to abstract himself from the world—he should by all means go to Lant Street.

LAPUTA. *U.T* xv.

LARKINS. Father of Jim. *S.B.B.*, Scenes xiii.

His line is coal and potatoes.

LARKINS. Jim, Horatio St. Julien. *S.B B.*, Scenes xiii.

LARKINS. Miss, the eldest. *D.C.* xviii.

Is not a little girl . . . not a chicken . . . perhaps the eldest Miss Larkins may be about thirty.

LARKINS. Mr. *D.C.* xviii.

A gruff old gentleman with a double chin, and one of his eyes immovable in his head.

LARNER. *M.P., S.R.*

LASCAR. *E.D.* i.

LATHARUTH. Habraham, A Jew. A client of Jaggers'. *G.E.* xx.

LATTER - DAY SAINTS. *U.T.* xx.

LAUNDRESS. Daughter of. *P.P.* xlvii.

LAUNDRESS. Mr. Perkers'. *P.P* xx.

A miserable-looking old woman . . . whose appearance, as well as the condition of the office (which she had by this time opened) indicated a rooted antipathy to the application of soap and water.

LAUNDRESSES. Slipshod, At Gray's Inn Square. *P.P.* liii.

LAUREAU. Village of. *C.S., M.f.T.S.* ii.

LAURIE. Sir P. *M.P., I. and C.*; *M.P., P.F.*

"**LAW.**" Mr. Grummer's name. *P.P.* xxiv.

Law, civil power, and exekative: them's my titles.

LAW. Name of the awful genie. *M.P., T.O.H.*

LAW IN ITS WIG. *M.P., T.T.C.D.*

LAWRENCE. Sir Thomas, Artist. *L.D.* x.

LAWYER. *N.N.* lix.

LAWYER. Attending deathbed of Nicholas Nickleby, Sen. *N.N.* i. Such things happen every day.

LAWYER. Jinkinson's. *M.H.C.* v.

LAWYERS. *M.P., D.V.*

LAWYER'S CLERKS. In Court of Chancery. *B.H.* i.

LAYARD. Mr. *M.P., S.F.A.*

LAYARDEEN. The troublesome. *M.P., T.O.H.*.

LAYMEN. *M.P., D.V.*

LAZZARONE. Capo. *P.F.I., R.D.*

LAZZARONI. Ragged. *P.F.I., R.D.*

LEAD MILLS. *O.T.* l.

LEADENHALL MARKET. *D. and S.* xxxix.; *M.P., I.S.H.W.*; *M.P., L.T.*,; *N.N.* xl.; *P.P.* xxxiii.; *R.P., B.S.*; *R.P., M.O.F.F.*

LEADENHALL STREET. *B.R.* xxxvii.; *C.S.*; *W.o.G.M.*

LEAKE COUNTY. *A.N.* xvii.

LEAMINGTON. *D. and S.* xx.

LEAMINGTON. Lodgings in. *D. and S.* xxi.

The Honourable Mrs. Skewton and her daughter resided, while at Leamington, in lodgings that were fashionable enough, and dear enough, but rather limited in point of space and conveniences—Mrs. Skewton, being in bed, had her feet in the window, and her head in the fireplace; while the Honourable Mrs. Skewton's maid was quartered in a closet within the drawing-room. Withers, the wan page, slept out of the house immediately under the tiles at a neighbouring milk-shop.

LEATH. Angela, Betrothed to the bashful man. *C.S., H.T.*

"**LEATHER BOTTLE.**" Cobham. *P.P.* xi.

A clean and commodious village alehouse.

Note.—The "Leather Bottle," an old-fashioned village inn, was a singular favourite with Dickens, both before and after he took up his residence at Gad's Hill Place. In his later years all his visitors had to be taken to Cobham.

"**LEATHER BOTTLE.**" Cobham, Dickens' Room. *P.P.* xi.

A long, low-roofed room, furnished with a number of high-backed, leather-cushioned chairs, of fantastic shapes, and embellished with a great variety of old portraits and roughly-coloured prints of some antiquity.

Note.—The room was not then called the Dickens' Room, of course; but although it was at one time in danger of being destroyed by fire, it still remains as it then was, with, perhaps, the only exception, of the prints, which have now been replaced with prints, drawings, etc., of Dickens and his characters. The "Leather Bottle" has now been restored and has proved to be a fourteenth century building.

LEATHER LANE. *B.R.* lxviii.

LEAVER. Mr. *S.Y.C.*

LEAVER. Mrs. *S.Y.C.*

LEAVER AND SONS. Messrs. *Mud. Pap.* ii.

LEAVING SHOP. A pawnbroker's. *O.M.F.* xxix.

LEBANON. Village of, near Belleville. *A.N.* xiii.

LECLERCQ. Miss Carlotta, as Marguerite. *M.P., N.T.*

LE DOUANIER. Monsieur. *U.T.* xvii.

L'ECU D'OR. Hôtel de *P.F.I., G.T.F.*

LEDBRAIN. Mr. *Mud. Pap.* i.

LEDBROOK. Miss, Member of Mr. V. Crummles' Company. *N.N.* xxiii.

Note.—A friend of Miss Snevellicci, and one of Mrs. Crummles' theatrical company.

LEE. *M.P., O.L.N.O.*

LEECH. Mr. John. *M.P., R.G.*

LEEDS. *R.P., O.O.S.*

LEEFORD. Mrs., Edward Leeford's mother. *O.T.* li.

LEEFORD. *See* Monks.

LEEFORD. Mr. *O.T.* xlix.

Note.—The betrayer of Agnes Fleming. The father of Monks and of Oliver Twist. He does not enter the story actively—only as a memory—as he was dead before Oliver's birth.

LEGACY DUTY OFFICE. *P.P.* lv.

LEGHORN. *D.C.* xxii; *R.P., P.M.T.P.*; *P.F.I.* ix.

LEGISLATIVE COUNCIL. *A.N.* ii.

LEICESTER FIELDS. *B.R.* lvi.

LEICESTERSHIRE. *N.N.* lx.

LEICESTER SQUARE. *B.H.* xxi.; *M.P., E.T.*; *R.P., A.P.A.*

LEIGHTON. *M.P., E.S.*

LEIPZIG. Poor of. *M.P., L.L.*

LEITH WALK. *P.P* xlix.

LEMON. Mark. *M.P., M.N.D.*; *M.P., N.S.*

LEMON. Mrs. Kept a preparatory establishment. *H.R.* iv.

LENVILLE. Mr., First Tragedy in Mr. Vincent Crummles' Company. *N.N.* xxiii.

A dark-complexioned man, inclining indeed to sallow, with long, thick, black hair, and very evident indications (although he was close-shaved) of a stiff beard, and whiskers of the same deep shade. His age did not appear to exceed thirty—his face was long, and very pale, from the constant application of stage paint. He wore a checked shirt, an old green coat with new gilt buttons, a neckerchief of broad red and green stripes, and full blue trousers; he carried, too, a common ash walking-stick.

Note.—Tragedian of Mr. Crummles' threatrical company. It was he who issued the cartel of defiance to Nicholas and was so summarily discomfited.

LENVILLE. Mrs., Member of Mr. V. Crummles' Company, and wife of Mr. Lenville. *N.N.*, xxiii.

In a very limp bonnett and veil.

LESBIA. *M.P., N.S.*

LESLIE. *M.P., O.L.N.O.*

LETHBRIDGE. Mr., Property man at Drury Lane Theatre. *R.P., D.W.T.T.*

L'ETOILE. Barrière de. *R.P., A.F.*

LEVI. Negro man; runaway slave. *A.N.* xvii.

LEWES. Mr. *B.H.*, Pref.

LEWIS. Mrs. A., As Madam Dor. *M.P., N.T.*

LEWISTON. *A.N.* xv.

LEWSOME. Mr. *M.C.* xxix.

Note.—The assistant of the medical man who supplied Jonas Chuzzlewit with the poison he intended for his grandfather Anthony. The suspicion of the purpose for which Jonas required the drug so preyed upon his mind that he made a voluntary confession of his part of the crime which he believed had been committed.

LIBRARY. The, Ramsgate. *S.B.B.*, Tales iv.

Was crowded. The same ladies, the same gentlemen, who had been on the sands, in the morning, and on the pier the day before.

LIBRARY. Ramsgate, One of the presiding goddesses of the. *S.B.B.*, Tales iv.

LIBRARY CART. Of Cheap Jack. Dr. Marigold. *C.S., D.M.*

LICENSED VICTUALLERS. The. *S.B.B.*, xxvi.

LIEUTENANT. A, In King Charles II's Army. *M.H.C.* ii.

Never a brave man. Married sister of his brother's wife, who murdered his nephew.

LIEUTENANT. Brother of, deceased. *M.H.C.* ii.

Married sister of lieutenant's wife.

LIEUTENANT. Deceased wife of brother of. *M.H.C.* ii.

LIEUTENANT. The, Mrs. Pott's brother. *P.P.* xviii.

LIFE. Name of bird. *B.H.* xiv.

LIFEBOAT. Peckham. *U.T.* xxxv.

LIFEGUARD. A, who taught fencing. *D. and S.* xxii.

LIFEGUARDS. A detachment of. *B.R.* xliii.

LIGHT JACK. *U.T.* v.

LIGHTERMAN'S ARMS. *Mud. Pap.*

LIGHTHOUSEMEN. Two spirits. *C.B., C.C., S.* iii.

LIGHTWOOD. Mortimer, A barrister. *O.M.F.* ii.

Another of Veneering's oldest friends, who never was in the house before, and appears not to want to come again (who sits disconsolate on Mrs. Veneering's left) who was inveigled by Lady Tippins (a friend of his boyhood) to come to these people's, and talk, and who won't talk.

Note.—Friend of Eugene Wrayburn. A solicitor employed by Mr. Boffin. A small income prevents his exerting himself in his profession, although he realizes more than his friend the need for some stability in life. He sticks to Eugene through his illness and the fight with society as represented by the Tippins, and decides to turn to and do something.

LIGNUM VITAE. Regimental nickname of Bagnet—*which see.*

LILIAN. William Fern's dead brother's child. An orphan. *C.B., C.* ii.

LILLE. *U.T.* xvii.

LILLERTON. Miss, Visiting Mr. and Mrs. Gabriel Parsons. *S.B.B.*, Tales x.

A lady— well educated; talks French; plays the piano, knows a good deal about flowers, and shells, and all that sort of thing; and has five hundred a year. A lady of very prim appearance and remarkably inanimate—her features might have been remarkably pretty when she was younger—her complexion—that of a well-made wax-doll.

LILLIE. Pet's deceased twin sister's name. *L.D.* xvi.

LILLIPUT. *U.T.* xv.

LILLYVICK. Mr., Uncle of Mrs. Kenwigs, a collector of water rates. *N.N* xiv

A short old gentleman in drabs and gaiters, with a face that might have been carved out of *lignum vitae*, for anything that appeared to the contrary.

Note.—The uncle of Mrs. Kenwigs. A water-rate collector from whom the Kenwigses have expectations. On this account he is treated by them with a deference which is ludicrous because it is studied and intentional. The collector marries Miss Petowker and disappoints them temporarily. Mrs. Lillyvick soon tires of her somewhat ponderous husband and elopes with a half-pay captain when Lillyvick returns to his relatives and casts off his wife for ever.

LIMBKINS. Mr., One of the Board. In the high chair. *O.T.* ii.
Note.—Chairman of the "Board" at the workhouse where Oliver was born.

LIMBURY. Mr. Peter. *M.P., I.S.H.W.*

LIME TREE LODGE. Groombridge Wells. *C.S., N.T.*, Act i.

LIMEHOUSE. *G.E.* xlv.; *M.P., C.J.*; *U.T.* xxxiv.

LIMEHOUSE CHURCH. *O.M.F.* vi.; *U.T.* xxxiii.

LIMEHOUSE HOLE. *D. and S.* lx.; *O.M.F.* xii.; *U.T.* xxix.

LIMERICK. *C.S., M.L. Leg.* i.

LINCOLNSHIRE. *B.H.* ii.; *C.S., M.L.Lo.* i; *M.P., E.S.*; *M.P., G.F.*

LINCOLN'S INN. *B.H.* i.
Lord High Chancellor's court situated in Lincoln's Inn.

LINCOLN'S INN. The old square. *B.H.* iii.
We passed into sudden quietude, under an old gateway, and drove on through a silent square until we came to an odd nook in a corner, where there was an entrance up a steep, broad flight of stairs, like an entrance to a church. And there really was a churchyard, outside under some cloisters, for I saw the gravestones from the staircase window.

LINCOLN'S INN FIELDS. *B.H.* x.; *B.R.* l.; *D.C.*, xxiv.; *P.P.* xliii.; *S.B.B.*, Scenes xvi.

LINCOLN'S INN FIELDS. Private hotel in. *D.C.* xxiii.
Where there was a stone staircase, and a convenient door in the roof.

LINCOLN'S INN GARDENS. *B.H.* x.

LINCOLN'S INN HALL. *B.H.* i.

LIND. Jenny. *M.P., T.D.*

LINDERWOOD. Lieut. *Mud. Pap.*

LINDERWOOD. Lieutenant, Officer of Marines in chase of pirates. *C.S., P.o.C.E.P.*

LINENDRAPER. Shopman of *B.R.*, Pref.

LINENDRAPER'S SHOP. *B.R.*, Pref.

LINENDRAPER'S SHOP. A dirty looking. *S.B.B.*, Tales v.

LINES. Chatham. *P.P.* iv.
A grand review . . . of half-a-dozen regiments . . . was to take place upon the lines.

LINKINWATER. Tim, Clerk of Cheeryble Brothers. *N.N.* xxxv.
Note.—The old clerk and ultimate partner of Cheeryble Brothers. He was at first doubtful about Nicholas, but quickly arrived at the conclusion that he would do for the office. He was a suitable character to associate with the genial and generous brothers. He married Miss La Creevy, much to Mrs. Nicklebys' disgust.

LINKINWATER'S. Tim, Sister. *N.N.* xxxvii.
Guest of Cheeryble Brothers.

LINNET. Thomas. *M.P., P.M.B.*

LINSEED. Duke of. *O.M.F.* xvii.

LINWOOD. Miss, *D.C.* xxxiii.; *R.P.P.A.*

LINX. Miss, A pupil of Miss Pupford. *C.S., T.T.G.* vi.

"**LION.**" Or "Lion and something Else." *D.C.* xi.
A miserable old public-house.

"**LION.**" Boots at the. *S.B.B.*, Tales viii.

LION HEART. A certain. *B.R.* iv.
Ready to become captain of certain reckless fellows.

LIONS. Friend of the, *M.P., T.L.*

LIRRIPER. Jemmy, Adopted grandson of Mrs. Lirriper. *C.S., M.L.Lo.* i.

LIRRIPER. Jemmy, Godson of the Major. *C.S., M.L.Lo.* i.

LIRRIPER. Joshua, Youngest brother of deceased. *C.S., M.L.Leg.* i.
Continually being summoned to the county court.

LIRRIPER. Mr., Deceased. *C.S., M.L.Lo.* i.

Was a handsome figure of a man, with a beaming eye and a voice as mellow as a musical instrument—in the commercial travelling line—behind-hand with the world and buried at Hatfield Church.

LIRRIPERS. Mrs., Lodgings. *C.S., M.L.Lo.* i.

Eighty-one Norfolk Street, Strand.

LIRRIPER. Mrs., Widow, and lodging-house keeper. *C.S., M.L.Lo.* i.

I am an old woman now and my good looks are gone, but that's me, my dear, over the plate warmer—and considered like.

LISSON GROVE. *S.B.B.*, Scenes xvii.

LIST. Isaac, Fellow-gambler with Mat. Jowl. *O.C.S.* xxix.

A slender figure stooping, and high in the shoulders—with a very ill-favoured face, and a most sinister and villanianous squint.

Note.—The companion of Jowl, *to which refer.*

LISTENER. New York, *M.C.* xvi.

LISTON. Mr. *S.Y.G.*

LITERARY AND SCIENTIFIC INSTITUTION. At Pavilionstone. *R.P., O.o.T.*

LITTIMER. Servant to Steerforth. *D.C.* xxi.

He was taciturn, soft-footed, very quiet in his manner, deferential, observant, always at hand when wanted, and never near when not wanted, but his great claim to consideration was his respectability. No one knew his Christian name. Distant and quiet as the North Pole.

Note.—Steerforth's servant was a capable hypocrite. After his master tires of Emily he proposes to marry her to Littimer. Littimer is last seen in the model prison in the next cell to that of Uriah Heep.

LITTLE BETHEL. *O.C.S.*, xxii.

LITTLE BRITAIN. *G.E.* xx.

LITTLE COLLEGE STREET. *P.P.* xxi.

LITTLE EYES. Nickname for Pubsey and Co.—*which see.*

LITTLE GOSLING STREET. Number thirty, London Docks. *L.D.* xxiv.

LITTLE HELEPHANT. The bar of. *D. and S.* lvi.

LITTLE RIFLE. The, The Kentucky Giant. *A.N.* xii.

LITTLE SAFFRON HILL. *O.T.* viii.

LITTLE TWIG STREET. No. 14. *M.P., U.N.*

LITTLE WINKLING STREET. *R.P., O.V.*

LIVELY. Mr., Respectable trader. *O.T.* xxvi.

Note.—A casual character who kept a receiver's shop in Field Lane, at the farther end.

LIVERER. Mr., The Marchioness' name for Mr. Swiveller—*which see.*

LIVERPOOL. *A.N.* i.; *B.H.* xxiv.; *C.S., H.T.*; *C.S., M.f.T.S.* ii.; *C.S.N.T.* Act ii.; *C.S., W.o.G.M.*; *H.T., G.* vii.; *L.D.* vii.; *M.C.* xiii.; *M.P., E.S.*; *M.P., R.T.*,; *M.P., S. Pigs*; *M.P., S.S.*; *R.P., B.S.*; *R.P., T.B.W.*; *R.P., T.D.P.*; *U.T.* ii.

LIVERPOOL MECHANICS' INSTITUTION. *M.P., E.A.S.*

LIVERY. Two tall young men in. *D. and S.* xxx.

Hired by Mrs. Skewton.

LIZ. Neighbour of Brickmaker. *B.H.* viii.

She has no kind of grace about her, but the grace of sympathy; but when she condoled with the woman, and her own tears fell, she wanted no beauty.

Note.—Wife of one of the brickmakers, and friend of Jenny.

LLANALLGO. *U.T.* ii.

LLANALLGO. Church at. *U.T.* ii.

A little church of great antiquity. The pulpit was gone, and other things usually belonging to the church were gone, owing to its living congregation having deserted it for the neighbouring schoolroom, and yielded it up to the dead. Forty-four ship-wrecked men and women lay here at one time, awaiting burial.

LLANDAFF. The Right Reverend the Bishop of. *N.N.* xxvii.

LLOYD'S. *S.B.B.*, Scenes ix.

LOAFING JACK. A, of the "Stars and Stripes." *U.T.* v.

With a long nose, lank cheek, high cheek-bones, and nothing soft about him but his cabbage-leaf hat.

LOBBS. Maria, Daughter of old Lobbs. *P.P.* xvii.

A prettier foot, a gayer heart, more dimpled face, or smarter form, never bounded so lightly over the earth they graced, as did those of "Maria Lobbs."

LOBBS. Old, The great saddler. *P.P.* xvii.

Who could have bought up the whole village at one stroke of his pen.

LOBBY. The, Of House of Commons. *S.B.B.*, Scenes xviii.

LOBLEY. Mr. Tartar's man. *E.D.* xxii.

He was a jolly-favoured man, with tawny hair and whiskers, and a big red face—the dead image of the sun in old woodcuts.

LOBSKIN. Signor, Singing-master at Minerva House. *S.B.B.*, Tales iii.

LOCH KATRINE. *M.P., I.*

LOCK LOMOND. *M.P., I.*

LOCK. House. *O.M.F.* xli.

LOCK. Plashwater Weir Mill. *O.M.F.* xliv.

Twenty mile and odd—call it five-and-twenty mile and odd—if you like—up-stream.

LOCK-UP-HOUSE. In vicinity of Chancery Lane. *S.B.B.*, Tales x.

LOCK-UP-HOUSE. Prisoner in, Ex-fruiterer, and then coal-dealer. *S.B.B.*, Tales x.

LOCK-UP-HOUSE. Prisoners. *S.B.B.*, Tales x.

In one of the boxes two men were playing at cribbage.—In another box, a stout, hearty-looking man of forty, eating some dinner which his wife, an equally comfortable-looking person had brought him.

LOCKHART. Mr., Scott's biographer. *M.P., S.P.*

LOCOCK. Dr. *M.P., B.A.*

L'OCTROI. Monsieur Le. *U.T.* xvii.

In his buttoned black surtout, with his note-book in his hand, and his tall black hat.

LODGE. At Newgate. *S.B.B.*, Scenes xxiv.

A whitewashed apartment.

LODGE. The. *P.P.* xlii.

LODGE. The, At Marshalesa. *L.D.* xviii.

LODGE. The, Residence of the Swidgers. *C.B., H.M.* i.

At students' college.

LODGER. Of Mrs. Bucket. *B.H.* xlix.

LODGER. Of Mrs. Raddle's. *P.P.* xlvi.

LODGER. Parlour, In Kenwigs'. *N.N.* xvi.

Empowered to treat, with the letting of a small back room on the second floor, reclaimed from the leads, and overlooking a soot-bespeckled prospect of tiles and chimney-pots. As a means of securing the punctual discharge of which service he was permitted to live rent free.

LODGER. Woman, In house for travellers. *S.B., H.M.* ii.

A young face, but one whose bloom and promise were all swept away. "My father was a gardener, far away in the country. He's dead to me."

LODGING-HOUSE. In Ramsgate, Rooms in (hired by the Tuggs). *S.B.B.*, Tales iv.

One ground floor sitting-room, and three cells with beds in them upstairs. Five guineas a week—with attendance (attendance means the privilege of ringing the bell as often as you like, for your own amusement).

LODGING-HOUSE. Travellers'. *E.D.* xiv.

LODGINGS FOR TRAVELLERS. *C.B., H.M.* ii.

LORD MAYOR. And court of Aldermen (1857). *M.P., S.F.A.*

LORD MAYOR. And Uncommon Counsellors. *M.C.* xxix.

LORD MAYOR [of London] 1850. *M.P., M.B.V.*

LORD MAYOR. Of London. *M.P., R.L.M.*

LORD MAYOR. Wholesale fruiterer. *M.H.C.* i.

A very substantial citizen indeed. His face was like the full moon in a fog, with two little holes punched out for his eyes, a very ripe pear stuck on for his nose, and a wide gash to serve for his mouth. He had once been a very lean, weazen little boy.

LORD MAYOR'S HEAD-FOOTMAN. The. *S.B.B., O.P.* i.

"**LORD.** My," A sweep on May Day. *S.B.B.*, Scenes xx.

Habited in a blue coat, and bright buttons, with gilt paper tacked over the seams, yellow knee-breeches, pink cotton stockings, and shoes: a cocked hat, ornamented with shreds of various coloured paper, on his head, a *bouquet* the size of a prize cauliflower in his button-hole, a long Belcher handkerchief in his right hand, and a thin cane in his left.

LORD. Noble, In House of Commons. *S.B.B.*, Scenes xviii.

LORD. Old, Of a great family. *N.N.* xviii.

Customer of Madame Mantalini and was going to marry a young lady.

LORD PRESIDENT. *B.R.* lxvii.

LORD WARDEN HOTEL. The, At Dover. *U.T.* xvii.

LORDS. House of. *M.H.C.* i.; *M.P., P.F.*; *S.B.B.*, Scenes xvi.

LORDS OF THE ADMIRALTY. The. *B.H.* xi.

LORENZO. Church of St. *P.F.I., G.A.N.*

LORN. Mr. *L.T.*

LORRY. Mr. Jarvis, of Tellson and Co's Bank. *T.T.C.* ii.

A gentleman of sixty, formally dressed in a brown suit of clothes, pretty well worn, but very well kept, with large square cuffs and large flaps to the pockets. He had a good leg and was a little vain of it.

Note.—Confidential clerk in Tellson's Bank. He is sent over to France in connection with the case of Dr. Manette and returns with him to England. He is a friend of the Manettes. He assists Lucy and her husband in the trials in Paris and escapes with them. In the "prophetic vision" he is seen ten years later passing peacefully away and leaving his goods to his friends.

LOSBERNE. Mr., A surgeon. *O.T.* xxix.

Known through a circuit of ten miles round as "The Doctor," had grown fat, more from good humour than from good living; and was as kind and hearty, and withal as eccentric an old bachelor, as will be found in five times that space, by any explorer alive.

Note.—A friend of the Maylies. The surgeon who was called in when Oliver was found shot after the attempted burglary. He was a bachelor, and like so many of Dicken's unmarried men, eccentric but kind-hearted. After Rose Maylie's marriage he settled his practice on his assistant and took a cottage outside the village of which his young friend [Harry Maylie] was pastor, and devoted himself to gardening, fishing, and carpentry work.

LOST. Mr., Of the Maze, Ware. *M.P., E.S.*

LOST AND LOST. Wool staplers. *M.P., E.S.*

LOUIS. A son of Madame Doche. *R.P., M.O.F.F.*

LOUIS. Belonging to inn in Switzerland. *C.S., H.T.*

LOUIS. Servant of Uncommercial Traveller. *U.T.* vii.

LOUISA. *S.Y.C.*

LOUISVILLE. *A.N.* xii.; *M.P., A.P.*

LOVE LANE. *C.S., H.T.*

"**LOVELY.**" A dog. *L.D.* x.

LOVETOWN. Mr. Alfred, *M.P., I.S.H.W.*

LOVETOWN. Mrs. *M.P., I S.H.W.*

LOWELL. Miss. *M.P., I.W.M.*

LOWELL. Mrs. *M.P., I.W.M.*

LOWELL. Prof. James Russell. *A.N.* iv.; *M.P., I.W.M.*

LOWESTOFT. *D.C.* ii.

We went to an hotel by the sea—David and Mr. Murdstone.

LOWFIELD. Miss. *S.Y.G.*

LOWTEN. Mr., Clerk to Mr. Perker. *P.P.* xx.

A puffy-faced young man.

Note.—Lowton was one of Mr. Perker's clerks and occupied a position somewhat in the nature of a confidential one. He was an example of a class of legal clerk now much rarer than in Dickens' times.

LOYAL. M., M. Loyal Devasseur. *R.P., O.F.W.*

LOYAL. Madame, Wife of M. Loyal. *R.P., O.F.W.*

An agreeable wife.

LUCAS. Solomon, Dealer in fancy dresses. *P.P.* xv.

His wardrobe was extensive—very extensive—not strictly classical, perhaps, not quite new, nor did it contain any one garment made precisely after the fashion of any age or time, but everything was more or less spangled; and what *can* be prettier than spangles.

LUCIFER. Sir, Sir Leicester Dedlock. *B.H.* ix.

LUCY. Only child of Mrs. Atherfield. *C.S., W.O.G.M.*

A little girl of three years old . . had a quantity of shining fair hair, clustering in curls all about her face.

LUD. King (Hudibras). *P.P.* xxxvi.

LUD-GATE. *M.H.C.* i.

LUDGATE HILL. *B.R.* lxvii.; *C.S., S.L.* iv.; *D.C.* xxx. *M.P., E.S.*; *M.P., T.D.*; *N.N.* xxxix.

LUDGATE HILL. A coffee-house on. *L.D.* iii.

LUFFY. *B.H.* xii.

LUFFEY. Mr., The highest ornament of the Dingley Dell Club. *P.P.* vii.

LUKIN. Young, Suitor of Mrs. Nickleby. *N.N.* xli.

LUMBEY. Doctor, Medical adviser to the Kenwigs. *N.N.* xxxvi.

A stout, bluff-looking gentleman, with no shirt collar, to speak of, and a beard which has been growing since yesterday morning; for Doctor Lumbey was popular, and the neighbourhood was prolific.

LUMMY. Ned, Of the Light Salisbury. *M.C.* xiii.

LUMPERS. Labourers employed to unload vessels. *R.P., D.W.T.T.*

LUMPS OF DELIGHT SHOP. *E.D.* iii.

"**LUNNON.**" *C.S., H.T.*

LUPIN. Mrs., Mistress of "Blue Dragon." *M.C.* iii.

In outward appearance just what a landlady should be: broad, buxom, comfortable, and good-looking, with a face a clear red and white, which by its jovial aspect at once bore testimony to her hearty participation in the good things of the larder and cellar, and to their thriving and healthful influences. She was a widow, but years ago had passed through her state of weeds, and burst into flower again—with roses on her ample skirts, and roses on her bodice, roses in her cap, roses in her cheeks—ay, and roses worth the gathering, too, on her lips. . . . She had a bright black eye, and jet black hair.

Note.—Mrs. Lupin was a picture of the typical landlady of an inn, as Dickens idealised them. She looked on Mark Tapley with very favourable eyes and regretted his departure for America. On his return they are married.

LUSANNE. *M.P., C.H.T.*

LUSHINGTON. Dr. *M.P., N.E.*

LUTH. Mr. Leary's learned dog. *H.T., G.* viii.

LYCEUM THEATRE. *M.P., M.M.*; *M.P., W.S.G.*; *R.P., B.S.*

LYNDHURST. Lord. *M.P., C.P.*

LYONS. *L.D.* xi.; *P.F.I., L.R.G.A.*

LYONS CATHEDRAL. *P.F.I., L.R.G.A.*

LYONS INN. *U.T.* xiv.

LYRIQUE. Paris. *M.P., W.*

LYTTON. Sir Edward Bulwer. *M.P., G.L.A.*

M

M. C. In linendraper's establishment. *S.B.B.*, Tales v.

The obsequious master of the ceremonies of the establishment, who, in his large white neckcloth and formal tie, looked like a bad portrait of a gentleman.

M. D. Little. *See* Marigold, Doctor. *C.S., D.M.*

M. J. Josiah. *A.N.* xvii.

M.P. An, In Bellamy's. *S.B.B.*, Scenes xviii.

A perfect picture of a regular *gourmand.*

M'ALLISTER. *A.N.* xvii.

MACAULAY. Mr. *M.P., I.*; *M.P., I M.*

MACBETH. Lady. *P.F.I., R.*

MACBETH. Lady, Character in play. *S.B.B.*, Scenes xiii.

The large woman, who is consulting the stage directions—always selected to play the part, because she is tall and stout.

MACCONNOCHIE. Captain. *M.P., P.P.*

MACCONNOCHIE'S SYSTEM. Captain. *M.P., H.H.W.*

MACCOORTS. The, Of MacCoort. *B.H.* xxx.

A great Highland family.

MACDOODLE. Charles, Of Macdoodle. *R.P., A.C.T.*

MACEY. Mr., Brother-in-law to Miss Maryon. *C.S., P.o.C.E.P.*

MACEY. Mrs., Miss Maryon's married sister. *C.S., P.o.C.E.P.*

MACFARREN. Mr. *M.P., M.M.*

MACINTOSH. Sir James. *M.P., I.M.*

M'KANE. *A.N.* xvii.

MACKIN. Mrs., Pawnbroker's customer. *S.B.B.*, Scenes xxiii.

A slipshod woman with two flat-irons in a basket.

MACLEAN. Governor. *M.P., N.E.*

MACLEAN. Mrs. *M.P., N.E.*

MACKLIN. Mrs., Of No. 4. *S.B.B.*, Scenes ii.

MACLISE. Daniel. *M.P., O.L.N.O.*; *M.P., S. for P.*; *M.P., S. of C.*

MACMANUS. Mr., A midshipman aboard the "Halsewell." *R.P., T.L.V.*

M'NEVILLE. Walter. *S.B.B.*, Tales iii.

MACREADY. *M.P., M.B.*; *M.P. P.P.D.*; *M.P., S.Q.F.*

MACSTINGER. Alexander, Son of Mrs. MacStinger. *D. and S.* xxv.

MACSTINGER. Charles. Son of Mrs. MacStinger. *D. and S.* xxxix.

MACSTINGER. Juliana, Daughter of Mrs. MacStinger. *D. and S.* xxv.

MACSTINGER. Mrs., Captain Cuttle's landlady. *D. and S.* ix.

A widow lady with her sleeves rolled up to her shoulders, and her arms frothy with soap-suds and smoking with hot water.

Note.—Captain Cuttle's landlady, He is particularly afraid of her, chiefly, apparently, because she is somewhat masterful. However, the captain succeeds in making a "moonlight flitting" without her knowledge. His precautions are only because the landlady would have prevented his going, and not because he was in her debt. Later on Mrs. MacStinger runs the captain to earth, and he is in danger of being taken back to bondage, but is rescued by Captain Bunsby. Captain Bunsby suffers the martyrdom of sacrifice, as Mrs. MacStinger marries him against his will.

MACSTINGERS. The little, Mrs. MacStinger's family. *D. and S.* ix.

MCWILLIAM. Dr. *M.P., N.E.*

MADDOX. John. *M.P., V.C.*

MADEIRA. *H.R.* iii.

MADGERS. Winifred, A girl of Mrs. Lirriper. *C.S., M.L. Leg.* i.

She was what is termed a Plymouth Sister. . . . A tidier young woman never came into a house.

MADNESS. Name of bird. *B.H.* xiv.

MADONNA DELLA GUARDIA. Chapel of. *P.F.I., G.A.N.*

MADRAS. *M.P., L.A.V.* ii.

MAG. Mary Ann. *M.P., E.S.*

MAGDALEN. *M.P., H.H.W.*; *M.P., I.M.*

MAGG. Mr., A vestryman. *R.P., O.V.*

MAGGIGG'S. Miss, Boarding establishment. *M.P., G.D.*

MAGGIORE. Lago. *P.F.I., V.M.M.S.S.*

"**MAGGY.**" Grand-daughter of my (Little Dorrit's) old nurse. *L.D.* ix.

She was about eight-and-twenty, with large bones, large features, large feet and hands, large eyes and no hair. Her large eyes were limpid and almost colourless; they seemed to be very little affected by light, and to stand unnaturally still. There was also that attentive listening expression in her face, which is seen in the faces of the blind, but she was not blind, having one tolerably serviceable eye. A great white cap, with a quantity of opaque frilling, that was always flapping about, apologised for Maggy's baldness.—The rest of her dress—had a strong resemblance to seaweed. Her shawl looked particularly like a tea-leaf, after long infusion.

Note.—Grandaughter of Mrs. Bangham. Attached to Little Dorrit. She goes to assist Mrs. Plornish, and reappears for the last time at Little Dorrit's wedding.

MAGICIAN. The African. *U.T.* xxvi.

Takes the cases of death and mourning under his supervision, and will frequently impoverish a whole family by his preposterous enchantments.

MAGISTRATE. A. *B.R.* xlix.

MAGISTRATE. County, *M.P., S.*

MAGISTRATE. Suburban, *U.T.* xxxvi.

MAGISTRATE. The, One of the Board. *O.T.* iii.

MAGISTRATES. At hospital. *S.B.B.*, Char. vi.

To take depositions of patient. One complained bitterly of the cold, and the other of absence of any news in the evening paper.

MAGISTRATES. Of Middlesex. *M.P., P.P.*

MAGNA CHARTA. *P.P.* xxiv.

MAGNIFICENT DISTANCES. The City of, Washington. *A.N.* viii.

MAGNUS. Mr., Peter. *P.P.* xxii.

A red-haired man with an inquisitive nose, mysterious-spoken personage, with a bird-like habit of giving his head a jerk every time he said anything. . . . "Curious circumstance about those initials, sir. You will observe P.M.—post meridian."

Note.—Mr. Peter Magnus travelled with Mr. Pickwick from London to Ipswich. The object of his visit to the ancient town was to propose to a lady who was stopping at the "Great White Horse," the hostel at which Mr. Pickwick and his fellow-traveller put up. After retiring for the night Mr. P. discovered he had left his watch downstairs. He returned for it. But having obtained it, he was unable to find his own room. At length he discovered one he believed to be his own. Then followed the tragic comedy of his adventure in the lady's bedroom. The sequel was that he and Tupman were haled before the Mayor of Ipswich on the charge of meditating a duel.

MAGOG. *M.P., G.A.*

"**MAGOG.**" The younger giant. *M.H.C.* i.

MAGPIE. In happy family. *M.P., R.H.F.*

"**MAGPIE AND STUMP.**" Inn. *P.P.* xx.

The weather-beaten signboard bore the half-obliterated resemblance of a magpie intently eyeing a streak of brown paint, which all the neighbours had been taught from infancy to consider as the "Stump."

MAGPIES. The Three. *O.M.F.* xvi.

MAGRA. The river. *P.F.I., R.P.S.*

MAGSMAN. A showman. *C.S., G.i.S.*

A grizzzled personage in velveteen with a face so cut up by the varieties of weather that he looked as if he had been tattooed.

MAGSMAN. House of. *C.S.*, *G.i.S.*

A wooden house on wheels. The wooden house was laid up in ordinary for the winter, near the mouth of a muddy creek.

MAGWITCH. Abel, *alias* Provis. Escaped convict. *G.E.* i.

A fearful man, all in coarse-grey with a great iron on his leg. A man with no hat, and with broken shoes, and with an old rag tied round his head—who limped and shivered and glared and growled.

Note.—Pip's convict. He escapes from the convict hulks, and when in a starving condition he meets Pip, he forces the boy, under threat of untold penalties, to procure food for him, together with a file. He is recaptured (partly) through the agency of Compeyson, to whom his evil career is largely due. He is transported, but in after years he amasses wealth in New South Wales, and anonymously through Jaggers, he makes a gentleman of Pip, with "great expectations." Later on he secretly returns to England under the name of Provis—Uncle Povis—but is recognised by Compeyson. Pip and his friends assist him in an attempt to escape, but their plan is frustrated. Compeyson is killed, and Magwitch so seriously injured that he dies in prison before his execution can be carried out; and ignorant of the fact that all his wealth has been forfeited.

MAID. Fanny's. *L.D.* xxxix.

MAID. Last new, Of the Nun's House. *E.D.* iii.

MAID. Miss Tox's. *D. and S.* x.

MAID. Of Mr. Jarndyce's household. *B.H.* vi.

MAID. Of Rokesmith. *O.M.F.* liv.

A fluttering young damsel, all pink and ribbons.

MAID. The Blue-eyed, Dover coach. *L.D.* iii.

MAIDEN LANE.

O.M.F. v.; *S.B.B.*, Scenes xx.

Inhabited by proprietors of donkey-carts, boilers of horse-flesh, makers of tiles, and sifters of cinders.

MAIDSTONE. *C.S.*, *P.o.C.E.P.*; *C.S.*, *S.P.T.* iii.

MAIDSTONE. (Jail.) *D.C.* xvi.

MAINE. *A.N.* iii.

MAIRIE. The. *C.S.*, *M.L.Leg.* i.

MAIRRWIE. The, At Sens. *C.S.*, *M.L.Leg.* i.

MAJESTY. His, On stage in Britannia. *U.T.* iv.

MAKER. Bonnet-shape. *S.B.B.*, Scenes iii.

MALABAR. *M.P.*, *L.A.V.* ii.

MALAKHOFF. *M.P.*, *B.A.*

MALAY. Sailor. *U.T.* xx.

MALAY PIRATES. *M.P.*, *P.F.*

MALCOLM. Character in play. *S.B.B.*, Scenes xiii.

Stupid-looking milksop, with light hair and bow legs—a kind of man you can warrant town-made.

MALDEN. Jack, Needy and idle. *D.C.* xvi.

Rather a shallow sort of gentleman, with a handsome face, a rapid utterance, and a bold, confident air.

Note.—Mrs. Strong's cousin. He is largely the cause of the temporary estrangement of Mrs. Strong from her husband. The doctor befriends him in every way, but always without any good effect on his dissolute relative.

MALDERTON. Mr. *S.B.B.*, Tales v.

A man whose whole scope of ideas was limited to Lloyd's, the Exchange, the India House, and the Bank. A few successful speculations had raised him from a situation of obscurity and comparative poverty to a state of affluence.

MALDERTON. Mr. Frederick. *S.B.B.*, Tales v.

Eldest son of Mr. and Mrs. Malderton.

In full dress costume, was the *beau ideal* of a smart waiter. Had lodgings of his own in town, always dressed according to the fashions of the months—went up the water twice a week in the season.

MALDERTON. Mr. Thomas. Younger son of Mr. and Mrs. Malderton. *S.B.B.*, Tales v.

With his white dress-stock, blue coat, bright buttons, and red watch-ribbon strongly resembled the portrait of that interesting, but rash, young gentleman, George Barnwell.

MALDERTON. Mrs. *S.B.B.*, Tales v.

A little fat woman like her eldest daughter multiplied by two.

MALDERTON. Miss Teresa, Elder daughter of Mr. and Mrs. Malderton. *S.B.B.*, Tales v.

A very little girl, rather fat, with vermillion cheeks but good-humoured, and still disengaged, although, to do her justice, the misfortune arose from no lack of perseverance on her part.

MALE. Elizabeth. *M.P., P.T.*

MALLARD. Mr., Clerk to Serjeant Snubbin. *P.P.* xxxi.

An elderly clerk, whose sleek appearance and heavy gold watch-chain, presented imposing indications of the extensive and lucrative practice of Serjeant Snubbin.

MALLET. Mr. *Mudfog Pap.* ii.

MALLEY. Mr. *O.M.F.* viii.

MALLOWFORD. Lord. *N.N.* li.

MALTA. *M.P., E.T.*

MALTA. Little, Daughter of Mr. and Mrs. Bagnet. *B.N.* xxvii.

MALTESE JACK. Visitor at " The Snug." *U.T.* v.

MALTHUS. A young Gradgrind. *H.T., S.* iv.

MALVERN. *M.P., M.N.D.*

MAMMAS. Matchmaking, Visitors in Assembly Rooms, Bath. *P.P.* xxxv.

MAN. Another, In chambers in Clifford's Inn. *P.P.* xxi.

Took the chambers, furnished them and went to live there. . . . Somehow or other he couldn't sleep

MAN. At the Morgue. *M.P., R.D.*

MAN. At the piano. *O.M.F.* xi.

A youngish, sallowish gentleman in spectacles, with a lumpy forehead.

MAN. Baked potatoe, *S.B.B.*, Scenes ii.

MAN. Capricious old, Wealthy relative of Jack Redburn, and his younger brother. *M.H.C.* ii.

MAN. Customer at ship chandler's. *D. and S.* iv.

Who came to ask change for a sovereign.

MAN. Dirty-faced, In blue apron. *S.B.B.*, Scenes viii.

In search of a will in Doctors' Commons.

MAN. Dull young. *M.P., S.S.A.*

MAN. Friend of John Podgers. *M.H.C.* iii.

A little man with a yellow face and a taunting nose and chin.

MAN. From Dombey's house. *D. and S.* xv.

MAN. From inn in Rochester. *C.S., S.P.T.* i.

With tray on his head containing vegetables and sundries.

MAN. From restaurant. *D. and S.* liv.

A bald man with a large beard.

MAN. From Shropshire. *See* Gridley, Mr.

MAN. Humpbacked. *O.T.* xxxii.

MAN. Husband of corpse. *O.T.* v.

Face was thin and very pale; his hair and head were grizzly; his eyes were bloodshot.

MAN. Ignorant. *M.P., T.O.H.*

MAN. In charge of three saddled horses. *M.H.C.* iii.

MAN. In uniform. *B.H.* lvii.

MAN. In the broker's shop. *S.B.B.*, Scenes v.

In the baked " jemmy " line, or the firewood or hearthstone line, or any other line which requires a floating capital of eighteen-pence or thereabouts.

MAN. In the Fleet. *P.P.* lxv.

MAN. In splendid armour, At Astley's. *S.B.B.*, Scenes xi.

MAN. Lame. *P.P.* xl.

MAN. Last drunken. *S.B.B.*, Scenes i.

Has just staggered heavily along, roaring out the drinking-song of the previous night.

MAN. Little, A visitor to Vauxhall Gardens. *S.B.B.*., Scenes xiv.

In faded black, with a dirty face and a rusty black neckerchief, with a red border, tied in a narrow wisp round his neck, who entered into conversation with everybody.

MAN. Little, ugly humpbacked. *O.T.* xxxii.

MAN. Long-legged young. *D.C.* xii.

MAN. Looking into church where Walter and Florence are married. *D. and S.* lvii.

With a wooden leg, chewing a faint apple and carrying a blue bag in his hand, looks in to see what is going on.

MAN. Merry-faced little. *M.P., P.M.B.*

MAN. Obnoxious young. *M.P., W.R.*

MAN. Old. *M.P., P.M.B.*

MAN. Old, A hard-featured, in Doctors' Commons, probably a money-lender. *S.B.B.*, Scenes viii.

A deeply wrinkled face—every wrinkle about his toothless mouth, and sharp, keen eyes, told of avarice and cunning. His clothes were nearly threadbare—from choice not from necessity. All his looks and gestures, down to the very small pinches of snuff, which he every now and then took from a little tin canister, told of wealth, and penury, and avarice.

MAN. Old, In the poor side of the Fleet. *P.P.* xlii.

Seated on a small wooden box, with his eyes rivited on the floor, his face settled into an expression of the deepest and most hopeless despair. A young girl, his little granddaughter, was hanging about him.

MAN. The old, Whose son is drowning. *P.P.* xxi.

The cause of Heyling's incarceration in the Marshalsea.

MAN. On swing-bridge over some docks in Thames. *U.T.* iii.

With a puffed, sallow face, and a figure all dirty and shiny and slimy, who may have been the youngest son of his filthy old Father Thames.

MAN. Poor, In distress in our parish. *S.B.B., O.P.* i.

Is summoned by—the parish. His goods are distrained, his wife dies— is buried by the parish—his children, they are taken care of by the parish. He is relieved by the parish—maintained in the parish asylum.

MAN. Prisoner, In the Fleet. *P.P.* xli.

His wife and a whole crowd of children might be seen making up a scanty bed on the ground, or upon a few chairs, for the younger ones to pass the night in.

MAN. Regular city, Owner of a garden. *S.B.B.*, Scenes ix.

He never does anything in it with his own hands; but he takes great pride in it notwithstanding —descants at considerable length upon its beauty and the cost of maintaining it. This is to impress you—with a due sense of the excellence of the garden, and the wealth of the owner.

MAN. Seafaring. *C.S., W.o.G.M.*

MAN. Shabby-genteel. *S.B.B.*, Char. x.

Reading in the British Museum —he always had before him a couple of shabby-genteel books—he used to sit all day, as close to the table as possible—to conceal the lack of buttons on his coat: with his old hat carefully deposited at his feet.

MAN. Tall, On horseback. *B.R.* lxvii.

Made a collection for the same purpose (the rioters) and refused to take anything but gold.

MAN. Ugly old. *D.C.* xiii.

MAN. Velveteen, A porter. *C.S., M.J.* ii.

Carrying his day's dinner in a small bundle that might have been larger, without suspicion of gluttony.

MAN. Very red-faced, Frequenting "The Peacock." *P.P.* xiv.

MAN. Wild. *M.P., F.L.*

MAN. With a wooden leg. *M.P., N.Y.D.*

MAN. Young, Frequenter of "Magpie and Stump." *P.P.* xx.

With a whisker, a squint, and an open shirt-collar (dirty).

MAN. Young, Hanged in Bishopsgate Street, father of. *B.R.* lxxvii.

Waited for him at the gallows, kissed him at the foot when he arrived, and sat there, on the ground till they took him down.

MAN. Young. In tea gardens. *S.B.B.*, Tales ix.

Keeping company with Uncle Bill's niece.

MAN. Young, One of the Gordon rioters. *B.R.* lxxvii.

Hanged in Bishopsgate Street.

MAN. Young, powerful, In brickmaker's. *B.H.* viii.

MAN. Young, Visitor to Bob Sawyer. *P.P.* xxxii.

Large-headed young man in a black wig.

MAN. Young, Wall-eyed. *C.S., S.P.T.* i.

Connected with the fly department of inn in Rochester.

MAN. Young, With donkey-cart. *D.C.* xii.

MAN OF ROSS = George Dolby. *M.P., I.W.M.*

MANCHESTER. *C.S.N.T.*, Act ii.; *M.P., E.S.*; *M.P., F.S.*; *M.P., G.F.*; *U.T.* xxiii.

MANCHESTER BUILDINGS. *N.N.* xvi.; *S.B.B.*, Scenes xviii.

Within the precincts of the ancient city of Westminster—is a narrow and dirty region, the sanctuary of the smaller members of Parliament in modern days. . . . If is comprised in one street of gloomy lodging-houses—from whose windows in vacation time there frown long, melancholy rows of bills "To Let."

MANCHESTER DELEGATES. *M.P., O.S.*

MANDANS. (Indians.) *M.P., E.T.*

MANDELL. D. J. *M.P., S.B.*

MANETTE. Dr. Alexandre, French prisoner. *T.T.C.* iv.

With his back towards the door, and his face towards the window, a white-haired man sat on a low bench, stooping forward and very busy, making shoes.

Note.—Physician unjustly incarcerated in the Bastille for eighteen years. He is found as a shoemaker in Paris, having been released on the eve of the Revolution. He is taken to England by Mr. Lorry and Lucie his daughter. There he regains the faculties which have left him in his long imprisonment, and even practises his profession. Lucie, his daughter, marries Charles Darnay, the son of the Marquis St. Evremonde. Darnay has resigned his estates to the country. He returns to Paris at the commencement of the Revolution to obtain the release of an old family servant, and is himself accused and thrown into prison. Dr. Manette follows and obtains his release in turn. But he is arrested again and convicted on the evidence of a document written by Dr. Mannette when he was in prison. Darnay is saved by the self-sacrifice of Carton, and Dr. Manette and his friends return to London, where the doctor forgets as far as possible the earlier happenings, and continues to practise medicine for many years.

MANETTE. Miss Lucie, Daughter of the rescued French prisoner. *T.T.C.* ii.

A young lady of not more than seventeen . . . with a slight, pretty figure, a quantity of golden hair, a pair of blue eyes, and a forehead with a singular capacity of lifting and knitting itself into an expression that was not quite one of perplexity, or wonder, or alarm, or merely of a bright fixed attention, though it included all the four expressions.

Note.—Daughter of Dr. Manette. Her mother dies before the opening of the story. Lucie goes to Paris, with Mr. Lorry to bring her father to London. On the journey she meets Darnay and is called as a witness in his trial for treason. She marries him later on. And when he is called to Paris and arrested there, she follows him with her father. Ultimately they succeed in escaping, and return to London, where they live happily.

MANGEL. Ralph. *M.P., P.M.B.*

MANN. Mrs., Matron of a branch workhouse. *O T* ii.

Where the parish authorities magnanimously and humanely resolved that Oliver should be "farmed." A parochial delegate, and a stipendiary.

Note.—The time-serving matron of the the branch workhouse, where the workhouse children are "farmed" for seven pence half-penny a week; of this sum Mrs. Mann appropriated the greater part to her own use.

MANNERS. Miss Julia. *S.B.B.*, Tales viii.

A buxom, richly-dressed female of about forty who by mistake eloped from Great Winglebury with Alexander Trott, and was married at Gretna Green.

MANNING. Mr. *M.P., D.M.*; *M.P., P.P.*

MANNING. Mrs., An emigrant. *R.P., T.D.P.*

MANNING. Sir Geoffrey, Friend of Pickwick's *P.P.* xviii.

MANNINGS. The, Husband and wife. (Criminals). *R.P., L.A.*

Hanging on the top of the entrance gateway of Horsemonger Jail.

"**MANOR FARM.**" In Muggleton. *P.P.* iv.

Scene of wedding of Bella and Trundle.

MANOR HOUSE.. Miss Havishams. *See* Satis House.

MANOR HOUSE. The old, The farmhouse. *R.P., D.W.I.F.*

MANSEL. Miss. *R.P., T.L.V.*

One of the five lady passengers on board the "Halsewell."

MANSFIELD. Lady. *B.R.* lxvi.

MANSFIELD. Lord. *B.R.* lxvi.

MANSION. Property of Michael Warden, Esq. *C.B., B.o.L.* iii.

MANSION HOUSE. *B.R.* lxi.; *M.H.C.* i.; *M.P., G.A.*; *M.P., R.L.M.*; *P.P.* xx.; *S.B.B.*, Scenes xvii.

MANTALINI. Husband of Madame Mantalini. *N.N.* x.

Dressed in a gorgeous morning gown, with a waistcoat, and Turkish trousers of the same pattern, a pink silk neckerchief, and bright green slippers, and had a very copious watch-chain wound round his body.

Note.—The man of fashion who lives on his wife's earnings as long as possible, but when she is made bankrupt separates from her. He is imprisoned, and released by a laundress who after the first blush has worn off her acquisition sets him to the mangle, where he is discovered turning the handle by Kate and Nicholas. Originally his name was Muntle, but obviously such a name was of no use to a fashionable man about town or to a high-class millinery and dressmaking business.

MANTALINI. Madam, Dressmaker. *N.N.* x.

A buxom person, handsomely dressed.

Note.—The dressmaker to whom Kate was sent by her uncle, Ralph Nickleby. She was made bankrupt by her husband's extravagance, and the business was acquired by her manageress.

MANTALINI'S SHOP. Ground floor of Madam. *N.N.* x.

Let off to an importer of otto-of roses.

MANTUA. *L.D.* xlv.; *P.F.I., V.M.M.S.S.*

MANUAL. A negro slave. *A.N.* xvii.

MAPLESONE. Julia. *S.B.B.*, Tales i.

Aged twenty-two. Afterwards Mrs. Simpson.

MAPLESONE. Matilda, Elder daughter of Mrs. Maplesone. *S.B.B.*, Tales i.

Aged twenty-five. Afterwards Mrs. Septimus Hicks.

MAPLESONE. Matilda, Mrs. Maplesone. *S.B.B.*, Tales i.

MARCHESE. Italian, The usual Guest of Mrs. Merdle. *L.D.* lv.

"**MARCHIONESS.**" Servant to the Brasses. *O.C.S.* xxxiv.

A small, slipshod girl in a dirty coarse apron and bib. . . . "Yes, I do plain cooking," replied the child. "I'm housemaid too; I do all the work in the house."

Note.—There is a good deal of mystery attached to the overworked and underfed drudge discovered by Dick Swiveller at the Brass' house in Bevis Marks. There is no solution of the mystery in the book, although it is hinted at: and Sally Brass is supposed to know a good deal more than she tells. Dick Swiveller and the Marchioness form a friendship, and when Dick is ill the Marchioness attends him. After his recovery Dick sends her to a school and finally marries her, when they go to live in a "little cottage at Hampstead."

MARGARET. Aunt, Guest at Christmas family party. *S.B.B.*, Char. ii.

Poor Aunt Margaret married a poor man—has been discarded by her friends—but Christmas coming round—the unkind feelings—have melted—like half-formed ice, beneath the morning sun.

MARGARET. Husband of Aunt. *S.B.B.*, Char. ii.

Turns out to be such a nice man, and so attentive to grandmama—such beautiful speeches and nice songs

MARGARET. Meg. *C.B., C., G.* iii.

MARGARET. Mr. Winkle Senior's maid. *P.P.* l.

MARGARET. Young child of. *C.S., M.f.T.S.* i.

MARGARET. Young widow. Hugh's widow. *C.S., M.f.T.S.* i.

MARGARETTA. Mrs. Frank Milvey. *O.M.F.* lxi.

MARGATE. C.S., *T.T.G.* vi.; *H.R.* iii.; *S.B.B.*, Scenes x.; *S.B.B.*, Tales iv.

MARGATE. Mayor of. *H.R.* iii.

MARGATE ROADS. *H.R.* iii.

MARGUERITE. *M.P., N.T.*

MARGUERITE. Miss, Niece of M. Obenreizer. *C.S., N.T.*, Act i.

The young lady wore an unusual quantity of fair bright hair, very prettily braided about a rather rounder white forehead than the average English type, and so her face might have been a shade rounder than the average English face, and her figure slightly rounder than the figure of the average English girl at nineteen.

MARIA. Runaway Negro woman slave. *A.N.* xvii.

MARIE. Jean. *M.P., N.T.*

MARIGOLD. Doctor, A Cheap Jack. *C.S., D.M.*

Born on the queen's highway, but it was the king's at that time, on a common—at present a middle-aged man of a broadish build, in cords, leggings, and a sleeved waistcoat, the string of which is always gone behind. "If I have a taste in point of personal jewelry, it is mother-of-pearl buttons."

MARIGOLD. Wife of Doctor. *C.S., D.M.*

She wasn't a bad wife, but she had a temper.

MARIGOLD. Willum, Father of Doctor Marigold, also a Cheap Jack. *C.S., D.M.*

MARINA. Caro Padre Abate. *M.P., L.L.*

MARINE STORE DEALERS. In Ratcliffe High Way. *S.B.B.*, Scenes xx

Here the wearing apparel is all nautical—large bunches of cotton pocket handkerchiefs, in colour and pattern unlike any one ever saw before—a few compasses, a small tray containing silver watches, in clumsy thick cases.

MARK LANE. The churches about. *U.T.* ix.

There was a dry whiff of wheat.

MARKER. Mrs. Wanting a cook. *N.N.* xvi.

Offers eighteen guineas; tea and sugar found. Two in family, and see very little company. Five servants kept. No man—no followers.

MARKET. Calf, *R.P., M.O.F.F.*

MARKET. Cattle, *R.P., M.O.F.F.*

MARKET. Covent Garden. *S.B.B.*, Scenes i.

Strewed with decayed cabbage leaves, broken hay-bands, and all the indescribable litter of a vegetable market.

MARKET. Sheep. *R.P., M.O.F.F.*

MARKET PLACE. Philadelphia. *A.N.* vii.

MARKET PLACE. Salisbury. *M.C.* v.

Being market-day—the thoroughfares about the market place—filled with carts, horses, donkeys, baskets, waggons, garden stuff, meat, tripe, pies, poultry, and hucksters' wares of every opposite description and possible variety of character.

MARKET TOWN. *B.H.* xviii.

A dull little town, with a church spire, and a market place, and a market cross, and one intensely sunny street, and a pond with an old horse cooling his legs in it, and a very few men sleepily lying and standing about in narrow little bits of shade.

MARKHAM. Steerforth's friend. *D.C.* xxiv.

Always spoke of himself indefinately, as a "man."

MARKLEHAM. Mrs., Mrs. Strong's mamma. *D.C.* vol. i., xvi.

MARKS. Will, John Podger's nephew. *M.H.C.* iii.

A wild, roving young fellow of twenty, who had been brought up in his uncle's house, and lived there still.

MARLBOROUGH. Downs, "In the direction of Bristol." *P.P.* xiv.

There are many pleasanter places, even in this dreary world, than Marlborough Downs, when it blows hard.

MARLBOROUGH HOUSE. *M.P.*, *S.D.C.*; *M.P.*, *S. for P.*; *M.P.*, *Th. Let.*

MARLEY. Scrooge and, Bill discounters. *C.B.*, *C.C.* s.i.

MARLEY. Late of Scrooge and Marley. *C.B.*, *C.C.* s.i.

Was as dead as a door-nail.

MARLOW. Alice, *See* Brown, Alice.

MAROON. Captain, Friend of Captain Barbary. *L.D.* xii.

A gentleman with tight drab legs, a rather old hat, a little hooked stick, and a blue neckerchief.

MARQUIS. *M.P.*, *T.T.*

"**MARQUIS OF GRANBY.** The," roadside public-house. *P.P.* xxvii.

MARROW BONES AND CLEAVERS. The, have got the scent of the marriage. *D. and S.* xxxi.

Put themselves in communication, through their chief, with Mr. Towlinson, to whom they offer terms to be bought off.

MARS. Sons of, Two former lovers of Mrs. Tetterby. *C.B.*, *H.M.* ii.

MARSEILLES. *L.D.* i.; *M.P.*, *W.*; *P.F.I.*, *G.T.F.*; *R.P.*, *M.O.F.F.*

MARSEILLES. Prison dungeon in. *L.D.* i.

A villanous prison. In one of its chambers, so repulsive a place that even the obtrusive stare (of the blazing sun) blinked at it, and left it to such refuse of reflected light as it could find for itself, were two men. Beside the two men, a notched and disfigured bench, immovable from the wall, with a draught-board rudely hacked upon it with a knife, a set of draughts, made of old buttons and soup-bones, a set of dominoes, two mats, and two or three wine bottles. The imprisoned air, the imprisoned light, the imprisoned damps, the imprisoned men, were all deteriorated by confinement.

MARSH GATE. *S.B.B.*, Scenes ii.

MARSHAL. The. *L.D.* vi.

MARSHALL. Mary, Betrothed to Richard Doubledick. *C.S.*, *S.P.T.* ii.

MARSHALL. Miss. *S.Y.G.*

MARSHALL. Mr. Matthew. *M.P.*, *F.L.*

MARSHALSEA. Errand bearers of the. *L.D.* ix.

MARSHALSEA. Go-betweens of the. *L.D.* ix.

MARSHALSEA. Father of the. *See* Dorrit, Mr. *L.D.* vi.

MARSHALSEA. Nondescript messengers of the. *L.D.* ix.

"**MARSHALSEA HOTEL.**" The. *L.D.* ix.

MARSHALSEA PLACE. *L.D.*, Pref.

The houses which I recognized, not only as the great block of the former prison, but as preserving the rooms that arose in my mind's eye, when I became Little Dorrit's biographer.

MARSHALSEA PRISON. *L.D.* vi.; *P.P.* xxi.

An oblong pile of barrack buildings, partitioned into squalid houses standing back to back, so that there were no back rooms; environed by a narrow-paved yard, hemmed in by high walls duly spiked at top. Itself a close and confined prison for debtors, it contained within it a much closer and more confined jail for smugglers—a blind alley some yard and a half wide, which formed the mysterious termination of the very limited skittle-ground in which Marshalsea debtors bowled down their troubles.

MARSHES. The, Marsh Country. *G.E.* i.

Down the river, within, as the river wound, twenty miles of the sea.

MARSHES. Pontine. *P.F.I.*, *R.D.*

MARSIGLIA. *L.D.* lviii.

MARTHA. Eldest daughter of Bob Cratchit. *C.B.*, *C.C.*, *S.* iii.

MARTHA. Aunt, Sister of Doctor Jeddler. *C.B.*, *B.O.L.* iii.

MARTHA. Inmate of workhouse. *O.T.* xxiii.

A withered old female pauper. Her body was bent by age; her limbs trembled with palsy; her face, distorted into a mumbling leer, resembled more the grotesque shaping of some wild pencil, than the work of Nature's hand.

MARTHA. John's daughter. *D. and S.* xxiv.

Her mother has been dead these ten year. . . . Ugly, misshapen. peevish, ill-conditioned, ragged, dirty—but beloved!

MARTHA. Maid to the Parsons. *S.B.B.*, Tales x.

MARTIGNY. *L.D.* xxxvii.

MARTIN. Miss, Client of. *S.B.B.*, Char. viii.

Lady in service, whose "missis" wouldn't allow a young girl to wear a short sleeve of an afternoon.

MARTIN. Amelia, The mistaken milliner. *S.B.B.*, Char. viii.

In a merino gown, of the newest fashion, black velvet bracelets on the genteelest principle, and other little elegancies.

MARTIN. Betsy, Convert to temperance. *P.P.* xxxiii.

Goes out charing and washing by the day, never had more than one eye, knows her mother drank stout, and shouldn't wonder if that caused it.

MARTIN. Betsy. *M.P.*, *L.*

MARTIN. Captain. *L.D.* xix.

A rather distinguished "collegian."

MARTIN. Jack, Bagman's uncle. *P.P.* xlix.

MARTIN. Miss, Young lady at the bar of dining-rooms, where Somebody's luggage was left. *C.S.*, *S.L.* i.

MARTIN. Servant to Mr. Allen's aunt. *P.P.* xlviii.

MARTIN. Sir Geoffrey Manning's gamekeeper—tall, raw-boned. *P.P.* xix.

MARTIN. Sir, Sir Martin Archer Shee. *M.P.*, *S.P.*

MARTIN. Tom, Butcher-prisoner in the Fleet. *P.P.* xli.

Clothed in a professional blue jean frock, and top boots with circular toes.

MARTIN'S. A friend of. *S.B.B.*, Char. viii.

Keeping company with a painter and decorator's journeyman.

MARTINEAU. Miss. *M.P.*, *P.P.*

MARTINS. *S.Y.G.*

MARTON. Schoolmaster. *O.C.S.* xxiv.

He was a pale, simple-looking man, of a spare and meagre habit, and sat among his flowers and beehives, smoking his pipe, in the little porch before the door.

Note.—The kindly old schoolmaster who befriends Nell and her grandfather on their travels and obtains for them their last post in the quiet village, in which he himself had been appointed clerk.

MARTYR. The Blessed, Charles I. *B.H.* vii.

MARWOOD. Good Mrs. Brown. *D. and S.* xxxiv.

MARY. *D. and S.* xxviii.

MARY. *P.P.* xli.

MARY. Another Seven Dials lady. *S.B.B.*, Scenes v.

MARY. Barmaid. *S.B.B.*, Scenes xxii.

MARY. Black girl runaway slave. *A.N.* xvii.

MARY. Daughter of drunkard. *S.B.B.*, Tales xii.

MARY. Daughter of John. *R.P., P.M.T.P.*

MARY. Handmaiden at "The Peacock." *P.P.* xiv.

MARY. Housemaid in pot-shop in Borough. *P.P.* lii.

MARY. Mrs. Perrybingle. *C.B., C.o.H.* i.

MARY. Negro girl slave. *A.N.* xvii.

MARY. Nupkins' maid servant. The pretty servant girl. *P.P.* xxv.

Note.—The appearance of the Pickwickians before the Mayor of Ipswich had another result than the exposure of Capt. Fitz-Marshall, as it was there Sam Weller first met Mary, the housemaid, whom he afterwards married. Mary also aided and abetted Arabella Allen in her runaway match with Mr. Winkle.

MARY. Servant at the Manor Farm, Dingley Dell. *P.P.* v.

MARY. Sweetheart of Captain Ravender. *C.S., W.o.G.M.*

She died six weeks before our marriage day—and she was golden if golden stands for good.

MARY. Visitor at Greenwich Fair. *S.B.B.*, Scenes xii.

MARY. Wife of George, Prisoner in Marshalsea—dying woman. *P.P.* xxi.

Let them lay me by my poor boy now.

MARY ANN. One of the presiding goddesses in library, Ramsgate, in maroon-coloured gowns. *S.B.B.*, Tales iv.

MARY ANNE. David and Dora's servant. *D.C.* xv.

She had a written character as large as a proclamation, and according to this document, could do everything of a domestic nature that ever I heard of, and a great many things that I never did hear of.

MARY ANNE. Favourite pupil of Miss Peecher. *O.M.F.* xviii.

Note.—Miss Peecher's maid and favourite. She conveyed intelligence of the happenings at Mr. Headstone's.

MARY ANNE. Wemmick's maid. *G.E.* xlv.

MARYLAND. *A.N.* viii.

MARYLEBONE. *D. and S.* xxx.; *M.P., S. Pigs.*

MARYLEBONE THEATRE. *M.P., V. and B.S.*

MARYON. Captain, Captain of the sloop "Christopher Colombus." *C.S., P.o.C.E.P.*

MARYON. Miss, Sister to Captain Maryon. *C.S., P.o.C.E.P.*

A beautiful young English lady, sister to the captain of our sloop.

MARYPOST. *L.T.* iii.

MASH. Master, Pupil of Mr. Barlow. *U.T.* xxxiii.

This young wretch wore buckles and powder.

MASK. The cavalier whose face was concealed under a black mask. *M.H.C.* iii.

"MASKERY'S MOST FEELING COACHMAN." *M.P., O.S.*

MASON. Monsieur, the tall and sallow. *U.T.* xviii.

MASON. The *D. and S.* xviii.

Sings and whistles as he chips out PAUL in the marble slab before him.

MASSACHUSETTS. *M.P., L.A.V.* ii.; *U.T.* iii.

MASSACHUSETTS JEMMY James T. Fields. *M.P., I.W.M.*

MAST-MAKER. Purchaser of the old boat. *D.C.* xxii.

MASTER. Deceased, of house which shall be nameless. *C.S., S.L.* i.

Was possessed of one of those unfortunate dispositions in which spirit turns to water, and rises in the ill-starred victim.

MASTER. Of servant of all work *S.B.B.*, Scenes i.

MASTER. The, Our friend. *M.P.*, *F.L.*

MASTER CARPENTERS' SOCIETY. *M.P.*, *R.T.*

MASTIFF. The. Evenson. *S.B.B.*, Tales i.

MATABOOS. A set of personages in Tonga Island. *U.T.* xxvi.

"**MATCHMAKER.**" The, A former Chuzzlewit. *M.C.* i.

A matron of such destructive principles, and so familiarised to the use and composition of inflammatory and combustible engines, that she was called the matchmaker, by which nickname and byword she is recognised in the family legends to this day.

MATE. Lock-keeper's. *O.M.F.* lvii.

MATHEWS. Thomas. *M.P.*, *L.A.V.* ii.

MATINTERS. Two Miss. *P.P.* xxxv.

Visitors at the Assembly Rooms, Bath.

MATRON. *C.S.*, *S.P.T.* i.

MATTHEWS. Servant of Mr. Gregsbury, M.P. *N.N.* xvi.

A very pale, shabby boy, who looked as if he had slept underground from his infancy—as very likely he had

MAWLS. Master, A pupil in our school. *R.P.*, *O.S.*

MAXBY. A day pupil at our school. *R.P.*, *O.S.*

MAXBY'S FATHER. *R.P.*, *O.S.*

MAXBY'S SISTERS. *R.P.*, *O.S.*

MAXEY. Caroline, A maid of Mrs. Lirriper's. *C.S.*, *M.L.Lo.* i.

Such a temper—a good-looking, black-eyed girl—and a comely-made girl to your cost when she did break out and laid about her.

MAXWELL. Mrs., Guest at christening party of the Kitterbells. *S.B.B.*, Tales xi.

MAY. Mr., As Tom, a waiter at the St. James's Arms. *M.P.*, *S.G.*

MAYDAY. Friend of Uncommercial Traveller. *U.T.* xix.

MAYES. Mr. *M.P.*, *P.T.*

MAYFAIR. *H.T.*, *S.* viii. ; *M.C.* xiii.

MAYLIE. Harry, Son of Mrs. Maylie. *O.T.* xxxiii.

About five-and-twenty years of age, and was of the middle height ; his countenance was frank and handsome, and his demeanour easy and prepossessing.

Note.—Mrs. Maylie's son. Originally destined for a prominent public career with Parliamentary prospects, he becomes pastor of a village church and marries Rose Maylie.

MAYLIE. Mrs., Lady of house attempted to be burgled. *O.T.* xxix.

Well advanced in years ; but the high-backed oaken chair in which she sat was not more upright than she. Dressed with the utmost nicety and precision, in a quaint mixture of bygone costume, with some slight concessions to the prevailing taste—she sat in a stately manner, with her hands folded.

Note.—Mrs. Maylie adopted Rose, and befriended Oliver Twist : beyond these she has no very important place in the story.

MAYLIE. Rose, Miss, Niece of Mrs. Maylie. *O.T.* xxix.

In the lovely bloom and springtime of womanhood—she was not past seventeen, cast in so slight and exquisite a mould ; so mild and gentle ; so pure and beautiful that earth seemed not her element.

Note.—Rose Maylie was discovered by Mrs. Maylie in the charge of some poor people, miserable and uncared for. Her condition is largely due to the machinations of Monks' mother. Mrs. Maylie took the child home and adopted her as her daughter. It is ultimately discovered that her real name is Rose Fleming ; that she is sister to Agnes Fleming, and therefore Oliver's aunt. She married Harry Maylie.

MAYOR. The, Of Eatanswill. *P.P.* xiii.

" May he never desert the nail and sarspan business."

MAYOR. The, Of Ipswich. *P.P.* xxiv.

MAYOR. The, Officers of. *P.P.* xiii.

MAYPOLE. HUGH. Ostler at Maypole. *See* Hugh.

MAYPOLE INN. The. *B.R.* i.

An old building, with more gable-ends than a lazy man would care to count on a sunny day; huge zigzag chimneys, out of which it seemed as though even smoke could not choose but come in more than naturally fantastic shapes—and vast stables gloomy, ruinous and empty. The place was said to have been built in the days of King Henry the Eighth; and there was a legend, not only that Queen Elizabeth had slept there one night—but that next morning, while standing on a mounting-block before the door with one foot in the stirrup, the virgin monarch had. . . boxed and cuffed an unlucky page for some neglect of duty . . . a very old house, perhaps as old as it claimed to be, and perhaps older, which will sometimes happen with houses of an uncertain, as with ladies of a certain, age.

MAYSVILLE. *A.N.* xvii.

MAZE. Ware. *M.P., E.S.*

M'CHOAKUMCHILD. Mr., A Schoolmaster. *H.T., S.* ii.

MEAGLES. Mr., Retired banker. *L.D.* ii.

Who never by any accident acquired any knowledge whatever of the language of any country into which he travelled.

Note.—Enters the story on numerous occasions; although not a chief actor in it. He is the father of Minnie. A retired banker who travels a good deal. Friend of Doyce, and of Arthur Clennam, and benefactor of Tatty Coram.

MEAGLES. Mrs., Wife of Mr., Meagles. *L.D.* ii.

Like Mr. Meagles, comely and healthy, with a pleasant English face, which had been looking at homely things for five-and-fifty years or more, and shone with a bright reflection of them.

MEAGLES. "Pet," Only daughter of Mr. and Mrs. *L.D.* ii.

About twenty. A fair girl with brown hair hanging free in natural ringlets. A lovely girl, with a frank face and wonderful eyes; so large, so soft, so bright, set to such perfection in her kind, good face. She was round, and fresh, and dimpled.

Note.—Daughter of the Meagles, Pet marries the young artist Harry Gowan, but is not very happy with him.

MEAGLE'S HOUSE. Mr. *L.D.* xvi.

A charming place—on the road by the river—It stood in a garden—and it was defended by a goodly show of handsome trees and spreading evergreens. It was made of an old brick house, of which a part had been altogether pulled down, and another part had been changed into the present cottage—within view was the peaceful river, and the ferry boat.

MEALMAN. Who supplies the Zoological Gardens. *M.P., G.H.*

MEALY POTATOES. *D.C.* xi.

MECCA. *R.P., O.H.F.*

MECHI. *R.P., B.S.*

MEDICAL CHOICE SPIRIT. *M.P., L.E.J.*

MEDICAL COLLEGE. Baltimore. *A.N.* ix.

MEDICAL STUDENT. *L.T.*

MEDICINE MAN. Of North American Indians. *U.T.* xxvi.

For his legal medicine, he sticks upon his head the hair of quadrupeds, and plasters the same with fats, and dirty white powder—and talks a gibberish.—For his religious medicine, he puts on puffy white sleeves, little black aprons, large black waistcoats—collarless coats, with medicine button-holes, medicine stockings and gaiters and shoes—and a highly grotesque medicinal hat.

MEDICINE MEN. Of civilisation. *U.T.* xxvi.

MEDITERRANEAN. *L.D.* liv.; *M.P., L.A.V.* ii.; *M.P., N.Y.D.*; *P.F.I., A.G.*; *U.T.* vii.

MEDIUM. A horrible. *M.P., S.B.*

MEDUSA. Bride's Aunt. *O.M.F.* x.

MEDWAY. *C.S.*; *S.P.T.* i.; *D.C.* xvii.; *P.P.* v.; *U.T.* xxiv.

The banks of the Medway, covered with cornfields and pastures, with here and there, a windmill, or a distant church.

MEDWIN. Mr. *M.P., S.S.*

MEEK. Augustus George, Son of Mr. and Mrs. Meek. *R.P., B.M.S.*

MEEK. George, Mr. Meek. *R.P., B.M.S.*

MEEK. Mrs., Wife of Mr. Meek. *R.P., B.M S.*

MEEK'S MOTHER. Mrs, *See* Bigby, Mrs.

MEGG. Mr., A vestryman. *R.P.,O.V.*

MEGGISSON'S. A lodging-house *U.T.* v.

MELBOURNE. Lord. *M.P., I.M.*

MELCHISEDECH'S. *B.H.* xxxiv.

'MELIA. Bill's wife. *G.E.* xx.

'MELIA. Housemaid of Dr. Blimber's. *D. and S.* xii.

A pretty young woman in leather gloves, cleaning a stove . . . tied some strings for Paul, aged six, . . . who couldn't dress himself easily, not being used to it . . . and further more, rubbed his hands to warm them; and gave him a kiss.

MELL. Mr. Charles, One of the masters at Salem House. *D.C.* v.

A gaunt, sallow young man, with hollow cheeks.

MELL. Mrs., Mother of Mr. Mell, and inmate of the almshouses. *D.C.* v.

MELLON. Mr. Alfred. *M.P., M.M.*

MELLON. Mrs. Alfred, As Sarah Goldstraw. *M.P., N.T.*

MELLOWS. J. Landlord of "Dolphin's Head." *U.T.* xxii.

MELLUKA. Miss, Polly's doll. *C.S., M.J.* iv.

MELTHAM. Major Banks. *H.D.* v.

MELTONBURY. *M.P., C. Pat.*

MELVILLE. Assumed name. *S.B.B.*, Scenes xiii.

MELVILLESON. Miss M. *B.H.* xxxii

Young lady of professional celebrity who assists at the Harmonic Meetings.

Note.—A casual character in the book. One of the entertainers at the "Sol's Arms." Her public name is Miss Melvinson, although she is married and the baby is carried to the "Sol's Arms" each night "to receive its natural nourishment."

MEMBER. A, Guest of Veneerings. *O.M.F.* ii.

MEN. *M.P., H.H.*

MEN. Amphibious-looking young. *S.B.B.*, Scenes x.

MEN. At sale of Dombey's furniture. *D. and S.* lix.

Stout men with napless hats on, look out of the bedroom windows, and cut jokes with friends in the streets—and sit upon everything within reach, mantelpieces included.

MEN. Blossom-faced, Undertakers' men. *O.M.F.* lix.

MEN. "**A DOZEN,**" Mr. Raddle. *P.P.* xxxii.

MEN. Middle-aged. *S.B.B.*, Scenes i.

Whose salaries have by no means increased in the same proportions as their families, plod steadily along, apparently with no object in view but the counting house.

MEN. Mr. Mould's. *M.C.* xix.

Found it necessary to drown their grief.

MEN. Of the House of Mr. John Jarndyce. *B.H.* xxxi.

MEN. Old, Seeing Mark Tapley off. *M.C.* vii.

MEN. One of the seven mild, Guest at Dombey's housewarming. *D. and S.* xxxvi.

MEN. Seven mild. Guests at Dombey's housewarming. *D. and S.* xxxvi.

MEN. Shabby-genteel, At Astley's. *S.B.B.*, Scenes xi.

In checked neckerchiefs and sallow linen—perhaps carrying under one arm a pair of stage shoes badly wrapped up in a piece of old newspaper.

MEN. Silly young, Visitors in Assembly Rooms, Bath. *P.P.* xxxv.

Lounging near the doors . . . displaying various varieties of puppyism and stupidity; amusing all sensible people near them with their folly and conceit.

MEN. Three or four, lounging about the stage-door. *S.B.B.*, Scenes xi.

With an indescribable public-house-parlour swagger.

MEN. Turnpike. *S.B.B.*, Scenes xii.

MEN. Two. *M.P.*, *N.T.*

MEN. Two, In Tea Gardens. *S.B.B.*, Scenes ix.

In blue coats and drab trousers smoking their pipes. Husbands of the two motherly-looking women.

MEN. Two or three, Prisoners in the poor side of the Fleet. *P.P.* xlii.

Congregated in a little knot and talking noisily among themselves.

MEN. Two stout, in centre box of private theatre. *S.B.B.*, Scenes xiii.

MEN. Two, Travellers in coach: in sky-blue and plum colour. *P.P.* xlix.

MEN. Washed, Twenty taking part in election. *P.P.* xiii.

MEN. Young, A group of three or four members of Mr. V. Crummles' Company. *N.N.* xxiii.

With lantern jaws, and thick eyebrows—they seemed to be of secondary importance.

MEN. Young, One of the—in livery in Brook Street. *D. and S.* xxxi.

Already smells of sherry, and his eyes have a tendency to become fixed in his head, and to stare at objects without seeing them.

MENAGERIES. Travelling, At Greenwich Fair. *S.B.B.*, Scenes xii.

MENAI STRAITS. *M.P.*, *C.C.*; *M.P.*, *E.T.*

MENDICANTS. Army of shabby. *L.D.* li.

MENDICITY SOCIETY. *R.P.*, *T.B.W.*

MERCANTILE JACK. Sailor on a merchantman. *U.T.* v.

MERCHANT. A, In Spitalfields. *U.T.* x.

A bow-legged character, with a flat and cushiony nose, like the last new strawberry.

MERCHANT. Kidney pie, *S.B.B.*, Scenes ii.

MERCURY. Another acquaintance of Sir Dedlock's Mercury. *B.H.* xvi.

MERCURY. Sir Leicester Dedlock's footman. *B.H.* xvi.

"Six foot two, I suppose?" says Mr. Bucket. "Three," says Mercury.

Note.—Sir Leicester Dedlock's footman. He has no other name and he is no more than a "super" in the story.

MERCY. Nurse of the Uncommercial traveller. *U.T.* xv.

MERDLE. Establishment in Harley Street. *L.D.* xxi.

Like unexceptionable Society, the opposing rows of houses—were very grim with one another.—Expressionless, uniform, twenty houses, all to be knocked at and rung at in the same form, all approachable by the same dull steps, all fended off by the same pattern railings, all with the same impracticable fire-escapes, the same inconvenient fixtures in their heads, and everything, without exception, to be taken at a high valuation.

MERDLE. Mr. *L.D.* xxi.

A man of prodigious enterprise; a Midas without the ears, who turned all he touched to gold. He was in everything good from banking to building. He was in Parliament of course. He was in the City necessarily. He was chairman of this, trustee of that, president of the other—he was a reserved man, with a broad, overhanging watchful head, that particular kind of dull-red colour in his cheeks which is rather stale than fresh, and a somewhat uneasy expression about his coat-cuffs, as if they were in his confidence, and had reasons for being anxious to hide his hands. The greatest forger and thief that ever cheated the gallows.

Note.—The wealthy financier. Father-in-law of Fanny Dorrit. He becomes a bankrupt and commits suicide. Amongst those who entrust their money to him and lose it are the Dorrits.

MERDLE. Mrs. *L.D.* xx.

She had large, unfeeling, handsome eyes, and dark, unfeeling, handsome hair, and a broad, unfeeling, handsome bosom. It was not a bosom to repose upon, but it was a capital bosom to hang jewels upon.

Note.—Wife of Mr. Merdle and mother of Mr. Sparkle, mother-in-law of Fanny Dorrit. She shines in society. Her son becomes entangled with Fanny in the early days, and she buys off the girl, but eventually, when the Dorrits come into money, Fanny marries the Sparkler. When Mr. Merdle fails, his wife receives the pity of Society and lives with her son.

MERDLE. Mrs., First husband of. Had been a colonel. *L.D.* xxi.

MEREDITH. Sir William. *B.R.* Pref.

MERITON. Mr. Henry. *R.P., T.L.V.* Second mate of the "Halsewell."

MERMAN. The, A gondolier. *L.D.* xlii.

MERMEN. Gondoliers. *L.D.* xlii.

"MERRIKER." *P.P.* xxxi.

MERRIWINKLE. Mr. and Mrs. *S.Y.C.*

MERSEY. The. *U.T.* v.

MERTON. Tommy, Pupil of Mr. Barlow. *U.T.* xxxiii.

MESHECK. A Jew in the bill-stealing way. *R.P., T.D.P.*

MESMEREST. Black. *R.P., O.o.S.*

MESROUR. *C.S., H.H.*

MESSENGER. From Somerset House. *S.B.B.*, Char. iii.

In a blue coat.

METHODISTICAL ORDER. One of. *P.P.* xxii.

A lanky chap with a red nose . . . The red-nosed man warn't by no means the sort of person you'd grub by contract.

METROPOLITAN IMPROVEMENT SOCIETY. *M.P., R.T.*

MEURICE HÔTEL. Calais. *P.F.I., G.T.F., U.T.* xvii.

MEWS. Two corner rooms over. *B.H.* xxxviii.

Residence of Mr. and Mrs. Prince Turveydrop.

MEWS STREET. Number twenty-four, Residence of Mr. Tite-Barnacle. *L.D.* x.

A squeezed house, with a ramshackle bowed front, little dingy windows, and a little dark area like a damp waistcoat-pocket. To the sense of smell the house was like a sort of bottle filled with strong distillation of mews; and when the footman opened the door, he seemed to take the stopper out.

MEXICO. *M.P., S.R.*

MEZZO. Giorno, Italian steam-packet. *R.P., P.M.T.P.*

MIBBS. "A very civil, worthy trader." *M.P., F.S.*

MIBBS. Young. *M.P., F.S.*

MIBBS' AUNT. Young. *M.P., F.S.*

MICAWBER. Master, Son of Micawber. *D.C.* xi.

MICAWBER. Miss, Daughter of Micawber. *D.C.* xi.

Aged about three.

MICAWBER. Mr., Agent for Murdstone and Grinby. *D.C.* xi.

A stoutish, middle-aged person in a brown surtout and black tights and shoes, with no more hair upon his head (which was a large one and very shining) than there is upon an egg, and a very extensive face.

Note.—Micawber is introduced as the landlord of David Copperfield when he is placed by his step-father in the congenial warehouse of Murdstone and Grinby. Even then he is in a state of impecuniosity and is waiting for "something to turn up." The only event that transpires is Mr. Micawbers' imprisonment for debt in the King's Bench Prison. He obtains his release under the Insolvent Debtor's Act, and proceeds to Plymouth. This does not induce anything to turn up, however, and he is next seen selling corn, or trying to, and then endeavours to get something in the coal trade on the Medway. Later on he enters Mr. Wickfield's office, under Uriah Heep. Uriah believes that Micawber's chronic shortness of money will make him a willing and a useful tool.

Micawber soon discovers what is expected of him, but instead of assisting in the evil schemes of his employer he quietly proceeds to collect all the evidence he can. This he communicates to Traddles. And at a general meeting at Mr. Wickfield's house. Uriah is denounced. As some recompense for this undoubted service, Micawber is enabled to emigrate to Australia. From a paper which David Copperfield receives from Mr. Peggotty we learn that Mr. Micawber prospered at Port Middlebay and became a magistrate.

MICAWBER. Mrs., Wife of Micawber. *D.C.* xi.

A thin and faded lady, not at all young.

MICAWBER. Mrs., Micawber's mamma. *D.C.* xii.

Departed this life before Mr. Micawber's difficulties commenced, or at least before they became pressing.

MICAWBER'S. Mrs., Twins. *D.C.* xi.

One of them was always taking refreshment.

MICAWBER. Wilkins. *D.C.* xii.

Eldest son of Micawber.

MICHAEL. Mr., The poor relation. *R.P., P.R.S.*

MICHAEL. Mr., A rogue. *R.P., D.W.I.F.*

MICHEL. An Iroquois hunter. *M.P., L.A. V.* i.

MIDDLE TEMPLE. *H.D.* iii.

MIDDLE TEMPLE GATE. *B.R.* xl.

MIDDLESEX. *B.R.*, xlviii.; *C.S., D.M.*; *C.S., N.T.* Act i; *M.P., C.P.*; *M.P.S.B.*; *M.P., W.M.*; *O.M.F.* xviii.; *S.B.B.*, Scenes xvii.

MIDDLESEX. Grand Jury. *M.P., S. Pigs.*

MIDDLESEX. House of Correction of. *M.P., C. and E.*

MIDDLESEX DUMPLING. Pugilist. *P.P.* xxiv.

MIDLAND COUNTIES. *U.T.* vi.

MIDSHIPMAN. The Wooden. *See* Gills' shop.

MIFF. Mr., Deceased husband of Mrs. Miff. *D. and S.* xxxi.

He held some bad opinions, it would seem, about free seats; and though Mrs. Miff hopes he may be gone upwards, she couldn't possibly undertake to say so.

MIFF. Mrs., Pew-opener. *D. and S.* xxxi.

The wheezy little pew-opener a mighty dry old lady, sparely dressed with not an inch of fulness anywhere about her. A vinegary face has Mrs. Miff, and a mortified bonnet, and eke a thirsty soul for sixpences and shillings.

MIGGOT. Mrs., Parkle's laundress. *U.T.* xiv.

MIGGS. Married sister of Miss. *B.R.* ix.

MIGGS. Miss, Domestic servant to the Vardens. *B.R.* vii.

A tall young lady, very much addicted to pattens in private life; slender and shrewish, of a rather uncomfortable figure, and though not absolutely ill-looking, of a sharp and acid visage.

Note.—Mrs. Varden's servant and maid-of-all-work. She ably seconds her mistress in her pretended indispositions, and together they render the old locksmith's life anything but pleasant. Miggs has her eye on Varden's apprentice Tappertit, and when he follows the rioters she leaves her mistress to act the part of guardian angel to Sim, who regards her with disfavour. After the riots she returns to her old situation. In the meantime, however, Mrs. Varden has undergone a change and her eyes have been opened regarding Miggs. The result is that the at one time indispensable companion is no longer required. She is appointed female turnkey at the Bridewell, a position for which her shrewish disposition is supposed to fit her. She retains the post for some thirty years, until she dies.

MIGGS. Nephew of. *B.R.* lxxx.

Born in Golden Lion Court, number twenty-sivin, and bred in the very shadow of the second bell-handle on the right-hand doorpost.

MIKE. Client of Jaggers. *G.E.* xx.

A gentleman with one eye, in a velveteen suit, and knee-breeches.

MILAN. *C.S.N.T.* Act ii.; *P.F.I.*, *V.M.M.S.S.*; *U.T.* iv.

MILE END. *B.H.* xiii.; *B.R.* lxi.; *P.P.* xxii.

MILES. Bob, A pickpocket. *R.P., D.W.I.F.*

MILES. Mr. Owen, Fourth member of Master Humphrey's Club. *M.H.C.* ii.

Once a very rich merchant—retired from business—an excellent man of sterling character: not of quick apprehension, and not without some amusing prejudices.

MILITARY. A strong body of. *B.R.* lxxvii.

MILITARY CHARACTER. A. *C.S., M.L. Leg.* i.

A military character in a sword and spurs and a cocked hat and yellow shoulder-belt, and long tags about him that he must have found inconvenient.

MILITIA. Northumberland. *B.R.* lxvii.

MILKMAN. A. *B.H.* iv.

MILKMAN. The. *O.M.F.* iv.

MILKMAN. Who supplies the Zoological Gardens. *M.P., G.H.*

MILKWASH. John. *S.Y.G.*

MILL. In Coketown. *H.T., S.* xi.

MILL. Paper. *O.M.F.* lvi.

MILL DAM ROAD. Boston. *M.P., I.W.M.*

MILL POND. *O.T.* l.

MILLBANK. *B.R.* lxxxii.; *D.C.* xviii.; *O.M.F.* xviii.; *R.P., O.B.*; *S.B.B.*, Scenes xvii.

MILLBANK STREET. *S.B.B.*, Scenes xviii.

MILLER. Joe. *C.B., C.C., S.* v.

MILLER. Joe. *M.P., W.H.*

MILLER. Mrs., Jane Ann, A widow *C.S., N.T.* Act i.

MILLER. Mr., Old acquaintance of Mr. Pickwick. *P.P.* xxviii.

The hard-headed old gentleman.

MILLER. The Hon. Mr. *M.C.* xxii.

MILLERS. The second nurse of the young Pockets. *G.E.* xxii.

MILLINER. The mistaken. *S.B.B.*, Char. viii.

MILLINER. Inmate of the Marshalsea. *L.D.* vii.

MILLINGTARY. The. *O.T.* vi.

MILLS. Miss Julia. *R.P., O.E.W.*

MILLS. Miss (Julia), Bosom friend of Dora Spenlow. *D.C.* iv.

Comparatively stricken in years . . . almost twenty . . . Having been unhappy in a misplaced affection, and being understood to have retired from the world, on her awful stock of experience, but still able to take a calm interest in the unblighted hopes and loves of youth.

MILLS. Mr., Father of Miss Mills. *D.C.* iv.

MILLS. Mr. *M.P., P.T.*

MILTON STREET. *S.B.B.*, Char. xi.

MILTON'S TOMB. Cripplegate. *U.T.* ix.

MILVEY. Mrs. Margaretta. *O.M.F.* ix.

Quite a young wife—a pretty, bright little woman, something worn by anxiety.

MILVEY. The Reverend Frank. *O.M.F.* ix.

He was quite a young man, expensively educated and wretchedly paid.

Note.—A secondary, but nevertheless an interesting character. He is consulted by the Boffins when they propose to adopt a child, and he reads the service at Betty Higden's burial. He is a hard-working, generous-minded curate.

MILVEY. Six children of the Rev. Frank. *O.M.F.* ix.

MIM. Proprietor of Travelling Show. *C.S., D.M.*

A very hoarse man—a ferocious swearer.

MIM. Step-daughter of. *C.S., D.M.*

Deaf and dumb. The poor girl had beautiful long dark hair, and was often pulled down by it and beaten.

MINCIN. Mr. *S.Y.G.*

MINCING LANE. *O.M.F.* iv.

MINCING LANE. One church near. *U.T.* ix.

Smelt like a druggist's drawer.

MINDERS. Nurse children. *O.M.F.* xvi.

In a corner below the mangle, on a couple of stools, sat two very little children: a boy and a girl.

MINDERSON. Mrs. *M.P., U.N.*

MINDING-SCHOOL. A. *O.M.F.* xvi.

MINE. The, On Silver Store Island. *C.S., P.o.C.E.P.*

A sunken block like a powder magazine—(a walled square of building, with a sort of pleasure ground inside) with a little square trench round it, and steps down to the door. The silver from the mine was stored there . . . brought over from the mainland.

MINERS. *C.B., C.C., S.* iii.

MINERS. Cornish. *C.S., H.T.*

Dancing before the Cornish inn by torchlight.

MINERVA. Esther. *B.H.* li.

MINISTER. Preaching at Britainnia Theatre on Sunday evening. *U.T.* iv.

I could not possibly say to myself that he expressed an understanding of the general mind and character of his audience—is it necessary or advisable to address such an audience continually as "fellow sinners"?

MINISTER OF STATE. *M.P.D.V.*

MINISTERIALISTS. In Parliament. *S.B.B.*, Scenes xviii.

MINISTERS. Three of his. *O.M.F.* liv.

Under-waiters at Greenwich Hotel.

MINNS. Mr. Augustus, A clerk in Somerset House. *S.B.B.*, Tales ii.

A bachelor of about forty, as he said—of about eight-and-forty as his friends said. He was always exceedingly clean, precise, and tidy; perhaps somewhat priggish, and the most retiring man in the world. Usually wore a brown frock-coat, without a wrinkle, light inexplicables without a spot, a neat neckerchief with a remarkably neat tie, and boots without a fault: he always carried a brown silk umbrella with an ivory handle.

MINOR CANON CORNER. *E.D.* vi.

A quiet place in the shadow of the Cathedral, which the cawing of the rooks, the echoing footsteps of rare passers, the sound of the Cathedral bell, or the roll of the Cathedral organ, seemed to render more quiet than absolute silence. Red-bricked walls harmoniously toned down in colour by time, strong rooted ivy, latticed windows, panelled rooms, big oaken beams and stone-walled gardens, where annual fruit yet ripened upon monkish trees.

MINORIES. The. *M.P., N.G.K.*; *R.P., D.W.I.F.*

MINT. The. *B.R.* lxvii.; *C.S., G.i.S.*; *M.C.* xxi.

MISANTHROPISTS. *S.B.B.*, Char. i.

Generally old fellows with white heads and red faces, addicted to port wine and Hessian boots—taking a great delight in thinking themselves unhappy, and making everyone that came near miserable—you may know them—at church by the pomposity with which they enter and the loud tone in which they repeat the responses—at parties, by their getting cross at whist, and hating music.

MISENO. *P.F.I., R.D.*

MISERERE. *P.F.I., R.*

MISSIONARY. A. *S.B.B., O.P.* vi.

MISSIS. My, Wife of Magwich. Molly, at Jaggers'. *G.E.* xlii.

MISSIS. Of Servant of all work. *S.B.B.*, Scenes i.

MISSIS. Our, Head of Refreshment Room at Mugby Junction. *C.S., M.J.* v.

MISSISSIPPI. *A.N.* x.; *M.C.* xvii.; *M.P., A.P.*; *M.P., E.T.*; *M.P., Y.M.C.*; *R.P., D.W.T.T.*; *U.T.* xvii.

MISSOURI. *A.N.* xvii.; *M.C.* xvii.; *M.P., A.P.*; *M.P., E.T.*; *U.T.* xx.

MISTAFOKS = Fox. *M.P., T.O.H.*

MISTAPIT = Pitt. *M.P., T.O.H.*

MISTASPEEKA = Chief of the office of the Royal Seraglio. *M.P., T.O.H.*

Speaker of the House of Commons.

MISTRESS. Mary's, Landlady of potshop in Borough. *P.P.* lii.

MISTRESS. My, Mother of Miss Wade's pupil. *L.D.* lvii.

MISTRESS. Of house which shall be nameless. *C.S., S.L.* i.

A widow in her fourth year.

MISTY. Messrs. *Mud.Pap.* ii.

MITCHELL. *M.P., F.L.*

MITCHELL. Mr. Manager of the Olympic. *A.N.* vi.

MITH. Sergeant, A detective. *R.P., T.D.P.*

A smooth-faced man with a fresh, bright complexion, and a strange air of simplicity, is a dab at house-breakers.

MITHERS. Client of Miss Moucher's. *D.C.* xxii.

MITHERS. Lady, Client of Miss Moucher's. *D.C.* xxii.

MITHERS' SCHOOL. *M.P., G.D.*

"**MITRE.**" The, An inn in cathedral town. *C.S., H.T.*

Where friends used to put up, and where we used to go to see parents, and to have salmon and fowls, and to be tipped.

MITTS. Mrs., A Titbull's Alms House inmate. *U.T.* xxvii.

A tidy, well-favoured woman.

MITTS. Mrs., Parlour of. *U.T.* xxvii.

A gloomy little chamber, but clean, with a mug of wallflower in the window. On the chimney-piece were two peacocks' feathers, a carved ship, a few shells, and a black profile with one eyelash;—her only son—cast away in China.

MIVINS. Mr., A prisoner in the Fleet. *P.P.* xli.

A man in a broad-skirted green coat, with corduroy knee-smalls and grey cotton stockings, was performing the most popular steps of a hornpipe, which, combined with the very appropriate character of his costume, was inexpressibly absurd.

MIZZLE. *B.H.* i.

MOB. Divisions of. *B.R.* xlix.

The London, Westminster, Southwark, and Scotch.

MOB. The swell, Pickpockets. *R.P., T.D.A.* ii.

MOBBS. Pupil at Dotheboys' Hall. *N.N.* viii.

"Mobbs' mother-in-law," said Squeers, "took to her bed on hearing that he wouldn't eat fat, and has been ill ever since. She wishes to know, by an early post, where he expects to go to, if he quarrels with his vittles.

MOCHA. *M.P., L.A.V.* ii.

MODDLE. Augustus, The youngest boarder at Todgers. *M.C.* xxxii.

MODEL. A, An artist's model. *R.P., G.o.A.*

MODEL PRISON. Pentonville. *M.P., P.P.*

MODENA. *P.F.I., P.M.B.*; *U.T.* xxviii.

MOFFIN. *O.M.F.* xxv.

MOGLEY. Suitor of Mrs. Nickleby. *N.N.* xli.

MOLA DI GAËTA. *P.F.I., R.D.*

MOLLY. Mr. Jaggers' housekeeper. *G.E.* xxvi.

About forty—rather tall, of a lithe, nimble figure, extremely pale, with large faded eyes, and a quantity of streaming hair—her lips—parted as if she were panting, and her face to bear a curious expression of suddenness and flutter. One wrist deeply scarred across and across.

Note.—Mr. Jaggers' housekeeper, Pip recognises in her Estella's mother.

MOLOCH. Little, Tetterby's baby. *C.B., H.M.* ii.

MOMUSES. Mississippi, Negro singers. *U.T.* xxxiii.

Nine dressed alike, in the black coat and trousers, white waistcoat, shirt-collar, and very large white tie and wristbands.

MONASTRY. Interior of. *M.P., N.T.*

MONASTRY RUIN. *E.D.* vi.

MONFLATHERS. Miss, Boarding school mistress. *O.C.S.* xxix.

MONKEY. Mr., Judge's rendering of Phunky. *P.P.* xxxiv.

MONKS. A confederate of Fagin. *O.T.* xxvi.

Note.—Monks was the name adopted by Edward Leeford when endeavouring to procure the ruin of Oliver Twist. Leeford's father had betrayed Agnes Fleming, although fully intending to marry her on his wife's death. He was, therefore Oliver's father; and Monks was Oliver's half-brother. Leeford, senior, died suddenly at Rome, and his wife and son destroyed his will leaving the bulk of his property to the girl he had wronged and the child Oliver which was to be born. The son Edward, at the age of eighteen, left his mother, after robbing her, and spent his money wildly and shamelessly. His mother, just before her death, disclosed the secret of the will,and bequeathed to him the letter she had withheld, together with her deadly hatred. Edward Leeford, or Monks, as he is more generally termed, entered into the object with wholehearted villany. He finds Oliver in Fagin's hands, and bribes the Jew to force him into crime. This evil design is frustrated largely by Nancy's evidence, and Monks is forced by Mr. Brownlow and the others to relinquish half the remainder of his father's large fortune to Oliver. The other moiety, amounting to little more than three thousand pounds, Monks retains. He emigrates to the New World, but soon returns to his former courses and ends his days in prison.

MONKS. Two. *M.P.*, *N.T.*

MONKS. Cappucini. *P.F.I.*, *A.G.*

MONKS' MOUND. The, Ancient Indian burial-place. *A.N.* xiii.

In memory of a body of fanatics of the order of La Trappe.

MONK'S VINEYARD. *E.D.* xii.

MONMOUTH STREET. *S.B.B.*, Scenes vi.

The only true and real emporium for secondhand wearing apparel. Venerable for its antiquity, and respectable for its usefulness.

MONMOUTH STREET. The inhabitants of. *S.B.B.*, Scenes vi.

A peaceable and retiring race, who immure themselves for the most part in deep cellars, or small back parlours, and who seldom come forth into the world, except in the dusk and coolness of the evening. Their countenances bear a thoughtful and dirty cast.

MONOMANIACS. *M.P.*, *G.B.*

MONT BLANC. *M.P.*, *L.A.V.* ii.

MONT BLANC. A good inn in the shadow of. *C.S.*, *H.T.*

Where one of the apartments has a zoological papering on the walls not so accurately joined—the elephant rejoices in a tiger's hind legs and tail, while the lion puts on a trunk and tusks.

MONT BLANC. Inn, In shadow of. *C.S.*, *H.T.*

Cheerful landlady, and honest landlord of.

MONTAGUE. Miss Julia, Singer at White Conduit. *S.B.B.*, Char. viii.

MONTAGUE. Mr. Basil. *M.P.*, *C.P.*

MONTAGUE. Mr. Wortley. *M.P.*, *T.O.H.*

MONTAGUE PLACE. Russell Square. *P.P.* xlvii,

MONTAGUE SQUARE. Mr. Jorkins' house near. *D.C.* vi.

MONTAGUE. Tigg, Esquire. *M.C.* xxvii.

MONTEFIAXHONE. *P.F.I.*, *R.P.S.*

MONTMARTRE. Abattoir. *R.P.*, *M.O.F.F.*

Surrounded by a high wall, and looking from the outside like a cavalry barrack.

MONTREAL. *A.N.* xv.

MONTROSE. *M.P.*, *E.S.*

MONUMENT. The. *B.R.*, xiii.; *M.C.* viii.; *O.M.F.* iii.; *R.P.P.R.S.*

MONUMENT. A church behind the, had a flavour of damaged oranges. *U.T.* ix.

MONUMENT YARD. *M.C.* xliv.

MOODLE. *B.H.* xii.

MOON. A physician. *R.P.*, *O.B.*

MOON. *M.P.*, *L.W.O.Y.*

MOON. *M.P.*, *W.*

MOON = Paris. *M.P.*, *R.D.*

MOONEY. Mr. *M.P., L.*

MOONEY. The active and intelligent beadle. *B.H.* xi.

MOONONIANS. Parisians. *M.P., R.D*

MOORE. Ralph. *M.P., N.E.*

MOORFIELDS. *L.D.* vii.

MOORFIELDS. House near. *B.R.*, lii.

They (the rioters) found in one of the rooms some canary birds in cages, and these they cast into the fire alive.—At the same house, one of the fellows—found a child's doll—a poor toy—which he exhibited at the window—as the image of some unholy saint, which the late occupants had worshipped.

MOORSHEAD. Captain. *M.P., L.A.V.* ii.

MOPES. Mr., The hermit. *C.S., T.T.G.* i.

Dressing himself in a blanket and skewer, and steeping himself in soot and grease, and other nastiness, had acquired great renown. A compound of Newgate, Bedlam, a Debtors' prison in the worst time, a chimney-sweep, a mudlark, and the noble savage.

MOPS. Fictitious name. *L.D.* vi.

MORAN AP KERRIG. Ancestor of Mrs. Woodcourt. *B.H.* xvii.

MORDLIN. Brother, Of the Ebenezer Temperance Association. *P.P.* xxxiii.

Had adapted the beautiful words of "Who hasn't heard of a jolly young waterman" to the tune of the Old Hundredth.

MORFIN. Mr., In Dombey and Son's office. *D. and S.* iv.

A cheerful-looking, hazel-eyed, elderly bachelor: gravely attired, as to his upper man in black; and as to his legs, in pepper-and-salt-colour. His hair was just touched here and there with specks of grey, as though the tread of time had splashed it: and his whiskers were already white.

Note.—Mr. Morfin is head clerk at Dombey and Son's. He is under James Carker, and sometimes overhears Carker and Mr. Dombey, although he adopts various artifices to inform them of his presence. He hears enough to make him friendly towards John Carker, the brother in disgrace. He is the "unknown friend" of Harriet Carker, whom he afterwards marries.

MORFIN. Mrs., née Harriet Carker. *D. and S.* lxii.

MORGAN. *S.Y.C.*

MORGUE. The, in Paris. *M.P. R.D.*; *P.F.I., G.T.F.*; *R.P., L.A.*; *U.T.* vii.

MORGUE. Two custodians of the. *U.T.* xviii.

MORGUE IN LONDON. Desolate open-air. *U.T.* xviii.

Right hand of Canal Bridge, near the cross-path to Chalk Farm—lying on the towing-path, with her face turned up towards us, a woman, dead a day or two, and under thirty, as I guessed, poorly dressed in black.

MORISON AND MOAT. Messrs. *M.P., Ag.Int.*

MORMON AGENT. The. *U.T.* xx.

A compactly-made, handsome man in black, rather short, with rich brown hair and beard, and clear bright eyes.

MORMON AGENTS. Two or three. *U.T.* xx.

MORTIMER. Assumed name of Mr. Micawber. *Which see.*

MORTIMER'S. Man. *O.M.F.* x.

Looking rather like a spurious Mephistopheles,

MOSELLE. The. *R.P., D.W.T.T.*

MOSES. *M.P., I.M.*

MOSES. E. and Son. *M.P., F.F.*

MOSES. (And Sons.) *M.P., S.D.C.*

MOSES AND SON. *R.P., B.S.*

MOSES AND SON. Messrs. *M.P., E.S.*

MOSQUITO SHORE. *C.S., P.o.C.E.P.*

MOTHER. Demonstrated by Goblin to Gabriel Grub. *P.P.* xxix.

Drew aside the window curtain, as if to look for some expected object.

MOTHER. Mr. Home's. *M.P.*, *M.M.*

MOTHER. Of discharged prisoner. *S.B.B.*, Scenes xxiv.

An elderly woman, of decent appearance, though evidently poor.

MOTHER. Of Monsieur Rigaud. *L.D.* i.

My mother was French by blood, English by birth.

MOTHER. Of Neckett's children. *B.H.* xv.

Died just after Emma was born.

MOTHER. Our, To the memory of *N.N.* xxxvii.

Toast of Cheeryble Brothers.

MOTHER. Our dear, Of the five sisters. *N.N.* vi.

MOULD. Mr., Undertaker. *M.C.* xix.

A little elderly gentleman, bald, and in a suit of black; with a notebook in his hand, a massive gold watch-chain dangling from his fob, and a face in which a queer attempt at melancholy was at odds with a smirk of satisfaction.

MOULD. Mrs., Wife of undertaker. *M.C.* xxv.

Was plumper than the two (daughters) together.

MOULD. Premises of Mr. *M.C.* xxv.

Nestled in a quiet corner, where the city strife became a drowsy hum, that sometimes rose, and sometimes fell, and sometimes ceased altogether. The light came sparkling in among the scarlet runners, as if the churchyard winked at Mr. Mould.

MOULD. The Misses, Daughters twain of Mr. Mould. *M.C.* xxv.

So round and chubby were their fair proportions, that they might have been the bodies once belonging to the angels' faces in the shop below, grown up, with other heads attached to them to make them mortal.

MOUNT MISERY. *M.P.*, *L.A.V.* ii.

MOUNT PLEASANT. *B.H.* xxi.

MOUNT VERNON. *A.N.* ix.

MOUNT VESUVIUS. *C.S.*, *S.L.* iii.

MOUNTAIN PASS. *M.P.*, *N.T.*

MOURNER. Chief. *C.B.*, *C.C.s.*i.

MOUSE. In "Happy Family." *M.P.*, *R.H.F.*

MOWATT. Mrs. Actress. *M.P.*, *V. and B.S.*

MOWCHER. Miss, Masseuse, etc. *D.C.* xxii.

A pursy dwarf of about forty or forty-five, with a very large head and face, a pair of roguish grey eyes, and such extremely little arms. Her chin, which was what is called a double chin, was so fat that it entirely swallowed up the strings of her bonnet, bow and all. Throat she had none, waist she had none, legs she had none worth mentioning. This lady dressed in an off-hand, easy style.

MOWCOP. *M.P.*, *E.S.*

MOZART. *M.P.*, *O.L.N.O.*

MUDBERRY. Mrs. *P.P.* xxxiv.

"Which kept a mangle."

MUDDLEBRANES. Mr. *Mud. Pap.* ii.

MUDFOG. *Mud. Pap.*

MUDFOG. *P.L.M.I.*

MUDFOG ASSOCIATION. *Mud.Pap.*

MUDGE. Jonas, Secretary of the Ebenezer Temperance Association. *P.P.* xxxiii.

Chandler's shopkeeper, an enthusiastic and disinterested vessel, who sold tea to the members.

Note.—Secretary of the Brick Lane Branch of the United Grand Junction Ebenezer Temperance Association, who was addicted to the immoderate consumption of toast and tea.

MUFF. Prof. *Mud. Pap.* i.

MUFFIN-BOY. The. *S.B.B.*, Scenes ii.

MUFFIN-MAKER. Former pastry-cook and. *E.D.* v.

MUFFY. *B.H.* xii.

MUGBY. The boy at refreshment room. *C.S.*, *M.J.* v.

He'll appear in an absent manner to survey the line through a transparent medium composed of your head and body, and he won't serve you as long as you can possibly bear it.

MUGBY HIGH STREET. *C.S., M.J.* ii.

MUGBY JUNCTION. *C.S., M.J.* i.

A place replete with shadowy shapes, this Mugby Junction in the small black hours of the four-and-twenty; mysterious goods trains, covered with palls, and gliding on like vast, wierd funerals. Red-hot embers showering out upon the ground.

MUGBY JUNCTION. Down refreshment room at. *C.S., M.J.* v.

Up in a corner—behind the bottles, among the glasses, bounded on the nor'west by the beer, stood pretty far to the right of a metallic object, that's at times the tea-urn and at times the soup-tureen—fended off from the traveller by a barrier of stale spong-cakes erected atop of the counter—you ask a boy so situated—for anything to drink—he'll try to seem not to hear you.

MUGBY JUNCTION. Lamps' cabin in. *C.S., M.J.* i.

A greasy little cabin it was, suggestive to the sense of smell, of a cabin in a whaler. But there was a bright fire burning in its rusty grate, and on the floor there stood a wooden stand of newly trimmed and lighted lamps ready for carriage service.

MUGGLETON. *P.P.* vii.

Everybody whose genius has a topographical bent knows perfectly well that Muggleton is a corporate town, with a mayor, burgesses, and freemen.

MUGGS. Sir A, *S.B.B.*, Tales iii.

MULATTO. A young, Pupil at our school. *R.P., O.S.*

MULBERRY. *See* Trotter, Job.

MULLINS. Jack. *O.M.F.* vi.

MULLIN'S MEADOWS. *P.P.* vi.

No better land in Kent.

MULLION. John. *C.S., W.o.G.M.*

One of crew of "Golden Mary."

MULLIT. Professor of Education; schoolmaster. *M.C.* xvi.

"Very short gentleman with red nose . . . he is a man of fine moral elements, Sir—has written some powerful pamphlets, under the name of "Suturb,' or Brutus reversed."

MULREADY. *M.P., O.L.N.O.*

MUMLER. Medium, a photographer. *M.P., R.S.D.*

MUNTLE. Mr. Mantalini. *Which see.*

MURDERER. Captain. Character in one of Nurse's Stories. *U.T.* xv.

An offshoot of the Bluebeard family—Captain Murderer's mission was matrimony—of a cannibal appetite with tender brides.

MURDERER. The. *C.S., D.M.P.*

MURDSTONE. Edward, Mrs. Copperfield's second husband. *D.C.* ii.

He had that kind of shallow black eye, which when it is abstracted, seems, from some peculiarity of light, to be disfigured, for a moment at a time, by a cast. His hair and whiskers were blacker and thicker, looked at so near, that even I had given them credit for being. His regular eyebrows, and the rich white, and black, and brown of his complexion—confound his complexion and his memory—made me think him, in spite of my misgivings, a very handsome man.

Note.—Mr. Murdstone marries Mrs. Copperfield and so becomes David's stepfather. With the assistance of his sister he endeavours to train his wife to be "firm." He succeeds so well in this that she dies, together with the baby that is born to them. David he endeavours to break. After his wife's death he marries again and carries out the same programme, accompanied by a fitting gloom and dark religious fanaticism, and reduces her to the condition of an incipient imbecile.

MURDSTONE. Miss Jane, Mr. Murdstone's sister. *D.C.* iv.

And a gloomy-looking lady she was . . . very heavy eyebrows, nearly meeting over her large nose, as if, being disabled by the wrongs of her sex from wearing whiskers, she had carried them to that account.

Note.—Mr. Murdstone's sister is a fitting assistant in the course of repression. She relieves the former Mrs. Copperfield of all housekeeping and dominates her and David. David again meets her as companion to Dora Spenlow.

MURDSTONE AND GRINBY. In the wine trade. *D.C.* x.

MURGATROYD. Mr. *M.R.B.*

MURPHY. *N.N.* ii.

MURPHY. Friend of Mrs. Nickleby. *N.N.* xxxvii.

MURPHY FAMILY. Tramps. *R.P., D.W.I.F.*

MURPHY'S TEMPERANCE HOTEL. Chapel Walks, Preston. *M.P., O.S.*

MURRAY. Honest, Publishers. *M.P., N.J.B.*

MUSES. Hall of the . *R.P., O.o.S.*

MUSEUM. The. *D.C.* xx.

MUSIC. Director of the. *S.B.B.*, Scenes xix.

In the blue coat and bright buttons.

MUSIC GALLERY. *N.N.* ii.

MUTANHED. Lord (young) of the élite of Bath. *P.P.* xxxv.

Splendidly dressed young man . . . with long hair and particularly small forehead. The richest man in Ba-ath at this moment.

MUTES. Two. *M.C.* xix.

Looking as mournful as could be reasonably expected of men with such a thriving job in hand.

MUTTON HILL. *O.T.* xi.

MUTUEL. Monsieur. *C.S., S.L.* ii.

A spectacled, snuffy, stooping old gentleman, in carpet shoes, and a cloth cap, with a peaked shade, a loose blue frock-coat reaching to his heels, a large limp white shirt-frill, and cravat to correspond, that is to say, white was the natural colour of his linen on Sundays, but it toned down with the week.

MUZZLE. Mr. Nupkins' footman. *P.C.* xxiv.

With a long body and short legs.

MYRA. Negro wench;. a slave. *A.N.* xvii.

MYSELF. A bashful man. *C.S.H.T.*

MYSTERY. Passenger in train. *R.P., A.F.*

Not young, not pretty, though still of an average candle-light passability.

N

NADGETT. Mr., Secret agent of the Anglo-Bengalee Disinterested Loan and Life Assurance Company. *M.C.* xxvii.

He was the man at a pound a week who made the inquiries—he was born to be secret. He was a short, dried-up, withered old man, who seemed to have secreted his very blood. How he lived was a secret, where he lived was a secret. In his musty old pocket-book he carried contradictory cards, in some of which he called himself a coal-merchant, in others a wine-merchant in others a commission-agent, in others a collector, in others an accountant: as if he didn't know the secret himself. He was mildewed, threadbare, shabby; always had flue upon his legs and back; and kept his linen so secret, by buttoning up and wrapping over, that he might have had none—perhaps he hadn't.

NAMBY. Sheriffs deputy. *P.P.* xl.

Dressed in a particularly gorgeous manner, with plenty of articles of jewellery about him— and a rough great-coat to crown the whole.

NAMELESSTON. Place of seaside resort. *U.T.* xxxii.

NAN. A female crimp. Dark Jack's delight. *U.T.* v.

His white un-lovely Nan.

NANCY. *U.T.* iii.

NANCY. *O.T.* ix.

Rather untidy about the shoes and stockings.

Note.—Nancy was a member of Fagin's gang, possibly the only one with any remaining feelings of humanity. She was devoted to Sikes and was the means of recapturing Oliver Twist after his escape from Fagin. It was she, however, who revealed Oliver's secret, and so made it possible to discover his parentage and restore his fortunes. She was spied upon whilst doing this. by Noah Claypole, who was watching her on Fagin's behalf. Fagin told Sikes, and Sikes brutally murdered the woman who was willing to do so much for him and beseeched him, even while he struck her, to go to foreign parts with her, where they could live a new life.

NANDY. Mr., John Edward, Mrs. Plornish's father. *L.D.* xxxi.

If he were ever a big old man, he has shrunk into a little old man. His coat is of a colour and cut that never was the mode anywhere, at any period. It has always large, dull metal buttons, similar to no other buttons—a thumbed and napless and yet an obdurate hat—his coarse shirt and his coarse neckcloth have co more individuality than his coat and hat; they have the same nharacter of not being his—of not being anybody's. . . . A poor little reedy piping old gentleman, like a worn-out bird who had been in the music-binding business—had retired of his own accord to the workhouse.

NAPIER. Admiral Sir Charles. *M.P.*, *N.G.K.*

NAPLES. M.*P.*, *N.G.K.*; *M.P.*, *W.H.*; *M.P.*, *W.M.*; *P.F.I.*, *R.D.*; *R.P.*, *O.F..W.*; *R.P.*, *P.M.I.P.*; *U.T.* iv.

NAPLES. King of. *P.F.I.*, *R.*

NAPOLEON. Spirit of. *M.P.*, *R.S.D.*

NAPOLEON BONAPARTE. *M.C.* iv; *O.M.F.* lvi; *R.P.*, *B.S.*; *R.P.*, *O.F.W.*

NATHAN. Messrs., In Titchbourne Street, Haymarket. *M.P.*, *I.M.*

NATHAN. Mr., The dresser in private theatre. *S.B.B.*, Scenes xiii.

A red-headed, red-whiskered Jew.

NATIONAL CINDER HEAP. Houses cf Parliament. *H.T.*, *R.* xi.

NATIONAL GALLERY. *U.T.* xxiii.

NATIONAL HOTEL. *M.C.* xxxiv.

"**NATIVE.** The," Dark servant of Major Bagstock's. *D. and S.* vii.

Note.—Major Bagstock's coloured servant. He was christened "The Native," by Miss Tox, and having no name to the Major, being called by any opprobrious term, he naturally becomes "the native" throughout. His last appearance is watching Dombey's house to satisfy the curiosity of his master.

NATURAL. A silly. *O.M.F.* xvi.

NAVAL OFFICER. An old—on half-pay. *S.B.B.*, *O.P.* ii.

His bluff and unceremonious behaviour disturbs the old lady's domestic economy—he will smoke cigars in the front court—and lifts up the old lady's knocker with his walking-stick—He attends every vestry meeting that is held; always opposes the constituted authorities of the parish, denounces the profligacy of the churchwardens, contests legal points against the vestry clerk, will make the tax-gatherer call for his money till he won't call any longer—then he sends it. Is a charitable, open-hearted fellow at bottom, after all.

NAVY ISLAND. *A.N.* xv.

NEAPOLITAN INN. Woman servant at. *U.T.* xxviii.

A bright, brown, plump little woman-servant.

NEAPOLITAN NOBILITY. *L.D.* li.

NECKETT. "A Follower." *B.H.* xiv.

"Industrious? He'd set upon a post at a street corner, eight or ten hours at a stretch, if he undertook to do it."

Note.—The Coavinses of Mr. Skimpole. He is sheriff's officer, but his duty, such as it is, he does well. He dies and leaves three children, who are befriended by Mr. Jarndyce.

NECKETT. CHARLOTTE. *B.H.* xv.

Note.—Eldest daughter of Coavinses, the sheriff's officer. She is introduced, after her father's death, working for her brother and baby sister, locking them up during her absence. Mr. Jarndyce visits them, with the result that little Emma is "took" care of by Mrs. Blinder, Tom is put to school, and Charley is sent as a "present" to Esther Summerson as her maid. Charley catches smallpox from Jo and gives it to Esther, who has nursed her, and Charley in turn nurses her mistress. She is eventually married to a miller well to do.

NECKETT. EMMA. *B.H.* xv.

Note.—Sister of "Charley" Neckett. She is a baby of eighteen months when she is first introduced, but the family is befriended by Mr. Jarndyce. And when "Charley" is married to the miller, Emma appears to take her place as maid to Esther.

NECKETT. Tom. *B.H.* xv.

A mite of a boy, some five or six years old, nursing and hushing a heavy child of eighteen months.

Note.—Son of the sheriff's officer. The family is befriended by Mr. Jarndyce and Tom is put to school. He is afterwards apprenticed to the well-to-do miller whom his sister marries; and is always falling in love and being ashamed of it.

NED. Chimney-sweep. *O.T.* xix.

NED. Negro man slave. *A.N.* xvii.

NED. Young boy of. *O.T.* xix.

NEESHAWTS. Dr. *Mud. Pap.* i.

NEGRO. At Pawkins. *M.C.* xvi.

In a soiled white jacket, busily engaged in placing on the tables two long rows of knives and forks, relieved by jugs of water, and as he travelled down one side of this festive board, he straightened with his dirty hands the dirtier cloth, which was all askew, and had not been removed since breakfast.

NEGRO SINGERS. *M.P., P.L.U.*

NEIGHBOUR. Our next door. *S.B.B., O.P.* vii.

NEIGHBOURS. Of Nicholas Nickleby, Senr. *N.N.* i.

NEIGHBOURS. Shy. *U.T.* x.

NEILL HOUSE. Hotel in Columbus. *A.N.* xiv.

Richly fitted with the polished wood of the black walnut.

NELL. Little. *See* Trent. Little Nell.

NELSON. *M.P., R.T.*; *M.P., T.O.P., U.T.* xv.

NEMO. *See* Hawdon, Captain.

NEPAULESE PRINCES. [In Vauxhall Gardens.] *M.P., R.H.F.*

NEPHEW. Pebbleson, Predecessors of Wilding and Co. *C.S., N.T.* Act i.

NEPHEW. Scrooge's, Son of Fan. *C.B., C.C., S.* ii.

NEUCHÂTEL. *C.S., N.T.* Act i.

NEUF. Pont. *P.F.I., G.T.F.*

NEVILLE. Mr., H. G. as George Vendale. *M.P., N.T.*

NEWARK. *N.N.* v.

NEW BOND STREET. *M.P., I.M.*

NEW BROMPTON. *P.P.* ii.

The streets present a lively and animated appearance occasioned chiefly by the conviviality of the military.

NEW BRUNSWICK. *R.P., T.D.P.*

NEWBURGH. The town of. *A.N.* xv.

NEW BURLINGTON STREET. *C.S., S.L.* iv.

NEW CHURCH. *S.B.B.*, Char. i.

NEWCOME. Clemency, *C.B., B.o.L.* i.

NEW CROSS STATION. *R.P., A.F.*

NEW CUT. *M.P., A.P.*

NEW ENGLAND. *A.N.* iii.

NEWGATE. *B.H.* xxvi; *B.R.* lviii.; *C.S., T.G.S.* i.; *G.E.* xx.; *M.P., C.P.*; *M.P., G.B.*; *M.P., N.G.K.*; *M.P., N.S.E.*; *M.P., R.G.*; *M.P., S.F.A.*; *M.P., W.S.G.*; *N.N.* iv.; *O.M.F.* xxii.; *O.T.* xi.; *P.P.*, xxi.; *R.P., L.A.*; *S.B.B.*, Scenes xvii.; *S.B.B.*, Scenes xxiv.; *S.B.B.*, Scenes xxv.; *T.T.C.*, Bk. ii.; Ch. ii.; *U.T.* xiii.

NEWGATE. Discharged prisoner from. *S.B.B.*, Scenes xxiv.

Had been long in prison, and had been ordered to be discharged that morning. He had formed dissolute connections: idleness had led to crime.

NEWGATE. Prisoner. *S.B.B.*, Scenes xxiv.

Boy of thirteen is tried, say for picking the pocket of some subject of Her Majesty. The boy is sentenced, perhaps. to seven years' transportation.

NEWGATE. Turnkey at. *S.B.B.*, Scenes xxiv.

An ill-looking fellow, in a broad-brimmed hat, belcher handkerchief and top-boots, with a brown coat—something between a great-coat and a sporting jacket on his back, and an immense key in his left hand.

NEWGATE MARKET. *B.H.* v.; *R.P., M.O.F.F.*; *R.P., T.D.P.*

NEWGATE PRISON. Condemned cell in. *S.B.B.*, Scenes xxv.

A stone dungeon, eight feet long by six wide, with a bench at the upper end, under which were a common rug, a bible, and prayer book. An iron candlestick fixed into the wall at side.—and a small high window . . . admitted air and light. It contained no other furniture of any description.

NEWGATE PRISON. Wardswomen and wardsmen of. *S.B.B.*, Scenes xxv.

Are all prisoners selected for good conduct. They alone are allowed the privilege of sleeping on bedsteads.

NEWGATE SCHOOL. *S.B.B.*, Scenes xxv.

A portion of the prison set apart for boys under fourteen. A tolerably sized room, in which were writing materials. Fourteen in all, some with shoes, some without; some in pinafores without jackets, others in jackets without pinafores and one in scarcely anything at all.—And fourteen such terrible little faces we never beheld. There was not one redeeming feature among them.

NEWGATE. The gibbet. *S.B.B.*, Scenes xxiv.

NEWGATE. Whipping place. *S.B.B.*, Scenes xxiv.

NEWGATE. Yard for men. *S.B.B.*, Scenes xxv.

In one of which—that towards Newgate Street—prisoners of the more respectable class are confined. The different wards necessarily partake of the same character. They are provided, like the wards on the women's side—the only very striking difference—is the utter absence of employment. Huddled together—by the fireside sit twenty men perhaps—all idle and listless—with the exception of a man reading an old newspaper.

NEWGATE STREET. *B.R.* lxiv.; *N.N.* xxvi.; *P.P.* xxxi.; *G.E.* xxxiii.

NEW HAMPSHIRE. *A.N.* iii.

NEW HAVEN. Known also as the City of Elms. *A.N.* v.

NEW INN. *M.P., B.S.*; *P.P.* xx.

NEW INN. Near R——. *R.P., T.D.P.*

NEW JERSEY. *R.P., T.D.P.*

NEWMAN STREET. *B.H.* xxiii.; *S.B.B.* Char. ix.

NEWMAN STREET. Mr. Turveydrop's Academy in. *B.H.* xiv.

NEWMARKET. *D.C.* xxv.; *R.P., A.C.T.*

NEW ORLEANS. *A.N.* iii.; *A.N.* xiv.; *M.P., A.P.*; *M.P., E.T.*

NEW OXFORD STREET. *R.P., D.W.I.F.*

NEW PAVILIONSTONE. *R.P., O.O.T.*

NEWPORT MARKET. *P.P.* xlix.; *R.P., M.O.F.F.*; *R.P., T.D.P.*

NEW RIVER. *B.R.* iv.

NEW RIVER 'ED. *D.C.* xxv.

A sort of private hotel and boarding 'ouse.

NEW RIVER HEAD. *B.R.* lxvii.

Detachment of soldiers were stationed to keep guard.

NEW ROAD. The. *S.B.B.*, Char. v.

NEW ROYAL ADELPHI THEATRE. *M.P., N.T.*

NEWSBOY. Uncommonly dirty. *M.C.* xvi.

NEW SOUTH WALES. *R.P., D.W.I.F.*; *R.P., P.M.T.P.*

NEW THERMOPYLAE. *M.C.* xxii.

NEWTON CENTRE. *M.P., I.W.M.*

NEWTON CONN. *M.P., S.B.*

NEW YORK. *A.N.* ii.; *C.S., H.H.*; *M.C.* xiii.; *M.P., C.P.*; *M.P., L.A.V.* ii.; *M.P., R.S.D.*;

M.P., S.B.; *M.P., W.R.*; *R.P., L.A.*, *R.P., T.D.P.*; *U.T.* xx.

NEW YORK. Bay of. *U.T.* xxxi.

NEW YORK. State. *R.P., T.D.P.*

NEW YORK. State House of. *M.C.* xvi.

"**NEW WHITE HART.**" An Inn. *U.T.* xxii.

Opposition house to the Dolphin.

NEW WORLD. The. *C.S., H.T.*

NEW ZEALAND. *B.H.* xxvii.; *C.S., N.T.* Act i.; *M.P., E.T.*; *M.P., R.I.*

NEXT DOOR NEIGHBOUR. Our. *S.B.B., O.P.* vii.

NIAGARA. *A.N.* xiv.; *R.P., D.W.T.T.*; *R.P., L.A.*

"**NIBBLING JOE.**" *M.P., O.S.*

NIBLOS. A small summer theatre—New York. *A.N.* vi.

NICE. *P.F.I., A.G.*

NICHOLAS. Butler at Bellamy's. *S.B.B.*, Scenes xviii.

Steady, honest-looking old fellow in black. An excellent servant is Nicholas, an unrivalled compounder of salad-dressing—an admirable preparer of soda-water and lemon—a special mixer of cold grog and punch—and, above all, an unequalled judge of cheese. His prim white neckerchief, with the wooden tie, into which it has been regularly folded for twenty years past, merging by degrees into a small-plaited shirt-frill—would give you a better idea of his character than a column of our poor description could convey.

NICK. Emperor of Russia. *M.P., B.S.*

NICKETS. Late owner of Bounderby's Retreat. *H.T., R.* vii.

NICKLEBY. Godfrey, Grandfather of Nicholas. *N.N.* i.

A worthy gentleman, who taking it into his head rather late in life that he must get married, and not being young enough, or rich enough to aspire to the hand of a lady of fortune, had wedded an old flame out of mere attachment. Mr. Nickleby's income at the time of his marriage fluctuated between sixty and eighty pounds per annum.

Note.—Father of Ralph and Nicholas Nickleby, senr.

NICKLEBY. Kate, Sister of Nicholas. *N.N.* i.

Fourteen, as near as we can guess.

Note.—Sister of Nicholas. She is placed by her uncle, Ralph Nickleby, with Madame Mantalini. She is the object of the undesirable attentions of some of Ralph's evil-minded clients. chiefly those of Sir Mulberry Hawk, who suffers at Nicholas' hand in consequence, Ultimately she marries Frank Cheeryble.

NICKLEBY. Mrs., Wife of Godfrey Nickleby. *N.N.* i.

After five years—presented her husband with a couple of sons.

NICKLEBY. Mrs., Mother of Nicholas. *N.N.* i.

Daughter of a neighbouring gentleman, a well-meaning woman enough, but weak withal. . . . She dearly loved her husband, and still doted on her children.

Note.—Mother of Kate and Nicholas; weak-minded and with a strong inclination to dwell on unimportant details. Her remarks were more often than not without point, and far beside the subject of conversation. She is devotedly attached to her son and daughter, although she is of little assistance to them, and accompanies them in their pursuit of fortune. She is firmly convinced that the mad gentleman next door to the house at Bow was reduced to that state of mind by her rejection of his addresses. She is highly indignant at Miss La Creevy's betrothal to Tim Linkinwater. After their marriages she sometimes resided with Nicholas, sometimes with Kate.

NICKLEBY. Nicholas, senr., Father of Nicholas. *N.N.* i.

Was of a timid and retiring disposition. Embraced his wife and children—solemnly commended them to the One who never deserted the widow and her fatherless children, and smiling gently on them—observed, that he thought he could fall asleep.

Note.—The father of Nicholas and Kate, brother of Ralph and the son of Godfrey. Left with a very small fortune, he speculated and lost what he had. He died and left his widow and son and daughter to the tender mercies of Ralph and the world.

NICKLEBY. Nicholas, Hero of tale. *N.N.* i.

About nineteen. His figure was somewhat slight, but manly and well-formed; and apart from all the grace of youth and comeliness, there was an emanation from the warm young heart in his look and bearing—bright with the light of intelligence and spirit. . . . First assistant master of Dotheboys' Hall.

Note.—The hero of the book. By his Father's unfortunate speculations he is reducedto poverty and faced with the problem of supporting himself and his mother and sister. They all come to London and attempt to interest Ralph Nickleby in their case. Nicholas is packed off to Squeers' school as usher. Kate is placed in Madame Mantalini's dressmaking establishment. Nicholas discovers early the state of things at the school, a state of things made worse for him by his rejection of the advances of Miss Sqeers. The end of it is that he thrashes Squeers and leaves the school accompanied by Smike. He returns to London, but finds it necessary to leave soon after. He reaches Portsmouth, meets Mr. Vincent Crummles, and joins the theatrical company. He makes a decided success in this until he is recalled to London by an urgent letter from Newman Noggs, relating to Kate. He removes his mother and sister from the charge, such as it is, of his uncle, and is fortunate enough to fall in with the Cheeryble brothers. From this point his success is unbroken. He rises in the estimation of the brothers, marries Madeline Bray, and buys a partnership in the business with her fortune.

NICKLEBY. Ralph, junr., Uncle of Nicholas. *N.N.* i.

Deduced from the tale (of his father's sufferings in his days of poverty) the two great morals that riches are the true source of happiness and power, and that it is lawful and just to accomplish their acquisition by all means short of felony . . . He wore a bottle-green spencer over a blue coat: a white waistcoat, grey mixture pantaloons, and Wellington boots drawn over them. The corner of a small plaited shirt-frill struggled out, as if insisting to show itself, from between his chin and the top button of his spencer . . . a long gold watchchain composed of a series of plain rings, which had its beginning at the handle of a gold repeater and its termination in two little keys . . . a sprinkling of powder on his head, as if to make himself look benevolent . . . something in his cold restless eye which seemed to tell of cunning that would announce itself in spite of him. The face of the old man was stern, hard-featured and forbidding. . . . The old man's eye was keen with the twinklings of avarice and cunning.

Note.—Uncle to Nicholas. A money-lender with a good and fashionable clientèle. The father of Smike, whom he believes dead. He obtains work, of a kind, for Nicholas and Kate when they come to London. But dislikes the former and endeavours in every way possible to thwart him and even to ruin his future. Eventually he finds his evil plans recoil on himself, and he hangs himself in his house in Golden Square. His relatives take no steps to secure his ill-gotten wealth, and it falls to the Crown.

NICKLEBY. Ralph Uncle of Godfrey Nickleby. *N.N.* i.

Left him (Mr. Godfrey Nickleby) the bulk of his little property, amounting in all to five thousand pounds sterling.

NICKS. Nehemiah. *M.P., F.F.*

NICOLL. *R.P., B.S.*

NIECES AND NEVYS. Of Cobbler's old gentleman. *P.P.* xliv.

NIGER. *M.P., N.E.*

NIGER. The, Left bank of. *B.H.* iv.

NIGHT-PORTER. In Lincoln's Inn. *B.H.* xxxii.

A solemn warder, with a mighty power of sleep, keeps guard in his lodge.

NIGHTINGALE. John. *M.P., P.M.B.*

NIGHTINGALE. Mr. *M.P., M.N.D.*

NILE. *H.T., G.* ii.; *M.P., E.T.*; *U.T.* xv.

NINER. Miss Margaret. *H.D.* iv.
Niece of Mr. Julius Slinkton.

NINEVEH. *M.P., N.J.B.*

NIPPER. Susan, Florence Dombey's nurse. *D. and S.* iii.
A short, brown, womanly girl of fourteen, with a little snub nose, and black eyes like jet beads.
Note.—Eventually Susan marries Toots

NISBETT. Mrs., Actress. *M.P., M.B.*

NIX. Mr. *R.P., D.W.I.F.*

NIXON. Mr. *S.B.B.*, Scenes xix.

NIXON. Mr. Charles. *S.B.B.*, Scenes xix.

NIXON. Mr. James. *S.B.B.*, Scenes xix.

NIXON. Mr. R. *P.P.* xliii.

NIXONS. The, Guests of the Gattletons. *S.B.B.*, Tales ix.

NOAKES. Mr. Percy, A law student. *S.B.B.* Tales vii.
Was what is generally termed a devilish good fellow. If any old lady whose son was in India gave a ball, Mr. Percy Noakes was master of the ceremonies—if any member of a friend's family died, Mr. Percy Noakes was invariably to be seen in the second mourning coach with a white handkerchief to his eyes, sobbing—like winkin . . . was smart, spoffish, and eight-and-twenty.

NOAKES. Mrs. *M.P., S.G.*

NOAKES AND STYLES. Messrs. *Mud. Pap.* ii.

NOBBS. *M.P., T.T.*

NOBLEMAN. A poor, Family of. *L.D.* lvii.
Miss Wade became governess to the family.

NOBLEMAN. Another, House of. *M.P., L.L.*

NOBLEMAN. English, Deceased.
Generous and gentle. *U.T.* xxiii.

NOBLEMAN. Good-natured. *M.P., L.L.*

NOBLEMAN. Mother of two daughters of poor. *L.D.* lvii.
Young and pretty.

NOBLEMAN. Two daughters of poor. *L.D.* lvii.
They were timid, but on the whole disposed to attach themselves to me.

NOBLEMAN'S FAMILY. Nurse in poor. *L.D.* lvii.
A rosy-faced woman.

NOBLEY. Lord. *M.C.* xxviii.

NOBODY. *M.P., N.S.E.*

NOBODY. *R.P., U.S.*
Lived on the bank of a mighty river, broad and deep . . . one of an immense family.

NOBODY'S MASTER. *R.P., U.S.*

NOBS. Old. Mr. Weller, senior. *Which see.*

NOCKEMORF. Sawyer late, *P.P.* xxxviii.

NODDY. Mr., Visitor, accompanying young man to Bob Sawyer's. *P.P.* xxxii.
A scorbutic youth in a long stock.

NOGGS. Newman, Clerk to Ralph Nickleby. *N.N.* ii.
A tall man of middle age, with two goggle eyes, whereof one was a fixture, a rubicund nose, a cadaverous face, and a suit of clothes (if the term be allowable when they suited him not at all) much the worse for wear, very much too small, and placed upon such a short allowance of buttons that it was marvellous how he contrived to keep them on. Kept his horses and hounds once—squandered his money, invested it anyhow, borrowed at interest, and in short made first a thorough fool of himself and then a beggar.
Note.—At one time a well-to-do gentleman in Yorkshire. But he squandered his money and eventually became clerk and general drudge to Ralph Nickleby. He is filled with the intention of exposing Ralph and his nefarious practices, and when Nicholas appears on the scene he befriends him. While Nicholas is away at Squeers' school and at Portsmouth he watches over Kate. It is largely through him that Nicholas and his friends are able to checkmate Ralph Nickleby. After the happy ending to the story he lives in a cottage close by Nicholas's house and delights in amusing the children.

NOGO. Prof. *Mud. Pap.* i.

NOLAND. Sir Thomas. *S.B.B.*, Tales v.

NOLLY. *O.T.* xiii.

NON-COMMISSIONED OFFICERS. Seven. *R.P., N.S.*
Nobodies.

NONDESCRIPT. The, Connected with the Marshalsea. *L.D.* ix.

NOODLE. *B.H.* xii.

NORAH. Sweetheart of Master Harry. *C.S., H.T.*
Long, bright, curling hair and sparkling eyes, in little sky-blue mantle.

NORE. The. *D. and S.* xv. ; *S.B.B.*, Tales vii. ; *U.T.* xxiv.

NORFOLK. *C.S., M.L.Lo.* i. ; *D.C.* xxxiv. ; *H.D.* iii.

NORFOLK. Duchess of. *M.P., C.C.*

NORFOLK ISLAND. *M.P., P.P.* ; *R.P., T.B.W.*

NORFOLK STREET. Strand. *C.S., M.L.Leg.* i.

NORMAN. The, William the Conqueror. *M.P., T.B.*

NORMANDY. Bonnet. *C.S., G.i.S.*

NORMANDY. Robert of. *M.P., F.C.*

NORRIS. Mr., Engaged in mercantile affairs. *M.C.* xvii.

NORRIS. Mr., Junior, Son of Mr. Norris. *M.C.* xvii.
A student at college.

NORRIS. The Misses, Daughters of Mr. Norris. *M.C.* xvii.
One eighteen, the other twenty—both very slender, but very pretty. They sang in all languages except their own.

NORRIS. Mrs. *M.C.* xvii.
Looked much older and more faded than she ought to have looked.

NORRIS. Mrs., Senior, Mother of Mr. Norris. *M.C.* xvii.
A little sharp-eyed, quick, old woman.

NORRIS. S. F. *M.P., S.B.*

NORTH BARRIER. *T.T.C.* bk. iii. ch. x.
The carriage left the street behind, passed the North Barrier, and emerged upon the country road. In Dr. Manette's story.

NORTH BRIDGE. *P.P.* xlix.

NORTH END. *O.T.* xlviii.

NORTH FORELAND. *R.P.*, ; *O.E.W.P.*

NORTH POINT. *A.N.* ix.

NORTH POLE. *B.H.* xviii. ; *M.P., R.T.* ; *O.M.F.* ii. ; *U.T.* xv.

NORTH SEA. *N.N.* xli.

NORTH TOWER. In the Bastille. *T.T.C.* bk. ii. ; ch. xxi.
Through gloomy vaults where the light of day had never shone, past hideous doors of dark dens and cages, down cavernous flights of steps, and again up steep, rugged ascents.

Note.—The North Tower was where Dr. Manette had been confined, in "One Hundred and Five."

NORTH-WESTERN LINE OF RAILWAY. L.N.W.R. *M.P., R.S.*

NORTHAMPTON. *S.U.T.H.* iii.

NORTHAMPTONSHIRE. *M.P., E.S.* ; *M.P., O.L., N.O.* ; *O.T.* liii. ; *R.P., T.D.P.*

NORTHFLEET. Kent. *O.M.F.* xii.

NORTHUMBERLAND HOUSE. In the Strand. *M.P., G.A., S.B.B.*, Scenes, iv.

NORTON. Charles Eliot. *M.P., I.W.M.*

NORTON. Mrs. *M.P., I.W.M.*

NORTON. Squire. *M.P., V.C.*

NORWEGIAN FROSTS. *U.T.* xxiv.

NORWICH. *D.C.* iii. ; *E.D.* ix. ; *M.P., W.* ; *P.P.* xiii.

NORWICH CASTLE. *M.P., U.N.*

NORWOOD. *D.C.* xxvi. ; *D. and S.* xxxiii. ; *U.T.* xiv.

NORWOOD ROAD. *D.C.* xxvi.

"NOT TIRED YET." *M.P., O.S.*

NOTRE DAME. *L.D.* liv. ; *R.P., M.O.F.F.* ; *U.T.* vii.

NOTTING HILL. *U.T.* x.

NO-ZOO. The Lord, Toby Chuzzlewit's grandfather. *M.C.* i.
It *has* been said—for human wickedness has no limits—that there

is no lord of that name—and that among the titles which have become extinct, none at all resembling this, even in sound, is to be discovered.

NUBBLES. Christopher, Shop-boy to Trent and then servant to the Garlands. *O.C.S.* i.

Kit was a shock-headed, shambling awkward lad with an uncommonly wide mouth.

Note.—Kit was errand-boy and shop-boy to Nell's grandfather. He is Nell's willing slave, but the grandfather takes it into his head that Kit has injured him and discharges him. Kit enters the employ of Mr. Garland, where he prospers. He is accused of theft, however, through the instrumentality of the Brasses and imprisoned. He is soon cleared, and his case arouses some interest, so that he is able to better his position. In the end he marries Barbara.

NUBBLES. Mrs., Kit's mother. *O.C.S.* x.

Wait till he's a widder and works like you do, and gets as little, and does as much, and keeps his spirits up the same.

Note.—Mrs. Nubbles is Kit's mother: a hardworking laundress, who is eventually placed out of the reach of want.

NUGENT. Lord. *M.P., C.P.*

NUMBER ONE. Another refractory in Wapping Workhouse. *U.T.* iii.

"NO. 20—COFFEE-ROOM FLIGHT." Prisoner in the Fleet. *P.P.* xli.

"Little dirty-faced man in the brown coat. If he got any wrinkles in his face they was stopped up with the dirt . . . he got into debt . . . and in course o' time he come here in consekens. It warn't much execution for nine pound nothin' multiplied by five for costs. He wos a very peaceful inoffendin' creetur—the turnkeys they got quite fond on him."

NO. 924. Cabdriver. *Refer to* Sam.

NUMSKULL. Sir Arrogant. *See* Dedlock, Sir Leicester.

NUPKINS. George, Principal Magistrate of Ipswich. *P.P.* xxiv.

As grand a personage as the fastest walker would find out, between sunrise and sunset, on the twenty-first of June, which being, according to the almanack, the longest day in the whole year, would naturally afford him the longest period for his search.

Note.—Mr. Nupkins was Mayor of Ipswich and therefore chief magistrate of the town. Miss Witherfield, the lady into whose bedroom Mr. Pickwick had accidentally strayed, lodged information with Mr. Nupkins that Mr. Pickwick was to fight a duel, with Mr. Tupman as his second. The two Pickwickians were accordingly arrested and carried before His Worship. The following proceedings are very diverting, as a skit on the ignorance of the elective magistracy. Mr. Pickwick and his friend owe their release to their knowledge of Jingle who, masquerading as Captain Fitz-Marshall, was intended for the "rich" husband of Miss Nupkins.

NUPKINS. Miss, Daughter of chief magistrate. *P.P.* xxv.

NUPKINS. Mrs., Wife of chief magistrate. *P.P.* xxv.

A majestic female in a pink gauze turban, and a light brown wig.

Note.—Mrs. Nupkins is one of Dickens' best examples of the lady who always knew a thing after it had happened.

NURSE. Attending deathbed of Nicholas Nickleby, senior. *N.N.* i.

NURSE. Moloch's. *C.B., H.M.* ii.

NURSE. The, Mrs. Kitterbell's. *S.B.B.*, Tales xi.

With a remarkably small parcel in her arms, packed up in a blue mantle trimmed with white fur.

NURSEMAIDS. Twenty, In Mr. Dombey's Street. *D. and S.* xxxi.

Have promised twenty families of little women, whose instinctive interest in nuptials dates from their cradles, that they shall go and see the marriage.

"**NUTMEG-GRATER.**" Landlord of the. *C.B., B.o.L.* iii.

"**NUTMEG GRATER.**" Roadside inn. *C.B., B.o.L.* iii.

Snugly sheltered behind a great elm-tree with a rare seat for idlers. . . . . the horse trough full of clear fresh water . . . the crimson curtains in the lower rooms, and the pure white hangings in the little bedchambers above, beckoned, Come in !

O

O——. Mr. *M.P., R.T.*

OAK LODGE. Camberwell. *S.B.B.*, Tales v.
Residence of the Maldertons.

OAKUM HEAD. Chief of Refractories. *U.T.* iii.

OBELISK. The. *C.S., S.L.* iii. ; *D.C.* xii. ; *U.T.* x.

OBENREIZER. Friend and Compatriot of. *C.S., N.T.* Act ii.
The friend's face was mouldy, and the friend's figure was fat. His age was suggestive of the autumnal period of human life.

OBENREIZER. M. Jules, Agent of " Defresnier et Cie."
C.S., N.T. Act i. ; *M.P.A.T.*
Champagne-making friends of Wilding and Co. . . . A black-haired young man of dark complexion. through whose swarthy skin no red glow ever shone. He was robustly made, well proportioned, and had handsome features.—If his lips could have been made a little thicker, and his neck much thinner, they would have found their want supplied.

OBENREIZER. Woman-servant of M. *C.S., N.T.* Act ii.

OBENREIZER'S HOUSE. *M.P., N.T.*

OBI. King. *M.P., N.E.*

O'BLEARY. Mr., Boarder at Mrs. Tibbs. *S.B.B.*, Tales i.
An Irishman, recently imported —had come over to England to be an apothecary, a clerk in a Government office, an actor, a reporter, or anything else that turned up—he was not particular—wore shepherd's plaid inexpressibles, and used to look under all the ladies' bonnets as he walked along the streets.

O'BOODLEOM. Irish member. *M.P., B.A.*

O'BRIEN. Mr., Passenger on Gravesend packet. *S.B.B.*, Scenes x.

OBSERVATORY. The. *O.M.F.* liv. *S.B.B.*, Scenes xii.

OBSERVATORY. A room in Gradgrind's house. *H.T., S.* xv.

OBSTACLE. The, The Obelisk. *C.S., S.L.* iii.

OCEAN CLIFFS. *M.P., T.O.P.*

O'CONNELL. Mr. *M.P., C.P.*

O'DONOVAN. Wife and daughter. Tramps. *R.P., D.W.I.F.*

OFFENDER. (Murdered person.) *M.P., F.N.P.*

O. F. F. I. C. E. =Antediluvian Cave. *M.P., T.O.H.*

OFFICER. Brother, Of soldier. *M.H.C.* ii.

OFFICER. Commanding, Of the Horse Guards. *B.R.* xlix.

OFFICER. From India on leave. *L.D.* ii.
Guest in Great Hotel in Marseilles.

OFFICER. In Doctors' Commons. *S.B.B.*, Scenes viii.
A little thin old man, with long grizzly hair—whose duty—was to ring a large handbell when the Court (Arches) opened in the morning, and who, for aught his appearance betokened to the contrary, might have been similarly employed for the last two centuries at least.

OFFICER. Militia. M.P. *S.B.B.*, Scenes xviii.
With a complexion almost as sallow as his linen, and whose large black moustache would give him the appearance of a figure in a hairdresser's window.—The most amusing person in the house—very punctual in his attendance, generally harmless, and always amusing.

OFFICER. Night. *M.P., S.S.U.*

OFFICER. Police. *O.T.* xi.
A bluff old fellow—kind hearted thief-taker.

OFFICER. Public, Guest of Veneerings. *O.M.F.* ii.

OFFICER. Sturdy old, of the Army. *M.H.C.* i.

OFFICER. Young. *M.P., L.L.*

OFFICER. Young, Of the audience in the theatre. *N.N.* xxiv.

Supposed to entertain a passion for Miss Snevelicci.

OFFICER OF THE COURT. In Doctors' Commons. *S.B.B.*, Scenes viii.

A fat-faced, smirking, civil-looking body, in a black gown, black kid gloves, knee-shorts, and silks, with his shirt-frill in his bosom, curls on his head, and a silver staff in his hand.

OFFICERS. Custom 'Us, Custom House Officers. *G.E.* liv.

OHIO. *M.P., S.B., R.P., D.W.T.T.*

OHIO. The. *A.N.* xi. ; *M.P., E.T.*

OJIBBEWAY BRIDE. *M.P., Th. Let.*

O'KILLAMOLLYBORE. Young. *M.P., C. Pat.*

OLD BAILEY. *A.N.* xiv. ; *B.R.* xxxix. ; *M.C.* ix. ; *M.P., A. in E.*; *M.P., C.P.* ; *M.P., Dr. C.* ; *M.P., D.M.* ; *M.P., L.E.J.* ; *M.P., N.S.E.* ; *M.P., P.L.U.* ; *M.P., T.D.* ; *P.P.* xxxiii. ; *T.T.C.* bk. ii. ch. ii., *U.T.* iii.

A vile place, in which most kinds of debauchery and villany were practised, and where dire diseases were bred. The court was all bestrewn with herbs and sprinkled with vinegar, as a precaution against gaol air and gaol fever.

OLD BOAR. The, Kept by a Watkins. *N.N.* xxiii.

" OLD BRICKS AND MORTAR." Crummles, Mr. V. *Which see.*

OLD BURLINGTON STREET. *U.T.* xvi.

OLD CHARON. *B.H.* xxxii.

OLD CURIOSITY SHOP. *O.C.S.*

The title-piece of the novel of the name. One of those receptacles for old and curious things which seem to crouch in odd corners.

OLD FILE. *L.D.* xlii.

OLD GOOSEBERRY. Fictitious name of donor of gift to the Father of the Marshalsea. *L.D.* vi.

OLD GRANITE STATE. *M.P., T.O.P.*

OLD HELL SHAFT. A disused pit. *H.T., G.* vi.

OLD HUMMUNS. *M.P., W.S.G.*

OLD KENT ROAD. *U.T.* vii.

OLD MINT. The, *R.P., D.W.I.F.*

OLD PALACE YARD. *U.T.* xiii.

OLD PANCRAS ROAD. *P.P.* xxi.

OLD ROYAL HOTEL. *P.P.* l.

OLD SQUARE. Lincoln's Inn. *B.H.* iii. *P.P.* xxxi.

OLIVES, MOUNT OF. *U.T.* iii.

OLD STREET ROAD. *B.H.* ix.

OLD 'UN. The, Mr. Gummidge. *D.C.* xxii.

OLYMPIC THEATRE. The, New York. *A.N.* vi. ; *U.T.* iv.

'OMAN. A young. *S.B.B.*, Scenes v.

" As takes in tambour work, and dresses quite genteel."

OMER. Minnie, Afterwards Mrs. Joram. *D.C.* ix.

OMER. Mr., Draper, tailor, haberdasher, funeral furnisher, etc. *D.C.* ix.

A fat, short-winded, merry-looking little old man in black, with rusty little bunches of ribbons at the knees of his breeches, black stockings, and broad-brimmed hat.

ONE. The Nobby Shropshire. *D. and S.* xxxii.

ONE HUNDRED AND FIVE. North Tower. *T.T.C.* bk. ii. ch. xx.

" Monsieur, it is a cell."

ONOWENEVER. Mrs. *U.T.* xix.

ONTARIO LAKE. *A.N.* xv.

"OODED WOMAN WITH A HOWL." Supposed ghost of the haunted house. *C.S., H.H.*

They say, in general, that she was murdered, and the howl he 'ooted the while.

'OOMAN. An old, In house in George's Yard. *S.B.B., O.P.* v.

"The ugliest and dirtiest I ever see. She cursed the little naked children as was rolling on the floor.

OPERA. *L.D.* xlii.; *M.C.* xxi.; *M.P., O.S.*

OPERA. French. *R.P., L.A.*

OPERA COLONNADE. *B.H.* xiv.

OPERA HOUSE. *P.P.* xli.

OPPOSITIONISTS. In Parliament. *S.B.B.*, Scense xviii.

ORANGE. Mr. *H.R.* iv.

ORANGE. Mrs. *H.R.* iii.

ORATOR. Celebrated, An Irishman. *S.B.B., O.P.* vi.

ORATOR. The parlour, Mr. Rogers. *S.B.B.*, Char. v.

ORCHESTRA. The. *S.B.B.*, Scenes xix.

ORCHESTRA. The, Mr. V. Crummles'. *N.N.* xxiv.

ORDINARY. Rev. *M.P., T.B.*

ORDINARY OF NEWGATE. Rev. *M.P., S.F.A.*

OREGON. *M.P., I.M.*

"**ORFLING.**" A, Servant to the Micawbers. *D.C.* xi.

ORLICK. Dolge, Journeyman of Joe Gargery's. *G.E.* xiv.

A broad-shouldered, loose-limbed, swarthy fellow of gr eat strength never in a hurry, and always slouching.

Note.—Joe Gargery's man. Enormously strong and with an unreasoning grudge against Pip and his sister. He kills Pip's sister and later on endeavours to do the same to Pip. The arrival of Herbert and others prevents the execution of the design.

ORPHAN BOY. The. *R P., A.C.T.*

ORSON. O'Bleary. *S.B.B.*, Tales i.

OSBORNE'S HOTEL. *P.P.* liv.

OSGOOD. James Ripley = The Boston Bantam. *M.P., I.W.M.*

OTAHEITE. *M.P., E.T.*; *M.P., L.A.V.* ii.

OTRANTO. Castle of. *P.F.I., R.D.*

OUR ENGLISH WATERING PLACE. *R.P., O.E.W.P.*

OUR FRENCH WATERING PLACE. *R.P., O.F.W.P.*

OUR SCHOOL. *R.P., O.S.*

OUTSIDES. Passengers outside on coach. *P.P.* xxxv.

OVERS. John. *M.P., Overs.* Working-man author.

OVERSEERS. The. *S.B.B., O.P.* i.

They are usually respectable tradesmen, who wear hats with brims inclined to flatness.

OVERTON. Joseph, Mayor of Great Winglebury. Solicitor. *S.B.B.*, Tales viii.

A sleek man—in drab shorts and continuations, black coat, neckcloth and gloves.

OVERTON. Mr. Owen, Mayor of a small town on the road to Gretna. *M.P., S.G.*

OWEN. John, Schoolboy. *O.C.S.* lii.

"A lad of good parts, sir, and frank honest temper."

OWEN. Mr. Robert. *M.P., S.B.*; *M.P., S.F.A.*

OWEN. Professor. *U.T.* xxix.

OWL. In "Happy Family." *M.P., R.H.F.*

OXENFORD. *M.P., V. and B.S.*

OXFORD. *M.P., I.M.F.*; *M.P., L.L.*; *M.P., T.O.H.*; *R.P., T.B.W.*

OXFORD. Colleges of. *M.P., L.W. O.Y.*

OXFORD. Member for the University of. *M.P., H.H.*

OXFORD MARKET. *D. and S.* xviii.

OXFORD ROAD. *B.R.*xvi; *P.P.* xxxiii.

OXFORD STREET. *B.H.* xiii.; *D.C.* xxviii.; *L.D.* xxvii.; *M.H.C.* i.; *M.P., N.Y.D.*; *M.P., P.F.*; *M.P., W.R.*; *N.N.* xxxv.; *R.P., D.W.I.F.*; *S.B.B.*, Scenes xv.; *S.B.B.*, Scenes xvi.; *S.B.B.*, Tales vii.; *T.T.C.* bk. ii. ch. vi; *U.T.* x.

OXFORD UNIVERSITY. *M.P., O.C.*

OXFORDSHIRE. *O.M.F.* xlii.

P

PA. Husband of lady in distress. *S.B.B., O.P.* v.

PAAP. Mr., Celebrated dwarf. *A.N.* v.

PACIFIC OCEAN. *N.N.* xli. ; *U.T.* xx.

PACKER. Client of Snagsby. *B.H.* x.

PACKER. Tom, In the Marines. *C.S., P.o.C.E.P.*

A wild, unsteady young fellow, son of a respectable shipwright—a good scholar who had been well brought up.

PACKET. The. *R.P., O.o.S.*

PADDINGTON. *S.B.B.,* Scenes xvii. ; *U.T.* iii.

PADDINGTON ROAD. *S.B.B.,* Scenes xvii.

PADUA. *P.F.I., A.I.D.*

PAESTUM. *P.F.I., R.D.*

PAGE. A, David Copperfield's. *D.C.* xix.

The principal function of this retainer was to quarrel with the cook; in which respect he was a perfect Whittington, without his cat, or the remotest chance of being made a Lord Mayor.

PAGE. A dissipated, Of the Pockets' *G.E.* xxiii

Who had nearly lost half his buttons at the gaming table.

PAILLASSE. *M.P., R.D.*

PAINE. Thomas, The spirit of. *M.P., S.B*

PAINTER AND DECORATOR'S JOURNEYMAN. *S.B.B.,* Char. viii.

Husband of Miss Martin's ·riend.

PAINTED GROUND. *P.P* xli.

From the fact of its walls having once displayed the semblances of various men-of-war in full sail, and other artistical effects, achieved in bygone times by some imprisoned draughtsman in his leisure hours.

PALACE. *M.H.C.* i.

PALACE. Farnese. *P.F.I., P.M.B.*

PALACE COURT. *L.D.* vii.

PALACE YARD. *B.R.* xliii. ; *M.P. O.C.* ; *O.M.F.* iii. ; *S.B.B.,* Scenes xviii.

PALACES. Royal. *B.R.* lxvii.

PALAIS ROYAL. *M.P., N.Y.D.* ; *R.P., A.F.* ; *U.T.* vii.

PALAIS ROYAL. Theatre of the *M.P., N.Y.D.*

PALEY. Poor. *M.P., R.S.D.*

PALL MALL. *C.S., G.i.S.* ; *C.S., W.o.G.M.* ; *M.C.* xxvii. ; *M.P., B.A.* ; *M.P., C.* ; *M.P., T.D.*; *O.M.F.* xliv. ; *R.P., B.S.* ; *S.B.B.,* Char. i. ; *U.T.* xvi.

PALL MALL. Clubmen of. *M.P., P.M.B.*

PALMAS. Cape. *M.P., N.E.*

PALMER. Mr. *M.P., B.A.* ; *M.P., M.P.* ; *M.P., S.F.A.*

PALMERSTON. Lord. *M.P., I.* ; *M.P., T.B.* ; *M.P., T.O.H.*

PANCKS. Mr., Mr. Casby's agent. *L.D.* xiii.

Short dark man—dressed in black and rusty iron-grey; had jet-black beads of eyes; a scrubby little black chin; wiry black hair striking out from his head in prongs, like forks or hairpins—dirty hands, and dirty broken nails—snorted and sniffed and puffed and blew, like a labouring steam-engine.

Note.—Mr. Casby's agent. He is moral whipping-boy to the Patriarch. He squeezes the tenants of Bleeding Heart Yard, who are quite sure that if only Mr. Casby knew he would disapprove. But when Pancks returns from collecting rents, the Patriarch grumbles because he has not squeezed enough. He assists very much in the discovery of Rigaud, and is a friend of Arthur Clennam. Before leaving Casby's employment he shows the Patriarch in his true colours to the people of the yard.

PANCRAS ROAD. *S.B.B.,* Char. iv.

PANGLOSS. Officer of Circumlocution Office. *U.T.* viii.

PANIZZI. Signor. *M.P., N.J.B.*

PANKEY. Miss, Boarder at Mrs. Pipchin's *D. and S.* viii.

A mild, little blue-eyed morsel of a child, who was shampooed every morning, and seemed in danger of being rubbed away altogether.

PANKEY'S FOLKS. The little, Boarders at Mrs. Pipchin's. *D. and S.* lix.

PANTALOON. On the stage in the Britannia. *U.T.* iv.

PANTHEON. At Rome. *P.F.I., R.*; *R.P., A.P.A.*

PAOLINA CAPELLA. A chapel. *P.F.I., R.*

PAPA'S. Grave, *S.B.B., O.P.* ii.

PAPER-BUILDINGS. *B.R.* xv.

A row of goodly tenements shaded in front by ancient trees, and looking at the back upon the Temple Gardens. *See also* Temple.

PAPERS. Boy at Smith's bookstall. *C.S., M.J.* v.

PARADIS. Hôtel du. *P.F.I., A.G.*

PARDIGGLE. Francis. *B.H.* viii.

PARDIGGLE. Mr. O. A., F.R.S., Husband of Mrs. Pardiggle. *B.H.* viii.

Mr. Pardiggle brings up the rear. . . . An obstinate-looking man with a large waistcoat and stubby hair.

Note.—A member of the charitable army who make a lot of noise and do little work. Occupies no important place in the story, and is chiefly of interest as the friend of the Jellybys.

PARDIGGLE. Mrs. Distinguished for rapacious benevolence. *B.H.* viii.

A formidable style of lady, with spectacles, a prominent nose, and a loud voice—I am a school lady, a visiting lady, a reading lady, a distributing lady, I am on the local Linen Box Committee, and many general committees.

Note.—Wife of Mr Pardiggle and like him. She makes her children charitable, much to their disgust.

PARENTS. Of pupil of Miss Wade. *L.D.* lvii.

Elderly people; people of station. and rich.

PARENTS OF PUPIL. Nephew of. *L.D.* lvii.

Whom they had brought up . . . he began to pay me attention.

PARIS. *B.H.* ii.; *B.R.* xliii.: *C.S., M.L. Leg* i.; *L.D.* xi.; *M.P. A. in E.*; *M.P., E.S.*; *M.P., I.*; *M.P., M.M.*; *M.P., N.J.B.*; *M.P., N.Y.D.*; *M.P., O.F.A.*; *M.P., T.O.H.*; *M.P., W.*; *O.M.F.* xii.; *P.F.I., G.T.F.*; *R.P., A.F.*; *R.P., L.A.*; *R.P., M.O.F.F.*; *R.P., O.o.T.*; *T.T.C., U.T.* iv.

PARIS. *Boulevarts* in. *U.T.* xxiii.

PARIS. Cafe of. *M.P., N.Y.D.*

PARIS. Inns of. *C.S., H.T.*

With the pretty apartment of four pieces up one hundred and seventy-five waxed stairs—and the not-too-much-for-dinner, considering the price.

PARIS. The Moon. *M.P., R.D.*

PARISH. Our, The parish. *S.B.B., O.P.* i.

How much is conveyed in these two short words "The Parish"—with how many tales of distress and misery of broken fortune and ruined hopes are they associated.

PARK. People's, Near Birmingham. *U.T.* xxiii.

PARK. The. *L.D.* x.; *O.M.F.* xxxv.; *P.P.* xxxv.; *R.P., P.R.S.*

PARK LANE. *L.D.* xxvii.; *M.C.* xiii.; *N.N.* xxxii.; *R.P., O.o.T.*

PARK. Mungo. *M.P., L.A.V.* ii.

PARK THEATRE. The, New York. *A.N.* vi.

PARKER. A constable. *R.P., D.W.I.F.*

PARKER. Mrs. Johnson. *S.B.B., O.P.* vi.

President of Ladies' Bible and Prayer-Book Distribution Society.

PARKER. Pilot. *R.P., D.W.I.F.*

PARKER. The Misses Johnson, (seven). *S.B.B., O.P.* vi.

Treasurers, auditors, and secretary of the Ladies' Bible and Prayer Book Distribution Society.

PARKER. Theodore. *M.P., S.B.*

PARKER. Uncle, Inhabitant of Corner House. *O.M.F.* v.

PARKER HOUSE. Boston. *M.P., I.W.M.*

PARKES, Phil, The Ranger. *B.R.* i.

PARKINS. *R.P., O.B.*

PARKINS. Mrs., Laundress of chambers in the Temple. *R.P., G.o.A.*

PARKINS. Porter of chambers. *R.P.*, *G.o.A.*

PARKINS' WIFE'S SISTER. *R.P.*, *O.B.*

PARKLE. H., A young barrister. *U.T.* xiv.

PARKS. The. *G.E.* xxii.

PARKS. The, The lungs of London. *S.B.B.*, Scenes xii.

PARKS. Your. *M.C.* xxi.

PARKSOP BROTHER. *G.S.E.* vi.

PARLIAMENT. Houses of = The club. *M.P.*, *N.G.K.*

PARLIAMENT. Of the United Kingdom. *M.C.* xvii. ; *R.P.*, *O.B.*

PARLIAMENT. Three members of, Attending public meeting at London Tavern. *N.N.* ii.

One Irish—one Scotch—the third who was at Crockford's all night . . . will certainly be with us to address the meeting. . . honourable gentleman in patent boots, lemon-coloured kid-gloves, and a fur coat-collar.

PARLIAMENT STREET. *B.R.* xliv. ; *M.P.*, *M.E.* ; *M.P.*, *R.T.* ; *R.P.*, *O.B.*

PARLIAMENTARY CINDER HEAP. Houses of Parliament. *H.T.*, *R.* ix.

PARLOURMAID. Mrs. Steerforth's *D.C.* xxix.

Modest little parlourmaid with blue ribbons in her cap.

PARLOUR-MAID-IN-CHIEF. The, of the Nuns' House. *E.D.* iii.

PARLOURS. Birmingham, Clubs. *R.P.*, *P.M.T.P.*

PARMA. *P.F.I.*, *P.M.B.* ; *U.T.* xxviii.

PARMARSTOON. Grand Vizier = Twirling Weathercock. Lord Palmerston. *M.P.*, *T.O.H.*

PARROT. In "Happy Family." *M.P.*, *R.H.F.*

PARRY. *M.P.*, *L.A.V.* ii. ; *M.P.*, *P.F.D.* ; *M.P.*, *V.C.*

PARSON. Miss Letitia, Pupil at Minerva House. *S.B.B.*, Tales iii.

PARSONAGE HOUSE. Formerly the Mr. Boythorn's residence. *B.H.* xviii.

With a lawn in front, a bright flower-garden at the side, with a well-stocked orchard and kitchen garden in the rear, enclosed by a venerable wall. The house—was a real old house, with settles in the chimney of the brick-floored kitchen, and great beams across the ceilings.

PARSONS. Mr., Gabriel, A rich sugar-baker. *S.B.B.*, Tales x.

A short, elderly gentleman, with a gruffish voice—who mistook rudeness for honesty, and abrupt bluntness for an open and candid manner.

PARSONS. Mrs. *S.Y.C.*

PARSONS. Mrs. Gabriel. *S.B.B.*, Tales x.

PARSONS. Two itinerant Methodist. *S.B.B.*, Tales xi.

PARTIES. Engaging boats at Searle's *S.B.B.*, Scenes x.

PARTRIDGE. Mr. *M.P.*, *S.B.*

PARTY. A regular, at Astley's. *S.B.B.*, Scenes xi.

At Easter or Midsummer holidays—Pa, Ma, nine or ten children, varying from five foot six to two foot eleven—from fourteen years of age to four.

PARVIS. Old Arson, Old resident of Laureau. *C.S.*, *M.f.T.S.* ii.

"One of old Parvis's fam'ly I reckon," said the captain, "kept a dry goods store in New York City, and realised a handsome competency by burning his house to ashes."

PASSENGER. A regular, Of omnibus. *S.B.B.*, Scenes xvi.

A little testy old man, with a powdered head, who always sits on the right-hand side of the door as you enter, with his hands folded on the top of his umbrella.

PASSENGER. Another regular, In omnibus. *S.B.B.*, Scenes xvi.

The shabby-genteel man with the green bag.

PASSENGER. Another regular, In omnibus. *S.B.B.*, Scenes xvi.

The stout gentleman in the white neckcloth, at the other end of the vehicle.

PASSENGER. Husband of a, On the "Screw." *M.C.* xvii.

Not altogether dead, sir, but he's had more fevers and agues than is quite reconcilable with being alive—a feeble old shadow came creeping down.

PASSENGER. In omnibus. *S.B.B.*, Tales xi.

A little prim, wheezing old gentleman.

PASSENGER. On board the "Esau Slodge." *M.C.* xxxiv.

A tall, thin gentleman—with a carpet-cap on, and a long loose coat of green baize, ornamented about the pockets with black velvet.

PASSENGER. On coach. *N.N.* v.

A hearty-looking gentleman with a very good-humoured face, and a very fresh colour.

PASSENGER. Of stage coach. *S.B.B.*, Scenes xvi.

A stout man, who had a glass of rum-and-water, warm, handed in at the window at every place where we changed.

PASSENGER. Outside, On early coach. *S.B.B.*, Scenes xv.

One old gentleman, and something in a cloak and cap, intended to represent a military officer.

PASSENGER. Outside. On early coach. *S.B.B.*, Scenes xv.

Thin young woman, cold and peevish—is got upon the roof, by dint of a great deal of pulling and pushing—and repays it by expressing her solemn conviction that she will never be able to get down again.

PASSENGERS. Coming in by early coach. *S.B.B.*, Scenes i.

Look blue and dismal.

PASSENGERS. Going out by early coach. *S.B.B.*, Scenes i.

Stare with astonishment at the passengers who are coming in by the early coach.

PASSENGERS. Inside, In early coach. *S.B.B.*, Scenes xv.

PASSENGERS. Of an omnibus. *S.B.B.*, Scenes xvi.

Change as often in the course of one journey as the figures in a kaleidoscope, and though not so glittering, are far more amusing.

PASSENGERS. Outside, On early coach. *S.B.B.*, Scenes xv.

Two young men with very long hair, to which the sleet has communicated the appearance of crystallised rats' tails.

PASSENGERS. Regular, In omnibus. *S.B.B.*, Scenes xvi.

Always take them up at the same places, and they generally occupy the same seats.

PASSENGERS. Woman and three children aboard the "Screw." *M.C.* xv.

Making the voyage by herself with these young impediments here, and going such a way at this time of the year to join her husband.—He's been away from her for two year—she's been very poor and lonely—looking forward to meeting him.

PASSNIDGE. Mr., Friend of Mr. Murdstone. *D.C.* ii.

PASTORAL GARDENS. *B.H.* xix.

PASTRYCOOK. In funereal room in Brook Street. *D. and S.* xxxi.

PAT. Mr. *M.P.*, *N.G.K.*

PATAGONIA. *M.P.*, *L.A.V.* i.

PATENT OFFICE. In Lincoln's Inn. *R.P.*, *P.M.T.P.*

PATENT OFFICE. The, Washington. *A.N.* viii.

PATIENT. First, Of young medical Practitioner. *S.B.B.*, *O.P.* i.

Stretched upon the bed, closely enveloped in a linen wrapper, and covered with blankets, lay a human form stiff and motionless. The head and face, which were those of a man, were uncovered, save by a bandage, which passed over the head and under the chin . . . The throat was swollen, and a livid mark encircled it. . . . One of the men who was hanged this morning.

PATIENT. The Hospital. *S.B.B.*, Char. vi.

PATRIARCH. Mr. Monomaniacal, *M.P.*, *G.B.*

PATRIARCH. The. *L.D.*, *I.* xiii.

PATRIOT. A certain. *M.C.* xxi.
Who had declared from his high place in the Legislature, that he and his friends would hang, without trial, any Abolitionist who might pay them a visit.

PATRONESSES. The lady. *S.B.B.*, Scenes xix.
Of Indigent Orphans' Friends' Benevolent Institution.

PATTEN-MAKERS. The, Worshipful Company of. *M.H.C.* i.

PATTY. Maiden sister of John. *C.S.*, *H.H.*
Eight-and-thirty, very handsome, sensible, and engaging—a woman of immense spirit.

PAUL. Jean. *M.P.*, *N.T.*

PAUL'S CHURCHYARD. *P.P.* xliv.
See also Doctors' Commons.

PAUL'S WORK. Canongate. *M.P.*, *S.P.*

PAVILIONSTONE. *R.P.*, *O.o.T.*
A little smuggling town.

PAVILIONSTONE STATION. *R.P.*, *O.o.T.*

PAVIOURS. Two, French-Flemish. *U.T.* xxv.

PAWKINS. Major, Husband of Mrs. Pawkins. *M.C.* xvi.
A gentleman of Pennsylvanian origin, was distinguished by a very large skull, and a great mass of yellow forehead;—a heavy eye, and a dull, slow manner. In commercial affairs he was a bold speculator—in plainer words, he had a most distinguished genius for swindling.

PAWKINS. Mrs., Kept a boarding-house . . . was very straight, bony, and silent. *M.C.* xvi.

PAWKINS'. Major, House. *M.C.* xvi.
A rather mean-looking house with jalousie blinds to every window; a flight of steps before the green street door; a shining white ornament on the rails on either side like a petrified pineapple, polished; a little oblong plate over the knocker, whereon the name of Pawkins was engraved.

PAWNBROKERS. Near King's Bench Prison. *S.B.B.*, Scenes xxi.
First watches and rings, then cloaks, coats, and all the more expensive articles of dress have found their way to the pawnbroker's. Dressing-cases, and writing-desks, too old to pawn, but too good to keep.

PAWNBROKER'S SHOP. Customers in. *S.B.B.*, Scenes xxiii.

PAWNBROKER'S SHOP. Little boxes in. *S.B.B.*, Scenes xxiii.
Little dens, or closets, which face the counter—here the more timid or respectable portion of the crowd shroud themselves from the notice of the remainder.

PAWNBROKER'S SHOP. The. *S.B.B.*, Scenes xxii.
Situated near Drury Lane, at the corner of a court, which affords a side entrance for the accommodation of such customers as may be desirous of avoiding the observation of the passers-by, or the chance of recognition in the public street. Tradition states that the transparency in the front door, which displays at night three red balls on a blue ground, once bore the words "Money advanced on plate, jewels, wearing apparel, and every description of property."

PAYNE. Surgeon. *P.P.* ii.
A portly personage in a braided surtout.
Note.—The fire-eating doctor who attended Dr. Slammer in the intended duel.

PAYNTER. My enemy. *M.P.*, *N.Y.D.*

PEACE. Name of Bird. *B.H.* xiv.

PEACE SOCIETY. *M.P.*, *P.F.*; *P.P.* xiii.; *N.N.* v.

PEACOAT. A Thames policeman. *R.P.*, *D.W.T.T.*

"**PEACOCK.**" The, An Inn. *C.S., H.T.*

A coaching-house at Islington.

PEAK. Mr. Chester's manservant. *B.R.* xxiii.

Note.—Sir John Chester's man-servant. He adapts himself so completely to his master's standard that on Sir John's death he decamps with everything portable and sets up as a man of fashion on his own account. His career in this rôle is not a long one, however, as he is apprehended and imprisoned.

"**PEAKS.** The," Former name of Bleak House. *B.H.* viii.

"**PEAL OF BELLS.**" Village alehouse. *C.S., T.T.G.*i.

"**PEAL OF BELLS.**" Landlord of the. *C.S., T.T. G* i.

PEASANT WOMAN. Owner of apartments to let. *L.D.* lvi.

Strong, cheerful—all stocking, petticoat, white cap, and ear-ring.

PEASANTS. *P.F.I.*

PEBBLESON. Nephew. *N.T.*, Act i.

PECKHAM. D. *and S.* iv.; *M.P., E.T.*; *M.P., W.R.*; *U.T.* vi.

PECKSNIFF. Mr. Seth, Architect and land surveyor. *M.C.* ii.

Was a moral man; a grave man, a man of noble sentiments, and speech. He was a most exemplary man: fuller of virtuous precepts than a copy-book. His hair just grizzled, with an iron-grey—stood bolt upright, or slightly drooped in kindred action with his heavy eyelids.—His very throat was moral. You saw a good deal of it. You looked over a very low fence of white cravat—and there it lay, a valley between two jutting heights of collar, serene and whiskerless before you.

Note.—Cousin of old Martin Chuzzlewit He is an architect and surveyor near Salisbury, living, however, on the labours and fees of his pupils and his reputation for respectability. He calls a meeting of the family at his house, while old Martin is lying ill at "The Dragon." Martin is the rich relative from whom all have expectations. Thinking to advance his interests with the old man, Pecksniff takes young Martin into his house to learn architecture. On a hint from old Martin that this course does not please him, he turns his young kinsman out of doors. Old Martin Chuzzlewit then comes to reside with him, and gives him to understand that he will inherit the largest portion of his wealth. He simulates senility and allows himself to be dominated by Pecksniff, who fawns on him and abases himself continually. On his return fromAmerica in company with Mark Tapley, young Martin finds Pecksniff receiving encomiums on the designs for a grammar school which Martin himself drew while he was with Pecksniff. This point of the story is somewhat impossible from a professional point of view, but it adds to the interest of the narrative and shows the development of Pecksniff's character. Still acting under the impression that he is studying the grandfather's desires, he repulses Martin. Ultimately his hypocrisy is laid bare by old Martin, his daughters are left unhappy and unfortunate, while he ends his days poverty-stricken under the curse of drink.

PECKSNIFF, Miss Charity, Daughter of Pecksniff. *M.C.* ii.

Miss Pecksniff's nose—was always very red at breakfast-time. For the most part, indeed, it wore at that season of the day a scraped and frosty look, as if it had been rasped; "Charity," said Mr. Pecksniff, "is remarkable for strong sense, and for rather a deep tone of sentiment."

Note.—The eldest daughter of Pecksniff was the replica of her father.Throughout our acquaintance with her she is a hypocritical shrew. She becomes betrothed to Mr. Moddle, one of Mrs. Todger's boarders. The house is furnished, the wedding breakfast is ready, and the guests, who have been invited by Cherry to witness her triumph are waiting, when a letter is received from Mr. Moddle announcing the fact that he has run away. Cherry is last seen in company with her father living on the charity of Tom Pinch.

PECKSNIFF. Miss Mercy, Younger daughter of Mr. Pecksniff. *M.C.* ii.

She was the most arch, and at the same time the most artless creature—she was too fresh and guileless, and too full of childlike vivacity—to wear combs in her hair, or to turn it up or to frizzle it or braid it. She wore it in a crop, a loosely flowing crop which had so many rows of curls in it, that the top row was only one curl. Moderately buxom was her shape, and quite womanly too; but sometimes she even wore a pinafore.

Note.—" Merry " Pecksniff, although filled with much the same falsities as her father, had some redeeming traits, or, at all events, she excites some sympathy on account of the terrible suffering she experienced after her marriage to Jonas Chuzzlewit. She enters into wedlock with him for a variety of reasons, none of which was a good one. After the wedding she sees her husband as he is, and he does not find it so very difficult a task to " break her spirit !" The trial purifies her nature, and she is last seen leaving Mrs. Todger's boarding-house with old Martin Chuzzlewit, who has determined to befriend her.

PEDDLE AND POOL. Solicitors. *L.D.* xxxvi.

PEDLAR'S ACRE. *S.B.B.*, Sc. iv.

PEECHER. Miss Emma, Schoolmistress. *O.M.F.* xviii.

Small, shining, neat, methodical, and buxom—cherry-cheeked and tuneful of voice.

Note.—Mistress in the girls' department at the school in which Bradley Headstone is master of the boys. She loves Bradley, but he has no affection for her, so she sighs in secret.

PEECHER. Miss, Schoolhouse of. *O.M.F.* xviii.

Her small official residence, with little windows like the eyes in needles, and little doors like the covers of schoolbooks—dusty little bit of garden attached.

PEEL. Mr. Frederick. *M.P., N.J.B.*, ; *M.P., C.P.*

PEEL. Sir Robert. *M.P., T.D.* ; *M.P., E.R.*

PEEPER. New York. *M.C.* xvi.

PEEPY. The honourable Miss. *R.P., O.E.W.*

The beauty of her day.

PEER. The old, Another frequenter of Bellamy's. *S.B.B.*, Scenes xviii.

Old man—his peerage is of comparatively recent date—has a huge tumbler of hot punch brought him.

PEERS. M.P.'s. *S.B.B.*, Scenes xviii.

PEERYBINGLE. Mr. John, Carrier. *C.B., C.o.H.* i.

Lumbering, slow, honest—so rough upon the surface, but so gentle at the core.

PEERYBINGLE. Mrs., Wife of Carrier Peerybingle. *C.B., C.o.H.* i.

Fair and young: though something of the dumpling shape.

PEERYBINGLE. Young, Infant son of carrier. *C.B., C.o.H.* ii.

PEFFER. Deceased partner of Peffer and Snagsby. *B.H.* x.

Has been recumbent this quarter of a century in the churchyard.

PEFFER AND SNAGSBY. Law stationers. *B.H.* x.

" **PEGASUS'S ARMS**." Public house. *H.T., S.* vi.

Underneath the winged horse, upon the signboard, " The Pegasus's Arms " was inscribed in Roman letters.

PEGG. A male crimp. *U.T.* v.

In a checked shirt, and without a coat.

PEGG. Mrs. Wife of Pegg, a female crimp. *U.T.* v.

A crouching old woman, like the picture of the Norwood gipsy in the old sixpenny dream-books.

PEGGOTTY. Clara, David's nurse. *D.C.* i.

There was a red velvet footstool in the best parlour, on which my mother had painted a nosegay. The ground-work of that stool and Peggotty's complexion appeared to me to be one and the same thing. The stool was smooth, and Peggotty was rough, but that made no difference.

Note.—Peggotty is the homely but kindly, good-hearted servant to Mrs. Copperfield, and nurse to David. On her mistress' marriage to Murdstone. she loses some of her influence, and when Mrs. Copperfield dies she is discharged. She then marries Barkis, the carrier. Barkis is somewhat miserly in his way and leaves Peggotty, on his death, with a fair sum. Part of this Peggotty wants to hand over to David on his Aunt's loss of fortune. Peggotty sticks to them in the end and " always . . . comes Peggotty, my good old nurse . . . accustomed to do needlework at night very close to the lamp."

PEGGOTTY. Daniel, Clara Peggotty's brother. *D.C.* ii.

A hairy man with a very good-natured face.

Note.—Brother of Peggotty, David's nurse. He lives at Yarmouth in a boat converted into a house, with his nephew Ham, his niece Emily, and Mrs. Gummidge He is first seen when David goes to Yarmouth while his mother is being married to Mr. Murdstone. Later on David visits them again with Steerforth. The latter brings about the ruin of Little Emily, and Dan'l sets forth to find her. He travels for months on his search, no one knows where, until David meets him in London one day and learns that he has travelled over a great part of the Continent, " mostly a-foot," in his search for his poor niece. Eventually he succeeds in finding her and they emigrate to Australia, where they prosper and Emily is able in some measure to forget the earlier happenings. Dan'l returns once to England and visits David.

PEGGOTTY. Ham, The intended husband of Little Em'ly. *D.C.* i.

A huge, strong fellow of six feet high, broad in proportion, and round-shouldered; but with a simpering boy's face and curly light hair.

Note.—Ham was Daniel's nephew. He is terribly upset when Emily runs away with Steerforth. When Steerforth and Emily part and the former is on his way to England the vessel is wrecked at Yarmouth. Ham attempts to rescue the passengers and endeavours to bring Steerforth to land. They are both drowned.

PEGGY. *C.S., G.i.S.*

PEGGY. King Watkins the First's Lord Chamberlain. *H.R.* ii.

PEGLER. Mrs., Bounderby's mother. *H.T., G.* v.

" I have never said I was your mother. I have admired you at a distance . . . only making the condition that I was to keep down in my own part."

PEGWELL BAY. *S.B.B.*, Tales iv.

PELL. Mr. Solomon, An attorney. *P.P.*, xliii.

A fat, flabby, pale man in a surtout, which looked green one moment and brown the next; with a velvet collar of the same chameleon tints. His forehead was narrow, his face wide, his head large, and his nose all on one side, as if Nature, indignant with the propensities she observed in him in his birth, had given it an angry tweak, which it had never recovered.

Note.—The rather disreputable attorney who undertook Sam Weller's " business " in confining himself in prison with Mr. Pickwick.

PELL. Mrs., A widow—deceased. *P.P.*, lv.

A splendid woman, with a noble shape, and a nose formed to command and be majestic.

PELTEER. *M.P., L.A.V.* i.

PELTIROGUS. Horatio, Supposed suitor for Kate Nickleby's hand. *N.N.* lv.

A young gentleman who might have been, at that time, about four years old, or thereabouts.

PELTIROGUSES. The. *N.N.* xlv.

PENITENTIARY. The. *S.B.B.*, Scenes x.

PENKRIDGE. *M.P., E.S.*

PENNSYLVANIA. *A.N.* xvii.; *M.P., P.P.*

PENREWEN. Old resident of Laureau. *C.S., M.f.T.S.* ii.

PENRITH. *C.S., W.O.G.M.*

PENSIONER. Greenwich, with an empty coat-sleeve. *U.T.* xxvii.

His coat-buttons were extremely bright, he wore his empty coat-sleeve in a graceful festoon, and he had a walking stick in his hand that must have cost money.

PENSIONER. Mrs. G., Late Mitts. Ex-occupant of Titbull's Almshouses. *U.T.* xxvii.

PENSIONERS. Old, Of Greenwich. *S.B.B.*, Scenes xii.

Who for the moderate charge of a penny exhibit the mast house, the Thames and shipping, the place where the men used to hang in chains, and other interesting sights, through a telescope.

PENSON. Mrs. W., as Mrs. Noakes. *M.P., S.G.*

PENTON PLACE. Pentonville. *B.H.* ix.

PENTONVILLE. *L.D.* xiii.; *M.P., P.F.*; *M.P., P.P.*; *O.T.* xii.; *P.P.* ii.; *S.B.B.*, Char. iv.; *S.B.B.*, Tales xi.; *U.T.* xiv.

PENZANCE. *C.S., M.F.S.* ii.

PEOPLE. Busy, Seeing Mark Tapley off. *M.C.* vii.

PEOPLE. Government office. *S.B.B., O.P.* vii.

In light drabs, and starched cravats, little, spare, priggish men.

PEOPLE. Married, At tea gardens. *S.B.B.*, Scenes ix.

PEOPLE. Of the United States. *M.P., Y.M.C.*

PEOPLE. On Sands at Ramsgate. *S.B..B*, Tales iv.

The ladies were employed in needlework, or watch-guard making or knitting, or reading novels; the gentlemen were reading newspapers and magazines; the children were digging holes in the sand. The nursemaids, with their youngest charges in their arms, were running in after the waves, and then running back with the waves after them.

PEOPLE. Several, Young and old. *M.C.* xxxi.

PEOPLE. Shabby-genteel. *S.B.B.*,, Char. x.

You meet them, every day, in the streets of London—they seem indigenous to the soil, and to belong as exclusively to London as its own smoke, or the dingy bricks and mortar. This shabby gentility is as purely local as the statue at Charing Cross or the pump at Aldgate. It is worthy of remark, too, that only men are shabby-genteel—a woman is always either dirty and slovenly—or neat and respectable, however poverty-stricken in appearance.

PEOPLE'S THEATRE = Eagle Saloon. *M.P., A.P.*

PEPLOW. Husband of Mrs. *S.B.B.*, Scenes ii.

PEPLOW. Master, Son of Mrs. Peplow. *S.B.B.*, Scenes ii.

PEPLOW. Mrs. *S.B.B.*, Scenes ii.

PEPPER. Pip's "Boots." *G.E.* xxvii.

Clothed him with a blue coat. canary waistcoat, white cravat, creamy breeches, and the boots already mentioned.

PEPS. Doctor Parker, Attending Mrs. Dombey. *D. and S.* i.

One of the court physicians, and a man of immense reputation for assisting at the increase of great families.

PEPYS. Mr. *M.P., L.L.*

PERCH. Mrs., Wife of Dombey's messenger. *D. and S.* xiii.

PERCH. The messenger at Dombey and Son's. *D. and S.* xiii.

Whose place was on a little bracket like a timepiece. When Perch saw Mr. Dombey come in—or rather when he felt that he was coming, for he had usually an instinctive sense of his approach—he hurried into Mr. Dombey's room, stirred the fire, quarried fresh coals from the bowels of the coal-box, hung the newspapers to air upon the fender, put the chair ready, and the screen in its place, and was round upon his heel on the instant of Mr. Dombey's entrance, to take his greatcoat and hat, and hang them up.

PERCY. Lord Algernon. *B.R.*, lxvii.

Commanding Northumberland militia.

PERCY STREET. *S.B.B.*, Char. ix.

PERKER. Mr., of Gray's Inn, Mr. Pickwick's lawyer. *P.P.* x.

He was a little, high-dried man, with a dark, squeezed-up face, and small, restless black eyes, that kept winking and twinkling, on each side of his little inquisitive nose, as if they were playing a perpetual game of peep-bo with that feature.

Note.—The little attorney who first appears as the election-agent of Slumkey, the "Blue" candidate in the Eatanswill election, and afterwards conducts Mr. Pickwick's side of the Bardell v. Pickwick case.

PERKINS. A general dealer. *C.S., H.H.*

PERKINS. Mrs. *B.H.* xi.

PERKINS. Mrs. *M.C.* xix.

PERKINS. Young. *B.H.* xi.

PERKINS'S BROTHER-IN-LAW. *C.S., H.H.*

A whip and harness-maker, who keeps the post office, and is under submission to a most rigorous wife of the Doubly Seceding Little Emmanuel persuasion.

PERKINS INSTITUTION and Massachusetts Asylum for the Blind at Boston. *A.N.* iii.

PERKINSOP. Mary Anne, Mrs. Lirriper's maid. *C.S., M.L.Lo.* i.

PERRIN BROTHERS. Clockmakers. *C.S., N.T.*, Act iv.

PERSIA. *M.P., S.R.*

PERSON. Hired by Smallweed. *B.H.* xxvi.

One of those extraordinary specimens of fungus that spring up spontaneously in the western streets of London.

PERSON. A roving, Member of Mr. V. Crummles' Company. *N.N.* xxiii.

In a rough great-coat, who strode up and down in front of the lamps, flourished a dress-cane, and rattling away in an undertone, with great vivacity—for the amusement of an ideal audience.

PERSONAGE. Elderly, Frequenting "The Peacock." *P.P.* xiv.

With a dirty face and a clay pipe.

PERSONAGES. Several, Eminent and distinguished. *P.P.* xlvii.

PERSONS. Another class of. *P.P.* xl.

Waiting to attend summonses their employers had taken out, which it was optional to the attorney on the other side to attend or not—and whose business it was, from time to time, to cry out the opposite attorney's name; to make certain that he was not in attendance without their knowledge.

PERT. Miss Scornful, Pussy. *E.D.* ii.

PERUGIA. *P.F.I., R.D.*

PESSELL AND MORTAIR. Messrs. *Mud. Pap.* ii.

PET. Family, A burglar. *O.T.* xxxi.

PETER. Lord. *S.B.B.*, Tales viii.

An imbecile lord, for whom Mr. Alexander Trott was mistaken.

PETER THE WILD BOY. *M.C.*, vii.

PETERSHAM. Surrey. *N.N.* l.

PETO AND BRASSEY. Messrs. *U.T.* xxiv.

PETOWKER. Miss, of the Theatre Royal, Drury Lane. *N.N.* xiv.

Young lady, daughter of a theatrical fireman, who "went on" in the pantomime, and had the greatest turn for the stage that was ever known.

Note.—A friend of the Kenwigses. Captivates Mr. Lillyvick, the collector, and marries him. But she tires of her husband and runs off with a half-pay Captain. Lillyvick utterly renounces her in the presence of the assembled Kenwigses.

PETTIFER. Tom., Captain Jorgan's Steward. *C.S., M.f. T.S.* i.

"Afraid of a sunstroke in England in November, Tom, that you wear your tropical hat, strongly paid outside and paper-lined inside, here?" said the captain. A man of a certain plump neatness, with a curly whisker, and elaborately nautical in a jacket, and shoes, and all things correspondent.

PEW-OPENER. In church where Paul Dombey was christened. *D. and S.* v.

A wheezy little pew-opener, afflicted with asthma—went about the building coughing like a grampus.

PEW-OPENER. Of church where Walter and Florence are married. *D. and S.* lvii.

A dusty old pew-opener, who only keeps herself, and finds that quite enough to do.

PEW-OPENER. The. *S.B.B., O.P.* vi.

PHANTOM. Image of Redlaw, Dead. *C.B., H.M.* i.

PHANTOM. Sister of, Late sister of Redlaw. *C.B., H.M.* i.

PHARISEE. Rev. Temple. *M.P., G.B.*

PHELPS. Dr., House of at Stratford, Connecticut. *M.P., R.S.D.*

PHELPS. Mr., Actor. *M.P., M.B.*

"**PHIB.**" Miss Squeers' handmaid. *N.N.*, xii.

The name "Phib" was used as a patronising abbreviation.

PHIBBS. Mr., Haberdasher. *R.P., T.D.A.* i.

PHIL. *B.H.* xxvi.

What with being scorched in an accident at a gasworks; and what with being blowed out of winder, case-filling at the firework business; I am ugly enough to be made a show on.

See Squod, Phil.

PHIL. Serving-man in Our School. *R.P., O.S.*

PHILADELPHIA. *A.N.* vii.; *M.P., I.W.M.*; *M.P., P.P.*; *M.P., S.B.*; *U.T.* xxiii.

PHILANTHROPISTS. Body of professing. *E.D.* vi.

PHILANTHROPISTS. Convened chief. *E.D.* vi.

Composite Committee of Central and District.

PHILANTHROPY. Haven of. *E.D.* vi.

PHILHARMONIC SOCIETY. *M.P., M.M.*

PHILLIPS. Mr. *M.P., E.T.*

PHILLIPS. Mr. Commissioner. *M.P., I.M.*

PHILLIPS. Mr. R., as Father Francis. *M.P., N.T.*

PHILLIPS. The Constable. *B.R.* lxi.

PHILOSEWERS. My friend. *M.P., P.M.B.*

PHOEBE. Lamps' daughter. *C.S., M.J.*, ii.

Lay on a couch that brought her face to a level with the window. The couch was white, and her simple dress or wrapper being light blue, like the band around her hair, she had an ethereal look, and a fanciful appearance of lying among clouds.

PHOEBE. Mother of, Deceased. *C.S., M.J.* iii.

Who died when she (Phoebe) was a year and two months old, was subject to very bad fits—she dropped the baby when "took."

PHOEBE. The biggest scholar of. *C.S., M.J.* iii.

The domestic of the cottage, had come to take active measures in it, attended by a pail that might have extinguished her, and a broom three times her height.

PHUNKY. Mr., junior, barrister for Pickwick. *P.P.*, xxxi.

Although an infant barrister, he was a full-grown man. He had a very nervous manner, and a painful hesitation in his speech; arising from the consciousness of being "kept down" by want of means, or interest, or connection, or impudence, as the case might be.

Note.—The "infant" barrister of little more than eight years standing—junior counsel with Sergeant Snubbin in Mr. Pickwick's case.

PHYSICIAN. The great. *L.D.* lxi.

PHYSICIAN. Famous. *L.D.* xxi.

In attendance on Mr. Merdle.

PHYSICIAN. Daughter of a. *C.S., S.L.* ii.

In an open carriage, with four gorgeously attired servitors—in massive gold ear-rings, and blue-feathered hat, shaded from the sun by two immense umbrellas of artificial roses.

PHYSICIAN'S GUESTS. At dinner party. *L.D.* lxi.

PHYSIOGNOMIST. The changer of countenances. *U.T.* xxv.

PIACENZA. *P.F.I., P.M.B.*

PIAZZA. *M.P., W.S.G.*

PIAZZA. Great, in Padua. *P.F.I., A.I.D.*

PIAZZA HOTEL. In Covent Garden. *D.C.* xxiii.; *U.T.* xiii.

PIAZZA. The, Parma. *P.F.I., P.M.B.*

PIAZZA. The, Rome. *P.F.I., R.*

PIAZZO OF THE GRAND DUKE. Florence. *P.F.I., R.D.*

PICCADILLY. *B.R.* lxvii. ; *C.S., S. L.* iii. ; *C. S., T. G. S.* i. ; *D. C.* xxviii. ; *M. P., A. P.* ; *M. P., N. J. B.* ; *M. P., T. D.* ; *M. P., T. T.* ; *N. N.* lxiv. ; *O. M. F.* x. ; *R. P., D. W. I. F.* ; *S. B. B.*, Scenes i.

PICHLYM. A chief of the Choctaw tribe of Indians. *A.N.* xii.

PICKFORD. *U.T.* xii.

PICKLE OF PORTICI. Mr., A tourist. *P.F.I., R.D.*

PICKLES. Mr., A fishmonger. *H.R.* ii.

PICKLESON. Rinaldo di Velasco. *C.S., D.M.*

PICKWICK. Samuel, General chairman and founder of the Pickwick Club, and central figure of the *Pickwick Papers.* *P.P.* i.

The eloquent Pickwick, with one hand gracefully concealed behind his coat-tails, and the other waving in the air, to assist his glowing declamation ; his elevated position revealing those tights and gaiters, which, had they clothed an ordinary man, might have passed without observation, but which, when Pickwick " clothed them "—if we may use the expression—inspired voluntary awe and respect.

Note.—The founder of the club from which the Papers take their rise. Originally a somewhat eccentric and almost unlovable character, he develops into a genial, jolly old gentleman. The gradual change was intentional, or at all events Dickens was aware of it. We are first introduced to the Chairman of the Pickwick Club, at a club meeting, but the fabric of the club as a vehicle for the episodes of the story is soon relinquished. The reason for this is soon explained in the preface to " Pickwick," but it is too lengthy for insertion here. When in London, Mr. Pickwick resided in Goswell Road, but except for the incident giving rise to the " Trial," neither the lodgings nor the landlady are essential. Most of the adventures take place in Kent, Bath, or in various parts of London. Reference may be made to the places the Pickwickians visited and the friends and enemies they met and made. The outline of the story, so far as it is a connected story and has an outline, is this : Mr. Pickwick, accompanied by Tupman, Snodgrass, and Winkle, sets out on his travels. Their first objective is Rochester, and the Three Towns. While attending a grand review at Chatham they meet Mr. Wardle and his family. (*See* Dingley Dell, and Muggleton). Later on they set out on an expedition to Eatanswill—*which see.* The breach of promise case between Mrs. Bardell and Mr. Pickwick is the most connected theme of the book, and is the medium for some of the best descriptions of law life and court practice of the time. The Bath expedition is of value, as it contains a small piece of corroborative evidence regarding the house in which Dickens spent the honeymoon of his marriage in 1836. The Manor House, at Chalk, is usually described as that in which the then young and little-known author spent his honeymoon and wrote some of the earlier chapters of Pickwick, but evidence, brought to light some years since, points to a small weather-boarded cottage not far distant fromthe Manor House, as the place. Stated succinctly, the evidence is as follows : Witnesses in the village of Chalk testified that no young married couple stayed at the Manor House in 1836, while such an event occurred at the cottage. The Manor House was then in the occupation of a French surgeon M. Lereaux, a gentleman of means who did not take lodgers, while Mrs Craddock, the landlady of the cottage did " do for them.!' The belief, the outcome of an ignorant mixing of the character with the author, still exists in the village, that Mr. Pickwick stayed at the unpretentious cottage. Mr. Pickwick refuses to pay costs and damages in the breach of promise case, and spends some time in the Fleet Prison. Dodson and Fogg, however, commit Mrs. Bardell to the same prison on her inability to pay her costs. This moves Mr. Pickwick to pay costs of both himself and Mrs. Bardell, and so effect the release of both. He resigns his membership of the Pickwick Club, which thereafter dissolves, and retires into private life at Dulwich.

PICKWICK. Samuel, And Fifth member of Master Humphrey's Club. *M.H.C.* iii.

An elderly gentleman—the sun shining on his bald head, his bland face, his bright spectacles, his fawn-coloured tights, and his black gaiters. He has a secret pride in his legs.

PICKWICK CLUB. The imaginary club of which Mr. Pickwick was Grand Chairman. *P.P.*

Note.—The club was the suggestion of Mr. Edward Chapman or of Mr. Seymour, and was introduced by Dickens with some reluctance. Its influence and importance become less as the narrative progresses.

PIDGER. Mr., Once a suitor of Lavinia Spenlow. *D.C.* xli.

Who played short whist and would have declared his passion, if he had not been cut short in his youth (at about sixty) by over-drinking his constitution, and overdoing an attempt to set it right again by swilling Bath water.

PIEDMONTESE. *M.P.*, *N.J.B.*

PIEDMONTESE OFFICERS. *P.F.I.*, *G.A.N.*

PIE-SHOP IN THE BOROUGH. Civil man in. *L.D.* lxx.

PIEMAN, A, Selling brandy-balls. *B.H.* xi.

PIEMEN. *S.B.B.*, Scenes i. Espiating on the excellence of their pastry.

PIER. Floating, at Greenwich. *O.M.F.*, liv.

PIERCE. Captain, Of the "Halsewell." *R.P.*, *T.L.V.*

PIERCE. Miss Mary, One of Captain Pierce's daughters. *R.P.*, *T.L.V.*

PIERCE. Two daughters of Captain. *R.P.*, *T.L.V.* On board the "Halsewell."

PIFF. Miss, Of Mugby Junction refreshment room staff. *C.S.*, *M.J.* v.

PIG AND TINDER-BOX. *Mud. Pap.* i.

PIG-FACED LADY. *N.N.* xlix.

PIGEON. Mr. John. *R.T.*, *T.D.P.*

PIGEON. Mr. Thomas, Tally-Ho Thompson. *R.T.*, *T.D.P.*

PIGGLEMU BUILDINGS. *R.P.*, *O.V.*

PILGRIMS. *P.F.I.*, *R.*

PILKINS. Mr., Family practitioner to the Dombeys. *D. and S.* i.

Who had regularly puffed the case for the last six weeks, among all his patients, friends, and acquaintances, as one to which he was in hourly expectations day and night of being summoned in conjunction with Doctor Parker Peps.

PIMIKIN AND THOMAS'S. "Out o' door." *P.P.* xx.

PIMLICO. *N.N.* xliv.

PINCH. Mr. Tom. *M.C.* ii.

An ungainly, awkward-looking man, extremely short-sighted, prematurely bald—dressed in a snuff-coloured suit of an uncouth make at the best, which, being shrunk with long wear, was twisted and tortured into all kinds of odd shapes; but notwithstanding his attire, his clumsy figure—and a ludicrous habit of thrusting his head forward—one would not have been disposed—to consider him a bad fellow by any means.

Note.—Tom Pinch was assistant and general factotum to Pecksniff. He was devoted to his master, whom he thought harshly judged by those who discovered his hypocrisy and his meanness of character. Later on, however, he himself sees Pecksniff in his true colours, and is discharged. He goes to London. Here he receives a mysterious appointment, through Mr. Fips, to arrange the library of an unknown benefactor. The "unknown" afterwards turns out to be old Martin Chuzzlewit.

PINCH. Ruth, Tom Pinch's sister. *M.C.* vi.

Was governess in a family, a lofty family; perhaps the wealthiest brass-and-copper founder's family known to mankind. . . . She had a good face; a very mild and prepossessing face; and a pretty little figure—slight and short, but remarkable for its neatness.

Note.—Ruth is governess in a brass-founder's family at Camberwell. While she is there Pecksniff and his daughters visit her, with a fitting show of condescension. This results in her dismissal, and she then keeps house for her brother Tom. Ultimately she marries John Westlock, a former pupil of Pecksniff.

PINDAR. Peter. *M.P., S.P.*

PINK. One of boat-crew training for racing. *S.B.B.*, Scenes x.

PIP. Mr., Threatrical Man. *M.C.* xxviii.

PIP. *See* Pirrip, Philip.

PIPCHIN. *M.P., N.Y.D.*

PIPCHIN. Mrs., Keeper of infantine boarding-house. *D. and S.* viii.

Who has for some time devoted all the energies of her mind, with the greatest success, to the study and treatment of infancy, and who has been extremely well connected. This celebrated Mrs. Pipchin was a marvellously ill-favoured, ill-conditioned old lady, of a stooping figure, with a mottled face, like bad marble, a hook nose, and a hard grey eye, that looked as if it might have been hammered at on an anvil without sustaining any injury.

PIPCHIN'S HUSBAND. Mrs. *D. and S.* viii.

Broke his heart—in pumping water out of the Peruvian mines.

PIPER. Alexander James, Son of Mrs. Piper. *B.H.* xi.

PIPER. Mr., Husband of Mrs. Piper. *B.H.* xi.

A cabinet maker.

PIPER. Mrs. Anastasia. *B.H.* xi.

PIPER. Professor. *M.C.* xxxiv.

PIPER. Young. *B.H.* xi.

PIPKIN. Mr. *Mud. Pap.* ii.

PIPKIN. Nathaniel. *P.P.* xvii.

Parish clerk of the little town at a considerable distance from London. A harmless, inoffensive, good-natured being, with a turned-up nose, and rather turned-in legs, a cast in his eye, and a halt in his gait, and he divided his time between the church and his school.

PIPS. Mr., Of Camberwell. *M.P., N.G.K.*

PIPSON. Miss, Pupil of Miss Griffin. *C.S., H.H.*

Having light curly hair and blue eyes.

PIRATES. Captain of the. *C.S., P. o. C.E.P.*

A Portuguese; a little man with very large ear-rings, under a very broad hat, and a great bright shawl twisted about his shoulders.

PIRATES. One of the. *C.S., P. o. C.E.P.*

One of the Convict Englishmen, with one eye, and patch across the nose.

PIRATES. The, Crowd of. *C.S., P. o. C.E.P.*

Malays, Dutch, Maltese, Greeks, Sambos, Negroes, and Convict Englishmen from the West India Islands, some Portuguese, and a few Spaniards.

PIRATE CHACE PARTY. The. *C.S., P. o. C.E.P.*

PIRRIP. Family name. *G.E.* i.

PIRRIP. Deceased father of Philip. *G.E.* i.

A square, stout, dark man, with curly black hair.

PIRRIP. Philip, an orphan. *G.E.* i.

Brought up "by hand" by his sister—apprenticed to his brother-in-law as blacksmith—then educated for "great expectations," which failed, and finally became first clerk and then partner in Clarriker and Co.

Note.—The principal character. He is introduced, as quite a little fellow, brought up "by hand"; an orphan living with his sister and her husband. His sister treats him unkindly, but as her husband suffers in the same way, Pip, as the boy was called, and he, become fast companions in spite of the difference between their ages. While still a child Pip meets an escaped convict in the marshes who compels him by threats to procure food and a file for him. Some time after he goes to Miss Havisham to play. He is then apprenticed to his brother-in-law. Following that he receives great assistance from an unknown benefactor through Jaggers. He receives a large allowance at once, with future "great expectations." After this good fortune he drifts away from his early friends. By the return of Magwitch he discovers that his unknown benefactor is not Miss Havisham, as he had thought, but the convict of his early childhood who has amassed wealth in New South

Wales. Pip conquers his disgust to a large extent. Magwitch is recaptured and sentenced to death. The sentence is not carried out as he dies in prison, but his wealth is forfeited to the Crown. Pip thus finds himself not only without money but heavily in debt. When he recovers from a severe illness, brought on by his devotion to Magwitch in prison, he sells everything for the benefit of his creditors, and, finding that Biddy has married Joe, accepts Herbert's offer of a clerkship in Clarriker and Co., and eventually becomes a partner in the firm. In the end he marries Estella.

PISA. *P.F.I., R.P.S.*

PITCAIRN'S ISLAND. *R.P., T.L.V.*

PITCHER. That young, A pupil of Squeers. *N.N.* vii.

PITCHLYNN. *A.N.* xii.

PITT. Miss Jane. *R.P., T.S.S*

PITT. William. *M.F.,F.O.E.G.* *See also* Mistapit.

PITTSBURG. *A.N.* vii.

PLACE. *C.S., S.L.* ii.

PLAINS. The. *U.T.* xx.

PLAINS OF ABRAHAM. Near Montreal. *A.N.* xv.

PLANTER'S HOUSE. A large hotel is S . Louis. *A.N.* xii.

PLASHWATER MILL WEIR LOCK. *O.M.F.* xli.

PLEADER. A special, from the Temple. *P.P.* xlvii.

PLORNISH. Mrs. Sally, Wife of Plornish. *L.D.* xii.

A young woman made somewhat slatternly in herself and her belongings by poverty, and so dragged at by poverty and the children together, that their united forces had already dragged her face into wrinkles.

PLORNISH. Thomas, Only a plasterer. *L.D.* ix.

A smooth-cheeked, fresh-coloured sandy-whiskered man of thirty. Long in the legs, yielding at the knees, foolish in the face, flannel-jacketed, lime-whitened.

Note.—A small plasterer making ends meet with difficulty. He lives in Bleeding Heart Yard, and is a tenant of Mr. Casby. They are befriended by Arthur Clennam, and when he is in a debtor's prison Mr. and Mrs. Plornish visit him.

PLORNISH'S HABITATION. In Bleeding Heart Yard. *L.D.* xii.

The last house in Bleeding Heart Yard—was a large house, let off to various tenants; but Plornish ingeniously hinted that he lived in the parlour, by means of a painted hand under his name, the forefinger of which—referred all inquirers to that apartment.

"PLOW AN' HARRER." *O.C.S.* xv.

"There's travellers' lodging, I know, at the Plow an' Harrer."

PLUCK. Mr., Guest of Ralph Nickleby. *N.N.*, xix.

A gentleman with a flushed face, and a flash air.

PLUMMER. Blind daughter of Caleb. *C.B., C.o.H.* ii.

PLUMMER. Caleb, A toymaker. *C.B., C.o.H.* i.

A little, meagre, thoughtful, dingy-faced man, who seemed to have made himself a great-coat from the sackcloth covering of some old box—upon the back of that garment, the inscription G. and T. in large capital letters. Also the word *Glass* in bold characters.

PLUMMER. Dear boy of Caleb. *C.B., C.o.H.* i.

PLUMMER. Mrs. Edward, Née May Fielding. *C.B. ,C.o.H.* iii.

PLUNDER. Name of a bird. *B.H.* xiv.

PLUNDERER. New York. *M.C.* xvi.

PLYMOUTH. *B.H.* xxxvi., *D.C.* xii.

PLYMOUTH HARBOUR. *B.H.* xiii.

PLYMOUTH SOUND. *M.P., N.E.*

PO. The. *P.F.I., T.B.F.*; *R.P.D.W.T.T.*

POBBS. Miss. *M.P.. T.T.*

POCKET. Fanny, Daughter of Mr. Matthew Pocket. *G.E.* xxiii.

POCKET. Joe, Son of Mr. Matthew Pocket. *G.E.* xxiii.

POCKET. Master Alick, Son of Matthew Pocket. *G.E.* xxii.

POCKET. Miss Jane, Daughter of Matthew Pocket. *G.E.* xxii.

POCKET. Mr. Herbert, "A prospective Insurer of Ships." *G.E.* xi.

A pale young gentleman with red eyelids and light hair—in a grey suit—with his elbows, knees, wrists and heels considerably in advance of the rest of him as to development.

Note.—Son of Matthew Pocket. First introduced as a pale young gentleman at Miss Havisham's who fights Pip. When Pip comes to London he lodges in Barnard's Inn with Herbert and they become very close friends. They both spend more than they should. Pip secures a partnership in Clarriker and Co., for Herbert, unknown to him. Herbert marries Clara Barley. They go abroad for the business.

POCKET. Mr. Matthew, Miss Havisham's cousin *G.E.* xviii.

A very young-looking man, in spite of his perplexities, and his very grey hair.

Note.—One of Miss Havisham's relatives—not of the self-seeking kind, and father of Herbert. Pip read with him for a time. Through Pip, Miss Havisham leaves him a cool four thousand.

POCKET. Mrs. Matthew. *G.E.* xxii.

Highly ornamental, but perfectly helpless and useless. . . . Only daughter of a certain quite accidentally deceased knight.

POCKET. Sarah. *G.E.* xi.

A little, dry, brown, corrugated old woman, with a small face that might have been made out of walnut-shells, and a large mouth like a cat's. without the whiskers.

Note.—One of Miss Havisham's fawning relatives. Left with " twenty-five pounds per annum fur to buy pills."

POCKET-BREACHES. Borough of. *O.M.F.* xx.

POCKET-BREACHES. Branch Station. *O.M.F.* xx.

POCKET-BREACHES. Market. *O.M.F.* xx.

Some onions and bootlaces under it [the town hall] which the legal gentleman says are a market.

POCKET-BREACHES. Town Hall of. *O.M.F.* xx.

A feeble little town hall on crutches.

PODDLES. The girl " minder." *O.M.F.* xvi.

PODDER. Mr., A most renowned member of the All-Muggletonians. *P.P.* vii.

PODGERS. John, A widower. *M.H.C.* iii.

Broad, sturdy, Dutch-built, short, and a very hard eater—a hard sleeper likewise. The people of Windsor—held that John Podgers was a man of strong sound sense—not what is called smart—but still a man of solid parts.

PODGERS. Mr. *L.T.* i.

POD'S END. *H.T., S.* v.

PODSNAP. Mr., In the marine insurance way. *O.M.F.* ii.

Two little light-coloured, wiry wings, one on either side of his else bald head, looking as like his hair-brushes as his hair, dissolving view of red beads on his forehead, large allowance of crumpled shirt-collar up behind.

Note.—The hook on which much of the book is hung, but of very little importance as an integral part of the story. He is last seen giving a dinner at which Eugene's marriage is discussed and condemned by the " voice " of society as represented by all present save Lightwood and Twemlow.

PODSNAP. Mrs. *O.M.F.* ii.

Fine woman—quantity of bone, neck and nostrils like a rocking-horse, hard-feature, majestic head-dress in which Podsnap has hung golden offerings.

PODSNAP. Miss Georgiana. *O.M.F.* xi.

An undersized damsel, with high shoulders, low spirits, chilled elbows, and a rasped surface of nose.

Note.—Popsnap's daughter. She was taken in hand by the Lammles. And was at one time in danger from their machinations.

POFFIN. *O.M.F.* xxv.

POGRAM. Elijah, Member of Congress. *M.C.* xxxiv.

He had straight black hair, parted up the middle of his head, and hanging down upon his coat ; a little fringe of hair upon his chin.

Note.—A member of Congress met with on Martin's travels in America.

POISSY. *R.P., M.O.F.F.*

POLCEVERA. The river. *P.F.I., G.A.N.*

POLICE. Assistant Commissioner of. *R.P., D.W.I.F.*

POLICE. Thames. *R.P., D.W.I.F.*

POLICE. The, An excellent force. *U.T.* xxxvi.

POLICE. The detective. *R.P., T.D.P.*

POLICE. The new. *S.B.B.*, Char. i.

POLICE COMMISSIONER. *M.P., S.F.A.*

POLICE FORCE. The Liverpool. *U.T.* v.

POLICE-OFFICE. *N.N.* lx.

POLICE-OFFICE. *S.B.B.*, Scenes xvii.

POLICE-OFFICERS. *O.T.* vi.

POLICE-OFFICERS. *S.B.*, Scenes xvii.

POLICE-OFFICERS. Two. *B.H.* lvii.

POLICE STATION. *O.M.F.* lxiii.

POLICE STATION. *U.T.* xxxvi.

POLICEMAN. *B.H.* xi.

With his shining hat, stiff stock, inflexible great-coat, stout belt and bracelet, and all things fitting, pursues his lounging way with a heavy tread, beating the palms of his white gloves one against the other.

POLICEMAN. *M.P., P.L.U.*

POLICEMAN. An accoucheur. *G.E.* iv.

POLICEMAN. Occasional. *S.B.B.*, Scenes i.

Listlessly gazing on the deserted prospect before him.

POLICEMEN. In attendance — in London Tavern. *N.N.* ii.

POLICEMEN. Two, on duty in the Good Hippotamus' den. *M.P., G.H.*

POLICINELLI. *P.F.I.; R.D.*

POLL. *D. and S.* xxviii.

POLL. A suicide. *U.T.* iii.

POLLY. Daughter of old sweetheart of Mr. Jackson (Barbox Brothers). *C.S., M.J.* iv.

POLLY. Schoolmaster's daughter. *C.S., M.L.Lo.* ii.

POLLY. Waitress at "Slap Bang." *B.H.* xx.

A bouncing young female of forty.

POLREATH. David, Old resident of Laureau. *C.S., M.f.T.S.* ii.

POLYGON. The. *B.H.* xliii.

POLYGON. The. *P.P.* liii.

POLYPHEMUS. The Private West India trader. *D. and S.* iv.

POLYTECHNIC INSTITUTION. In Regent Street. *M.P., A.P.*; *M.P., R.S.D.*

POMPEII. *P.F.I., R.D.*; *U.T.* xxviii.

POMPEY. A negro fellow—slave. *A.N.* xvii.

PONT ESPRIT. *L.D.* xi.

POODLE. *B.H.* xii.

POOL. Lower. Below Bridge. *G.E.* xlvi.

POOL. The. *S.B.B.*, Tales vii.

POONEY. Mr., C. D. S. *M.P., W.R.*

POOR-HOUSE. The, The House. *O.M.F.* xvi.

POOR-LAW COMMISSIONERS. *M.P., P.T.*

POOR-LAW INSPECTOR. *M.P., P.T.*

POPE. Alexander. *M.C.* xxxvii.

POPE. Alick = Man of Ross. *M.P., I.W.M.*

POPE. The. *P.F.I.R.*

POPE OF ROME. In 1850. *M.P., L.W.O.Y.*

POPES. The Palace of the. *P.F.I., L.R.G.A.*

POPLAR. *M.P., C.J.*; *M.P., I.S.H.W.*

POPLAR. At house in. *C.S., W.O.G.M.*

Taken care of and kept shipshape by an old lady, who was my mother's maid before I was born.

POPLAR WALK. Stamford Hill. *S.B.B.*, Tales ii.

POPLARS. The, The Haunted House. *C.S., H.H.*

A solitary house, standing in a sadly neglected garden—a house of about the time of George the Second—as stiff, as cold, as formal, and in as bad taste as could possibly be desired—was much too closely and heavily shadowed by trees—there were six tall poplars before the front windows.

POPOLO. Piazza del. *P.F.I., R.*

PORDAGE. Mr., Clerk and supercargo. *C.S., P.o.C.E.P.*

PORDAGE. Mr., Commissioner of Silver-Store Island. *C.S., P.o.C.E.P.*

A stiff-jointed, high-nosed old gentleman, without an ounce of fat on him, of a very angry temper and a very sallow complexion.

PORDAGE. Mrs., Wife of Commissioner Pordage. *C.S.,P.o.C.E.P.*

Making allowance for difference of sex, was much the same.

PORK PIE. A spirit. *M.P., W.R.*

PORKENHAM. Miss, Bosom friend of the Nupkins. *P.P.* xxv.

PORKENHAM. Mrs., Bosom friend of the Nupkins. *P.P.* xxv.

PORKENHAM. Old, Husband of Mrs. Porkenham. *P.P.* xxv.

Opposition magisterial party.

PORKIN AND SNOB. *P.P.* xl.

PORT. A spirit. *M.P., W.R.*

PORT. The, In French watering-place. *R.P., O.F.W.*

PORT HOPE. *A.N.* xv.

PORT LEOPOLD HARBOUR. *M.P., E.T.*

PORT MIDDLEBAY HARBOUR. *D.C.* xxxiv.

PORT NICHOLSON. Cook's Straits. *M.P., E.T.*

PORT ROYAL. *C.S., P.o.C.E.P.*

PORTA CAPUANA. Church by the. *P.F.I., R.D.*

PORTE ST. MARTIN. Paris. *M.P., W.*

PORTER. *S.B.B.,* Scenes iii.

PORTER. *D. and S.* lv.

At the iron gate which shut the courtyard from the street.

PORTER. At Mansion House. *B.R.* lxi.

PORTER. At Mugby Junction. *C.S., M.J.* i.

PORTER. Carrying Nicholas' luggage to coach to Yorkshire. *N.N.* v.

Had evidently been spending the night in a stable, and taking his breakfast at a pump.

PORTER. Head. *C.S., M.J.* iii.

PORTER. Kentucky giant. *A.N.* xii.

Seven feet eight inches in his stockings.

PORTER. Miss Emma, Daughter of Mrs. Porter. *S.B.B.,* Tales ix.

PORTER, Mrs. Joseph, A gossip. *S.B.B.,* Tales ix.

The good folks of Clapham and its vicinity stood very much in awe of scandal and sarcasm, and thus Mrs. Porter was courted and flattered and caressed.

PORTER. The under, Of the Anglo-Bengalee Disinterested Loan and Life Assurance Company. *M.C.* xxvii.

PORTER FELLOW. *L.D.* x.

PORTERS. At Gray's Inn Square. *P.P.* liii.

PORTERS. Foolish Mr. *E.D.* iii.

A certain finished gentleman.

PORTERS AND WAREHOUSEMEN. *N.N.* xxxvii.

Of Cheeryble Brothers.

PORTERS. Warehouse. *R.P., T.D.P.*

PORTLAND. A suburb of Louisville. *A.N.* xii.

PORTLAND PLACE. *D. and S.* iii.; *M.P., P.F.*; *O.M.F.* xlix.

PORTLAND STREET. *M.P., W.R.*; *S.B.B* Tales vii.

PORTMAN SQUARE. *M.P., C.*; *O.M.F.* xi.

PORTSMOUTH. *N.N.* xxii; *U.T.* v.

PORTSMOUTH YARD. *C.S., P.o.C.E.P.*; *M.P., N.G.R.*.

PORTUGAL. *P.F.I., G.A.N.*

PORTUGAL STREET. *P.P.* xliii.

PORTUGUESE CAPTAIN. *C.S., P.o.C.E.P.* i.

POSILIPO. Grotto of. *P.F.I., R.D.*

POSTBOY. *P.P.* l.

POSTBOY. (Of the Village) The. *B.R.* lxi.

A soft-hearted, good-for-nothing vagabond kind of a fellow.

POSTBOY. The. *B.H.* vi.

POSTBOYS. *P.P.* xiii.

POSTBOYS. At the "Great White Horse." *P.P.* xxiv.

POST-CHAISE. Owner of and tenant. *U.T.* xxii.

A little spare man who sat breaking stones by the roadside.

POST-OFFICE. *M.P.*, *M.E.R.*

POST-OFFICE. Bury. *P.P.* xviii.

POST-OFFICE. Leith Walk, waste ground. *P.P.* xlix.

An enclosure belonging to some wheelwright, who contracted with the Post-Office for the purchase of old, worn-out mailcoaches. My uncle was a very enthusiastic, emphatic sort of person—finding he could not find a good peep between the palings—he got over them, and sitting himself down—began to contemplate the mail-coaches.

POST-OFFICE. The. *M.H.C.* i.

POST-OFFICE. The. *N.N.* xxxix.

POST-OFFICE. The General. *E.D.* xxiii.

POST-OFFICE. Washington. *A.N.* viii.

POSTE. Malle. *P.F.I.*, *G.T.F.*

POSTE-RESTANTE. *L.D.* ii.

POSTERITY. *M.P.*, *P.A.P.*

POSTHOUSE. *P.F.I.*, *G.T.F.*

POSTILION. *B.H.* vi.

POSTILIONS. *P.F.I.*, *G.T.F.*

POSTMAN. *P.P.* liii.

POSTMAN. *U.T.* ii.

POSTMASTER GENERAL. *M.P.*, *M.E.R.*

POTATOES. Mealy, Another boy at Murdstone and Grinby's. *D.C.* xi.

Complexion pale or mealy.

POTATOES. Mealy's father. *D.C.* xi.

A waterman who had the additional distinction of being a fireman, and was engaged at one of the large theatres.

POTATOES. Mealy's sister. *D.C.* xi.

Who did Imps in the pantomimes.

POT-BOY. *S.B.B.*, Scenes v.

POTBOY. *B.H.* xi.

POTBOY. Of, The Six Jolly Fellowship Porters. *O.M.F.* vi.

White-aproned—with his shirt-sleeves arranged in a tight roll on each bare shoulder.

POTKINS. William—Waiter of the "Blue Boar." *G.E.* lviii.

POTOMAC. Creek. *A.N.* ix.

POTOMAC RIVER. *A.N.* viii.

POTT. Misses, Daughters of Mrs. Pott. *P.P.* xv.

Here are my little girls said Minerva, pointing towards a couple of full-grown young ladies, of whom one might be about twenty, and the other a year or two older, dressed in very juvenile costumes.

POTT. Mr., Editor of *Eatanswill Gazette*. *P.P.* xiii.

A tall, thin man with a sandy-coloured head inclined to baldness, and a face in which solemn importance was blended with a look of unfathomable profundity.

Note.—Editor of the *Eatanswill Gazette*. Bitter enemy of Mr. Slurk, editor of the *Eatanswill Independent*. They meet accidentally at the "Saracen's Head," Towester, and "have it out," but being prevented by Sam Weller, they continue the combat in their respective papers.

POTT. Mrs., Wife of editor of *Eatanswill Gazette*. *P.P.* xiii.

"The feminine Pott," wearied with politics and quarrels with *The Independent*.

POTTER. Colonel Robert. *A.N.* xvii.

POTTER. Thomas, A Clerk in the City. *S.B.B.*, Char. xi.

There was a spice of romance in Mr. Smither's disposition—which stood out in fine relief against the off-hand, dashing, amateur-pick-pocket-sort-of-manner of Mr. Potter.

POTTERIES. The. *U.T.* x.

POTTERSON. Job, Ship's steward. *O.M.F.* iii.

Note.—Brother of Miss Abbey Potterson. Having been steward of the ship on which John Harmon returned from Africa, he is able to identify him in John Rokesmith. It is to be inferred that Job takes over the "Six Jolly Fellowship Porters" in the future.

POTTERSON. Miss Abbey, Sole Proprietor and Manager of the "Six Jolly Fellowship Porters." *O.M.F.* vi.

A tall, upright, well-favoured woman, though severe of countenance—more the air of a schoolmistress than mistress of the "Six Jolly Fellowship Porters."

Note.—The landlady of the "Six Jolly Fellowship Porters." She befriends Lizzie Hexam in her trouble when her father is accused of the murder of John Harmon. She enters casually into the book when John Rokesmith is identified at the "Porters."

POTTINGTON. *M.P., B.A.*

POUCH'S. Jo, Widow. *B.H.* xxvii.

POULTRY. The. *B.R.* lxvii.

POUNCERBY. Squire. *U.T.* xi.

"**POWDER.**" Mr. Merdles' footman. *L.D.* xxi.

POWLERS. Relations of Mrs. Sparsit. *H.T., S.* vii.

The Powlers were an ancient stock who could trace themselves so exceedingly far back that it was not surprising if they sometimes lost themselves.

PRACTITIONER. Young medical. *S.B..B,* Tales vi.

Recently established in business . . . began to wonder when his first patient would appear.

PRAIRIE. La. *A.N.* xv.

PRAISER. A, A poet. *R.P., T.N.S.* Singing the praises of his chief.

PRANTA DEL MONTE. *P.F.I., R.*

PRATCHETT. Mr., Husband of Mrs. Pratchett in Australia. *C.S., S.L.* i.

PRATCHETT. Mrs., Head chambermaid. *C.S., S.L.* i.

PRATT. Messrs., In Bond Street. *M.P., I.M.*

PRATT. Parley P., A Mormon. *U.T.* xx.

PRATT'S SHOP. For sale of armour. *R.P., G.o.A.*

PRAYMIAH = The Talkative Barber. The Prime Minister. *M.P., T.O.H.*

PRECEDENT. Name of a bird. *B.H.* xiv.

PRECINCTS. The. *E.D.* xiv. Never particularly well-lighted.

PRE-GALILEO BROTHERHOOD. *M.P., O.L.N.O.*

PRE-GOWER AND PRE-CHAUCER BROTHERHOOD. *M.P., O.L.N.O.*

PRE - HENRY - THE - SEVENTH BROTHERHOOD. *M.P., O.L.N.O.*

PRE-NEWTONIAN BROTHERHOOD. *M.P.. O.L.N.O.*

PRE-PERSPECTIVE BROTHERHOOD. *M.P., O.L.N.O.*

PRE-RAPHAEL BROTHERHOOD. *M.P., O.L.N.O.*

PREMIER. *M.P., I.*

'PRENTICE KNIGHTS. Secret Society of *B.R.* viii.

PREROGATIVE OFFICE. In Doctors' Commons. *S.B.B.,* Scenes viii.

A long, busy-looking place, partitioned off, on either side, into a variety of little boxes, in which a few clerks were engaged in copying or examining deeds.

PRESBYTERIAN BROTHER. *M.P., S.B.*

PRESCOTT. Mr. *M.P., I.C.*; *M.P., L.A.V.* ii.

PRESIDENT. *M.P., Y.M.C.*

PRESIDENT. *T.T.C.* bk. iii. ch. vi.

PRESS-ROOM. In Newgate Prison. *S.B.B.,* Scenes xxv.

Immediately on your right as you enter is a building containing the press-room, day-room and cells. It (the press-room) is a long, sombre room, with two windows sunk into the stone wall, and here the wretched men are pinioned on the morning of their execution, before being removed towards the scaffold.

PRESTON. *G.S.E.* iii.; *M.P., O.S.*

PRESTON COTTON LORDS. *M.P., O.S.*

PRESTON MASTERS. *M.P., O.S.*

PRESTON OPERATIVES. *M.P., O.S.*

PREVENTIVE STATION. Naval officer of the. *R.P., O.E.W.*

With that bright mixture of blue coat, buff waistcoat, black neckerchief, and gold epaulette.

PRICE. Under arrest. *P.P.* xl.

A coarse, vulgar young man of about thirty, with a sallow face and a harsh voice.

PRICE. 'Tilda, Friend of Miss Fanny Squeers. *N.N.* ix.

A miller's daughter of only eighteen, who had contracted herself to the son of a small corn-factor, residing in the nearest market town. She was pretty, and a coquette, too, in her small way.

Note.—A miller's pretty daughter. She marries John Browdie. She is a friend of Fanny Squeers, who is exceedingly jealous of her good fortune in securing a husband. Miss Price takes a great delight in furthering the " suit " of Nicholas with Miss Squeers, which exists only in Miss Squeers' imagination. 'Tilda, however, proves a good friend to Nicholas, together with her husband; and they befriend the boys of Squeers's school after the last and only " break up " of Dotheboys' Hall.

PRIEST. *L.D.* lv.

He was an ugly priest by torchlight; of a lowering aspect, with an overhanging brow.

PRIEST. A. *B.R.* lxi.

A mild old man—whose chapel was destroyed.

PRIESTS. *M.P., D.V.*

PRIESTS. *P.F.I., T.R.P.*

PRIG. Mrs., Betsey, Nurse from Batholomew's. *M.C.* xxv.

" The best of creeturs, but she is otherwise engaged at night " . . . of the Gamp guild, but not so fat; and her voice was deeper, and more like a man's—she had also a beard.

Note.—Betsey Prig was a companion character to Mrs. Gamp, and in, fact, they " nurse together, turn and turn about." Her character is of secondary importance, and for that reason is not so detailed. She is last seen making a violent exit from Mrs. Gamp's room after a quarrel over poor old Chuffey.

PRIME MINISTER. *M.H.C.* i.; *M.P., G.B., M.P., W.*

PRIMROSE HILL TUNNEL. *M.P., O.S.*

PRINCE. English. *M.P., L.W.O.Y.*

PRINCE. The. *M.P., F.O.E.G.*

PRINCE CONSORT. *M.P., T.B.*

PRINCE OF WALES. *M.P., N.E.*; *M.P., T.B.*

PRINCE REGENT. The. *M.P., C.P.*; *N.N.* xxxvii.

PRINCESS. Of Little Dorrit's tale to Maggy. *L.D.* xxiv.

PRINCESS'S ARMS. In Princess's Place. *D. and S.* vii.

Much resorted to by splendid footmen. A sedan chair was kept inside the railing before the Princess's Arms, but it had never come out within the memory of man—and on fine mornings the top of every rail was decorated with a pewter-pot.

PRINCESS'S CHAPEL. In Princess's Place. *D. and S.* vii.

With a tinkling bell, where sometimes as many as five-and-twenty people attended service on a Sunday.

PRINCESS'S PLACE. *D. and S.* vii.

It was not exactly a court, and it was not exactly a yard, but it was the Dullest of No-Thoroughfares, rendered anxious and haggard by distant double knocks. The name of this retirement, where grass grew between the chinks in the stone pavement, was Princess's Place.

PRINGLE. Mr., The butcher. *M.P. S.P.*

PRISCILLA. Mrs. Jellyby's maidservant. *B.H.* iv.

A young woman, with a swelled face bound up in a flannel bandage, blowing the fire of the drawing-room. The young woman waited (at dinner) and dropped everything on the table wherever it happened to go, and never moved it again till she put it on the stairs.

PRISON. *B.H.* liii.
A large prison, with many courts and passages so like one another, and so uniformly paved. . . . In an arched room, by himself, like a cellar upstairs: with walls so glaringly white, that they made the massive iron window bars and iron-bound door even more profoundly black than they were, we found the trooper.

PRISON PHILANTHROPIST. *M.P., M.P.*

PRISONER. *M.P., S.*

PRISONER. A debtor friend of doctor in Marshalsea. *L.D.* vi.
Was in the positive degree of hoarseness, puffiness, red-facedness, all fours, tobacco, dirt, and brandy.

PRISONER. A doomed wretch, in Newgate. Two sons of, (Rioters). *B.R.* lxiv.
Heard, or fancied they heard, their father's voice—one mounted on the shoulders of the other, tried to clamber up the face of the high wall At last they cleft their way among the mob about the door—and were seen in—yes, the fire, striving to prize it down with crow-bars.

PRISONER. A sallow, In Court of Chancery. *B.H.* i.
Has come up, in custody, for the half-dozenth time, to make a personal application "to purge himself of his contempt" (a solitary surviving executor who has fallen into a state of conglomeration about accounts of which it is not pretended he had ever any knowledge).

PRISONER. Condemned to death. *S.B.B.*, Scenes xxiv.
How restlessly he has been engaged —in forming all sorts of fantastic figures with the herbs which are strewed upon the ledge (in the dock) before him.

PRISONER. In the Fleet. *P.P.* xli.
Another man, evidently very drunk, who had probably been tumbled into bed by his companions, was sitting up between the sheets, warbling as much as he could recollect of a comic song, with the most intensely sentimental feeling and expression.

PRISONER. The Italian Giovanni Carlavero. *U.T.* xxviii.

PRISONERS. About to enter prison van. *S.B.B.*, Char. xii.
Boys of ten, as hardened in vice as men of fifty—a houseless vagrant going joyfully to prison as a place of food and shelter, handcuffed to a man whose prospects were ruined, character lost, and family rendered destitute by his first offence.

PRISONERS. About to enter prison van. *S.B.B.*, Char. xii.
A couple of girls, of whom the elder could not be more than sixteen, and the younger of whom had certainly not attained her fourteenth year.

PRISONERS. At Newgate in the Press-room. *S.B.B.*, Scenes xxv.
Three men—the fate of one of these prisoners was uncertain—the other two had nothing to expect from the mercy of the Crown. "The first man had been a soldier of the Foot Guards."

PRISONERS. Certain English. *C.S., P.o.C.E.P.*

PRISONERS. In new jail at Clerkenwell. *B.R.*, lxvi.

PRISONERS. The gentlemen, in Marshalsea. *L.D.* vi.

PRISONS. *C.B., C.C., S.*I.

PRISONS. Mamertine. *P.F.I., R.*

PRITCHARD. Mr., As the second husband. *M.P., N.T.*

PRIVATE HOUSE. A, in Princess's Place. *D. and S.* vii.
Tenanted by a retired butler, who had married a housekeeper—at this other private house, apartments were let furnished.

PRIVY COUNCIL. *B.R.* lxvii.; *M.P., C.P.*; *M.P., R.H.F.*

PRIVY SEAL. Clerk of the Lord Keeper of the. *R.P., P.M.T.P.*

PRIVY SEAL. Lord Keeper of. *R.P., P.M.T.P.*

PRIVY SEAL OFFICE. *R.P., P.M.T.P.*

PROCESSION. Funeral to Protestant Cemetery near Italian City. *U.T.* xxvi.

I. Mr. Kindheart, much abashed, on an immense grey horse.

II. A bright yellow coach and pair, driven by a coachman in bright red velvet knee-breeches and waistcoat. Both coach-doors kept open by the coffin, which was on its side within, and sticking out at each.

III. The mourner for whom the coach was intended, walking in the dust.

IV. Concealed behind a roadside well, the unintelligible upholsterer (who had made the arrangements) admiring.

PROCTER. Miss Adelaide Anne. *M.P., A.A.P.*

PROCTER. Mrs. *M.P., A.A.P.*

PROCTER'S. Miss, Sister. *M.P., A.A.P.*

PROCTOR. A. *C.S., S.P.T.* i.

PROCTORS. The, In Doctors' Commons. *S.B.B.*, Scenes viii.

Very self-important-looking personages, in stiff neckcloths, and black gowns with white fur collars.

PRODGIT. Mrs., A Maternity Nurse, *R.P., B.M.S.*

She wore a black bonnet of large dimensions, and was copious in figure.

PROPRIETOR. Irish. *M.P., C.P.*

PROPRIETOR. Of hairdresser's establishment. *N.N.* lii.

Wore very glossy hair, with a narrow walk straight down the middle, and a profusion of flat, circular curls on both sides.

PROPRIETOR. Proprietor of gambling booth *N.N.*l.

A tall, fat, long-bodied man, buttoned up to the throat in a light green coat, which made his body look still longer than it was. He wore, besides, drab breeches, and gaiters, a white neckerchief, and a broad-brimmed white hat.

PROPRIETORS OF DONKEYS. Deputy. *S.B.B.*, Tales iv. Donkey boys.

PROSECUTOR. *M.P., W.M.*

PROSEE. Mr., eminent counsel. *P.P.* xlvii.

PROSPECT PLACE. Poplar. *M.P., I.S.H.W.*

PROSS. Miss, Miss Manette's nurse and attendant. *T.T.C.* iv.

A wild-looking woman, all of a red colour . . . dressed in some extraordinary tight-fitting fashion. . . . "I really think this must be a man!" was Mr. Lorry's breathless reflection.

Note.—Miss Lucie Manette's maid and sister of Barsad. She accompanies Lucie to Paris, and when her mistress and her husband escape she covers their retreat. While doing this she is assailed by Madame Defarge, who endeavours to force her way into the room where she believes the fugitives are hidden. Madame Defarge draws a pistol, but as she fires it, Miss Pross strikes her arm and the charge kills "The Tigress." Miss Pross locks the room, throws the key into the river, and succeeds in making good her escape, but she is rendered stone deaf.

PROSS. Solomon. The degraded brother of Miss Pross.

There never was, nor will be, but one man worthy of Ladybird, said Miss Pross, "and that was my brother Solomon, if he hadn't made a mistake in life."

Note.—Pross was the real name of John Barsad. Brother of Miss Pross whom he defrauds of her money. When he enters the story he is a spy and the principal witness against Darnay. He is seen again a spy in Paris, and then as a turnkey in the Conciergerie, where he is utilized in Darnay's escape. It is understood that he eventually suffers death from the guillotine.

PROTESTANT ASSOCIATION. The Great—of England. *B.R.* xxxviii.

PROUT. Mr. *M.P., E.T.*

PROVIS. *See* Magwitch, Abel.

PROWLER. Mr. *M.P., B.A.*

PRUFFLE. Scientific gentleman's servant. *P.P.* xxxix.

PRUSSIA. *M.P., C.P.*

PRUSSIA. King of. *M.P., L.A.V.* ii.

PUBLEEK. Or the many-headed. *M.P., T.O.H.*; *M.P., T.O.P.*
The Public.

PUBLIC COMPANIES. *D. and S.* xxv.

PUBLIC HOUSE. Just opposite the Insolvent Court. *P.P.* xliii.

PUBLIC HOUSE. *D.C.* xi.

PUBLIC HOUSE. A low dingy.
In Seven Dials. *S.B.B.*, Scenes v.

PUBLIC HOUSE. An old, quiet, decent. *S.B.B.*, Char. v.
A modest public house of the old school, with a little old bar—a snug little room with a cheerful fire, protected by a large screen.

PUBLIC HOUSE. Little Roadside. *P.P.* v.
A litttle roadside public-house, with two elm-trees, a horse-trough and a sign-post in front.
Note.—The Sir John Falstaff, which was probably intended, stands opposite Gad's Hill Place.

PUBLIC HOUSE. Obscure, Proprietor of. *M.C.* xiii.
In a fur cap, who was taking down the shutters.

PUBLIC HOUSE. Small. *O.T.* xlviii.

PUBLICAN. The. *M.H.C.* i.

PUBLICCASH. The Dowager Marchioness of. *S.B.B.*, Tales i.

PUBSEY AND CO. *See* Fledgeby, Young.

PUDDING SHOP. Close to St. Martin's Church. *D.C.* xi.

PUDDING SHOP. Good, In Strand. *D.C.* xi.

PUFFER. Princess, The opium dealer. *E.D.* xxiii.
As ugly and withered as one of the fantastic carvings on the upper brackets of the stall seats.

PUFFY. *B.H.* xii.

PUGIN. Mr. *M.P., O.L.N.O.*

PUGSTYLES. Mr., Heading a deputation to Mr. Gregsbury, M.P.
A plump old gentleman. *N.N.* xvi.

PUMBLECHOOK. Premises of Mr. *G.E.* viii.
In the High Street of the market town, . . . were of a peppercorny and farinaceous character, as the premises of a corn-chandler and seedsman should be.

PUMBLECHOOK. Uncle, Joe Gargery's Uncle, a well-to-do, corn-chandler. *G.E.* iv.
A large, hard-breathing, middle-aged, slow man, with a mouth like a fish, dull staring eyes, and sandy hair standing upright as if he had just been all but choked and had that moment come to.
Note.—Joe Gargery's uncle. A corn-chandler and seedsman "Up-town." He takes Pip to Miss Havisham and "takes him into custody" with a sort of proprietary right. When Pip comes into his money and expectations Uncle Pumblechook abases himself. Orlick and others break into the shop, rob the till, give Pumblechook "a dozen," and stuff his mouth with "hardy annuals." When Pip returns, Pumblechook is as obnoxious in another way. His humility becomes patronising pity for Pip's reduced circumstances—circumstances brought on through Providence by Pip's ingratitude to him.

PUMKINSKULL. Prof. *Mud. Pap.* ii.

PUMP. Titbull's in Titbull's Almshouses. *U.T.* xxvii.
Which stands with its back to the thoroughfare just inside the gate (of court of Titbull's Almshouses), and has a conceited air of reviewing Titbull's pensioners.

PUMP. [Trough]. *P.C.* lii.

PUMP-ROOM. The. *D. and S.* xxi.

PUMP-ROOM. The Great—Bath. *P.P.* xxxv.

PUMPION. Alexander. *M.P., W.R.*

PUMPION. Widow. *M.P., W.R.*

PUNCH. *M.P., O.S.*

PUNCH. *M.P., R.G.*

PUNCH'S OPERA. Proprietor of. *M.P., G.H.*

PUPFORD. Assistant of Miss. *C.S., T.T.G.* vi.
With the Parisian accent—never conversed with a Parisian, and was never out of England—except once in the foreign waters which ebb and flow two miles off Margate.

PUPFORD. Cook, of Miss. *C.S., T.T.G.* vi.

PUPFORD. Establishment of Miss. *C.S.*, *T.T.G.* vi.

For six young ladies of tender years, in an establishment of a compact nature, an establishment in miniature, quite a pocket establishment.

PUPFORD. Housemaid of Miss. *C.S.*, *T T.G.* vi.

PUPFORD. Miss, Schoolmistress. *C.S.*, *T.T.G.* vi.

When Miss Pupford and her assistant first foregathered is not known to men, or pupils. A belief would have established itself—that the two once went to school together—were it not for the audacity of imagining Miss Pupford born without mittens—a front—a bit of gold wire among her front teeth, and little dabs of powder on her neat little face and nose.

PUPIL. Of Miss Wade's. *L.D.* lvii.

A girl of fifteen.

PUPIL. Of special pleader. *P.P.* xlvii.

Who had written a lively book about the law of demises, with a vast quantity of marginal notes and references.

PUPKER. Sir Matthew, Chairman of United Metropolitan Improved Hot Muffin and Crumpet Baking and Punctual Delivery Company. *N.N.* ii.

Had a little round head with a flaxen wig on the top of it.

PURBECK. Island of. *R.P.*, *T.L.V.*

PURBLIND. Mr. *Mud. Pap.* ii.

PURDAY. Captain (the old Naval officer on half pay). *S.B.B.*, *O.P.* iv.

PURSE-BEARER. The Lord Chancellor's. *R.P.*, *P.M.T.P.*

PUSSEY = Dr. Pusey. *M.P.*, *A.J.B.*

PUTNEY. Formal, precise, composed and quiet. *D.C.* ix.; *L.D.* xvi.; *M.H.C.* iii. ; *M.P.*, *L.H.*

PYEGRAVE. Charley, client of Miss Mowcher's. In the Life Guards. *D.C.* xxii.

PYKE. Mr., Guest of Ralph Nickleby. *N.N.* xix.

A sharp-faced gentleman.

PYRAMIDS. *R.P.*, *M.F.F.* ; *U.T.* ix

Q

QUACK DOCTOR. *M.P.*, *M.M.*

QUADRANT, THE. *S.B.B.*, Char. I.

QUAKER HOSPITAL. In Philadelphia. *A.N.* vii.

Not sectarian in the great benefits it confers.

QUALE. Mr. *B.H.* iv.

With large shining knobs for temples, and his hair all brushed to the back of his head.

Note.—Friend of Mrs. Jellyby and intimately concerned with her philanthropic objects. He is also a prospective candidate for Caddy's hand, which she refuses.

QUALITY. Person of. *M.P.*, *N.J.B.*

QUALITY COURT. (Chancery Lane). *B.H.* viii.

QUANKO SAMBO. Bowler in Jingle's West Indian cricket match *P.P.* vii.

QUAPAW INDIANS. *A.N.* xvii.

QUARL. Philip, Gifts on Christmas tree. *R.P.*, *A.C.T.*

QUARLL. Philip. *M.C.* v.

QUEBEC. *A.N.* xv., and *M.P.*, *L.A.V.* ii.

QUEEN SQUARE. *B.H.* xviii. ; *P.P.* xxxv. ; and *R.P.*, *B.S.*

QUEEN'S PALACE. *B.R.*, lxvii. ; *M.P.*, *B.A.* ; *M.P.*, *W.H.*

QUEENSTOWN. *A.N.*, xv. ; *U.T.* ii.

QUEENSTOWN HARBOUR. *U.T.* xxxi.

QUEER CLIENT. Prisoner in Marshalsea. *P.P.* xxi.

QUEER COMPANY. The Queer Hall of some. *U.T.* xxi.

Gives upon a churchyard.

QUEERSPECK. Prof. *Mud. Pap.* i.

QUICKEAR. Of Liverpool Police Force. *U.T.* v.

QUILP. Daniel, Trent's evil spirit. *O.C.S.* iii.

An elderly man of remarkably hard features and forbidding aspect, and so low in stature as to be quite a dwarf, though his head and face were large enough for the body of a giant. His eyes were restless, sly, and cunning.

Note.—Quilp was the malignant dwarf—the evil geni of the story. He lent money to Nell's grandfather and then turned them into the street. He had Sampson Brass under his thumb and compelled him to do the dirty work. He had a pretty wife whose life he made one long spell of terror. Tom Scott, his errand boy, was the only being with whom there could be said to be any sympathy. Quilp's end is a violent one: he falls from his own wharf into the river and is drowned, when attempting to escape from the police officers. Having had no time to make his will his wife inherits his property.

QUILP. Mrs., Betsy, the dwarf's wife. *O.C.S.* iii.

"Pretty Mrs. Quilp, obedient, timid, loving Mrs. Quilp," A pretty, little, mild-spoken, blue-eyed woman.

Note.—The wife of the evil dwarf. A pretty, little, mild woman who paid for her folly in a state of constant fear of her deformed husband. She inherits his wealth and marries again.

QUILP'S BOY. *See* Scott, Tom.

QUILP'S WHARF. *O.C.S.* iv.

On the Surrey side of the river was a small, rat-infested, dreary yard . . . in which were a little wooden counting-house . . . a few fragments of rusty anchors; several large iron rings; some piles of rotten wood; and two or three heaps of old sheet-copper.

QUIN. *M.P., R.S.L.*

QUINCH. Mrs., Eldest occupant of Titbull's Almshouses. *U.T.* xxvii.

QUINION. Mr., Manager of Murdstone's wine business. *D.C.* ii.

Note.—Quinion, the manager at Murdstone and Grinby's, is first seen at Lowestoft, before Murdstone's marriage with Mrs. Copperfield. After that he is seen as head of the warehouse, where David is placed by his stepfather. Quinion is not unkind, but the nature of the work makes it impossible for the sensitive boy to endure it. Quinion drops out of the story after David runs away from the warehouse.

QUODLE. *B.H.* xii.

R

R. Y. *C.S., S.L.* iv.

RABBI. Chief, Office of the. *U.T.* ii.

RABBIT DEALERS. *S.B.*, Scenes v.

RACHAEL. A mill hand. *H.T., S.* x.

A quiet oval face, dark and rather delicate, irradiated by a pair of very gentle eyes, and further set off by the perfect order of her shining black hair. It was not a face in its first bloom. She was a woman of five-and-thirty years of age.

Note.—Rachael was the friend of Stephen Blackpool, although she was unable to marry him, as his wife, a dissolute woman, was alive. When Stephen is accused of the bank theft, Rachael protested his innocence. When Stephen did not return, she was certain that something had befallen him, and it was through her that he was discovered injured at the bottom of the old shaft.

RACHAEL. Mrs., *See* Chadband, Mrs.

RACHAEL. Mrs., Daughter of. *B.H.* iii.

RACHAEL. Mrs., Servant of Miss Barbary. *B.H.* iii.

RACHEL. "A negro woman" slave. *A.N.* xvii.

RADCLIFFE. Mrs. *S.B.B.*, Scenes xxiv.

RADDLE. "Misses" (Mrs.) Bob Sawyer's landlady. *P.P.* xxxii.

A little, fierce woman.

RADDLE. Mr., Husband of Mrs. Raddle. *P.P.* xxxii.

My husband sits sleeping downstairs and taking no more notice than if I was a dog in the street. A base, faint-hearted, timorous wretch.

RADDLE. Mrs. *P.P.* xlvi.

RADFOOT. George, Third mate on board ship. *O.M.F.* xxix.

RADICALS. In Parliament. *S.B.B.*, Scenes xviii.

RADICOFANI. *P.F.I., R.P.S.*

RADLEY. Mr., Of the Adelphi Hotel. *A.N.* i.

RAGFAIR. *L.D.* ix.

RAGGED SCHOOL. *U.T.* ii.

RAGGED SCHOOL. West Street, Saffron Hill. *M.P., S.S.U.*

RAGGED SCHOOLS. *M.P., C. and E.*

RAGLAN. Lord. *M.P., S.F.A.*

RAGS. Name of a bird. *B.H.* xiv.

RAILWAY. Northern. *C.S., H.T.*

RAILWAY ARMS. The. *D. and S.* vi.

RAILWAY EATING-HOUSE. The. *D. and S.* vi.

RAILWAY HAM, BEEF, AND GERMAN SAUSAGE WAREHOUSE. *M.P., U.N.*

RAILWAY HAT AND TRAVELLING CAP DEPOT — HAIRCUTTING SALOON—IRONMONGERY, NAIL AND TOOL WAREHOUSE—BAKERY—OYSTER ROOMS AND GENERAL SHELL-FISH SHOP—MEDICAL HALL—HOSIERY AND TRAVELLING OUTFITTING ESTABLISHMENT — RAILWAY HOTEL (late " Norwich Castle "). *M.P., U.N.*

RAILWAY PASSENGERS ASSURANCE COMPANY. *M.P., E.S.*

RAILWAY PIE-SHOP. *M.P., U.N.*

RAILWAY PORTER. Begging Letter Writer. *R.P., T.B.W.*

RAILWAY TAVERN. *M.P., U.N.*

RAINBIRD. Alice, A schoolgirl, aged seven *H.R.* i.

RAINFORTH. Miss, As Lucy Benson. *M.P., V.C.*

RAIRYGANOO. Sally, One of Mrs. Lirriper's maids, still suspect of Irish extraction. *C.S., M.L. Leg.* i.

RAMES. William, Second mate of the " Golden Mary." *C.S., W.o.G.M.*

RAMPART. Sir Charles. *S.B.B.*, Tales i.

Commanding officer in volunteers in Mr. Tibb's unfinished tale.

RAMSEY. Mr., Client of Dodson and Fogg. *P.P.*, xx.

That chap as we issued the writ against at Camberwell. A precious seedy-looking customer.

RAMSGATE. Allowed by the Tuggs's to be just the place of all others. *S.B.B.*, Tales iv.

RAMSGATE PIER. *S.B.B.*, Tales iv.

RANDAL. Runaway slave of J. Surgette. *A.N.* xvii.

RANDOLPH. Assumed name. *S.B.B.*, Scenes xiii.

RANDOM. Hon. Charles. *M.P., C. Pat.*

RANELAGH. *T.T.C.* bk. ii., ch. xii.

Mr. Stryver inaugurated the Long Vacation with a formal proposal to take Miss Manette to Vauxhall Gardens, that failing, to Ranelagh.

RANGOON. *M.P., L.A.V.* ii.

RANK AND FILE. 130 Nobodies. *R.P., N.S.*

RANKIN. Mr. *M.P., Th. Let.*

RANSOM AND CO. *M.P., I.*

RAPHAEL. *M.P., O.L.N.O.*

RAPPER. A, One of a sect. *C.S., H.H.*

A fellow-traveller in a coach, a goggle-eyed gentleman of a perplexed aspect.

RARX. Mr., Passenger on " Golden Mary." *C.S.,, W.o.G.M.*

An old gentleman, a good deal like a hawk if his eyes had been better and not so red. Not a pleasant man to look at, nor yet to talk to—a sordid and selfish character.

RATCLIFFE. *D. and S.* xxiii. ; *O.M.F.* iii. ; *O.T.* xiii. ; *U.T.* xxx.

A squalid maze of streets, courts, and alleys of miserable houses let out in single rooms.

RATCLIFF HIGHWAY. *R.P., D.W.T.T.* : *S.B.B.*, Scenes xxi.

That reservoir of dirt, drunkenness and drabs : thieves, oysters, baked potatoes and pickled salmon.

RATS CASTLE. *R.P., O.D.*

RAVEN. In the Happy Family. *M.P., P.F.*

RAVENDER. Father of William George. *C.S., W.o.G.M.*

RAVENDER. William George, Captain of the " Golden Mary." *C.S.* ; *W.o.G.M.*

Apprenticed to the sea when twelve years old. Part-owner of a smart schooner.

RAVENGLASS. *M.P.*, *E.S.*

RAYBROCK. Alfred, A young fisherman. *C.S.*, *M.f.T.S.* i.
Of two or three-and-twenty, in the rough sea-dress of his craft, with a brown face, dark curling hair, and bright, modest eyes, under his sou'wester hat, and with a frank, but simple and retiring, manner.

RAYBROCK. Father of Hugh and Alfred. *C.S.*, *M.f.T.S.* i.
Had been a small tradesman.

RAYBROCK. Hugh, Fisherman. *C.S.*, *M.f.T.S.* v.
Returned from desert island, where he was supposed to be drowned.

RAYBROCK. Jorgan, Son of Alfred and Kitty. *C.S.*, *M.f.T.S.* v.
A rosy little boy.

RAYBROCK. Mrs., Draper and also post office. *C.S.*, *M.f.T.S.* i.
A comely, elderly woman, short of stature, plump of form, sparkling and dark of eye.

RAYBROCK. Private sitting-room of Mrs. *C.S.*, *M.f.T.S.* i.
Little, low backroom—decorated with divers plants in pots, tea-trays, old China teapots and punch-bowls—which was at once the private sitting-room of the Raybrock family, and the inner cabinet of the post office.

REACH. Some, Down the river. *D. and S.* xix.

READE. Mr. *M.P.*, *M.E.R.*

READING. *B.H.* iii.; *M.P.*, *I.S.H.W.*; *M.P.*, *P.P.*

REBBECK. Mr. *M.P.*, *P.T.*

RECEIVER. The, In the cause. *B.H.* i.

RECKLESS GUESSER. *M.P.*, *S.S.U.*

RECORDER. For the City of London. *M.H.C.* i.
A man of education and birth, of the Honourable Society of the Middle Temple, barrister-at-Law.

RECORDER OF LONDON. In 1811. *M.P.*, *C.P.*

RED. One of boating-crew training for race. *S.B.B.*, Scenes x.

RED LION SQUARE. *M.P.*, *G.A.*

RED MAN. Red Indian. *A.N.*, xii.

RED SEA. *M.P.*, *H.H.*

RED TAPE. *M.P.*, *R.T.*
See also Circumlocution Office, and Scarli Tapa.

REDAN. *M.P.*, *B.A.*

REDBURN. Brother of Jack. Master Humphrey. *M.H.C.* ii.

REDBURN. Jack, Member of Master Humphrey's Club. *M.H.C.* ii.
Master Humphrey's librarian, secretary, steward, and first minister—something of a musician, author, actor, painter, very much of a carpenter, and an extraordinary gardener. He wears a quantity of iron-grey hair. We seldom see him in any other garment than an old spectral dressing-gown, with very disproportionate pockets.

REDBURN. Younger brother of Jack. *M.H.C.* vi.

REDFORTH. Bob, Cousin of William Tinkling. *H.R.*i.

REDFORTH. Lieut.-Col. Robin. *H.R.* i.

REDLAW. Mr., The haunted man. *C.B.*, *H.M.* i.
A learned man in chemistry, and a teacher.

REDMAYNE'S. *S.B.B.*, Tales v.

RED 'US. The. *S.B.B.*, Scenes x.

REEFAWM =Light of reason. Youngest and fairest of all the Sultan's wives. *M.P.*, *T.O.H.* Reform.

REFORM CLUB. *M.P.*, *B.A.*

REFORM CLUB-HOUSE. *R.P.*, *B.S.*

REFORM PARTY. *See* Reefawm.

REFRACTORIES. Inmates of Refractory Ward of Wapping Workhouse. *U.T.* iii.
Picking oakum in a small room giving on a yard. They sat in line on a form, with their backs to a window; before them, a table, and their work. The oldest refractory was, say twenty; youngest refractory, say sixteen.

REFRESHMENT ROOM. At Mugby Junction. *C.S.*, *M.J.* v.

REFRESHMENTERS. At Mugby Junction. *C.S., M.J.* v.
Ockipying the only proudly independent footing on the line.

REFUGE FOR THE DESTITUTE. New York. *A.N.* vi.

REGENCY PARK. *P.P.* xlv.

REGENT STREET. *M.P., A.P.*; *M.P., P.F.*; *M.P., R.D.*; *N.N.* x.; *S.B.B.*, Char. i.; *S.B.B.*, Scenes xvi.; *U.T.* xvi.

REGENT'S CANAL. *U.T.* vi.

REGENT'S PARK. *M.P., F'L.*; *M.P., P.F.*; *U.T.* xviii.

REGIMENTAL BANDS. Of Stepney Union. *U.T.* xxix.

REGISTRAR. The, In Chancery Court. *B.H.* i.

REGISTRAR. The, In Doctors' Commons. *S.B.B.*, Scenes viii.
An individual in an armchair, and a wig.

REGISTRAR-GENERAL *M.P., F.N.P.*

REGONDI Signor Giulio. *M.P., M.M.*

REID Dr. *M.P., N.E.*

REIGATE *U.T.* xi.

REIGATE STATION. *R.P., A.F.*

RELATION. Poor, Of John. *R.P., P.R.S.*
Nobody's enemy but my own.

RELATION. Poor, Of Ralph Nickleby, senr. *N.N.* i.
To whom he (Ralph Nickleby senr.) paid a weekly allowance of three shillings and sixpence

RELATIONS. Poor, A couple of. *P.P.* xxviii.
At wedding of Bella and Trundle.

REPORTERS. Of Court of Chancery. *B.H.* i.

REPORTERS. Of the newspapers. *B.H.* i.

REPRESENTATIVES. House of, Washington. *A.N.* iii.
A beautiful and spacious hall, of semicircular shape, supported by handsome pillars.

" **RESERVE.**" Detective. *O.M.F.* iii.

RESINA. *P.F.I., R.D.*

REST. Name of bird. *B.H.* xiv.

RESTORER. *M.P., N.Y.D.*

RETAINER. Fifth—of Veneerings. With a mournful air. *O.M.F.* ii.

RETAINERS OF VENEERINGS. Four. *O.M.F.* ii.
Pigeon-breasted—in plain clothes.

RETREAT. Mr. Bounderby's. *H.T., R.* vii.
About fifteen miles from Coketown.

RETREATS. *U.T.* xxvii.
There is a tendency in these pieces of architecture to shoot upward unexpectedly.

REVEREND. The, Master of school. *R.P., T.S.S.*

REVIEWER. The, *M.P., M.E.R.*

REYNOLDS. Miss, Pupil at the Nun's House. *E.D.* ix.

RHINE. The restless inns upon the. *C.S., H.T.*; *C.S., N.T.* Act. iii.; *M.P., A.P.*; *P.F.I., V.M.M., S.S.*; *R.P., D.W.T.T.*
Where your going to bed—appears to be the tocsin for everybody else's getting up—and where in the table d'hôte room—one knot of stoutish men, entirely dressed in jewels and dirt—will remain all night, clinking glasses and singing.

RHODE ISLAND. *A.N.* vi.

RHONE. The. *C.S., N.T.* Act iii.; *P.F.I., L.R.G.A.*

RIAH. Mr. *O.M.T.* xxii.
An old Jewish man in an ancient coat, long of skirt, and wide of pocket. A venerable man bald and shining at the top of his head, with long grey hair flowing down at its sides and mingling with his beard.

Note.—The Jew who, as the tool of Fascination Fledgeby, acts as Pubsey and Co. While he is a noble character, he is considered " a regular Jew " when he is doing the work of his employer. He befriends Lizzie Hexam and assists her to employment at the up-river mill. He arrives at the conclusion that he is doing his race an injustice so long as he remains Pubsey and Co., and gives Fledgeby notice. After that he takes up his residence with Jenny Wren.

RIALTO. The. *L.D.* xli.
RIBBLE. River. *G.S.E.* v.
RICHARD I. King *M.P., C.C.*
RICHARD II. *B.H.* Pref.
RICHARD III. *S.B.B.*, Scenes xiii.
RICHARD IV. *P.P.* xxv.
RICHARD. Brother of one of the wrecked and drowned from the "Royal Charter." *U.T.* ii.
RICHARD. Meg's sweetheart. *C.B., C.C.* i.

A handsome, well-made, powerful youngster—with eyes that sparkled like the red-hot droppings from a furnace fire; black hair that curled about his swarthy temples rarely—and a smile.

RICHARD. Richard Doubledick. *C.S., S.P.T.* ii.
RICHARD. Waiter at Saracen's Head. *N.N.* iv.
"**RICHARDS.**" *See* Toodle, Mrs.
RICHARDSON. Mr. *M.P., J.G.*
RICHARDSON. Sir John. *M.P., L.A.V.* i.
RICHARDSON'S. The Booth at Greenwich Fair. *S.B.B.*, Scenes xii.

Where you have a melodrama, a pantomime, a comic song, an overture, and some incidental music, all done in five-and-twenty minutes.

RICHMOND. Earl of. *S.B.B.*, Scenes xiii.
RICHMOND. *A.N.* ii.; *G.E.* xxxiii.; *O.M.F.* li.; *P.P.* lvii.; *S.B.B.*, Scenes vi.; *S.B.B.*, Scenes x.
RICHMOND. The terrace at. *P.P.* lvii.
RICHMOND. (U.S.A.) *A.N.* viii.
RICHMOND HILL. *M.P., I.*
RICKITTS. Little, A pupil at the Nuns' House. *E.D.* xiii.
RIDERHOOD. Home of. *O.M.F.* xxix.

In Limehouse Hole, among the riggers, and the mast, oar and block makers, and the boat-builders and the sail-lofts.

RIDERHOOD. Miss Pleasant, An unlicensed pawnbroker, and daughter of Rogue Riderhood. *O.M.F.* xxix.

In her four-and-twentieth year of life—possessed of what is colloquially termed a swivel eye—she was otherwise not positively ill-looking, though anxious, meagre, of a muddy complexion, and looking as old again as she really was.

Note.—Rogue Riderhood's daughter. She is first seen managing her father's house and acting as "an unlicensed pawnbroker" upon the smallest of small scales. Eventually she marries Mr. Venus.

RIDERHOOD. Mrs., The late. *O.M.F.* xxix.

Mother of Pleasant Riderhood.

RIDERHOOD. Roger, A waterside man. *O.M.F.* vi.

With a squinting leer, who fumbled at an old sodden fur cap, formless and mangy, that looked like a furry animal, dog or cat, puppy or kitten, drowned and decaying.

Note.—A Thames "night-bird" of ill-fame. John Harmon is maltreated in the Rogue's house. The "secret" of the book is the identity of the murdered man. But Riderhood lodges an accusation of the crime against Gaffer Hexam, for the purpose of obtaining the reward offered by Mr. Boffin. The death of Hexam deprives him of this, which leaves him with a feeling of decided injury. Rogue Riderhood becomes a lock-keeper at Plashwater Weir, and discovers Bradley Headstone's attempted murder of Eugene Wrayburn. He blackmails Bradley and persecutes him until the schoolmaster turns in desperation and drowns both the Rogue and himself in the lock.

RIDING-MASTER. At Astley's. *S.B.B.* Scenes xi.

None of your second-rate riding-masters—but the regular gentleman attendant on the principal riders, who always wears a military uniform with a tablecloth inside the breast of the coat, in which costume he forcibly reminds one of a fowl trussed for roasting.

RIGAUD. Late, Madame, Widow of M. Henri Barronneau. *L.D.* i.

One night Madame Rigaud and myself were walking—on a height overhanging the sea—I remonstrated on the want of duty and devotion—

Madame Rigaud retorted—I retorted—Mme. Rigaud leaped over, dashing herself to death.

RIGAUD, Monsieur. *L.D.*i.

He had a hook nose, handsome after its kind, but too high between the eyes, by probably just as much as his eyes were too near to one another. For the rest he was large and tall in frame, had thin lips where his thick moustache showed them at all, and a quantity of dry hair, of no definable colour, in its shaggy state, but shot with red. The hand—was unusually small and plump; would have been unusually white, but for the prison grime. When (he) laughed, a change took place in his face, which was more remarkable than prepossessing. His moustache went up under his nose, and his nose came down over his moustache in a very sinister and cruel manner.

"I myself was born in Belgium—call me thirty-five years of age—have been treated and respected like a gentleman everywhere."

Note.—First seen in prison on a charge of killing his wife. He escapes, however, and makes his way to England, where he is closely entangled in the story. He is a polished scoundrel living on his wits. He obtains possession of the box of papers confided to Ephraim Flintwich by his brother Jeremiah, and endeavours to extract money from Mrs. Clennam by threatening exposure. He dose not succeed, however, and dies in the ruins of Mrs. Clennam's house, which falls on him.

RIGAUD. *M.P., M.E.R.*

RIOTERS. Of the Gordon Riots. *B.R.* lxiii.

RIOTERS. Two. *B.R.* lxxvii.

Were to die before the prison.... who had been concerned in the attack upon it.

RIVER. The. *S.B.B.*, Scenes x.

RIVIERA. The. *P.F.I., G.A.N.*

RIVOLI. Rue de. *P.F.I., G.T.F.*; *R.P., A.F.*; *U.T.* vii.

ROADS. The, within twelve miles of London. *B.R.* ii.

Were at that time ill paved, seldom repaired, and very badly made.

ROBBERS. Captain of the *M.P., T.O.H.*

ROBBERS. Forty. *M.P., T.O.H.*

ROBBINS. Mr.. A bank officer. *A.N.*; xvii.

ROBBS. *M.P., T.T.*

ROBEMAKER. Two daughters of, Combing their curls. *B.H.* x.

ROBERT. Uncle, Husband of Aunt Jane, guest at Christmas family party. *S.B.B.*, Char. ii.

ROBERTS. *M.P., O.L.N.O.*

ROBERTSON. Mr. Peter. *M.P., S.P.*

ROBIN. Cecil. *M.P., P.M.B.*

ROBIN HOOD. A toy. *R.P.; A.C.T.*

ROBINS. Mr. Auctioneer. *S.B.B.*, Tales. i.

ROBINSON. Mr., Who married one of the Miss Willises. *S.B.B., O.P.* iii.

A gentleman in a public office, with a good salary, and a little property of his own beside—dressed in a light blue coat and double-milled kersey pantaloons, white neckerchief, pumps, and dress-gloves.

ROBINSON. Mrs., The youngest Miss Willis. *S.B.B., O.P.* iii.

ROBINSON. Mrs. Tibb's servant. *S.B.B.*, Tales i.

ROBINSON. Rival wit at counting-house. *D. and S.* li.

ROBINSON. Robinson Crusce. *D.C.* v.; *P.P.* vii.; *S.B.B., O.P.*ii. *U.T.* xv.

ROBINSON CRUSOE. Gift on Christmas tree. *R.P., A.C.T.*

ROBINSON CRUSOE'S ISLAND. *U.T.* xv.

ROCHESTER. *C.S., S.P.T.* i.; *D.C.* xiii.; *L.D.* liv.; *P.P.* ii.. *U.T.* vii;

The commodities chiefly exposed for sale in the public streets are marine stores, hardbake, apples, flat fish, and oysters.

See also Cloisterham.

ROCHESTER. High street of. *C.S., S.P.T.* i.

Full of gables, with old beams and timbers, carved into strange faces. It is oddly garnished with a queer old clock that projects over the pavement out of a grave, red-brick building—dark apertures in its walls—the ruin looks as if rooks and daws had pecked its eyes out.

ROCHESTER. Minor Canons' residences in. *C.S., S.P.T.* iii.

A wonderfully quaint row of red-brick tenements. They had odd little porches over the doors, like sounding-boards over old pulpits.

See also Minor Canon Corner.

ROCHESTER. The old gates of the city of. *C.S., S.P.T.* iii.

ROCHESTER. Strood, etc. *P.P.* ii.

The principal productions of these towns appear to be soldiers, sailors, Jews, chalk, shrimps, officers, and dockyard men.

ROCHESTER BRIDGE. *P.P.* ii.

ROCHESTER CASTLE. *P.P.* ii. *C.S., S.P.T.* i.

Frowning walls—tottering arches dark nooks—crumbling staircases.

ROCHESTER CATHEDRAL. *C.S., S.P.T.* i. ; *P.P.* ii.

Earthy smell—little Saxon doors —confessionals like money-takers' boxes at theatres.

ROCKINGHAM. Lord. *B.R.* lxvii.

ROCKINGHAM. Marquis of. *M.P., A. in E.*

ROCKY MOUNTAINS. *M.P., T.O.P.* ; *O.M.F.* viii.

RODOLH. Mr. Jennings, vocal a musical friend of Journeyman Painters. *S.B.B.*, Char. viii.

RODOLPH. Mrs. Jennings, musical friend of journeyman painter. *S.B.B.*, Char. viii.

ROE. Richard. *M.P., L.E.J.*

ROE FAMILY. The only female member of the. *B.H.* xx.

ROEBUCK. Mr. *M.P., T.B.* ; *M.P., T.T.*

ROGERS. Friend of Mrs. Nickleby. *N.N.* xxxvii.

A lady in our neighbourhood when we lived near Dawlish.

ROGERS. Johnny, Workhouse inmate. *R.P., W.I.A.*

ROGERS. Mr. *M.P., F.L.*

ROGERS. Mr., A policeman. *R.P., D.W.I.F.*

ROGERS. Mr., The parlour orator. *S.B.B.*, Char. v.

A stoutish man of about forty, whose short, stiff, black hair curled closely round a broad, high forehead, and a face to which something besides water and exercise had communicated a rather inflamed appearance.

ROGERS. Mr., Third mate of the "Halsewell." *R.P., T.L.V.*

ROGERS. Mrs., Mrs. Raddles, lodger. *P.P.* xlvi.

ROGUE. A. *C.S., S.P.T.* i.

ROKER. Mr. Tom, Gentleman who had accompanied Mr. Pickwick into the prison. *P.P.* xli.

ROKESMITH. *See* Harmon John.

ROKESMITH. Mrs., John. *See* Wilfer, Bella.

ROLLAND. Partner of Defresnier et cie. *C.S., N.T.* Act ii.

ROLLS YARD. *B.H.* x.

ROMAN BATH. In one of the streets out of the Strand. *D.C.* vi.

ROMANO CAMPAGNA. *P.F.I., R.P.S.*

ROMANS. Sulky. *P.F.I., R.*

ROME. *B.H.* Pref. ; *L.D.* xlvii. ; *P.F.I., R.* ; *P.F.I., R.P.S.* ; *R.P., L.A.* ; *U.T.* ix.

ROME. Catacombs of. *P.F.I., R.*

ROMER. Mr. R., As first husband. *M.P., N.T.*

ROMILLY. Lawyer. *M.P., C.P.*

ROMILLY. Sir Samuel. *B.R.* Pref.

RONCIGLIONE. *P.F.I., R.P.S.*

ROOD LANE. London. *M.P., E.T.*

ROOKERY. At Blunderstone, in Suffolk, David's birthplace. *D.C.* i.

ROOKERY. The. *S.B.B.*, Scenes xxii.

That classical spot adjoining the Brewery at the bottom of Tottenham Court Road. The filthy and miserable appearance of this part of London can hardly be imagined by those who have not witnessed it. Wretched houses with broken windows patched with rags and paper: every room let to a different family and in some instances to two or even three—fruit and "sweet stuff" manufacturers in the cellars, barbers and red-herring vendors in the front parlours, cobblers in the back; a bird-fancier in the first floor, three families on the second, starvation in the attics, Irishmen in the passage, a musician in the front kitchen, a charwoman with five hungry children in the back—filth everywhere.

"ROOMS." Master of the. *R.P., O.E.W.*
Wears knee-breeches.

ROOMS. The Assembly Rooms. *R.P., O.E.W.*

ROPE-WALK. Old Green Copper. *G.E.* xlvi.

ROSA. A dark-eyed, dark-haired, shy village beauty. *B.H.* vii.

Note.—A maid whom Mrs. Rouncewell takes young to train. Watt Rouncewell falls in love with her, but there are difficulties. Eventually, however, Rosa leaves for a year's polishing in Germany before marrying Watt.

ROSA. Father of. [Rosa Bud] *E.D.* ix.
Died brokenhearted on first anniversary of that (the accidental drowning of his wife) hard day.

ROSA. Mother of. *E.D.* ix.
A pretty little creature—brought home in her father's arms, drowned.

ROSA VILLA. Clapham Rise. *S.B.B.*, Tales ix.
In occupation of Mr. Gattleton—usually so neat and tidy, was regularly turned out o' windows in preparation for private theatricals.

ROSE. *M.P., V.C.*

ROSE. Enemy of Col. Potter. *A.N.* xvii.

ROSE. Oliver Twist's aunt. *O.T.* li.

ROSES AND DIAMONDS. Jemmy. *C.S., M.L.Lo.* i.

ROSINA. *M.P., M.N.D.*

ROSS. Mr. *A.N.* xvii.

ROSS. Sir James. *M.P., E.T.*

ROSSINI. Signor. *M.P., M.M.*

ROTHERHITHE. *M.P., G.B.*; *O.T.* l.
To reach this place the visitor has to penetrate through a maze of close, narrow, and muddy streets. The cheapest and least delicate provisions are heaped in the shop; the coarsest and commonest articles of wearing apparel dangle at the salesman's door, and stream from the house parapet and windows.

ROTHSCHILD. *M.P., G.A.*

ROTHSCHILDS. *M.P., F.L.*

ROTTEN GRAY'S INN LANE. *R.P., D.W.I.F.*

ROTTINGDEAN. *D. and S.* viii.

ROUGE ET NOIRE. Demented woman. *M.P., W.S.G.*

ROUNCEWELL. An Ironmaster. Son of Sir Leicester Dedlock's housekeeper. *B.H.* xxvii.
A little over fifty, perhaps, of a good figure, like his mother; has a clear voice, a broad forehead, from which his dark hair has retired, and a shrewd, though open face. A responsible-looking gentleman dressed in black, portly enough, but strong and active.

Note.—Son of Mrs. Rouncewell. He stays in England and prospers as an ironmaster. It is his son Watt who is betrothed to Rosa.

ROUNCEWELL. Children of the ironmaster. *B.H.* lxiii.

ROUNCEWELL. Mr. George, Ex-trooper, and shooting-gallery owner. *B.H.* vii.
A swarthy man of fifty; well made and good looking; with crisp dark hair, bright eyes, and a broad chest. His sinewy and powerful hands, as sunburnt as his face, have evidently been used to a pretty rough life.

Note.—Rouncewell is first seen as the keeper of a shooting range. It transpires that he is the son of the Dedlock's housekeeper. Eventually he becomes a companion-servant to Sir Leicester Dedlock.

ROUNCEWELL. Mr., Husband of Mrs. Rouncewell. *B.H.* vii.

Died some time before the decease of the pretty fashion of pigtails.

ROUNCEWELL. Mrs., House-keeper at Chesney Wold. *B.H.* vii.

A fine old lady, handsome, stately, wonderfully neat—and has such a back and such a stomacher, that if her stays should turn out when she dies to have been a broad old-fashioned family fire-grate, nobody who knows her would have cause to be surprised.

Note.—Housekeeper at Chesney Wold. Mother of George and the ironmaster. She is devoted to the Dedlock family, and when the story closes she is still seen "harder of hearing," but looking after her duties.

ROUNCEWELL. Mrs., Wife of the ironmaster. *B.H.* lxii.

ROUNCEWELL, WATT *B.H.* vii.

Note.—Son of the Ironmaster and grandson of Mrs. Rouncewell. He meets Rosa at Chesney Wold and falls in love with her. There are difficulties in the way. But she is eventually sent to Germany "to be polished up" as the intended wife of Watt.

ROVINGHAMS. Commission merchants. *L.D.* v.

All our consignments have long been made to Rovinghams', the commission merchants and—as a check upon them, and in the stewardship of my father's resources, your judgment and watchfulness have been actively exerted.

ROWDY JOURNAL. New York. *M.C.* xvi.

ROYAL ACADEMY OF ARTS. *M.P., O.L.N.O.*; *R.P., G.o.A.*

ROYAL ACADEMY OF MUSIC. *M.P., O.L.N.O.*

ROYAL ALMACKS. *M.C.* xxi.

ROYAL COLLEGE OF SURGEONS. *M.P., O.L.N.O.*

ROYAL EXCHANGE. *B.R.* lxvii.; *C.S., W.o.G.M.*; *D. and S.* iv.; *M.P., I.*; *M.P., W.*; *R.P., B.S.*; *U.T.* vi.

ROYAL FREE HOSPITAL. Gray's Inn Road. *M.P., V.D.*

ROYAL GEORGE. Dover. *T.T.C.*, bk. i. ch. iv.

ROYAL GEORGE. The, Hotel. *C.B., C.o.H.*; *R.P., A.F.*; *S.B.B.*, Tales x.

ROYAL HÔTEL. The, Angaishee Ouse Calais. *U.T.* xvii.

ROYAL HOTEL. *P.P.* xxxvii.

ROYAL HOTEL. Leamington. *D. and S.* xx.

ROYAL ITALIAN OPERA. *U.T.* iv.

ROYAL OLD DUST BIN. Dining-rooms. *C.S., S.L.* i.

ROYALE. Rue. *R.P., O.o.S.*

RUDDLE. Mortgage of. *N.N.* ii.

RUDGE. Barnaby. *B.R.* i.

His hair, of which he had a great profusion, was red, and hanging in disorder about his face and shoulders.—His dress was of green clumsily trimmed here and there—with gaudy lace; brightest where the cloth was most worn and soiled. A pair of tawdry ruffles dangled at his wrists. He had ornamented his hat with a cluster of peacocks' feathers—girt to his side was the steel hilt of an old sword without blade or scabbard. When her son was born he bore upon his wrist what seemed a smear of blood but half washed out.

Note.—The title-character of the story. A shrewd, kindly, but half-witted youth, with a deep knowledge of, and love for, wild life: deeply exercised in mind as to what makes the stars shine. He is watched over by his mother. His closest companion, after his raven, is Maypole Hugh, like whom he is strong and muscular. He is embroiled with the rioters, and on the suppression of the disturbances he is sentenced to death, but is pardoned, as the result of Varden's efforts on his behalf. Afterwards he settles down on the Maypole farm and improves in mind and intellect. But the wild scenes in London have had so much effect on his mind that he will never after enter London.

RUDGE. Mr., Steward of Reuben Harewood. *B.R.* i.

Whose body — scarcely to be recognised by his clothes and the watch and ring he wore—was found at the bottom of a piece of water in the grounds, with a deep gash in his breast where he had been stabbed with a knife.

Note.—Barnaby's father. He was formerly steward to Reuben Haredale. Mr. Haredale was murdered and Rudge fled. A dead body, so disfigured as to be unrecognisable, is discovered, and it is supposed to be that of Rudge the murderer. Later on he returns and pesters his wife in secret. It is discovered by others that he is alive, and his identity established. It is proved not only that he murdered Mr. Haredale, but also that the death of the man whose body was taken for that of Rudge himself, was due to him, and he is executed.

RUDGE. Mrs. Mary, Barnaby's mother. *B.R.* iv.

About forty—perhaps two or three years older—with a cheerful aspect, and a face that had once been pretty.

Note.—Mother of Barnaby. She watches over her son, and her whole life is devoted to keeping him away from his father and out of his clutches : and with this end in view, she is reduced to all kinds of stratagems.

RUDGE ROW. *R.P., B.S.*

RUFFIAN NUMBER ONE. *U.T.* xxxvi.

A shirking fellow of five-and-twenty, in an ill-favoured, and ill-savoured suit.

RUFFIAN, NUMBER TWO. *U.T.* xxxvi.

A burly brute of five-and-thirty, in a tall stiff hat, is a composite, as to his clothes, of betting and fighting man ; is whiskered—has insolent and cruel eyes ; large shoulders ; strong legs, booted and tipped for kicking.

RUFFIAN. The. *U.T.* xxxvi.

Always a ruffian, always a thief.

RUFFIANISM. Preparatory schools of. *U.T.* xxxvi.

RUGBY. *M.P., E.S.* ; *M.P., L.L.* ; *M.P., O.S.*

RUGG. Miss Anastasia, Daughter of Rugg. *L.D.* xxv.

A lady of a little property, which she had acquired—by having her heart severely lacerated—found it necessary to proceed at law to recover damages for a breach of promise of marriage.—Had little nankeen spots, like shirt-buttons, all over her face, and whose yellow tresses were rather scrubby than luxuriant.

RUGG. Mr., Mr. Panck's landlord. *L.D.* xxv.

General agent, accountant, debts recovered, had a round white visage, as if all his blushes had been drawn out of him long ago—a ragged yellow head like a worn-out hearth broom.

Note.—Pancks' landlord. He is Arthur Clennam's professional adviser in his financial reverses.

RUIN. Name of a bird. *B.H.* xiv.

RULE OFFICE. *B.H.* x.

RULER. Gentleman, Landlord of lodging-house. *N.N.* xlvi.

Who was smoking hard in front parlour (though it was not yet (noon).

RULES. The, Of the King's Bench Prison. A certain liberty adjoining the prison. *N.N.* xlvi. ; *S.B.B.*, Scenes xxi.

Comprising some dozen streets in which debtors who can raise money to pay large fees, from which their creditors do *not* derive any benefit, are permitted to reside by the wise provisions of the same enlightened laws, which leaves the debtor who can raise no money, to starve in jail, without the food, clothing, lodging or warmth which are provided for felons convicted of the most atrocious crimes that can disgrace humanity. There were small gardens in front—which served as pens for the dust to collect in.

RUMMUN. Prof. *Mud. Pap.* ii.

RUNAWAYS. Some five-and-forty. *B.R.* xxxiii.

Varying from six years old to twelve.

RUSH. Murderer. *M.P., D.M.*

RUSSELL. Lord John. *M.P., N.E.* ; *M.P., T.B.*

RUSSELL. (Mr. W. H.) *M.P., B.A.*

RUSSELL SQUARE. *N.N.* xxxvii. ; *S.B.B.*, Char i.

RUSSIA. *M.P.*, *C.P.* ; *M.P.*, *N.G.K.* ; *M.P.*, *W.* ; *M.P.*, *W.H.* ; *U.T.* vii.

RUSSIA. Czar of. *M.P.*, *R.S.D.*

" **RUSSIA.**" First officer of steamer. *U.T.* xxxi.

" **RUSSIA.**" Second officer of steamer. *U.T.* xxxi.

" **RUSSIA.**" Third officer of steamer. *U.T.* xxxi.

Posted at the stern rail with a lantern.

" **RUSTIC LODGE.**" Near Reading. *M.P.*, *I.S.H.W.*

RUTLANDSHIRE. *C.S.*, *M.L.Lo.* ii.

RYDE. *N.N.* xxv.

S

S. Mrs. *M.P.*, *S.B.*

SACKVILLE STREET. *O.M.F.* x.

SACRISTAN. The. *P.F.I.*, *L.R.G.A.*

SADDLER. The. *G.E.* viii.

SADLER'S WELLS. *S.B.B.*, Scenes xiii.

SADLER'S WELLS THEATRE. *O.T.* viii.

SAFE. John, Engine-driver. *M.P.*, *R.S.*

SAFFRON HILL. *B.H.* xxvi ; *M.P.*, *C. and E.* ; *M.P.*, *S.S.U.* ; *O.T.* viii.

SAGE. *M.P.*, *P.M.B.*

SAGE. Dick. *M.P.*, *G.D.*

SAGGERS. Mrs., Eldest but one of occupants of Titbull's Almshouses. *U.T.* xxvii.

SAILOR. *M.P.*, *G.F.*

SAILOR. Body of a. *O.M.F.* iii.

With two anchors and a flag and G.F.T. on his arm.

ST. AGATA. *P.F.I.*, *R.D.*

ST. ALBAN'S. *B.H.* vi. ; *D.C.* xxiv. ; *M.P.*, *F.C.*, *O.T.* xlviii. ; *U.T.* xi.

ST. ALPHAGE. Canterbury. *D.C.* xvi.

ST. ANDREW'S. Churchyard of. *B.H.* x.

ST. ANDREW'S, HOLBORN. *O.T.* xxi.

ST. ANGELO. *P.F.I.*, *R.D.*

ST. ANGELO. Bridge of. *P.F.I.*, *R.*

ST. ANGELO. Castle of. *P.F.I.*, *R.*

ST. ANNE'S VILLAS. *M.P.*, *N.S.*

ST. ANTOINE. A suburb of Paris. *T.T.C.* v.

Cold, dirt, sickness, ignorance, and want, were the lords in waiting on the saintly presence.

ST. BARTHOLOMEW. Hospital of *L.D.* xiii. ; *R.P.*, *T.D.P.*

ST. BARTHOLOMEW. Surgeon of. *L.D.* xiii.

ST. BENEDICT. *N.N.* vi.

SAINT BLANK'S HOSPITAL. House surgeon of. *R.P.*, *T.D.A.* iii.

SAINT BLANK'S HOSPITAL. Secretary of. *R.P.*, *T.D.A.* iii.

ST. BLANK'S HOSPITAL. A student. *R.P.*, *T.D.A.* iii.

A tallish, good looking young man of one or two and twenty, with a light whisker.

SAINT BLANK'S HOSPITAL. Treasurer of. *R.P.*, *T.D.A.* iii.

S. CARLINO THEATRE. *P.F.I.*, *R.D.*

S. CARLO. Theatre of. *P.F.I.*, *R.D.*

ST. CATHERINE'S DOCKS. *U.T.* xxviii.

ST. CLAIR. Assumed name. *S.B.B.*, Scenes xiii.

ST. CLEMENT'S CHURCH. *P.P.* xxiii. ; *S.B.B.*, *O.P.* vii.

ST. CLEMENT'S DANES. *C.S.*, *M L.Lo.* i.

SANTA CROCE. Church of. *P.F.I.*, *R.D.*

SAINT DUNSTAN. *B.R.* xl. ; *M.H.C.* iii.

ST. DUNSTAN'S. The figures at. *M.P.*, *G.A.*

ST. EVREMONDE. Marquis de. *T.T.C.*, bk. ii., ch. xxiv.

A man of about sixty, handsomely dressed, haughty in manner, and with a face like a fine mask.

Note.—Uncle of Charles Darnay. He rides over a child and kills it in the streets of Paris. Gaspard, the father, follows him to his chateau and kills him. On the night before his murder his nephew arrives from London to visit him.

ST. EVREMONDE. Marquis. *T.T.C.* bk. iii., ch. x.
Note.—The father of Charles Darnay and twin brother of the monseigneur of the story. Dead when he is mentioned first.

ST. EVREMONDE. Marquis. *See also* Darnay, Charles, who succeeded his uncle, when Monsieur the Marquis was murdered.

ST. EVREMONDE. Marquise. *T.T.C.*, Bk. iii., ch. x.
Note.—Mother of Charles Darnay. She visited Dr. Manette after he had learned the secret of her husband and his brother.

ST. GEORGE OF SOUTHWARK. *L.D.* xiv.; *R.P., D.W.I.F.*

ST. GEORGE'S CHAPEL. Windsor *M.P., C.C.*; *M.P., T.D.*

SAINT GEORGE'S CHURCH. *L.D.* vi.; *N.N.* xxi.; *P.P.* xxi.; *U.T.* iii.

SAINT GEORGE'S CHURCH. Clerk of. *L.D.*lxx.

ST. GEORGE'S CHURCH. Hart Street. *S.B.B.*, Tales xi.

ST. GEORGE'S FIELDS. Southwark. *B.R.*, xlviii.; *M.P., G.F.*; *M.P., S.B.*; *N.N.* xlvi.; *P.P* xliii.; *S.B.B.* xxvii.; *U.T.* x. Really fields at that time.

ST. GEORGE'S GALLERY. *R.P., T.N.S.*

ST. GEORGE'S-IN-THE-EAST. *U.T.* iii.

ST. GERMAIN. *M.P., L.A.V.* i.; *P.F.I., R.D.*

ST. GILES. *B.R.* xliv.; *M.P., G.A.*; *P.F.I., A.G.*; *P.F.I., R.D.*; *R.P., D.W.I.F.*; *S.B.B.*, Scenes v.; *S.B.B.*, Scenes xxii.; *S.B.B.*, Tales xi.; *U.T.* x.

ST. GILES STATION HOUSE. *R.P., D.W.I.F.*

SAN GIOVANNI DECOLLATO. Church of. *P.F.I., R.*

ST. GIOVANNI AND ST. PAOLO. Church of. *P.F.I., R.*

ST. GOTTHARD PASS. *C.S., N.T.*, Act iii.

ST. HELENA. *M.P., L.A.V.* ii.

ST. HONORÉ. Rue. *U.T.* vii.

ST. JACQUE DE LA BOUCHERIE, Tower of. *U.T.* xviii.

ST. JAMES'S. *C.S., M.L.Lo.* i.; *M.P. F.C.*; *O.M.F.* ii.; *U.T.* iii.

SAINT JAMES'. Court of. *B.H.* xii.; *M.C.* xvi.

ST. JAMES'S ARMS. Chambermaid at the. *M.P., S.G.*

ST. JAMES'S ARMS. In a small town of the road to Gretna. *M.P., S.G.*

ST. JAMES'S CLUB-HOUSE. *N.N.* I.

ST. JAMES'S PARISH. *M.P., N.Y.D.*; *N.N.* iv.; *U.T.* xxiii. Where bell wires are esteemed as convenient toothpicks.

ST. JAMES'S PARK. *M.C.* xiv.; *M.P., F.N.P.*; *M.P., Th. Let.*; *N.N.* xliv.; *S.B.B.*, char. i.

ST. JAMES' SQUARE. *B.R.* lxx.; *M.C.* xxvii.; *O.M.F.* ii.

ST. JAMES'S STREET. *C.S., T.G.S.* i.; *H.T., G.* iii.; *R.P., O.B.*

ST. JAMES'S THEATRE. *M.P., I.S.H.W.*; *M.P., V.C.*; *R.P., F.*

ST. JANUARIUS'S GALLERY. *M.P., T.B.*

ST. JOHN S. *A.N.* xv.

ST. JOHN'S ROAD. *O.T.* viii.

ST. JULIEN HORATON, alias Jem Larkins. *S.B.B.*, Scenes xii. In the white hat and checked shirt, brown coat and brass buttons lounging behind the stage box—his line is genteel comedy.

ST. JUSTE. *C.S., M.f.T.S.* ii.

ST. LAWRENCE. *A.N.* xv.; *R.P., D.W.T.T.*

ST. LOUIS. *A.N.* xii.; *U.T.* xx.

ST. LUKE'S HOSPITAL. *U.T.* iv.

ST. LUKE'S WORKHOUSE. *D.C.* xi.

ST. MAGNUS. *O. T.* xlvi.

ST. MARGARET'S CHURCH. *S.B.B.*, Scenes xviii.

SANTA MARIA DELLA CONSOLAZIONE. Church of. *P.F.I., R.*

SANTA MARIA DELLE GRAZIE. Convent of. *P.F.I., V.M.M.S.S.*

ST. MARK'S CATHEDRAL. Venice, *C.S., H.T.*

ST. MARTIN'S CHURCH *B.R.*, xliv.; *P.F.I.*, *G.A.N.*; *S.B.B.*, Char. i.; *U.T.* xiii.

ST. MARTIN'S COURT. *O.C.S.* i. Think of a sick man, in such a place as St. Martin's Court.

ST. MARTIN'S HALL. Long Acre. *M.P.*, *S.F.A.*

SAINT MARTIN'S LANE. *D.C.* xi. Leading down to Strand.

ST. MARTIN'S-LE-GRAND. *M.P.*, *M.E.R.*; *P.P.* ii.

ST. MARY IN THE STRAND. *U.T.* xiv.

ST. MARY'S ABBEY. *N.N.* vi.

ST. MARY AXE. *O.M.F.* bk.2.ch.v.

ST. MILDRED'S CHURCH. *B.R.* lxvii.

SAINT OMER'S. *B.R.* xliii.

ST. PANCRAS. The old church burial-ground. *T.T.C.*, bk. ii., ch. xiv. Far off in the fields.
Note.—Cly's pseudo burial of paving stones took place here.

ST. PANCRAS BOARD OF GUARDIANS. *M.P.*, *S. Pigs.*

ST. PANCRAS NEW CHURCH. *S.B.B.*, *T.* i.

ST. PANCRAS WORKHOUSE. *M.P.*, *P.P.*

ST. PAUL'S. *B.H.* xix.; *B.R.* xxii.; *C.S.*, *N.T.*, *O.*; *D.C.* iv.; *G.E.* xx.; *L.D.* iii.; *M.C.* xxxviii.; *M.H.C.* i.; *M.P.*, *A. in E.*; *M.P.*, *C.*; *M.P.*, *G.A.*; *M.P.*, *G.B.*; *M.P.*, *P.A.P.*; *M.P.*, *P.F.*; *M.P.*, *T.D.*; *M.P.*, *R.S.D.*; *M.P.*, *V. and B.S.*; *N.N.* xlv.; *O.M.F.* xxxiv.

ST. PAUL'S CHURCHYARD. *B.R.* xxxvii.; *C.B.*, *C.C.*, *S.* i.; *M.H.C.* i.; *O.M.F.*, viii.; *P.F.I.*, *R.P.S.*; *R.P.*, *B.S.*; *S.B.B.*, Scenes iii.

ST. PÈLAGIE. *R.P.*, *O.o.S.*

ST. PETER. Church of. *L.D.* xliii.; *M.P.*, *V. and B.S.*, *P.F.I.*, *R.*; *R.P.*, *O.B.*; *U.T.* ix.

ST. PETER'S. Great Piazza of. *P.F.I.*, *R.*

ST. PETERSBURG. *L.D.* xvi.

SAN PETRONIO. Church of. *P.F.I.*, *T.B.F.*

SAN PIETRO CATHEDRAL. Mantua. *P.F.I.*, *V.M.M.S.S.*

SAN REMO. *P.F.I.*, *G.A.N.*

ST. SAVIOUR'S. Southwark. *O.T.* xlvi.; *U.T.* ix.

SAN SEBASTIANO. Church of *P.F.I.*, *R.*

ST. SEPULCHRE'S. *B.R.* lxiv.; *N.N.* iv.; *U.T.* xiii.

ST. SIMON WITHOUT. *P.P.* xlv.

ST. STEFANS ROTONDO. *P.F.I.*, *R.*

ST. STEPHEN. *M.P.*, *P.P.*

SAINT THOMAS'S STREET. *N.N.* xxiii.

SAINT WALKER WITHIN. *P.P.* xlv.

ST. YTRES. M. Latour de. *M.P.*, *V. and B.S.*

SALA. Madam, as Julia Dobbs. *M.P.*, *S.G.*

SALA. Madam, as Mrs. Peter Limbury. *M.P.*, *I.S.H.W.*

SALCY. Monsieur P., Travelling showman. *U.T.* xxv.

SALCY. The family P. *U.T.* xxv. Fathers, mothers, sisters, brothers, uncles, and aunts—so fat and so ike one another.

SALEM. Massachusetts, United States. *C.S.*, *M.f.T.S.* ii.

SALEM HOUSE. School. *D.C.* v. Down by Blackheath . . . enclosed with a high brick wall and looked very dull.

SALISBURY. *M.C.* ii.

SALISBURY. Bishop of. *M.P.*, *R.S.D.*

SALISBURY ARMS. The. *C.S.*, *M.L.Lo.* i.

SALISBURY CATHEDRAL. *M.C.* ii.

SALISBURY PLAIN. *C.S.*, *H.T.*; *U.T.* xx.

SALISBURY POST OFFICE. *M.C.* ix.

SALLE DE LA QUESTION. *P.F.I.*, *L.R.G.A.*

SALLY. Compeyson's wife. *G.E.* xlii.

SALLY. Negro slave. *A.N.* xvii.

SALLY. Nurse in Foundling Hospital. *C.S., N T., O.*

SALLY. Old, Dying inmate of workhouse. *O.T.* xxiii.

Nursed a pretty young creetur that was brought into the House with her feet cut and bruised with walking—she gave birth to a boy and died. They *called* him Oliver.

Note.—The pauper nurse who robs Oliver's mother when she dies in the workhouse.

SALLY. Uncle Bill's niece. *S.B.B.*, Scenes ix.

SALOON. Haircutting, Overlooking Mr. Dombey's room. *D. and S.* xiii.

Where a waxen effigy, bald as a Mussulman in the morning—covered after eleven o'clock in the day with luxuriant hair and whiskers in the latest Christian fashion.

SALOON. Oyster, waitress in. *S.B.B.*, Char. vii.

Of about five-and-twenty, all in blue—splendid creature, charming face, and lovely figure.

SALTINE. Gorge of the. *P.F.I., V.M.M.S.S.*

SALVATORE, SIGNIOR. Head guide *P.F.I., R.D.*

SALWANNERS. The, The Savannah. *B.R.* lxxii.

SAM. Cab-driver. *P.P.* ii.

SAM. Mr. Pecksniff's hostler. *M.C.* v.

SAM. Slave. *A.N.* xvii.

SAMBO PILOT. Christian King George. *C.S., P.o.C.E.P.*

SAMBOS. Natives of Silver Store Island. *C.S., P.o.C.E.P.*

Half-negro and half-Indian.

SAMPSON. George, Sweetheart of Bella, and afterwards of Lavinia Wilfer. *O.M.F.* iv.

Note.—A young man, a kind of pet poodle belonging to the Wilfers. At the opening of the story he is begining to become devoted to Bella, but transfers his adoration to her sister, when she is adopted by the Boffins. It would perhaps be better to say that, deeming it likely that another pet poodle in the family would be difficult to obtain, Lavinia took him over. He is left paying a visit to his future sister-in-law in her "marble halls."

SAMPSON. Mr., Chief manager of an insurance office. *H.D.* i

SAMPSON'S AUNT. *O.M.F.* lv.

SANDERS. Mrs., particular acquaintance of Mrs. Bardell. *P.P.* xxvi.

A big, fat, heavy-faced personage.

SANFORD. Master Harry, Pupil of Mr. Barlow. *U.T.* xxxiii.

SANDGATE-BY-THE-SEA. *M.P., S.F.A.*

SANDHURST. *M.P., G.D.*

SANDUSKY. *A.N.* xiv.

SANGAR POINT. *C.S., W.o.G.M.*

SANTENSE'S. Madame. *O.M.F.* xi.

SAONE. The river. *L.D.* xi. ; *R.P., D.W.T.T.*

Like a sullied looking-glass in a gloomy place, reflected the clouds heavily; and the low banks leaned over here and there, as if they were half-curious, and half-afraid, to see their darkening pictures in the water.

SAPPER. A huge-bearded. *U.T.* vii.

SAPSEA. Maid of Mr. *E.D.* iv.

SAPSEA. Mr. Thomas, Auctioneer. *E.D.* iv.

Dresses as the Dean—has been bowed to for the Dean—spoken to as my Lord, under the impression that he was the Bishop—without his chaplain. Much nearer sixty years of age than fifty, with flowing outline of stomach—reputed to be rich.

Note.—The pompous Mayor of Cloisterham. An auctioneer reputed to be rich. He may be considered almost as one of the auxiliary characters of the book, as, so far as the story goes, he occupies a quite subsidiary place. When introduced he is composing an epitaph for his wife's tomb, as follows:

Ethelinda,
Reverential Wife of
Mr. Thomas Sapsea,
Auctioneer, valuer, estate agent, etc.,
of this city.
Whose knowledge of the world,
Though somewhat extensive.
Never brought him acquainted with
A spirit

More capable of
Looking up to him.
Stranger, pause
And ask thyself the Question,
Canst thou do likewise /
If not,
With a blush retire.

At the last mention in the book he has just made the acquaintance of Datchery.

SAPSEA. The late Mrs., Ethelinda. *E.D.* iv.

" **SARACEN'S HEAD.**" Snow Hill. *N.N.* iii.; *O.M.F.* xlix.; *U.T.* iii.

" **SARACEN'S HEAD.**" Towcester. *P.P.* li.

" Everything clean and comfortable. Wery good little dinner, sir, they can get ready in half an hour —pair of fowls, sir, and a weal cutlet; French beans, taturs, tart, and tidiness."

SARAH. *P.P.* xli.

SARAH. Domestic at Westgate House. *P.P.* xvi.

SARAH. Maid of old lady. *S.B.B.*, *O.P.* ii.

SARAH. Seven Dials lady. *S.B.B.*, Scenes v.

SARAH'S SON'S HEAD. *See* Saracen's Head.

SATIS HOUSE. The Manor House. *G.E.* viii.

SAUNDERS. *S.Y.C.*.

SAUNDERS. Robt. L. *M.P.*, *O.C.*

SAVAGE. A baby; a waif. *C.B.*, *H.M.* i.

A creature more like a young wild animal than a young child—a bundle of tatters, held by a hand, in size and form almost an infant's, but in its greedy—clutch, a bald old man's—a face rounded and smoothed by some half-dozen years, but—twisted by the experience of a life. Bright eyes, but not youthful —naked feet, beautiful in their childish delicacy—ugly in the blood and dirt that cracked upon them.

SAVAGE. The noble. *R.T.*, *T.N.S.*

SAVANNAH. The. *B.R.* lxxii.

SAVILLE. Sir George. *B.R.* lvi.

SAVILLE ROW. *U.T.* xvi.

SAVIOUR. The. *M.P.*, *I.M.*

SAWBONES. A couple of surgeons. *See* Allen Benjamin, and Sawyer Bob.

SAWYER. Bob, Very particular friend of Mr. Benjamin Allen. *P.P.* xxx.

Wore a pair of plaid trousers, and a large double-breasted waistcoat; out of doors he carried a stick with a big top. He eschewed gloves, and looked upon the whole, something like a dissipated Robinson Crusoe.

Note.—A medical student, friend of Benjamin Allen. He sets up as a chemist-medical-practitioner in Bristol, but in spite of many artful dodges, does not succeed. He eventually passes through the Gazette and accompanies Benjamin Allen to Bengal in the service of the East India Company.

SAWYER. Mr. *M.R.B.*

SAWYER. Visitor to Bob. *P.P.* xxxii.

Prim personage in clean linen and cloth boots.

SCADDER. Mr. Zephaniah, Agent for the Eden Settlement. *M.C.* xxi.

He was a gaunt man in a huge straw hat, and a coat of green stuff —he had no cravat and wore his shirt-collar wide open; so that every time he spoke something was seen to twitch and jerk up in his throat like the little hammers in a harpischord when the notes are struck. Two grey eyes lurked deep within this agent's head but one of them had no sight in it, and stood stockstill. Each long black hair upon his head hung down as straight as any plummet-line; but rumpled tufts were on the arches of his eyes.

Note.—This land-agent was a typical real estate swindler. While he does not lie enough perhaps to bring him within the American law of the time, he conveys the impression that Eden is a thriving city, and sells Martin Chuzzlewit a " lot " of fifty acres. The " city " turns out to be all in the future, its present consisting of a few log huts; the property, a morass, and the population a handful of broken settlers dying under the ravages of fever.

SCADGERS. Lady, Great-aunt of Mrs. Sparsit. *H.T.*, *S.* vii.

An immensely fat old woman, with an inordinate appetite for butcher's meat, and a mysterious leg which had now refused to get out of bed for fourteen years.

SCALA. Santa, or Holy Staircase. *P.F.I.*, *R.*

SCALEY. Mr., A bailiff. *N.N.* xxi.

Proprietor of a white hat, and a red neckerchief, and a broad round face, and a large head, and part of a green coat.

SCALP. An Indian chief. *A.N.* ix.

SCARBOROUGH. *D. and S.* xxi.; *H.D.* iv.

SCARLI TAPA. *M.P.*, *T O.H.*

Red tape.

SCARLI TAPA. Son of. *M.P.*, *T.O.H.*

SCARLI TAPA. Wife of. *M.P.*, *T.O.H.*

SCAVENGERS. Theatre of the. *M.P.*, *N.Y.D.*

SCEAUX. *R.P.*, *M.O.F.F.*

SCHLESINGER. Mr. *M.P.*, *I.W.M.*

SCHŎN. Mr., Missionary. *M.P.*, *N.E.*

SCHOOL. *O.C.S.* xxiv.

SCHOOL. *R.P.*, *S.S.*

SCHOOL. High, Cloisterham. *E.D.* xiv.

SCHOOL. In Canterbury. *D.C.* xvi.

A grave building in a courtyard with a learned air about it.

SCHOOL. Ladies, late shop. *S.B.B.*, Scenes iii.

SCHOOL. Our. *R.P.*, *O.S.*

SCHOOLBOYS. Three or four. *S.B.B.*, Scenes i.

On a stolen bathing expedition.

SCHOOLMASTER. *O.C.S.* xxiv.

SCHOOLMASTER. At the Tooting Farm. *M.P.*, *P.S.*

SCHOOLMASTER. Former, of Scrooge. *C.B.*, *C.C.*, *S.* ii.

SCHOOLMASTER. Our. *S.B.B.*, *O.P.* i.

One of those men one occasionally hears of on whom misfortune seems to have set her mark. His talents were great; his disposition easy, generous, and liberal. His friends profited by the one, and abused the other. He is an old man now. He had never cared for himself, the only being who had cared for him—was spared to him no longer—meek, uncomplaining and zealous.

SCHOOLS. Day, In Seven Dials. *S.B.B.*, Scenes v.

SCHUTZ. Mr., A passenger on the "Halsewell." *R.P.*, *T.L.V.*

SCIENTIFIC GENTLEMAN. *P.P.* xxxix.

An elderly gentleman of scientific attainments, writing a philosophical treatise. In the agonies of composition, the elderly gentleman looked sometimes at the carpet, sometimes at the ceiling, and sometimes at the wall.

SCIENTIFIC SHOEING - SMITH AND VETERINARY SURGEON. *U.T.* xxii.

SCOTCH FELLOWS. Three or four, Guests of the Baillie. *P.P.* lxix.

Stout, bushy-eyebrowed, canny old Scotch fellows that the Baillie had got together to do honour to my uncle.

SCOTLAND. *B.R.* lxxxii.; *M.P.*, *A. in E.*; *M.P.*, *O.C.*; *M.P.*, *R.S.*

SCOTLAND YARD. *S.B.B.*, Scenes iv.

SCOTT. Miss. *M.P.*, *S.P.*

SCOTT. Sir Walter. *M.P.*, *M.B.*; *M.P.*, *S.P.*

SCOTT. Tom, Quilp's boy. *O.C.S.* l.

Note.—Quilp's errand-boy. He is nearly as eccentric as Quilp himself, which may account for the affection or sympathy existing between them, in spite of Quilp's brutality to him. On Quilp's death he becomes an Italian tumbler, thus putting to effective use the accomplishment he had acquired and used for Quilp's annoyance.

SCOUTS. Hangers-on and outsiders about Doctors' Commons. *D.C.* x.

SCRADGER. Mr. *M.P.*, *W.H.*

SCREWZER. Tommy. *D. and S.* lxi.

A man of an extremely bilious habit.

SCRIVENS. *M.P.*, *C. Pat.*

SCROGGINS. Sir Giles. *M.P.*, *W.*

SCROGGINS AND PAYNE. Messrs. Solicitors. *S.B.B.*, Tales vii.

SCROOGE. Counting-house of old. *C.B.*, *C.C.*, *S.* i.

The door of Scrooge's counting-house was open that he might keep his eye upon his clerk, who, in a dismal little cell beyond, a sort of tank, was copying letters.

SCROOGE. Ebenezer. Of Scrooge and Marley. On 'change. *C.B.*, *C.C.*, *S.* i.

A squeezing, wrenching, grasping, scraping, clutching, covetous old sinner. Hard and sharp as flint—secret—and solitary as an oyster. The cold within him froze his old features, nipped his pointed nose, shrivelled his cheek, stiffened his gait; made his eyes red, his thin lips blue, and spoke out shrewdly in his grating voice.

SCROOGE. Father of. *C.B.*, *C.C.*, *S.* ii.

SCROOGE. Niece by marriage of. *C.B.*, *C.C.*, *S.* iii.

SCROOGE. Ruin of school attended by. *C.B.*, *C.C.S.* ii.

SCROOGE. Spirit of sister of. *C.B.*, *C.C.*, *S.* i.

SCROOGE'S CHAMBERS. *C.B.*, *C.C.*, *S.* i.

A gloomy suite of rooms, in a lowering pile of building up a yard. It was old enough—and dreary enough, for nobody lived in it but Scrooge, the other rooms being all let out as offices.

SCROOGE'S NEPHEW. *C.B.*, *C.C.*, *S.* i.

SCROOGE'S NIECE'S SISTER. *C.B.*, *C.C.*, *S.* iii.

The plump one with the lace tucker.

SCUTARI. *M.P.*, *S.F.A.*; *M.P.*, *T.T.*

SEA-CAPTAIN. *M.P.*, *L.E.J.*

SEACOMBE. *R.P.*, *T.L.V.*

SEALER. Deputy. *R.P.*, *P.M.T.P.*

SEAMAN. Rough. *M.P.*, *S.W.*

SEAMAN'S BOARDING-HOUSE. *O.M.F.* xxix.

SEAMAN'S HOMES. *U.T.* v.

SEAMSTRESS. Little. *T.T.C.*, bk.iii., ch. xiii.

SEAPORT. (Chatham.) *M.P.*, *N.Y.D.*

SEARLE'S YARD. Boating establishment. *S.B.B.*, Scenes x.

SEBASTOPOOL. *M.P.*, *T.O.P.*; *M.P.*, *T.T.*

SEBASTOPOL. Boulevard de. *U.T.* xviii.

SECRETARY. Pickwick Club. *P.P.* i.

SECRETARY TO THE POST-OFFICE. *M.P.*, *M.E.R.*

SEDAN-CHAIR. Bearers of., *P.P.* xxxvi.

One short fat chairman, and one long thin one.

SEINE. The. *R.P.*, *D.W.T.T.*

SELF AND CRAGGS. Snitchey and Craggs. *C.B.*, *B.o.L.* i.

SEMANDRÈ. *M.P.*, *L.A.V.* i.

SEMINARY. National. *S.B.B.*, *O.P.* vi.

SEMINARY. Thieves' kitchen and. *R.P.*, *D.W.I.F.*

SEMPRONIUS. Mr., Son of Gattleton. *S.B.B.*, Tales ix.

SEN' GEORGE'S CHANNEL. *D. and S.* xxiii.

SENATE. The, "A dignified and decorous body." *A.N.* iii.; *M.P.*, *Y.M.C.*

SENATOR. A certain. *M.P.*, *W.*

SENECAS. Indians. *A.N.* xvii.

SENEGAL. *M.P.*, *L.A.V.* ii.

SENIOR UNITED SERVICE CLUB HOUSE. *M.P.*, *B.A.*

SENS. *C.S.*, *M.L. Leg.* i.; *P.F.I.*, *G.T.F.*

SENTRY. At Chatham Dockyard,. *U.T.* xxiv.

SEPTIMUS. Nephew of Mr. Booley, *M.P.*, *E.T.*

SERAGLIO. *C.S.*, *H.H.*

SERAPHINA. Daughter of schoolmaster. *C.S.*, *M.L.Lo.* ii.

Had brown hair all curling beautifully.

SERAPHINA. Lady. *L.D.* xvii.

SERGEANT. *G.E.* v.

SERGEANT. Recruiting. *B.R.* xxxi.

SERGEANT. Returned from India. *U.T.* viii.

A man of very intelligent countenance.

SERJAMESES STREET. St. James' Street. *U.T.* xvi.

SERJEANT-AT-ARMS. *S.B.B.*, Scenes xviii.

SERJEANT'S INN. *P.P.* xl.

SERJEANTS. Three. *P.P.* xxxiv.

SERVANT. *M.P.*, *L.*

SERVANT. Another, of J.P. *B.R.* xlvii.

SERVANT. At the Warren. *B.R.* xiv.

SERVANT. In livery of old gentleman. *S.B.B.*, *O.P.*, v.

SERVANT. John. *M.P.*, *I.S.H.W.*

SERVANT. Lodger's, Of Mrs. Raddles. *P.P.* xlvi.

SERVANT. Miss Madeline Bray's. *N.N.* xlvi.

SERVANT. Mr. Boythorn's man. *B.H.* ix.

SERVANT. Of Catholic gentleman. *B.R.* lxi.

SERVANT. Of Mr. and Mrs. Parsons. *S.B.B.*, Tales x.

A middle-aged female.

SERVANT. Shivering, Of passenger by early coach. *S.B.B.*, Scenes xvi.

SERVANT GIRL. *M.P.*, *N.Y.D.*

SERVANT GIRL. Of the Wilfers. *O.M.F.* iv.

SERVANT GIRL. Of lady in distress. *S.B.B.*, *O.P.* v.

SERVANT GIRL. Young, Employed by Squeers. *N.N.* vii.

SERVANT MAID. Of Miss Havisham. *G.E.* xxix.

SERVANTS. *S.B.B.*, Scenes i.

SERVANTS. Of all work. *S.B.B.*, Scenes i.

SERVANTS. Of hotel in Brook Street. *L.D.* lii.

SERVANTS. Of Mr. John Jarndyce. *B.H.* xxxi.

SERVANTS. Two female, Of Mrs. Tibbs. *S.B.B.*, Tales i.

SESSIONS HOUSE. The. *B.R.* lxv.

SESSIONS HOUSE. Wards of. *S.B.B.* Scenes xxv.

There are several (wards) in this part of the building but a description of one is a description of the whole. A spacious, bare, whitewashed apartment, lighted of course, by windows looking into the interior of the prison—a large fire with a deal table before it—along both sides of the room ran a shelf, below it, a row of large hooks—on each of which was hung the sleeping mat of a prisoner, her rug and blanket on the shelf above.

SESSIONS HOUSE PRISON YARD. *S.B.B.*, Scenes xxv.

One side of this yard is railed off, at a considerable distance, and formed into a kind of iron cage, about five feet ten inches in height, roofed at the top, and defended in front by iron bars, from which the friends of the female prisoners communicate with them.

SESSIONS HOUSE PRISON YARD. Another prisoner in. *S.B.B.*, Scenes xxv.

A squalid-looking woman, in a slovenly, thick-bordered cap, with her arms mufiled in a large red shawl.

SESSION HOUSE PRISON YARD. A visitor in. *S.B.B.*, Scenes xxv.

A yellow, haggard, decrepit old woman, in a tattered gown that had once been black, and the remains of an old straw bonnet, with faded ribbons of the same hue.

SESSIONS HOUSE YARD. Prisoner's visitor. *S.B.B.*, Scenes xxv.

Thinly clad, and shaking with the cold. Barely past her childhood, it required but a glance to discover that she was one of those children, born and bred in neglect and vice, who have never known what childhood is.

SESSIONS HOUSE PRISON YARD. Prisoner in. *S.B.B.*, Scenes xxv.

A young girl—of about two-and-twenty. A good-looking, robust female, with a profusion of hair streaming about in the wind—for she had no bonnet on—and a man's silk pocket-handkerchief loosely thrown over a most ample pair of shoulders. Hardened beyond all hope of redemption, she listened doggedly to her mother's entreaties.

" **SETTING MOON.**" The, Public-house. *R.P., T.D.P.*

SETTLER. Eldest son of, In Eden. *M.C.* xxiii.

Has a chill upon him, and is lying wrapped up in the blankets.

SETTLER. In Eden. *M.C.* xxiii.

He was pale and worn, and—his anxious eye was deeply sunken in his head. His dress of home-spun blue hung about him in rags, his feet and head were bare.

SETTLER'S YOUNGEST SON. In Eden. *M.C.* xxiii.

SETTLERS. At Eden Settlement. *M.C.* xxiii.

Some half dozen men—wan and forlorn to look at, but ready enough to assist. They shook their heads in speaking of the Settlement. Those who had the means of going away had all deserted it. They who were left had lost their wives, their children, friends, or brothers there, and suffered much themselves.

" **SEVEN BELLS.**" The, An inn. *R.P., T.S.S.*

SEVEN DIALS. *A.N.* vi. ; *M.P., S.D.C.* ; *N.N.* lxiv. ; *R.P., B.S.* ; *S.B.B.*, Scenes v.

Where is there such another maze of streets, courts, lanes, and alleys? The streets and courts dart in all directions until they are lost in the unwholesome vapour which hangs over the house-tops, and renders the dirty perspective uncertain and confined.

SEVEN HILLS. *L.D.* li.

SEWER. New York. *M.C.* xvi.

SEWERS. Hon. Board of Commissioners of. *M.P., L.W.O.Y.*

SEXTON. *L.D.* xiv.

SEXTON. *O.C.S.* xxv.

SEXTON. At church where Paul was christened. *D. and S.* v.

SEXTON. Of church where Walter and Florence are married. *D. and S.* lvii.

The shabby little old man, ringer of the disappointed bell, is standing in the porch, and has put his hat in the font, for he is quite at home there, being sexton.

SEYMOUR. Lord, Member for Totnes. *M.P., I.W.M.*

SHABBY-GENTEEL MAN. *S.B.B.*, Char. x.

Clad in an old rusty and thread-bare black cloth, which shines with constant wear as if it had been bees-waxed. The trousers tightly strapped down, partly for the look of the thing and partly to keep his old shoes from slipping off at the heels—his yellowish-white neckerchief is carefully pinned up, to conceal the tattered garment underneath, and his hands are encased in the remains of an old pair of beaver gloves—you may set him down as a shabby-genteel man.

SHADWELL CHURCH. *U.T.* xx.

SHAFTESBURY. Lord. *U.T.* xvi.

SHAKER. A grim old. *A.N.* xv.

" **SHAKER VILLAGE.** The." Peopled by " shakers." *A.N.* xv.

SHAKESPEARE. *A.N.* vii. ; *D. and S.* lxi. ; *E.D.* ix. ; *L.D.* xii. ; *M.P E.S.* ; *M.P., G.D.* ; *M.P., O.F.A.* ; *M.P., S.* ; *M.P., R.S.L.* ; *M.P., P.S.* ; *M.P., R.G.* ; *M.P., W.* ; *O.M.F.* ii. ; *P.P.* xli. ; *R.P., T.B.W.* ; *R.P., T.N.S.* ; *U.T.* iv.

SHALLOW FAMILY. Justices. *M.P., S.D.C.*

SHANKLIN. *O.M.F.* x.

SHARKEY. A. C., *A.N.* xvii.

SHARP. Mr., First master at Salem House. *D.C.* vi.

Mr. Mell took his meals with the boys, but Mr. Sharp dined and supped at Mr. Creakle's table. He was a limp, delicate-looking gentleman, I thought, with a good deal of nose.

SHARPER. Abandoned. *M.P., T.T.C.D.*

SHARPEYE. Of Liverpool police force. *U.T.* v.

SHAWNEES. Indians. *A.N.* xvii.

"**SHED.**" A, near Maiden Lane. *S.B.B.*, Scenes xx.

A wooden house with windows stuffed with rags and paper, and a small yard at the side, with one dust-cart, two baskets, a few shovels, and little heaps of cinders, and fragments of china, and tiles, scattered about it.

SHEEN AND GLOSS. Mercers. *B.H.* ii.

SHEEPSKIN. Name of a bird. *B.H.* xiv.

SHEERNESS. *C.S., S.P.T.* iii.

SHE-GOBLIN. *P.F.I., L.R.G.A.*

SHELLEY. The grave of. *P.F.I., R.*

SHEPHERD. Miss, A boarder at the Misses Nettingall's establishment. *D.C.* xviii.

A little girl, in a spencer, with a round face, and curly flaxen hair.

SHEPHERD. The, Methodistical. *P.P.* xxii.

"A great fat chap in black, with a great white face, and a smilin' avay like clockwork."

SHEPHERDSON. Mr., A butcher thief. *R.P., T.D.P.*

SHEPPERTON. *O.T.* xxi.

SHERMAN. Captain, Commander of the steamboat "Burlington." *A.N.* xv.

SHERRIFF. A. *M.H.C.* i.

SHERRIFFS. The. *D. and S.* xxv.

SHERRIFFS. The. *S.B.B.*, Scenes xxiv.

SHERRIFFS'. The. *S.B.B.*, Scenes xix.

SHINY WILLIAM. Deputy hostler at the "Bull Inn," Rochester. *P.P.* v.

"**SHIP.**" Landlord of the. *G.E.* liv.

A weakly, meditative man, with a pale eye.

"**SHIP.**" The. A public-house. *G.E.* liv.

SHOE LANE. *M.P., J.S.P.*; *S.B.B.*, Scenes xvi.

"**SHOEMAKER.**" *M.P., O.S.*

SHOOTER'S HILL. *C.S., H.T.*; *P.P.* lvii.; *T.T.C.* ii.; *U.T.* vii.

SHOOTING GALLERY. George's. *B.H.* xxi.

A great brick building, composed of bare walls, floors, roof-rafters, and skylights.

SHOP. Barber's, Child at. *C.S., S.L.* ii.

A mere baby—dressed in the close white linen cap, which small French country children wear—and a frock of homespun blue, that had no shape except where it was tied round her little fat throat.

SHOP. Chandler's, In Seven Dials. *S.B.B.*, Scenes v.

SHOP. Converted into two. *S.B.B.*, Scenes iii.

One a bonnet-shape maker's, the other was opened by a tobacconist, who also dealt in walking-sticks and Sunday Newspapers.

SHOP. Empty, in Dover. Where David rested. *D.C.* xiii.

SHOP. Handsome, originally private house. *S.B.B.*, Scenes iii.

Linen-drapery and haberdashery.

SHOP. Lumps of delight. *E.D.* iii.

SHOP. One, A Sample of the rest. *S.B.B.*, Scenes iii.

Originally a substantial, good-looking private house.

SHOP. Our, Schoolroom at Dotheboys' Hall. *N.N.* viii.

A bare and dirty room, with a couple of windows, whereof a tenth part might be of glass, the remainder being stopped up with old copy-books and paper. There were a couple of long, old, rickety desks, cut and notched, and inked, and damaged in every possible way; two or three forms, a detached desk for Squeers; and another for his assistant. The ceiling was supported, like that of a barn, by cross beams and rafters; and the walls were so stained and discoloured, that it was impossible to tell whether they had ever been touched with paint or whitewash.

SHOP. Proprietor—and Co. *S.B.B.*, Scenes iii.

Did nothing but walk up and down the shop, and hand seats to the ladies.

SHOP. Tobacconist's. *S.B.B.*, Scenes iii.

Succeeded by a theatrical hairdresser.

SHOP. Young men in. *S.B.B.*, Scenes iii.

Such elegant men.

SHOPBOYS. Patrons of private theatres. *S.B.B.*, Scenes xiii.

Who now and then mistake their masters' money for their own.

SHOPMAN. Mr. Pumblechook's. *G.E.* viii.

SHOPMEN. *S.B.B.*, Scenes i.

Engaged in cleaning and decking the windows for the day.

SHOPS. Gin, In the rookery. *S.B.B.*, Scenes xxii.

All is light and brilliancy. The gay building with the fantastically ornamented parapet, the illuminated clock, the plate-glass windows surrounded by stucco rosettes, and its profusion of gaslights in richly-gilt burners, is perfectly dazzling. A bar of French polished mahogany, elegantly carved, extends the whole width of the place.

SHOPS. Twenty. *S.B.B.*, Scenes iii.

Which we are quite sure have paid no taxes for the last six years.

SHORE. Jane. *R.P.*, *A.C.T.*

SHOREDITCH. *O.T.* xxi. : *R.P.*, *B.S.*

SHOREDITCH CHURCH. *M.P.*, *A.P.*

SHORT. One of prisoners taken by pirates. *C.S.*, *P.o.C.E.P.*

SHORT. Trotters. " Punch " showman. *See* Harris.

SHORTHAND WRITERS. In High Court of Chancery. *B.H.* i.

SHORT-TIMERS. School-children. *U.T.* xxix.

SHOT TOWER. *S.B.B.*, Scenes iv.

SHOW-TRAMP. *U.T.* xi.

SHREWSBURY SCHOOL. *T.T.C.* bk. ii. ; ch. iii.

The old Sydney Carton of old Shrewsbury School.

SHROPSHIRE. *D. and S.* xxxvi.

SHYLOCK. *G.E.* xliii. ; *P.F.I.*, *A.I.D.*

SIBTHORP. Great. *M.P.*, *S. for P.*

SIBYL. Temple of the. *P.F.I.*, *R.*

SIDDONS. Mrs. *M.P.*, *S.P.*

SIDNEY. Master, As Little Walter Wilding. *M.P.*, *N.T.*

SIDNEY. Mr., As John Johnson. *M.P.*, *S.G.*

SIENA. *P.F.I.*, *R.P.S.*

SIERRA LEONE. *M.P.*, *N.E.*

SIGHT. Goblin, Elfin creatures of the Bells. *C.B.*, *C.*, q. iii.

Leaping, flying, dropping, pouring from the Bells without a pause.

SIGNALL HILL. *C.S.*, *P.o.C.E.P.*

SIGNAL-BOX. *C.S.*, *T.G.S.* ii.

There was a fire, a desk for an official book in which he had to make certain entries, a telegraphic instrument with its dial, face, and needles.

SIGNALMAN. The. *C.S.*, *T.G.S.* ii.

A dark sallow man, with a dark beard and rather heavy eyebrows.

SIGNET. Clerk of the. *R.P.*, *P.M.T.P.*

SIGNET OFFICE. *R.P.*, *P.M.T.P.*

SIKES. Bill, A burglar. *O.T.* xiii.

A stoutly-built fellow of about five-and-thirty, in a black velveteen coat, very soiled drab breeches, lace-up half-boots, and grey cotton stockings, which inclosed a bulky pair of legs, with large swelling calves. He had a brown hat on his head, and a dirty belcher handkerchief round his neck.

Note.—Sikes with his mistress Nancy are the two figures which do most to carry out Dickens' object in writing this story of crime. Sikes is the most villainous character of the whole gang, of whom even Fagin is afraid. He is common thief, burglar, and becomes a murderer. As he first enters the story he receives the sprinkled contents of a pot of beer in his face. The pot was thrown by Fagin at the Artful Dodger. Sikes plans to carry out a burglary at Mrs. Maylie's house, and Fagin sends Oliver with him and Toby Crackit, to crawl through the window and to open the door. The scheme miscarries and Oliver is snatched from Fagin's clutches. Nancy discloses the secret to Rose Maylie, and Fagin, who discovers what he thinks is the girl's treachery, tells Sikes. The Burglar beats out Nancy's brains with his pistol and club. He immediately escapes to the country. But everywhere he goes he feels himeslf marked, and he returns to one of the thieves' haunts, on Jacob's Island bordering on the Folly Ditch. His former friends shrink from him, however, and Charley Bates shrieks for the police from the window. Sikes seeing all other means of escape cut off, attempted to leave by the ditch. He fastened one end of his rope round the chimney stack, and was adjusting the other in a loop beneath his armpits, when he glanced up and saw, in imagination, Nancy's eyes. He staggered and lost his balance, and the noose tightened round his neck as he fell for thirty-five feet. His dog attempted to jump to him and fell into the ditch, where he was killed.

SILENT GENTLEMAN. Interviewing Martin. *M.C.* xxii.

With glazed and fishy eyes, and only one button on his waistcoat (which was a very large metal one, and shone prodigiously) got behind the door, and stood there, like a clock, long after everybody else was gone.

SILSILEH. *M.P., E.T.*

SILVER-STORE. The Island of. *C.S., P.o.C.E.P.*

SILVER STREET. Golden Square. *N.N.* vii.

SILVERMAN. George, An orphan. *G.S.E.* i.

A worldly little devil was my mother's name for me.

SILVERSMITHS. In Chalons. *L.D.* xi.

SILVIA. *C.S., G.S.E.* v.

SIMKIN AND GREEN'S MANAGING CLERK. *P.P.* xx.

SIMMERY. Mr. *P.P.* lv.

SIMMONDS. Miss, In Madame Mantalini's employ. *N.N.* xviii.

SIMMONS. Mrs. Henrietta, Another of Mrs. Quilp's visitors. *O.C.S.* iv.

SIMMONS. The parish beadle. *S.B.B., O.P.* i.

Perhaps the most important member of the local administration. The dignity of his office is never impaired by the absence of efforts on his part to maintain it. On Sunday in his state-coat and cocked hat with a large-headed staff for show in his left hand, and a small cane for use in his right. . . With the glare of the eye peculiar to beadles.

SIMMONS. William, van driver. *M.C.* xiii.

A red-faced, burly young fellow; smart in his way, and with a good-humoured countenance—his spruce appearance was sufficiently explained by his connection with a large stage-coaching establishment.

SIMON. Negro man slave. *A.N.* xvii.

SIMON. Servant of J.P. *B.R.* xlvii.

SIMPLON. Pass. *C.S., N.T.* Act iii.; *L.D.* xxxix.; *P.F.I., V.M.M.S.S.*

SIMPSON. Mr., A Boarder at Mrs. Tibb's. *S.B.B.*, Tales i.

As empty-headed as the great bell of St. Paul's; always dressed according to the caricatures published in the monthly fashions; obtained engagement at a fashionable hairdresser's.

SIMPSON. Mr., Prisoner in the Fleet. *P.P.* xlii.

Leaning out of the window as far as he could without overbalancing himself, endeavouring, with great perseverance, to spit upon the crown of the hat of a personal friend on the parade below.

SIMPSON. Mr. Shepherdson. *R.P., T.D.P.*

SIMPSON. The late Mr. *S.B.B.*, Scenes xiv.

SIMSON. Mr., One of steam excursion party. *S.B.B.*, Tales vii.

SINBAD THE SAILOR. *M.P., G.A.*

SING. HE, Mandarin passenger. *M.P., C.J.*

SING. SAM, *M.P., C.J.*

SING SING. Prison for the State at. *A.N.* vi.

SINGER. At harmonic meeting. *S.B.B.*, Scenes ii.

Stout man with the small voice with brown small surtout, white stockings and shoes, is in the comic line.

SINGER. Comic. *S.B.B.*, Scenes xi.

The public-house chairman.

SINGERS. Four something-ean : in the costume of their country. *P.P* xv.

SINGLE GENTLEMAN. Lodger wanted by the City Clerk. *S.B.B.*, *O.P.* vii.

Good-humoured looking gentleman of about five-and-thirty—invited friends home, who used to come at ten o'clock and begin to get happy about the small hours.

SIR SOMEBODY'S HEAD. A public-house. *S.B.B.*, Char. vii.

SISTINE CHAPEL. *P.F.I.*, *R.*

SISTER. A little. *M.P.*, *N.Y.D.*

SISTER. Of Mr. Allen's aunt. *P.P.* xlviii.

Who keeps the large boarding-school just beyond the third mile-stone—where there is a very large laburnum tree and an oak gate.

SISTER. Tim Linkinwater's. *N.N.* lxiii.

The chubby old lady.

SISTER. Twin (deceased) of Pet's. *L.D.* ii.

Who died when we could just see her eyes—exactly like Pet's—above the table, as she stood on tiptoe holding by it.

SISTER OF MRS. KENWIG'S. *N.N.* xi.

Sister of Mrs. Kenwigs—quite a beauty.

SISTERS. The Weird, Characters of play. *S.B.B.*, Scenes xiii.

Three uncouth-looking figures, with broken clothes-props in their hands, who are drinking gin and water out of a pint pot.

SISTERS OF YORK. Five. *N.N.* vi.

Tall stately figures, with dark flashing eyes and hair of jet ; dignity and grace were in their every movement ; and the fame of their great beauty had spread through all the country round.

" **SITTERS.**" Two, Passengers in four-oared galley. *G.E.* liv.

SITTINGBOURNE. *L.D.* liv.

" **SIX JOLLY FELLOWSHIP-PORTERS.**" *O.M.F.* iii.

A tavern of dropsical appearance, had long settled down into a state of hale infirmity. In its whole constitution it had not a straight floor, and hardly a straight line, but it had outlasted many a better trimmed building. Externally it was a narrow, lopsided, wooden jumble of corpulent windows, heaped one upon the other.

SIX MILE ISLAND. *A.N.* xvii.

SKELETON. A living, Exhibited at Greenwich Fair. *S.B.B.*, Scenes xii.

SKETTLES. Lady, Wife of Sir Barnet. *D. and S.* xiv.

SKETTLES. Master, Prospective pupil at Dr. Blimber's. *D. and S.* xiv.

Revenging himself for the studies to come, on the plum-cake.

SKETTLES. Sir Barnet, Guest of Dr. Blimber. *D. and S.* xiv.

In the House of Commons, and of whom Mr Feeder said that when he *did* catch the speaker's eye (which he had been expected to do for three or four years) it was anticipated that he would rather touch up the radicals.

SKETTLES. Residence of. *D. and S.* xxiii.

A pretty villa at Fulham, on the banks of the Thames, which was one of the most desirable residences in the world when a rowing match happened to be going past, but had its little inconveniences at other times, among which may be enumerated the occasional appearance of the river in the drawing-room, and the contemporaneous disappearance of the lawn and shrubbery.

SKEWTON. Friends of Mrs. *D. and S.* xxxvi.

Guests at Dombey's housewarming.

With the same bright bloom on their complexion, and very precious necklaces on very withered necks.

SKEWTON. The Honourable Mrs. Mrs. Granger's mama. *D. and S.* xxi.

Although the lady was not young, she was very blooming in the face—quite rosy—and her dress and attitude were perfectly juvenile, her age, which was about seventy—her dress would have been youthful for twenty-seven. . . . What I have ever sighed for has been to retreat to a Swiss farm, and live entirely surrounded by cows—and china.

SKIDDAW. *L.T.* i.

SKIFFINS. An acccountant and agent, Miss Skiffin's brother. *G.E.* xxxvii.

SKIFFINS. Miss. *G.E.* xxxvii.

Was of a wooden appearance—the cut of her dress from the waist upwards, both before and behind, made her figure very like a boy's kite—her gown a little too decidedly orange, and her gloves a little too decidedly green.

SKIMPIN. Mr., Serjeant Buzfuz' junior barrister for Bardell. *P.P.* xxxiv.

SKIMPOLE. Arethusa. *B.H.* xliii.

" My beauty daughter—plays and sings odds and ends like her father."

SKIMPOLE. Children of Harold. *B.H.* vi.

SKIMPOLE. Harold, A musical man, and an artist too *B.H.* vi.; *M.P., L.H.*

" At least as old as I am "—but in simplicity, and freshness, and enthusiasm, and a fine inaptitude for all worldly affairs—a perfect child. A little bright creature, with a rather large head; but a delicate face, and a sweet voice—had more the appearance of a damaged young man than a well-preserved elderly one.

Note.—A friend of Mr. Jarndyce, upon whom he sponges. He is without principle and effects an absolute childishness about money, with the result that he is selfish. Originally a medical man, he has not sufficient strength of character to do anything. A coolness arose between him and Mr. Jarndyce, but his later history is given in brief. He died some five years afterwards, leaving a diary and letters behind him which were published.

SKIMPOLE. Kitty. *B.H.* xliii.

" My comedy daughter—sings a little, but don't play."

SKIMPOLE. Laura. *B.H.* xliii.

" My sentiment daughter—plays a little, but don't sing."

SKIMPOLE. Mrs., Wife of Harold Skimpole. *B.H.* xliii.

Who had once been a beauty, but was now a delicate, high-nosed invalid, suffering under a complication of disorders.

SKIM'S. Mrs., Private hotel and commercial lodging-house. *M.P., L.T.*

SKIRMISHERS. Refractories in Wapping workhouse. *U.T.* iii.

" **SKYLARK.**" Mr. *D.C.* ii.

A very nice man, with a very large head of red hair. . . . I thought " Skylark " was his name; and that as he lived on board ship, and hadn't a street door to put his name on, he put it on his chest instead.

SLACKBRIDGE. *H.T., R.* iv.

Chairman of United Aggregate Tribunal.

SLADDERY. Mr., Librarian. *B.H.* ii.

SLAMJAM COFFEE HOUSE. *C.S., S.L.* i.

SLAMMER. Mr., Surgeon to the 97th. Chatham Barracks. *P.P.* ii.

A little fat man, with a ring of upright black hair round his head, and an extensive bald plain on the top of it. The doctor took snuff with everybody, chatted with everybody, laughed, danced, made jokes, played whist, did everything, and was everywhere, at the Charity Ball, Rochester.

Note.—The surgeon of the Ninety-seventh Regiment, who feels himself affronted by Mr. Jingle in the affections of a wealthy widow. Jingle is dressed in Winkle's Pickwick coat, and as Jingle refuses his name, the doctor has only the evidence of the coat to go upon. Winkle receives the doctor's challenge to fight a duel, and supposes he was drunk. The affair goes as far as Winkle on the field with his eyes shut ready to fire, when Dr. Slammer of the ninety-seventh finds that Mr. Winkle is not the man. The affair was arranged, and the whole party left the field in a much more lively manner than they proceeded to it.

SLAMMONS, Mr. *See* Smike.

SLANG. Lord. *S.Y.C.*

SLAP. *M.P., M.N.D.*

"**SLAP BANG.**" A dining-house. *B.H.* xx.

SLAPPENBACHENHAUSEN. Baron. *S.B.B.*, Tales i.

SLASHER. Surgeon at St. Bartholomew's. *P.P.* xxxii.

Took a boy's leg out of the socket last week, boy ate five apples, and a gingerbread cake, exactly two minutes after it was all over—and he'd tell his mother if they didn't begin.

SLAUGHTER. Lieutenant, Friend of Captain Waters. *S.B.B.*, Tales iv.

SLAUGHTER. Mrs., Greengrocer, etc., of Great Twig Street. *M.P., A.N.*

SLAUGHTER. Young. *M.P., A.N.*

SLAUGHTER-HOUSES. *R.P., M.O.F.F.*

SLEARY. Miss Josephine, Daughter of Sleary. *H.T., S.* iii.

A pretty, fair-haired girl of eighteen—tied on a horse at two years old—had made a will at twelve—expressive of her desire to be drawn to the grave by two piebald ponies.

SLEARY. Owner of a circus. *H.T., S.* iii.

A stout modern statue—with one fixed eye, and one loose eye, and a voice (if it can be called so) like the efforts of a broken old pair of bellows, a flabby surface, and a muddled head which was never sober, and never drunk.

Note.—Proprietor of Sleary's Circus. He is kindly and gentle. When Tom Gradgrind's guilt is discovered, he hides the culprit, and when he is detected in his disguise, Sleary enables him to escape out of the country.

SLEEK. Dr., Of the City-free. *U.T.* xix.

SLEEPY HOLLOW. *A.N.* xv.

SLEIGHT. Hannah. *M.P., P.T.*

SLIDERSKEW. Peg, Arthur Gride's servant. *N.N.* li.

A short, thin, weasen, blear-eyed old woman, palsy-stricken and hideously ugly, wiping her shrivelled face upon her dirty apron.

Note.—Housekeeper to Arthur Gride, the Miserly usurer. She steals his box of documents in revenge for what she thought she had suffered at his hands. Squeers makes friends with her to obtain documents relating to Madeline Bray's fortune. In the end she "went beyond the seas" and never returned.

SLIMMERY. Frank, Friend of Wilkins Flasher, Esq. *P.P.* lv.

A very smart young gentleman, who wore his hat on his right whisker, killing flies with a ruler. Both gentlemen had very open waistcoats and very rolling collars,—very small boots—very big rings—very little watches—very large guard-chains and symmetrical inexpressibles, and scented pocket-handkerchiefs.

"**SLINGO.**" Dealer in horses. *L.D.* vii.

SLINKTON. Mr. Julius, A murderer. *H.D.* ii.

About forty or so, dark, exceedingly well dressed in black, being in mourning. His hair, which was elaborately brushed and oiled, was parted straight up the middle.

SLITHERS. Mr., Barber. *M.H.C.* i.

A very brisk, active little man, for he is, as it were, chubby all over, without being stout or unwieldy.

SLIVERSTONE. Mr. *S.Y.C.*

SLIVERSTONE. Mrs. *S.Y.C.*

SLOANE STREET. *N.N.* xxi.

SLOGGINS. *M.P., G.B.*; *M.P., N.G.K.*; and *M.P., S.F.A.*

SLOPPY. A love-child. *O M.F.* xvi.

A very long boy, with a very little head, and an open mouth of disproportionate capacity—parents never known—was brought up in the House. Too much of him longwise, too little of him broadwise.

Note.—First introduced "turning" [the mangle] for Betty Higden. He has been a street child, brought up at the workhouse and taken charge of by Betty. He is not very bright, but is assisted by the Boffin's and taught woodwork. He is last seen visiting Jenny Wren, promising to come again and to make her several things as specimens of his craft.

SLOTH. Mr. Wombwell's. *M.P., G.H.*

SLOUT. Mr. *O.T.* xxvii.

SLOWBOY. Maternal and paternal parents of Tilly Slowboy. *C.B., C.o.H.*

Were alike unknown to fame.

SLOWBOY. Miss, Tilly Slowboy. *C.B., C. o. H.* i.

Of a spare straight shape—insomuch that her garments appeared to be in constant danger of sliding off these sharp pegs, her shoulders.

SLUDBERRY. Complainant in brawling case. *S.B.B.*, Scenes viii.

SLUDBERRY. Thomas. *S.B.B.*, Scenes viii.

SLUDGE. A murderer. *R.P., O.B.*

SLUFFEN. Mr., A master sweep. *S.B.B.*, Scenes xx.

SLUG. Mr. *Mud. Pap.* i.

SLUM. Mr., A military gentleman, a poet. *O.C.S.* xxviii.

"Ask the perfumers, ask the blacking-makers, ask the hatters, ask the lottery office-keepers--ask any man among 'em what my poetry has done for him, and mark my words he blesses the name of Slum. . . . Then upon my soul and honour, ma'am, you'll find in a certain angle of that dreary pile, called Poet's Corner, a few smaller names than Slum."

SLUMKEY. The, Hon. Samuel of Slumkey Hall. *P.P.* xiii.

Blue candidate for Parliament for Eatanswill, in top boots, and blue neckerchief, patted the babies on the head, kissed one of 'em.

SLUMKEY'S MAN. Agent. *P.P.* xiii.

SLUMMERY. Mr. *S.Y.C.*

SLUMMINTOWKENS. Friends of the Nupkins. *P.P.* xxv.

SLURK. *P.P.* li.

Note.—Editor of the *Eatanswill Independnt*, and on that account the opponent of Mr. Pott.

SLY. Mr., Of "King's Arms" and Royal Hotel. *C.S., D.M.*

SLYBOOTS. A, Mr. Krook. *B.H.* xxxii.

SLYME. Chevy. *M.C.* iv.

Perpetually round the corner. Wrapped in an old blue camlet cloak with a lining of faded scarlet. His sharp features being much pinched and nipped by long waiting in the cold, and his straggling red whiskers and frowzy hair being more than usually dishevelled from the same cause; he certainly looked rather unwholesome and uncomfortable than Shakespearian or Miltonic —"Too insolent to lick the hand that fed him in his need, yet cur enough to bite and tear it in the dark."

Note.—A kinsman of old Martin Chuzzlewit and, like so many of his relatives, with an eye on the old man's money. He engages in several occupations, but is a general failure. He is last seen as a police officer engaged in the arrest of Jonas Chuzzlewit. He says he has taken up the work to shame old Martin.

SMALDER GIRLS. The, Acquaintances of cousin Feenix. *D. and S.* xli.

SMALLCHECK. Sam Weller's name for gamekeeper. *P.P.* xix.

A half-booted leather-leggined boy.

SMALLWEED. Judith, Twin sister of Bartholomew Smallweed. *B.H.* xxi.

Never owned a doll—never played at any game.

SMALLWEED. Joshua, Grandfather Smallweed. *B.H.* xxi.

"He's a leech in his disposition, he's a screw and a wice in his actions, a snake in his twistings, and a lobster in his claws.'"

Note.—Relation of Krook. A discounter of bills, etc. He endeavours to blackmail Sir Leicester Dedlock, and finds a will in old Krooks' papers relating to the Jarndyce case which he disposes of to Bucket for Mr. Jarndyce.

SMALLWEED. Mrs., senior, grandmother of Bartholomew Smallweed. *B.H.* xxi.

An eternal disposition to fall asleep over the fire, and into it.

Note.—Of little more importance in the history than as a foil to show off the eccentricities of her husband, old grandfather Smallweed.

SMALLWEED. Young Bartholomew clerk in Kenge and Carboys. *B.H.* xx.

He is something under fifteen, and an old limb of the law. A town made article of small stature and weazen features; but may be perceived from a considerable distance by means of his very tall hat.

Note.—Smallweed's grandson and sister of Judy. Friend of Mr. Guppy. They call out to some extent over the letters which Lady Dedlock wants destroyed.

SMANGLE. Mr. Prisoner in the Fleet. *P.P.* xli.

An admirable specimen of a class of gentry which never can be seen in full perfection but in such places. A tall fellow, with an olive complexion, long dark hair, and very thick bushy whiskers meeting under his chin. He wore no neckerchief—on his head he wore one of the common eighteenpenny French skull caps, with a gawdy tassel dangling therefrom, very happily in keeping with a common fustian coat. His legs, which were long, were afflicted with weakness . . . graced a pair of Oxford mixture trousers.

SMAUKER. John, One of a select company of Bath Footmen. *P.P.* xxvii.

Note.—Bantam's footman who introduced Sam Weller to the select company of Bath footmen in the small parlour of the greengrocer's shop.

SMART. Tom, Friend of Bagman's uncle. Of the great commercial house of Bilson and Slum. *P.P.* xiv.

Tom sometimes had an unpleasant knack of swearing.

Note.—Introduced in the "Bagman's Story." Prevents the marriage of Jinkins with the landlady of the inn by marrying her himself.

SMIF. Putnam. *M.C.* xxii.

SMIFSER. Suitor of Mrs. Nickleby. *N.N.* xli.

SMIGGERS. Joseph, Esq. Perpetual Vice-President of the Pickwick Club. *P.P.* i.

SMIKE. Mother of. *N.N.* ix.

Secret marriage—the result of this private marriage was a son. The child was put out to nurse, a long way off; his mother never saw him but once or twice, and then by stealth.

SMIKE. Squeers' boy, An orphan pupil. *N.N.* vii.

A tall, lean boy with a lantern in his hand. Although he could not have been less than eighteen or nineteen years old, and was tall for that age, he wore a skeleton suit, such as is usually put upon very little boys, and which, though most absurdly short in the arms and legs, was quite wide enough for his attenuated frame. He was lame.

Note.—First met with at Squeers' school in Yorkshire, a poor drudge half-witted through cruelty and privation. Nicholas feels compassion for him, and when, after an escape and recapture, Squeers proceeds to flog him, Nicholas interferes. Nicholas leaves Dotheboys' Hall and travels towards London; on the way he finds Smike and is persuaded to take him. They reach London but leave it again for Portsmouth where Smike becomes a fellow member of Crummles' theatrical company with Nicholas. Away from the reign of terror at Squeers, Smike, though simple, is willing and devoted. They return to London, and Smike is again captured by Squeers, but he escapes with the assistance of John Browdie and returns to Nicholas, who refuses to give him up. His early hardships have undermined his constitution and broken his spirit; and though the latter might mend, the former was past it and he dies. It transpires that Smike was the son of Ralph Nickleby. Brooker, at one time clerk to Ralph, had placed the boy in Squeer's hands, and told the father he was dead. The regret and remorse had something to do with Ralph's death at his own hands.

SMITH. *M.P., C.*

SMITH. Adam, A young Gradgrind. *H.T., S.* v.

SMITH. Captain Aaron. *N.P., P.F.*

SMITH. Fixem. *S.B.B., O.P.* v.

SMITH. Job. *M P., N.G.K.*

SMITH. Joe, The prophet. *U.T.* xx.

SMITH. Miss, As Fanny Wilson. *M.P., S.G.*; *M.P., V.C.*

SMITH. Mr. *Mud. Pap.* ii.

SMITH. Mr. *S.B.B.*, Scenes xix.

SMITH. Mr. Albert. *M.P., L.A.V.* ii.

SMITH. Mr., A clerk. *S.B.B.*, Char. i.

A tall, thin, pale person, in a black coat, scanty grey trousers, little pinched-up gaiters, and brown beaver gloves. He had an umbrella in his hand—not for use, for the day was fine—but evidently, because he always carried one to the office in the morning.

SMITH. Mr., C. F., as Jean Marie. *M.P., N.T.*

SMITH. Mr., Our new member. *S.B.B.*, Scenes xviii.

SMITH. Mr. Samuel, Salesman in linen-draper's, in silk department. *S.B.B.*, Tales v.

Alias Horatio Sparkins.

SMITH. Sydney. *M.P., M.E.R.*; *M.P., S.D.C.*

SMITH. T. Southwood. *M.P., O.C.*; *M.P., R.T.*

SMITH AND ELDER. Messrs., of Cornhill. *H.T., S.* v.

SMITH, PAYNE AND SMITH. *M.P., G.A.*; *M.P., I.*; *U.T.* xxi.

SMITH SQUARE. *O.M.F.* xviii.

SMITHERS. Miss, A lady boarder at Westgate House. *P.P.* xvi.

SMITHERS. Miss Emily, Pupil at Minerva House. *S.B.B.*, Tales iii.

The belle of the house.

SMITHERS. Mr. *M.P., F.C.*

SMITHERS. Robert, A clerk in the City. *S.B.B.*, Char. xi.

Generally appeared in public in a surtout and shoes— a rough blue coat with wooden buttons, made upon the fireman's principle, a low crowned flower-pot-saucer-shaped hat.

SMITHERS AND PRICE'S. Chancery. *P.P.* xx.

SMITHFIELD MARKET. *B.R.* xviii.; *G.E.* xx.; *L.D.* xiii.; *M.P., L.T.*; *N.N.* iv.; *O.T.* xvi; *R.P., M.O.F.F.*; *R.P., T.D.P.*; *U.T.* xxxiv.

It was market morning. The ground was covered, nearly ankle deep, with filth and mire; a thick steam perpetually rising from the reeking bodies of the cattle, and mingling with the fog,which seemed to rest upon the chimney-tops, hung heavily above. Countrymen, butchers, drovers, boys, thieves, idlers, and vagabonds of every low grade were mingled together in a mass.

SMITHICK AND WATERSBY. Merchant house. Of Liverpool. *C.S., W.o.G.M.*

SMITHIE. Miss. *P.P.* ii.

Present at the Charity Ball, Rochester.

SMITHIE. Mrs., Wife of Mr. Smithie. *P.P.* ii.

Present at the Charity Ball, Rochester.

SMITHIE. Mr., Something in the Dockyard. *P.P.* ii.

Present at the Charity Ball, Rochester.

SMITH'S BOOKSTALL. At Mugby. *C.S.,M.J.* v.

SMITHS. The, Guests of the Gattletons. *S.B.B.*, Tales ix.

SMIVEY. Chicken. *M.C.* xiii.

SMOLLETT'S GRAVE. Leghorn. *P.F.I.*, *R.P.S.*

SMORLTORK. Count, A literary man. *P.P.* xv.

A well-whiskered individual in a foreign uniform. The famous foreigner—gathering materials for his great work on England.

SMOUCH. *P.P.* xl.

Man in the brown coat—troubled with a hoarse cough.

SMUGGINS. Mr., Another artist. *S.B.B.*, Scenes ii.

Sings a comic song.

SNAGGY BAR. On Ohio River. *M.P.*, *E.T.*

SNAGSBY. Mr., Law stationer. *B.H.* x.

A mild, bald, timid man, with a shining head and a scrubby clump of black hair, sticking out at the back —in grey shop coat and black calico sleeves.

Note.—Law stationer in Cook's Court, Cursitor Street. He is intimately wrapped up, much against his desire, in the Dedlock mystery, and is worried by his wife, who becomes intensely jealous of his secrecy. This does a good deal of harm to the others, but when things are cleared up, her husband is exonerated in her eyes by Bucket, and she shows contrition.

SNAGSBY. Mrs., Niece of Mr. Peffer. *B.H.* x.

Something too violently compressed about the waist, and with a sharp nose like a sharp autumn evening.

SNAP. Betsy, Uncle Chill's domestic. *R.P.*, *P.R.S.*

A withered, hard-favoured yellow old woman—our only domestic.

SNAPPER. Mr., Emphatic gentleman. *M.P.*, *O.S.*

SNAWLEY. Mr., Stepfather—or "father-in-law" of two boys, pupils of Squeers, in the oil and colour way. *N.N.* iv.

A sleek, fat-nosed man, clad in sombre garments, and long black gaiters, and bearing in his countenance an expression of much mortification and sanctity.

Note.—Snawley is first seen placing his two stepsons with Squeers. He is a man of a similar kidney to Squeers, and the future of the poor boys is well understood between them. He is employed by Ralph Nickleby to personate the father of Smike, but the scheme fails, and he laid bare the plans of the two principal schemers.

SNEVELLICCI. Miss, Member of Mr. V. Crummles' Company. *N.N.* xxiii.

Who could do anything from a medley dance to Lady Macbeth—always played some part in blue silk knee-smalls, at her benefit—glancing from the depths of her coal-scuttle bonnet.

Note.—Miss Snevellicci was one of the leading ladies in Crummles' theatrical company. She was very much smitten with Nicholas, who did not reciprocate her feeling.

SNEVELLICCI. Mr. *N.N.* xxx.

Note.—Father of Miss Snevellicci, much addicted to drink.

SNEWKES. Mr. *N.N.* xiv.

Supposed to entertain honorable designs upon last lady mentioned (sister of Mrs. Kenwigs).

SNICKS. Mr., The life office secretary. *P.P.* xlvii.

SNIFF. Mrs., Wife of Sniff. One of refreshment room staff at Mugby Junction. *C.S.*, *M.J.* v.

"She's the one with the small waist buckled in tight at front, and with lace cuffs at her wrists, which she puts on the edge of the counter before her, and stands a smoothing while the public foams."

"**SNIGGLE AND BLINK.**" *P.P.* xl.

SNIGGS. Mr. *Mud. Pap.*

SNIGSWORTH. Lord. Twemlow's relative. *O.M.F.* ii.

SNIGSWORTHY PARK. *O.M.F.* ii.

SNIPE. Honourable Wilmot, Ensign 97. *P.P.* ii.

Great family—Snipes—very.

Note.—The "little boy with the light hair and pink eyes" at the charity ball at the "Bull inn."

SNITCHEY. Mr. A lawyer. *C.B.*, *B.o.L.* i.

Like a magpie, or raven, only not so sleek.

SNITCHEY. Mrs., Wife of Mr. Snitchey. *C.B., B.o.L.* ii.

The feather of a bird of Paradise in Mrs. Snitchey's turban trembled, as if the bird were alive again

SNITCHEY. Jonathan, Mr. Snitchey. *C.B., B.o.L.* i.

SNITCHEY AND CRAGGS. Lawyers. *C.B., B.o.L.* i.

SNITCHEY AND CRAGGS. Office of. *C.B., B.o.L.* ii.

SNOADY. *M.P., L.T.*

SNOBB. Mr., The Honourable, Guest of Ralph Nickleby. *N.N.* xix.

A gentleman with the neck of a stork and the legs of no animal in particular.

SNOBEE. Mr. *S.B.B.,* Char. iii.

SNOBS. Subjects of Prince Bull. *R.P., P.B.*

SNODGRASS. Augustus, Member of the Pickwick Club. *P.P.* i.

The poetic Snodgrass . . . enveloped in a mysterious blue coat with a canine-skin collar.

Note.—One of the Pickwickians, a member of the corresponding society of the club, who accompanied Mr. Pickwick. He married Emily Wardle and settled on a small farm at Dingley Dell, which they cultivated more for occupation than profit. And Mr. Snodgrass, being occasionally abstracted and melancholy, is . . . reputed a great poet among his friends and acquaintance.

"**SNOOKS.**" Fictitious name of correspondent leaving gift with Father of Marshalsea. *L.D.* vi.

SNORE. Prof. *Mud. Pap.* i.

SNORFLERER. Lady. *S.Y.C.*

SNORRIDGE BOTTOM. *C.S.*; *P.o.C.E.P.*

SNOW HILL. *B.R.* lxvii.; *L.D.* xiii.; *N.N.* iii.; *O.T.* xxvi.; *R.P., M.O.F.F.*; *S.B.B.,* Tales xi.

SNOW. Tom, Black steward of "Golden Mary." *C.S.*; *W.o.G.M.*

SNUBBIN. Serjeant, Barrister. *P.P.* xxxi.

A sallow-faced, sallow-complexioned man of about five-and-forty—or as the novels say he might be fifty. His hair was thin and weak. He had that dull looking boiled eye which would have been sufficient without the additional eyeglass which dangled from a broad black riband round his neck, to warn a stranger that he was near sighted.

Note.—Snubbin was "for the plaintiff" in Bardell v. Pickwick. A counsel very much in demand and well aware of his own worth, though abstracted, and careless of other matters.

SNUFFIM. Sir Tumley, Mrs. Wititterly's doctor. *N.N.* xxi.

SNUFFLETOFFLE. Mr. *Mud. Pap.* ii.

"**SNUG.**" A singing house. *U.T.* v.

About the room some amazing coffee-coloured pictures varnished an inch deep, and some stuffed creatures in cases.

SNUGGERY. The. *P.P.* xlii.

SNUGGERY. The, In the Marshalsea. *L.D.* vi.

SNUGGERY. Barmaid of. *L.D.* viii.

SNUGGERY. Potboy of. *L.D.* viii.

SNUGGERY. Waiter of. *L.D.* viii.

SNUGGERY. Landlord of. *L.D.* viii.

SNUGGERY. The Tavern establishment at the upper end of prison. *L.D.* viii.

Where the collegians had just vacated their social evening club.

SNUGGLEWOOD. A physician. *R.P., O.B.*

SNUPHANUPH. The Dowager Lady. *P.P.* xxxv.

SO AND SO. Mr. and Mrs., Guests of the old lady. *S.B.B., O.P.* ii.

SOBBS. *M.P., T.T.*

SOCIAL OYSTERS. Private club. *M.P., E.T.*

SOCIEETEE. Prince, Ward of the Genie Law. *M.P., T.O.H.*

SOCIETY FOR THE PROPAGATION OF THE GOSPEL IN FOREIGN PARTS. *B.H.* xvi.

SOCIETY FOR THE SUPPRESSION OF VICE. *S.B.B.,* Tales xi.

SOCIETY OF WELLDOING. *R.P., O.F.W.*

Who are active all the summer, and give the proceeds of their good works to the poor.

SOEMUP. Dr. *Mud. Pap.* ii.

SOHO. District of London.
C.S., *N.T.*, Act i. *M.P.*, *G.F.*; *N.N.* lxiv.

A curious colony of mountaineers, has long been enclosed within that small flat—district. Swiss watchmakers, Swiss silver-chasers, Swiss jewellers, Swiss importers of Swiss musical boxes, and Swiss toys of various kinds—Swiss professors of music, painting and languages. Swiss artificers—Swiss laundresses--shabby Swiss eating-houses, coffee-houses, and lodging-houses.

SOHO SQUARE. *B.H.* xxiii.; *C.S.*, *N.T.*, Act i.; *M.P.*, *N.Y.D.*; *T.T.C.*, bk. ii., ch. vi.

The quiet lodgings of Dr. Manette were in a quiet street-corner not far from Soho Square.

SOLA ACQUA. *P.F.I.*, *G.A.N.*

SOLDIER. Irish, In workhouse in Liverpool. *U.T.* viii.

The dismalest skeleton—the ghost of a soldier.

SOLDIERS. *G.E.* v.

SOLDIERS. *P.F.I.*, *G.T.F.*

SOLDIERS. Guard of, and Officer in command of. *L.D.* i.

A stout, serviceable, profoundly calm man, with his drawn sword in his hand, smoking a cigar.

SOLDIERS. Two, Billeted on Madame Bouclet. *C.S.*, *S.L.* ii.

SOLICITOR. *N.N.* ii.

SOLICITOR-GENERAL.
T.T.C., bk. ii., ch. iii.; *U.T.* xi.

SOLICITOR-GENERAL. In 1830. *M.P.*, *C.P.*

SOLICITOR'S BOYS. *B.H.* i.

SOLICITORS. Three. *P.P.* xlvii.

SOLICITORS. Various, in the cause in Chancery High Court. *B.H.* i.

Ranged in a line, in a long matted well (but you might look in vain for Truth at the bottom of it).

SOLOMONS. Owner of an assumed name. *S.B.B.*, Scenes xiii.

SOLS. Mr., Toots' name for Gills, Sol, *which see.*

"**SOL'S ARMS.**" The. *B.H.* xi.

"**SOL'S ARMS.**" The potboy of the. *B.H.* xxxii.

SOLVENT COURT. *P.P.* lv.

SOME ONE. Shadow of. *L.D.* xxiv.

Who had gone by long before. Character in Little Dorrit's tale to Maggy.

SOMEBODY. *M.P.*, *G.A.*

SOMEBODY. *M.P.*, *N.S.E.*

SOMEBODY. Another guest of Ralph Nickleby. *N.N.* xix.

Who appeared to be a makeweight.

SOMEBODY. Madame, Entertainer in Vauxhall Gardens.
S.B.B., Scenes xiv.

SOMEBODY. Owner of left luggage. *C.S.*, *S.L.* i.

SOMEBODY ELSE. Mr. and Mrs., Guests of the old lady.
S.B.B., *O.P.* ii.

SOMERSET HOUSE. *M.P.*, *C.P.*; *M.P.*, *R.D.*; *R.P.*, *D.W.T.T.*; *R.P.*, *P.M.T.P.*; *S.B.B.*, Char. iii.

SOMERSETSHIRE. *C.S.*, *S.P.T.* ii.

SOMERSTOWN. *B.H.* xliii.; *M. P.*, *G. F.*; *N. N.* xxxviii.; *P. P.* xx.; *S. B. B.*, Scenes i.; *S. B. B.*, Scenes xx.; *U. T.* x.

SON. Only, Of "cause" of Haying's incarceration. *P.P.* xxi.

Dying before his father's eyes.

SOPHIA. Eldest pupil of Miss Pinch. *M.C.* ix.

A premature little woman of thirteen years old, who had already arrived at such a pitch of whalebone and education that she had nothing girlish about her.

Note.—The brass-founder's daughter and Ruth Pinch's pupil. A child who has been spoiled by her parents and following their example, despises her governess.

SOPHIA. Mr. Pocket's housemaid. *G.E.* xxiii.

SOPHONISBA. *C.S.*, *G.i.S.*

SOPHRONIA. *See* Marchioness.

SOPHY. Adopted daughter of Doctor Marigold. *C.S.*, *D.M.*

SOPHY. Daughter of. *C.S., D.M.* She can speak.

SOPHY. Husband of. *C.S., D.M.* (Also deaf and dumb).

SOPHY. Willing, Mrs. Lirriper's maid. *C.S., M.L.Lo.* i.

Upon her knees scrubbing early and late and ever cheerful, but always smiling with a black face.

SORDUST. *M.P., C.Pat.*

SORRENTO. *P.F.I., R.D.*

SOUDAN. *M.P., N.E.*

SOULS OF THE DEAD. *M.P., R.S.D.*

SOUTH COUNTRY. *B.H.* xxiii.

SOUTH - EASTERN RAILWAY COMPANY. *R.P., O.o.T.*

SOUTH KENSINGTON MUSEUM. *M.P., C.H.T.*; *M.P., L.*

SOUTH SEA HOUSE. *M.P., G.A.*

SOUTH SEA ISLANDS. *R.P., D.W.I.F.*

SOUTH SQUARE. Late Holborn Court. *P.P.* xxxi.

SOUTHAMPTON. *D. and S.* xxxii.; *N.N.* xxiii.

SOUTHAMPTON BUILDINGS. Chancery Lane. *R.P., P.M.T.P.*

SOUTHAMPTON STREET. *E.D.* xxii.

SOUTHCOTE. Mrs. *A.N.* xviii.

SOUTHCOTE. Mrs. *R.P., B.L.W.* Wife of a begging-letter writer

SOUTHERN STATES. *A.N.* iii.

SOUTHWARK. *B.R.* v.; *L.D.* vi.; *M.P., F.S.*; *M.P., S.B.*; *O.T.* l.; *P.P.* xxxii.; *R.P.*; *D.W.T.T.*; *U.T.* ix.

SOUTHWARK BRIDGE. *O.M.F.* i.; *R.P., D.W.T.T.*

SOVEREIGN LADY OF OUR ISLE. *M.P., T.B.*

SOWERBERRY. Mr., Parochial undertaker. *O.T.* iv.

A tall, gaunt, large-jointed man, attired in a suit of threadbare black, with darned cotton stockings of the same colour, and shoes to answer. His features were not naturally intended to wear a smiling aspect, but he was in general rather given to professional jocosity.

Note.—The undertaker to whom Oliver was "apprenticed." He was somewhat kindly disposed towards the boy if only for business purposes; kindly disposed, that is, compared with most of the others who were connected with parochial authority. To satisfy his wife he is obliged to thrash Oliver severely, and this, together with the other insults and injuries, causes the boy to run away.

SOWERBERRY. Mrs., Undertaker's wife. *O.T.* iv.

A short, thin, squeezed-up woman, with a vixenish countenance.

Note.—The wife of the undertaker. She had a violent dislike to Oliver; and fed him on scraps and refuse.

SOWNDS. Mr., The beadle. *D. and S.* xxxi.

Sitting in the sun upon the church steps—seldom does anything else, except, in cold weather, sitting by the fire.

SOWSTER. *Mud. Pap.* ii.

SPADA. PALAZZO. *P.F.I., R.*

SPAGNA. Piazza di. *P.F.I., R.*

SPAIN. *M.P., C.P.*; *P.F.I., G.A.N.*; *U.T.* xv.

SPANIARD. A. *M.P., L.L.*

SPANIARDS. Courteous, In nursery tale. *U.T.* xv.

"**SPANIARDS.**" The, At Hampstead. Tea gardens. *P.P.* xlvi.

SPANISH FRIAR. *M.P., Dr. C.*

SPANISH JACK. Visitor at the "Snug." *U.T.* v.

With curls of black hair, rings in his ears, and a knife not far from his hand if you got into trouble with him.

SPANISH MAIN. The. *R.P., O.S.*

SPARKE. Thomas, Fireman. *M.P., R.S.*

SPARKINS. Horatio, Mr. Smith. *S.B.B.*, Tales v.

Young man with the black whiskers and the white cravat.

SPARKLER. Colonel, Deceased. *L.D.* xxi.

Mrs. Merdle's first husband.

SPARKLER. T. =Dickens, Charles. *M.P., N.S.*

SPARKLER. Mr. Edmund, Son of Mrs. Merdle. *L.D.* xxi.

He was of a chuckle-headed, high-shouldered make, with a general appearance of being, not so much a young man, as a swelled boy. Monomaniacal in offering marriage to all manner of undesirable young ladies, and in remarking of every successive young lady to whom he tendered a matrimonial proposal, that she was a " doosed fine gal—well educated too—with no biggodd nonsense about her."

Note.—Mrs. Merdle's son by her former husband. He has an unfortunate propensity for wanting to marry most of the girls he meets. In this way he becomes entangled with Fanny Dorrit while she is a ballet dancer. He is extricated by his mother. But when the Dorrits come into their estate, he again meets Fanny and eventually marries her.

SPARKS. Tom. *M.R., S.G.*

SPARROW. *M.P., O.S.*

SPARROW. *M.P., R.H.F.*

SPARSIT. Mr., Deceased. *H.T., S.* vii.

Had been by the mother's side, what Mrs. Sparsit called a " Powler."

SPARSIT. Mrs., Housekeeper to Mr. Bounderby. *H.T., S.* vii.

In her elderly days, with the Coriolanian style of nose, and the dense black eyebrows which had captivated Sparsit. Had not only seen better days, but was highly connected.

Note.—Mr. Bounderby's housekeeper with very high connections. Owing to her indiscretion in discovering Bounderby's mother in old Mrs. Pegler she is discharged.

SPARTA. *A.N.* xvii.

SPATTER. John, Partner of Mr. Michael. *R.P., P.R.S.*

Who had been my clerk.

SPEAKER. The. *B.H.* lviii. ; *M.P., F.C.* ; *S.B.B.*, Scenes xiv. ; *S.B.B.* Scenes xviii. ; *U.T.* xxvi.

SPECIAL CONSTABLE. *P.P.* xxv.

SPECTRE. *C.S., H.H.*

SPECTRE. A. *C.S., T.G.S.* ii.

Standing by the red light near the tunnel.

SPECTRE. The. *C.B., H.M.* i.

SPECKS. Joe, A doctor in Dullborough. *U.T.* xii.

SPECKS. Junior, Barrister-at-law. Son of Joe Specks. *U.T.* xii.

SPECKS. Mrs., Née Lucy Green. *U.T.* xii.

SPECULATOR. *M.P., G.D.*

SPEECHLESS FRIEND. *N.T.*, Act ii.

SPEEDIE. Dr. *L.T.* ii.

SPENLOW. Dora, Mr. Spenlow's daughter. *D.C.* xxvi.

A fairy, a sylph.

Note.—The daughter of Mr. Spenlow, of Spenlow and Jorkins, falls in love with David Copperfield as David falls in love with her. There appears little prospect of the realization of their hope, however, until the death of Dora's father, leaving her with a small inheritance to the care of his two sisters. After this Dora becomes the " child-wife " ; and she and David set up house. He endeavours to teach her how to manage the housekeeping and other duties, but without success, and eventually relinquishes the attempt. It is not very long before her health breaks down and she dies.

SPENLOW. Misses, Maiden sisters of Mr. Spenlow. *D.C.* xxxiii.

Who lived at Putney, and who had not held any other than chance communication with their brother for many years. Dry elderly ladies dressed in black.

SPENLOW. Mr., Attorney. *D.C.* xxxiii.

In a black gown trimmed with white fur. . . . A little light-haired gentleman, with undeniable boots, and the stiffest of white cravats and shirt-collars. He was buttoned up mighty trim and tight, and must have taken a great deal of pains with his whiskers, which were accurately curled. He was got up with such care, and was so stiff, that he could hardly bend himself ; being obliged, when he glanced at some papers on his desk, after sitting down in his chair, to move his whole body, from the bottom of his spine, like Punch.

Note.—A partner in the firm of Spenlow and Jorkins, proctors in Doctors' Commons, to whom David Copperfield is articled. He uses Jorkins' name as a convenience when anything unpleasant has to be done, notably in his refusal to cancel David's articles and refund his aunt's £1,000. He dies, and contrary to expectations, leaves only a small property.

SPENLOW AND JORKINS. Attorneys in office in Doctors' Commons. *D.C.* xxiii.

SPEZZIA. *P.F.I., R.P.S.*

SPIDER. The. *See* Drummle, Bentley.

SPIKE PARK. *P.P.* xlii.

SPIKER. Mr. Henry, Solicitor to something or somebody remotely connected with the Treasury. *D.C.* xxv.

So cold a man, that his head instead of being grey, seemed to be sprinkled with hoar-frost.

SPIKER. Mrs. Henry. *D.C.* xxv.

A very awful lady in a black velvet dress, and a great black velvet hat.

SPILLER. Portrait by, Of Pecksniff *M.C.* xxiv.

SPINACH. Name of a bird *B.H.* xiv.

SPINE. John, celebrated novelist. *R.P., O.B.*

SPIRIT. An anonymous. *M.P., S.B.*

SPIRIT. The. *M.P., D.V.*

SPIRIT OF THE FORT. Boy emerging from the Fort. *U.T.* xxiv.

SPIRITS. Three. *C.B., C.C., S.* ii.

SPIRITS. First of the three. *C.B., C.C., S.* ii.

A strange figure—like a child, yet not so like a child as like an old man, viewed through some supernatural medium.

SPIRITS. The second of the three. *C.B., C.C., S.* iii.

Clothed in one simple green robe, or mantle, bordered with white fur—hung so loosely—that its capacious breast was bare. Its feet—were also bare—and on its head—no other covering than a holly wreath, set here and there with shining icicles,—girded round its middle was an antique scabbard; but no sword was in it.

SPIRITS. The third of the. *C.B., C.C., S.* iv.

The phantom—shrouded in a deep black garment, which concealed its head, its face, its form, and left nothing of it visible save one outstretched hand. It was tall and stately.

SPITALFIELDS. *O.T.* xix.; *R.P., M.O.F.F.*; *U.T.* x.

SPITHEAD. *R.P., A.F.*; *U.T.* xv.

SPITHERS. The new attorney-general. *M.P., G.D.*

SPODGER. Miss. *M.P., L.E.J.*

SPODGER. Mr. *M.P., L.E.J.*

SPODGER. Mr. B. *M.P., L.E.J.*

SPOFFINS. *O.M.F.* xxv.

SPOKER. Bust by. Of Pecksniff. *M.C.* xxiv.

SPOTTED BABY. The, One of Magsman's troup. *C.S., G.i.S.*

SPOTTLETOES. Mr., Husband of Martin Chuzzlewit's niece. *M.C.* iv.

"Spottletoe married my father's brother's child, didn't he? and Mrs. Spottletoes is Chuzzlewit's own niece, isn't she," said Chevy Slyme, Esquire who was so bald and had such big whiskers.

SPOTTLETOES. Mrs., Wife of Mr. Spottletoes, and niece of Martin Chuzzlewit. *M.C.* iv.

Much too slim for her years, and of a poetical constitution, was accustomed to inform her more intimate friends that the said whiskers (Mr. Spottletoes'), was the lodestar of her existence.

"**SPREAD EAGLE.**" *M.P., E.S.*

SPRING GARDENS. *S.B.B.*, Char. ix.

SPRINGFIELD. *A.N.* v.

SPRITES. On stage in Britannia. *U.T.* iv.

SPRODGKIN. Mrs. Sally, A widow. *O.M.F.* lxi.

Member of the Reverend Frank's congregation, made a point of distinguishing herself in that body by conspicuously weeping at everything, however cheering, said by the Reverend Frank.

SPROUSTON. *M.P., E.S.*

SPRUGGINS. Candidate for post of beadle, with ten small children (two of them twins), and a wife. *S.B.B., O.P.* iv.

A little thin man, in rusty black, with a long, pale face, and a countenance expressive of care and fatigue.

SPUNGING HOUSE. A lock-up house. *S.B.B.*, Tales x.

SPYERS. Jim, Police officer. *O.T.* xxxi.

SQUARE. The. *D.C.* xxx.

SQUARE. The. *N.N.* xxxvii.

SQUEERS. Junior, Son of Squeers. *N.N.* viii.

A striking likeness of his father, his chief amusement was to tread upon the other boys' toes.

Note.—Young Wackford followed closely in his father's footsteps and delighted to inflict his own small but ingenious tortures on the boys, besides wearing the clothes sent them.

SQUEERS. Miss Fanny, Daughter of Squeers. *N.N.* ix.

In her three-and-twentieth year—not tall like her mother, but short like her father; from the former she inherited a voice of harsh quality; from the latter a remarkable expression of the right eye, something akin to having none at all—her hair—it had more than a tinge of red—curled in five distinct rows—and arranged dexterously over the doubtful eye.

Note.—Fanny Squeers combined the bad qualities of both parents. She fell in love (so far as the term can be used in this way) with Nicholas, but when he rejected her advances her affection turned to hate. She was a friend of 'Tilda Price, although she was bitterly jealous of the miller's daughter.

SQUEERS. Mr. Wackford, Master of Dotheboys' Hall. *N.N.* iv.

He had but one eye—unquestionably useful—but decidedly not ornamental; being of a greenish-grey, and in shape resembling the fanlight of a street door. The blank side of his face was much wrinkled and puckered up, which gave him a very sinister appearance, especially when he smiled. His hair was very flat and shiny, save at the ends—brushed up very stiffly from a low protruding forehead. He was about two or three and fifty—a trifle below the middle size—wore a white neckerchief with long ends, and a suit of scholastic black—his coat-sleeves a great deal too long, and his trousers a great deal too short.

Note.—Squeers was a schoolmaster of the type then prevalent in Yorkshire. He took little boys without any qualifications for educating them, partially starved them and brutally ill-treated them. Unfortunately for him he engages Nicholas Nickleby as usher. When Squeers is about to flog Smike, Nicholas soundly trounces him. This enrages Squeers, who assists Ralph in his plans to ruin Nicholas. These plans fail, however, and Squeers is transported. When this happens his school is broken up with great rejoicing by the boys.

SQUEERS. Mrs., Wife of Mr. Squeers. *N.N.* iv.

"You will have a father in me, my dears, and a mother in Mrs. Squeers." Of a large, raw-boned figure, about half a head taller than Mr. Squeers, dressed in a dimity night-jacket; with her hair in papers—she had also a dirty nightcap on, relieved by a yellow cotton handkerchief, which tied it under the chin.

Note.—Wife of Squeers, an able assistant in his career of cruelty.

SQUIRES. Olympia. *U.T.* xix.

Childhood's sweetheart of the Uncommercial Traveller.

SQUOD. Phil, Custodian of George's gallery in George's absence. *B.H.* xxi.

A little grotesque man, with a large head—is dressed something like a gunsmith, in a green baize apron and cap; and his face and hands are dirty with gunpowder—with a face all crushed together, who appears, from a certain blue and speckled appearance that one of his cheeks presents, to have been blown up, in the way of business at some odd time or times—is lame, though able to move very quickly.

Note.—A man picked out of the gutter, employed by Mr. Geogre in his shooting gallery, and afterwards accompanies him to Chesney Wold.

STABBER. New York. *M.C.* xvi.

STABBER'S BAND. *M.P., A.N.*

STABLES. The Honourable Bob. *B.H.* ii.

Who can make warm mashes with the skill of a veterinary surgeon, and is a better shot than most gamekeepers.

STAFFORD. *M.P., J.T.*

STAFFORDSHIRE. *R.P., A.P.A.*

STAGE-COACH HOUSE. An old *U.T.* xxii.

STAGG. Proprietor of cellar near Barbican. *B.R.* viii.

Wore an old tie-wig as bare and frowsy as a stunted hearthbroom. His eyes were closed, but had they been wide open it would have been easy to tell, from the attentive expression of his face—that he was blind.

Note.—Stagg keeps an underground drinking den. It is here that Simon Tappertit and his "United Bull-Dogs" foregather. Deprived of sight, his other senses become abnormally developed.

STAGG'S GARDENS. *D. and S.* vi.

In a suburb, known by the inhabitants of Stagg's Gardens, by the name of Camberling Town. It was a little row of houses, with little squalid patches of ground before them, fenced off with old doors, barrel staves, scraps of tarpaulin and dead bushes; with bottomless tin kettles and exhausted iron fenders thrust into the gaps. Here the Stagg's gardeners trained scarlet beans, kept fowls and rabbits, erected rotten summer-houses (one was an old boat), dried clothes and smoked pipes.

STAINES. *O.M.F.* xli.

STALKER. Inspector, A detective. *R.T., T.D.P.*

A shrewd hard-headed Scotchman—in appearance not at all unlike a very cute, thoroughly trained schoolmaster.

STALKER. Mrs., A thief. *R.P., D.W.I.F.*

STAMFORD. *N.N.* v.

STAMFORD HILL. *S.B.B.* Scenes ix.

STAMFORD STREET. *R.P., D.W.T.T.*

STANFIELD. *M.P., O.L.N.O.*

STANFIELD. Mr. Clarkson. *M.P., A.P.*; *M.P., L.S.*

STANGER. Dr. *M.P., N.E.*

STANLEY. Lord. *S.B B.*, Scenes xiii.

STANLEY. Lord, An M.P. *S.B.B.*, Scenes xviii.

STANLEY. Sir Hubert. *D. and S.* i.

STAPLE. Mr., A Dingley Deller. *P.P.* vii.

STAPLE INN. Holborn. *B.H.* x.; *E.D.* xi.

One of the nooks, where a few smoky sparrows twitter in smoky trees, as though they called to one another "Let us play at country," and where a few feet of garden mould, and a few yards of gravel enable them to do that refreshing violence to their tiny understandings.

STAR. Eastern, East London Children's Hospital. *U.T.* xxxiv.

STARELEIGH. Mr. Justice, Judge in Bardell *v.* Pickwick. *P.P.* xxxiv.

Who sat in the absence of the Chief Justice, occasioned by indisposition. So fat that he seemed all face and waistcoat. He rolled in, upon two little turned legs, and having bobbed gravely to the bar—

put his legs underneath his table, and his three-cornered hat upon it.

STARGAZER. Emma. *M.P., L.*

STARGAZER. Master Galileo Isaac Newton Hamstead. *M.P., L.*

STARGAZER. Mr. *M.P., L.*

STARLING. Alfred. *C.S., H.H.*

An uncommonly agreeable young fellow of eight-and-twenty.

STARLING. Mrs. *S.Y.C., L.C.*

STARTOP. *G.E.* xxiii.

He had a woman's delicacy of feature.

Note.—Friend of Pip's boarding at Mr. Pocket's. He introduces Pip and Herbert to the "Finches of the Grove." He is also a party in the attempted escape of Magwitch from England. The story leaves him after the overturning of the boat.

STATE HOSPITAL FOR THE INSANE. S. Boston. *A.N.* iii.

STATE HOUSE. The. *A.N.* iii.

STATE PAPER OFFICE. *M.P., W.R.*

STATESMAN. Great. *M.P., L.W.O.Y.*

STATION HOUSE. *S.B.B.*, Char. xi.

STATIONER. Eldest, Daughter of fancy. *S.B.B.*, Scenes iii.

Occupant of shop.

STATIONER'S HALL. *U.T.* ix.

STEADIMAN. John, Chief officer of the "Golden Mary." *C.S., W.o.G.M.*

Aged thirty-two—a brisk, bright, blue-eyed fellow, a very neat figure, and rather under the middle size—a face that pleased everybody, and that all children took to.

STEAM PACKET WHARF. *S.B.B.*, Tales vii.

STEELE. Tom, A suicide. *R.P., D.W.T.T.*

STEEPWAYS. Village of. *C.S., M.f.T.S.* i.

There was no road in it, there was no wheeled vehicle in it, there was not a level yard in it. From the seabeach to the cliff top two irregular rows of white houses. The old pack-saddle—flourished here intact. Strings of pack-horses and pack-donkeys toiled slowly up the staves of the ladders, bearing fish, coal, and such other cargo as was unshipping at the pier.—The rough, sea-bleached boulders of which the pier was made, and the whiter boulders of the shore, were brown with drying nets.

STEERFORTH. James, Head boy at Salem House. *D.C.* v.

Before this boy, who was reputed to be a great scholar, and was very good looking, and at least half a dozen years my senior, I was carried as before a magistrate.

Note.—The head pupil at Salem House when David Copperfield enters it. For certain reasons he enjoys immunity from punishment and presumes accordingly, but his engaging manners make him a prime favourite. He drops out of the story after David's leaving the school until David returns to London some years later. He visits Mr. Peggotty at Yarmouth with David, and entices Emily away. They live abroad at various places, but in the end Steerforth desires to turn her over to his valet, Littimer, and deserts her. The ship on which he returns to England is wrecked off the Yarmouth coast. Ham Peggotty endeavours unsuccessfully to attempt a rescue and meets his death. The stranger whom he swam to rescue is washed ashore, dead, and is found to be Steerforth.

STEERFORTH. Mrs., Steerforth's mother. *D.C.* xx.

An elderly lady, with a proud carriage and a handsome face, who lived in an old brick house at Highgate on the summit of a hill.

Ntoe.—Mrs. Steerforth, with a blind love for her son, is nevertheless eventually estranged from him; and she is last seen broken and mentally deranged.

STELLA. Violetta, of the Italian Opera. *O.C.S.* xl.

STEPFATHER. Of Neville and Helena (deceased). *E.D.* vii.

STEPHENSON. Mr., Engineer. *M.P., C.C.*, ; *M.P., S.*

STEPNEY. *M.P., C.J.*

STEPNEY FIELDS. *O.M.F.* xv.

STEPNEY PAUPER UNION. *U.T.* xxix.

STEPNEY STATION. *U.T.* xxxiv.

STEVENS. Billy, Inmate of workhouse. *R.P., W.I.A.W.*

STEWARD. In Clifford's Inn. *P.P.* xxi.

Thought he had run away: opened the door, and put a bill up.

STEWARDS. Fourteen, At Guildhall. *S.B.B.*, Scenes xix.

Each with a long wand in his hand, like the evil genius in the pantomime.

STIFFIN'S ACRE. Great Winglebury. *S.B.B.*, Tales viii.

STIGGINS. Mr. *P.P.* xxvii.

Prim-faced, red-nosed man, with a long thin countenance, and a semi-rattlesnake sort of eye—rather sharp but decidedly bad.

Note.—The shepherd was very much addicted to pineapple rum and water. He "led" a flock of silly women, one of them Mrs. "Tony" Weller. With his humbug he so prevailed on her that she made old Weller's life miserable at home. Old Weller on one occasion makes him drunk when he has to attend a monthly meeting of the Brick Lane Branch, with results highly entertaining to Sam Weller and his father. Ultimately the shepherd is literally kicked out of the Marquis of Granby by Tony Weller.

STILL-BORN BABY. A. *L.D.* xxv.

STILTSTALKING. Augustus. *L.D.* xxvi.

STILTSTALKING. Lord Lancaster. *L.D.* xxvi.

A grey old gentleman of dignified and sullen appearance—in a ponderous white cravat, like a stiff snow-drift. He shaded the dinner, cooled the wines, chilled the gravy, and blighted the vegetables.

STILTSTALKING. Tom, Dick, or Harry. *L.D.* xxvi.

STILTSTALKING. Tudor. *L.D.* xxvi.

STILTSTALKINGS. Branch of the. *L.D.* x.

Who are better endowed in a sanguineous point of view than with real or personal property.

STOCK EXCHANGE. *P.P.* lv.

STOCKHOLM. Academy of. *M.P., L.L.*

STOCKPORT. *M.P., O.S.*

STOCKWELL GHOST. *M.P., R.S.D.*

STOKE. *R.P., A.P.A.*

STOKE NEWINGTON. *U.T.* xii.

STOKER. Mrs., As the first wife. *M.P., N.T.*

STOKES. *M.P., C.*

STOKES. Mr. Martin. *M.P., V.C.*

STONE. *L.D.* xxv.

STONE. Mr. *M.P., C.*

STONE JUG. The. *O.T.* xliii.

STONE LODGE. Mr. Gradgrind's house. *H.T., S.* iii.

A great square house with a heavy portico darkening the principal windows—six windows on this side of the door—six on that—a total of twelve in this wing, a total of twelve in the other wing; four-and-twenty carried over to the back wings.

STONEBREAKER. Owner of old post chaise. *U.T.* xxii.

STONEHENGE. *C.S., H.T.* : *U.T.* i.

STOUT. Mr., Master of workhouse. *O.T.* xxvii.

STOWELL. Rev. Hugh. *M.P., P.F.*

STOWMARKET. *M.P., E.C.*

STRADA BALBI. *P.F.I., A.G.*

STRADA NUOVA. *P.F.I., A.G.*

STRADELLA. *P.F.I., P.M.B.*

STRAGGLERS. Uncouth, interviewing Martin. *M.C.* xxii.

Men of a ghostly kind, who being in, didn't know how to get out again.

STRAND. *B.H.* xix. ; *B.R.* xv. ; *C.S., M.L.Lo.* i. ; *C.S., S.L.* i. ; *M.C.* xlviii. ; *M.P., G.A.* ; *M.P., M.E.R.* ; *M.P., N.E.* ; *M.P., O.C.* ; *M.P., R.D.* ; *M.P., R.H.F.* ; *M.P., T.D.* ; *N.N.* iii. ; *O.C.S.* viii. ; *R.P., P.M.T.P.* ; *R.P., T.D.P.* ; *S.B.B.*, Char. i. ; *T.T.C.* bk. ii., ch. xiv. ; *U.T.* xxxiv.

STRAND BRIDGE. A toll-taker. *R.P., D.W.T.T.*

Muffled up to the eyes in a thick shawl, and amply great-coated, and fur-capped.

STRAND LANE. *S.B.B.*, Tales vii.

STRANDENHEIM. A shopkeeper. *U.T.* vii.

He wore a velvet skull-cap, and looked usurious and rich. A large-lipped, pear-nosed old man, with white hair, and keen eyes.

STRANDENHEIM'S HOUSKEEPER. *U.T.* vii.

Far from young, but of a comely presence—was cheerily dressed, had a fan in her hand, and wore large gold earrings and a large gold cross.

STRANGE GENTLEMAN. *M.P., S.G.*

STRANGER. Ancient. *C.B., C.o.H.* i.

Who had long white hair, good features, singularly bold and well defined for an old man, and dark, bright, penetrating eyes. His garb was very quaint and odd—a long way behind the time. In his hand he held a great brown club, or walking-stick; and striking this upon the floor, it fell asunder, and became a chair.

STRANGER. Nobleman. *M.H.C.* i.

STRANGERS' GALLERY. Door-keeper of. *S.B.B.*, Scenes xviii. Tall stout man in black.

STRANGERS' GALLERY. In House of Commons. *M.P., P.L.U.*; *S.B.B.*, Scenes xviii.

STRANGER'S GRAVE. The, New York. *A.N.* vi.

STRANGERS. At sale of Dombey's furniture. *D. and S.* lix.

Fluffy and snuffy strangers, stare into the kitchen range, as curiously as into the attic clothes-press.

STRASBOURG. *C.S., N.T.*, Act. iii.; *R.P., M.O.F.F.*; *U.T.* vii.

STRATFORD. Mr. *N.N.* xxvii.

STRATFORD-UPON-AVON. *M.P., E.S.*; *U.T.* xix.

STRAW. Sergeant, A detective. *R.P., T.D.P.*

A little wiry sergeant.

STREAKER. Housemaid. *C.S., H.H.*

STREET. A stately. *M.P., G.D.*

STREET-BREAKFAST. A coffee-stall near Temple Bar. *S.B.B.*, Tales vii.

The coffee was boiling over a charcoal fire, and large slices of bread-and-butter were piled one upon the other, like deals in a timber yard.

STREETS. Of London, In the night. *B.R.* xvi.

It would be difficult for the beholder to recognize his most familiar walks in the altered aspect of little more than half a century ago. They were all, from the broadest and best, to the narrowest, and least frequented, very dark. It is no wonder that with these favouring circumstances–street robberies, often accompanied by cruel wounds—should have been of nightly occurrence, in the very heart of London.

STREETS. The, London, night. *S.B.B.*, Scenes ii.

On a dull, dark, murky winter's night, when there is just enough damp gently stealing down to make the pavement greasy, without cleansing it of any of its impurities.

STREETS. The (morning), London. *S.B.B.*, Scenes i.

An air of cold, solitary desolation about the noiseless streets, which we are accustomed to see thronged at other times by a busy, eager crowd.

STRICKLAND. Mr., As old Benson. *M.P., V.C.*

STRONG. Doctor, Schoolmaster. *D.C.* xvi.

Looking almost as rusty as the tall iron rails, and gates outside the house: his clothes not particularly well brushed, and his hair not particularly well combed.

Note.—Dr. Strong is the master of the school at Canterbury to which David Copperfield is sent by his aunt. He is engaged on the compilation of a monumental dictionary which might be completed " in one thousand six hundred and forty nine years, counting from the Doctor's last, or sixty-second, birthday." At the time the story leaves him he has reached the letter "D." His enemies endeavour to sow discord between him and his young wife, but without success. He relinquishes the school, going to live at Highgate. When Betsey Trotwood's reverse of fortune occurs, David Copperfield goes to Dr. Strong's to assist him.

STRONG. Mrs., Dr. Strong's young wife. *D.C.* xvi.

Note.—The young and beautiful wife of Dr. Strong. She had been formerly inclined towards Jack Maldon, her cousin, but came to the conclusion that there could be no happiness in an unsuitable union. Jack, however, continues to make love to Mrs. Strong, even while he is accepting the doctor's gifts and assistance. The doctor declines to mistrust his wife, and is eventually justified, as she confesses to him, and the cloud between them is removed.

STRONG WIND. *M.P., Th. Let.*

STROOD. *P.P.* ii.

The smell which pervades the streets must be exceedingly delicious to those who are extremely fond of smoking. The principal productions of these towns appear to be soldiers, sailors, Jews, chalk, shrimps, officers, and dockyard men.

STROUD. *See* Strood.

STRUGGLES. Mr., Player in the Dingley Dell Club. *P.P.* vii.

Note.—An All Muggleton cricketer.

STRUMPINGTON. *M.P., C.P.*

STRYVER. C. J., Counsel for Darnay at Old Bailey. *T.T.C.*, bk. ii., ch. iii.

A man of little more than thirty, but looking twenty years older than he was, stout, loud, red, bluff, and free from any drawback of delicacy.

Note.—Counsel for Charles Darnay in his trial for treason. He was the friend and employer of Sydney Carton, who "did" his cases. He finds that single life loses its attractions, and proposes to marry Lucie Manette. But he "counts his chickens" too soon, as Mr. Lorry assures him he has no chance with the young lady. Stryver thereupon faces about and makes believe that the young lady wanted him, and he had thought better of it. Stryver of the King's Bench bar passes out of the story quite casually.

STRYVER. Mrs. *T.T.C.*, bk. ii., ch. xxi.

STUBBS. Mrs., Mr. Percy Noaks' laundress. *S.B.B.*, Tales vii.

A dirty old woman, with an inflamed countenance.

STUCCONIA. *O.M.F.* x.

STUMPINGTON. Loid. *M.P., C.P.*

STUMPS. Bill, A labouring man. *P.P.* xi.

The man who was reported to have said he was responsible for the letters on the famous stone.

STUMPY AND DEACON. *P.P.*, xl.

STYLES. John. *M.P., P.P.*

STYLES' SISTER. John. *M.P., P.P.*

SUBURBS. The. *S.B.B.*, Scenes ii.

SUDBURY. *S.B.B.*, Tales x.

SUE. A suicide. *U.T.* iii.

SUEZ. *M.P., E.T.*

SUFFOLK. *C.S., D.M.*; *D.C.* xxxiv.; *M.P., E.C.*; *M.P., F.S.*; *S.B.B.*, Tales x.

SUFFOLK BANTAM. Pugilist. *P.P.* xxiv.

SUGAR BAKERS. German. *R.P., D.W.I.F.*

SUITOR. Another, Ruined in Chancery Court. *B.H.* i.

SULLIWIN. Mrs. Sarah. *S.B.B.*, Scenes v.

SULLIWIN. One of boating-crew training for race. *S.B.B.*, Scenes x.

SULLY. Mr., A distinguished American artist. *A.N.* vii.

SUMMERSON. Esther, An orphan niece of Miss Barbary. *B.H.* iii.

I was brought up, from my earliest remembrance—by my godmother.

Note.—She is the narrator of portions of the story, and is in many ways the central figure in the narrative. She is introduced early into the book, and the secret of her birth is well kept. This secret is that she is the illegitimate daughter of Lady Dedlock and Captain Hawdon, before the former married and became Lady Dedlock. She is all that a woman is supposed to be, modest but capable, and as a result she is respected and admired by all and consulted by many of her more intimate friends. She is the particular friend of Ada Clare and of Richard Carstone.

Mr. William Guppy, of Kenge and Carboy's proposes to her, but is rejected. She is attacked by smallpox and her good looks suffer. After this Guppy is afraid he may be held to his earlier promise. John Jarndyce, the friend and employer of Esther, wishes to marry her, but she ultimately becomes the wife of Allan Woodcourt.

SUMMERSON. Mother of Esther. *B.H.* iii.

SUN STREET. *O.T.* xxi.

SUNBURY CHURCH. *O.T.* xxi.

SUNDERLAND. Mr., The mesmeriser. *M.P., S.B.*

SUNDERLAND. The John of. *G.E.* liv.

SUPERANNUATED WIDOWS. *B.H.* viii.

SUPERINTENDENT. Mr., Of Liverpool police force. *U.T.* v.

A tall, well-looking, well set-up man of soldierly bearing, with a cavalry air, a good chest, and a resolute, but not by any means ungentle face.

SUPERINTENDENTS. *M.P., H.H.W.*

SUPREME COURT. At Washington. *A.N.* iii.

SURAT. *M.P., L.A.V.* ii.

SURFACE. Joseph. *M.P., S. for P.*

SURGEON. A. *M.C.* xlii.

SURGEON. A, At pit-mouth. *H.T., G.* vi.

Who brought some wine and medicines.

SURGEON. Parish. *O.T.* i.

SURGEON'S HALL. *B.H.* xiii. ; *B.R.* lxxv.

SURGETTE. James, Plantation owner. *A.N.* xvii.

SURINAM. *M.P., L.A.V.* ii.

SURREY. *B.H.* xxvii. ; *B.R.* xlviii. ; *C.S., H.T.* ; *C.S., M.L.Lo.* ; *D.C.* xi. ; *G. E.* xxxiii. ; *O. M. F.* i. ; *R. P.* ; *B. S.* ; *S. B. B.*, Scenes iii. ; *U.T.* xi.

SURREY CANAL *U.T.* vi.

SURREY HILLS. The. *L.D.* lv. ; *U.T.* xxxv.

SURREY THEATRE. *M.P., A.P.*

SURREY ZOOLOGICAL. Keepers at. *M.P. G.H.*

SURROGATE'S. *D.C.* iv.

SUSAN. *M.P., M.N.D.*

SUSAN. Mrs. Mann's Domestic. *O.T.* ii.

SUSANNAH. *M.P., S.R.*

SUSQUEHANNA. *A.N.* ix.

SUSSEX. Duke of. *M.P., C.C.* ; *M.P., T.D.*

SUSSEX. *U.T.* xi.

SUSSEX COAST. *D. and S.* xvii.

SUSSEX COUNTY HOSPITAL. *U.T.* xi.

SWALLOW. Mr. *B.H.* iv.

SWALLOW. Owner of a chaise. *N.N.* xiii.

SWALLOW. Rev. Single. *M.P., G.B.*

SWALLOW STREET. *B.R.* xxxvii.

SWALLOWFLY. Our good friend, *M.P., G.D.*

"**SWAN.**" At Wolverhampton. *M.P., F. and S.*

"**SWAN.**" The, A public house. *S.B.B.*, Tales ii.

SWEDEN. *M.P., C.E.*

SWEDEN. Poor of. *M.P., L.L.*

SWEEDLEPIPE. Paul, Barber and bird-fancier. *M.C.* xxvi.

A little elderly man, with a clammy right hand, from which even rabbits and birds could not remove the smell of shaving soap —wore in his sporting character, a velveteen coat, a great deal of blue stocking, ankle boots, a neckerchief of some bright colour, and a very tall hat. Pursuing his more quiet occupation of barber, he generally subsided into an apron not over clean, a flannel jacket, and corduroy knee shorts.

Note.—Mrs. Gamp's landlord, and friend of Bailey. He was barber and bird-fancier. He leaves the story in company with Mrs. Gamp, and Bailey, whom he vows he will take into partnership.

SWEENEY. Mrs. A laundress of chambers. *U.T.* xiv.

In figure extremely like an old family umbrella—in figure, colour, texture and smell. The tip-top complicated abomination of stockings, skirts, bonnet, limpness, looseness, and larceny.

SWEENEY. The late Mr. *U.T.* xiv.

Was a ticket-porter of the Honourable Society of Gray's Inn.

SWEEP. A little, Afterwards a master sweep. *S.B.B.*, Scenes xi.

With curly hair and white teeth. He believed " he'd been born in the vurkis, but h'd never know'd his father."

SWEEP. Little. *S.B.B.*, Scenes i.

Knocked and rung till his arms ache—sits patiently down on the door step.

SWEEP, CHIMNEY. *U.T.* xxxvi.

SWEEPS. The, On first of May, *S.B.B.*, Scenes xx

Got the dancing to themselves, and handed it down.

SWEET WILLIAM. Travelling showman. *O.C.S.* xix.

Probably as a satire upon his ugliness . . . as if he had rather deranged the natural expression of his countenance by putting small leaden lozenges into his eyes and bringing them out at his mouth.

SWEETHEARTS. At tea gardens. *S.B.B.*, Scenes ix.

SWIDGER. Charley, Junior. *C.B.*, *H.M.* i.

Nephew of Mrs. William Swidger.

SWIDGER. George, Eldest son of Mr. Philip. *C.B.*, *H.M.* i.

SWIDGER. Mr., Senior. Father of Mr. William Swidger. *C.B.*, *H.M.* i.

SWIDGER. Mr. William, Gatekeeper at student's college. *C.B.*, *H.M.* i.

A fresh-coloured busy man.

SWIFT. *M.P.*, *W.S.G.*

SWILLENHAUSEN. Baron Von. *N.N.* vi.

SWILLS. Little, Comic vocalist. *B.H.* xi.

A chubby little man in a large shirt collar, with a moist eye, and an inflamed nose.

SWINDON. *M.P.*, *E.S.*

SWISS. *M.P.*, *N.J.B.*

SWISS GUARD. The Pope's. *P.F.I.*, *R.*

SWITZERLAND. *C.S.*, *N.T.*, Act i. ; *M.P.*, *A.J.B.* ; *M.P.*, *I.* ; *P.F.I.* ; *R.P.*, *L.A.* : *R.P.*, *O.B.* ; *U.T.* vii.

SWITZERLAND. A little inn in. *C.S.*, *H.T.*

A very homely place, in a village of one narrow zigzag street—you went in at the main door through the cow-house, and among the mules, and dogs, and fowls, before ascending a great bare staircase to the rooms ; which were all of unpainted wood—like rough packing-cases.

SWIVELLER. Rebecca, Dick Swiveller's aunt. *O.C.S.* lxvi.

Spinster, deceased, of Cheselbourne in Dorsetshire.

SWIVELLER. Richard, The friend of Frederick Trent. *O.C.S.* ii.

At length there sauntered up, on the opposite side of the way—with a bad pretence of passing by accident—a figure conspicuous for its dirty smartness, which, after a great many frowns and jerks of the head, in resistance of the invitation, ultimately crossed the road and was brought into the shop.

Note.—Dick, the founder of the " Glorious Apollers," is first introduced as the friend of Frederick Trent. Dick is persuaded by Trent into an attempt to marry Nell for the sake of the money it is supposed she will receive from her grandfather. The scheme is frustrated. by the flight of Nell with the old man Dick is engaged by Sampson Brass as clerk at the instance of Quilp. While at Bevis Marks he makes the acquaintance of the Marchioness. The Marchioness nurses Dick through a serious illness, and is the means of clearing Kit Nubbles of the charge of theft. Dick enters into an annuity of a hundred and fifty pounds a year, and puts the Marchioness to school for some six years and then marries her."

SWOSHLE. Mrs. Henry George Alfred, née Tapkins. *O.M.F.* xvii.

SWOSSER. Captain, Of the Royal Navy. *B.H.* xiii.

First husband of Mrs. Badger.

SYDENHAM. Exhibition at. *M.P.*, *N.G.K.*

SYDNEY. *M.P.*, *C.* ; *R.P.*, *P.M.T.P.*

SYDNEY COLLEGE. Committee of. *M.P.*, *C.*

SYLVIA. Farmer's daughter. *G.S.E.* v.

SYMONDS' INN. Chancery Lane. *B.H.* xxxix.

A little, pale, wall-eyed, woebegone inn, like a large dustbin, of two compartments and a sifter.

T

TABBY. Miss Griffin's servant. *C.S.*, *H.H.*

Upon whose face there was always more or less blacklead.

TABERNACLE CHAPEL. Finsbury. *M.P.*, *R.S.D.*

TABLE ROCK. *A.N.* xiv.

TABLEWICK. Mrs. *S.Y.C.*

TACKER. One of Mr. Mould's assistants. *M.C.* xix.

His chief mourner in fact—an obese person, with his waistcoat in closer connection with his legs than is quite reconcilable with the established ideas of grace; with that cast of feature which is figuratively called a bottle nose; and with a face covered all over with pimples. . . . Who from his great experience in the performance of funerals, would have made an excellent pantomime actor.

TACKLETON. Gruff and Tackleton. *C.B.*, *C.o.H.* i.

A man whose vocation had been quite misunderstood by his parents and guardians. . . . He despised all toys. . . . What he was in toys, he was in other things. He delighted in his malice to insinuate grim expressions into the faces of brown-paper farmers who drove pigs to market.—You may easily suppose, therefore, that within the great green cape—there was buttoned up to the chin, an uncommonly pleasant fellow; and that he was about—as agreeable a companion as ever stood in a pair of bull-headed looking boots with mahogany coloured tops. He always had one eye wide open, and one eye nearly shut.

TADGER. Brother, Member of Ebenezer Temperance Association. *P.P.* xxxiii.

A little emphatic man, with a bald head and drab shorts.

Note.—Brother Tadger introduced Mr. Stiggins in an inebriated state to the meeting of the Brick Lane Branch—and was knocked down the ladder.

TAILOR AND FAMILY. Of the audience in theatre. *N.N.* xxiv.

TAIT. Mr., Of Edinburgh. *M.P.*, *Overs.*

TALA. Mungongo. *N.T.* xxvi.

TALFOURD. Mr. Justice. *M.P.*, *J.T.*

TALLOW CHANDLER S COMPANY. *M.P.*, *M.B.V.*

TALLY-HO. Thompson. *R.P.*, *T.D.P.*

TAMAROO. Successor to Bailey at Todger's. *M.C.* xxxii.

This ancient female had been engaged, in fulfilment of a vow, registered by Mrs. Todgers, that no more boys should darken the commercial doors; and she was chiefly remarkable for a total absence of all comprehension upon every subject whatever. She was a perfect tomb for messages and small parcels.

TAMBOUR-WORKER. A. *L.D.* xii.

A spinster, and romantic, still lodging in the yard.

TAMPLE. Bob. *M.P.*, *G.D.*

TANGLE. Mr. *B.H.* i.

TANK. The, Clerk's room in Scrooge's counting-house. *C.B.*, *C.C.*, s. i.

TAP. The, Inn attached to coach office. *S.B.B.*, Scenes xv.

TAPAAN ZEE. *A.N.* xv.

TAPE. A tyrannical old godmother. *R.P.*, *P.B.*

TAPENHAM. Mr. *M.P.*, *C.Pat.*

TAPKINS. Felix. *M.P.I.S.H.W.*

TAPKINS. Miss. *O.M.F.* xvii.

TAPKINS. Miss Antonia. *O.M.F.* xvii.

TAPKINS. Miss Euphemia. *O.M.F.* xvii.

TAPKINS. Miss Frederica. *O.M.F.* xvii.

TAPKINS. Miss Malvina. *O.M.F.* xvii.

TAPKINS. Mrs. *O.M.F.* xvii.

TAPLEY. Mark. *M.C.* v.

A young fellow of some five or six and twenty perhaps, and was dressed in such a free and fly-away fashion, that the long ends of his loose red neckcloth were streaming out behind him as often as before; and the bunch of bright winter berries in the buttonhole of his velveteen coat was as visible—as if he had worn that garment wrong side foremost. "I'm a Kentish man by birth."

Note.—Hostler at the "Blue Dragon." His spirits rose in adversity, and he was always on the outlook for greater misery, that he could be the more jolly. A whimsical, kind-hearted character. Believing that there will be some opportunity of shining under adverse circumstances he accompanies Martin Chuzzlewit to America. There he is the constant friend, although he takes the position of a servant. He nurses Martin through the fever at Eden—a place where he thinks he really can rise superior—and then takes the same complaint himself. After his second recovery they return to England; and Mark both witnesses and takes a great part in the retribution that overtakes Pecksniff. Eventually he marries Mrs. Lupin of the "Blue Dragon," and changes the name of the inn to the "Jolly Tapley."

TAPLIN. Mr. H., Comic singer of White Conduit. *S.B.B.*, Char. viii.

TAPPERTIT. Simon, Apprentice to Gabriel Varden. *B.R.* iv.

An old fashioned, thin-faced, sleek haired, sharp nosed, small eyed little fellow, very little more than five feet high—a figure, which was well enough formed, though somewhat of the leanest, for which he entertained the highest admiration—his legs, in knee-breeches, were perfect curiosities of littleness. . . . In years just twenty, in his looks much older, and in conceit at least two hundred.

Note.—Mr. Varden's apprentice. He makes himself a duplicate key and goes out at night to meetings of the "United Bull-dogs." The "Bull-Dogs" are a body of apprentices banded together to suppress their masters and elevate themselves to their former state—a state of independence, holidays and a participation in innumerable rows! Sim fancies himself in love with Dolly Varden and becomes the desperate and unscrupulous rival, so far as his spirit permits the expansion of these qualities, of Joe Willet. On the other hand, Miggs, Mrs. Varden's servant, covets his hand and his heart. As founder and captain of the "United Bull-Dogs," Simon takes part in the Gordon Riots. During the disturbances he is shot and his legs are crushed. He is eventually discharged with two wooden legs, and set up in business as a shoe black. His military and other customers become so numerous that he engages two assistants and marries the relict of a rag-and-bone merchant. With a due regard to the marriage vows he endeavours to enforce the obedience of his spouse; while she, taking advantage of his infirmity, retaliates by abstracting his wooden legs.

TAPPERTIT. Two apprentices of Simon. *B.R.* lxxxii.

In business as shoeblack.

TAPPERTIT. Simon, Wife of. *B.R.* lxxxii.

Widow of an eminent bone-and-rag collector.

TAPPLETON. Lieutenant, Dr. Slammer's Friend. *P.P.* ii.

Note.—The officer who arranged the details of Dr. Slammer's intended duel with Mr. Winkle.

TARTAR. A, Mr. Boythorn. *B.H.* ix.

TARTAR. Chambers of Mr. *E.D.* xxii.

His sitting-room was like the admiral's cabin, his bath-room was like a dairy, his sleeping chamber fitted all about with lockers and drawers, was like a seedsman's shop.

TARTAR. Retired naval lieutenant. *E.D.* xvii.

A handsome gentleman, with a young face, but with an older figure in its robustness and its breadth of shoulder; say a man of eight-and-twenty, or at the utmost thirty, so extremely sunburnt that the contrast between his brown visage and the white forehead, shaded out of doors by his hat, and the glimpses of white throat would have been almost ludicrous, but for his broad temples, bright blue eyes, clustering brown hair, and laughing teeth.

Note.—A retired lieutenant, who has inherited a fortune and occupies chambers close to those of Neville Landless in Staple Inn. He only appears towards the end of the book and makes the acquaintance of Neville and of Rosa Bud. It seems probable that the author intended him to occupy an important post in the remainder of the story.

TARTARS. Kingdom of. *M.P., T.O.H.*

TARTARY. *H.T., S.* xv.

TARTARY. Emperor of. *N.N.* xli.

TARTER. Bob, First boy at school. *R.P., T.S.S.*

TARTER. Father of Bob. *R.P., T.S.S.*

TASSO'S PRISON. *P.F.I., T.B.F.*

TATE. Mr. Nahum. *M.P., R.S.L.*

TATERS. Charles. *M.P., P.M.B.*

TATHAM. Mrs. *S.B.B.*, Scenes xxiii.

Customer of pawnbroker, pawning clothes.

TATT. Mr. *R.P., T.D.A.* ii.

TATTLESNIVEL. A town. *M.P., T.B.*

TATTLESNIVELLIAN. Outraged, *M.P., T.B.*

TATTYCORAM. Miss Meagle's maid. From the Foundling Hospital. *L.D.* ii.

A handsome girl with lustrous dark hair and eyes, and very neatly dressed.

Note.—Originally a foundling, but at the time of the story maid or companion to Minnie Meagles. She is, however, jealous and passionate. And in the belief that she is becoming more independent she runs away to Miss Wade. This is not very sucessful, and she returns to her old master with the iron box he has been scouring Europe for as an intercession.

TAUNTON. Captain. *C.S., S.P.T.* ii.

Whose eyes—were bright, handsome dark eyes—what are called laughing eyes generally, and, when serious, rather steady than severe.

TAUNTON. Miss Emily. *S.B.B.*, Tales vii.

Elder daughter of Mrs. Taunton.

TAUNTON. Miss Sophia. *S.B.B.*, Tales vii.

TAUNTON. Mrs. *S.B.B.*, Tales vii.

A good-looking widow of fifty, with the form of a giantess, and the mind of a child. The pursuit of pleasure, and some means of killing time, were the sole end of her existence. She doted on her daughters, who were as frivolous as herself.

TAUNTON. Mrs., Mother of Captain Taunton. *C.S., S.P.T.* ii.

A widow.

TAUNTON. Servant of Mrs. *C.S., S.P.T.* ii.

TAUNTON. Vale of. *B.H.* xxxvii.; *N.N.* xxxv.

TAUNTONS. Family of. *S.B.B.*, Tales vii.

TAVERN. *T.T.C.*, bk. ii., ch. iv.

TAVERN. A. *M.H.C.* ii.

TAVERN. Waiter of. *M.H.C.* ii.

TAVISTOCK SQUARE. *P.P.* xxxi.

TAVISTOCK STREET. Covent Garden. *S.B.B.*, Tales ii.

TAWELL. *M.P., I.M.*

TAX-GATHERER. *N.N.* ii.

TAX-GATHERER. *M.P., P.L.U.*

TAXEDTAURUS = Fleeced Bull, King of Persia. *M.P., F.O.H.*

People of England subjected to excessive taxation.

TAYLOR. John, A Mormon. *U.T.* xx.

TAYLOR. Mr., A preacher. *A.N.* iii.

Once a mariner—a weatherbeaten, hard-featured man.

TE' PALAZZO. (Mantua.) *P.F.I., V.M.M.S.S.*

TEACHER. Pupil, *M.P., S.S.U.*

TEACHERS. *M.P., D.V.*

TEETOTAL SOCIETY. Of Coketown. *H.T., S.* v.

TELBIN. Mr. *M.P., C.M.B.*

TELLSON'S BANK. By Temple Bar. *T.T.C.*, ii.

Tellson's wanted no light, Tellson's wanted no embellishment.

Note.—The bank at which Mr. Lorry was confidential clerk; and at which Cruncher was messenger.

TELLSON'S BANK. French branch. *T.T.C.*, bk. iii., ch. ii.

Established in the St. Germain quarter of Paris, in a wing of a large house.

" **TEMERAIRE.**" Coffee-room of. *U.T.* xxxii.

Crumbs on all the tables—stuffy, soupy, airless atmosphere, stale leavings everywhere about.

" **TEMERAIRE.**" Hotel at Namelesston. *U.T.* xxxii.

" **TEMERAIRE.**" Page at, Youth in livery. *U.T.* xxxii.

" **TEMERAIRE.**" Two ladies in bar of. *U.T.* xxxii.

Who were keeping the books.

" **TEMERAIRE.**" Waiters at. *U.T.* xxxii.

Who was not the waiter who ought to wait upon us, and who didn't.

TEMPLE. Middle. *M.H.C.* i.

TEMPLE. The. *B.H.* xix. ; *B.R.* xv. ; *C.S., H.T.* ; *G.E.* xxxix ; *M.C.* xxxviii. ; *O.M.F.* viii. ; *P.P.* xxxi. ; *R.P., B.S.* ; *R.P., G.O.A.* ; *S.B.B.*, Tales iv. ; *T.T.C.*, bk. ii., ch. iii. ; *U.T.* xiv.

TEMPLE BAR. *B.H.* i. ; *B.R.* viii. ; *C.S., T.G.S.* i ; *L.D.*, liii. ; *M.H.C.* i. ; *M.P.. G.A.* ; *M.P., T.D.* ; *M.P., W.* ; *O.M.F.* xliv. ; *R.P., P.M.T.P.*

TEMPLE CHURCH. *O.M.F.* xii.

TEMPLE GARDENS. *B.R.* xv. ; *C.S., H.T.*

TEMPLE GATE. *G.E.* xlv.

" **TEMPLE OF EQUALITY.**" Washington. *A.N.* viii.

TEMPLE OF VESTA. The. *L.D.* li.

TEMPLE STAIRS. *E.D.* xxii. ; *G.E.* xlvii.

TEMPLE WATCHMEN. One of our. *C.S., H.T.*

TENANT. Solitary, Prisoner in the Fleet. *P.P.* xli.

Poring, by the light of a feeble tallow candle, over a bundle of soiled and tattered papers.

TENANT IN CLIFFORD'S INN. Top set. *P.P.* xxi.

Shut himself up in his bedroom closet, and took a dose of arsenic.

TENTERDEN. Lord. *M.P., C.P.*

TERNI. Falls of. *P.F.I., R.D.*

TERRACINA. *P.F.I., R.D.*

TESTATOR. Mysterious visitor to Mr. *U.T.* xiv.

A man who stooped—with very high shoulders, a very narrow chest, and a very red nose. He was wrapped in a long, threadbare black coat, fastened up the front with more pins than buttons.

TESTATOR. Tenant of chambers in Lyons Inn. *U.T.* xiv.

TETTERBY. Adolphus, Eldest son of Tetterby. *C.B., H.M.* ii.

Also in the newspaper line of life, being employed, by a more thriving firm than his father and Co., to vend newspapers at a railway station—and his shrill little voice—as well known as the panting of the locomotives.

TETTERBY. Children of. *C.B., H.M.* ii.

Seven boys and one girl.

TETTERBY. Johnny, Second son of Tetterby. *C.B., H.M.* ii.

Considerably affected in his knees by the weight of a large baby, which he was supposed—to be hushing to sleep.

TETTERBY. Mr., A newsvendor. *C.B., H.M.* ii.

TETTERBY. Mrs., Wife of Mr. Tetterby. *C.B., H.M.* ii.

The process of induction, by which Mr. Tetterby had come to the conclusion that his wife was a little woman, was his own secret. She would have made two editions of himself easily.

TETTERBY AND CO. *C.B., H.M.* ii.

TETTERBY'S BABY. Daughter of Tetterby. *C.B., H.M.* ii.

TEWKESBURY. At the Hop Pole. *P.P.* l.

TEXAS. *N.N.* xiv.

THACKERAY. Mr., W. M. *M.P., I.M.T.* ; *M.P., M.E.R.*

THAMES. *A.N.* ii. ; *B.R.* xv. ; *C.S., N.T.,* Act i. ; *C.S., S.L.* iii. ; *G.E.* liv. ; *M.H.C.* i. ; *M.P., E.T.* ; *M.P., H.H.* ; *O.M.F.* i. ; *P.P.* xxi. ; *R.P., B.S.P.* ; *R.P., D.W.T.T.* ; *S.B.B.,* Scenes x ; *U.T.* iii.

THAMES POLICE OFFICE. *S.B.B.,* Tales vii.

THAMES STREET. *B.R.* xiii. ; *D. and S.* vi. ; *N.N.* xi.

THANET. Isle of. *U.T.* xvi.

THATMAN. Propective M.P. *U.T.* xxx.

THAVIES INN. *B.H.* iv.

THEATRE. City. *S.B.B.,* Char. xi.

THEATRE. Gentlemen of the. *L.D.* xx.

Some half-dozen close-shaved gentlemen, with their hats very strangely on, who were lounging about the door.

THEATRE. Manager of a private. *S.B.B.,* Scenes xiii.

He is all affability when he knows you well—or in other words when he has pocketed your money once, and entertains confident hopes of doing so again.

THEATRE. Private. *S.B.B.,* Scenes xiii.

The little narrow passages beneath the stage are neither especially clean nor too brilliantly lighted; and the absence of any flooring, together with the damp mildewy smell which pervades the place, does not conduce—to their comfortable appearance.

THEATRE. Proprietor of a private. *S.B.B.,* Scenes xiii.

May be an ex-scene painter, a low coffee-house keeper, a disappointed eighth-rate actor, a retired smuggler, or uncertificated bankrupt.

THEATRE EMPLOYE. *L.D.* xx.

A sprightly gentleman with a quantity of long black hair.

THEATRE FRANÇAIS. *M.P., W.* ; *R.P., T.N.S.*

THEATRE OF PUPPETS. The, Or Marionetti. *P.F.I., G.A.N.*

THEATRE OF VARIETIES. *M.P., N.Y.D.*

THEATRES. Penny, in Seven Dials. *S.B.B.,* Scenes v.

THEATRES. Principal patrons of private, dirty boys. *S.B.B.,* Scenes xiii.

THEBES. *M.P., E.T.*

THEOPHILE. Corporal. *C.S., S.L.* ii.

Devoted to little Bebelle . . . walking with little Bebelle . . . brought his breakfast into the place, and shared it there with Bebelle. Always Corporal and always Bebelle.

THICKNESS. Mr. *M.R.B.*

THIEF. The. *U.T.* xxxvi.

Always a thief, always a ruffian.

THIRSTY WOMAN OF TUTBURY. *N.N.* xlix.

THISMAN. Prospective M.P. *U.T.* xxx.

THISTLEWOOD. *M.P., S. for P.*

THOM. Mr., Of Canterbury. *A.N.* xviii.

THOMAS. Groom in Sir Leicester Dedlock's household. *B.H.* xl.

THOMAS. Mr. Mortimer Knag's boy. *N.N.* xviii.

A boy nearly half as tall as a shutter.

THOMAS. Pastrycook. *S.B.B.,* Tales ix.

THOMAS. Tom. *C.S., S.L.* iii.
"I was the real artist of Piccadilly, I was the real artist of Waterloo Road, I am the only artist of all those pavement-subjects—I do 'em and I let 'em out."

THOMAS. Waiter at "Winglebury Arms." *S.B.B.*, Tales viii.

THOMAS. Waterman. *O.M.F.* xv.

THOMPSON. Bill, Actor in Victoria Gallery. *S.B.B.*, Scenes ii.

THOMPSON. Daughter of. *R.P., T.D.P.*

THOMPSON. Harry, Bather at Ramsgate. *S.B.B.*, Tales iv. Friend of Captain Waters.

THOMPSON. Julia. *S.Y.G.*

THOMPSON. Mr. *S.B.B.*, Scenes v.

THOMPSON. Mr. *M.P., S.P.*

THOMPSON. Mrs. *S.Y.G.*

THOMPSON. Mrs., Wife of Thompson. *R.P., T.D.P.*

THOMPSON. Tally Ho, Horse-stealer. *R.P., T.D.P.*

THOMPSON'S. *S.B.B., O.P.* v.

THOMPSON'S. Great room. *S.B.B.*, Scenes ix.

THOMPSON'S WIFE. *R.P., T.D.P.*

THOMSON. Owner of an assumed name. *S.B.B.*, Scenes xiii.

THOMSON. Sir John, An M.P., with the yellow gloves. *S.B.B.*, Scenes xviii.

THOMSON. T. R. H. *M.P., N.E.*

THOROUGHFARE. No, A court in City of London. *C.S., N.T.*, Act i.
A courtyard diverging from a steep, a slippery, and a winding street connecting Tower Street with the Middlesex shore of the Thames.

THOROUGHGOOD AND WHITING. Bill-printers. *R.P., B.S.*

THREADNEEDLE STREET. *C.S., D.M.P.*; *N.N.* xxxv.; *S.B.B.*, Tales ii.

THREADNEEDLE STREET. Old Lady in. *M.P., F.L.*

"**THREE CRIPPLES.**" Landlord of *O.T.* xxvi.

"**THREE JOLLY BARGEMEN.**" The, Public-house. *G.E.* x.
"There was a bar—with some alarmingly long chalk scores in it on the wall at the side of the door, which seemed to me to be never paid off."
Note.—The inn to which Orlick went to eat his dinner.

THREE KINGS. Hotel of the, At Bâle. *P.F.I., V.M.M.S.S.*

THREE PROVINCIAL BROTHERS. Café of the. *M.P., N.Y.D.*

THROSTLETOWN. Delegate from *M.P., O.S.*

THROWER. A, Worker in pottery. *R.P., P.A.*

THRUSH. William. *M.P., P.M.B.*

THUGS. *M.P., S.F.A.*

THUMB. The Hon. T. Barnum. *M.P., R.S.D.*

THURSTON. Samuel, A young duellist, aged fifteen. *A.N.* xvii.

THURTELL. Mr. *M.P., T.F.*

THURTELL. Murderer. *M.P., D.M.*

TIBBS. Mr., Husband of Mrs. Tibbs. *S.B.B.*, Tales i.
Had very short legs, but by way of indemnification, his face was peculiarly long. He was to his wife what the 0 is in 90—of some importance *with* her—nothing without her. . . . He always went out at ten o'clock in the morning, and returned at five in the afternoon, with an exceedingly dirty face.

TIBER. The. *P.F.I., R.*; *R.P., D.W.T.T.*

TICKET PORTER. *D. and S.* xiii.
If he were not absent on a job, ran officiously before to open Mr. Dombey's office door, and hold it open, with his hat off, while he entered.

TICKIT. Grandchild of Mrs. *L.D.* xxvii.

TICKIT. Mrs., Cook and housekeeper to the Meagles family when the family were at home, and housekeeper only when the family were away. *L.D.* xvi.

TICKLE. Mr. *Mud. Pap.* ii.

TICKNOR. Howard Malcolm. *M.P., I.W.M.*

TICKNOR. Mrs. *M.P., I.W.M.*

TIDDY. Doll. *M.P., C.P.*

TIDDYPOT. Avestryman. *R.P.,O.V.*

TIER-RANGERS. Water-thieves. *R.P., D.W.T.T.*

TIESOLE. *P.F.I., R.D.*

TIFFEY. Mr., Spenlow and Jorkins' clerk. *D.C.* xxvi.

A dry little man who wore a stiff brown wig that looked as if it were made of gingerbread.

TIFFIN. U.S.A. *N.N.* xiv.

TIGG. Montague. *M.C.* iv.

The gentleman was of that order of appearance, which is currently termed shabby-genteel—his fingers were a long way out of his gloves, and the soles of his feet were at an inconvenient distance from the upper leather of his boots. His nether garments were of a bluish-grey—and were so stretched and strained in a tough conflict between his braces and straps, that they appeared every moment in danger of flying asunder at the knees. His coat, in colour blue and of a military cut, was buttoned, and frogged up to the chin. His hat had arrived at such a pass that it would have been hard to determine whether it was originally white or black. He wore a moustache—a shaggy moustache too.

Note.—Friend of Chevy Slyme. A self-reliant but impecunious knave. He enters into partnership with Crimple, and together they float the Anglo-Bengalee Disinterested Loan and Life Insurance Company—a bigger swindle than any he had previously engaged in. Learning that Jonas Chuzzlewit had made an attempt to poison his father, he uses the knowledge to compel Jonas to enter the firm, to invest his own money in it, and to persuade Pecksniff to do the same. Jonas turns at length and murders Tigg. The crime is discovered and the murderer arrested.

TIGGIN AND WELPS. In the calico and waistcoat piece line. *P.P.* xlix.

Employer of Bagman's uncle.

"**TILTED WAGON.**" An inn. *E.D.* xv.

A cool establishment on the top of a hill.

TIM. Fat clerk of Cheeryble brothers. *N.N.* xxxv.

A fat, elderly, large-faced clerk, with silver spectacles, and a powdered head.

TIM. Tiny, Cripple son of Bob Cratchit. *C.B., C.C., S.* iii.; and *M.P., I.W.M.*

He bore a little crutch, and had his limbs supported by an iron frame.

TIMBERED. Mr. *Mud. Pap.* i.

TIMBERRY. Mr. Snittle, Actor. *N.N.* xlviii.

Member of Mr. Vincent Crummles' Company.

TIMKINS. Candidate for Beadle's post. *S.B.B., O.P.* iv.

TIMSON. Coach-owner. *U.T.* xii.

TIMSON. Uncle of Mr. *S.B.B.*, Tales x.

TIMSON. The Reverend Charles. *S.B.B.*, Tales x.

TINKER. A. *D.C.* xiii.

Most ferocious-looking ruffian.

TINKER. A dusky. *C.S., T.T.G.* i.

Who had got to work upon some villager's pot or kettle, and was working briskly. . . . How should such as me get on, if we *was* particular as to weather? There's something good in all weathers. If it don't happen to be good for my work to-day, it's good for some other man's to-day, and will come round to me to-morrow.

TINKER. Travelling. *O.T.* xxviii.

Who had been sleeping in an outhouse . . . on Mrs. Maylie's premises.

TINKLER. Mr., Mr. Dorrit's valet. *L.D.* xli.

TINKLING. Esq., William, A schoolboy aged eight. *H.R., P.* i.

TIP. Mr. Gabblewig's "tiger." *M.P., M.N.D.*

TIPKINS. Churchwarden. *D.C.* xxix.

TIPKISSON. A constituent. *R.P.*, *O.H.F.*

TIPP. Another packer in Murdstone and Grinby's. *D.C.* xi.

TIPPIN. Master, Son of Mrs. Tippin. *S.B.B.*, Tales iv.

TIPPIN. Miss, Daughter of Mrs. Tippin. *S.B.B.*, Tales iv.

TIPPIN. Mr., Husband of Mrs. Tippin. *S.B.B.*, Tales iv.

TIPPIN. Mrs., Of the London theatres. *S.B.B.*, Tales iv. Sings in Ramsgate Library.

TIPPINS. Lady, Guest of Veneerings. *O.M.F.* ii.

With an immense, obtruse, drab, oblong face, like a face in a tablespoon, and a dyed "Long Walk" up the top of her head, as a convenient approach to the bunch of false hair behind.

Note.—Merely a "hook" in the story. She is present at the meetings of Society as represented by dinners at Veneering's and Podsnap's. She is last seen on one of those occasions eliciting the "voice" of Society in a verdict on Wrayburn's marriage.

TIPPINS. Sir Thomas. *O.M.F.* x. Knighted in mistake for somebody else.

"**TIPPINGS.**" A branch of the spiritual proceedings. *M.P.*, *S.B.*

TIPSLARK. Suitor of Mrs. Nickleby. *N.N.* xli.

TIPSTAFF. The. *P.P.* xl.

TISHER. Mrs., A deferential widow. *E.D.* iii.

With a weak back, a chronic sigh, and a suppressed voice, who looks after the ladies' wardrobes, and leads them to infer that she has seen better days.

TITBULL. Sampson, Founder of Titbull's Almshouses. *U.T.* xx.

TITBULL'S ALMSHOUSES. No. 7. *U.T.* xxvii.

A tall, straight, sallow lady, who never speaks to anybody, who is surrounded by a superstitious halo of lost wealth, who does her household work in housemaid's gloves, and who is secretly much deferred to; though openly cavilled at—and it has obscurely leaked out that this old lady has a son, grandson, nephew, or other relative, who is a "Contractor," and who would think it nothing of a job to knock down Titbull's, pack it off into Cornwall, and knock it together again.

An immense sensation was caused by a gipsy-party calling in a spring-van, to take this old lady up to go for a day's pleasure into Epping Forest.

TITBULL'S ALMSHOUSES. Occupants of. *U.T.* xxvii.

Two old men. They are little, stooping, blear-eyed old men of cheerful countenance, and they hobble up and down the courtyard wagging their chins and talking together quite gaily. They live next door to one another, and take it by turns to read—the newest newspaper they can get, and they play cribbage at night.

TITCHBOURNE STREET. Haymarket. *M.P.*, *I.M.*

TITIAN. *M.P.*, *O.L.N.O.*

TITUS. Triumphal Arches of. *P.F.I.*, *R.*

TIVERTON HIGHWAY. *M.P.*, *N.J.B.*

TIVOLI. *P.F.I.*, *R.*

TIX. Mr., A bailiff. *N.N.* xxi.

TOASTMASTER. At public dinner. *S.B.B.*, Scenes xix. With stentorian lungs.

TOBACCO DEALERS. In Chalons. *L.D.* xi.

TOBAGO. *O.M.F.* ii.

TOBBS. *M.P.*, *T.T.*

TOCKAHOOPO INDIANS. *B.H.* viii.

TODD. Mr., Baker. *S.B.B.*, Scenes i.

TODD'S YOUNG MAN. *S.B.B.*, Scenes i.

Almost as good-looking and fascinating as the baker himself; fond of mails, but more of females.

TODDLES. The boy "Minder." *O.M.F.* xvi.

TODDYHIGH. Joe, Poor boy with the Mayor. *M.H.C.* i.

Not over and above well dressed, with sunburnt face and grey hair.

TODGERS. M., Proprietress of commercial boarding-house. *M.C.* viii.

Rather a bony and hard-featured lady, with a row of curls in front of her head, shaped like little barrels of beer; and on the top of it something made of net—you couldn' call it a cap exactly—which looked like a black cobweb. She had a little basket on her arm, and in it a bunch of keys, that jingled as she came.

Note.—Mrs. Todgers kept a boarding-house. So far as the fact that she is the landlady of a boarding-house will admit of it, she is kind-hearted, and warmly befriends Mercy Pecksniff, then Mrs. Jonas Chuzzlewit, after the suicide of her husband. She is last seen at Cherry Pecksniff's "wedding" party.

"**TODGERS'S.**" Commercial boarding house. *M.C.* x.

TOFTS. Mary. *N.N.* xviii.

TOLLMAN. The. *M.C.* v.

A crusty customer, always smoking solitary pipes in a windsor chair.

TOLLMAN'S CHILDREN. *M.C.* v.

TOLLMAN'S WIFE. *M.C.* v.

TOM. *M.P., S.G.*

TOM. *M.P., S.R.*

TOM. *P.P.* iv.

TOM. Another assistant of Mr. Mould. *M.C.* xix.

TOM. Attendant at the "Leather Bottle." *P.P.* xi.

TOM. Captain, Prisoner in Newgate. *G.E.* xxxii.

TOM. Chemist's boy. *P.P.* xxxviii,

In a sober grey livery, and a gold-laced hat.

TOM. Clerk in general agency office. *N.N.* xvi.

A lean youth with cunning eyes, and a protruding chin.

Note.—The clerk at the registry office to which Nicholas applies for a position. He is overheard by Frank Cheeryble "insulting a young lady" and promptly punished, and in leaving the house of refreshment he leaves the story, never having been anything more than a subsidiary character.

TOM. Coachman of the Dover Mail. *T.T.C.* ii.

TOM. Detective. *S.B.B.*, Tales xii.

TOM. Driver of chaise. *S.B.B.*, Tales viii.

TOM. Driver of omnibus. *S.B.B.*, Tales xi.

TOM. Driver of train which killed the signalman, who saw the spectre. *C.S., T.G.S.* ii.

TOM. Gardener working for Mr. Parsons. *S.B.B.*, Tales x.

In a blue apron, who let himself out to do the ornamental for half-a-crown a day, and his "keep."

TOM. Gattleton's man. *S.B.B.*, Tales ix.

TOM. Honest, An M.P. *S.B.B.*, Scenes xviii.

The smart-looking fellow in the black coat with velvet facings, and cuffs, who wears his *D'Orsay* hat so rakishly.

TOM. Kentucky, Runaway slave of J. Surgette. *A.N.* xvii.

TOM. Mr. Peggotty's brother-in-law. *D.C.* iii.

"—Dead, Mr. Peggotty?" I hinted, after another respectful silence. "Drown dead," said Mr. Peggotty.

TOM. Mulatto. *A.N.* xvii.

TOM. One of boating-party. *S.B.B.*, Scenes x.

TOM. Tom Pettifer Ho. *C.S., M.f.T.S.* i.

TOM. Uncle, Pawnbroker. *P.P.* xlii.

TOM. Young man in the art line. *C.S., S.L.* iii.

Of that easy disposition, that I lie abed till it's absolutely necessary to get up and earn something, and then I lie abed again until I have spent it.

TOM. Young medical practitioner's boy. *S.B.B.*, Tales vi.

TOM TEA-KETTLE. *M.P., N.E.*

TOM THUMB. General. *M.P., Th. Let.*

TOM TIDDLER'S GROUND. Ruined hermitage in. *C.S., T.T.G.* i.

A dwelling-house, sufficiently substantial, all the window-glass of which—abolished, and all the windows of which were barred across with rough-split logs of trees nailed over them on the outside.

TOM-ALL-ALONE'S. A ruinous place. *B.H.* xvi.

In a black, dilapidated street—crazy houses were seized upon, when their decay was far advanced, by some bold vagrants, who, after establishing their own possession, took to letting them out in lodgings. These tumbling tenements contain, by night, a swarm of misery This desirable property is in Chancery, of course.

TOM'S COFFEE-HOUSE. *M.P., E.S.*

TOM'S WIFE. *G.E.* xi.

TOMBS. Old, of Rome. *L.D.* li.

TOMBS. The, New York Prison. *A.N.* vi.; *R.P., T.D.P.*

TOMKINS. The lady abbess of Westgate House. *P.P.* xvi.

TOMKINS. Charles. *M.P., S.G.*

TOMKINS. A pupil at Dotheboys' Hall. *N.N.* xiii.

TOMPKINS. Mr. *S.B.B.*, Scenes xix.

TOMKINS. Mr. Alfred, Boarder at Mrs. Tibbs. *S.B.B.*, Tales i.

Clerk in a wine-house—a connoisseur in paintings, and had a wonderful eye for the picturesque.

TOMLINSON. Mr., As a monk. *M.P., N.T.*

TOMLINSON. Mrs., The post-office keeper. *P.P.* ii.

Seemed, by mutual consent, to have been chosen the leader of the trade party, at the Charity Ball, Rochester.

TOMMY. Little greengrocer with a chubby face. *S.B.B.*, Char. iii.

TOMMY. Waterman. *P.P.* ii.

A strange specimen of the human race, in a sack-cloth coat, and apron of the same, with a brass label and number round his neck.

TOMPION CLOCK. Pump Room, Bath. *P.P.* xxvi.

TONGA ISLANDERS. *U.T.* xxvi.

TONY. Young, Grandson of old Weller, and son of Sam. *M.H.C.* iii.

A playin' with a quart pot—and smoking a bit of fire-wood and sayin' "Now I'm grandfather."

TOODLE. Mr., A stoker, Mrs. Toodle's husband. *D. and S.* ii.

He was a strong, loose, round-shouldered, shuffling, shaggy fellow, on whom his clothes sat negligently; with a good deal of hair and whisker, deepened in its natural tint, perhaps, by smoke and coal dust: hard knotty hands: and a square forehead, as coarse in grain as the bark of an oak.

TOODLE. Mrs. Polly, Foster-mother to Paul Dombey. *D. and S.* ii.

Mother of five children—youngest six weeks. . . .

TOODLES JUNIOR. Biler, otherwise Rob, otherwise Grinder. *D. and S.* xxii.

A strong-built lad of fifteen, with a round red face, a round sleek head, round black eyes, round limbs, and round body, who to carry out the general rotundity of his appearance, had a round hat in his hand, without a particle of brim to it—a velveteen jacket and trousers very much the worse for wear, a particularly small red waistcoat like a gorget, an interval of blue check, and the hat before mentioned.

TOODLESES. Two, Youngest children of Mr. and Mrs. Toodles. *D. and S.* ii.

Two rosiest of the apple-faced family.

TOOKE. Thomas. *M.P., O.C.*

TOOLEY STREET. *B.R.* lxvii. ; *H.T., S.* iii. ; *M.P., I.* ; *M.P., S. Pigs.*

TOORELL. Dr. *Mud. Pap.* i.

TOOTING. *B.H.* x. ; *M.P., P.T.* ; *M.P., T.F.* ; *M.P., V.D.* ; *R.P., W.I.A.W.*

TOOTLE. Tom. *O.M.F.* vi.

TOOTLEUM-BOOTS. Mrs. Lemon's baby. *H.R.* iv.

TOOTS. Another little stranger. *D. and S.* lxii.

TOOTS. Florence, Daughter of Toots. *D. and S.* lxii.

TOOTS. Mrs., *Née* Nipper, Susan. *D. and S.* lx.

TOOTS. P., Head boy at Dr. Blimber's. *D. and S.* xi.

When he began to have whiskers he left off having brains : young Toots was, at any rate, possessed of the gruffest of voices, and the shrillest of minds ; sticking ornamental pins into his shirt, and keeping a ring in his waistcoat-pocket to put on his little finger by stealth, when the pupils went out walking.

TOOTS. Susan, Daughter of Toots. *D. and S.* lxii.

TOOZELLEM. The Honourable Clementina. *L.D.* xvii.

TOPE. Mr., Chief verger and showman of the Cathedral. *E.D.* ii.

Note.—Verger of the cathedral at Cloisterham, whose grammar requires and receives correction by Mr Crisparkle.

TOPE. Mrs., Wife of the verger. A comely dame. *E.D.* ii.

TOPHANA. In the Western handicap. *M.P.. B.S.*

TOPPER. Guest of Scrooge's Nephew *C.B., C.C., S.* iii.

Had his eye on one of Scrooge's niece's sisters.

TOPPITT. Literary lady. *M.C.* xxxiv.

Wore a brown wig of uncommon size.

TORIES. In Parliament. *S.B.B.*, Scenes xviii.

TORLONIA BANK. The. *L.D.* li.

TORONTO. *A.N.* xv.

TORRAZZO. The, Cremona. *P.F.I., V.M.M.S.S.*

TORRE DEL GRECO. *P.F.I., R.D.*

TOTNES. *M.P., N.G.K.*

TOTT. Mrs. Bell. *C.S., P.o.C.E.P.*

Widow of a non-commissioned officer of the Line. She had got married and widowed at St. Vincent, with only a few months between the two events. With a bright pair of eyes, rather a neat little foot and figure, and rather a neat little turned-up nose.

TOTTENHAM COURT ROAD. *B.R.* xliv. ; *M.P., M.E.* ; *M.P., M.E.R.* ; *S.B.B.*, Scenes vii. ; *S.B.B.*, Tales v.

TOTTLE. Mr. Watkins. *S.B.B.*, Tales x.

He was about fifty years of age, stood four foot six inches and three-quarters in his socks—for he never stood in stockings at all—plump, clean, and rosy—had long lived in a state of single blessedness, as bachelors say, or single cursedness, as spinsters think.

TOULON. *P.F.I., V.M.M.S.S.*

TOWCESTER. *P.P.* li.

TOWER. Cathedral. *E.D.* iii.

Its hoarse rooks hovering about—its hoarser and less distinct rooks in the stalls far beneath.

TOWER. Leaning, Pisa. *P.F.I., R.P.S.*

TOWER. Moorish. In Vauxhall Gardens. *S.B.B.*, Scenes xiv.

That wooden shed with a door in the centre, and daubs of crimson and yellow all round, like a gigantic watchcase.

TOWER. The, Of London. *B.R.* lxvii. ; *M.C.* xi. ; *O.M.F.* iii. ; *U.T.* xxxi.

Fortified, the drawbridges were raised, the cannon loaded and pointed, and two regiments of artillery busied in strengthening the fortress and preparing it for defence.

TOWER. White. *G.E.* liv

TOWER HILL. *O.C.S.* iii. ; *O.M.F.* xxv. ; *R.P., D.W.T.T.*

TOWER STAIRS. *B.R.* li.

TOWER STREET. *B.R.* xxxi. ; *C.S., N.T.*, Act. i

TOWER STREET. Church near. *U.T.* ix.

There was often a subtle flavour of wine : sometimes of tea.

TOWLER. Private John, Of the 2nd Grenadier Guards. *M.P., R.T.*

TOWLINSON. Manservant in Dombey's household. *D. and S.* v.

TOWN. Country. *O.C.S.* xix.

TOWN. High, Overlooking French watering-place. *R.P., O.F.W.*

An old walled town—on the top of a hill.—There is a charming walk, arched and shaded by trees—whence you get glimpses of the streets below, and changing views of the other town, and of the river, and of the hills, and of the sea.

TOWN. Small, on the road to Gretna. *M.P., S.P.*

TOWN. Small English country. *B.R.* xlv.

The inhabitants supported themselves by the labour of their hands in plaiting, and preparing straw for those who made bonnets and other articles of dress and ornament from their material.

TOWN ARMS. Eatanswill. *P.P.* xii.

TOWN HALL. *G.E.* xiii.

A queer place—with higher pews in it than a church—and with some shining black portraits on the walls, which my unartistic eye regarded as a composition of hardbake and sticking-plaister.

TOWN HALL. *O.C.S.* xxvii.

TOWN HALL. Ipswich. *P.P.* xxii.

TOWNSHEND. Chauncy Hare. *M.P., C.H.T.*

TOX. Miss, Very particular friend of Mrs. Chick. *D. and S.* i.

A long, lean figure wearing such a faded air, that she seemed not to have been made in what linen-drapers call "fast colours" originally, and to have, little by little, washed out. Had the softest voice that ever was heard—nose, stupendously aquiline, had a little knob, in the very centre or keystone of the bridge, whence it tended downwards towards her face, as in an invincible determination never to turn up at anything. Miss Tox's dress—had a certain character of angularity and scantiness — when fully dressed she wore round her neck the barrenest of lockets, representing a fishy old eye.

TOX'S HOUSE. Miss, In Princess's Place. *D. and S.* vii.

A dark little house, that had been squeezed, at some remote period of English history, into a fashionable neighbourhood at the west end of the town, where it stood in the shade like a poor relation, looked coldly down upon by mighty mansions. Perhaps there never was a smaller entry, and staircase, than the entry and staircase of Miss Tox's house—it was the most inconvenient little house in England, but then—"what a situation." The dingy tenement—was her own.

TOYNBEE. Mr. *M.P., R.T.*

TOZER. Pupil of Dr. Blimber. *D. and S.* xii.

Whose shirt-collar curled up to the lobes of his ears.

TOZER. Mrs., Mother of pupil of Dr. Blimber's. *D. and S.* xiv.

TPSCHOFFKI. Major. *C.S., G.i.S.*

TRABB. Mr., Tailor. *G.E.* xix.

A prosperous bachelor.

Note.—Tailor and undertaker in "Up-town." He officiates at Pip's sister's funeral.

TRABB'S BOY. Shopboy to Trabb. *G.E.* xix.

The most audacious boy in all the country side.

Note.—The tailor's errand-boy. He annoys Pip exceedingly at various times. But is instrumental in saving Pip from Orlick.

TRACEY. Mr., Prison Governor. *M.P., C. and E.*

TRADDLES. David's friend and old schoolmate. *D.C.* v.

Note.—Traddles enters the scene as a schoolfellow of David Copperfield at Salem House. Later on when David returns to London from Dover he finds Traddles lodging with the Micawbers, and looking forward to his marriage, some day, with the "dearest girl in the world." He has a hard time and "reads" with difficulty, but ultimately succeeds. He is married and sets up house in chambers in Holborn Court, where he is surrounded with the sisters of the dearest girl in the world. The story leaves him near the top of the tree, expecting his appointment as a judge, still surrounded by the sisters. He is largely instrumental earlier in the story in freeing Mr. Wickfield from the clutches of Uriah Heep.

TRADESMAN. Accommodating. *D. and S.* xxx.

Who lent out all sorts of articles to the nobility and gentry, from a service of plate to an army of footmen.

TRADESMEN'S MORAL ASSOCIATIVE BETTING CLUB. *M.P., B.S.*

TRAFALGAR SQUARE. *M.P., R.H.F.* ; *R.P., B.S.* ; *U.T.* xxiii.

TRAGEDIAN. The leading. *S.B.B.*, Scenes xi.

Identified with drunkenness and distress.

TRAGEDIANS. The, At Astley's. *S.B.B.*, Scenes xi.

TRAMP. Another kind of. *U.T.* xi.

Got up like a countryman.

TRAMP. Bricklayer. *U.T.* xi.

TRAMP. Educated. *U.T.* xi.

Who pretends to have been a gentleman—educated at Trinity College, Cambridge.

TRAMP. Handicraft men. *U.T.* xi.

TRAMP. No occupation whatever. *U.T.* xi.

He generally represents himself, in a vague way, as looking out for a job of work; but he never did work, he never does, and he never will.

TRAMP. Slinking. *U.T.* xi.

TRAMP CHILDREN. *U.T.* xi.

Attired in a handful of rags.

"**TRAMPERS.**" Lottery Commissioners billstickers. *R.P., B.S.*

TRAMPFOOT. Of Liverpool police force. *U.T.* v.

TRAMPING SAILOR. *U.T.* xi.

TRAMPING SOLDIER. *U.T.* xi.

TRAMPS. *U.T.* xi.

TRAMPS. Harvest. *U.T.* xi.

TRAMPS. Haymaking. *U.T.* xi.

TRAMPS. Hopping. *U.T.* xi.

TRANSCENDENTALISTS. Sect of philosophers. *A.N.* iii.

TRATTORIE. Suburban. *P.F.I., G.A.N.*

TRAVELLER. *S.S., T.T.G.* i.

TRAVELLER. Demented, in train. *R.P., A.F.*

TRAVELLER. Grandfather at Christmas party. *R.P., T.C.S.*

Set out upon a journey. It was a magic journey.

TRAVELLER. Guest in great hotel in Marseilles. *L.D.* ii.

A clerical English husband in a meek strait-waistcoat, on a wedding trip with his young wife.

TRAVELLER. In coach with Esther Summerson. *B.H.* iii.

TRAVELLER. In hotel in Marseilles. *L.D.* ii.

A deaf old English mother, tough in travel, with a very decidedly grown up daughter indeed.

TRAVELLER. In hotel in Marseilles. *L.D.* ii.

Went sketching about the universe in the expectation of ultimately toning herself off into the married state.

TRAVELLER. Jaded. *E.D.* i.

TRAVELLER. Mr., The traveller. *C.S., T.T.G.* i.

TRAVELLER. Resting at "The Nutmeg Grater." *C.B., B.o.L.* iii.

Attired in mourning, and cloaked and booted like a rider on horseback—an easy, well-knit figure of a man in the prime of life. His face, much browned by the sun, was shaded by a quantity of dark hair, and he wore a moustache.

TRAVELLER. Uncommercial. *U.T.* i.

When I go upon my journeys, I am not usually rated at a low figure in the bill—when I come home from my journeys, I never get any commission—I am both a town traveller, and a country traveller, and am always on the road—I travel for the great house of Human Interest Brothers.

TRAVELLERS. For pleasure. *L.D.* ii.

Guests in great hotel in Marseilles.

TRAVELLERS. Guests in great hotel in Marseilles. *L.D.* ii.

Merchants in the Greek and Turkey trades.

TRAVELLERS. On business. *L.D.* ii.

Guests in great hotel in Marseilles.

TRAVELLERS. Six poor. *C.S., S.P.T.* i.

A very decent man, with his arm in a sling, a little sailor-boy, a mere child, a shabby-genteel personage, with a dry suspicious look; the absent buttons on his waistcoat eked out with red tape. A foreigner by birth, but an Englishman in speech, who carried his pipe in the band of his hat.

TRAVELLERS. Third party of. *L.D.* xxxvii.

Four in number: a plethoric, hungry, and silent German tutor in spectacles, on a tour with three young men, his pupils, all plethoric, hungry, and silent, and all in spectacles.

TRAVELLERS. Two, At hotel at Martigny. *L.D.* xxxix.

Mrs. Merdle and Mr. Sparklei.

TRAVELLERS' COFFEE-HOUSE. In Coketown. *H.T., R.* vi.

A nice clean house.

TRAVELLERS' TWOPENNY. *E.D.* v.

" **TREASURY.**" Guest of Mr. Merdle. *L.D.* xxi.

TREASURY. *M.P., R.T.*

TREASURY. The. Washington. *A.N.* viii.

TREATY OF AMIENS. *A.N.* xi.

TREDGEAR. John, Old resident of Laureau. *C.S., M.f.T.S.* ii.

TREGARTHEN. Mr., Father of Kitty. *C.S., M.f.T.S.* ii.

A Cornishman—a rather infirm man, but could scarcely be called old yet, with an agreeable face, and a promising air of making the best of things.

TREMONT HOUSE. An hotel. *A.N.* ii.

TRENCK. Baron. *M.P., W.S.G.*

TRENT. Frederick, Little Nell's brother. *O.C.S.* ii.

" A profligate, sir, who has forfeited every claim not only upon those who have the misfortune to be of his blood, but upon society, which knows nothing of him but his misdeeds."

Note.—Little Nell's profligate brother. He plans to marry her to his friend Dick Swiveller for the sake of the money he believes their grandfather to have. He falls in with a gang of sharpers and gamblers. Then goes abroad and continues the same course of life. His body is recognised at that hospital in Paris where the drowned are laid out to be owned.

TRENT. Little Nell's grandfather. *O.C.S.* i.

He was a little old man with long grey hair . . . though much altered by age, " I fancied I could recognise in his spare and slender form something of that delicate mould which I had noticed in the child."

TRENT. Little Nell. The principal figure in the story. *O.C.S.* i.

" She put her hand in mine, as confidently as if she had known me from her cradle . . . child she certainly was, although I thought it probable from what I could make out that her very small and delicate frame imparted a peculiar youthfulness to her appearance."

Note.—The heroine of the story is one of Dickens' most touching and pathetic characters. She lives with her grandfather in the Old Curiosity Shop. After they are turned out by Quilp, of whom the old man has borrowed money for gambling, Nellie and her grandfather leave London on foot, tramping through the country in an endeavour to find a refuge. They find many strange people on the road. Codlin and Short, the men with the "Punch," are perhaps the most lifelike characters of this miscellaneous collection. They get the idea that there will be some reward obtainable for information regarding the wanderers. Nellie guesses at something of the sort and manages to slip away from them. After this the travellers make the acquaintance of Mrs. Jarley, of Jarley's waxworks. This good woman befriends them and employs Little Nell to exhibit the figures in her show to visitors. Little Nell and her grandfather are caught in a thunderstorm one evening and take refuge in a public house, "The Valiant Soldier," Here they find three men playing cards, and the old man's dominant passion is roused. Little Nell is unable to deter him from playing, and finds him on another occasion playing with the same gang, and being persuaded to rob Mrs. Jarley. Nellie can see only one path open—"to again wander forth"; this they do. They again meet with the poor schoolmaster, who is instrumental in obtaining a post for them in the same village as that to which he has been appointed clerk. They enter upon the quiet peaceful life with thanksgiving, but Nellie's health has been destroyed, and she sinks and dies and is buried in the old church. The direction of Nell's flight has been much discussed, but it cannot be laid down with certainty.

TRENT. Valley of the Sparkling. *R.P.*, *A.P.A.*

TRESHAM. Beatrice's husband. *C.S.*, *M.J.* iv.

TRESSEL. *S.B.B.*, Scenes xiii.

TRIMMER. Mr. *N.N.* xxxv.

Getting up a subscription for the widow and family of a man who was killed in the East India Docks this morning. "Smashed, sir, by a cask of sugar."

TRING. *M.P.*, *E.S.*

TRINITY HOUSE. *O.M.F.* xxv.

TRINKLE. Mr., Upholsterer. *R.P.*, *T.D.A.* i.

TROTT. Alexander—mistaken for another. *S.B.B.*, Tales viii.

A young man, had highly promising whiskers, an undeniable tailor, and an insinuating address—he wanted nothing but valour, and who wants that with three thousand a year. Party to a duel which never came off, and taken by force to Gretna Green in mistake for Lord Peter.

TROTTER. Job. *P.P.* xvi.

Young fellow in mulberry-coloured livery, who had a large, sallow, ugly face, very sunken eyes, and a gigantic head, from which depended a quantity of lank black hair.

Note.—Job Trotter is a curious character. An abnormal cunning is united with an unwavering devotion to Jingle, his master and companion. He first enters the story in connexion with Jingle's bogus attempt to enter the bonds of matrimony. He shares Jingle's fortunes even to a debtor's prison—the Fleet—and finally accompanies him to the West Indies.

TROTTER. Captain H. D. *M.P.*, *N.E.*

TROTTLE. *C.S.*, *G.i.S.*

TROTWOOD. Betsey Trotwood's husband. *D.C.* xviii.

"The time was, Trot, when she believed in that man most entirely. He repaid her by breaking her fortune . . . married another woman, became an adventurer, a gambler and a cheat . . . and I believed him—I was a fool!—to be the soul of honour."

Note.—Miss Betsey Trotwood's husband occupies a mysterious position of anonymity until near the end of the book, when he dies. Although handsome and pleasing, he treats his wife cruelly, and they separate. He sinks low in the social scale, and periodically pesters Miss Betsey for money, which she, foolishly, she admits, gives him.

TROTWOOD. Betsey (Copperfield), god-daughter of Betsey Trotwood. *D.C.* xxxv.

TROTWOOD. Miss Betsey, David's great-aunt. *D.C.* i.

"My aunt was a tall, hard-featured lady, but by no means ill-looking. There was inflexibility in her face, in her voice, in her gait and carriage; but her . . . features were rather handsome than otherwise, though unbending and austere.'

Note.—David Copperfield's paternal aunt is so disappointed at his birth that he is not a girl, that she does not go near the family after her eccentric departure from the "Rookery." When David runs away from his uncongenial employment in London, however, he goes to her at Dover. She befriends him, puts him to a good school in Canterbury, and pays for his articles with a firm of proctors in Doctors' Commons. She loses her money, however, and they have to economise. Accompanied by Mr. Dick she comes to London to David. Together they make the best of the changed circumstances, although she still acts the part of staunch friend to David. It transpires that she had been married to a ne'er-do-well, who habitually obtained money from her. She is left in the story "in stronger spectacles, an old woman of fourscore years and more, but upright yet, and a steady walker of six miles at a stretch in winter weather."

TROWZE. Miss. *M.P., U.N.*

TROWZE. Mrs. *M.P., U.N.*

TROY. *M.P., S.B.*

TRUCK. Mr. *Mud. Pap.* i.

TRUCKERS. Less thieves than smugglers. *R.P., D.W.T.T.*

TRUEFITT'S. Mr., The excellent hairdresser's. *U.T.* xvi.

TRUMAN, HANBURY AND BUXTON. *D.C.* xxviii.; *M.P. U.N.*

TRUMBULL. Colonel, An artist and member of Washington's staff. *A.N.* viii.

TRUNDLE. Mr., The future husband of Isabella Wardle. *P.P.* iv.

Note.—A curiosity in the book, as although several times on the stage, he has never a "speaking part." He marries Miss Isabella Wardle quite prosaically.

TRUSTEE. Witty. *M.P., L.E.J.*

TRUSTEES. Ballantyne. *M.P., S.P.*

TRUSTEES. Of Titbull's Almshouses. *U.T.* xxvii.

TUCKETT'S TERRACE. *R.P., O.V.*

TUCKLE. Mr., Footman. *P.P.* xxxvii.

A stoutish gentleman in a bright crimson coat, with long tails, vividly red breeches, and a cocked hat.

TUFNELL. Mr., School inspector. *U.T.* xxix.

TUGBY. Former porter of Sir Joseph Bowley. *C.B., C.,* q. iv.

Mrs. Chickenstalker's partner in the general line.

TUGBY. Mrs., Late Chickenstalker. *C.B., C.,* q. iv.

TUGGS. Joseph, A grocer. *S.B.B.,* Tales iv.

A little dark-faced man, with shiny hair, twinkling eyes, short legs, and a body of very considerable thickness.

TUGGS. Miss Charlotte, Only daughter of Mr. and Mrs. Tuggs. *S.B.B.,* Tales iv.

The form of—fast ripening into—luxuriant plumpness.

TUGGS. Mrs., Wife of Joseph Tuggs. *S.B.B.,* Tales iv.

The figure of the amiable Mrs. Tuggs—if not perfectly symmetrical, was decidedly comfortable.

TUGGS. Simon, Only son of Mr. Tuggs. *S.B.B.,* Tales iv.

There was that elongation in his thoughtful face, and that tendency to weakness in his interesting legs, which tell so forcibly of a great mind and romantic disposition. He usually appeared in public in capacious shoes with black cotton stockings—was observed to be particularly attached to a black glazed stock, without tie or ornament of any description.

TUILERIES. The. *M.P., R.S.D.*; *U.T.* vii.

TULKINGHORN. Mr. *B.H.* ii.

The old gentleman is rusty to look at . . . wears knee-breeches tied with ribbons, and gaiters or stockings: and reputed to have made good thrift out of aristocratic marriage settlements.

Note.—Family lawyer of Sir Leicester Dedlock. He is constantly appearing and reappearing in the story, but the chief fact is that he becomes cognisant of some of the particulars of Lady Dedlock's secret. He threatens to reveal his knowledge to her husband. As a result she leaves home and dies. Mr. Tulkinghorn is found dead—shot; and Lady Dedlock and Mr. George are suspected, but Inspector Bucket traces the crime to Mademoiselle Hortense,

TULKINGHORN'S CHAMBERS. *B.H.* ii.

TULRUMBLE. Master. *Mud. Pap.*

TULRUMBLE. Mr. *Mud. Pap.*

TULRUMBLE. Mrs. *Mud. Pap.*

" **TUMBLER'S ARMS.**" The. *G.E.* xiii.

TUNBRIDGE. *R.P.*, *A.F.*

TUNGAY. Factotum at Salem House. *D.C.* v.

We were surveyed when we rang the bell by a surly face, which I found, on the door being opened, belonged to a stout man with a bull-neck, a wooden leg, overhanging temples, and his hair cut close all round his head.

TUPMAN. Tracy, Member of the Pickwick Club. *P.P.* i.

The too susceptible Tupman, who to the wisdom and experience of maturer years superadded the enthusiasm and ardour of a boy, in the most interesting and pardonable of human weaknesses—love. Time and feeding had expanded that once romantic form.

Note.—Tupman supplies the amatory character of the members of the Corresponding Society of the Pickwick Club. Tupman is easily led into a predicament by the machinations of Jingle, and goes to Cobham with the object of "hastening altogether" from the world. The Pickwickians find him preparing to do so by dining off roast fowl, bacon, ale, etc. He never proposed again. however, and finally took lodgings at Richmond, where he enjoys the admiration of the elderly ladies.

TUPPINTOCK'S GARDENS. Liggs Walk, Clapham Rise. *C.S.*, *H.H.*

TUPPLE. Mr., Junior clerk in Somerset House. *S.B.B.*, Char. iii.

A tidy sort of young man, with a tendency to colds and corns—a perfect ladies' man—such a delightful companion—delightful partner—makes one of the most brilliant and poetical speeches that can possibly by imagined.

TURIN. *M.P.*, *A.A.P.*

TURKEY. *M.P.*, *B.S.*; *P.P.* xxiii.

TURNCOCK. Attached to the waterworks. *D.C.* xxviii.; *M.P.W.*

TURNER. *M.P.*. *O.L.N.O.*

TURNKEY. At Marshalsea. *L.D.* vi.

Practical Turnkey. . . . Godfather to Little Dorrit. Time went on and the Turnkey began to fail. "When I'm off the lock for good and all, you'll be the father of the Marshalsea."

TURNKEY. In Fleet Prison. *P.P.* xl.

Stout turnkey—sat down and looked at him carelessly from time to time.

TURNKEY. In Fleet Prison *P.P.*xl.

A long, thin man—thrust his hand beneath his coat-tails, and planting himself opposite, took a long view of him."

TURNKEY. Third, Of Fleet Prison. *P.P.* xl.

Rather surly-looking gentleman, who had apparently been disturbed at his tea—stationed himself close to Mr. Pickwick, and resting his hands on his hips, inspected him narrowly.

TURNKEYS. The, Of Newgate. *B.R.* lxxiv.

TURNPIKE-KEEPER. A cobbler. *U.T.* xxii.

Unable to get a living out of the tolls, plied the trade of a cobbler.

TURNPIKE-KEEPER. Children of. Sunburnt, dusty. *U.T.* xxii.

TURNPIKE-KEEPER. Wife of. Sold ginger-beer. *U.T.* xxii.

TURNPIKE HO. *U.C.* xxxi.

TURTLE. Great, An Indian chief. *A.N.* ix.

TURVEYDROP. Mother of one of apprentices of. *B.H.* xxxviii.

The melancholy boy's mother kept a ginger-beer shop.

TURVEYDROP. Mr. Prince, Junior. *B.H.* xiv.

Christened Prince, in remembrance of the Prince Regent.

A little blue-eyed fair man of youthful appearance, with flaxen hair parted in the middle, and curling at the ends all round his head.

Note.—The son of Mr. Turveydrop. He maintains his father. And, when he marries Caddy Jellyby, they continue to do it together. They prosper, however, and Caddy is last seen with her own little carriage, working hard, but living in a better part of the town.

TURVEYDROP. Mr., Senior, A widower. *B.H.* xiv.

A very gentlemanly man indeed; celebrated, almost everywhere, for his deportment . . . with a false complexion, false teeth, false whiskers, and a wig. He had a fur collar—a padded breast to his coat, which only wanted a star or a broad blue ribbon to be complete.

Note.—Father of Prince Turveydrop. He lived on his deportment—and his son. He had married a little dancing-mistress, whom he had allowed to work herself to death; and continued the same course with his son. When his son married he still lived with them and on them. The book leaves him exhibiting his deportment about town in the same old way.

TURVEYDROP. Mrs. *See* Jellyby, Caddy.

TURVEYDROP'S APPRENTICES. *B.H.* xxxviii.

Four—one indoor, and three out. One melancholy boy—waltzing alone in the empty kitchen. Two other boys—and one dirty little limp girl in a gauzy dress, such a precocious little girl with a dowdy bonnet on. When our outdoor apprentices ring us up in the mornings I am actually reminded of the sweep.

TURVEYDROP S DAUGHTER. Little Esther. *B.H.* l.

A tiny old-faced mite, with a countenance that seemed to be scarcely anything but cap-border, and a lean, long-fingered hand, always clenched under its chin.

TUSCAN VILLAGES. *P.F.I.*, *R.P.S.*

TUSCANY. *M.P.C.P.*; *P.F.I.*, *R.D.*; *U.T.* xxviii.

TUSCANY. Dukes of. *P.F.I.*, *R.P.S.*

TUSCULUM. Ruins of. *P.F.I.*, *R.*

TUSSAUD. Madame. *R.P.*, *B.S.*

TUSSAUD'S WAXWORK. Madam. *M.P.*, *I.M.*

TUTBURY. *See* Thirsty woman of Tutbury.

TWEMLOW. Melvin, First cousin of Lord Snigsworth. *O.M.F.* ii.

Grey, dry, polite, susceptible to east wind. First-gentleman-in-Europe collar and cravat, cheeks drawn in as if he had made a great effort to retire into himself some years ago, and had got so far, and never got any further.

Note.—First cousin to Lord Snigsworth, upon whose generosity he lives. He is a member of "society" as represented by the dinners of the Veneerings and the Podsnaps. He is unassuming, but because of his relationship is "in demand" with society. He is last seen at a dinner at Veneering's defending Wrayburn's marriage to Lizzie.

TWICKENHAM. *L.D.*, bk. i.,Ch. xvi.

TWIGGER. Mr. *Mud. Pap.*

TWIGGER. Mrs. *Mud. Pap.*

TWINKLETON. Miss. *E.D.* iii.

Every night the moment the young ladies have retired to rest, does Miss Twinkleton smarten up her curls a little, brighten up her eyes a little, and become a sprightlier Miss Twinkleton than the young ladies have ever seen.

Note.—Mistress of the Nuns' House boarding-school. She becomes companion to Rosa Bud when the girls run away from Cloisterham to avoid Jasper's attentions, and carries out a brisk warfare with the Billickin, the landlady.

TWIST. Oliver, Born in a workhouse. *O.T.* i.

There was considerable difficulty in inducing Oliver to take upon himself the office of respiration. Oliver Twist's ninth birthday found him a pale, thin child, somewhat diminutive in stature, and decidedly small in circumference—nature or inheritance had implanted a good sturdy spirit in Oliver's breast.

Note.—The chief character of the book. He is the son of Agnes Fleming and Leeford (the elder), born and bred a "workhouse brat." He was apprenticed to Sowerby, an undertaker; but ran away to London. On the road he met the Artful Dodger who took him to Fagin. Fagin kept a thieves' school in Saffron Hill, and considered Oliver a suitable scholar. Monks, Oliver's half-brother, discovers him later and bribes Fagin to make a thief of the boy—to bring him to the foot of the gallows. This Fagin had already endeavoured to do. On the first morning out Oliver was chased, captured and falsely charged with stealing. He is sentenced to imprisonment by Fang, the magistrate, but is released on the testimony of the bookseller, who saw the theft committed by the Dodger. Mr. Brownlow took him home, and later, to show his trust in him, sent him with books and money to the bookseller. While on the errand he is recaptured by Nancy. He is then used by Sikes and Toby Crackit "in cracking the Chertsey Crib." But endeavouring to alarm the household, already alarmed, he is shot, and eventually taken care of by Mrs. Maylie. Nancy revealed enough of the secrets she has learned to enable Oliver's new friends to discover his parentage and to make Monks share the remainder of his father's fortune with him. Through Monks it is discovered that Rose Maylie is really Oliver's aunt.

TWO ROBINS INN. *L.T.* ii.

TYBURN. *B.R.*, Pref.; *P.P.* xliii.

TY KONG. *M.P.*, *C.J.*

TYLER'S TIGER. Mr. *M.P.*, *G.H.*

U

UMBRELLA-TAKER. *M.P.*, *P.L.U.*

UMTARGARTIE. A witch. *R.P.*, *T.N.S.*

UNCLE. Bagman's uncle. *P.P.* xlix.

Found it was grey morning, and he was sitting in the wheelwright's yard, on the box of an old Edinburgh mail, shivering with the cold and wet, and stamping his feet to warm them.

UNCLE. My, Of Diggory Chuzzlewit. *M.C.* i.

I have bestowed upon that irresistible uncle of mine everything I ever possessed—with the exception of the suit of clothes I carry about with me, the whole of my wearing apparel is at my uncle's. This gentleman's patronage and influence must have been very extensive, for his nephew writes, "His interest is too high." "It is too much," and the like.

UNCLE. Of Tozer, pupil of Dr. Blimber's. *D. and S.* xiv.

Who not only volunteered examinations of him, in the holidays, on abstruse points, but twisted innocent events and things, and wrenched them to the same fell purpose.

UNCLE GEORGE. Your, Spectre created by Mr. F.'s aunt. *L.D.* xxiii.

Nobody ever knew—whose uncle George was referred to, or what spectral presence might be invoked under that appellation.

UNCLE TOM. Thomas Balderstone. *S.B.B.*, Tales ix.

Very rich, and exceedingly fond of his nephews and nieces: as a matter of course, therefore, an object of great importance in his own family. Always in a good temper, always talking—wore top boots on all occasions—remembered all the principal plays of Shakespeare.

UNCOMMERCIAL. Mr., The Uncommercial Traveller. *U.T.* xx.

UNCOMMERCIAL TRAVELLER'S LODGINGS. In Arcadian London. *U.T.* xvi.

My lodgings are at a hatter's—my own hatter's.

UNDERRY. Mr., A solicitor. *C.S.*, *H.H.*

UNDERTAKER. *C.B., C.C., S.* i.

UNDERTAKER'S MAN. Phantom. Phantom undertaker's man in faded black. *C.B., C.C., S.* iv.

" **UNION.**" The, Workhouse. *L.D.* xxxi. ; *C.B., C.C., S.* i.

UNION HALL. *R.P., T.D.A.* i.

UNITARIAN CHURCH. In St. Louis. *A.N.* xii.

UNITED AGGREGATE TRIBUNAL. *H.T., R.* iv.

UNITED AGGREGATE TRIBUNAL. President of. *H.T.*, R. iv.

UNITED BULL DOGS. The. *B.R.* xxxvi. Formerly the 'Prentice Knights.

UNITED KINGDOM. *M.P., N.J.B.* ; *M.P., R.T.*

UNITED PICKWICKIANS. The Pickwick Club. *P.P.* i.

UNITED STATES. *A.N.* ; *B.R.* lxxii. ; *C.S., H.T.* ; *C.S., M.J.* iv. ; *H.R.* iii. ; *M.C.* xii. ; *M.P., A. in E.* ; *M.P., B.A.* ; *M.P., C.P.* ; *M.P., F.F.* ; *M.P., I.C.* ; *M.P., L.A.V.* ii. ; *M.P., L.H.* ; *M.P., N.G.K.* ; *M.P., N.S.E.* ; *M.P., O.F.A.* ; *M.P., P.P.* ; *M.P., R.S.D.* ; *M.P., T.O.P.* ; *M.P., Y.M.C.* ; *N.N.* xviii. ; *P.P.* liii. ; *R.P., T.D.P.* ; *U.T.* x.

UNITED STATES. Delegate from. *M.P., F.F.*

UNITED STATES. Inns of. *C.S., H.T.*

UNITED STATES BANK. Philadelphia. *A.N.* vii.

UNIVERSITIES. Criminal Court. *U.T.* xxxvi.

UNIVERSITIES. *See also* separate names.

UNIVERSITY. Old, In Padua. *P.F.I., A.I.D.*

UNKNOWNS. Attendant, At wedding. *O.M.F.* x.

UPPER SERVANT'S HALL. House of Commons. *M.P., B.S.*

UPPER SEYMOUR STREET. Portman Square. *M.P., C.*

UPTOWN. Scene of Pip's origin. *G.E.* i.

UPWICH. Richard, Greengrocer, juryman. *P.P.* xxxiv.

URANUS. *M.P., W.*

URBINO. *M.P., O.L.N.O.*

USHER. At Our School. *R.P., O.S.*

UTAH. *U.T.* xx.

UXBRIDGE. *C.S., D.M.* ; *D.C.* xix.

V

VAGRANT. Houseless. *S.B.B.* viii. Coiled up his chilly limbs in some paved corner, to dream of food and warmth.

VALE OF HEALTH. *O.T.* xlviii.

VALENTINE. A toy. *R.P., A.C.T.*

VALENTINE. Private. *C.S., S.L.* ii. Acting as sole housemaid, valet, cook-steward, and nurse in the family of Monsieur le Capitaine de la Cour.

VALET. Mr. Dorrit's. *L.D.* xxxix.

VALEXO. Rinaldo di, The giant belonging to Mine. *C.S., D.M.P.*

" **VALIANT SOLDIER.**" By Jem Groves. Public-house and gambling den. *O.C.S.* xxix. Where have you come from, if you don't know the " Valiant Soldier " as well as the Church catechism ?

VALMONTONE. *P.F.I., R.D.*

VAN DIEMEN'S LAND. *C.S., W.o.G.M.*

VARDEN. Dolly. *B.R.* iii. A face lighted up by the lovliest pair of sparkling eyes—the face of a pretty, laughing girl, dimpled, fresh, and healthful—in a smart little cherry-coloured mantle, with a hood of the same drawn over her head, and on the top of that hood, a little straw hat, with cherry-coloured ribbons, and worn the merest trifle on one side—a cruel little muff, and a heartrending pair of shoes.

Note.—The daughter of the old locksmith resembles her father rather than her mother in disposition, and renders the old man's life much more endurable than it would otherwise have been. She is the companion-friend of Miss Emma Haredale. Eventually she marries Joe Willet.

VARDEN. Gabriel. A locksmith. *B.R.* ii.

A round, red-faced, sturdy yeoman, with a double chin, and a voice husky with good living, good sleeping, good humour, and good health. He was past the prime of life—bluff, hale, hearty, and in a green old age—muffled up in divers coats and handkerchiefs—one of which, passed over his crown—secured his three-cornered hat and bob-wig from blowing off his head.

Note.—The locksmith's was one of those hearty, kindly characters in the delineation of which Dickens was so successful. He was father to Dolly, master of Tim Tappertit, friend of Mr. Willet, and benefactor of many of the characters of the story. In the commencement he suffers from his wife's meagrims, but he is finally left happy and comfortable.

VARDEN. Martha, Wife of Gabriel Varden. *B.R.* ii.

A lady of what is commonly called uncertain temper—who did not want for personal attractions, being plump and buxom to look at, though, like her fair daughter, somewhat short in stature.

Note.—Mr. Varden's wife is first seen as the shrew, but she ultimately becomes a good and attentive wife.

VARDEN. Mother-in-law of. Dead twenty years. *B.R.* iii.

VARIÉTÉS. Paris. *M.P., W.*

VARNA. *M.P.,N.G.K.*; *M.P.,S.F.A.*

VATICAN. The. *L.D.* xliii. ; *M.P,. T.O.H.* ; *P.F.I.*

VAUDEVILLES. Theatre of. *M.P., N.Y.D.*

VAUXHALL. *B R.* xli. ; *R.P., D.W.T.T.*

VAUXHALL BRIDGE. *C.S., S.L.* iii. ; *O.M.F.* xviii. ; *S.B.B.*, Scenes x.

VAUXHALL GARDENS. *M.P., R.H.F.* ; *P.F.I., G.A.N.* ; *S.B.B.*, Scenes xiv. ; *T.T.C.* bk. ii. ch. xii.

VAUXHALL GARDENS. Visitors to. *S.B.B.*, Scenes xiv.

Gentleman, with his wife and children and mother, and wife's sister, and a host of female friends, in all the gentility of white pocket-handkerchiefs, frills, and spencers.

VECCHIO. Palazzo. *P.F.I., R.D.*

VECCHIO. Ponte. *P.F.I., R.D.*

VECK. Margaret, Toby Veck's daughter. *C.B., C.* q. i.

VECK. Toby, Porter. *C.B., C.* q. i.

A very small, spare old man. He was a very Hercules—in his good intentions. He loved to earn his money–was very poor–and couldn't well afford to part with a delight—to believe—that he was worth his salt. Toby trotted—making with his leaky shoes a crooked line of slushy footprints in the mire—blowing on his chilly hands—poorly defended from the searching cold by threadbare mufflers of grey worsted—his cane beneath his arm.

VEFOUR. Café. *M.P., N.Y.D.*

VELINO. River. *P.F.I., R.D.*

VENDALE. Master George, Partner in Wilding and Co. *C.S., N.T.*, Act i.

A brown-cheeked, handsome fellow—with a quick, determined eye and an impulsive manner.

VENDALE. Marguerite, Wife of George Vendale. *C.S.,N.T.*, Act iv.

VENDERS. Flat fish, oyster, and fruit. *S.B.B.*, Scenes ii.

VENDOME PLACE. *R.P., A.F.*

VENEERING. Mr. Hamilton, Of Chicksey, Veneering and Stobbles. *O.M.F.* ii.

Forty, wavy-haired, dark, tending to corpulence, sly, mysterious, filmy—a kind of sufficiently well-looking veiled prophet, not prophesying.

Once traveller, or commission agent of Chicksey and Stobbles—signalised his accession to supreme power, by bringing into the business a quantity of plate-glass window, and French mahogany partition, and a gleaming and enormous door-plate.

Note.—As the name denotes these people were of recent manufacture and a "trifle sticky." He had been commission agent in Chicksey and Stobbles, but in time he becomes the firm. His dinners are the media for advancing the story on several occasions. He enters Parliament for a rotten borough, but eventually becomes bankrupt, and retires to Calais, where the family live on Mrs. Veneering's jewels.

VENEERING. Mr., and Mrs., Baby of. *O.M.F.* ii.

A bran-new baby.

VENEERING. Mrs. Anastatia. *O.M.F.* ii.

Fair, acquiline-nosed and fingered, not so much light hair as she might have, gorgeous in raiment and jewels, enthusiastic, propitiatory, conscious that a corner of her husband's veil is over herself.

VENEERING'S. House of. *O.M.F.* ii.

A bran-new house in a bran-new quarter of London.

VENEERING'S. Nurse of Mrs. *O.M.F.* xx.

VENGEANCE. The, A woman revolutionist. *T.T.C.*, bk.ii.,ch.xxi.

The short, rather plump wife of a starved grocer.

Note.—Friend of Madame Defarge. She not only takes a leading part in the Revolution, but she enjoys intensely the executions. And she is left in the story gloating over the execution of Sydney Carton Darnay, but bewailing the absence of Madame Defarge. In the "prophetic vision" she is executed later on by the guillotine

VENICE. *L.D.* xxxix. ; *P.F.I.*, *A.I.D.* ; *R.P.*, *D.W.T.T.*

VENICE. The inns of. *C.S.*, *H.T.*

With the cry of the gondolier below.

VENNING. Mrs., Inhabitant of Silver Store Island. *C.S.*, *P.O.C.E.P.*

A handsome, elderly lady.

VENTRILOQUIST. *U.T.* xxv.

Thin and sallow, and of a weakly aspect.

VENUS. Mr., Preserver of animals and birds. *O.M.F.* vii.

A sallow face with weak eyes, surmounted by a tangle of reddish-dusty hair—no cravat on—no coat on—only a loose waistcoat over his yellow linen. His eyes are like the overtired eyes of an engraver, but he's not that ; his expression and stoop are like those of a shoemaker, but he is not that.

Note.—Friend of Silas Wegg. Silas takes Venus into his confidence and together they explore and examine the dust mounds. Venus allows Wegg to think he is with him in his scheme for blackmailing Mr. Boffin, but he early becomes disgusted with its meanness and dishonesty and reveals it to Mr. Boffin. He is a taxidermist and "articulator" in Clerkenwell in love with Pleasant Riderhood, whom he eventually marries.

VERBOSITY. Member for. *R.P.*, *O.H.M.*

VERDI. Signor. *M.P.*, *M.M.*

VEREY. Café. *M.P.*, *N.Y.D.*

VERGER. The. *C.S.*, *S.P.T.* i.

VERISOPHT. Frederick Lord, Guest of Ralph Nickleby. *N.N.* xix.

The gentleman exhibited a suit of clothes, of the most superlative cut, and a pair of whiskers of similar quality, a moustache, a head of hair, and a young face.

Note. —One of Sir Mulberry Hawk's fledglings whom he designs to pluck. He quarrels with his mentor over Kate Nickleby and is killed in a duel with Sir Mulberry.

VERITY. Mr. *G.S.E.* iv.

VERMONT. *A.N.* iii.

VERNON. Mr. *M.P.*, *G.F.*

VERONA. *P.F.I.*, *V.M.M.S.S.*

VERULAM BUILDINGS. *U.T.* xiv.

VERULAM WALL. Old. *B.H.* xliii.

VESTRIS. Madame. *R.P.*, *B.S.*

VESTRY. Our. *R.P.*, *O.V.*

VESTRY-CLERK. The, An attorney. *S.B.B.*, *O.P.* i.

A short, pudgy little man, in black, with a thick watch-chain of considerable length, terminating in two large seals and a key.

VESUVIUS. Mount. *D.C.* xxiii.; *P.F.I.*, *R.P.S.*; *R.P.*, *L.A.*

VETCHES. Edward. *M.P.*, *P.M.B.*

VETERINARY COLLEGE. *D.C.* xxvii.

VETERINARY HOSPITAL. *P.P.* xxi.

VETTURINO. Half-French, half-Italian. *P.F.I.*, *G.A.N.*

VEVAY. *C.S.*, *N.T.*, Act iii.

VEVAY. The town of. *P.F.I.*, *V.M.M.S.S.*

VHOLES. Jane. *B.H.* xxxvii.

VHOLES. Mr., A widower — a lawyer. *B.H.* xxxvii.

A sallow man with pinched lips that looked as if they were cold, a red eruption here and there upon his face, tall and thin, about fifty years of age, high-shouldered, and stooping. Dressed in black, black-gloved, and buttoned to the chin.

Note.—Richard Carstone's solicitor in the great Chancery suit. He does not appear to do much, and Richard is encouraged in his unfortunate pursuit of a myth.

VIA GREGORIANA. *L.D.* xlvii.

VIA SACRA. *P.F.I.*, *R.*

VICAR GENERAL'S OFFICE. *D.C.* iv.

VICAR OF WAKEFIELD. *M.P.*, *F.F.*

VICAR'S FAMILY. *M.P.*, *E.C.*

VICE CHAMBERLAIN. [Of Queen Adelaide.] *M.P.*, *C.C.*

VICKSBURG. *A.N.* xvii.

VICOLI OF VIENNA. *M.P.*, *N.G.K.*

VICTORIA. Queen of England. *M.C.* xxi.; *M.P.*, *C.C.*; *M.P.*, *E.T.*; *M.P.*, *G.L.A.*; *M.P.*, *N.E.*; *M.P.*, *N.G.K.*; *M.P.*, *O.L.N.O.*; *M.P.* *T.B.*; *R.P.*, *P.M.T.P.*

VICTORIA GALLERY. *S.B.B.*, Scenes ii.

VICTORIA THEATRE. *M.P.*, *A.P.*, *S.B.B.*, Scenes ii.

VICTUALLER. Mr. Licensed, Host of the "Snug." *U.T.* v.

A sharp and watchful man—attended to his business himself, he said. Always on the spot.

VIDE POCHE. Carondelet. *A.N.* xiv.

VILDSPARK. Tom, Case of manslaughter quoted by Sam Weller. *P.P.* xxxiii.

VILLAGE. An English. *M.P.*, *V.C.*

VILLAGE. Pip's home. *G.E.* i.

VILLAGERS. *T.T.C.*, bk. ii., ch. viii.

VILLAGES. Swiss. *P.F.I.*, *V.M.M.S.S.*

VILLAIN. The greatest = William Bousefield. *M.P.*, *D.M.*

VILLE. Hotel de. *U.T.* xviii.

VILSON. *P.P.* xxxix.

VINES. The, An open green in Rochester. *C.S.*, *S.P.T.* iii.

VINYARD. James R. *A.N.* xvii. Member from Grant County.

VINING. Miss, Actress. *M.P.*, *V. and B.S.*

VINTNERS' COMPANY. *C.S.*, *N.T.*, Act i.

VIRGILIANA. Piazza (Mantua). *P.F.I.*, *V.M.M.S.S.*

VIRGINIA. (U.S.A.) *A.N.* viii.; *M.P.*, *V. and B.S.*

VIRGINIUS. *M.P.*, *V. and B.S.*

VISCOUNT. A certain. *M.C.* xxviii.

VISITOR. One other. *M.P.*, *P.L.U.*

VISITOR. To bar-parlour. *S.B.B.*, Char. iii.

An elderly gentleman with a white head and broad-brimmed brown hat.

VISITORS. Female, At Manor Farm. *P.P.* xxviii.

VISITORS. To Martin in room of state of National Hotel. *M.C.* xxii.

One after another, dozen after dozen, score after score—all shaking hands with Martin. Such varieties of hands, the thick, the thin, the long, the short, the fat, the lean—the hot, the cold, the dry, the moist, the flabby—such diversities of grasp.

VITERBO. *P.F.I.*, *R.*; *P.F.I.*, *R.P.S.*

VOIGT. Maître, Chief notary of Neuchâtel. *C.S.*, *N.T.*, Act iv.

Professionally and personally, the notary was a popular citizen. His long brown frock coat and his black scull-cap, were among the institutions of the place; and he carried a snuff-box which, in point of size, was popularly believed to be without parallel in Europe.

VOIGT. Maître, Room of. *C.S., N.T.*, Act iv.

A bright and varnished little room, with panelled walls, like a toy chamber. According to the seasons of the year, roses, sun-flowers, holly-hocks, peeped in at the windows. A large musical box on the chimney-piece often trilled away—had to be stopped by force on the entrance of a client, and irrepressibly broke out again the moment his back was turned.

VOLUMNIA'S MAID. *B.H.* lviii.

VOLUNTEERS. Royal East London. *B.R.* xli.

VOTERS. With blue cockades. *P.P.* xiii.

VUFFIN. Mr., Travelling showman. *O.C.S.* xix.

The proprietor of a giant, and a little lady without legs or arms.

W

WAAGEN. Dr. *M.P., P.L.U.*

WACKLES. Miss Jane. *O.C.S.* viii.

"The art of needlework, marking and samplery, by Miss Jane Wackles," at the Ladies' Seminary, Miss Jane numbered scarcely sixteen years.

WACKLES. Miss Melissa. *O.C.S.* viii.

"English grammar, composition, geography and the use of the dumb-bells, by Melissa Wackles," at the Ladies' Seminary. Miss Melissa verged on the autumnal.

WACKLES. Miss Sophia, afterwards Mrs. Chegg. *O.C.S.* vii.

"She's all my fancy painted her, sir, that's what she is."

WACKLES. Mrs. *O.C.S.* viii.

"Corporal punishment, fasting, torturing and other terrors," by Mrs. Wackles, at the Ladies' Seminary.

WADE. Miss. *L.D.* ii.

A handsome young English-woman, travelling quite alone, who had a proud observant face—so still and scornful, set off by the arched dark eyebrows, and the folds of dark hair. Although not an open face, there was no pretence in it.

Note.—She inveigles Tattycoram away from the Meagles and retains her by force of character. Tattycoram is very miserable, however, and runs away from her to return to the Meagles.

WAGGONER. Of Mr. Jarndyce's waggon. *B.H.* vi.

WAGGONER. The sleepy. *S.B.B.*, Scenes i.

WAGGONER'S BOY. *S.B.B.*, Scenes i.

Luxuriously stretched on the top of the fruit-baskets, forgets his curiosity to behold the wonders of London.

WAGHORN. Mr. *Mud. Pap.* i.

WAITER. *D.C.* v.

WAITER. *D. and S.* lv.

WAITER. *M.P., L.T.*

WAITER. At Bachelors' Inns at Temple Bar. *M.C.* xlv.

In white waistcoat, never surprised—a grave man, and noiseless.

WAITER. At coffee-house in Ludgate Hill. *L.D.* iii.

WAITER. At famous inn—in Salisbury. *M.C.* xii.

WAITER. At old Royal Hotel. *P.P.* l.

WAITER. At the Spaniards' tea garden. *P.P.* xlvi.

WAITER. Come of a family of waiters. *C.S., S.L.* i.

WAITER. In restaurant. *P.P.* xliv.

WAITER. Innocent young, in hotel at Greenwich. *O.M.F.* liv.

With weakish legs, as yet unversed in the wiles of waiterhood, and but too evidently of a romantic temperament—finding, by ill fortune, a piece of orange flower somewhere in the lobbies—approached—and placed it on Bella's right hand.

WAITER. Live, Of "White Horse Cellar." *P.P.* xxxv.
Which article is kept in a small kennel for washing glasses, in a corner of the compartment.

WAITER. Non-resident, Laundress' daughter's husband. *P.P.* xlvii.

WAITER. Of "The Bush." *P.P.* xlviii.

WAITER. Representative of waiter of tavern. *M.H.C.* ii.
A poor, lean, hungry man.

WAITERING. Father of the, Old Charles. *C.S., S.L.* i.

WAITERS. At the "Great White Horse." *P.P.* xxiv.

WAITERS. Hired. *P.P.* xv.
A dozen in the costume of their country—and very dirty costume too.

WAITERS. Two, At Guildhall. *S.B.B.*, Scenes xix.

WAITERS. Two, At "The Peacock." *P.P.* xiii.
"Pumpin' over the independent woters as supped there last night."

WAITING MAIDS. Of Dorrit's party. *L.D.* xxxvii.

WAITRESS. *U.T.* xxii.

WAITRESS. A, Sister of waiter. *C.S., S.L.* i.

WAITS. The. *C.S., S.P.T.* iii.

WAITS. The. *R.P., A.C.T.*

WAKEFIELD. Mr., *M.P., C.P.*

WAKEFIELDS. The. *S.B.B.*, Tales vii.
Mr. Wakefield, Mrs. Wakefield, and Miss Wakefield of the steam excursion party.

WAKLEY. Mr. *M.P., P.T.*

WAKLEY. Mr., Late coroner. *U.T.* xviii.
Nobly patient and humane.

WALCOT SQUARE. Lambeth. *B.H.* lxiv.

WALDENGARVER. Mr., An actor at a small provincial theatre. *G.E.* xxxi.

WALES. *C.S., M.J.* iv.; *M.P., E.S.*; *M.P., R.S.*; *U.T.* ii.

WALES. Young Prince of. *B.R.* lxxviii.

WALKER. A crimp. *U.T.* v.

WALKER. Mick, Regular boy at Murdstone and Grinby's. *D.C.* xi.

WALKER. Mr. *S.B.B.*, Scenes xix..
Auditor of indigent Orphans Friends' Benevolent Institution.

WALKER. Mr., Prisoner in lock-up-house. *S.B.B.*, Tales x.
A horsedealer from Islington.

WALKER. Mr. H. Tailor; convert to temperance. *P.P.* xxxiii.
When in better circumstances, owns to have been in the constant habit of drinking ale and beer . . . is now out of work and penniless, has nothing but cold water to drink, and never feels thirsty.

WALKER. Mrs., At No. 5. *S.B.B.*, Scenes ii.

WALKER. Mrs., Convert to temperance. *P.P.* xxxiii.

WALKER. Mr. and Mrs., Children of. *P.P.* xxxiii.

WALKER. Owner of an assumd name. *S.B.B.*, Scenes xiii.

WALKER. Secret name. *N.N.* ii.

WALL STREET. New York. *A.N.* vi.
The Stock Exchange and Lombard Street of New York.

WALLACE. Mr., Member for Greenock. *M.P., M.E.R.*

WALLACE. Mr. Vincent. *M.P., M.M.*

WALMER. Mr., Father of Master Harry. *C.S., H.T.*
A gentleman of spirit, and good-looking, and held his head up when he walked, and had what you may call fire about him.

WALMERS. Master Harry. *C.S., H.T.*

WALTER. An Indian merchant. *R.P., A.C.T.*

WALTER. Edward M'Neville, Theodosius' butler. *S.B.B.*, Tales iii.

WALTERS. Charley, Inmate of workhouse. *R.P., W.I.A.W.*

WALTON. *O.M.F.* xli.

WALWORTH. *G.E.* xxiv. ; *S.B.B.*, Tales vi. ; *U.T.* vi.

WALWORTH. House of patient in. *S.B.B.*, Tales vi.

A small low building, one storey above the ground—an old yellow curtain was closely drawn across the window upstairs, and the parlour shutters were closed, but not fastened. The house was detached from any other.

WALWORTH. Inmate of patient's house in. *S.B.B.*, Tales vi.

A tall, ill-favoured man, with black hair, and a face (as the surgeon declared afterwards), as pale and haggard as the countenance of any dead man he ever saw.

WANDSWORTH. *C.S.*, *D.M.* ; *S.B.B.*, Tales v.

WANT. Name of a bird. *B.H.* xiv.

WAPPING. *B.R.* liii. ; *C.S.*, *M.f.T.S.* v. ; *H.T.*, *S.* vi. *M.P.*, *G.A.* ; *O.M.F.* xxix. ; *U.T.* iii.

WAPPING OLD STAIRS. *U.T.* iii.

WAPPING WORKHOUSE. East end of London. *U.T.* iii.

WAPPING WORKHOUSE. Matron of. *U.T.* iii.

Very bright and nimble—quick, active little figure and intelligent eyes.

WAPPING WORKHOUSE. Two aged inmates of. *U.T.* iii.

Sitting by the fire (in one large ward) in armchairs of distinction—were two old women—the younger of the two, just turned ninety, was deaf, but not very—in her early time she had nursed a child—now another old woman, more infirm than herself, inhabiting the very same chamber. The elder of this pair, ninety-three —was a bright-eyed old soul, really not deaf—and amazingly conversational.

WAPPING WORKHOUSE. Two inmates of ward for idiotic and imbecile. *U.T.* iii.

Two old ladies in a condition of feeble dignity, which was surely the very last and lowest reduction of self-complacency, to be found in this wonderful humanity of ours.

WAPPING WORKHOUSE. Wardswoman of ward for idiotic and imbecile. *U.T.* iii.

An elderly able-bodied pauperess, with a large upper lip, and an air of repressing and saving her strength biding her time for catching or holding somebody—a reduced member of my honourable friend Mrs. Gamp's family

WAR HATCHET. An Indian chief. *A.N.* ix.

WAR OFFICE. *B.R.* xxxi.

WARDEN. Of Fleet Prison. *P.P.* xl.

WARDEN. Master detective. *S.B.B.*, Tales xii.

WARDEN. Mr., A client of Snitchey and Craggs. *C.B.*, *B.o.L.* ii.

A man of thirty, or about that time of life, negligently dressed, and somewhat haggard in the face, but well-made, well-attired, and well-looking.

WARDEN. Wife of Michael. *Née* Marion Jeddler. *C.B.*, *B.o.L.*

WARDLE. Emily, Wardle's daughter. *P.P.* iv.

Note.—Daughter of Mr. Wardle. Marries Mr. Snodgrass and settles down on a farm at Dingley Dell.

WARDLE. Isabella, Wardle's daughter. Married Mr. Trundle. *P.P.* iv.

WARDLE. Mr. *P.P.* iv.

In an open barouche . . . stood a stout old gentleman, in a blue coat and bright buttons, corduroy breeches and top boots.

Note.—Wardle's is a pleasing picture of the old English yeoman farmer—jovial in spirits and substantial in body and purse. He has two daughters who are the means of affording many interesting incidents and adventures. Mr. Snodgrass marries Emily, and Isabella is wedded to Mr. Trundle. Tupman falls in love with Wardle's sister Rachel. Jingle supplants him and elopes, giving rise to the famous episode of the chase from Muggleton to London, which results in the discovery of Sam Weller. Wardle is a good friend to the Pickwickians, who visit him on occasion at the Manor Farm, Dingley Dell. Mr. Wardle and the Pickwickians meet at the grand review at Rochester. Wardle is left in the midst of Snodgrass' wedding festivities.

WARDLE. Mrs., Mr. Wardle's mother. *P.P.* vi.

A very old lady, in a lofty cap and a faded silk gown.

Note.—Old Wardle's mother. She is deaf, but affects to be more deaf than she really is. She is seventy-three years of age.

WARDLE. Miss Rachel, Wardle's sister; a "lady of doubtful age." *P.P.* iv.

"She's a miss, she is; and yet she ain't a miss—eh, sir, eh?"

Note.—Mr. Wardle's sister. She displays a shrewish jealousy of her nieces. Tupman falls in love with her. But Jingle by a clever ruse transfers her affections to himself. They elope together. Pickwick and Wardle pursue them, but the chaise breaks down, and the fugitives escape. They are discovered at the White Hart Inn in the Borough in time for the marriage to be prevented. Jingle is bought off for £120, and Miss Rachel returns to Dingley Dell.

WARDOUR STREET. *M.P., I.M.*

WARDS City. *B.R.* lxvii.

WARE. *M.P., E.S.*

"**WAREHOUSE.** The," Of Mr. Mortimer Knag. *N.N.* xviii.

About the size of three Hackney carriages.

WARNER. Captain. *M.P., G.D.*

WARREN. An engine driver. *A.N.* iii.

WARREN. Mr. *M.P., E.T.*

WARREN. Mr. *S.B.B.*, Scenes v.

WARREN. The. *B.R.* i.

A large old red brick mansion, a dreary, silent building, with echoing courtyards, desolated turret chambers, and whole suites of rooms shut up and mouldering to ruin.

WARREN STREET. *M.P., M.E.*

"**WARWICK.** The Earl of," A pickpocket. *R.P., D.W.I.F.*

"**WARWICK ARMS.**" An inn. *R.P., T.D.P.*

WARWICK CASTLE. *D. and S.* xxvi.

WARWICK LANE. *R.P., M.O.F.F.*

WARWICK STREET. *B.R.* l.

WARWICKSHIRE. *D. and S.* lviii.; *T.T.C.*, bk. ii. ch. xviii.

WASHINGTON. Negro man slave. *A.N.* xvii.

WASHINGTON. Auxiliary Temperance Societies. *A.N.* xi.

WASHINGTON. "The city of magnificent distances." *A.N.* iii.; *M.P., I.C.*

WASHINGTON MONUMENT. Baltimore. *A.N.* ix.

"**WASP.**" Passenger in train. *R.P., A.F.*

WASTE. Name of a bird. *B.H.* xiv.

WATCH. Mr. Weller's, A Kitchen club in Master Humphrey's. *M.H.C.* v.

Consisting of the housekeeper, the barber and Mr. Weller and Sam.

WATCHMAKER. The. *G.E.* viii.

WATCHMAN. A. *B.R.* lxi.

WATCHMEN. Temple, One of. *C.S., H.T.*

WATERBROOK. Mr., Mr. Wickfield's agent. *D.C.* xxv.

A middle-aged gentleman with a sore throat and a good deal of shirt-collar, who only wanted a black nose to be the portrait of a pug dog.

WATERBROOK. Mrs. *D.C.* xxv.

A large lady—or who wore a large dress, I don't exactly know which was dress and which was lady.

WATERHOUSE. Pegg. *U.T.* v.

WATERING PLACE. Our English. *R.P., O.E.W.*

Sky, sea, beach, and village, lie as still before us as if they were sitting for the picture.

WATERING PLACE. Our French. *R.P., O.F.W.P.*

WATERLILY. Hotel at Malvern. *M.P., M.D.*

WATERLOO. *A.N.* xvii.; *C.S., S.L.* iii.; *M.P., G.D.*

WATERLOO BRIDGE. *B.H.* xxi.; *M.P., G.F.*; *P.P.* xvi.; *R.P., D.W.T.T.*; *S.B.B.*, Scenes xiii.; *S.B.B.*, Tales xii.; *U.T.* x.

WATERLOO PLACE. *S.B.B.*, Scenes xv.

WATERLOO ROAD. *C.S., S.L.* iii.; *R.P., B.S.*: *R.P., D.W.T.T.*; *U.T.* xxxvi.

WATERMAN. *S.B.B.*, Scenes vii.

Dancing the "double shuffle" to keep his feet warm.

WATERMAN. With one eye. *D. and S.* xix.

Had made the captain out some mile and half off, and had been exchanging unintelligible roars with him ever since.

WATERMEN. *S.B.B.*, Scenes ii.

With dim lanterns in their hands, and large brass plates upon their breasts—retire to their watering-houses, to solace themselves with the creature comforts of pipes and purl.

WATERMEN. Thames. *U.T.* xiv.

WATERS. Captain Walter *S.B.B.*, Tales iv.

A stoutish, military-looking gentleman in a blue surtout buttoned up to his chin, and white trousers chained down to the soles of his boots.

WATERS. Companion to a married lady. *N.N.* xxi.

WATERS. Mrs. Captain. *S.B.B.*, Tales iv.

Black-eyed young lady.

WATERSIDE - -LABOURERS. At Ratcliff. *U.T.* xxx.

Occupants of single rooms.

WATERTOAST GAZETTE. Two gentlemen from the. *M.C.* xxii.

Had come express to get the matter for an article on Martin—one took him below the waist; one above.

WATKINS. Mr., Kate Nickleby's godfather. *N.N.* xviii.

Said he was very sorry he couldn't repay the fifty pounds just then—should take it very unkind if we didn't buy you a silver coral and put it down to his old account.

WATKINS. The, Who kept "The Old Boar." *N.N.* xviii.

WATKINS THE FIRST. King. *H.R.* ii.

WATKINS THE FIRST. Queen of. *H.R.* ii.

WATSONS. *S.Y.G.*

WATT. *M.P., S.*

WATTS. The tomb of Master Richard. *C.S., S.P.T.* i.

With the effigy of worthy master Richard starting out of it like a ship's figure head.

WATTS. Worshipful Master Richard. *C.S., S.P.T.* i.

WATTS' CHARITY. *C.S., S.P.T.*

A clean white house, of a staid and venerable air, with an arched door, choice long low lattice windows, and a roof of three gables.

WATTS' CHARITY. Daughter of matron off. *C.S., S.P.T.* i.

WATTS' CHARITY. Matron of. *C.S., S.P.T.* i.

A decent body, of wholesome matronly appearance—a mighty civil person.

WATTY. Mr., A bankrupt. *P.P.* xxxi.

A rustily-clad, miserable-looking man in boots with tops, and gloves without fingers. There were traces of privation and suffering—almost of despair, in his lank and careworn countenance.

Note.—Mr. Perker's bankrupt client; to whom his lawyer is not at home. Cf. with the chancery characters of Bleak House.

WAYFARER. Hungry. *S.B.B.*, Scenes ii.

WEBB. Lieutenant. *M.P., N.E.*

WEBSTER. *M.P., O.L.N.O.*

WEBSTER. Mr. *A.N.* xiv.

WEBSTER. Mr. Benjamin, as Joey Ladle. *M.P., N.T.*

WEDGINGTON. Master B., Aged ten months. *R.P., O.o.S.*

WEDGINGTON. Mr. B., An actor. *R.P., O.o.S.*

WEDGINGTON. Mrs, B., An actress. *R.P., O.o.S.*

WEDLAKE. Mary *M.P., F.F.*

WEEDLE. Anastasia, Emigrant. *U.T.* xx.

With Mrs. Jobson. A pretty girl in a bright garibaldi.

WEEVLE. *See* Jobling, Tony.

WEGG. Silas. *O.M.F.* v.

A man with a wooden leg (had sat for some years) with his remaining foot in a basket in cold weather, picking up a living in this wise. Every morning—he stumped to the corner, carrying a chair, a clothes-horse, a pair of trestles, a board, a basket, and an umbrella, all strapped together. The board and trestles became a counter—the basket supplied the fruit and sweets he offered for sale upon it, and became a foot-warmer. The unfolded clothes-horse displayed a choice collection of half-penny ballads. All weathers saw the man at his post, When the weather was wet, he put up his umbrella over his stock-in-trade, not over himself. In front of his sale board hung a little placard, like a kettle-holder, bearing the inscription—

Errands gone
On with fi
Delity By
Ladies and Gentlemen
I remain
Your humble Servt
Silas Wegg.

Note.—Introduced as a stall-keeper in the vicinity of Cavendish Square. Mr. Boffin is attracted by the collection of ballads which flanks the fruit and gingerbread, and hires the vendor for two hours every evening to read to him. Wegg is an illiterate rascal. Being put in charge of the Bower he discovers a will later than that proved by Mr. Boffin. By this he hopes to keep the Golden Dustman's nose to the grindstone, i.e., to extract from him all or most of the money Boffin has inherited. Boffin allows him to continue under this delusion for for some time, Mr. Venus having betrayed him because of the meanness of his scheme, and then greatly surprising him by showing that he was cognisant of the scheme, and proving the existence of a will still later than that discovered by Wegg. Silas, no longer a thriving "literary man with a wooden leg," then returns to selling fruit and gingerbread.

WELBECK STREET. *B.R.* lii.

WELLER. Mrs, *P.P.* xx.

"There never was a nicer woman as a widder than that 'ere second wentur of mine. All I can say on her now is, that as she was such an uncommon pleasant widder, it's a great pity she ever changed her condition. She don't act as a vife. Take example by your father, my boy, and be wery careful o' widders all your life."

Note.—The buxom widow Mrs. Clarke, whom Tony Weller married. She is grossly imposed upon by the hypocritical shepherd, the Rev. Stiggins, who drinks unlimited pineapple-rum at the "Marquis of Granby." Mrs. Weller's public-house. Mrs. Weller thinks her husband a reprobate and renders his life miserable. She catches cold whilst "settin too long on the damp grass in the rain a-hearin' of a shepherd who warn't able to leave off till late at night owen to his havin' vound his-self up vith brandy and water," and dies regretting that she hasn't looked after Tony better.

WELLER. Sam. *M.H.C.* iii.; *P.P.* x.

Habited in a coarse-striped waistcoat, with black calico sleeves, and blue glass buttons; drab breeches and leggings.

Note.—Next to Pickwick, Sam Weller is the most important character in the book. He is first met with cleaning boots at the "White Hart" inn, Borough. Mr. Pickwick is very favourably impressed and engages him as his servant. Sam then accompanies the Pickwickians on their travels. He is an amusing and invaluable witness in the trial Bardell v. Pickwick. He is instrumental in discovering Jingle's machinations. When Mr. Pickwick elects to go into the Fleet Prison rather than pay costs and damages, Sam arranges for his own committal to the same prison. When Pickwick is exposing Jingle to the Mayor of Ipswich, Sam meets Mary, the housemaid, with whose charms he is very much struck. When Mr. Pickwick settles down at Dulwich, Sam refuses to leave him, but after two years Mary is promoted to the position of housekeeper to Mr. Pickwick and she and Sam are married. According to Sam himself, he was turned out on the streets at a tender age for his education, with the result that he is full of a shrewd, quaint humour. He afterwards reappeared in "Master Humphrey's Clock."

WELLER. Tony, Sam Weller's father. *M.H.C.* iii. ; *P.P.* x.

Stout, red-faced, elderly man . . . A raythe r stout gen'lm'n of eight-and-fifty. His face had expanded under the influence of good living—and its bold, fleshy curves had so far extended beyond the limits originally assigned them, that unless you took a full view of his countenance in front, it was difficult to distinguish more than the extreme tip of a very rubicund nose.

Note.—As Sam is typical of London life below stairs, so his father is representative of the coachmen who were displaced by the coming of the railways. His second wife is the only one we are made acquainted with. She was a widow, and landlady of the "Marquis of Granby." Tony Weller looks upon himself as an awful example to all young men of the effects of marrying a "vidder"; and repeatedly warns his son against women in general and widows in particular. Eventually he is compelled, by gout, to relinquish his coach. But the contents of his pocket-book have been so well invested for him by Mr. Pickwick "that he had a handsome independence to retire on."

WELLESLEY. Sir A., Duke of Wellington. *M.P., T.D.*

WELLINGTON. Duke of. *M.P., E.S.* ; *M.P., E.T.* ; *M.P., R.T.* ; *M.P., S.F.A.* ; *M.P., T.D.* ; *M.T., T.O.P.*

WELLINGTON STREET. *R.P., T.D.P.*

WELLS, TUNBRIDGE. *E.D.* iii.

WELSH COAST. *U.T.* xxxi.

WELSH MOUNTAINS. *C.S., W.o.G.M.*

WEMMICK. Mr., Mr. Jaggers' clerk. *G.E.* xxi.

A dry man, rather short in stature, with a square wooden face, whose expression seemed to have been imperfectly chipped out with a dull-edged chisel. There were some marks in it that might have been dimples—but which—were only dints. He wore at least four mourning rings, besides a brooch representing a lady and a weeping willow at a tomb with an urn on it. Several rings and seals hung at his watchchain. He had glittering eyes—small, keen and black.

Note.—Jaggers' clerk. In business he matches his master, but, like him, he is good-hearted. Wemmick holds the money for Pip, and a friendship grows up between them. Pip goes out to the Castle at Walworth, where he sees the senior Mr. Wemmick and Miss Skiffins, whom Mr. Wemmick marries.

WEMMICK. Mrs., *née* Skiffins. *G.E.* lv.

WEMMICK. Senr. *G.E.* xxv.

Note.—The father of Mr. John Wemmick. Known as "The aged,"

WEMMICK'S HOUSE. In Walworth. *G.E.* xxv.

A little wooden cottage in the midst of plots of garden, and the top of it was cut out and painted like a battery mounted with guns, with the queerest Gothic windows, and a Gothic door, almost too small to get in at.

WENTWORTH STREET. *R.P., D.W.I.F.*

WEST. An artist. *A.N.* vii.

WEST. Dame, The grandmother of the schoolmaster's favourite scholar. *O.C.S.* xxv.

WEST BROMWICH. *R.P., P.M.T.P.*

WEST END. *C.S., S.L.* iv. ; *N.N.* xi. ; *R.P., B.S.*

WEST-ENDERS. *N.N.* xxxvii.

WEST INDIA DOCKS. *M.P., C.J.*

WEST INDIES. *B.R.* lxxviii ; *C.S., P.o.C.E.P.* ; *C.S., W.o.G.M.*; *D. and S.* xiii. ; *M.P., C.J.* ; *M.P. L.T.* ; *N.N.* xxxvii. ; *O.T.* xiv. ; *P.P.*xxvii. ; *R.P., T.S.S.* ; *U.T.*xix.

WEST RIDING. *N.N.*xxxv.

WEST STREET. Saffron Hill. *M.P., C. and E.* ; *M.P., S.S.U.*

WEST TWENTY - SIXTH STREET. No. 78. *M.P., S.B.*

WESTERN ROAD. *M.C.* xlii.

WESTERN OCEAN. *M.P., L.A.V.* ii.

WESTGATE HOUSE. Establishment for young ladies. *P.P* .xvi.
Consisting of the spinster lady of the establishment, three teachers, five female servants, and thirty boarders.

WESTLOCK. John, Pupil of Pecksniffs'. *M.C.* ii.
A good-looking youth, newly arrived at man's estate.
Note.—John was one of those pupils of Picksniff who found him out. He left his mentor and prospered. He was a staunch friend of Tom Pinch, and a friend of old Martin Chuzzlewit. He eventually marries Ruth, Tom's sister.

WESTMINSTER. *B.R.* xxxviii. ; *M.P., H.H.* ; *M.P., O.C.* ; *M.P., S.S.* ; *N.N.* xxxvii. ; *O.M.F.* iii. ; *R.P.,G.o.A.* ; *R.P.,T.D.P.* ; *U.T.*iii.

WESTMINSTER. Great conservator of the peace at. *S.B.B.*, Scenes xviii.
Stout man, with a hoarse voice, in the blue coat, queer crowned, broad-brimmed hat, white corduroy breeches, and great boots.

WESTMINSTER ABBEY. *G.E.* xxii. ; *L.D.* xv. ; *O.M.F.* vi. ; *U.T.* xiii.

WESTMINSTER AND BLACKFRIARS' BRIDGES. *L.D.* xli.

WESTMINSTER BRIDGE. *B.R.* xlvii. ; *O.M.F.* xviii. ; *R.P.,P.R.S.* ; *S.B.B.*, Scenes x. ; *U.T.* xiii.

WESTMINSTER BRIDGE ROAD. *M.P., M.B.V.*

WESTMINSTER HALL. *B.H.* xix. ; *B.R.* lxvii. ; *D.C.* xxx ; *L.D.* lxi ; *M.P., M.E.* ; *M.P., P.F.* ; *M.P., S. of C.* ; *O.M.F.* xxi. ; *R.P., G.o.A.*

WESTMINSTER MARKET. *M.P., O.C.*

WESTMINSTER SCHOOL. *H.T., R.* vii. ; *N.N.* xvii.

WESTWOOD. Mr., Friend of Sir Mulberry Hawk. *N.N.* l.

WHARF. A. *D. and S.* xix.

WHARF. A, Opening on the Thames—behind the old dingy house. *N.N.* xi.
A picture of cold, silent decay. . . . An empty dog-kennel, some bones of animals, fragments of iron hoops, and staves of old casks, lay strewn about, but no life was stirring there.

WHARF. Spigwiffin's. *N.N.* xxvi.

WHARTON. Mr. Granville, George Silverman's pupil. *G.S.E.* ix.

WHATELEY. Archbishop. *M.P., P.P.*

WHAT'S-HER-NAME. Mrs. *U.T.* xii.
A lodger at greengrocer's shop in High Street, Dullborough.

WHAT'S-HIS-NAME. Pupil at Dotheboys' Hall. *N.N.* vii.

WHEELWRIGHTS. Seeing Mark Tapley off. *M.C.* vii.

WHEEZY. Prof. *Mud. Pap.* i.

WHELKS. Joe. *M.P., A.P.*

WHIFF. Miss, Of Mugby Junction Refreshment-room staff. *C.S., M.J.* v.

WHIFFERS. Mr., Footman. *P.P.* xxxvii.
Gentleman in orange-coloured plush.

WHIFFIN. The town crier of Eatanswill. *P.P.* xiii.

WHIFFLER. Mr. *S.Y.C.*

WHIFFLER. Mrs. *S.Y.C.*

WHIGS. In House of Parliament. *S.B.B.*, Scenes xviii.

WHILKS. Mr. *M.C.* xix.

WHIMPLE. Mrs. *G.E.* xlvi.
An elderly woman of pleasant and thriving appearance.

WHIP. The. *B.H.* lviii.

WHIPPERS-IN. M,P.'s. *S.B.B.*, Scenes xviii.

WHISKER. Red, One of party picnicing near Guildford. *D.C.* iv.
Pretended he could make a salad and voted himself into the charge of the wine-cellar, which he constructed being an ingenious beast, in the hollow trunk of a tree.

WHISTLING SHOP. *P.P.* xliv.

WHITBY. *D. and S.* xv.

WHITE. Betsy, A female crimp. *U.T.* v.

WHITE. Constable. *R.P., D.W.I.F.*

WHITE. One of Mrs. Lemon's pupils. *H.R.* iv.

WHITE. One of the "Army." *S.B.B.*, Scenes xiii.

WHITE. Young, At gasfitter's. *S.B.B.*, Char. ix.

WHITE HART. Bath. *P.P.* xxxv.

WHITE HART. Borough. *P.P.* x.

WHITE HOUSE. *A.N.* viii.

WHITEBAIT-HOUSE. Blackwall. *M.P., C.J.*

WHITECHAPEL. *B.R.* iv.; *C.B., C.C.*, s. iii.; *M.P., F.S.*; *M.P., G.B.*; *M.P., N.S.L.*; *M.P., T.O.P.*; *O.T.* xix.; *P.P.* xx.; *R.P., B.S.*; *R.P., D.W.T.T.*; *R.P., M.o.F.F.*; *U.T.* x.

WHITECHAPEL CHURCH. *U.T.* iii.

WHITECHAPEL WORKHOUSE. *M.P., N.S.L.*

WHITE CONDUIT CONCERT HALL. *S.B.B.*, Char. viii.

WHITE CONDUIT HOUSE. *S.B.B.*, Scenes xix.

WHITECROSS STREET. *P.P.* xl.

WHITEFRIARS. *B.H.* xxvii. *G.E.* xliv.; *S.B.B.*, Tales xii.

WHITEFRIARS. *See also* Hanging-sword-alley.

WHITEHALL. *A.N.* xv.; *M.P., F.F.*; *M.P., O.C.*; *P.P.* ii.; *R.P., P.M.T.D.*

WHITE HART INN. High Street, Borough. *P.P.* v.

A great, rambling, queer, old place, with galleries, and passages, and staircases, wide enough to furnish materials for a hundred ghost stories.

WHITE HORSE CELLAR. *B.H.* iii.; *P.P.* xxxv.

Starting place for coach for Bath.

WHITE HOUSE. Grogus's. *S.B.B.*, Tales ii.

WHITE LION. The. *O.M.F.* xli.

WHITE RIDING HOOD. *U.T.* xxxvi.

WHITE WOMAN. *M.P., W.S.S.*

WHITENED SEPULCHRES. Hon. Member for. *M.P., S.S.*

WHITFIELD TABERNACLE. *M.P., N.Y.D.*

WHITROSE. Lady Belinda *O.M.F.* xxxv.

WHITTINGTON. *M.P., B.M.V.*

WHITYBROWN. Bellringer of an old City church. *U.T.*ix.

WICKAM. Mrs., Paul's nurse. *D. and S.* viii.

Mrs. Wickam was a waiter's wife—which would seem equivalent to being any other man's widow—whose application for an engagement—had been favourably considered, on account of the apparent impossibility of her having any followers, or any one to follow—was a meek woman, of a fair complexion, with her eyes always elevated, and her head always drooping; who was always ready to pity herself, or to be pitied, or to pity anybody else.

WICKFIELD. Agnes, Mr. Wickfield's daughter. *D.C.* xv.

Her face was quite bright and happy, there was a tranquility about it, and about her—a quiet, good, calm spirit.

Note.—Agnes is David's "sister" during his schooldays at Canterbury, and his counsellor afterwards. Uriah Heep designs to marry her but fails; and her father's name is cleared. Eventually she marries David.

WICKFIELD. Mr., A lawyer. *D.C.* xv.

A gentleman with grey hair (though not by any means an old man) and black eyebrows.

Note.—Mr. Wickfield is a Canterbury lawyer, legal adviser and friend of Betsey Trotwood. He is entirely wrapped up in his daughter Agnes, but after his wife's death he loses spirits and drinks rather more port than is necessary. Uriah Heep is clerk in the office, but as Mr. Wickfield's infirmity increases he gains a greater ascendency. But his machinations are defeated and Mr. Wickfield is rescued from him.

WICKFIELD. Mrs., Agnes' dead mother. *D.C.* xxxi.

She married me in opposition to her father's wish, and he renounced her. She prayed him to forgive her before my Agnes came into the world. He was a very hard man, and her mother had long been dead. He repulsed her. He broke her heart.

WICKS. Mr., Clerk of Dodson and Fogg. *P.P.* xx.

In a brown coat, and brass buttons inky drabs, and bluchers.

" **WIDEAWAKE.**" *L.D.* vi.

WIDGER. Mr. Bobtail. *S.Y.C.*

WIDGER. Mrs. Bobtail. *S.Y.C.*

WIDOW. Dreary, Pew-opener. *O.M.F.* x.

Whose left hand appears to be in a state of acute rheumatism, but is in fact voluntarily doubled up to act as a moneybox.

WIDOW. Landlady of inn in Marlborough Downs. *P.P.* xiv.

Buxom . . . of somewhere about eight-and-forty or thereabouts, with a face as comfortable as the bar.

WIDOW. Next lodger of City clerk. *S.B.B., O.P.* vii.

WIDOW. Son of. *S.B.B., O.P.* vii.

Earned, by copying writings, and translating for booksellers. Nature had set that unearthly light in his plaintive face, which is the beacon of her worst disease.

WIDOW LADY. Cross. *M.P., F.F.*

WIELD. Inspector Charley, A detective. *R.P., T.D.P.*

A middle-aged man, of a portly presence, with a large, moist, knowing eye.

WIFE. Country manager's. *M.P., G.F.*

WIFE. First. *M.P., N.T.*

WIFE. Of J. P. *B.R.* xlvii.

A lady who had the appearance of being delicate in health, and not too happy.

WIFE. Of prisoner in the Fleet. *P.P.* xli.

WIFE. Second. *M.P., N.T.*

WIFE. Young, Of clerical English traveller. *L.D.* ii.

WIGAN. *M.P., F.S.*

WIGGS AND CO. Owners of the " Polyphemus." *D. and S.* iv.

WIGS. Name of a bird. *B.H.* xiv.

WIGSBY. Mr. *Mud. Pap.* i.

WIGSBY. Mr., A vestryman. *R.P., O.V.*

WIGTON. *L.T.* ii.

WIGZELL. J. *M.P., U.N.*

WILBURN. John. *A.N.* xvii.

WILDE. Sir Thomas. *M.P., M.E.R.*

" **WILD BEAST SHOWS.**" Travelling menageries. *S.B.B.*, Scenes xii.

WILD LODGE. East Cliff. *R.P., O.o.S.*

WILDERNESS. *See* Quilp's Wharf.

" **WILDERNESS WALK,**" *R.P., O.V.*

WILDING. Little Walter. *M.P., N.T.*

WILDING. Mr. Walter, Of Wilding and Co. *C.S., N.T.*, Act i.

An innocent, open-speaking, unused-looking man, with a remarkably pink-and-white complexion, and a figure much too bulky for so young a man, though of a good stature. With crispy, curling brown hair, and amiable, bright blue eyes.

WILDING. Walter, The second so-named foundling. *C.S., N.T.*, Act i.

There was a question that day about naming an infant, a boy, who had just been received. We generally named them out of the Directory. One of the gentlemen who managed the hospital happened to be looking over the Register. " He noticed that the name of the baby who had been adopted (Walter Wilding was scratched out, for the reason that the child had been removed from our care. " Here is a name to let," he said, " give it to the new foundling who has been received to-day."—You, sir, were that child.

WILDING AND CO. Mansion of. *C.S., N.T.*, Act i.

It really had been a mansion in

the days when merchants inhabited the City, and had a ceremonious shelter to the doorway without visible support, like the sounding board over an old pulpit. It had also a number of long, narrow strips of window, so dispersed in its grave brick front as to render it symmetrically ugly. It had also, on its roof, a cupola with a bell in it.

WILDING AND CO. Wine merchants. *C.S.*, *N.T.*, Act i.

WILDING'S HOUSE. *M.P.*, *N.T.*

WILFER. Bella, *O.M.F.* iv.

Note.—Left in John Harmon's will, like his other goods, to his son. She is adopted by the Boffins, and there meets the secretary, John Rokesmith. She marries him and afterwards discovers that he is the John Harmon of the will. She is the spoiled daughter of Reginald Wilfer, although in the testing she is proved to be true gold.

WILFER. Lavinia. *O.M.F.* iv.

Note.—Daughter of Reginald Wilfer and younger sister of Bella. She is jealous of her sister's good fortune. She has no respect for her mother, and has not her sister's love for their father. After Bella leaves home, Lavvy takes Geogre Sampson "in tow."

WILFER. John. *O.M.F.* iv.

WILFER. Mrs., Wife of R. Wilfer. *O.M.F.* iv.

A tall woman and an angular —much given to tying up her head in a pockethandkerchief knotted under the chin. This headgear, in conjunction with a pair of gloves worn within doors, she seemed to consider as at once a kind of armour against misfortune—and as a species of full dress.

WILFER. Reginald, A poor clerk. *O.M.F.* iv.

His black hat was brown before he could afford a coat, his pantaloons were white at the seams and knees before he could buy a pair of boots, his boots had worn out before he could treat himself to new pantaloons.

Note.—Bella's father has several nicknames, amongst them, "The Cherub," and "Rumty." He is greatly at his wife's mercy and something of a nonentity in his home. Bella loves him and gives him several treats. He is appointed secretary in place of Rokesmith, when Rokesmith reveals himself as John Harmon.

WILKINS. Captain Boldwig's sub-gardener. *P.P.* xix.

WILKINS. Dick, *C.B.*, *C.C.*, *S.* ii.

WILKINS. Mrs. *M.C.* xlix.

WILKINS. Mr. Samuel, A journeyman carpenter. *S.B.B.*, Char. iv.

Below the middle size—bordering perhaps upon the dwarfish. His face was round and shining, and his hair carefully twisted into the outer corner of each eye till it formed a variety of that description of semi-curls usually known as "aggerawaters."

WILKS. Mrs. *M.C.* xix.

WILKS. Thomas Egerton. *M.P.*, *J.S.*

To . . . was confided the M.S. of Grimaldi's life and adventures.

WILL. *M.P.S.G.*

WILL. Uncle, William Fern. *C.B.*, *C.*, q. ii.

WILL OFFICE. *P.P.* lv.

WILLET. Joe, Son of John Willet. *B.R.* i.

A broad-shouldered, strapping young fellow of twenty, whom it pleased his father still to consider a little boy, and to treat accordingly . . . enrolled among the gallant defenders of his native land. . . . I am a poor, maimed, discharged soldier.

Note.—The son of John Willet and his assistant in the "Maypole." He resents his father's treatment of him, however, and enlists in the Army. During the war in America he lost an arm at the seige of Savannah—which arm Dickens seems to be rather uncertain. He returns to England at the time of the Riots and proves of the utmost assistance to his friends. He marries Dolly Varden, and after his father's death inherits his wealth and becomes a man of great consequence in the district.

WILLET. Joe and Dolly, Children of. *B.R.* lxxxii.

A red-faced little boy, a red-faced little girl, another red-faced little boy—more small Joes, and small Dollys than could be easily counted.

WILLET. John, Landlord of the "Maypole." *B.R.* i.

A burly, large-headed man, with a fat face, which betokened profound obstinacy and slowness of apprehension, combined with a very strong reliance upon his own merits—a pair of dull, fish-like eyes.

Note.—The honest landlord of the 'Maypole" inn was so obtuse, and his density was only equalled by his obstinacy and ignorance. After Joe's return from the "Salwanners" he is so surprised that he never really recovers, although he is inordinately proud of his son, and still more proud ot his loss of an arm—in the "Salwanners." When he dies it is found that he has left even more money than was generally supposed.

WILLET. Mrs. Joe, *Née* Varden, Dolly, *which see.*

WILLIAM. *D.C.* xix.

WILLIAM. Mrs., Mrs. Swidger. *C.B., H.M.* i.

WILLIAM. One of visitors to Astley's. *S.B.B.*, Scenes xi.

Encouraged in his impertinence.

WILLIAM. Shiny, *See* Shiny William.

WILLIAM. Sir Mulberry Hawks' groom. *N.N.* xxxii.

WILLIAM. Son of the drunkard. *S.B.B.*, Tales xii.

A young man of about two-and-twenty, miserably clad in an old coarse jacket and trousers.

WILLIAM. Son of the widow. *S.B.B., O.P.* vii.

WILLIAM. Waiter. *D.C.* v.

He was a twinkling-eyed, pimple-faced man, with his hair standing upright all over his head.

Note.—This was the waiter who ate David's dinner and drank David's ale.

WILLIAM. Waiter at "Blue Boar." *G.E.* lviii.

WILLIAM. Waiter at "Saracen's Head." *N.N.* v.

WILLIAMS. A constable. *R.P., D.W.I.F.*

WILLIAMS, WILLIAM. *O.M.F.* vi.

WILLIAMSON. Mrs., Landlady of "Winglebury Arms." *S.B.B.*, Tales viii.

WILLIAMSON. Mr., As John, a waiter at the "St James's Arms." *M.P., S.G.*

WILLING. Sophy. *C.S.M.L.Lo.*

WILLING MIND. The. *D.C.* iii.

Mr. Peggotty went occasionally to a public-house called "The Willing Mind."

WILLIS. Miss, The eldest. *S.B.B., O.P.* iii.

WILLIS. Mr., A prisoner in lock-up-house. *S.B.B.*, Tales x.

A young fellow of vulgar manners, dressed in the very extreme of the prevailing fashion—with a lighted cigar in his mouth.

WILLIS. Mrs., Kate. *S.B.B., O.P.* iii.

WILLIS. The second Miss. *S.B.B., O.P.* iii.

WILLISES. The four Miss. *S.B.B., O.P.* iii.

Were far from juvenile.

WILLISES. The two other Miss. *S.B.B., O.P.* iii.

Used to "play duets on the piano."

WILLMORE. Mr. Graham. *M.P., L.E.J.*

WILLY. The brother of Little Nell's friend. *O.C.S.* lv.

Willy went away to join the angels; but if he had known how I should miss him, he never would have left me, I am sure.

WILSON. Police-officer. *S.B.B.*, Scenes xviii.

WILSON. Fanny. *M.P., S.G.*

WILSON. Mary. *M.P., S.G.*

WILSON. Miss, Pupil at Minerva House. *S.B.B.*, Tales iii.

The ugliest girl in Hammersmith.

WILSON. Mr. *M.P.. F.C.*

WILSON. Mr. *S.B.B.*, Char. iii.

WILSON. Mr. *S.B.B.*, Scenes xix.

WILSON. Mr., Friend of the Gattletons. *S.B.B.*, Tales ix.

WILSON. Mr., Godfather to the Kitterbells' baby. *S.B.B.*, Tales xi.

WILSON. Mrs., Godmother to the Kitterbells' baby. *S.B.B.*, Tales xi.

WILSON. Professor. *M.P.*, *S.P.*

WILTSHIRE. Farm in. *M.C.* xiii.

WILTSHIRE. Hanger on at inn down in. *C.S.*, *H.T.*

A supernaturally preserved Druid I believe him to have been—with long white hair, and a filmy blue eye always looking afar off, who claimed to have been a shepherd.

WILTSHIRE. Inn down in. *C.S.*, *H.T.*

WILTSHIRE. Labourer emigrant. *U.T.* xx.

A simple, fresh-coloured farm labourer, of eight-and-thirty.

WILTSHIRE LABOURERS. *M.P.*, *W.L.*

WILTSHIRE VILLAGE. *M.C.* ii.

The declining sun, struggling through the mist which had obscured it all day looked brightly down upon a little Wiltshire village. The wet grass sparkled in the light; the scanty patches of verdure in the hedges—took heart, and brightened up. The birds began to chirp and twitter on the naked boughs. The vane upon the tapering spire of the old church glistened from its lofty station.

WILTSHIREMAN. Cheeseman. *R.P.*, *T.S.S.*

WIMPOLE STREET. *U.T.* xvi.

"**WIN THE DAY.**" *M.P.*, *O.S.*

WINCH. Mr. *M.P.*, *P.T.*

WINCHESTER. *B.H.* iv.; *N.N.* xxix.

WINDER. At last shift. *M.P.*, *O.S.*

WINDERMERE. *M.P.*, *E.S.*

WINDMILL. The old, Hexam's dwelling-place. *O.M.F.* xii.

WINDMILL HILL. *S.U.T.H.* i.

WINDSOR. *B.H.* iii.; *C.S.*, *D.M.P.*; *M.C.* xxi; *M.H.C.* iii.; *M.P.*, *C.C.*; *M.P.*, *E.S.*; *M.P.* *S.D.C.*; *M.P.*, *T.D.*; *R.P.*, *A.F.*; *R.P.*, *O.o.T.*; *U.T.* x.

WINDSOR PAVILION. *M.C.* xxi.

WINDSOR TERRACE. City Road. *D.C.* xi.

Micawber's address. His house in Windsor Terrace which was shabby like himself, but also, like himself, made all the show it could.

WINE MERCHANT'S. Courtyard in. *M.P.*, *N.T.*

WINE VAULTS. Keepers of. *S.B.B.*, Scenes xxii.

WINGLEBURY. Great, The little town of. *S.B.B.*, Tales viii.

Is exactly forty-two miles and three-quarters from Hyde Park Corner. It has a long, straggling, quiet High Street.

WINGLEBURY. Little. *S.B.B.*, Tales viii.

Down some cross-roads about two miles off—Great Winglebury.

WINGLEBURY. Mayor of, *S.B.B.*, Tales viii.

WINGLEBURY. Post office of Great. *S.B.B.*, Tales viii.

WINGLEBURY. Town hall of Great. *S.B.B.*, Tales viii.

Half way up (High Street) with a great black and white clock.

"**WINGLEBURY ARMS.**" The, Inn. *S.B.B.*, Tales viii.

In the centre of the High Street opposite the small building with the big clock, is the principal inn of Great Winglebury—the commercial inn, posting-house, and excise office. Blue house at every election, and judges' house at every assizes. A large house with a red brick and stone front; a pretty, spacious hall, ornamented with evergreen plants.

"**WINGLEBURY ARMS.**" Four stout waiters of. *S.B.B.*, Tales viii.

"**WINGLEBURY ARMS.**" Landlady of. *S.B.B.*, Tales viii.

WINKLE. Mr., A wharfinger. *P.P.* l.

Note.—Mr. Winkle, Senior, the father of Nathaniel, was a wharfinger at Birmingham, was precise and business-like and naturally resented his son's marriage to Arabella Allen. Arabella herself conquers him, however, and he takes his son back to favour.

WINKLE. Nathaniel, Member of the Pickwick Club. *P.P.* i.

In a new green shooting-coat, plaid neckerchief, and closely-fitting drabs.

Note.—One of the members of the corresponding society of the Pickwick Club who accompanied Mr. Pickwick on his expeditions of research. Mr. Winkle's desires to be a sportsman are greater than his skill, and he has an unfortunate habit of making others think he is one, with humiliating results to himself. He is challenged to fight a duel by Dr. Slammer, although he has no knowledge of firearms. Happily the doctor discovers that Winkle is "not the man," and the event terminates happily for everyone. To Winkle was due the invention of the Pickwick Coat with the "P. C." buttons. Winkle marries Arabella Allen quietly without consulting his father, upon whom he is dependent. A reconciliation is effected, however, and Nathaniel becomes London agent for his father, discards the Pickwick coat, and "presented all the external appearance of a civilised Christian ever afterwards."

WINKLE. Private residence of Mr. *P.P.* l.

In a quiet, substantial-looking street, stood an old red-brick house with three steps before the door, and a brass plate upon it, bearing in fat Roman capitals the words 'Mr. Winkle." The steps were very white, and the bricks were very red.

WINKS. *See* Deputy.

WIRY TARRIER. Licensed house. *M.P., G.B.*

WISBOTTLE. Mr., Boarder at Mrs. Tibbs. *S.B.B.*, Tales i.

A high tory—clerk in the Woods and Forests Office—knew the peerage by heart—had a good set of teeth and a capital tailor.

WISCONSIN. *A.N.* xvii.

WISCONSIN. Legislative Hall. *A.N.* xvii.

WISEMAN. Dr. *M.P., F.F.*

WISEMAN. Master = Cardinal Wiseman. *M.P., A.J.B.*

WISEMAN. Nicholas. *M.P., L.W.O.Y.*

WISK. Miss, Fiancée of Mr. Quale. *B.H.* xxx.

WIT. Of counting-house of Dombey. *D. and S.* li.

Reconciliation is established—between the acknowledged wit of the counting-house and an aspiring rival, with whom he has been at deadly feud for months.

WITCH. First, In Liverpool, in common lodging-house. *U.T.* v. Making "money-bags."

WITCH. Second, In Liverpool, common lodging-house. *U.T.* v.

WITCH. Third, In Liverpool, in common lodging-house. *U.T.* v

WITCHEM. Sergeant, A detective. *R.P., T.D.P.*

Marked with the smallpox. . . . He might have sat for Wilkie for the soldier in the reading of the will.

WITHERDEN. Mr., Notary. *O.C.S.* xiv.

Short, chubby, fresh-coloured, brisk, and pompous.

Note.—The notary to whom Abel Garland was articled: and largely instrumental in securing the downfall of Sampson Brass.

WITHERFIELD. Miss, Middle-aged lady. *P.P* xxiv.

Mr. Pickwick had no sooner put on his spectacles than he at once recognised in the future Mrs. Magnus, the lady into whose room he had so unwarrantably intruded on the previous night.

Note—Miss Witherfield was the lady whom Mr. Magnus came to propose to and in whose room Mr. Pickwick had the night adventure.

WITHERS. Mrs. Skewton's page. *D. and S.* xxi.

The chair (in which Mrs. Skewton was seated) having stopped, the motive power became visible in the shape of a flushed page—who seemed to have in part out grown and in part out-pushed his strength, for when he stood upright he was tall, wan, and thin.

WITHERS'S. At Brighton. *M.P., G.D.*

WITITTERLY. Henry. *N.N.* xxi.
An important gentleman of about eight-and-thirty, of rather plebeian countenance, and with a very light head of hair.

Note.—The husband of Mrs. Wititterley. He supports his wife in her affected airs and simulated delicacy without any regard for the feelings of others.

WITITTERLY. Mrs., Julia. *N.N.* xxi.
The lady had an air of sweet insipidity, and a face of engaging paleness; there was a faded look about her.

Note.—The soul-ful lady to whom Kate Nickleby acts as companion.

WIX. Mr. *R.P., D.W.I.F.*

WIZZLE. Mr., One of steam excursion party. *S.B.B.*, Tales vii.

WOBBLER. Mr., Of Secretarial Department in Circumlocution Office. *L.D.* x.
Polishing a gun-barrel on his pocket-handkerchief.

WOLF. Mr., Literary character. *M.C.* xxviii.

WOLVERHAMPTON. *M.P., F. and S.*; *M.P., L.S.*; *R.P., A.C.T.*

WOMAN. *L.D.* xiv.
She was young—and neither ugly nor wicked looking. She spoke coarsely, but with no naturally coarse voice; there was even something musical in its sound.

WOMAN. Customer at ship chandler's. *D. and S.* iv.
Came to ask the way to Mile-End Turnpike.

WOMAN. Deceased husband of. *S.B.B., O.P.* i.
Died in the hospital.

WOMAN. Fat old, A nurse. *S.B.B., O.P.*, iii.
In a cloak and nightcap, with a bundle in one hand and a pair of patterns in the other.

WOMAN. In tea gardens. *S.B.B.*, Scenes ix.

WOMAN. Miserable-looking, A widow. *S.B.B., O.P.* i.
Represents a case of extreme destitution.

WOMAN. Old. *M.P., G.D.*

WOMAN. Old, In Marshalsea. *L.D.* lxv.
Who arranged Mr. Clennam's rooms in the Marshalsea.

WOMAN. Old, Mother of corpse. *O.T.* v.

WOMAN. Old, very dirty, very wrinkled and dry. *L.D.* xxvii.

WOMAN. One worthy. *B.H.* xxxi.
To assist in nursing Charley.

WOMAN. Outside the workhouse. *M.P., N.S.L.*

WOMAN. Prisoner's wife in the poor side of the Fleet. *P.P.* xlii.
Watering, with great solicitude, the wretched stump of a dried-up, withered plant, which, it was plain to see, could never send forth a green leaf again; too true an emblem perhaps, of the office she had come there to discharge.

WOMAN. Selling flowers. *D. and S.* xv.

WOMAN. Serving at Bank. *H.T., R.* i.

WOMAN. Sister of man hanged. *M.H.C.* iii.
Whole appearance most dejected, wretched and forlorn.

WOMAN. Strong-minded. *M.C.* xliv.

WOMAN. Widow of man hanged. *M.H.C.* iii.
Deadly pale—garments wet and torn—hair dishevelled and streaming in the wind.

WOMAN. Wretched, With an infant in her arms. *S.B.B.*, Scenes ii.
Round whose meagre figure the remnant of her own scanty shawl is carefully wrapped . . . has been attempting to sing some popular ballad, in the hope of wringing a few pence from the compassionate passers-by.

WOMAN. Young. *P.P.* xxxviii.

WOMAN. Young, Wife of a prisoner in the Fleet. *P.P.* xli.
With a child in her arms, who seemed scarcely able to crawl, from emaciation, and misery, was walking

up and down the passage in conversation with her husband, who had no other place to see her in.

WOMBWELL'S KEEPERS. Mr. *M.P., G.H.*

WOMEN. Basket. *S.B.B.*, Scenes i.

WOMEN. Five, Outside the workhouse. *M.P., N.S.L.*

WOMEN. Two motherly-looking, *S.B.B.*, Scenes ix.

In smart pelisses, chatting confidentially—in admiration of the little boy who belongs to one of them.

WOMEN. Old, On board Gravesend packet. *S.B.B.*, Scenes x.

Who had brought large wicker hand-baskets with them.

WOMEN. Strong young, Applicants to General Agency Office. *N.N.* xvi.

Some half dozen strong young women, each with pattens and an umbrella.

WOOD. Mr. *M.P., C.C.*

WOOD. In which Jonas murdered Montague. *M.C.* xlvii.

WOOD OF BOLOGNE. *M.P., N.Y.D.*

WOOD STREET. *G.E.* xx. ; *L.D.* xiii.

WOODCOURT. Allan, Miss Flite's physician. *B.H.* xiv.

The kindset physician in the college.

Note.—At first a naval surgeon. But practising in London he comes in contact with Jo, the Snagsbys and others, and so occupies a rather important position, and eventually marries Esther Summerson.

WOODCOURT. Children of Allan and Esther. *B.H.* lxvii.

WOODCOURT. Esther, *Née* Hawdon. *See* Summerson, Esther.

WOODCOURT. Mr., Deceased. *B.H.* xxx.

Served his king and country as an officer in the Royal Highlanders, and he died on the field.

WOODCOURT. Mrs., Mother of Allan Woodcourt. *B.H.* xvii.

She was a pretty old lady, with bright black eyes, but she seemed proud.

Note.—Mother of Allan Woodcourt; a Welsh lady with the utmost reverence for her ancestry. She thinks Esther has no ancestry, but she ultimately gets to love her.

WOODENCONSE. Mr. *Mud. Pap.* i.

WOODS. Prison in the, Of the pirates. *C.S., P.o.C.E.P.*

WOODS AND FORESTS OFFICE. *M.P., R.T.*

WOODSTOCK COMMISSIONERS. *M.P., R.S.D.*

WOOL-DEALER. Son of a Warwickshire, *R.P., N.S.*

WOOLFORD. Miss, Lady equestrian, at Astley's. *S.B.B.*, Scenes xi.

WOOLWICH. *B.R.* lxvii. ; *M.P.*, *N.E.* ; *U.T.* v.

WOOLWICH. Young, Son of the Bagnets. *B.H.* xxvii.

Got an engagement, with his father, at the theayter, to play the fife in a military piece.

WOPSLE. Mr., Church clerk. *G.E.* iv.

United to a large Roman nose, and a large and shining fore-head, had a deep voice which he was uncommonly fond of.

Note.—Friend of Pip's sister. He lives over his great-aunt's shop, and once a quarter he examines her scholars by acting before them. He is parish clerk, but he relinquishes that and takes to the London stage, where he meets with no very brilliant success.

WORCESTER. *A.N.* v. ; *M.P., E.S.*

WORKHOUSE. Common to most towns. *O.T.* i.

In this workhouse was born the item of mortality . . . whose name is prefixed to the head of this chapter (Oliver Twist).

WORKHOUSE. Master of, in Liverpool. *U.T.* viii.

WORKHOUSE. Master of the. *S.B.B., O.P.* i.

We should think he had been an inferior sort of an attorney's clerk, or else the master of a national school. His income is small, certainly, as the rusty black coat and threadbare velvet collar demonstrate: but then he lives free of house-rent, has a limited allowance of coals and candles. He is a tall, thin, bony man, always wears shoes and black cotton stockings with his surtout.

WORKHOUSE. Master of, in St. George's-in-the-East. *U.T.* iii.

WORKHOUSE. Metropolitan. *R.P.*, *W.i.a.W.*

WORKHOUSE. Pauper in, in St. George's-in-the-East. *U.T.* iii.

WORKHOUSE. Refuge for the destitute. *N.N.* xx.

WORKMAN. A, In Dr. Blimber's *D. and S.* xiv.

There was something the matter with the great clock; and a workman on a pair of steps had taken its face off, and was poking instruments into the works by the light of a candle. The workman on the steps was very civil.

"**WORKS.**" The, Of Daniel Doyce and Clennam. *L.D.* xxiii.

The little counting-house reserved for his (Daniel Doyce's) own occupation, was a room of wood and glass at the end of a long low workshop.

WORSHIPFUL COMPANY. Master and wardens of. *D. and S.* lvii.

Inscription about what the masters and wardens of the Worshipful Company did in one thousand six hundred and ninety-four (in the church where Walter and Florence were married).

WOSKY. Mr., Attending Mrs. Bloss. *S.B.B.*, Tales i.

A little man with a red face—dressed, of course, in black, with a stiff white handkerchief—had a very good practice, and plenty of money, which he had amassed by invariably humouring the worst fancies of all the females of all the families he had ever been introduced to.

WOZENHAM. Miss, Lodging-house keeper. *C.S.*, *M.L.Lo.* i.

With a cast in the eye, and a bag of bones—her father having failed in pork.

WRAYBURN. Eugene. *O.M.F.* ii.

In susceptibility to boredom . . . I assure you I am the most consistent of mankind.

Note.—Friend of Mortimer Lightwood, aimless and indolent. He accompanies Mortimer in the Harmon case and meets Lizzie Hexam. He is attracted by her, and without knowing why, or where his action will lead, he makes her aquaintance and interests himself in improving her education. He takes a delight in tormenting Bradley Headstone, To avoid Headstone, and so save Wrayburn from his madness, Lizzie leaves London. Eugene traces her, however, and is in turn followed by Bradley, who attempts to murder him. Lizzie saves Eugene, however, and although it is expected that he will die, he marries Lizzie as the only reparation he can make. He does not die, however, although it is some time before he recovers, and is left in the story determined to stand and fight, for his wife's sake.

WRAYBURN. Eugene, Eldest brother of. *O.M.F.* xii.

Heir to the family embarrassments—we call it before company, the family estates.

WRAYBURN. Eugene, Respected father of. *O.M.F.* xii.

WRAYBURN. Eugene, Second brother of. *O.M.F.* xii.

A little pillar of the Church.

WAYBURN. Eugene, Third brother of. *O.M.F.* xii.

Pitchforked into the navy.

WRAYBURN. Eugene, Youngest brother of. *O.M.F.* xii.

It was settled—that he should have a mechanical genius.

WRAYBURN. Mrs. Eugene, *Née* Lizzie Hexam. *Which see.*

WREN. Miss Jenny. *See* Cleaver, Fanny.

WRETCHES. Four doomed. In Newgate. *B.R.* lxiv.

Who were to suffer death—could be plainly heard—crying—that the flames would shortly reach them—and that with as much distraction—

as though each had an honoured happy life before him, instead of eight-and-forty hours of miserable imprisonment, and a violent death.

WRIGHTS'. Inn "next door" to "Bull" Inn, Rochester. *P.P.* ii.

WRITER. The begging-letter. *R.P., B.L.W.*

Has been in the army, the navy, the Church, and the law.

WRYMUG. Mrs., Applicant for cook at general agency office. *N.N.* xvi.

Pleasant place, Finsbury—wages twelve guineas. No tea, no sugar—serious family.

WUGSBY. Jane. *P.P.* xxxv.

The prettier and younger daughter.

WUGSBY. Mrs. Colonel, One of whist party at Assembly Rooms, Bath. *P.P.* xxxv.

Of an ancient and whist-like appearance.

WURZEL. Roger. *M.P., P.M.B.*

WYE. *M.P., I.W.M.*

WYNFORD. Lord. *M.P., C.P.*

X

X. Right Hon. Mr. *M.P., R.T.*

XAVIER. Saint Francis, Cathedral dedicated to in St. Louis. *A.N.* xii.

Y

Y—. Earl. *M.P., R.T.*

YALE COLLEGE. New Haven. *A.N.* v.

YARD. The. *See* Chatham Dockyard.

YARMOUTH. *D.C.* ii.

Then there's the sea; and the boats and ships; and the fishermen; and the beach.

YARMOUTH ROADS. *U.T.* xvii.

YAWLER. Schoolfellow of Traddles. *D.C.* xxvii.

With his nose on one side . . . A professional man who had been at Salem House.

YAWYAWAH. Captain of the robbers. *M.P., T.O.H.*

YELLOW. Another boating man. *S.B.B.*, Scenes x.

YELLOW DWARF. A toy. *R.P., A.C.T.*

YELLOW STONE BUFFS. *M.P., A.P.*

YORK. *C.S., H.T.*; *N.N.* vi.; *L.D.* xxv.

YORK. (U.S.A.) *A.N.* ix.

YORK MINSTER. *N.N.* vi.

YORKSHIRE. *B.H.*, lx.; *C.S., H.T.*; *G.E.*; *H.T., R.* xi.; *M.P., P.F. and S. R.*; *O.M.F.* x.; *R.P., A.C.T. and B.S.*; *U.T.* x.

YOUNG. Brigham, A Morman. *U.T.* xx.

YOUNG ENGLAND. *M.P., A.J.B.*

YOUTH. From a library. *D. and S.* xii.

A white-haired youth, in a black calico apron.

YOUTH. Name of a bird. *B.H.* xiv.

Z

"Z." *M.P., F.N.P.*

Z——. Lord. *M.P., R.T.*

"ZAMIEL." Passenger in train. *R.P., A.F.*

ZOBBS. *M.P., T.T.*

ZOOLOGICAL GARDENS. Regent's Park. *M.P., F. of the L. and M.P., P.F.*; *U.T.*xxiv.

Originals and Prototypes

of

Characters and Places

in the

Works of Charles Dickens.

INDEX TO ORIGINALS.

THE pursuit of originals seems to have had a fascination for many readers of Dickens's works. So far as topography is concerned, there is some foundation to go upon, because the Novelist generally described and utilized actual places and buildings seen by or known to him ; and, provided proper investigation is made, with due regard to Dickens's own descriptions, there is a reasonable chance of discovering the real places he had in mind.

Unfortunately, proper investigation has not always been carried out, if one may judge by the result, and I think a considerable number of so-called originals is very doubtful, or even without any foundation whatever.

Most writers on Dickens Topography have been content to place on record that "it is said to be the original" without giving any reference to the originator of the statement, or the grounds upon which he made it. It is therefore not possible to judge whether it has any foundation, or was made on false or insufficient evidence.

In the following pages I have given references where possible. These may not, and, in many instances are not the earliest statements or suggestions, but are the earliest I have found. The reader can, at all events, refer to publications in which more detail is given, and thus form some opinion as to the value or otherwise of the evidence upon which an 'original' is based.

Originals of Characters depicted in the novels are on still less solid ground. Numerous "originals" have been confidently put forward, apparently on no more substantial basis than a real or fancied resemblance. Dickens's characters are alive to-day, and examples are to be met with in real life. I once knew Mr. Vincent Crummles and his talented family quite well; Miss Moncher passes my house regularly; and I am acquainted rather intimately with Mr. Sapsea. The present-day Sapsea, however, if faithfully described as Dickens could have described him, would be regarded by the modern critic as a gross exaggeration of Mr. Sapsea of Cloisterham, and an impossible character.

Dickens's characters were types of human beings of his day, and probably several men or women, with varied characteristics, went to the making of each. In my opinion, very few indeed were founded upon any one person.

In *David Copperfield*, to some extent the hero was Dickens himself, inasmuch as the author was writing much from his own early life. Possibly *Little Dorrit* and *Great Expectations* were also founded in part upon his own experiences and aspirations, and in that sense may perhaps be regarded as continuations of his autobiography. Micawber, in many respects, was founded upon his father, whilst certain traits in the character of his mother are depicted in Mrs. Nickleby and Mrs. Reginald Wilfer, but to assume that Micawber was John Dickens, or that Mrs. Wilfer was the author's mother, is erroneous. In the same sense, Maria Beadnell was undoubtedly the original of Dora Spenlow, Flora Finching and perhaps other heroines in the novels, but I think the attributes of the characters founded upon Maria Beadnell were not so much those of the lady herself as those with which Dickens invested her, in his imagination.

This list of originals is probably far from complete, but, in general, places and people mentioned in Dickens's Works under their real names, have been purposely omitted.

W. L. G.

Abbey Town. *P.P.* Original was very possibly Town Malling, where the remains of the Abbey still stand. Other suggestions are Canterbury, Maidstone and Rochester.

Abercrombie (Helen) Said to be the prototype of the poisoned girl in *Hunted Down.* Ref. *Dickensian* VIII. 318.

Acton Street. Gray's Inn Road. In *Little Dorrit* Mr. Casby is described as living in a street off Gray's Inn Road, which had set off from that thoroughfare with the intention of running at one heat down into the valley and up again to the top of Pentonville Hill, but which had run itself out of breath in twenty yards, and had stood still ever since. In the "London of Dickens" Mr. Dexter says there is no such place in that part now, but Dickens may have meant either Acton Street or Swinton Street, both of which run down into the valley.

Adelphi Hotel. In *American Notes* the reference is to the Adelphi Hotel, Liverpool. In *Mrs. Lirriper's Legacy* the reference is to the Adelphi Hotel, Strand, London.

Adelphi Hotel. Situated at the corner of John and Adam Streets in the Adelphi. It was the Osborne's hotel mentioned in the *Pickwick Papers.* First opened in 1777 as the Adelphi New Tavern and Coffee House. Ref. *Inns and Taverns of Pickwick.*

Agent. Insolvent Debtors' Court. See Garland.

Ah Sing. See New Court.

Alamode Beef-House. *D.C.* See Johnson's, Clare market.

Ale-house at East Winterslow. Suggested by R. Allbut as the original of the "Half Moon and Seven Stars," where Mr. Tigg and Chevy Slyme were to be found. (*M.C.*)

Ale (Genuine stunning). *D.C.* See Red Lion, Parliament Street

Allen (Gordon). According to Sir Edward Clarke, K.C., the original of Sydney Carton, (*T.T.C.*) was Gordon Allen, an English barrister who practised for some years at Wellington, New Zealand. He was formerly associated with Edwin James, a barrister who sat for Stryver, Q.C., on Dickens's own admission. Edwin James was detected in roguery and disbarred, and soon afterwards Gordon Allen was found almost starving in his chambers. The generosity of his brother barristers provided him with books, clothing, and means to start a new career in another land. Ref. *Dickens and the Law, Cornhill,* May 1914; *Dickensian* X., 144, 301 Dickens said that the plot of *A Tale of Two Cities* occurred to him while he was acting in the play called "The Frozen Deep." The sacrifice of Richard Wardour in that play, appears to have been the suggestion for the character of Sydney Carton, and probably Dickens had no living prototype in mind. There have been many instances of living people strongly resembling the characters created by Dickens, but it is very doubtful if the author knew of, or had ever heard of these persons.

Allington Weir. Possibly the Cloisterham Weir of *Edwin Drood.* Other suggestions have been East Farleigh and Snodland. With regard to the latter, it has been stated that this was the most probable, but there happens to be no weir at Snodland, and it is not known that there ever was one. Dickens probably had some weir on the Medway in mind, but there is no certainty as to which of several it was. See also Lock-gates, Strood.

All Hallows. Staining. Mark Lane. Suggested by Mr. F. S. Johnson as the rank and hemmed-in Churchyard where Ebenezer Scrooge was shewn his own grave by the last of the Spirits. (*C.C.*). The Church of All Hallows, Staining (*Stein,* or *Stane,* to distinguish it from timber-built structures), was dedicated to All Saints, and was of very old foundation. It was so decayed in the seventeenth century that it fell down in 1669. It was rebuilt in 1674, and demolished in 1870. The squat, square tower, however, was left standing, and still remains, in accordance with an old covenant between the Ecclesiastical Commissioners and the Cloth-Workers Company. This Churchyard may be the one Dickens meant. Equally, he may have had in mind the place mentioned in *Bleak House.* "A worthy place, walled in by houses; over-run by grass and weeds—choked up by too much burying."

Alms-houses. Cobham. See Vintners' Alms-houses.

Robert Langton said there is little doubt that Cobham College was in Dickens's mind when he wrote the lines "When in rustic places, the last glimmerings of daylight died away from the ends of Avenues," etc. (*Haunted Man, i*). The passage, with its reference to parks and woods and high fern; the mists rising from dyke and river; and the lights in old halls and cottage windows, may be a description of Cobham and its neighbourhood, and probably is so, but the Alms-houses themselves do not seem to be particularly indicated.

Amesbury. House at. See St. Mary's Grange.

Anglers' Inn. *O.M.F.*
See Red Lion, Henley.

Appollo. See Glorious Appollers.

Arabin (Sergt.) A well known counsel said to be the original of Sergt. Snubbin, leading Counsel for the defendant in the trial Bardell *v.* Pickwick, (*P.P.*) Lucidity of expression does not appear to have been a strong point with him. Ref. *Observer*, Ap. 3, 1921.

Assembly Rooms. *O.E.W.P.* These were in Nuckall's Place, Broadstairs. Afterwards the Assembly Rooms were converted into a Club.

Atkinson (Miss). See Pig-faced Lady.

Austin Friars. According to J. Ardach (*Dickensian* XX., 204), No. 21 Austin Friars, an old Dutch merchant's house and place of business (demolished in 1888) would have served very well for the premises of Ebenezer Scrooge (*C.C.*); and mentions that part of Scrooge's kitchen was lined with Dutch tiles. The quotation is not correct. Dickens said the *fireplace* (not the kitchen) was an old one, built by some Dutch merchant long ago, and paved all round with quaint Dutch tiles. The house in Austin Friars may have had such a one as Dickens pictured, but it did not agree with the book as to locality. Scrooge's warehouse must have been near to Cornhill, because Bob Cratchit went down a slide there, twenty times, before running home to Camden Town; and the gruff old bell, peeping down slyly at Scrooge out of the Gothic window of an ancient church tower, was probably that of St. Michael's, Cornhill. Mr. Fips's chambers were in Austin Friars. (*M.C.*)

Aylesford Bridge, over the Medway. Suggested as the "wooden bridge" against which the curious little green box on four wheels, containing Mr. Pickwick and his friends, was dashed to pieces by the runaway horse, on the first journey to Dingley Dell. Aylesford bridge, however, is a stone bridge, and the fact that it is practically in Aylesford village makes it highly improbable that Dickens meant this bridge. Mr. Pickwick would never have led that wretched horse for miles and miles, after an accident here, for he could have left it immediately at any one of the two or three inns at Aylesford. It is much more likely that the "wooden bridge" Dickens had in mind was a wooden railing separating the road from a pond, several examples of which are still to be found in the neighbourhood of Cobham, Singlewell, and Sole Street.

Aylesford Bridge has also been suggested as the bridge mentioned in *Great Expectations*, chap. 46, but this is obviously quite wrong, and without the slightest foundation.

Baker's Chop House. Change Alley.
Suggested by Mr. F. S. Johnson as the original of the melancholy tavern where Scrooge took his melancholy dinner. (*C.C.*) It was as likely a place as any in the City, and was a noted Chop house for over a century. One of the waiters there, familiarly known as James, had been in the service of the house for many years, and his portrait in oils was hung in one of the rooms. The building has now been demolished.
See also Austin Friars.

Baker's Trap (*U. T.*). See Gravel Lane Bridge.

Baldwin (Joe). *See* Weller (Sam).

Bardell (Mrs.). (*P. P.*). See Ellis (Ann).

Barker. A carrier of Blundeston in Suffolk, is stated to be the original of Barkis, the carrier of *David Copperfield.*
Another writer says the original was Blake, a carrier at Blundeston. Ref. *T. P.'s Weekly*, Oct. 21, 1904.
See also Originals founded on names.

Barnacle (L. D.) *See* Originals founded upon names.

Barnes (Richard). Probably the original of John Browdie (*N.N.*). Richard Barnes was an attorney in Barnard Castle, and of six similar professional men, he was the only one who was agent for Charles Smithson, Dickens's professional friend who gave him the letters of introduction. Naturally Smithson would refer Dickens to his own agent, rather than to a strange lawyer, when applied to for a letter of introduction to a local practitioner. Barnes died in 1863.
Ref. *Dickensian* XI., 296. *With Dickens in Yorkshire.*
See also Todd (Thos.), Brownie (John) and S—— (John).

Barkis (D. C.). See Barker.

Bantam (Angelo Cyrus). (*P.P.*). See Jervois (Mr.), also Queen's Square, Bath

Barrow (Janet). An aunt of Dickens, and a painter of miniatures. Suggested by F. C. Kitton as the original of Miss La Creevy (*N.N.*). Like the good-natured little portrait painter, Mrs. Barrow was a vivacious, kindly woman, and rather witty. Ref. *T. Ps.' Weekly*, Oct. 21, 1904.

Battens (Mr.). (*U.T.*). A Titbull Pensioner. See Originals founded upon names.

Battery (Old). (*G.E.*). See Cliffe Fort.

Battle Bridge, over the Fleet river. Near the place where Boffin's Bower, or Harmony Jail was. (*O.M.F.*) Mr. Boffin said it was nigh upon a odd mile, or say and a quarter, if you like, up Maiden Lane, Battle Bridge. Maiden Lane is now known as York Road, and there used to be huge mounds of rubbish in the neighbourhood, as described by Dickens. Afterwards the site was covered by various factories of the bone-boiling type, and in part by the Great Northern Railway. Ref. *Dickensian* X., 207, XVII., 189.

Probably Dickens derived his impressions of the Battle Bridge district when living at Somers Town, as a boy.

Bayham Street (No. 141), Camden Town. Suggested as the house of the Cratchit family (*C.C.*). The Dickens family lived here in 1823, when the novelist was about eleven years old, and his description of Bob Cratchit's house may have been a recollection of his boyhood's home. In many respects 141, Bayham Street conformed to the description. St. Stephen's Church in Camden Street, not far away, which was built in 1823, might have been the church Bob Cratchit attended with Tiny Tim, on the Xmas day. Ref. *Dickensian* V., 183.

Bayham Street Almshouses. See Vintners' Almshouses.

Beacon at Cliffe Creek, Lower Thames. Original of the Beacon on the Marshes (*G.E.*). The early type of Beacon on the Thames consisted of an elevated iron cage in which a bon-fire, or flare, could be lighted as an alarm signal. In later times they were used as navigation marks, and the iron cages were gradually replaced by skeleton iron balls. The beacon at Cliffe Creek was the successor of one of the two earliest erected by Richard II. about the year 1377. It stood on the north side of the entrance to the Creek until 1925. Very few beacons now survive and those remaining have skeleton balls instead of the original iron cage which Dickens described as " an ugly thing when you were near it, like an unhooped cask on a pole." Ref. *Dickensian* XXII., 110.

Beadnell (George). Banker, of Lombard Street, and father of Maria Beadnell, the object of Dickens's first love. It has been said that he was the original of the benevolent-looking old humbug Mr. Casby, of *Little Dorrit*, but the claim is not very convincing. Also that he was the original of Mr. Spenlow (*D.C.*)—probably suggested by the parallel that he was the father of Maria Beadnell, as Mr. Spenlow was the father of Dora. Ref. *The Beadnell Letters*.

Beadnell (Maria). Daughter of George Beadnell, banker, of Lombard Street. The original of Dora Spenlow (*D.C.*), Flora Finching (*L.D.*), Dolly Varden (*B.R.*), and, according to Edwin Pugh, Estella (*G.E.*). She was the original in the sense that she was the heroine of Dickens's own early romance, but he gave these different characters attributes which existed in his own mind, rather than those she actually possessed. Dickens met Miss Beadnell when he was a youth of 17, and instantly conceived a deep and romantic but unrequited passion for her, which influenced the whole of his life and, to a considerable extent, his writings. He idealized her as Dolly Varden and as Dora Spenlow, but years after his dismissal, when he met her again as Mrs. Henry Winter, the glamour had departed and he portrayed her, though still tenderly, as Flora Finching. In *Little Dorrit* he put Arthur Clennam in what had been his own place and experience. Ref. *Forster's Life of Dickens*.

Beadnell's Bank. See Child's Bank.

Bear Hotel, Malling. Suggested as the original of the Blue Lion at Muggleton. The Swan at Malling has been claimed to be the Blue Lion of the *Pickwick Papers*, but the Swan is in a side road, of less importance in Dickens's time than it is now. The Bear is in the centre of the Market place, and on the Authority of Mr. Rust, of Birling, was the only Inn at Malling containing a room large enough for the Cricket Club dinner.

Beaufort Arms, Bath. Said to be the scene of the footmen's cold swarry which Sam Weller attended (*P.P.*). The Beaufort Arms was probably a rendezvous of the Bath footmen at the time Dickens visited the city, but that it represents the small greengrocer's shop to which Sam Weller accompanied Mr. John Smawker, is more than doubtful. It has, however, been stated that the Beaufort Arms *was* a greengrocer's shop before it was a tavern, but there seems to be no proof of this, and B. W. Matz thought it was more likely to have been the public-house from which the liquors for the festivity were fetched. Ref. *Inns and Taverns of Pickwick*.

Bell Inn, Berkeley Heath. On the high road between Bristol and Gloucester. The Inn where Mr. Pickwick, Bob Sawyer, and Mr. Benjamin Allen halted for lunch and to change horses, on the journey from Bristol to Birmingham, to interview the elder Mr. Winkle (*P.P.*). It is now a private house. The signpost remains, but the sign-board itself has disappeared. This sign-board used to announce that " Charles Dickens and party lunched here in 1827," which, of course, was not a fact; the party was only a fictitious one in the pages of *Pickwick*. Ref. *Inns and Taverns of Pickwick* ; *The Pickwick Pilgrimages*.

BERWICK (Mary). (*M.P., A.A.P.*) See Procter (Adelaide Ann).

BEVIS MARKS. (*O.C.S*). It has been suggested that the house occupied by Sampson Brass may have been No. 10.

BILLICKINS. (*E.D.*). See Southampton Street.

BILL STUMPS. (*P.P.*). The incident of the discovery of the stone at Cobham bearing the cryptic inscription which the envious Mr. Blotton of Aldgate translated as " Bill Stumps, his mark " is said to be founded upon Chatterton's " Memoirs of a Sad Dog." It has also been said to be derived from Kit's Coty house, a cromlech on the Chatham-Maidstone road, but what the connection may be is not at all clear. In 1779 a stone inscribed with Roman capitals was discovered in the lime quarries, near Paris, and its inscription puzzled the learned men of Paris, until an old man explained that it was merely a direction-post for the people who brought donkeys with baskets for lime (Ici le chemin des Anes). Ref. *Dr. Phipson " The Storm and its portents,"* 1878.

BIRLING PLACE. A fine old Tudor farmhouse, situated just below the North Downs at Birling, Kent, has been suggested by Mr. S. J. Rust as the original of Dingley Dell. (*P.P.*). This house fits the description in the *Pickwick Papers* both externally and internally, and its approach is exactly as described in the book. One of its chief claims rests upon the close agreement between the character of the road from Rochester and the description of the route taken by the Pickwickians. In this respect, no other suggested route is so good. Birling is about 12 miles from Rochester, and after passing the back lanes near Cobham, where we are told Mr. Pickwick dropped his whip, the road is a country lane passing through some beautiful country, and almost without a habitation upon it, even to-day, until the White Horse Inn at Harvel is reached. This inn would, in Pickwick's time, have answered admirably for the inn where the red-headed man refused to take charge of the horse. It was a way-side inn (since rebuilt), with elm trees and a horse-trough in front of it. From the inn, a further lonely walk brings one to the top of the North Downs, and at the bottom of a steep hill on the South side, a narrow lane branches off to the farm, which was the original home of the Neville family. The large pond, close to the house, is now drained, but was skated upon in living memory. Birling village, with its old Church on a hillock in the middle of the village, is about a mile further south, and 2½ miles from Malling, which, on this assumption would be Muggleton, (which see). Ref, *Dickensian* XXIV., 225.

BIRT (Dr. I.) Stated to be the original of Dr. Strong (*D.C.*). The Rev. I. Birt, M.A., of Christ Church, Oxford, was the first Head-master of the King's School, Canterbury, to take his Doctorate while in office (1822). His character exactly fitted Dickens's description of Dr. Strong. He was also a musician, and Dr. Strong was " very fond of music." Dr. Birt died at Faversham in 1847 Ref. *Canterbury and Charles Dickens.*

BIRMINGHAM, Little Nell's route in. (*O.C.S.*). Wilmot Corfield considers that Little Nell and her grandfather disembarked from the canal boat at the Old Wharf ; and that the " dirty lane leading to a crowded street," which they traversed, was the canal side-track leading out through one of the gates into Paradise Street. Ref. *Dickensian* VIII., 236.

See also Gas Street, Birmingham.

BISHOP'S COURT, Chancery Lane. Krook's rag and bottle shop where Nemo died and Miss Flite lived, was on the right-hand side of Bishop's Court, opposite the " Ship " public-house, near Chichester Rents. Both shop and public-house were demolished in 1896. Ref. " *London," Dec.*, 1896.

BLACKING FACTORY. Original of Murdstone and Grinby's wine warehouse (*D.C.*) Warren's Blacking Factory, where Dickens worked for some time as a boy, was near Hungerford Bridge, Charing Cross. When Hungerford market was demolished to make room for the railway station in 1863, Hungerford Bridge was moved to Clifton, and is now the Suspension Bridge over the Avon. Ref. *Dickensian* VII., 264 ; XX., 13.

According to Forster, James Lamert and his cousin started the factory at 30, Hungerford Stairs, in opposition to the original Warren.

BLACKLEY (ALDERMAN). The Lord Mayor who retreated to his bedroom at the Mansion House rather than have anything to do with Mr. Haredale or the rioters (*B.R.*), is said to have been Alderman Blackley. Another version gives the name of the Lord Mayor as Alderman Kennett.

BLACK LION INN, Whitechapel. Where Joe Willet disposed of a frugal dinner, before directing his steps towards the locksmith's house, attracted by the eyes of blooming Dolly Varden (*B.R.*). The Black Lion in Whitechapel has disappeared, but the yard of the Inn, still bearing the name, remains.

BLAKE, Carrier. See Barker.

BLANDOIS (Monsieur). (*L.D.*). See Wainwright (T. G.).

BLEAK HALL, Kemsworth, Herts. Suggested by the Rev. H. Bodel Smith as the original of Bleak House (*B.H.*). It has many features in common with Dickens's description, but it is not so near to St. Albans as the novel indicates. The chief items of similarity to the Bleak House of the story are (1) it has three peaks; (2) it is on a hill and approached by a long drive; (3) it is near to a brickfield. Mr. Tyrrell has, however, pointed out that Bleak Hall is too far from St. Albans, and the features which give it similarity to the Bleak House of the novel were added after Dickens had described the house. At the time *Bleak House* was written, Bleak Hall consisted of three cottages, and it was not named Bleak Hall until after alterations in the summer of 1852, which was after the publication of the earlier portions of *Bleak House*. Ref. *Dickensian* XV., 197; XVI., 40.

BLEAK HOUSE. (*B.H.*).
See Bleak Hall.
Also Gombards Road, St. Albans.
Nast Hyde.
Fort House, Broadstairs.
Cobley's Farm, Finchley.

BLEWBERRY JONES. (*O.M.F.*). The prototype of the miser, called by Bella Wilfer "Blackberry Jones," is stated to have been the Rev. Morgan Jones, curate of the parish church at Blewberry for 40 years. In all that time he wore only one coat, and the only time he renewed his head-gear was by exchange with a scare-crow. As the reverend miser was connected with Blewberry until about the year 1830, it is quite possible that Dickens had heard about him and that he was the Blewberry Jones, the reading of whose history aloud to Mr. Boffin had such a disastrous moral effect upon Mr. Silas Wegg. Ref. *Daily Telegraph*, 13/2/1914.

BLIMBER'S (Dr.) ACADEMY. (*D. & S.*). See Chichester House, Brighton.

BLUE BOAR (G. E.). See Bull Hotel, Rochester.

BLUE BOAR, Whitechapel. The inn to which David Copperfield came from Yarmouth. "We approached London by degrees and got in due time to the inn, in the Whitechapel district. I forget whether it was the 'Blue Bull' or the 'Blue Boar,' but I know it was the Blue something, and that its likeness was painted on the back of the coach."

The "Blue Boar" was next to the "Bull," and its site is now marked by a sculptured effigy of a Boar, with gilded tusks, built into the wall of a tobacco factory. Ref. *Dickensian* I., 238

BLUE DRAGON. (*M.C.*). *See* George Inn, Amesbury.

BLUE LION, Muggleton. (*P.P.*). See Swan Hotel, Malling; also Bear Hotel, Malling.

BLUNDESTON, Suffolk. Original of Blunderstone. (*D.C.*). The Rectory, from the windows of which the churchyard can be seen, still boasts a "rookery" of elms, with no rooks, and, according to B. W. Matz and Dr. John Bately of Gorleston, there are the strongest reasons to believe that the Rectory was the "Rookery" of *David Copperfield*, although Blundeston Hall has been claimed to be the original. The ground of this claim is that the interior of the Hall coincides more nearly with Dickens's description. On the other hand, neither the graveyard nor the sun-dial over the church porch can be seen from the Hall, as they can from the Rectory, and in other geographical respects the Hall can have no claim. Blundeston Church is an ancient little edifice with a round tower, probably Saxon. The sun-dial seen by little David Copperfield is over the church door. The high-backed pews he spoke of have been removed, but through a window we can still see the Rectory, as did Peggoty, who liked to make herself as sure as she could that it was not being robbed nor in flames.

The village inn at Blundeston is the "Plough," from whence Mr. Barkis was wont to start on his rounds. Ref. *Dickensian* II., 153.

It has been suggested that the Church at Blunderstone might have been the old Parish Church at Chatham, but it is not understood why the suggestion is made.

BLUNDESTON HALL. See Blundeston.

BLUNDERSTONE. (*D.C.*). See Blundeston.

BOARDING SCHOOL, Bury St. Edmunds. See Westgate House.

BOAT-HOUSE AT GRAVESEND. On the bank of the Canal at Gravesend, there is a quaint little cottage consisting of an inverted fishing boat supported on low walls of brick-work. The boat itself is 30 feet long, and forms an upper Chamber, lighted by a small window cut in the stern, where the rudder used to be; and is very like Phiz's original drawings of Peggotty's house in *David Copperfield*. A guide to Gravesend, printed in 1844, described it as the *old* boat-built cottage bordering the Canal, so that it was probably in existence and known to

Dickens, either when he was staying at Chalk in 1836, or when he stayed with Forster at a nearby hotel in 1841. This cottage is a real ship on dry land, and if Dickens derived the idea of Peggotty's house from a real original, it is very likely that he had this boathouse in mind when he wrote *David Copperfield* in 1849.

See also: Sharman's Hut, Yarmouth.

BOATMEN. (*O.E.w.P.*). See Ford (Harry).

BOFFIN NICHODEMUS. (*O.M.F.*). See Dodd.

BOFFIN'S BOWER. (*O.M.F.*). See Battle Bridge.

BOMPAS (Sergt.). Original of Sergt. Buzfuz (*P.P.*). Mr. Fitzgerald, in *Bozland* cites a much more recent breach of promise case than Mr. Pickwick's, to show that the methods of Sergt. Buzfuz still survive. "Not long since, in Mr. Justice Lawrence's Court the late Sergt. Buzfuz reappeared in the flesh and began his speech by declaring that not merely in the whole course of his professional experience, but never at any time had facts more painful been brought before a jury." He went on to say: "The plaintiff, gentlemen, the plaintiff was a young lady, the daughter of a gentleman deceased, who was at one time in the War Office. She lived with her mother and her two sisters in the peaceful and innocent atmosphere of a small preparatory school at Thornton Heath. Gentlemen, she was a young girl, she knew nothing of London life; she had been delicately and tenderly nurtured by a loving mother in a quiet country house. Knowing nothing and suspecting nothing of evil or deceit, she got into a train for London Bridge, not knowing that in the same carriage was a person, whom, for brevity, *I will call a Man* !'" Ref. *The Dickens Originals*.

BOOKSTALL KEEPER. (*O.T.*). The original of the book-stall keeper who spoke for Oliver at the Police Court in Hatton Garden, has been identified by someone as the owner of a book-shop in Hampstead Road where Dickens was sometimes sent by his father, when they lived at Bayham Street.

BOOT TAVERN, Cromer Street, Gray's Inn Road. The inn mentioned in *Barnaby Rudge* was not an imaginative place, but actually existed in the fields at the back of the Foundling Hospital, as described. In 1780 it was the headquarters of the Gordon rioters, and at that time was in a solitary neighbourhood, and approachable only by a dark and narrow lane.

Cattermole's drawing of the Boot Tavern in *Barnaby Rudge* was copied from an etching of 1780, and is a pretty faithful picture of the inn as it was at that time. The tavern was kept by the Speedy family for several generations, and was rebuilt by Peter Speedy in 1801. In 1908, his great grandson, Harry Speedy, was the host. Ref. *Dickensian* IV., 258

BOOT (ALFRED). Butler to the Grant Bros. of Manchester. According to Edwin Pugh, he was the original of David, the apoplectic butler who produced the double-diamond port. (*N.N.*). Dickens met the Grant Bros. in Manchester, and may have seen and utilized their butler, but *The Dickens Originals* is not always to be relied upon.

BOTTOM INN (Gravel Hill), near Petersfield. Original of the little inn, 12 miles from Portsmouth, where Nicholas Nickleby met and supped with Mr. Vincent Crummles. (*N.N.*). Dickens did not name the inn, but C. G. Harper says, from the author's very accurate description, there can be no question as to the identical spot Dickens had in mind. The building is now a game-keeper's cottage. Ref. *Dickensian Inns and Taverns*.

BOULOGNE. The original of "Our French Watering Place." (*R.P.*).

BOWES ACADEMY, near Greta Bridge, Yorkshire. The original of Dotheboys Hall (*N.N.*). It was the so-called scholastic establishment of William Shaw, a well-known Yorkshire schoolmaster who was the prototype of Squeers. Dickens's picture of Dotheboys Hall agrees in many respects with the building at the western end of the village of Bowes, which, however, has since been altered. The old schoolroom at the rear of the premises has been taken down, and other structural changes made to convert the place to its present use as a private house; but the original pump in the yard, with its well-worn stone trough, at which Smike and his unfortunate school-mates performed their morning ablutions—when the pump was not "froze"—still remains. Ref. *With Dickens in Yorkshire*.

BOYTHORNE (LAURENCE). (*B.H.*). See Landor (Walter Savage).

BRASS (SAMPSON). (*O.C.S.*). See Tinsley Also Bevis Marks.

BRAY (MADELINE). (*N.N.*). See Hogarth Mary).

Also Originals founded upon names.

BRICK LANE, Commercial Street, E. Mission room at. The original of the Brick Lane Branch of the United Grand Junction Ebenezer Temperance Association (*P.P.*). The building, and the ladder down which Brother Tadger was precipitated, still exist, but the mission room is really at the bottom, and not at the top of the ladder. Ref. *Dickensian* I., 234.

See also Hanbury Street.

Bridge of Sighs. See Gravel Lane Bridge.

Bridge over Canal. (*O.C.S.*). See Gas Street.

Brisac (**Walter de**). See Rudge (Barnaby).

British Association for the Advancement of Science. If has been suggested that the *Mudfog Association* was a skit on this.

Broad Row, Yarmouth. See Middlegate Street.

Broadstairs. The original of "Our English Watering Place" (*R.P.*). The Assembly Rooms mentioned were in Nuckall's Place. Afterwards the Assembly Rooms became a Club.

Broadstairs (Cottage at). See Strong (Mary).

Broad Street, Soho. See Kenwigs family.

Browdie (**John**). (*N.N.*).
See Barnes (Richard).
Todd (Thomas).
Brownie (John).
S—— (John).

Brownlow (Mr.). (*O.T.*). See Craven Street.

Brown (Dr. **John**). The original of Joe Specks, mentioned in *Dulborough Town.* (*U.T.*). Dr. Brown was one of Dickens's school-fellows at Giles' school, Chatham, and later had his surgery in Rochester High Street, on the site of the present new Co-operative building. For some years before his death, Dr. Brown had a framed and glazed reprint of Dickens's account of their meeting hanging in his hall.

Brownie (**John**). Said to be the original of John Browdie. (*N.N.*). He had a gargantuan appetite, a boisterous laugh, and a loud broad Yorkshire brogue. It is claimed that he met Dickens at Barnard Castle, and that when *Nicholas Nickleby* was published, the author presented him with a specially bound copy, which is still preserved in the family. Without further details of Brownie and his occupation, it is not possible to determine whether this claim has any foundation or not. Ref. *T. P.'s Weekly, Aug.* 4, 1905.

Bucket (**Inspector**). (*B.H.*). See Field (Inspector).

Buckingham Street, Strand. York House, No. 15, has been identified as the original of the house where David Copperfield lodged with Mrs. Crupp. Dickens himself lodged here on first leaving his father's home in Bentinck Street. He was then 22 years of age and employed on the staff of the *Morning Chronicle.* He remained at York House for a short time, moving to 13, Furnival's Inn about Christmas, 1834. Peter the Great at one time occupied rooms in York House, as also did Henry Fielding and William Black. The house was swept away some years since. Ref. *Dickensian* II., 309; VII., 101.

Buck Inn, Yarmouth. Arriving at Yarmouth, David Copperfield found Ham waiting for him at the public-house which was the stopping-place of the Blunderstone carrier. (*D.C.*). Dickens did not mention the name of the public-house, but the Buck Inn, which still exists in the market square was undoubtedly the identical house where Barkis came to a halt at Yarmouth. Ref. *Dickensian Inns and Taverns.*

Budden. The original of Joe the fat boy at Manor Farm (*P.P.*), was the son of James Budden, who kept the Red Lion hotel at the corner of Military Road and High Street, Chatham. Various other originals have been claimed, some of them on behalf of people who were probably not born at the time *Pickwick* was written.

According to the *Western Morning News* of June, 1910, the original of the fat boy was a servant at the Turk's Head Inn at Exeter. Another claim, put forward in the *Manchester Guardian,* in April, 1905, was that Charles Peace, the murderer, alias Richard Cockerill, was the original of the fat boy, on his own statement. Neither of these two claims deserves any consideration whatever.

Buffaloes (Ancient Order of). See Glorious Apollers.

Bugsby's Marsh. See Quilp's Wharf.

Bull Inn, Birdcage Alley. Original of the sequestered tavern in Southwark referred to by Dickens in *Household Words* (*On duty with Inspector Field*). The Bull, or old Black Bull, was known in 1746 as the "Warm Harbour," and figured under that name in a play called "The Old Mint of Southwark," at the Queen's Theatre in 1848. The *London Journal* of 1862 described the house as the "Red Bull" and spoke of its thatched roof and latticed windows, and its over-hanging porch supported by a row of stumpy pillars. In *Household Words* Dickens described this porch as a low colonade. Ref. *Dickensian* XII., 14, 164.

Bull Inn, Leadenhall Street. Possibly the Blue Boar frequented by the Elder Mr. Weller, and where his son indited the famous valentine. (*P.P.*). Ref. *Inns and Taverns of Pickwick.*

Bull Hotel, Rochester. Figures under its own name in *The Pickwick Papers*, and is the original of the Winglebury Arms (*S. by B.*) and the Blue Boar (*G.E.*) The entrance, staircase, and rambling passages of the inn are much the same as when Dickens described them. The ball-room still contains the elevated den in which the musicians were securely confined, on the occasion when Winkle and Jingle attended an Assembly, but the room itself has been somewhat altered. The red benches and the hanging glass chandeliers have been removed to make way for electric lights and modern furniture. The coffee-room on the ground floor has also been altered since the time Mr. Pickwick and his friends dined there, and Pip and Bentley Drummle pretended not to know each other. The commercial room, on the other side of the Archway, was converted into a restaurant some years since. Above this, and partly over the archway, is the room in which Pip's apprenticeship dinner was held, and Mr. Wopsle gave them Collins's Ode with such tremendous effect. Room No. 17, on the first floor, is pointed out as Mr. Pickwick's room. This is the room Dickens himself sometimes occupied (see *The Seven Poor Travellers*). Rooms 13 and 19 are inter-communicating and are traditionally assigned to Messrs. Winkle and Tupman. The indifferent chamber allotted to Pip, after his fall from Great Expectations, was one of three chambers up the yard over the coach-houses or stables, which could be reached by a wooden staircase from the yard.

Bull Inn, 25 Aldgate. The starting place of Mr. Pickwick's journey to Ipswich. It stood where Aldgate Avenue now is, and in 1827 was kept by Ann Nelson. There was a room in the inn specially reserved for coachmen and guards, more exclusive than the commercial rooms of the old bagman days. Ref. *Dickensian* I., 237

Burial Ground. (*B.H.*). See Russell Court.

Burnham. See Cobtree Hall.

Bush Hotel, Bristol. (*P.P.*). Until 1864, this stood on the site of the present Lloyd's Bank, near the Guildhall. Ref. *Pickwick Pilgrimages*.

Burnett (Harry). The deformed son of Dickens's sister Fanny. Original of Paul Dombey (*D. & S.*), if a strong impression prevailing in Manchester circles can be accepted as proof. It has, however, been stated that Dickens himself told his sister that her son was the original of Paul Dombey. Little Burnett had a spinal deformity, and had been taken to Brighton, as little Paul is represented to have been. He is said to have been a singular child, meditative and odd, and Dickens may have been attracted by him as reflecting something of his own childish character. Like Paul Dombey, Harry Burnett died young. Ref. *Dickensian* VI, 9; VII., 21.

Burnett (Henry). According to Edwin Pugh, in *The Dickens Originals* Dickens's brother-in-law, Henry Burnett was his ideal man, and was the original of Nicholas Nickleby (*N.N.*) Harry Maylie (*O.T.*), Edward Chester (*B.R.*), Tom Pinch (*M.C.*), and Walter Gay (*D. & S.*). Burnett seems to have been accepted by some of Dickens's intimates as the original of Nicholas Nickleby, but there is no real ground for suggesting him as the original of the other characters mentioned. Pugh simply says: "and if Nicholas Nickleby, why not Harry Maylie, Edward Chester, Tom Pinch, and Walter Gay?" The Burnetts lived in Upper Brook Street, Manchester, and in the *Palatine Notebook* for 1883, a writer said that there was a strong impression in Manchester circles that Henry Burnett was the ideal of Nicholas Nickleby.

Bury St. Edmunds. See Sudbury.

Bushey. Suggested as the country town where the races were, on an open heath on a hill, a full mile from the town. (*O.C.S.*). See also London to Tong.

Butler's Wharf. See Quilp's Wharf.

Buzfuz (Sergeant). (*P.P.*). See Bompas (Sergeant).

Cairo, Illinois. The original of the dismal swamp called "Eden" to which Martin Chuzzlewit and Mark Tapley were induced to go. Cairo has since developed into the ideal town which Mr. Scadder visualised. Ref. *The Dickens Encyclopaedia*; Forster's *Life of Dickens*, I.

Campbell (Mrs.). A former well-known resident of Leamington. Said to be the original of Mrs. Skewton (*D. & S.*), but the original reference has not been found.

Canterbury. See Abbey Town.

Carker (Death of). (*D. & S.*). See Paddock Wood.

Carlisle House, Carlisle Street. Identified by R. Allbut and Snowden Ward as the original of Dr. Manette's house in Soho. (*T.T.C.*). Carlisle House was originally the town house of the Howards, Earls of Carlisle, and was built in 1690. In Dickens's time it was let out in tenements. In 1895, Rose Street, in the same district, was re-named Manette Street, to commemorate the association of the neighbourhood with the Doctor of the Bastile. Ref. *Dickensian* I., 208; XXI., 96, 159.

CARNABY STREET. See Kenwigs family.

CARTON (SYDNEY). (*T.T.C.*). See Allen (Gordon).

CASBY (CHRISTOPHER). (*L.D.*). See Beadnell (George).

CASBY'S HOUSE. (*L.D.*). See Acton Street.

CASTLE HOTEL, Coventry. The inn at Coventry where Mr. Pickwick stopped to change horses, on the journey from Birmingham, is not named in the *Pickwick Papers*, but may have been the Castle Hotel. It was the scene of a public dinner to Dickens in 1858, when he was presented with a gold repeater watch in recognition of his reading of the *Christmas Carol* in aid of the Coventry Institute. Ref. *Inns and Taverns of Pickwick*.

CATHARINE WHEEL INN, Beckhampton. See Shepherd's Shore.

CEMETERY GATE. See Chertsey Gate.

CHAIRMEN AT BATH. (*P.P.*). The two chairmen, one short and fat, and the other long and thin, mentioned in chap. xxxvi. of *Pickwick Papers*, are said to have been real and well-known people. If so, it is barely possible that Dickens may have seen them in his reporting days at Bath, but considerable evidence has been adduced to indicate that the author of *Pickwick* obtained most of his descriptions of Bath from a guide book. Ref. *Dickensian* XXIII., 181.

CHANDOS STREET. The warehouse, connected with the blacking factory at Hungerford Bridge, was in Chandos Street, on a site now occupied by the Civil Service Stores. Here young Dickens, in company with Bob Fagin and other boys, used to tie up pots of blacking "near the second window as you come from Bedford Street."

See also Blacking Factory.

CHAPMAN (LACEY). A butcher of Canterbury, and belonging to a Gravesend family. Said to be probably the original of Tracy Tupman (*P.P.*), but on very doubtful premises. Another suggestion put forward as Tupman's original is a middle-aged man named Winter, who used to ogle the ladies in Hyde Park. A more than doubtful suggestion.

CHAPMAN (THOMAS). A City merchant, and chairman at Lloyds. Claimed to be the original of Mr. Dombey (*D. & S.*), but Forster distinctly denies this and characterises it as an absurd invention. Ref. Forster's *Life of Dickens*.

CHARACTER "originals." A number of fictitious characters in the works of various authors has been put forward from time to time as Dickens originals.

John Brodie recalls Scott's Dandy Dinmont.

Sam Weller recalls Andrew Fairservice in *Rob Roy*.

Ralph Nickleby recalls Gilbert Glossin in *Guy Mannering*.

Squeers recalls Dick Hatteraick in the same book, etc., etc.

These, and others like them, appear to amount to a charge of plagiarism against Dickens, and nothing else.

CHARLES STREET. (*U.T.*). Was the last street at the north-west end of Long Acre. It has been re-named Arne Street. Ref. *Dickensian* VIII., 221.

CHATHAM. See Rochester.

CHATHAM MECHANICS' Institution. See Rochester.

CHATHAM PARISH CHURCH. See Blundeston and Providence Chapel.

CHATTERTON. See Bill Stumps.

CHEERYBLE BROS. (*N.N.*). See Grant Bros.

CHERTSEY GATE, Rochester Cathedral. The gate-house in which John Jasper lodged. (*E.D.*). It has been stated that the description in *Edwin Drood* includes some features of the Priory Gate and the Deanery Gate, but what those features are is not stated, and the writer cannot agree that the book description includes anything but the Chertsey Gate on the High Street.

Sir Luke Fildes, in one of his illustrations in *Edwin Drood* places the Priory Gate where the Chertsey Gate should be, possibly because he made the drawing in London from detached sketches, and mistook the positions of the two gates. Ref. *Dickensian* XXIII. 157.

CHESHIRE CHEESE, Fleet Street. The tavern to which Sydney Carton conducted Charles Darnay to dine, after the latter's acquital at the Old Bailey. (*T.T.C.*). The tavern is approached from Fleet Street by a covered passage—Wine Office Court—and a tablet in the dining-room professes to show where Carton and Darnay sat. Mr. I. Ardagh says, however, that the original of the tavern in the *Tale of Two Cities* was the Cock, which until 1887 stood at the opposite side of the street, near Chancery Lane. The Cock was also approached by a wooden covered passage. Mr. Ardagh adds that his opinion was supported by Percy Fitzgerald. Ref. *Dickensian* XXIII., 209.

CHESNEY WOLD. (*B.H.*). See Rockingham Castle.

CHESTER (SIR JOHN). (*B.R.*). See Chesterfield (Lord).

Chester (Edward). (*B.R.*). See Burnett (Henry).

Chesterfield (Lord). The original of Sir John Chester. (*B.R.*). Ref. *The Dickens Originals.*

If true, the identification was not founded upon personal appearance or character, but only on a similarity between Lord Chesterfield's letters and the sayings of Sir John Chester.

Chichester House, Brighton. The corner house at the west end of Chichester Terrace is claimed to be the original of Dr. Blimber's Academy. (*D.& S.*). It justifies Dickens's description as a "mighty fine house, fronting the sea." It was the academy of the Rev. George Proctor, D.D. between 1839 and 1846, and was identified by Dickens's friend Harrison Ainsworth as Dr. Blimber's house.

In 1901 Miss Boyle published *Mary Boyle, her Book*, in which she suggested Wick House, the residence and school of the Rev. Dr. Everard, as Blimber's academy. There was another Mr. Everard conducting an academy at 21 and 22, Sussex Square, but he must not be confused with Dr. Everard of Wick House. Wick House looks towards the sea but is ten minutes walk from the front, and in 1837 the sea view was intercepted by buildings. Miss Boyles' suggestion arose from her schoolgirl recollections of Dr. Everard's academy, but most Dickens topographers are satisfied that the real original of Blimber's was Chichester House. Ref. *Dickensian* VI., 255; XIX., 158; XX., 90; *The Dickens Originals.*

Chicken (Richard). Sometime clerk on the North Eastern Railway, and living in the Skeldegate district of York. Mr. T. P. Cooper has been at considerable pains to prove that Chicken was the original of Mr. Micawber (*D.C.*). Over 100 of his letters have been preserved, all couched in the florid style of those written by Micawber, and it is stated that he knew Dickens's brother Alfred, and met the novelist in York. Chicken's letters give the impression that if he were not the original of Micawber, he ought to have been; but Forster distinctly records that the character of Micawber was founded chiefly upon the novelist's father, John Dickens. Ref. *The Real Micawber*; *Dickensian* XVI., 148.

Chicksey Veneering and Stobbles. (*O.M.F.*). See Mincing Lane.

Children's Hospital. (*O.M.F.*). See Hospital for Children, Great Ormonde Street.

Child's Bank. Temple Bar. Original of Tellson's Bank. (*T.T.C.*). Child's Bank was an old-fashioned tall and narrow building in Fleet Street, adjoining Temple Bar. There is an excellent drawing of it by Finney, in 1855. As Dickens described Tellson's Bank as being in Fleet Street, next to Temple Bar, and Child's Bank was, and is on the spot, one would think there could be no doubt about the original. Nevertheless, other banks have been claimed to be the original of Tellson's. According to Edwin Pugh it was Beadnell's Bank in Lombard Street; and other suggestions are Gosling's Bank, and Child's Bank in Middle Temple Lane. Ref. *Dickensian* X., 263; *The Dickens Originals*; *Bohemian Days in Fleet Street*, 1913.

Chillip (Dr.). (*D.C.*). Said to have been founded upon the Doctor who attended the Dickens family at Devonshire terrace; but the evidence is not known. Dickens lived at Devonshire Terrace about 1839, and *David Copperfield* was published in 1850.

Chimes (The). (*C.B., C.*). See St. Dunstan's Church.

Chivery (John). (*L.D.*). See Union Road.

Chumley. See Weller (Tony).

Church (*R.P., C.d.of S.*). See Providence Chapel.

Church (Little Nell's). (*O.C.S.*). See Tong. Also Minster Abbey.

Church (Marriage of Bella Wilfer). (*O.M.F.*). See St. Alphage's Church.

Church House, Highgate. The old brick, Georgian house in South Grove, now called Church House, was suggested by Mr. Tyrrell as the home of Mrs. Steerforth (*D.C.*). It corresponds in almost every particular with Dickens's description (the buildings now separating it from a side lane were not there in the Copperfield days), and was very probably the house Dickens had in mind. He was well acquainted with Highgate and "hung out" at the Red Lion in 1832-3, when staying with his father, who had temporary lodgings at Mrs. Goodman's, next door to the Red Lion at Highgate. Ref. *Dickensian* VIII., 93.

Church on the Marshes. (*G.E.*). See Cooling. Also Lower Higham.

Church Street, Ipswich. See Green Gate.

Church Street, Millbank. Now Dean Stanley Street. A large house at the corner of this street and Smith Square now covers the site of the dolls' dress-maker's home. Ref. *The London of Dickens.*

CHURCH (HIDEOUS). (*O.M.F.*). See St. John the Evangelist.

CHURCHYARD. See Cooling and Lower Higham.

CITY VOLUNTEERS. See Royal East London Volunteers.

CLARE (ADA). (*B.H.*). See Hogarth (Mary).

CLARENDON PARK. Between Winterslow and Salisbury. Suggested by R. Allbut as the place where Jonas Chuzzlewit murdered Montagu Tigg (*M.C.*). In the earlier years of last century, he says the Park was more like a plantation or wood, and "doubtless it was the place intended by Dickens." This identification, however, depended entirely on the contention that the Blue Dragon of *Martin Chuzzlewit* was the Lion's Head at Winterslow, and this contention was shown by Dr. Gibbons to be wrong.

See also Lion's Head Inn.

CLARKE (Thos.). See Tom-all-alones.

CLARIDGE'S HOTEL, Brook Street. Claridge's, or Mivart's hotel is stated to be probably the scene of Nicholas Nickleby's encounter with Sir Mulberry Hawk on the occasion when the latter was damaged by the accident to his gig.

CLENNAM (Mrs.). (*L.D.*). The original idea for this character is contained in Dickens's note-book. "Bed-ridden (or room-ridden) twenty five-and-twenty years. Any length of time. As to most things, kept at a stand-still all the while. Thinking of altered streets as the old streets. Changed things as the unchanged things. The youth or girl I quarrelled with all those years ago, as the same youth and girl now. Brought out of doors by an unexpected exercise of my latent strength of character, and then how strange!" Ref. Forster's *Life of Dickens.*

See also Upper Thames Street.

CLIFFE (FORGE AT). See Forge at Chalk.

CLIFFE FORT, Thames Marshes. On the site of an old battery or bulwark erected by Henry VIII. in 1539. The old bulwark was the original of the old Battery in which Pip and Joe Gargery sometimes pursued their studies. (*G.E.*). Cliffe Fort was built by General Gordon (Gordon of Khartoum) in 1869-1870, about 10 years after Dickens wrote *Great Expectations.* Ref. *Dickensian* XXII., 111.

CLIFTON SUSPENSION BRIDGE, Bristol. Formerly Old Hungerford Bridge, Charing Cross.

See also Blacking Factory.

CLOISTERHAM. (*E.D.*). See Rochester.

CLOISTERHAM WEIR. (*E.D.*). See Allington.

CLOVELLY, Devon. Original of the village of Steepways. (*Message from the Sea*). Dickens and Wilkie Collins visited Clovelly in November, 1860, for the purpose of obtaining local colour for the forthcoming Xmas story in *All the Year Round*; and the description of the village in chapter 1 was a faithful picture of the real place. This chapter was written by Dickens. The little fishing village on the Devonshire coast remains to-day very much as it was when Captain Jorgan viewed it from the little harbour wall. Ref. *Dickensian* X., 128.

COACH AND HORSES, Strood Hill. Suggested by Mr. Harris as the original of the "Tilted Wagon" Inn. (*E.D.*). B. W. Matz in *Dickensian Inns and Taverns* merely records this statement without comment, but the writer cannot accept the identification, for several reasons, and believes that the original of the Tilted Wagon has yet to be found.

COACH OFFICE in "Our Town." (*G.E.*). In 1838, the coach office at Rochester was at 24, High Street, close to the Bull Inn (Blue Boar), and belonged to Messrs. Edwards and Chaplin, coach proprietors. The building has now a modern brick front and is a druggist's shop, but the back of the premises is still much as it was when Dickens wrote *Great Expectations,* although what was the coach-yard has been built upon.

COAVINSES. (*B.H.*). See Sloman.

COBBOLD (Mrs.). See Monckton (Hon. Miss).

COBHAM HALL, Kent. The seat of the Earl of Darnley. This was the Hall the stable clock of which was repaired by the clock-mending tramp. (*U. T. Tramps*).

COBHAM COLLEGE. See Vintners' Almshouses.

COBLEY'S FARM, Finchley. Suggested original of Bleak House. (*B.H.*). Dickens stayed there once or twice, but the place has no connection with the venue of the story and is certainly not Mr. Jardyce's Bleak House.

COBTREE HALL. Usually considered to be the original of Manor Farm, Dingley Dell. (*P.P.*). Cobtree Hall was first identified by Hughes or Hammond Hall, on the suggestion of the late Mr. Cobb of Rochester, as being of a character to fit Dickens's description of the Wardle's home. It is, however, open to considerable doubt. Cobtree is about seven miles from Rochester on the main road to Maidstone, a road and district Dickens was not acquainted with when he wrote the *Pickwick Papers,* for, in a letter to Forster more than twenty years afterwards, he said he had just discovered that the road from Maidstone to Rochester was one of the prettiest in Kent. In *My Father as I knew him* Miss Mamie Dickens says he pointed out to her the exact spot where Mr. Pickwick dropped his whip, in one of the back lanes near Cobham, which is not on the road to Cobtree, though it is possible, of course, to recross the Medway and get back to that place, by a very roundabout way, via Aylesford Bridge. The first cheap edition of *Pickwick* contained some drawings by Onwhyn, some of them said to have been made " on the spot." These were made in 1837, many years before Hammond Hall's identification of Cobtree. The sketches show a typical Kentish farm which might be one of almost any number which existed, and some of which still exist, with pond, rookery, and all. In *The Inns and Taverns of Pickwick* B. W. Matz says that until the vexed question of Muggleton is settled the identity of the Blue Lion Inn cannot be verified. This applies equally to Cobtree Hall.

Other suggested originals of Dingley Dell are Burham, and Frindsbury Manor House, near Rochester. Also Northfleet (if Muggleton be Gravesend). It is suggested somewhere that the jingle of the name given to the Wardle's home might have been derived from Singlewell, a little hamlet between Gravesend and Cobham and close to Chalk, where Dickens was staying when he wrote the earlier chapters of *Pickwick*. See also Birling Place.

COCKERILL (Richard). See Budden.

COCK TAVERN. See Cheshire Cheese.

CODLIN, Showman. (*O.C.S.*). See Willis (Tom).

COFFEE HOUSE, Covent Garden. (*B.R.*). See Tom's Coffee House.

COFFEE HOUSE on Ludgate Hill. (*L.D.*). See London Coffee House.

COKE TOWN. (*H.T.*). See Manchester.

COLE. See Weller (Tony).

COLLEGE YARD GATE. See Chertsey Gate.

COLLINS (WILKIE). Dickens's companion on the lazy tour in the North of England (*L.T.*) and dubbed Thomas Idle by the author.

COMMERCIAL STREET. See Cooking Depôt

CONSTANT COMPANION. (C. *d. of a S.*). Probably one of Dickens's sisters. Harriet Ellen Dickens has been suggested.

CONVICT PRISON, Chatham (Site of). See Tom-all-alones.

COOK'S COURT, Cursitor Street. (*B.H.*). See Took's Court.

COOKING DEPÔT (Self-supporting). (*U. T.*). Originally a four-storey warehouse at the corner of Commercial Street and Flower and Dean Streets. Up to the early eighties it was a cooking depôt for the workers of the district. Ref. *Dickensian* I., 235.

COOLING. Cooling church-yard is said to be the place where Pip first encountered the escaped convict. (*G.E.*). This is on the authority of John Forster, who said Dickens told him he meant to make Cooling Castle and Church the scene of his new story. He may, however, have altered his mind at the last moment, as he certainly did in the cases of *Edwin Drood* and *Martin Chuzzlewit*. In the latter case, Forster says Dickens intended the scene to be in Cornwall, but altered his mind at the last minute in favour of a Wiltshire village. The row of little gravestones mentioned in *Great Expectations* is certainly in Cooling Churchyard, but in no other respect do the church and hamlet of Cooling bear the slightest resemblance to the church and village of the story. Ref. *Dickensian* XX., 131, 214; XXI., 13, 100.

See also Lower Higham.

COOPER (Mrs. M. A.). According to Edwin Pugh, the original of Little Dorrit. (*L.D.*). The statement that Dickens gave her the name "Little Dorrit" when they were both living in Somer's Town, is not very credible. Dickens was then 17 years of age, and he wrote *Little Dorrit* when 43. The claim on behalf of Mrs. Cooper is one of numerous irresponsible statements that are so difficult to kill, when once circulated. Ref. *Dickensian* VIII., 317.

CORN EXCHANGE, Rochester. The grave red-brick building, out of which projected a queer old clock, as if Time carried on business there, and hung out his sign. (*U.T.*).

Also the small Town-Hall of Great Winglebury. See also Rochester.

COTTAGE AT BOW (Mrs. Nickleby's). (*N.N.*) See Grove Hall Estate.

COUNTY INN, Canterbury. The original of the inn where Mr. Dick stayed (*D.C.*) is said to be the Fountain Hotel, in St. Margaret's Street, for the reason that it was referred to in the Coaching days as *the* county inn. Ref. *Dickensian Inns and Taverns*.

Mr. T. W. Tyrrell dissents from this. There was, and is, a County Inn at Canterbury. In his MS., Dickens wrote the word with a capital C, but it was printed with a small letter, and the mistake has never been rectified.

Another suggestion is the Fleur de de Lys in the High Street.

COUNTY TOWN. (*O.C.S.*). See Bushey.

Coventry. Percy Fitzgerald was satisfied that Coventry was the town in which Mrs. Jarley exhibited the waxworks the night after encountering little Nell and her grandfather. (*O.C.S.*). Little Nell is described as wandering about the town at night, and hiding herself in the shadow of an old gateway, on catching sight of Quilp. This old gateway is locally believed to be one which still stands in Much Park Street. Ref. *Dickensian* II., 132.

The claim is, however, rejected by Mr. Nowell of Coventry, and Mr. Dexter suggests Warwick as the real original. Refs. *The England of Dickens, Coventry Herald, Dec.* 15., 1922.

Coventry (Inn at). (*P.P.*). See Castle Hotel, Coventry.

Craven Street, Strand. No. 39 has been identified as the original of Mr. Brownlow's house. (*O.T.*). Craven Street also at one time possessed at No. 8 the door-knocker which suggested the fancy of Scrooge's knocker changing into Marley's face; but the lady who resided at No. 8 in 1899 took it from the door to prevent its being photographed. The knocker was originally fixed by Dr. David Rees, who lived at No. 8 from 1841-1863. There is an excellent photograph, by Mr. Tyrrell, of this curious knocker in the *Dickensian* of 1924. Ref. *Dickensian* XX., 203.

Cratchit (Bob). (*C.C.*). See Bayham Street.

Creakle (Mr.). (*D.C.*). See Jones.

Crescent (The), Bath. (*P.P.*). Nos. 15 and 16 were the only houses in the Crescent which let apartments at the time of Pickwick. Mr. Winkle must therefore have lodged here, when he ran round the Crescent one night in his night-gear. In the *Pickwick Papers* the landlady's name was Craddock, and this was the real name of the person with whom Mr. and Mrs. Dickens lodged, when spending their honeymoon at Chalk, in 1836.

Crisparkle (Rev. S.). (*E.D.*). See Minor Canon Row.

Crooked Billet (*B.R.*). The inn mentioned in *Barnaby Rudge* as the headquarters of the recruiting sergeant from whom Joe Willet took the King's shilling, was stated by Forster, and also by Mr. Dexter, to have been an inn at No. 1, Tower Hill, at the corner of the Minories. Ref. *The London of Dickens.*

According to Mr. T. W. Tyrrell, however, it was not actually at the corner of the Minories; and B. W. Matz states that there was until 1912 an old weather-beaten inn called the Crooked Billet at No. 1, Little Town Hill, at the corner of Shorter Street. Ref. *Dickensian Inns and Taverns.*

Crown and Anchor, Yarmouth. See Duke's Head, Yarmouth.

Crown Inn, Rochester. Identified as the "Crozier" where Datchery announced himself as an idle dog living on his means. (*E.D.*). The "Crown" was at one time known as Wright's Hotel, and was referred to by Mr. Jingle as "Dear, very !" (*P.P.*). Ref. *Inns and Taverns of Pickwick.*

The statement has been made that the original of the "Crozier" was the Mitre Hotel, Rochester, on the site of the present Capital and Counties Bank. There never was a Mitre Hotel in Rochester, and the Capital and Counties Bank (Lloyd's) is the building which was formerly the house of Sir Richard Head, from which house King James II. escaped to France in 1688.

Crozier Hotel, Cloisterham. (*E.D.*). See Crown Inn, Rochester.

Crummles (Vincent). (*N.N.*). See Davenport.

Crummles' (Vincent) Lodgings at Portsmouth. See Thomas Street Portsmouth.

Crupp (Mrs.). (*D.C.*). *See* Buckingham Street.

Curtriss's Coffee House. See Tom's Coffee House.

Cuttle (Captain). (*D. & S.*). See Grove Place.

Cute (Alderman). (*C.B., C.*). See Laurie (Sir Peter).

Dancer (Daniel). (*O.M.F.*). The miser whose history was studied by Mr. Boffin, with the aid of his literary man, Silas Wegg, was a real person of that name. He was born at Weald, Harrow, in 1716, and died in 1794. Ref. *The Dickens Encyclopaedia.*

Dartle (Rosa). (*D.C.*). See Originals founded upon names.

Davenport. A well-known lessee and actor-manager, who, with his wife and daughter, played at various provincial theatres about the time *Nicholas Nickleby* was written. The family have been claimed to be the originals of Mr. and Mrs. Crummles and the infant "phenomena," but on doubtful premises. Ref. *Daily Telegraph,* Dec., 1904.

The fact that the career of the Davenports had some resemblance to that of Mr. Crummles does not make them the originals of that character and his family. Many years ago, but, of course, long after *Nicholas Nickleby,* the writer was personally acquainted with a prosperous theatrical family who travelled about with their own company and a portable theatre. The father acted the heavy tragedian; his wife officiated in the box office and took leading lady parts; whilst the younger of the two sons was pitch-forked into every play possible as an infant prodigy. These people, who were exceedingly generous and charitable, if uneducated, were so exactly like the Crummles family that they might have stepped straight out of the pages of *Nicholas Nickleby* and showed, once more, that Dickens's characters are not overdrawn, but are founded on real life.

Quite recently the Davenport story has been re-stated by Mr. Frederick Harker, and this has elicited a vigorous denial of any truth whatever in the suggestion, from Sir Henry F. Dickens. Ref. *Sunday Times*, July 24, 1927.

DAVID. Butler to Cheeryble Bros. (*N.N.*). See Boot (Alfred).

DEANERY GATE, Rochester. See Chertsey Gate.

DE BRISAC (WALTER). See Rudge (Barnaby).

DEDLOCK (Lady). See Watson (Hon. Mrs.).

DEDLOCK ARMS. (*B.H.*). See Sondes Arms, Rockingham.

DENNIS (NED). (*B.R.*). See Originals founded upon names.

DIBABSES (The). (*N.N.*). See Mile End Cottage.

DICKENS (Charles). See Index to originals. Providence Chapel. Goodchild Francis.

DICKENS (FANNY). Mr. Pugh, in *The Dickens Originals* says that Fanny Dickens was the original of Fanny Dorrit. (*L.D.*). Mr. Pugh is ingenious in discovering originals of Dickens's characters, but there seems to be very little similarity between the attributes of Fanny Dorrit and Dickens's real sister.

It has also been somewhat feebly suggested that Dickens's sister Fanny and her husband Henry Burnett were the originals of Caddy Jellyby and Prince Turveydrop, on the ground that the Burnetts had some resemblance to the characters.

DICKENS (Harriet Ellen). See Constant Companion.

DICKENS (JOHN). See Chicken (Richard). John Dickens has also been suggested as the original of Mr. Dorrit, and possibly the character was, in part, founded upon him.

DICKENS (Mrs. JOHN). There seems to be little doubt that Dickens's mother served as a model upon which Mrs. Nickleby (*N.N.*) and Mrs. R. Wilfer (*O.M.F.*) were, to some extent, founded

DINGLEY DELL. (*P.P.*). See Cobtree Hall.

See also Parrock Hall, and Birling Place.

DR. JOHNSON'S BUILDINGS, Inner Temple. According to Sir Edward Clarke, the chambers of Stryver, Q.C., were at No. 2. Ref. *Cornhill Magazine*, May 1914.

DODD (Mr.), a dust contractor. Original of Nicodemus Boffin. (*O.M.F.*). The story of Boffin, told by Dickens, was substantially correct. Mr. Dodd had a daughter who was sought in marriage, and on the bridal morning her father said the only present he could give her was one of his dust heaps. The bridegroom accepted what he thought was a very bad bargain, but eventually sold the heap to a contractor for £10,000. Ref. *The Dickens Originals*.

DODSON AND FOGG. (*P.P.*). See Freeman's Court.

DOLLY VARDEN. (*B.R.*). See Beadnell (Maria).

DOMBEY (FLORENCE). (*D. & S.*). See Hogarth (Mary).

DOMBEY (Mr.). (*D. & S.*). See Chapman (Thomas).

See also Mansfield Street.

DOMBEY (PAUL). (*D. & S.*). See Burnett (Harry).

See also Marylebone Church.

DORKING. See Marquis of Granby.

DORRETT. See Originals founded on names.

DORRIT (AMY) (Little Dorrit). (*L.D.*). See Haymen (Mrs.)
Cooper (Mrs. M. A.)
Mitton (Mary Ann)

DORRIT (FANNY). (*L.D.*). See Dickens (Fanny).

DOTHEBOYS HALL. (*N.N.*). See Bowes Academy.

DOVER. See Market Place, Dover.

DOWLER (*P.P.*). See Forster (John).

DOWLING (VINCENT). See originals founded on names.

DROOD MYSTERY. Some years since it was stated that the origin of Dickens's plot (*E.D.*) had been traced to an actual case in Rochester. The story was that a bachelor living in the High Street was trustee for his nephew. The nephew went to the West Indies but returned unexpectedly. Shortly afterwards he disappeared, and sometime later the skeleton of a young man was found close by. This naturally led to the conclusion that the uncle had murdered his nephew and buried the body. The writer has been unable to find the original statement or to obtain any confirmation of the story.

DRUMMOND, (ROSE EMMA). To whom Dickens sat for his portrait in 1835. Miss Drummond may possibly have been the original of Miss La Creevy, in

Nicholas Nickleby, in so far as the character had any real prototype. Ref. *The Dickens Originals*.

See also Barrow (Janet).

DUKE'S HEAD, Yarmouth. Identified as the original of the inn where David Copperfield met William, the friendly waiter, who assisted him with his meal and particularly befriended him by "taking off" the ale which was too strong for the boy. (*D.C.*). The Duke's Head was the principal coaching inn at Yarmouth, and well-known to Dickens. Ref. *Dickensian Inns and Taverns*.

Another suggestion is the Crown and Anchor Inn.

DUKE OF YORK INN. The "old beef-steak house," at the foot of Gadshill, on the Dover Road, is probably the Inn Dickens referred to as the tavern which no man possessed of a penny, had ever been known to pass in hot weather. (*U.T. Tramps*). The house has been re-built since Dickens's time, but the trimmed limes and the cool well still stand in front of the tavern.

See also Half-way House (*G.E.*).

DULLBOROUGH (*U.T.*). See Rochester.

DULWICH (House at). See Pickwick's Cottage.

DUNSTABLE. See Luton.

DURDLE'S YARD. (*E.D.*). Hopkins and Reade, in *The Dickens Atlas*, place Durdle's cottage and stone-mason's yard on Rochester Esplanade, facing the river, practically where the ruins of Sir John de Cobham's bridge chapel (built 1396) stand. This is evidently a mistake. Mr. Carden, in *The Murder of Edwin Drood*, suggests that Durdle's yard, where Jasper's attention was drawn to the lime, was adjoining the old Deanery. There was undoubtedly a small builder's yard there at one time, but the writer has always identified Durdle's place with a stone-mason's yard and small tumble-down stone cottage in Crow Lane, or Maidstone Road, immediately behind what was, in Dickens's day, the White Duck taven, or "Traveller's two-penny." This was close to the old City wall, just across the lane, with open access to it before the present Baptist Institute was built; and Durdle's cottage was supposed to have been built of stones stolen from the City wall. The cottage and yard disappeared some years since, when a furniture depository was built on the site, but is well-remembered by many people, besides the writer. Durdles himself was a real person, though not of that name. He was a well-known drunken German stone-mason who used to potter about the Cathedral at all hours, with his dinner in a bundle.

EAST FARLEIGH. See Allington Weir.

EASTGATE HOUSE, Rochester. The Nuns' House and Miss Twinkleton's academy for young ladies. (*E.D.*). It is now a museum but was at one time an academy for young ladies, and the brass plate so inscribed is preserved in the Dickens room on the ground floor.

See also High Street, Rochester.

EATANSWILL. (*P.P.*). See Sudbury.

EATON SOCON. Original of Eton Slocomb. (*N.N.*).

See also Sudbury.

EASY ROW, Birmingham. Original of the elder Mr. Winkle's house. (*P.P.*). At the corner of Easy Row and Edmund Street. Dickens described it as "In a quiet substantial-looking street stood an old red-brick house with three steps before the door, and a brass-plate upon it, bearing, in fat Roman capitals, the words 'Mr. Winkle.'" The house identified had seven steps before the door, but otherwise fitted the description. Ref. *Dickensian* III., 130.

This house was demolished in 1913, and No. 11, Easy Row now claims the distinction, and has the necessary three steps.

Eden. (*M.C.*). See Cairo.

EIGHT BELLS INN, Hatfield. Original of the small public house into which Bill Sykes crept, with his limping and lame dog following, after the murder of Nancy. (*O.T.*). Here he met the pedlar with the infallible composition for removing blood stains. The Eight Bells still stands near the bottom of the narrow descending street in Hatfield where Dickens placed it in the story. Ref. *Dickensian Inns and Taverns*.

ELLIS (Mr.), of the firm of Ellis and Blackman, solicitors, by whom Dickens was employed in his early days as lawyer's clerk. Mr. Ellis is said to be the original of Mr. Perker, the attorney in the *Pickwick Papers*. Ref. *The Dickens Originals*.

ELLIS (MRS. ANN). According to a writer in *T. P.'s Weekly*, Oct., 1904, the original of Mrs. Bardell, of Goswell Street (*P.P.*). Mrs. Ellis was the proprietor of an eating-house near Doctor's Commons. As the writer referred to merely offered the bare statement, without evidence, it is not possible to accept it.

ELTON (ESTHER). Said to be the original of Esther Summerson. (*B.H.*). Miss Elton was the daughter of a friend of Dickens, and married a Mr. Nash. Her son was the Revd. James A. Nash, sometime chaplain of Marylebone workhouse. Ref. *The People*, Mar. 23, 1913.

Another original of Esther Summerson is stated to be Miss Sophia Iselin, the poetess. Ref. *T.P.'s Weekly*, Oct., 1904.

EMANUEL CHURCH, Camberwell. See St. Giles', Camberwell.

ESTELLA. (*G.E.*). See Beadnell (Maria).

EVERARD (Dr.). See Blimber (Dr.).

EXCHEQUER COFFEE HOUSE. (*O.M.F.*). The Exchequer Coffee House at which Mr. Julius Handford was staying, according to the information he gave to Mr. Inspector at the quiet police station in Limehouse, does not now exist. It has been stated that there was no such place and that it existed only in Dickens's imagination, but it was actually the Exchequer hotel and tavern at No. 1, New Palace Yard, in 1850 and later, as shown by the London Directories of that time.

FAGIN, THE JEW. (*O.T.*).
See Solomons (Iky) and
Originals founded upon names.

FAIRSERVICE (ANDREW). See Weller (Sam).

FALCON HOTEL, Aldersgate Street. Suggested as the traveller's lodging house where John Jasper stayed on his visits to the opium den. (*E D*)

FALSTAFF (SIR JOHN) INN, Gadshill. Has been suggested as the way-side public-house, with two elm trees, and a horse-trough in front of it, where Mr. Pickwick tried to get rid of the led horse, on the way to Dingley Dell. The grounds on which the suggestion was made were that Muggleton may have been Gravesend, and that Dickens was very familar with the Falstaff Inn, which stands nearly opposite Gadhill Place. Gravesend probably entered into the description of Muggleton, but, geographically, the town is very unlikely. There were, and still are, two or three plane trees in front of the Falstaff, but no sign in front of it, although there is a modern horsetrough across the road.

FANG (Mr.). (*O.T.*). See Laing (Mr.).

FARLEIGH. See Allington Weir.

FARMHOUSE IN THE BOROUGH. Mentioned in *Household Words*, 1851, "On duty with Inspector Field." The house was situated in what is now Disney Street, a turning out of Harrow Road, and a little north of Marshalsea Road. Some time since it was used as a mission. Ref. *Dickensian* XI., 316.

FAT BOY. (*P.P.*). See Budden.

FAVERSHAM. See Muggleton.

FETTER LANE. No. 24, Fetter Lane has been stated to be the original of the Old Curiosity Shop (*O.C.S.*), but on what ground is not known.

FIELD (INSPECTOR). Original of Inspector Bucket. (*B.H.*). He also figures in the *Reprinted Pieces* as Detective Wield. Edwin Pugh says: "But all that Inspector Field provided was the clothes—it was Dickens who filled those clothes with the concentrated essence of that modern wonder-worker who bulks so large in so many tales, and whom we know most familiarly as Sherlock Holmes." Ref. *The Dickens Originals*.

FINCHING (FLORA). (*L.D.*). See Beadnell (Maria).

FIPS (Mr.). (*M.C.*). See Pump Court.

FLEUR DE LYS HOTEL. See Country Inn, Canterbury.

FLITE (Miss). (*B.H.*).
See Sant (Miss).
Templar (Sally).
Littlewood (Miss).

FOLKESTONE. See Pavilion Hotel.

FORD (HARRY). A boatman of Broadstairs, claimed to be the original of the boatman mentioned in *Our English Watering Place*. Dickens, however, spoke of the " boatman " in the collective sense, and not of any particular person.

FORGE (JOE GARGERY'S). (*G.E.*). See Forge at Chalk.

FORGE AT CHALK. The undoubted original of Joe Gargery's forge, where Pip lived with his married sister. (*G.E.*). This is the only forge in the marsh country which agrees at all with the description in the novel, and it agrees in every particular. Kitton and Snowden Ward identified different cottages at Cooling as the original of Joe Gargery's forge, and Mr. Smetham has cited certain deeds as proof that one of them was once a forge. Neither of these cottages was ever a forge, although one of them was called " The Forge " for the reason that it was built in 1881 on a piece of land upon which a farmer had previously kept a small portable smith's hearth. Canon Burnham, in his *Dickens and Kent* accepted a suggestion that the original was the forge at Cliffe, but there seems to be no grounds for this suggestion except that there was a forge there and never was one at Cooling, and that Cliffe is in the marsh country. There was also a forge at Lower Higham when Dickens wrote *Great Expectations*, but it did not agree with the description in the book. Mr. O. Mullender, the blacksmith at Chalk, was very well known to Dickens, and often took part in cricket matches and other festivities at Gadshill. Ref. *Dickensian* II., 87; III., 247; IV., 121; XXI., 101; XXII., 284.

Forster (**John**). According to Percy Fitzgerald, the original on whom Dowler was founded. (*P.P.*). Ref. *Pickwickian Studies*.

Also the original of Podsnap. (*O.M.F.*) Ref. *The Dickens Originals*.

Foster (**John**). See Pickwick (Samuel).

Fort House, Broadstairs. Often stated to be the original of Bleak House. (*B.H.*). Fort House is now named " Bleak House "—a tribute to Dickens, but although the author lived there during the summer of 1850, it has not the slightest claim to being in any way connected with the story. Ref. *The Kent of Dickens*.

Fountain Hotel, Canterbury. See County Inn, Canterbury.

Fox Court, Holborn. Mr. Roffey states that the Thieves' Kitchen mentioned in the reprinted piece *On Duty with Inspector Field*, was about the centre of this Court. It was demolished somewhere about the year 1884. Ref. *Dickensian*, XXI., 158.

Fox-under-the-Hill. The public-house referred to by Mr. Roker as the spot where Tom Martin whopped the coal-heaver (*P.P.*) was on the Thames water-side, at the bottom of Ivy Lane, in the Adelphi. It was known to Dickens in his blacking-warehouse days at Hungerford stairs, and he records in his biography that one of his favourite localities was a little public-house by the water-side, called the Fox-under-the hill; and he had a recollection of sitting on a bench outside, one fine evening, looking at some coal-heavers dancing in front of the house. Robert Allbut identified the Fox-under-the-hill as the tavern where young Martin Chuzzlewit stayed, and was visited by Mark Tapley. (*M.C.*). Ref. *Inns and Taverns of Pickwick*.

Freeman's Court, in which was the office of Messrs. Dodson & Fogg. (*P.P.*). Both Kitton and Snowden Ward asserted that there was no such place as Freeman's Court, and it has been suggested that Newman's Court, Cornhill was the original, but any map of London of the Pickwick period will show Freeman's Court, close to the Royal Exchange. It was between Nos. 83 and 84, Cornhill, on the left-hand side going eastwards. Mr. Tyrrell says it was demolished when the present Royal Exchange was built, about 1840. Ref. *Dickensian*, V., 192, 224.

Friar Bacon. (*M.P.*, *P.M.B.*). See Lawes (Sir J. B.).

Friend of Lions. (*M.P.*, *T.L.*). Possibly Sir Edwin Landseer.

Frindsbury Manor. See Cobtree Hall.

Frozen Deep (The). See Allen (Gordon).

Furnival's Inn. See South Square.

Gamp (Mrs.). (*M.C.*). The prototype of Mrs. Gamp was a real nurse who was engaged to attend Miss Meredith, the friend and companion of the Baroness Burdett Coutts. This was in the winter of 1842-3, when Miss Meredith had a severe illness. The nurse's characteristics were found to be of too exciting a nature for a sick-room, but her ways and habits would have been highly diverting anywhere else. Afterwards, Miss Burdett Coutts and Miss Meredith related to Dickens many anecdotes of their trying experiences, with the result that he created Mrs. Gamp for *Martin Chuzzlewit*, which he was writing at the time. Among the peculiarities of the real Mrs. Gamp was a habit of slowly sliding her nose backwards and forwards along the top of a tall fender, a habit which Dickens utilized. Ref. *Dickensian* XXIII., 27.

Gargery's Forge. See Forge at Chalk.

Garland Family. (*O.C.S.*). Originals of. The family with whom Dickens lodged in Lant Street, Borough, in the days when John Dickens was confined in the Marshalsea prison. Charles's landlord was himself an agent of the insolvent debtors' court. He was lame, but a fat, good-natured, kind old gentleman. His wife was also very good-natured, and they had an innocent grown-up son, also lame. The whole family was exceedingly kind to the boy-lodger, and on one occasion were all three about his bed all night when he had one of his attacks of spasms. Forster says this was told him by Dickens after the family were all dead, but adds that they live still, in another form, very pleasantly as the Garland family in the *Old Curiosity Shop*.

Gaselee (Sir **Stephen**). Mr. Justice Gaselee was the original of the little fat judge who presided at the trial Bardell *v.* Pickwick, and who was called " Justice Stareleigh " by Dickens. Ref. *The Dickens Originals*.

Gas Street Bridge, Birmingham. Said to be the bridge at which little Nell and her grandfather left the canal boat. (*O.C.S.*). They crossed a busy thoroughfare (Broad Street) and passed down a winding lane (St. Martin's Lane) on their way to the Black Country. Ref. *Dickensian* III., 130.

See also Birmingham, Little Nell's route in.

Gashford. (*B.R.*). See Watson (Robert).

Gay (**Walter**). (*D. & S.*). See Burnett (Henry).

Gaydon. A Village nine miles from Warwick. Probably where Little Nell and her grandfather fell in with Mrs. Jarley. (*O.C.S.*). Ref. *The England of Dickens.*

GEORGE INN, Amesbury. Original of the "Blue Dragon." (*M.C.*). Snowden Ward identified Amesbury as the village of the story. The turnpike house, where Tom Pinch left his box, was still in existence, and the Church, where he played the organ, was rightly situated. Although there is no walk through the wood from the house selected as Mr. Pecksniff's, there is a path through a little plantation making a short cut to the church. Amesbury also fits into the story in regard to the coach route from London. (*Dickensian Inns and Taverns*). C. G. Harper considered the "Blue Dragon" to be a composite picture of the "George" at Amesbury, and the "Green Dragon" at Alderbury. Ref. *Dickensian* I., 119.
See also Green Dragon, Alderbury.
Lion's Head, Winterslow.
Green Dragon, Market Lavington.

GEORGE INN, Greta Bridge. According to T. P. Cooper, the original of the Holly Tree Inn at which the traveller was snowed up, in the Christmas story *The Holly Tree.* Ref. *With Dickens in Yorkshire.*

GEORGE INN, SOUTHWARK. This was *not* the original of the White Hart in the Borough, where Sam Weller was first encountered by Mr. Pickwick (*P.P.*), although it has repeatedly been stated to be so. The White Hart Inn existed at the time, and exactly where Dickens said it was. Ref. *Inns and Taverns of Pickwick.*

GEORGE HOTEL, High Street, Salisbury Identified by Snowden Ward as the inn where Tom Pinch and Martin Chuzzlewit first met. (*M.C.*). Ref. *Dickensian Inns and Taverns.*

GEORGE AND NEW INN, Greta Bridge. (*N.N.*). There is some confusion as to the identity of the inn where Squeers and Nicholas Nickleby, with the new pupils, were set down at the end of their long coach journey from London. In *Dickensian Inns and Taverns*, B. W. Matz says the George Inn, close to the bridge, was the place, and suggests that Dickens combined the names of two inns, viz.: the *George Inn* and the *New Inn*, some half a mile distant. There is an inn called the "Unicorn," but originally known as the "George," at the village of Bowes, and this has been repeatedly suggested as the inn Dickens meant, as it is close to Bowes Academy. This is, however, a strong argument against its identification, as, in that case, there was no need for the boys to be put in the luggage cart, whilst Nickleby and Squeers went in the chaise. Squeers said Dothebys Hall was about three miles from the inn. Mr. T. P. Cooper says the oldest inn at Greta Bridge was the "George," on the north side of the bridge, but it ceased to be a licensed house about 1826, when the "New Inn" was built about half a mile away. This inn was also known as the "George," and as the "George and New Inn," and became the most important coaching inn of the district, the landlord, George Martin, being also postmaster. It is now a farmhouse, and has reverted to its original name, "Thorpe Grange," but it seems to be clear that the "George and New Inn," about half-a-mile from the bridge, was the real place and that Dickens gave it its correct name. He also made play with the name of the landlord, when he makes Mrs. Squeers say: "Now if you take the chaise and go one road, and I borrow *Swallow's* chaise and go the other, what with keeping our eyes open and asking questions, one or other of us is pretty certain to lay hold of him." Ref. *Dickensian* VII., 10; XX., 74; *Dickensian Inns and Taverns.*

GEORGE THE FOURTH. See Magpie and Stumps.

GERRARD STREET, Soho. Mr. Jaggers lived in Gerrard Street, but there is little evidence in the book (*G.E.*) to show which was the house. Dickens's uncle Thos. Barrow lived at No. 10, and this may have been the house the novelist had in mind.

GIBBET ON THE MARSHES. (*G.E.*). In the early years of the 19th century there were still several gibbets, on which the bodies of pirates were exposed, along the lower reaches of the Thames, but it has not been found that there was such a gibbet on the Cliffe marshes where Dickens undoubtedly placed it in *Great Expectations.* In his boyhood, there was such a gibbet on the Medway, nearly opposite Chatham Dockyard, which Dickens must often have seen on his rambles or when visiting his father at the Navy Pay Office, assuming it was there in 1820 as is asserted. It is probable he had this gibbet in mind when writing the opening chapter of *Great Expectations.* An old print depicting Her Majesty's navy at Chatham in 1702-1714 shows the gibbet, with the body of an executed pirate hanging from it, very distinctly; and Dickens may quite well have seen a copy of the print. Ref. *Dickensian* XXII., 111.

GIBSON (MARY). See Weller (Mary).

GILLS (SOL). (*D.& S.*). See Leadenhall Street.

Glorious Apollers. (*O.C.S.*). In the early part of the 19th century, a song book entitled "Opollo" was published. On every page there was a toast or sentiment, appropriate or otherwise, and Mr. Dick Swiveller perhaps quoted from this book. It has also been said that the Glorious Apollers was founded upon the Ancient Order of Buffaloes, but this suggestion does not appear to be worth much.

Golden Cross Hotel. (*P.P.*), (*D.C.*). In Dickens's boyhood the "Golden Cross" was, perhaps, the most important coaching inn of West London. It stood at Charing Cross about eighty feet north-east of Charles the First's statue. In the early part of the nineteenth century the main structure, or at any rate the frontage, was replaced by a new front of gothic design but the site was not altered. The Gothic building did not remain very long, for in 1827 it was purchased by the Government, and, with other buildings, was demolished about 1830 to make room for the Charing Cross improvements. In 1831-1832 the sign and the business were transferred to a site between St. Martin's church and the Strand, where the present "Golden Cross" remains. Dickens was well-acquainted with the old "Golden Cross" in his young days, but whether in the second chapter of *Pickwick* he had in mind the Gothic-fronted inn, or the older one, is not of much consequence as they were both on the same site. According to Wilmot Corfield the older building (or "Canalletto" Inn) was demolished in 1811, in which case Dickens could never have seen it. In *David Copperfield* he described the Gothic "Golden Cross," in what is now Trafalgar Square, and from its windows David peeped out at the statue of King Charles, on his way down to breakfast with Steerforth. The present "Golden Cross" hotel in the Strand has no association with Dickens, except in name. Ref. *Dickensian* XI., 91, 158.

Golden Square. No. 7 was probably the house Dickens had in mind as the residence of Ralph Nickleby. (*N.N.*). It has now disappeared. Ref. *Dickensian* XVI., 30.

Goldsmith (Oliver). Suggested as the original of Mr. Mell, the flute-playing usher at Mr. Creakle's academy (*D.C.*). In early life Oliver Goldsmith was employed as an usher in a school at Peckham, and his chief hobby was playing the flute. Forster's *Life of Oliver Goldsmith* was published in 1848, and Dicken's commenced *David Copperfield* in the spring of 1849. Ref. *Dickensian* XVI., 133.

It has also been stated that Mr. Mell was founded upon Mr. Taylor, the English master at Wellington House Academy, when Dickens was at school there.

Gombards Road, St. Albans. An old Georgian house in this road has been identified as the original of Bleak House. (*B.H.*). Its geographical position is fairly correct, but the house itself, both externally and internally, has no resemblance whatever to the Bleak House of the story, and cannot therefore be accepted. The description in the book is much too minute and circumstantial to be purely imaginary, and there must have been a real original, but, so far, it has not been discovered.

See also Bleak Hall, and Nast Hyde.

Goodchild (Francis). (*L.T.*) Dickens himself.

Goswell Street. (*P.P.*). Now Goswell Road. The Goswell Street of Mr. Pickwick was that portion of Goswell Road which runs from the Barbican to Percival Street. Ref. *Pickwich Pilgrimages.*

Gordon (Lord George). (*B.R.*). See Welbeck Street.

Gosling's Bank. See Child's Bank.

Grant (William and David), of Manchester and Ramsbottom. Originals of the Brothers Cheeryble. (*N.N.*). Dickens first met them in Manchester in 1838. They were wealthy merchants who used their means for the benefit of their less fortunate fellow-men. James Nasmyth, the famous engineer, was one who had been helped by them in his early youth, and in his autobiography he wrote of the Grant brothers: "In the course of many long years of industry, enterprise and benevolence, they earned the goodwill of thousands, the gratitude of many, and the respect of all who knew them. I was only one of many who had cause to remember them with gratefulness." William Grant, the elder of the two brothers died in 1842 at the age of 73, and a tablet to his memory is erected in St. Andrew's Presbyterian Church, Ramsbottom. The younger brother, Daniel, died in 1855. Dickens was in America when he heard that William Grant had died, and thus wrote from Niagara Falls: "One of the noble hearts who sat for the Cheeryble Bros. If I had been in England I would certainly have gone into mourning for the loss of such a glorious life." The characters of the Cheeryble Bros., as portrayed in *Nicholas Nickleby* were true to life, and in no wise overdrawn. The warehouse of the Grant Bros. was in Canon Street, Manchester, and was in existence until a few years since, being named "Cheeryble House." Ref. Forster's *Life of Dickens*; *Dickensian* I., 94.

See also Hollingworth Bros.

GRAHAM (MARY). (*M.C.*). See Hogarth (Mary).

GRAPES INN, Limehouse. The original of the Six Jolly Fellowship Porters. (*O.M.F.*). Dickens's description of this tavern agrees very closely indeed with the "Grapes" which has been generally accepted as the original of the "Porters," but Mr. H. E. Popham, in his recently published *Guide to London Taverns*, makes the rather startling statement that "most students of Dickens are agreed that the novelist had in mind the "Prospect of Whitby," when describing the Six Jolly Fellowship Porters in *Our Mutual Friend*. The "Prospect of Whitby" is a picturesque inn on the riverside at Shadwell. Ref. *Dickensian Inns and Taverns*; *The Guide to London Taverns*.

GRAVEL LANE BRIDGE, St. George's in the East. Locally known as the "Bridge of Sighs," from the number of suicides committed therefrom. It spans the "Baker's Trap," mentioned in the *Uncommercial Traveller*. In the article on "Wapping Workhouse," Dickens says he found himself on a swinging-bridge, looking down at some dark locks in some dirty water, and asking a creature remotely in the likeness of a young man what it called the place, was told it was Mr. Baker's trap. "'A common place for suicide,' said I, looking down at the locks. 'Sue,' returned the ghost, with a stare, 'Yes! and Poll, likewise Emily, and Nancy, and Jane . . . and all the biling, ketches off their bonnets or shorls, takes a run and headers down here, they doos. Always a-headering down here, they is. Like one o'clock.'" Ref. *Dickensian* II., 42.

GRAVESEND. See Muggleton.

Gravesend has also been suggested as the Market Town of *Great Expectations*, but the book contains convincing evidence that the town was Rochester.

GREAT WHITE HORSE, Ipswich. (*P.P.*). The Great White Horse Hotel, with its leaden effigy of a white horse over the doorway, still stands in Tavern Street, Ipswich. In most respects, it hardly differs from Dickens's description of it in the *Pickwick Papers*, except that it does not deserve the disparaging remarks made by Mr. Pickwick. The bedroom in which occurred the adventure with the lady in curl-papers, still preserves its early Victorian character and is apparently to-day exactly as Dickens described it about 1837. Dickens himself stayed at the hotel when reporting an election at Ipswich in 1835.

GREAT ST. ANDREWS STREET, Seven Dials. See Willis (J.).

GREAT WINGLEBURY. (*S.B.B.*). See Rochester.

GREEN DRAGON, Market Lavington. Suggested as the original of the "Blue Dragon" (*M.C.*), but no convincing evidence is afforded. Schomberg considered that Dickens had no particular tavern in mind. Ref. *Dickensian* I., 222.

See also George Inn, Amesbury.

GREEN DRAGON, Alderbury. Claimed to be the original of the "Blue Dragon." (*M.C.*). It is a village ale-house, as described in the novel, but could not have afforded accommodation for post-chaise travellers such as old Martin Chuzzlewit and Mary. Nevertheless, these travellers did not put up at the village ale-house for choice. The gentleman was taken ill upon the road, and had to seek the first house that offered. Ref. *Dickensian* I., 119.

The George Inn, Amesbury, is more generally accepted as the true original of the "Blue Dragon."

See also George Inn, Amesbury.

GREEN DRAGON, Gracechurch Street. Suggested as the Blue Boar. (*P.P.* XXXIII), but a more likely inn was the Bull in Leadenhall Street.

GREEN MAN INN, Leytonstone. Original of the half-way house between Chigwell and London. (*B.R.*). It stands near to the present-day railway station. Ref. *Dickensian Inns and Taverns*.

GREEN (LUCY). (*U. T.* xii.). See Stroughill (Lucy).

GREEN GATE. (*P.P.*). At Mr. Nupkin's residence, where Sam Weller encountered the surly groom, is believed locally to be a gate adjoining the churchyard (St. Clement's ?), Ipswich.

GREEN (MISS), who married Joe Specks. (*U. T.*). See Stroughill (Lucy).

GREEN (POL.). See Originals founded on names.

GREEN STREET, Leicester Square. R. Allbut stated in *Rambles with Charles Dickens* (1894) that No. 10, Green Street at the corner of Green and Castle Streets, was the original of the Old Curiosity Shop (*O.C.S.*). A lady, personally acquainted with the novelist, told him she was once taken there by Dickens himself, who described it to her as the home of Little Nell, pointing out an inner room, divided from the shop by a glass partition, as her bedroom. The lady's name was not stated and the identification depends entirely upon her word. Whether it be accepted or not, it may not be out of place to repeat here what has so often been said, viz.: that the Old Curiosity Shop in Portsmouth Street is *not* the original of the shop Dickens wrote about. Ref. *Dickensian* VI., 44.

GRIP, THE RAVEN. (*B.R.*). The originals upon which Barnaby's raven were founded were two ravens which belonged to Dickens himself at different times. One of them died in 1841, and the other in 1845.

GROVE HALL ESTATE, Bow. It is generally believed that the little cottage at Bow to which Nicholas Nickleby took his mother and sister to live in, and where Mrs. Nickleby had an amusing adventure with the mad gentleman next door, had its original on this estate. The estate was sold for building purposes in 1906 and is now fully built upon. The identification of the locality was so far considered to be proved, that a writer in the *London Argus* suggested that some large-hearted and rich person should come forward and save the historic site. Ref. *Dickensian* II., 227.

It must, however, be said that the Grove Hall Estate was doubtful, for internal evidence in *Nicholas Nickleby* indicates that the cottage was on the main road.

GROVE PLACE, Stepney. Suggested as the original of Brig place, where Captain Cuttle lodged with the terrible Mrs. McStinger. In 1912 Grove Place was re-named Cuttle Place, in honour of the faithful Captain. Ref. *Dickensian* VIII., 172

GUILDHALL, Rochester. See High Street, Rochester.

GUY, EARL OF WARWICK. See Half-way House. (*G.E.*).

HALF MOON AND SEVEN-STARS. (*M.C.*). See Ale-house, East Winterslow.

HALF-WAY HOUSE. (*B.R.*). See Green Man, Leytonstone.

HALF-WAY HOUSE. (*G.E.*). The half-way house where Pip breakfasted one day, afterwards completing the journey to the market town (Rochester) on foot. has been stated to be the "Duke of York," or "Old Beefsteak" house, half-way between Gravesend and Rochester. There is no justification for this identification. Chapters 28 and 49 of *Great Expectations* make it quite clear that the half-way house was a long way back on the Dover Road towards London, and the writer has satisfied himself by close investigation that the half-way house Dickens had in mind was the "Guy, Earl of Warwick" Inn, the half-way house between London and Gravesend, and the house which Captain Bunsby of the "Cautious Clara" once had his eye upon when delivering a weighty opinion in the parlour behind Sol Gill's instrument shop in Leadenhall Street. The "Guy, Earl of Warwick" was a very ancient tavern at the eastern extremity of Welling, below Shooter's Hill. It has recently been pulled down and re-built some little distance to the east of the former site.

HALL. (*U. T. Tramps*). See Cobham Hall.

HALL (SAMUEL CARTER). Born 1822, died 1889. He was the original on which Mr. Pecksniff was founded (*M.C.*), and was publicly hailed as such when he lectured in America. Percy Fitzgerald, having heard Dickens speak of Samuel Hall, thought the theory of his being the original of Pecksniff not very far-fetched. Hall was for some time gallery reporter for the *New Times*. It has also been suggested that the original of Pecksniff was Pugin the Architect.

HANBURY STREET, Christ Church Hall. Claimed to be the scene of the United Grand Junction Ebenezer Temperance meetings. (*P.P.*). The only ground for the claim appears to be that there is a tradition that Dickens frequented the place and made it the scene of Brother Stiggins's exploit. Ref. *Dickensian* III., 67, 103.

See also Brick Lane.

HAREDALE (EMMA). (*B.R.*). See Hogarth (Mary).

HARLEY STREET. Mr. Merdle's house was the handsomest house in Harley Street, Cavendish Square.

HARRIS (SHOWMAN). (*O.C.S.*). See Tubby.

HATTON GARDEN, No. 54. See Police Court.

HAVISHAM (Miss). (*G.E.*). The character of Miss Havisham is said to have been founded on a real case in Australia. The lady resided in a large old-fashioned house on the Kettle Estate at Newtown, a suburb of Sydney, and it is stated that being jilted on her marriage morning, she remained a voluntary prisoner in her own room, with all her wedding finery scattered around her, until her death. The story goes that an Australian in England related the incident to Dickens, who created Miss Havisham from this material. No dates have, however, been given of the occurrences referred to, and the only authority is a statement to the above effect in an Australian newspaper.

An echo of Miss Havisham's case was also cited in 1916, in the person of a Mr. Nation, who died in 1914. It was stated that he also was jilted on his wedding-day, and left the house he had prepared for his bride, in Queen's Gate, entirely neglected and shut up until his death. This story seems to have been denied by a relative of Mr. Nation, and is probably a myth. Another similar case was given by the *Daily Mirror* in 1914. This was a lady named Miss Christina Witland, of Stockholm, Sweden. Her marriage was broken off on the wedding-day, and for seventy-five years she lived alone in the house, seeing nobody but her servants. Like Miss Havisham, she shut out all daylight from her rooms, which were lighted by candles.

The above cases, if authentic, only prove that the character of Miss Havisham was not the gross exaggeration it has often been said to be, but had its counterpart in real life. Ref. *Dickensian* II., 298; X., 132; XII., 262, 304.

HAYES (Mrs.). Stated to be the original of Polly Toodle, Paul Dombey's nurse. (*D. & S.*). In her early life she was in the service of Mrs. Henry Burnett, Dickens's sister Fanny, at Manchester; and the novelist "frequently told her he had used her for a character in more than one of his books." The last statement is rather difficult to accept.

The late B. M. Matz strongly asserted that there was no truth in the suggestion and that Mrs. Hayes was certainly ***not*** the original of Polly Toodle. Ref. *Dickensian* III., 73; VIII., 317.

HAYDON (Benjamin). An artist, of Plymouth and Exeter. Said to be the original of Harold Skimpole. (*B.H.*). Ref. *Western Morning News*, June, 1910.

If this Haydon were the artist who executed a bust of John Dickens, the novelist certainly used one of his traits in creating Harold Skimpole, for in a letter to Leigh Hunt he said: "The diary-writing I took from Haydon, not from you"; but this does not make Haydon the original of Skimpole. Forster records Haydon's death and Dickens's offer to give £5 if a subscription were started, but no other particulars.

HAYMEN (Mrs.), of Southsea. Claimed to be the original of Little Dorrit. (*L.D.*). It was also freely stated in the press, at the time of her death, that her brother was the original of Paul Dombey and also of Tiny Tim. Both claims are without any foundation and not worth considering. Ref. *Dickensian* VI., 256.

See also Cooper (Mrs.).

HEEP (Mrs.), house of. (*D.C.*). See North Lane, Canterbury.

HENLEY LOCK. See Hurley Lock.

HEXAM (Gaffer). (*O.M.F.*). The originals who suggested the characters of Gaffer Hexam and his son Charlie, were seen casually by Dickens in Chatham. In a letter to John Forster he said: "I must use, somehow, the uneducated father and the educated boy in spectacles whom Leach and I saw at Chatham.'

HIGH STREET, Rochester. Opposite Eastgate House there is a row of three old gabled houses. the lower floors of which are used as shops. The one at the western end and occupied by a firm of auctioneers, is the original of Mr. Pumblechook's corn and seed premises. (*G.E.*). At the time the book was written, this shop was occupied by a corn and seedsman named William Fairbairn, and the rows of little seed drawers mentioned by Pip, actually existed in the shop, just as described. The three houses were originally one mansion, the date on one of the gables being 1684, and communicating doors still connect the upper rooms. There is a commemorative tablet on the building but it is on the eastern or wrong end. The same house, used for Pumblechook's premises, was also the original of Mr. Sapsea's house in *Edwin Drood*. The carved figure of an auctioneer in his pulpit was not at this place but was taken from a real figure which was over the door of an auctioneer's rooms at St. Margaret's Banks, now a savings Bank.

Rochester High Street contains many buildings associated with Dickens, such as the Bull Hotel (*Pickwick*); The Guildhall (*Great Expectations*); Jasper's gate house, and Eastgate House (*Edwin Drood*). Watt's Charity (*Seven Poor Travellers*); etc.

HIGHAM. See Lower Higham.

HIGHAM (Forge at). See Forge at Chalk.

HIGDEN (BETTY). (*O.M.F.*). See Rigden (Martha).

HOCKLEY-IN-THE-HOLE. See Oliver Twist. Route to London.

HOGARTH (Georgina). Suggested as the original of Agnes Wickfield. (*D.C.*). Ref. *Evening News and Evening Mail*, Nov. 6, 1909.

See also Hogarth (Mary).

HOGARTH (Mary). According to Edwin Pugh, the original of Ada Clare (*B.H.*), Rose Maylie (*O.T.*), Kate Nickleby (*N.N.*), Madeline Bray (*N.N.*), Emma Haredale (*B.R.*), Mary Graham (*M.C.*), Florence Dombey (*D. & S.*), Agnes Wickfield (*D.C.*), Little Nell (*O.C.S.*), and Lucie Manette (*T.T.C.*). Pugh appears to found this opinion upon the fact that these characters all have something in common, and belong to what he calls "that galaxy of amazing dolls." That Dickens had the death of his sister-in-law before him when he described the death of Little Nell, is evident from his letters to Forster.

HOLLINGWORTH BROS., of Turkey Mill, Maidstone. Stated by a writer in the *Kent Messenger*, in 1920, to have been the originals of the Cheeryble Bros. (*N.N.*). The worthy brothers Hollingworth may have been as generous and warm-hearted as stated, and to have handed down their fame to our day, as the writer remarks, but there is not the slightest justification for claiming them as the originals of Dicken's Cheeryble Bros., who were the Grant Bros. of Manchester, on the author's own authority.

See Grant (William and Daniel).

HOLLY TREE INN. (*C.S.*, *H.T.*). See George Inn, Greta Bridge.

HORN COFFEE HOUSE. (*P.P.*). As Dickens knew it, the Horn Coffee House and Tavern was a narrow-fronted brick building, with extensive cellars, on the east side of Godliman Street, Doctors' Commons—a street now leading from St. Paul's Churchyard to Queen Victoria Street. It was about six doors from Carter lane, and dated from shortly after the Fire of London. In Robson's *London Directory* for 1819, it was referred to as "Sam Lovegrove, wine merchant, Horn Tavern and Coffee House, 10, Godliman Street, Doctors' Commons." Ref. *Dickensian* XXII., 101.

HORSE AND GROOM, Portugal Street. The public-house opposite the Insolvent Debtor's Court where Mr. Weller consulted the Lord Chancellor's great friend Mr. Solomon Pell. (*P.P.*). The site of the "Horse and Groom" is now covered by Messrs. W. H. Smith & Sons' buildings. Ref. *Inns and Taverns of Pickwick.*

HORSE-SHOE AND CASTLE INN. The inn at Cooling has been stated to be the original of the "Three Jolly Bargemen" (*G.E.*), presumably because Cooling was thought to be the village of the story. The "Horse-Shoe and Castle" does not agree with the book, even if the hamlet of Cooling be considered to be where Pip lived. The only topographical reference to the position of the inn is contained in the words "Thus we came to the village. The way we approached it took us past the 'Three Jolly Bargemen.'" There is only one way of approach to Cooling, and the "Horse-Shoe and Castle" is at the far end of the hamlet. Ref. *Dickensian* XXII., 237.

HORTENSE (Mdlle.). (*B.H.*). See Manning (Mrs.).

HOSPITAL FOR CHILDREN, Great Ormonde Street. The Hospital in which Little Johnnie died. (*O.M.F.*). Also, possibly, the one so feelingly referred to by Maggie, as the place where "chicking" was to be had (*L.D.*).

Dickens took great interest in this hospital, and in 1859 made a most moving appeal on its behalf, at a public dinner at which he took the chair. The immediate response to that appeal was an addition to the funds of £3,000, subscribed on the spot, but Dickens did not stop there. He put the crown upon this good work by shortly afterwards giving a public reading of *A Christmas Carol* for the benefit of the hospital.

HOTEL (HANDSOME). (*N.N.*). See Claridge's Hotel.

HOTEL, Greenwich. (Wedding breakfast of Bella). (*O.M.F.*). See Ship Hotel, Greenwich.

HOUNDSDITCH CHURCH. (*U. T.*). See St. Botolph's Church.

HULKS, OR PRISON SHIP. (*G.E.*). Internal evidence shows that Dickens placed the "Wicked Noah's Ark," moored off the mud-bank of the lower Thames, at Egypt Bay on the Cooling marshes. At the time there was a hulk on the spot, but it was a Coastguard Hulk, and not a convict ship. There were also at Egypt Bay a wooden guard-hut and a landing stage, as described in the book. In Dickens's boyhood there were three convict hulks lying in the River Medway, off Upnor Castle, below Chatham Dockyard; and he must have been familiar with the appearance of these ships and of the convicts brought down by coach to be imprisoned in them. It is considered that the description of the hulks and convicts was taken from Dickens's recollections of his young days, but for the purpose of the story he utilized the existing coast-guard hulk, hut and landing-stage at Egypt Bay on the Thames. Ref. *Dickensian* XXII., 182.

HUMPHREY (MASTER). (*M.H.C.*). Master Thomas Humphrey, the clock in the doorway of whose shop at Barnard Castle attracted Dickens's attention, was born in 1787. He was apprenticed in 1806 to Robert Thwaites, a watch and clock-maker of Barnard Castle, and commenced business on his own account in 1815 in Amen Corner, next to the Churchyard. Here he exhibited the clock (made by his son) which Dickens saw and utilized as the title of *Master Humphrey's Clock*. It is a curious coincidence that Richard Barnes, the attorney, was a sub-tenant of Thomas Humphrey, and had his offices behind and above the clock-maker's shop. (See Barnes (Richard). Ref. *With Dickens in Yorkshire.*

HUNGERFORD MARKET. On the site of the present Charing Cross railway station. See Blacking Factory.

HUNT (LEIGH). When creating the character of Harold Skimpole, in *Bleak House,* Dickens made use of some of the peculiarities of Leigh Hunt, and, although Hunt himself appeared not to notice the similarity, his many friends did notice it and some of them remonstrated with Dickens. Accordingly, he toned down those characteristics which were particularly reminiscent of Leigh Hunt, but eventually the friends of the latter pointed out to him the similarity between himself and Dickens's Harold Skimpole. Having perceived this, he was much annoyed, and Dickens therefore wrote him an apology for the liberty he had taken, and an explanation. Ref. Forster's *Life of Dickens* ; *Dickensian III.*, 116.

HUNTER (Mrs. LEO). (*P.P.*). See Monckton (Hon. Miss).

HURLEY LOCK. Stated by various writers to be the original of Plashwater Weir Mill Lock. (*O.M.F.*). Others have given the original as Henley Lock, perhaps a misprint for Hurley.

IDLE (Thomas). (Lazy Tour). See Collins (Wilkie).

INN, A famous. See White Hart, Salisbury.

INN, Roadside. See Bottom Inn.

INN OF MINOR REPUTATION. ((*G.E.*). See Mitre Hotel, Chatham.

INSOLVENT DEBTORS' COURT. (*P.P.*). Described as a lofty room, ill-lighted and worse ventilated. It was in Portugal Street, and was afterwards used as the old Bankruptcy Court, and later, as the Westminster County Court. Ref. *Dickensian* V., 72.

IPSWICH. See Sudbury.

IRON BRIDGE. (*L.D.*). See Southwark Bridge.

ISELIN (Sophia). See Elton (Esther).

JACOB'S ISLAND. (*O.T.*). The scene of Bill Sykes's death was accurately described by Dickens in *Oliver Twist,* and even the house was one actually frequented by thieves, hiding from the police. An old L.C.C. plan, dated April 5, 1855, was discovered in 1917 by Mr. G. W. Mitchell, an official in Bermondsey Town Hall, and a copy was presented to the Dickens Fellowship. The plan shows the old mill stream at Jacob's Island, and a corner house on its bank is marked "Bill Sykes's house." It is evident that in 1855 the actual place was generally identified. Ref. *Dickensian* XIV., 184.

JAGGERS (Mr.). (*G.E.*). See Lewis (J. G.).
Gerrard Street, Soho.

JAMES (EDWIN). Original of Stryver, Q.C. (*T.T.C*). Dickens met him only once, in connection with an unfortunate quarrel between Thackeray and Edmund Yates. This was a few months before Stryver, Q.C. appeared in the pages of a *Tale of Two Cities,* and Yates says Dickens admitted he was a likeness of Edwin James. James was afterwards disbarred and disappeared entirely. Ref. *Dickensian* X., 301.

JARNDYCE AND JARNDYCE. (*B.H.*). Forster states that Dickens's description of this Chancery suit was founded upon a tract issued by Challinor. This was a pamphlet, published in 1849, by William Challinor, solicitor ; and entitled "The Court of Chancery ; its inherent defects." According to Edwin Pugh, the actual suit related to the estate of a Mr. Jennings, or Jennans, of Acton, Suffolk, who died in 1798. As late as 1878, this case was still before the Court. The case of Gridley, which Dickens declared was in no essential altered from one of actual occurrence, has been traced to the action Cook *v.* Fymney, in 1844. Ref. *Dickensian* XIII., 16.

JASPER (JOHN). (*E.D.*). See Originals founded upon names.

JASPER'S GATE-HOUSE. (*E.D.*). See Chertsey Gate.

JELLYBY (Caddy). (*B.H.*). See Dickens (Fanny).

JENNENS V. JENNENS. See Jarndyce and Jarndyce.

JERUSALEM BUILDINGS. (*C.B., H.M.*). See Jerusalem Passage.

JERUSALEM PASSAGE. In St. John's Square, Clerkenwell, may possibly be the Jerusalem Buildings mentioned in the *Haunted Man.*

JERVOIS (Mr.), of 21, Portland Place, Bath. Master of Ceremonies at the time *Pickwick Papers* were published. Original of Angelo Cyrus Bantam, Esq. Dickens, however, made the character reside at Queen's Square, where Eleazer Pickwick, brother of Moses, the coach proprietor, was living in 1837. At this time a Mr. A. Snodgrass was residing at 16, Trim Street, Bath. Ref. *The Pickwick Pilgrimages.*

JESSOP (Mrs.), of Malton, Yorks. Said to be the original of the redoubtable Mrs. McStinger, Captain Cuttle's landlady. Ref. *Leeds Mercury,* 20 Jan., 1912.
This identification is not absolutely impossible. Dickens certainly visited his friend Smithson at Malton.

JINGLE (ALFRED). (*P.P.*). There was probably no definite original of this character, but in 1814 there appeared a little volume entitled "The General Post Bag; or, News Foreign and Domestic," by Humphrey Hedgehog, Esq., in which the conversation was carried on in the jerky, laconic style of Mr. Alfred Jingle of No Hall, Nowhere. E.g.: "Mails robbed—bags dropped—picked up by different people—contents scattered about country—took a journey—popped into roadside public-house—" etc. It is not suggested that Dickens plagiarized Humphrey Hedgehog, Esq., it is only mentioned as a curious coincidence. Ref. *Dickensian* VII., 100.

Jingle is also stated to be founded on a fellow clerk of Dickens, at Ellis and Blackman's, named Potter.

JIP. (*D.C.*). The original of Dora's Jip, is said to have been a little dog, called "Daphne," belonging to Maria Beadnell; but on what authority is not known.

JOE, THE CROSSING SWEEPER. (*B.H.*). See Ruby (George).

JOHNSON'S, Claremarket. Suggested as the Alamode Beef-house where David Copperfield once went to dine. Apparently Johnson's was known as "The New Thirteen Canons."

JOHNSTONE'S OPIUM DEN. In a garret off Ratcliff Highway. Stated by Charles Dickens the younger to be the place referred to in *Edwin Drood*. In the *Dictionary of London*, 1879, issued from the office of *All the Year Round*, he said, under the heading "Opium dens"—"The best known of these justly-named "dens" is that of one Johnstone, who lives in a garret off Radcliff Highway. This is the place referred to in *The Mystery of Edwin Drood*." Ref. *Dickensian* XIII., 49.

JONES (Mr.). Headmaster of Wellington House Academy when Dickens attended the school in 1824. Stated to have been the original of Mr. Creakle, head-master at Salem House. (*D.C.*). Ref. *The Dickens Encyclopedia*.

JORGAN (Capt.). (*M.f. Sea*). See Morgan (Captain).

KENNETT (ALDERMAN). See Blackley (Alderman).

KENNETT INN, Beckhampton. See Shepherd's Shore.

KENWIGS family. Lodgings. (*N.N.*). According to R. Allbut, in *Rambles in Dickensland*, the Kenwigs family lodged at 48, Carnaby Street, but Mr. T. W. Tyrrell suggests, with more reason, that the place was one of a row of old houses in Broad Street, Soho. He also suggests that the same setting was used in *David Copperfield* for the lodging of Martha. Ref. *Dickensian* XVI., 30.

KENT STREET, Borough. (*U. T.*). In the *Uncommercial Traveller* Dickens says: "Except in the Haymarket, which is the worst kept part of London, and about Kent Street in the Borough, and along a portion of the line of the Old Kent Road, the peace was seldom violently broken." Kent Street was renamed Tabard Street between 1880 and 1890, and a great part of it has been demolished. Ref. *Dickensian* VIII., 221.

KING'S ARMS, Dorking. See Marquis of Granby.

KING'S HEAD, Chigwell. Generally considered to be the original of the Maypole. (*B.R.*). B. W. Matz remarks that there is, or was, a real Maypole Inn at Chigwell Row, which may have suggested the name to Dickens, but that is all it can claim. Ref. *Dickensian Inns and Taverns*.

In a letter to Forster, Dickens wrote about "such a delicious old Inn, opposite the churchyard." Recently, however, Mr. Wintersgill has put forward a claim for the old Maypole at Chigwell Row, supported by evidence that Dickens moved the King's Head at Chigwell to the site of the Maypole at Chigwell Row, as a more suitable locality for the story. Ref. *Dickensian* XXIII., 122.

KING'S HEAD, DORKING. See Marquis of Granby.

KING'S HEAD, Dover. This old coaching inn was stated by B. W. Matz, in the *Dickensian* of 1908 to be the inn which Dickens described in a *Tale of Two Cities* as the "Royal George." In his *Dickensian Inns and Taverns* (1922) the same writer said this identification was due to R. Allbut, but he himself considered it incorrect, and that the original of the hotel where Mr. Lorry arrived after his mail- coach journey from London, was the "Ship." A good many of Mr. Allbut's identifications appear to the present writer to be rather unsatisfactory and to require further proof.

KING'S SCHOOL, Canterbury. See Lady Wootton's Green.

KITS COTY. See Bill Stumps.

KIT'S LODGING HOUSE. See White Duck, Rochester.

KNOCKER (Marley's). See Craven Street.

KROOK'S RAG SHOP. (*B.H.*). See Bishop's Court.

LA CREEVY (Miss). (*N.N.*).
See Drummond (Rose E.).
Barrow (Janet).

LADY WOOTTON'S GREEN, Canterbury. No. 1 is said to be the house where Dr. Strong was supposed to live. (*D.C.*). Ref. *The Kent of Dickens*; *The Dickens Atlas*.

This identification, however, has always appeared to be doubtful, and the Rev. Gordon Wilson, of Canterbury, says there are many reasons which make it impossible and even absurd. The Head-master of the King's School lived in a house next to the school itself, and in *David Copperfield* Dickens indicates this quite plainly—" The school-room was a pretty large hall on the quietest side of the house . . . commanding a peep of an old secluded garden belonging to the Doctor, where the peaches were ripening on the sunny south wall." Ref. *Canterbury and Charles Dickens*.

LAING (Mr.) Magistrate at Hatton Garden Police Office. Original of Mr. Fang, the magistrate before whom Oliver Twist was brought on a charge of pocket-picking. (*O.T.*). Forster records that Dickens wrote to Mr. Haines, a gentleman connected with the courts: " In my next number of *Oliver Twist* I must have a magistrate; and casting about for a magistrate whose harshness and insolence would render him a fit subject to be shown up, I have as a necessary consequence stumbled upon Mr. Laing of Hatton Garden celebrity." He went on to suggest that he might be smuggled into the Police Office, under Mr. Haines's auspices, in order to study the magistrate's personal appearance and manner. This, says Forster, was done.

LAMERT (George). See Blacking Factory.

LAMERT (JAMES). Dickens's uncle by marriage. Generally considered to be the original of Dr. Slammer of the 97th. (*P.P.*). It has also been stated that a certain Dr. Sam Piper, of the Provisional Battalion, Chatham, recognised himself in the fiery little Doctor who had the altercation with Mr. Jingle on the staircase of the Bull Hotel, Rochester.

See also Blacking Factory.

LANDLESS (NEVILLE and HELENA). (*E.D.*) Said to be founded on two mulattoes who were pupils at Wellington House Academy when Dickens was a schoolboy there. Probably more than doubtful.

LANDOR (WALTER SAVAGE). Original of Laurence Boythorne. (*B.H.*). A great friend of Dickens, who sometimes visited him at 35, St. James' Square, Bath. During one visit in 1840, with his wife, Maclise and Forster, Dickens conceived the story of Little Nell, which afterwards appeared in the *Old Curiosity Shop*. Landor's house is now marked by a tablet, which was unveiled by Percy Fitzgerald on Feb. 7, 1903. Ref. Forster's *Life of Dickens*; *Dickensian* II., 151.

LANDSEER (Sir E.). See: Friend of Lions.

LARKIN (Miss). (*D.C.*). See Originals founded upon names.

LASCAR SAL. See New Court.

LAWES (Sir JOHN BENNETT). Founder of a temperate (not temperance) Club for Agricultural Labourers, and probably the poor man's friend referred to in the *Poor Man's Beer* (*M.P.*) as Friar Bacon.

LAURIE (Sir PETER). Original of Alderman Cute. (*C.B.*, *C.*). Like the character depicted in the *Chimes*, Sir Peter Laurie always expressed a strong determination to put down offences, especially suicide, by the most drastic methods. Ref. *The Dickens Originals*.

LEADENHALL STREET. No. 157, Leadenhall Street, was the original of Soll Gill's instrument shop. (*D. & S.*). The site is now occupied by Insurance Offices.

LEWIS (J. G.). Suggested by Sir Edward Clarke as the original of Mr. Jaggers. (*G.E.*). In 1860, Lewis was the best-known attorney in the class of work Mr. Jaggers engaged in. For twenty-five years his offices were at 10, Ely Place. Ref. *Dickens Centenary Souvenir*.

LIGHTHOUSE. (*C.C.*). See Longships Lighthouse.

LIME-KILN ON THE MARSHES. (*G.E.*). The original of the little lime-kiln near the sluice house to which Pip was decoyed by Orlick, has been identified as one which stood by the side of the marsh road from Cliffe to Cliffe Creek. For many years the kiln was buried in undergrowth and forgotten, but was discovered and cleared of bushes, etc., in 1924. Since then, the ruins of the old lime-house, which stood by the kiln, have been demolished and the flint walls used for mending the road. Ref. *Dickensian* XXII., 184.

LINCOLN'S INN FIELDS. No. 58, in which John Forster lived, was the house described in *Bleak House* as that of Mr. Tulkinghorn, the family lawyer of Sir Leicester Dedlock, Bart. Ref. *Dickensian* I., 200.

LINKINWATER (TIM). (*N.N.*). It is stated that the original of this character was an old and valued clerk in the employ of the Grant Bros., of Manchester. Ref. *The Dickens Encyclopaedia*.

The Grant Bros. were undoubtedly the originals of the Brothers Cheeryble, but it seems to be very unlikely that Dickens would found both Linkinwater, and David, the butler, on the actual servants of those brothers.

See Boot (Alfred).

Lion's Head Inn, Winterslow. Suggested by R. Allbut as the original of the "Blue Dragon" (*M.C.*), chiefly from considerations of the routes of the Quicksilver coach from London to Exeter. Mr. Gibbons, however, showed later that Allbut was wrong in this. The Quicksilver coach ran from 1837 onwards, via Amesbury, and not via Winterslow Corner. Ref. *Dickensian* I., 192, 222, 250. In *The England of Dickens*, Mr. Dexter votes for Winterslow as the Wiltshire village of the story, and the Lion's Head Inn as the original of the Blue Dragon.

See also George Inn, Amesbury.

Little Bethel. (*O.C.S.*). See Orange Street Chapel.

Little Inn, Canterbury. (*D.C.*). See Sun Inn, Canterbury.

Little Inn, Hungerford Stairs. (*D.C.*). See Swan Inn, Hungerford Stairs.

Little Inn on the Portsmouth Road. (*N.N.*). See Bottom Inn.

Little Nell. (*O.C.S.*).
See Hogarth (Mary).
Tice (Harriet Lucy).

Littlewood (Miss). Stated to be the original of Miss Flite. (*B.H.*). She lived in Chichester Rents, and had delusions similar to those of little Miss Flite. This person seems to be a replica of Miss Sant, and possibly the two are really one. Ref. *The Dickens Encyclopaedia*.

Lobster Smack Inn, Canvey Island. The original of the River-side Inn to which Magwitch was taken by boat from London. (*G.E.*). In chapter 54 of *Great Expectations*, this boat journey is minutely and circumstantially described and is as accurate as a guide-book. So much so, that from the description in the novel, any Thames pilot can at once name the part of the river referred to ; and by following Dickens's pictures of the river and its banks one is inevitably led to the river-side inn still standing where he said it did. Pip's boat is made to follow the correct course of a rowing boat against the flood tide, and this knowledge Dickens obtained in May, 1861, when he chartered a small steamer from Blackwall to Southend especially to ascertain the proper course of such a boat, and what objects and adventures might be met with on the way. Forster tells us that his keen observation of the river and its banks was busy all the time. The Lobster Smack Inn at Hole Haven is exactly in accordance with Dickens's description both of its exterior and interior, particularly in the significant phrase "a light and a roof." and it is on the proper side of the river for Magwitch to be picked up by the foreign steamer. This could not be done anywhere on the south side of the river, owing to extensive shoals and mud-banks in those "broad and solitary reaches" where the riverside inn was found.

Dickens described the inn as being rather a dirty place, but whatever it was in his day, it is clean enough now, and is a favourite resort for local yachtsmen. Ref. *Dickensian* XXII., 31.

See also Ship and Lobster, Gravesend.

Lock Gates, Strood. The lock-gates of the Gravesend and Rochester canal at Strood, have been suggested by Mr. Cobbett Barker as the "Weir" Dickens had in mind when writing *Edwin Drood*. These gates are a short distance from the North side of Rochester Bridge and sufficiently near for Mr. Crisparkle's morning swim. There is no real weir within several miles of Rochester.

See also Allington Weir.

Lodging House (Travellers). (*E.D.*). See Falcon Hotel.

Lombard Street, Portsmouth. A street crossing the High Street, in which was the old Theatre. In this street Miss Snevillici lodged when Nicholas Nickleby called upon her in connection with her benefit performances at the theatre. (*N.N.*).

London to Tong. (*O.C.S.*). Mr. Dexter suggests a well-reasoned route by which Little Nell and her grandfather travelled from the Old Curiosity Shop in London, to Tong in Shropshire. The stages of the journey are given as Uxbridge, Aylesbury, Buckingham. Banbury, Warmington, Warwick, Birmingham, Wolverhampton and Tong. Ref. *The England of Dickens*.

London Coffee House, Ludgate Hill. Original of the Coffee House in the window of which Arthur Clennan sat on the doleful Sunday evening, on his first arrival in London from abroad. (*L.D.*). The church bells which urged the populace to come to church so insistently, were those of St. Martin's, next door. Ref. *Dickensian* XI., 290 ; XXII., 190.

Until 1867 the London Coffee House occupied Nos. 42, 44 and 46, Ludgate Hill, and reached to the corner of Old Bailey.

Longships Lighthouse. Cornwall. Probably the lighthouse mentioned in a *Christmas Carol*.

Looney. Beadle in Salisbury Square. Said to be the original of Mooney, who aspired to see himself in print as the active and intelligent Beadle of the district' (*B.H.*). Looney was Beadle at Salisbury Square about the time *Bleak House* was written. He was rather feeble-minded, and was the butt of all the errand-boys of the neighbourhood. Ref. *Dickensian* XV., 198; "*My Life's Pilgrimage*"—Catling.

LORD MAYOR. (*B.R.*). See Blackley, (Alderman).

LOUGHTON HALL, Essex. Was probably the original of The Warren. (*B.R.*). It was a large, irregular building, surrounded by very beautiful rural scenery, and was the residence of a Mrs. Whittaker until it was burned down in 1836. Ref. *Dickensian* XIV., 278; XV., 51.

LOWER HIGHAM. The originals of the church and village on the marshes. (*G.E.*). The row of "lozenge" gravestones is imported from Cooling. Joe Gargery's forge is transplanted from Chalk, and the gibbet and prison-ship are taken from the Medway at Chatham, but for the rest, the churchyard, village and marshes described in the book are almost an exact picture of Lower Higham on the Thames. Ref. *Dickensian* V., 68; XX., 131, 214; XXI., 100.

See also Cooling.

LUCAS (JAMES). The Hertfordshire hermit, locally known as "Mad Lucas," lived at Red Coats Green, Knebworth. Supposed to be the original of Mr. Mopes, the miserly hermit in *Tom Tiddler's Ground*. Ref. *The Dickens Country*; *Dickensian* IV., 194.

LUPIN (Mrs.). (*M.C.*). See Samuel (Mrs.).

LUTON, Beds. Probably the small country town where the people lived by straw-plaiting, and where Mrs. Rudge and Barnaby lived under an assumed name. Here they were visited by Stagg, the blind informer. (*B.R.*).

Another suggested town is Dunstable, but this seems to be less likely.

MACKAY (JOHN). A tutor at Shaw's Bowes Academy, and said to have been generally recognised as the original of Nicholas Nickleby. (*N.N.*). Ref. *Dickensian* VII., 11.

MAIDSTONE.
See Abbey Town.
Muggleton.

MAGNUS (LAZARUS). See Originals founded on names.

MAGPIE AND STUMP. (*P.P.*). The original might have been either the "George the Fourth," Claremarket, or the "Old Black Jack," in Portsmouth Street. Both were demolished in 1896. Ref. *Inns and Taverns of Pickwick*.

It is said there used to be a "Magpie and Stump" in Fetter Lane, and if so, Dickens may have taken the name of Mr. Lowten's favourite house from it.

MALLING (West, or Town), Kent. See Abbey Town.

MALT SHOVEL INN, Chatham. The lines Dickens described as being on the sign of the Pegasus Arms in *Hard Times* were probably copied from the old inn sign of the "Malt Shovel," which formerly stood at the foot of Chatham Hill. Ref. *Dickensian Inns and Taverns*.

The original of the mean little public-house, with red lights in its windows, which Dickens called the "Pegasus' Arms," has not been found. It might be almost any little inn in any Lancashire town.

See also Manchester.

MANAGER (Louisvillian). See Quilp.

MANCHESTER. Generally supposed to be the original of Coke Town (*H.T.*), but B. W. Matz thought it was a composite picture, with a good deal of Preston in it, and possibly other manufacturing towns. The writer, who is familiar with many Lancashire towns, can see nothing of Manchester in the picture of Coke Town, and little, if any, of Preston. From Dickens's description of the town, it is much more likely to have been either Rochdale or Oldham.

MANETTE (Dr.). (*T.T.C.*). See Carlisle House.

MANETTE (LUCIE). (*T.T.C.*).
See Hogarth (Mary).
Stroughill (Lucy).

MANNING (Mrs.). Stated by Edwin Pugh to be the original of Mdlle Hortense. (*B.H.*). Mrs. Manning was a notorious murdress, hanged at Horsemonger Lane Jail in 1849.

MANSFIELD STREET. The house at the corner of Mansfield Street and Queen Anne Street, between Portland Place and Bryanstone Square, has been identified as the house of Mr. Dombey (*D. & S.*), but this is considered to be very doubtful.

MANTALINI (Madame). (*N.N.*). See Wigmore Street.

MARCHIONESS (The). (*O.C.S.*). The Marchioness of the *Old Curiosity Shop* was founded upon an orphan girl from Chatham Workhouse, who was taken to London as servant by John Dickens, when he migrated from Chatham in 1823. The real marchioness, with her sharp little worldly ways, did actually toil in the basement kitchen of 141, Bayham Street, Camden Town. Ref. *Dickensian* V., 184; Forster's *Life of Dickens*.

MARKET HARBOROUGH. Said to be the native town of Oliver Twist. (*O.T.*). Others say Peterborough. Others think the town described by Dickens was as likely as not Chatham, though transferred to the Midlands.

MARKET SQUARE, Dover. The steps on which David Copperfield rested, while he was in search of his aunt, Miss Trotwood, were those of Mr. Igglesden's baker's shop at the corner of the Market Square and Castle Street. The shop has been replaced by a modern building by the present owners, Messrs. Igglesden and Greaves, but in Dickens's time it was a plain-fronted, old-fashioned shop, with a small-paned bow-window, and the door approached by a rather steep flight of eight stone steps. It was these steps on which David is represented to have rested. The present building bears a tablet commemorating the fictitious event, but does not claim that David spent the penny given to him by a good-natured fly-driver, in the purchase of a loaf at the establishment. Ref. *Dickensian* IV., 242.

MARKET TOWN. (*G.E.*). See Rochester.

MARQUIS OF AILSBURY, Clatford. See Wagon and Horses, Beckhampton.

MARQUIS OF GRANBY, Dorking. (*P.P.*). R. Allbut (1897) claimed to have discovered the original of Mrs. Weller's hostelry in the High Street, opposite the Post Office at Dorking. Only a part of it, used as a grocer's shop, then remained. According to Matz, there were two inns at Dorking, the "King's Head," and the "King's Arms," and of the two, he considered the latter to be the more likely original of the "Marquis of Granby."

MARSHALSEA. (*L.D.*). The debtors' prison in which Mr. Dorrit was confined was built about 1811. The older prison stood between Newcomen Street (formerly King Street) and Mermaid Court, and not so near the Church as the remains of Little Dorrit's prison stand. Ref. *Dickensian* XXI., 43.

MARSH MILL, Henley. Said to be the original of the paper mill where Lizzie Hexam was employed, when she rescued Eugene Wraybourn from the river.

MARY. Housemaid. (*P.P.*). See Weller (Mary).

MARYLEBONE CHURCH. Suggested as the church where Paul Dombey was christened. (*D. & S.*).

MAYLIE (HARRY). (*O.T.*). See Burnett (Henry).

MAYLIE (ROSE). (*O.T.*). See HOGARTH (Mary).

MAYPOLE INN. (*B.R.*). See King's Head Chigwell.

MAYPOLE INN, Chigwell Row. See King's Head, Chigwell.

MCSTINGER (Mrs.). (*D. & S.*)' See Jessup (Mrs.).

MEDICAL ATTENDANT. See Chillip (Dr.)

MELL (Mr.). (*D.C.*). See Goldsmith (Oliver).

MERDLE (Mr.). (*L.D.*).
See Sadlier (John).
Harley Street.

MICAWBER (Mr.). (*D.C.*).
See Chicken (Richard).
Bayham Street.

MICROSCOPE, GAS MAGNIFYING. (*P.P.*). The "double million magnifyin' gas microscope of hextra power," mentioned by Sam Weller at the trial Bardell *v.* Pickwick, was a topical reference to a "new gas microscope, with magnifying powers of two million and a half," which was exhibited in Bond Street in 1833, and was considered to be a wonderful discovery or invention. Ref. *Dickensian* XII., 326.

MIDDLEGATE STREET, Yarmouth. No. 74 was suggested by Dr. John Bately as the original of Mr. Omer's shop. (*D.C.*). In 1909 it was still in existence, and was a very old-fashioned shop with bow windows on either side of the door. Curiously enough, it was occupied by a carpenter and builder, and the sign-board over the door bore the words "Funerals furnished completely." Ref. *Dickensian* V., 237.

Incidentally it may be mentioned that the name of Omer is not unknown in Kent, and can still be seen on the sign of a Rochester tradesman.

MILE END COTTAGE, Alpington. Said to be the beautiful little thatched house where Mrs. Nickleby recollected the Dibabses lived, and where the earwigs fell into one's tea on a summer evening. The identification is a very possible one.

MILES (WILLIAM). Verger, for many years at Rochester Cathedral, is believed to be the original of Mr. Tope, the verger at Cloisterham Cathedral. (*E.D.*). Mr. Miles was born in 1816, and died in 1908, after being connected with the cathedral for seventy-five years. Mrs. Tope's house, where Datchery lodged, adjoins Jasper's Gate-house on the east side, and is now a tea-shop, but little altered. Ref. *Lloyd's Weekly News*, March, 1908.

MINCING LANE. The offices of Chicksey, Veneering and Stobbles were probably next to Dunston Court, four doors from the corner of Fenchurch Street. Ref. *The London of Dickens*.

MINOR CANON ROW, Rochester. Mr. Chrisparkle lived here. (*E.D.*). The second house from the eastern side is thought to be the home of the China Shepherdess. The *Dickens Atlas* names No. 7. In the Notes and plans for *Edwin Drood*, written by Dickens for his own guidance, there is a note, "Minor Canon Corner, the closet I remember there, as a child." To this may be referred Mrs. Crisparkle's wonderful spice-closet.

MINORIES. See Wooden Midshipman.

MINSTER ABBEY, Sheppey Island. Suggested by a writer in the *Antiquary*, of March, 1910, as the church where Little Nell died. (*O.C.S.*). The suggestion depends upon certain graves at Minster which are apparently referred to in the story. The action of the tale, however, is against it, and in favour of Tong Church, in Shropshire.

MISS TWINKLETON'S ACADEMY. (*E.D.*). See Eastgate House.

MITFORD (MARY RUSSELL). According to the *Daily Chronicle*, of Jan. 4, 1909, Jenny Wren, the doll's dressmaker in *Our Mutual Friend*, had a prototype in real life. About 130 years since Mary Mitford lived, in a small Dorsetshire town, with her father, who was an inveterate drunkard, and whom she called "her bad boy." Miss Mitford was the authoress of "*Our Village*."

MITRE HOTEL, Chatham. Probably the original of the inn of minor reputation at which Pip dined on one occasion. (*G.E.*). In Dickens's time there was a small six-sided common room, adjoining the bar, furnished with dark and heavy furniture of somewhat clerical design and appearance. There does not seem to have been any similar common room at any of the hotels or inns in Rochester. Dickens was very familiar with the common room at the Mitre, which he often visited with his father, as a boy. The Mitre was almost certainly the inn mentioned in the *Holy Tree* as the inn at the Cathedral town where he went to school. It is there described as having an ecclesiastical appearance, and a bar which was the next best thing to a Bishopric—it was so snug.

MITRE HOTEL, Rochester. See Crown Inn, Rochester.

MITTON (MARY ANN). Said to be the original of Amy Dorrit. (*L.D.*). Ref. *Dickens Encyclopaedia*.

MITTON (THOMAS). Dickens's solicitor and former school-fellow has been stated to be the original of Simon Tappertit. (*B.R.*). and Wemmick. (*G.E.*), but on what eveidence is not known. The two characters are so dissimilar that it is difficult to imagine them as derived from the same original.

MIVART'S OR CLARIDGE'S HOTEL. Percy Fitzgerald, in *Bozland*, considered that this was the handsome hotel where Nicholas Nickleby had the encounter with Sir Mulberry Hawk. (*N.N.*).

MONCKTON (Hon. Miss). Lady Cook. According to Edwin Pugh, the original of Mrs. Leo Hunter, the gifted authoress of an "Ode to an Expiring Frog." (*P.P.*). A Mrs. Somerville Wood has also been stated to be the original, as well as Mrs. John Cobbold, of The Cliff, Ipswich. Probably none of these originals is correct. Ref. *The Dickens Originals*; *T. P.'s Weekly*, Oct., 1904; *Daily Chronicle*, Jan., 1922.

MONK'S VINEYARD. (*E.D.*). See Vines (The), Rochester.

MONUMENT SQUARE. Original of Monument Yard. (*M.C.*)

MOONEY, THE BEADLE. (*B.H.*). See Looney.

MOORE (ANN). The thirsty woman of Tutbury, mentioned by Mrs. Nickleby during her lamentations, on the occasion of the mad gentleman next door being found in the chimney, is said to have been a certain Ann Moore, the fasting woman of Tutbury.

MOPES (Mr.). (*T.T.G.*). See Lucas (James).

MORGAN (Captain). Original of Captain Jorgan. (*C.B.*, *M. Sea*). Capt. Morgan, an American seaman, was an old friend of Dickens, who, in a letter to him, said: "I hope you will have seen the Christmas number of *All the Year Round*. Here and there in the description of the sea-going hero, I have given a touch or two of remembrance of somebody you know; very heartily desiring that thousands of people may have some faint reflection of the pleasure I have for many years derived from the contemplation of a most amiable nature and most remarkable man." Ref. *Dickensian* XIV., 209.

MOUCHER (Miss). (*D.C.*). See Seymour Hill (Mrs.)

MUCKING FLAT LIGHTHOUSE. Is the lighthouse mentioned in *Great Expectations* as a "squat shoal lighthouse, stranded in the mud on stilts and crutches." It is a curious little iron structure on open piles, built in 1851, on the mud flats at the north end of the Lower Hope, on the Thames, and some five or six miles below Gravesend. There was no other lighthouse, after passing Gravesend, except the Chapman, a somewhat similar structure a long way down sea reach. Mucking lighthouse agreed exactly with Dickens's description, and the stoney spit on which the boat party landed can easily be identified close by. The light has not been used since the beginning of the Great War in 1914. Ref. *Dickensian* XXII., 32.

MUDFOG. (*Mud. Pap.*). See Rochester.

MUDFOG ASSOCIATION. (*Mud. Pap.*). See British Association.

MUGGLETON. (*P.P.*). There is a considerable diversity of opinion as to the original of the town of Muggleton, and the question is not yet settled. In the *Inns and Taverns of Pickwick*, Matz says that, so far, no topographer has discovered which corporate town it was. Mr. Dexter appears to incline to the belief that Muggleton was Maidstone. Maidstone has a jail, and a jail forms part of the tale "The Convict's return"; but the story does not indicate that the jail was actually at Muggleton. Other towns suggested are Town Malling, and Gravesend. The former fits the description very well from the geographical and other points of view, particularly with regard to the cricket ground. But the rather derisive account of Muggleton seems to be very largely derived from the corporate town of Gravesend, which is still known as the "Ancient and Loyal Borough."

Dickens was staying at Chalk, close to Gravesend, when he wrote the earlier chapters of *Pickwick*, and, of course, knew Gravesend very well. It is commonly known that he did not like Gravesend, which adds some point to the sarcastic description of Muggleton in *Pickwick*.

Other suggested originals of Muggleton, like Faversham and Tenterden, cannot be considered, in the absence of references to the evidence adduced.

MULATTOES, at Wellington House School. See Landless.

MURDSTONE AND GRINBY, wine warehouse. (*D.C.*). See Blacking Factory.

NAST HYDE. A house on the St. Alban's-Hatfield Road suggested by Mr. W. C. Day as possibly the original of Bleak House. (*B.H.*). It appears to fit the description very well, but has not yet been definitely accepted.

NEWMAN (Mrs.). Reputed to be the original of the Old Lady mentioned in *Our Parish*. (*S.B.B.*). She lived at No. 5, Ordnance Terrace, Chatham, when the Dickens family lived at No. 2.

NEWMAN STREET. Mr. Turveydrop's Academy for Dancing and Deportment (*B.H.*) was at No. 26, and in 1905 was still next door to a mews, and had a long dancing room extending behind it. Ref. *Dickensian* I., 203.

NEWMAN'S COURT. See Freeman's Court.

NEW COURT, St. George's in the East. The actual opium den described in *Edwin Drood* is said to be one which was kept by a certain Lascar Sal in this Court (now demolished). It was visited by Dickens more than once, and in the summer of 1869 he took his American friend J. T. Fields to see it. The John Chinaman mentioned in the book was George Ah Sing, who kept a rival opium den at 131, Cornwall Street, St. George's in the East. He died in Jan., 1890. Lascar Sal was living in 1875. Ref. *Dickensian* XII., 21; XV., 59.

See also Johnstone's opium den.

NEW THIRTEEN CANONS. See Johnson's, Clare Market.

NICKLEBY (KATE). (*N.N.*). See Hogarth (Mary).

NICKLEBY (Mrs.). (*N.N.*). See Dickens (Mrs. John).

NICKLEBY (Nicholas). (*N.N.*).
See Burnett (Henry).
Mackay (John).

NOGGS (NEWMAN). (*N.N.*). See Nott (Newman).

NORTHFLEET, Kent. See Cobtree Hall.

NORTH LANE, Canterbury. The original of the little house in which Uriah Heap's mother dwelt (*D.C.*) has been identified as a small house in North Lane, Canterbury. There is, however, considerable doubt about its being anything more than a mere guess.

NORWICH. See Sudbury.

NOTT (NEWMAN). A ne-er-do-weel who called regularly at Messrs. Ellis & Blackman's offices in South Square for a weekly allowance from a wealthy relative, when Dickens was employed there. Said to be the original of Newman Noggs. (*N.N.*). Ref. *The Dickens Originals*.

It has also been claimed that the original of Newman Noggs was a well-known character at Barnard Castle.

NUCKALL'S PLACE, Broadstairs. See Assembly Rooms.

OLD BLACK JACK. See Magpie and Stump.

OLD CHEQUERS INN, Lower Higham. The original of the "Three Jolly Bargemen." (*G.E.*). The old inn, on the site of the present modern building, was demolished in 1900-1. It was a weather-boarded old inn with red-tiled roof and tall chimneys, and agreed in character and situation with the description in *Great Expectations*. Ref. *Dickensian* XXII., 237.

OLD CURIOSITY SHOP. (*O.C.S.*).
See Green Street.
Fetter Lane.

OLD CURIOSITY SHOP. Portsmouth Street See Green Street.

OLDHAM. See Manchester.

OLD LADY. (*S. B. B.*, *O.P.*). See Newman (Mrs.).

OLD SHIP TAVERN. At the corner of Chichester Rents, Chancery Lane. It was the original of the "Sol's Arms," where the inquest on Nemo was held, and where Little Squills officiated at the harmonic evening afterwards. (*B.H.*) The *Dickens Atlas* gives No. 7 as the place. Ref. *Dickensian Inns and Taverns*.

Old Square, Lincoln's Inn. On the authority of the *Dickens Atlas*, No. 13 was the office of Messrs Kenge and Carboy. (*B.H.*).

Oliver Twist. (*O.T.*). See Market Harborough.

Oliver Twist. Route to London. (*O.T.*). Part of the route of Oliver and his escort Mr. John Dawkins is thus described: "They crossed from the "Angel" into St. John's Road, struck down the small street which terminates at Sadler's Wells Theatre, through Exmouth Street and Coppice Row, down the little court by the side of the Workhouse, across the classic ground which once bore the name of Hockley-in-the-Hole, thence into Little Saffron Hill, and so into Saffron Hill the Great."

The small street which terminates at Sadler's Wells Theatre is Arlington Street, and the little Court by the side of the Workhouse is Crawford Passage. Coppice Row disappeared in 1860, but it ran from the end of Exmouth Street, down what is now Farringdon Road, to the "Butchers' Arms," at the back of which was Hockley-in-the-Hole. Ref. *Dickensian* VIII., 75; IX., 298.

Opium Den. (*E.D.*).
See New Court, St. George's in the East. Johnstone's opium den.

Orange Street Chapel, Leicester Square Suggested by Wilmot Corfield as the original of Little Bethel. (*O.C.S.*). He rejects the claim of Zoar Chapel, Goodman's Fields, and adduces considerable argument in favour of the chapel in Orange Street. Whilst the identification cannot be definitely established, there is much reason to believe that the Little Bethel was somewhere in the neighbourhood of Leicester Square and Green Street. Ref. *Dickensian* IX., 268.

See also Zoar Chapel.

Osborne's Hotel. (*P.P.*). See Adelphi Hotel.

Originals founded upon Names. Suggested originals of Dickens's characters, founded merely upon a similarity of name, are numerous, and probably have no foundation whatever. Dickens used names to suit his characters and most of them are to be found in the London Directory. Examples of these so-called originals are:—

Barkis (*D.C.*). Original Barker, carrier of Blundeston.

Dowler (*P.P.*). Original Vincent Dowling, an associate of Dickens, on a reporting expedition to Bath.

Dorrit (*L.D.*). Original Dorrett, a prisoner in the King's Bench.

Peter Magnus (*P.P.*). Original Lazarus Magnus of Chatham.

Rigaud (*L.D.*). Original General Rigaud.

Snodgrass (*P.P.*). Original Gabriel Snodgrass. Also name founded on Snodland, a village in Kent.

Mr. Struggles (*P.P.*). Original George Stroughill.

Edwin Drood (*E.D.*). Original Edwin Trood, landlord of the Falstaff Inn.

Barnacle (*L.D.*). A person of that name lived in Bath

Battens (*Mr.*) (*U.T.*). The name of a former Mayor of Rochester.

Bray (*Madeline*) (*N.N.*). Taken from the name of one of Dickens's schoolfellows at Wellington House Academy

Dartle (*Rosa*). The name is said to be an old Rochester one.

Jasper (*John*). A name still to be found in Rochester.

Larkins (*Miss*) (*D.C.*). Suggested that Dickens took the name from a monument erected to the memory of Charles Larkin, at Higham.

Sowerberry (*Mr.*) (*O.T.*). This name occurs in the Church registers at Chatham.

Stiggins (*Bro.*). (*P.P.*). The name is found at Higham.

Twist (*Oliver*) (*O.T.*). In the Salford Register of Births there is an entry recording the birth of John Twist, son of Oliver Twist, on May 6, 1567, but it is extremely doubtful that Dickens ever saw or heard of it.

The name of *Fagin* was taken from the surname of a fellow-worker at the Hungerford Market Blacking Factory, but only the name. The cognomen of *Dennis*, the hangman in *Barnaby Rudge*, was a real one, as, apparently the hangman at the time of the Gordon riots was a certain John Dennis, but the resemblance probably went no farther than the name.

Our English Watering Place. (*R.P.*). See Broadstairs.

Our French Watering Place. (*R.P.*). See Boulogne.

Paddock Wood Station. According to Canon Benham, and others, this was the scene of Carker's terrible death. (*D. & S.*). Ref. *Dickensian* III., 247.

Pageant House. See Westgate House.

Paper Mill. (*O.M.F.*). See Marsh Mill.

Park Street, Bristol. An old-fashioned chemist's shop at the bottom of this street, was suggested by O. Sack as the original of Bob Sawyer's establishment: "Something between a shop and a private house." (*P.P.*). About the time of Mr. Winkle's supposed visit Park Street was very different from what it is now, and was made up of private houses with small bow windows to the front parlours. Sack's identification can only be regarded as a conjectural one, as there is nothing in *Pickwick* to indicate the exact locality. Ref. *Dickensian* VII., 260.

PARISH CHURCH, Chatham. See Blundeston.

PARROCK HALL, Gravesend. One of the suggestions of the original of Dingley Dell (*P.P.*). Other suggestions are Northfleet, Burham, and Frindsbury Manor Farm, near Rochester. The name of Dingley Dell it is said may have been suggested by Singlewell, a hamlet between Gravesend and Cobham.

PAVILION HOTEL, Folkestone. The hotel called " Pavilionstone " in *Out of Town.* On one occasion Dickens wrote: " A thoroughly good inn, in the days of coaching and posting, was a noble place. But no such inn would have been equal to the reception of four or five hundred people, all of them wet through, and half of them dead sick, every day in the year. This is where we shine in our Pavilionstone Hotel."

PAVILIONSTONE HOTEL. (*O. of T.*). See Pavilion Hotel, Folkestone.

PEACE (Charles). See Budden.

PEAL O' BELLS INN. (*T.T.G.*). See White Hart, Stevenage.

PECKSNIFF (Mr.). (*M.C.*). See Hall (Samuel Carter).

PECKSNIFF'S HOUSE. (*M.C.*). See St. Mary's Grange.

PEGASUS' ARMS. (*H.T.*). See Malt Shovel, Chatham.

PEGGOTTY. (*D.C.*). See Weller (Mary).

PEGGOTTY'S HOME. (*D.C.*). See Sharman's Hut. Also Boat House at Gravesend.

PERKER (Mr.). (*P.P.*). See Ellis.

PETERBOROUGH. See Market Harborough

PHIL. See Squod (Phil.).

PIAZZA HOTEL, Covent Garden. (*D.C.*). The hotel mentioned by Steerforth as where he was going to breakfast with one of his friends, was the coffee-house at the north-eastern angle of Covent Garden Piazza. It was a favourite resort of actors at one time. Ref. *Dickensian Inns and Taverns.*

PICKWICK'S COTTAGE at Dulwich. (*P.P.*). A certain cottage on the outskirts of Dulwich has been claimed to be the house to which Mr. Pickwick retired after his wanderings. It was a square plain-looking house surrounded by a garden, but there is no real evidence that Dickens meant this, or any other actual cottage. The illustration of the house at Dulwich, by T. Onwhyn in 1837, has no resemblance whatever to the house claimed,, and Charles Dickens, junior, asserted that his father had no real house in his mind.

PICKWICK (SAMUEL). (*P.P.*). Mr. Pickwick was purely an imaginary character, but the figure, as depicted by Seymour, was stated by Mr. Chapman, of Chapman & Hall, to have been copied from John Foster, of Richmond, a friend of his partner. A claim that Mr. Pickwick and his adventures were invented by Seymour (the artist who illustrated the first number), was dealt with by Dickens in his Preface to the first cheap edition of *Pickwick.*

PIG-FACED LADY. (*N.N.*). The pig-faced lady mentioned by Mrs. Nickleby, in the course of her lamentation, is stated to have been a Miss Atkinson, but the authority is not known.

PINCH (TOM). (*M.C.*). See Burnett (Henry).

PINCH (TOM). Lodgings. (*M.C.*). See Terrett's Place.

PINCHIN (Mrs.). (*D. & S.*). See Roylance (Mrs.)

PIPER (Dr. Sam.). See Lamert (James).

P. J. T. (*E.D.*). See Staple Inn.

PLASHWATER WEIR MILL LOCK. (*O.M.F.*). See Hurley Lock.

PLOUGH INN, Blundeston. Probably the inn from which Mr. Barkis, the carrier, was made to start on his rounds. (*D.C.*). David pictured the parlour of the inn as the room where Commodore Trunnion held that Club with Mr. Pickle. Ref. *Dickensian Inns and Taverns.*

PODSNAP (Mr.). (*O.M.F.*). See Forster (John).

POISONED GIRL. (*H.D.*). See Abercrombie (Miss Helen).

POLICE COURT, Hatton Garden. (*O.T.*). Mr. Laing's Court in Hatton Garden was at No. 54, not at No. 53, as sometimes stated. In the ground floor of No. 54 was the panelling on the walls mentioned by Dickens, and a reference to the law lists of the period unmistakeably establishes No. 54 as the correct building. Ref. *Dickensian* X., 48.

POMFRET ARMS, Towcester. The original of the " Saracen's Head," where the fracas between Mr. Pott of the " Eatanswill Gazette," and Mr. Slurk of the " Independent " took place. (*P.P.*). The " Pomfret Arms " was originally called the " Saracen's Head " and was so known in 1827-8, the period of *Pickwick*, so Dickens was historically correct in giving it that name. Ref. *Inns and Taverns of Pickwick.*

PORTER (Mrs. JOSEPH). (*S.B.B.*) See Porter Leigh (Mrs. John).

PORTER LEIGH (Mrs. JOHN). Said to have been the original of Mrs. Joseph Porter in the sketch of that title (*Sketches by Boz*). She was the wife of a corn dealer living at Lea Bridge Road, Lower Clapton from 1828-1833. Ref. *The Beadnell Letters*.

POTTER. See Jingle (Alfred).

PRESTON. See Manchester.

PRINCESS PUFFER. (*E.D.*). Supposed to be founded on Lascar Sal, keeper of an opium den visited by Dickens. See New Court, St. George's in the East.

PRIOR. See Quilp.

PRIORY GATE, Rochester. See Chertsey Gate.

PROCTER (Adelaide Ann). Writer of poems in *Household Words* under the assumed name of Mary Berwick. Afterwards Dickens discovered that Mary Berwick was Adelaide Procter, daughter of his old friend Barry Cornwall.

PROSPECT OF WHITBY. See Grapes Inn, Limehouse.

PROVIDENCE CHAPEL, Chatham. The church over which the Child (Dickens ?) and his sister saw the Star (*C. d. of a Star*), has been stated to be the Parish Church at Chatham.

As Dickens lived at St. Mary's Place, on the Brook, between the ages of 4 and nine, when he left Chatham, and the house on the Brook adjoined Mr. Giles's Baptist Chapel, it seems more likely that this chapel was the "Church" over which the Star was seen.

PUBLIC-HOUSE OPPOSITE INSOLVENT DEBTORS' COURT. (*P.P.*). See Horse and Groom.

PUCKLER-MUSKAU (Prince). Said to be the original of Count Smaltork, one of the guests at Mrs. Leo Hunter's garden party. No evidence of identity adduced. Ref. *T. P.'s Weekly*, Oct., 1904.

PUGIN, architect. See Hall (Samuel Carter).

PUMBLECHOOK'S PREMISES. (*G.E.*). See High Street, Rochester.

PUMP COURT. It has been stated that the chambers of Mr. Fips, the solicitor of old Martin Chuzzlewit, were probably in Pump Court, but on what grounds this statement is made is difficult to understand. Dickens said Mr. Fips's chambers were in Austin Friars, and there seems to be no object in looking elsewhere.

PYECROFT HOUSE, Chertsey. The house burgled by Bill Sykes and Toby Cratchit, unwillingly assisted by Oliver Twist. (*O.T.*). Pyecroft House was an eighteenth century red-brick mansion standing in a lane at the end of Pyecroft Street Chertsey. The grounds were enclosed by a high wall, as described in the story. Ref. *Dickensian* I., 262.

The pantry window through which Oliver Twist was supposed to have been pushed by the burglar, is at present lent to Dickens House, Doughty Street.

QUEEN ANNE STREET. See Mansfield Street.

QUEEN'S HEAD, Canterbury. See Sun Inn.

QUEEN'S SQUARE, Bath. House of Angelo Cyrus Bantam, Esq. (*P.P.*). The entrance has a square portico and side columns. At the house next door to it there is still preserved a large screen, bearing the name Moses Pickwick and the date 1830, that once stood in the office of the "White Hart," where the Pickwickians put up, on their arrival in Bath. Ref. *Dickensian* II., 150.

QUEER CLIENT. Tale of. (*P.P.*). See Shorne Churchyard.

QUILP. (*O.C.S.*). An American paper claimed that the original of this character was a theatrical manager at Louisville. The original, however, followed the character, for *Old Curiosity Shop* was published in 1840-41, and Dickens's first visit to America was in 1842.

According to a writer in *The Times* of Sept. 7, 1913, the original of Quilp was a man named Prior, of Bath, who hired out donkeys for children's rides. He said that Dickens was introduced to Prior by the Dowager Lady Graves-Sawle.

QUILP'S HOUSE. (*O.C.S.*). See Tower Hill.

QUILP'S WHARF. (*O.C.S.*). On the Surrey side of the River, close to the end of Tower Bridge. The site was afterwards occupied by Butler's Wharf. The river foreshore on which Quilp's drowned body was cast ashore is supposed to be Bugsby's Marsh, but it is not known on what evidence.

RAVEN. See Grip.

RECTORY BLUNDESTON. See Blundeston.

RED LION, Bevis Marks. Confidently stated to be the inn frequented by Dick Swiveller. (*O.C.S.*). Ref. *Dickensian Inns and Taverns*.

RED LION INN, Barnet. Said to be the inn where Oliver Twist and the Artful Dodger regaled themselves, after their first meeting by the roadside. (*O.T.*). Probably not correct. Also suggested as the inn where Esther Summerson hired a carriage for Bleak House. (*B.H.*). Ref. *Dickensian Inns and Taverns*.

RED LION INN, Hampton. Hampton was the country town from which Betty Higden fled in terror from her questioners. (*O.M.F.*). She had seen the "Sign of the 'White Lion' hanging across the road, and the fluttering market booths, and the old grey church." According to B. W. Matz, there is no doubt this little town was Hampton, although Dickens gave it no name. Ref. *Dickensian Inns and Taverns.*

RED LION INN, Henley. The Angler's inn to which the injured Eugene Wraybourne was taken, after he had been battered down by Bradley Headstone. (*O.M.F.*).

The inn, which is on the west bank of the river Thames, and north of the bridge, was a favourite resort of anglers. The patch of lawn sloping down to the river coincides with the book description. Ref. *Dickensian Inns and Taverns*

RED LION HOTEL, 48, Parliament Street. The scene of the incident of the "genuine stunning ale." Forster tells us this was an actual occurrence in Dickens's blacking warehouse days, and that the place was a public-house in Parliament Street, at the corner of a short street leading to Cannon Row. Afterwards, the author utilized the incident in *David Copperfield.* The existing building is not the actual tavern described, although on the same site. The old Red Lion of Dickens's boyhood was demolished about the year 1848.

REGENT HOTEL, Leamington. Stated to be the Royal Hotel of *Dombey & Son.*, but there was Copp's Royal Hotel, Leamington.

RESTORATION HOUSE, Rochester. The Satis house of *Great Expectations.* It is the finest specimen of an Elizabethan house in Rochester. Built in the form of the letter E, in 1580-1600, it takes its name from the fact that Charles the Second slept in it the night before the Restoration, in 1660. The room he occupied is still called the King's room, and is a fine panelled apartment on the first floor, with a secret passage leading from it to the roof and to the garden. The King's room is probably the room Dickens assigned to Miss Havisham, for the large drawing-room in which the decaying wedding feast was laid out is directly opposite, across a broad landing on the grand staircase. This landing is mentioned two or three times in the book. In Dickens's time there was a disused brewery in the grounds, partly on the site of a modern chapel, and a detached house, corresponding to the house that looked as if it might belong to the manager or head clerk of the extinct brewery, still stands inside the high wall surrounding the grounds.

RIGAUD (General). See Originals founded on names.

RIGDEN (Martha). Suggested as the original of Betty Higden. (*O.M.F.*). She was Postmistress at Higham during Dickens's residence at Gadshill Place and died in Strood Infirmary, at the age of 85, in 1920. Probably she frequently came in contact with Dickens but there is no evidence that she was the original of old Betty Higden. Ref. *Dickensian* XVI., 119.

RIVER-SIDE INN. (*G.E.*).
See Lobster Smack, Canvey Island.
Ship and Lobster, Gravesend.

ROCHESTER, Kent. Original of Cloisterham. (*E.D.*). Also the Market Town (*G.E.*). With Chatham, it figured as Mud-fog (*Mud-pap.*), and as Great Winglebury (*S.B.B.*). It was also obviously the Dullborough of Dickens's boyhood, together with Chatham. (*U.T.*). The S.E.R. railway station was at Chatham, and the Dullborough Mechanics' Institution was the Chatham Institute. The Dullborough Town Hall and the great Winglebury Town Hall are frequently stated to be the Rochester Corn Exchange, but this must be a mistake. the "moon-faced" clock is that of the Corn Exchange, but the Town Hall at Rochester is the Guildhall, built 1687.

ROCHESTER BRIDGE. The bridge which Dickens always had in his mind's eye, when referring to Rochester Bridge, was the old stone bridge built in 1387 and demolished in 1856, when the iron bridge replaced it. The stone bridge crossed the river about forty yards above Watling Street, the continuity of which was not restored till the opening of the iron bridge. It was the stone bridge of Dickens's earlier life from which Mr. Pickwick viewed the city of Rochester, and over which David Copperfield limped one Sunday evening after getting through three and twenty miles of dusty travel on the Dover Road.

ROCHDALE. See Manchester.

ROCKINGHAM CASTLE, Northamptonshire. Original of Chesney Wold, Sir Leicester Dedlock's place in Lincolnshire. (*B.H.*). Rockingham Castle, which Dickens visited several times, was the home of his friends the Watsons, and, according to Snowden Ward, all the important features of Chesney Wold can be recognised in the Castle and neighbouring village of Rockingham. The keeper's lodge, where Lady Dedlock, Esther, and her guardian sheltered from the thunderstorm; the steep village street leading to the "Dedlock Arms" (Sondes Arms); the ghost's walk; the sun-dial and stable clock; Mr. Tulkinghorn's room in the tower, with the leads on which he walked; the parsonage house where Lawrence Boythorn lived; and other features can all be recognised. Ref. *Dickensian* I., 202.

ROOKERY (The). (*D.C.*). See Blundeston.

ROYAL EAST LONDON VOLUNTEERS. (*B.R.*) The earliest volunteers were the train bands. The early "Volunteers" were formed about 1794 and were disbanded soon after the fall of Napoleon. In 1859 the Volunteer force was revived, to be succeeded by Lord Haldane's Territorial force in 1908. The period of *Barnaby Rudge* is 1775, and it is not certain which Volunteers Dickens referred to as the Royal East London, in which Gabriel Varden served. Possibly the Honourable Artillery Company, which was in existence long before the early volunteers of the Napoleonic Wars.

ROYAL GEORGE HOTEL, Dover. (*T.T.C.*). See King's Head, Dover.

ROYAL HOTEL, Bath. (*P.P.*). See York House.

ROYAL HOTEL, Birmingham. (*P.P.*). This hotel, where Mr. Pickwick once put up, is in Temple Row. Externally it has been considerably altered. Prior to a banquet at the hotel in 1853, Dickens was presented with a silver salver and a diamond ring, by the Society of Arts. Ref. *Dickensian* XXIII., 152.

ROYAL HOTEL, Leamington. (*D. & S.*). See Regent Hotel.

ROYLANCE (Mrs.). Of Little College Street, Camden Town, was the original of Mrs. Pipchin, with whom Paul Dombey resided for a time. In a letter to John Forster, Dickens said "The key of the house" (Gower Street) "was sent back to the landlord and I was handed over as a lodger to a reduced old lady, long known to our family, in Little College Street, Camden Town, who took children in to board; and who, with few alterations and embellishments, unconsciously began to sit for Mrs. Pipchin in "Dombey" when she took in me. Ref. Forster's *Life of Dickens*.

RUBY (George). Suggested as the original of Joe, the crossing sweeper, in *Bleak House*. George Ruby, a boy of 14 years old, was put into the witness box at the Guildhall on Jan. 8, 1850, to give evidence in an assault case. In reply to the presiding Alderman, he said he did not know what an oath was. He could not read, and did not know what prayers meant. He had heard of the Devil, but did not know him. All he knew was how to sweep a crossing. Ref. *Dickensian* VIII., 246.

RUDGE (BARNABY). (*B.R.*). Said to have been founded upon a half-witted young man named Walter de Brisac, who lived at Chatham. The original authority for this statement has not been found, but it is thought to be very doubtful. *Barnaby Rudge* was written in 1841. Walter de Brisac died in 1893, so he was presumably a very young man indeed if Dickens knew him in 1823, between which date and the date of the story he was very unlikely to have seen or heard of him.

RUSSELL COURT Burial Ground. Original of the City burial ground of *Bleak House*. It was attached to the church of St. Mary le Strand, and situated north of the Strand, near Drury Lane Theatre. It was converted into a recreation ground in 1886, and the whole locality is changed from what it was when Dickens described it. York Street East now traverses the cemetery where Nemo was buried in a pauper's grave. Ref. *Dickensian* VII., 161.

See also St. Clement Danes.

S—— (JOHN), of Brondeswood. Suggested by F. C. Kitton as the original of John Browdie (*N.N.*), on what evidence is not known.

SADLIER (JOHN). The character of Mr. Merdle (*L.D.*) is stated to have been founded on John Sadlier, M.P. for Carlow, and at one time a Junior Lord of the Treasury. After his suicide on Hampstead Heath it was found that he had been swindling for years. Among other frauds were £150,000 on the Royal Swedish Railway, of which he was Chairman, and £200,000 on the Tipperary Joint Stock Bank, of which he was also the Chairman. Ref. *Daily Chronicle*, Feb. 17, 1914.

Sadlier's career was very similar to that of Mr. Merdle in *Little Dorrit*, but he was not the only one, and there have been several Mr. Merdles before and since Dickens wrote this book.

ST. ALPHAGE'S CHURCH, Greenwich. Said to be the church where Bella Wilfer was married to John Rokesmith. (*O.M.F.*).

ST. ANN'S CHURCH, Soho. Probably the church in which Lucie Manette was married to Charles Darnay, or Evrèmonde. (*T.T.C.*). At the period of the story, the church was without its present steeple, which was built in 1802.

ST. BOTOLPH'S CHURCH. Probably the Houndsditch Church mentioned in *The Uncommercial Traveller* (XXXV.).

ST. CLEMENT DANES. Burial ground said to have been in Dickens's mind when he wrote *Bleak House*. In 1850 there was some agitation about the state of certain graveyards in London, and a bill was introduced in Parliament for the abolition of intramural interments. The churchyard of St. Clement Danes was described as a cholera nursery, and Dickens himself drew attention to the disgraceful state of the burial ground of St. Giles' in the Fields, where there had been 12,000 burials in three and a half years.

Ref. *Dickensian* VIII., 193.

It is generally agreed, however, that the burial ground, with its reeking little tunnel, in which Nemo was interred, and where Lady Dedlock died, was the one in Russell Court.

See also Russell Court.

St. Dunstan's Church, Fleet Street. The chimes of this church were those from which the Christmas Book took its title. Ref. *The London of Dickens*.

St. Dunstan's Street, Canterbury. No. 71 is generally pointed out as the house of Mr. Wickfield (*D.C.*), but the authority is not known.

St. George's Church, Camberwell. See St. Giles', Camberwell.

Saint Ghastly Grim. (*U.T.*). See St. Olave's, Hart Street.

St. Giles', Camberwell. According to Mr. Tyrrell, the old Parish Church of St. Giles', Camberwell, was where Wemmick was married to Miss Skiffins. (*G.E.*). It was burned down in 1841. Robert Allbut identified Emanuel Church as the place of Wemmick's marriage, but Emmanuel Church was not built until 1841, and the period of the story was about 1820-23. F. Fitch (*Dickensian* IV., 125) disagreed with Allbut and suggested St. George's Church, Camberwell, built 1822. This was not far from the Surrey canal, where a good deal of angling was done at one time, and this may have suggested Wemmick's queer fancy for a fishing-rod on the memorable occasion.

St. John the Evangelist. The Church of St. John the Evangelist in Smith Square, Millbank, is the very hideous church, with four towers at the four corners, generally resembling some petrified monster on its back, with its legs in the air. (*O.M.F.*).

St. Mary's Grange, Alderbury. A red-brick mansion built by Pugin the famous architect. It stood about half-a-mile from Alderbury and about three miles from Salisbury, and was suggested by C. G. Harper as the original of Pecksniff's house. (*M.C.*). On the other hand, Snowden Ward identified an old mansion on the Wilsford Road, Amesbury—eight miles from Salisbury—as Mr. Pecksniff's house, and this was apparently accepted by the late B. W. Matz. The description of Pecksniff's house in *Martin Chuzzlewit* does not, however, convey the idea of a large mansion, such as the above suggested originals, and there seems to be considerable doubt that Dickens meant either of them. Ref. *Dickensian* I., 119; *Dickensian Inns and Taverns*.

St. Michael's Church, Cornhill. See Austin Friars.

St. Peter's Churchyard, Cornhill. The churchyard in a paved square court, with a raised bank of earth, about breast high, in the middle, enclosed by iron rails, where Bradley Headstone, schoolmaster, made his vehement declaration of love to Lizzie Hexam. *O.M.F.* Ref. *The London of Dickens*.

The churchyard is still almost exactly as Dickens described it.

St. Stephen's Church, Camden Town. See Bayham Street.

St. Olave's, Hart Street, E.C. The churchyard which Dickens, in *The City of the Absent*, called the churchyard of Saint Ghastly Grim. It is a small churchyard in the heart of the City, and, in Dickens's words, has a ferocious, strong, spiked gate, like a jail.

Salem House School. (*D.C.*). See Wellington House Academy.

Samuel (Mrs.). The landlady of the cottage at Alpington which Dickens took for his parents, is said to have been the original of Mrs. Lupin, the buxom landlady of the "Blue Dragon" in *Martin Chuzzlewit*. The only authority for this appears to be the bare statement by a writer in the *Western Morning News*, in 1910.

Sandling. See Dingley Dell.

Sant (Miss). Suggested original of Miss Flite. (*B.H.*). She is said to have paid regular daily visits to Doctors' Commons to search for particulars of a large estate to which she was firmly convinced she was entitled. She arrived every day at 10 o'clock, carrying a paper parcel which she called her deeds of title, and never left until the office closed at 4 o'clock in the afternoon The years in which this harmless little old woman conducted her searches are not stated, but if early enough, Miss Sant might well have sat for poor little Miss Flite, whom she certainly closely resembled. Ref. *Dickensian* XXI., 28.

See also Templar (Sally).
Littlewood (Miss).

Sapsea's House. (*E.D.*). See High Street, Rochester.

Sapsea (Mr.). (*E.D.*). See Thomas (Jesse).

Satis House. (*G.E.*). See Restoration House, Rochester.

Saracen's Head, Towcester. (*P.P.*). See Pomfret Arms, Towcester.

Saracen's Head, Snow Hill. (*N.N.*). The inn where Mr. Squeers stayed when in town, and to which the jolly Yorkshireman John Browdie took his bride, was leased to Messrs Ormiston and Glass for business purposes in 1912. Although the present building is not the original Saracen's Head, the owners have commemorated its association with Dickens by placing a bust of the novelist over the doorway, and life-sized figures of Nicholas Nickleby and Wackford Squeers on either side. According to Mr. Roffey, the present building is not actually on the site of the Saracen's Head (which he says was where the new Police Station is). Mr. Hayward says the inn was at the top of Snow Hill, adjoining St. Sepulchre's Church, but Mr. Dexter states it was three doors from the Church. This is correct. Refs. *Dickensian* VIII., 87; *Dickens Encyclopaedia*; *The London of Dickens*.

SAWYER, LATE NOCKEMORF. (*P.P.*). See Park Street, Bristol.

SCHOOL (Mr. Giles's), at Chatham. The school which Dickens attended as a boy, at Chatham, was in Clover Lane, now Railway Street. Afterwards Mr. Giles moved to the corner of Rhode Street and Best Street, off the New Road.

SCHOOL (Our). (*R.P., O.S.*). See Wellington House Academy.

SCROOGE (EBENEZER). (*C.C.*). See Austin Friars.

SENS, France. About seventy miles from Paris, on the road to Switzerland. The continental town to which Mrs. Lirriper and the Major, with Jimmy, went to see the invalid. (*Mrs. L.'s Legacy*). The description of the Cathedral had an inaccuracy very unusual with Dickens. He said it was "two-towered," whereas it has only one tower, with another tower atop, like a sort of stone pulpit. The hotel where Mrs. Lirriper stayed was probably the Hotel de L'Ecu. It has a good view of the Cathedral, a balcony all round the first floor, and a courtyard, all as described. Ref. *Dickensian* XXIII., 201.

SEYMOUR HILL (Mrs.). A chiropodist of 6, York Gate, was stated in *The Town*, of Nov., 1838, to be the original of Miss Mowcher. (*D.C.*). Pugh repeats this in his *Dickens Originals*. Forster does not name her, but there seems to have been a real original of Miss Mowcher for he says she wrote to Dickens complaining that he had put her in his book.

SHARMAN'S HUT, Yarmouth. Said to have been the original of Peggotty's boat-hut on the sands at Yarmouth. (*D.C.*). Sharman was the custodian of the Nelson Monument and lived for many years in the hut, fashioned by himself, which had the appearance of being half ship and half shed, much sunk in the sand. There is no evidence that Dickens ever saw this hut, which was demolished in 1845, but he is stated to have met Sharman in 1848, and may have glorified the hut he heard about into a real vessel, which Sharman's hut did not really warrant. Another claimant to be the original of Peggotty's home, has been put forward in favour of a shanty which used to stand in Camden Road, but its authenticity is strongly denied by Dr. Bately. Ref. *Dickensian* V., 236. Both of these identifications are considered to be unsatisfactory.

See also Boat House at Gravesend.

SHAW (WILLIAM). Prototype of Wackford Squeers. (*N.N.*). Shaw was a notorious Yorkshire schoolmaster whom Dickens visited with Hablot K. Browne in the winter of 1837-38. He was an unprincipled London schemer who had opened a school at Bowes, on the distant Yorkshire moors. He kept cows and pigs and the scholars were usefully employed on the farm. In Dickens's diary, under the date Feb. 3rd, there is an entry which reads: "Shaw, the schoolmaster we saw to-day, is the man in whose school several boys went blind some time since, from gross neglect. The case was tried and the verdict went against him. It must have been between 1823 and 1826. Look this out in the newspapers." The cases here referred to were tried in October, 1823, and resulted in verdicts with £300 damages against Shaw. It is only fair to say that many other schoolmasters in that district were equally infamous, and when depicting Squeers Dickens intended to pillory the whole class and abolish the system of boy-farming. Ref. Forster's *Life of Dickens*; *With Dickens in Yorkshire*; *Letter from Dickens to Mrs. Hall, Dec.*, 1838.

SHEPHERD'S SHORE, Inn at. Said to be the original of the inn mentioned in the Bagman's story. (*P.P.*). According to the Rev. A. C. Smith, all North Wiltshiremen at once identified this inn as the scene of Tom Smart's adventure. From Beckhampton to Shepherd's Shore there is a three-mile stretch of as howling a wilderness as you may find anywhere, and from Shepherd's Shore towards Devizes another two miles of equally exposed road. Ref. *Dickensian* I., 244.

Other suggestions are the "Catherine Wheel" and the "Kennet Inn," both at Beckhampton.

See also Wagon and Horses, Beckhampton.

Ship and Lobster Tavern, Gravesend. Suggested by Frost in 1881 as the original of the Riverside Inn of *Great Expectations*. On his own showing, Frost was only in Gravesend half a day, and in the evening he walked along the river bank till he came to the "Ship and Lobster," opposite the official anchorage for ships and about three-quarters of a mile below Gravesend. "This," said Frost, "we decided must be the Riverside Inn of *Great Expectations*," but offered no reasons whatever for his guess. For anything he knew, there might have been half-a-dozen inns by the river more like the "Ship" inn of the story, and really were one or two which would better fit the description of the inn. Since Frost, other people have endeavoured to provide arguments in support of his wild guess, but no argument will make the "Ship and Lobster" fit Dickens's descriptions, which, after all, are the only true guide. The whole of chapter 54 of *Great Expectations* is quite irreconcilable with, and against the "Ship and Lobster." In its favour, however, it has been stated that there actually was a "Jack" employed there, just like the "Jack" of the story. If true, and Dickens knew the man before he wrote the novel, it is conceivable that he modelled his "Jack" upon this man, but that does not prove that he took the inn where the man was actually employed. It has also been urged that the tides and currents in the river frequently cause the bodies of drowned persons to be cast ashore near the "Ship and Lobster." Ref. *Dickensian* XXII., 31

See also Lobster Smack Inn.

Ship Hotel, Greenwich. Said to be the hotel where the wedding breakfast was held, after the marriage of Bella Wilfer, at which his Grace the Archbishop officiated. (*O.M.F.*).

Shop (Mr. **Omer's**). (*D.C.*). See Middlegate Street, Yarmouth.

Shorne Churchyard. There is very little doubt that the churchyard referred to in the "Tale of a Queer Client" (*P.P.*), as "one of the most peaceful and secluded churchyards in Kent," was the churchyard at Shorne, a village about two miles from Gravesend, and one of Dickens's favourite spots.

Singlewell, Kent. See Cobtree Hall.

Six Jolly Fellowship Porters. (*O.M.F.*). See Grapes Inn, Limehouse.

Skewton (Mrs.). (*D. & S.*). See Campbell.

Skiffins (Miss). (*G.E.*). Whilst no original of this virtuous character is known, it is interesting to hear that Dickens possibly adopted her name from the sign-board of a shop which was close to the back lanes, ditches and little gardens of Walworth. At the time Mr. Wemmick was supposed to inhabit his castle there a greengrocer named Skiffins carried on business in the Kent Road. Ref. *Dickensian* III., 307.

Skimpin (Mr.). (*P.P.*). See Wilkins.

Skimpole (**Harold**). (*B.H.*).
See Hunt (Leigh).
Haydon (Benjamin).

Slammer (Dr.). (*P.P.*). See Lamert (James).

Slinkton (**Julius**). (*H.D.*). See Wainwright (T. G.).

Sloman. Sloman's Spunging House at No. 2, Cursitor Street, has been stated to be the original of "*Coavinses*," so-called by Mr. Skimpole in *Bleak House*. Ref. *The Dickens Encyclopaedia*.

Sluice-Gate Hut, Cliffe Marshes. Probably the sluice-house to which Pip was decoyed by Orlick. (*G.E.*). It still stands on the bank of the filled-in canal which once connected a lime quarry with Cliffe Creek, where the lime was loaded into Thames barges. The last man to work the sluice-gates on the canal stated that the hut was there, and used by him, sixty odd years ago. Ref. *Dickensian* XXII., 185.

Sluice-House. (*G.E.*). See Sluice-Gate Hut, Cliffe Marshes.

Slum (Mr.). (*O.C.S.*). The first study for this character was founded upon one of the poets employed by the Blacking concern in Chandos Street, when Dickens worked there, as a boy. Ref. Forster's *Life of Dickens*.

Smart (**Tom**). Scene of his Adventure. (*P.P.*). See Wagon and Horses, Beckhampton.

Smike. (*N.N.*). More than one prototype of this pathetic character in *Nicholas Nickleby* has been put forward as the original on which the character was founded. Mr. E. Hardy, in 1911 confidently asserted that the original of Smike was a boy named Smith, whom he recollected personally. According to the late Peter Ball, who published a "History of Blackley" in 1892, a certain Bold Cooke of that neighbourhood who had been a pupil at Bowes Academy, said that Smike was a fellow-pupil of his and belonged to Higher Broughton, in Manchester. This boy actually ran away from the school because of the master's brutality, but was captured and unmercifully flogged two or three times in the presence of all the trembling boys. Cooke further said that the scholars were ill-fed, and plied with disgusting doses of brimstone and treacle; had no fire in the depth of winter, and were obliged to wash their faces with clay, in lieu of soap. All this may be true, but as regards Smike, Dickens's own words prove that he was a purely imaginary character suggested by a gravestone in Bowes churchyard. Writing to Mrs. Hall in December, 1838, he said: "There is an old Church near the School, and the first gravestone I stumbled on that dreary winter afternoon, was placed above the grave of a boy, 18 long years old, who had died suddenly—died at that wretched place. I think his ghost put Smike into my head, upon the spot." Ref. *Dickensian* VII., 11, 155; *Daily Telegraph*, Sept. 3, 1915.

SMORLTORK (Count). (*P.P.*). See Puckler-Muskau (Prince).

SNODGRASS (GABRIEL). See Originals founded on names.

SNODLAND, Kent. See Allington Weir.

SNOLLEDGE BOTTOM (commonly known as Snorridge Bottom). A long, deep valley or gulley between two ridges of high ground on the east side of the Chatham-Maidstone Road. The valley is mainly grazing land for cattle and sheep, but there are a few cherry orchards here and there. One of them is immediately behind Snodhurst Farm, which may have been the farm at which Gil Davis was employed. (*The Perils of Certain English Prisoners*). Ref. *Dickensian* XXII., 226.

SNORRIDGE BOTTOM. (*Perils of Certain English Prisoners*). See Snolledge Bottom.

SNUBBIN (Sergt.). (*P.P.*). See Arabin (Sergt.).

SOLOMONS (IKY). Suggested as the probable original upon whom Fagin the Jew was founded. (*O.T.*). Solomons was a notorious receiver of stolen property, and was in Newgate prison in 1831. Major Arthur Griffiths, sometime Governor of Newgate, gives a full account of Iky Solomon's career in *The Chronicles of Newgate*. In 1830, a play called "Van Diemen's Land" was produced at the Surrey Theatre. One of the characters in the play was named Barney Fence, a jew. After Iky Solomons had been tried and convicted, this play was revived, but Barney Fence was re-named Iky Solomons. It has been suggested that Dickens founded Fagin on the character in the play. Ref. *John o' London's Weekly*, Jan. 22, 1921.

SOL'S ARMS. (*B.H.*). See Old Ship Tavern.

SONDES ARMS, Rockingham. Original of the "Dedlock Arms" (*B.H.*). The "Sondes Arms," in Rockingham village, dates from 1763. Ref. *Dickensian Inns and Taverns*.

SOUTHAMPTON STREET, W.C. The original of "Billickins's" (*E.D.*) is said to be No. 20, Southampton Street. Ref. *The London of Dickens*.

SOUTHGATE HOUSE. *See* Westgate House.

SOUTH SQUARE, Gray's Inn. Formerly Holborn Court. At No. 2 were the Chambers of Tommy Traddles (*D.C.*). Traddle's chambers have also been said to be Dickens's own chambers in Furnival's Inn.

SOUTHWARK BRIDGE. The iron bridge of *Little Dorrit*. It was opened in 1819, and rebuilt about the year 1919.

SOWERBERRY (Mr.). (*O.T.*). See Originals founded upon names.

SPECKS (JOE). (*U.T.*). (Dulborough Town). See Brown (Dr. John).

SPENLOW (Dora). (*D.C.*). See Beadnell (Maria).

SPENLOW (Mr.). (*D.C.*). See Beadnell (George).

SPONG (W.). Of Cobtree Hall, near Maidstone. Said to be the original of old Mr. Wardle of Manor Farm (*P.P.*) but, in the writer's opinion, on very doubtful authority. In *The Pickwick Pilgrimages*, Mr. Dexter remarks that Dickens may possibly have met Mr. Spong and visited him at his house, driving over from Chalk, when staying there on his honeymoon. This would account for Mamie Dickens's statement about the back road from Rochester; but when we consider Dickens's position at the time of his marriage, and the improbability of his being acquainted with county families at that time, the suggestion does not seem to be very feasible.

SPRIGWIFFIN'S WHARF. See Upper Thames Street.

SQUARE (The), in which was the business house of the Cheeryble Bros. (*N.N.*). See Square (The), Ramsbottom.

SQUARE (The), Ramsbottom. The works of the Brothers Grant at Ramsbottom were called "The Square," and it has been suggested that the description of the Cheeryble Bros.' warehouse as in a small square in the City of London was deceptive. This seems to be very far-fetched. It is generally thought that the house of Cheeryble was somewhere between Threadneedle Street, Cornhill, Finch Lane, and Bishopsgate.

SQUAT, SHOAL LIGHTHOUSE. (*G.E.*). See Mucking Flat Lighthouse.

Squod (Phil). (*B.H.*). Supposed to be founded on an attendant or porter, named Phil, at Wellington House Academy.

Squeers (Wackford). (*N.N.*). See Shaw (William).

Staple Inn. The letters P.J.T. presented in black-and-white over the ugly portal of a set of chambers in the little quadrangle of Staple Inn, which Dickens surmised might haply have meant " Perhaps John Thomas," or " Perhaps Joe Tyler," are the initials of President James Taylor, 1747. Ref. *The London of Dickens.*

Star Hotel, Yarmouth. Supposed to be the hotel where David Copperfield and Steerforth met the volatile MissMowcher Ref. *Dickensian Inns and Taverns.*

Stareleigh (Mr. Justice). (*P.P.*). See Gaselee (Sir Stephen).

Steepways. (*M. from the Sea*). See Clovelly.

Steerforth (Mrs.). house of. (*D.C.*). See Church House, Highgate.

Steerforth. (*D.C.*). See Stroughill (George).

Stiggins Bro. (*P.P.*). See Originals founded upon names.

Strong (Dr.). (*D.C.*).
See Birt (Rev. J.).
Lady Wootton's Green.

Strong (Miss Mary). The original of Betsy Trotwood (*D.C.*) on the authority of Charles Dickens, junior. Miss Strong resided in a double-fronted cottage in Nuttall's Place, on the sea front at Broadstairs, and was firmly convinced that she had a right to prevent the passage of donkeys past her door. In pursuance of this conviction she used to harry the donkey-drivers with a hearth-broom. The *Dickens Atlas* gives Miss Trotwood's probable location as Priory Hill, Dover,but Dickens appears to have transferred the Broadstairs cottage to that town, in accordance with his frequent practice. Ref. *Dickensian* IV., 240.

Stroughill (George). A Companion of Dickens's boyhood. He lived at No. 1, Ordnance Terrace, Chatham, when the Dickens family were at No. 11. The character of Steerforth (*D.C.*) is stated to have been founded upon him. His sister Lucy is also said to have served as the model for some of the novelist's female characters, including the child in the *Wreck of the Golden Mary*, but although the bare statements have been repeatedly made, the writer has been unable to find any reference to the originator.

See also Originals founded on names.

Stroughill (Lucy). Generally considered to be the original of Lucy Green, who married Joe [Specks (*U.T.*). The Stroughills were among Dickens's early friends and neighbours at Ordnance Terrace, Chatham, and the identification may quite possibly be correct, but the originator is not known, and his evidence may, or may not be convincing.

Also said to be the original of Lucie Manette. (*T.T.C.*).

Stryver, Q.C. (*T.T.C.*). See James (Edwin).

Stryver's Chambers. (*T.T.C.*). See Dr. Johnson's Buildings.

Sudbury, Suffolk. Original of Eatanswill. (*P.P.*). Dickens reported an election here in 1834 or 1835, and said " open house is kept at all the inns in the town ; the voters are seen reeling about the streets in a beastly state of intoxication. Cooping and other manœuvres have been resorted to to procure voters." The " Rose and Crown " Inn situated in King Street, close to the Market Place, was the headquarters of the Blue faction at this election, and evidently stands for the Town Arms, Eatanswill. The old " Rose and Crown " was unfortunately destroyed by fire in January, 1922. The " Peacock," where Messrs. Winkle and Snodgrass put up, might have been the " Four Swans " hotel in North Street. The name Eatanswill may possibly have been suggested to Dickens by Eaton Socon, a signpost bearing that name, which he would have passed on his coach journeys, stands 55½ miles down the Great North Road. Ref. *Dickensian* III., 117, 133 ; IV., 75.

Other claimants to being the original of Eatanswill are Bury St. Edmunds, Ipswich and Norwich. It is generally agreed, however, that the evidence is all in favour of Sudbury.

Summerson (Esther). (*B.H.*). See Elton (Esther).

Sun Inn, Canterbury. This quaint little hostel in Sun Street is usually stated to be the original of the little Inn where Mr. and Mrs. Micawber received David Copperfield. The inn sign claims that the place was made famous by Dickens in his rambles in Kent, whatever that may mean. Another claimant to be the original of Micawber's little inn is the " Queen's Head," at the corner of Watling Street and St. Margaret's Street. Neither of these identifications can be said to have been substantiated, and further investigation is required.

Surrey Theatre. Possibly the theatre where Frederick Dorrit played the clarionette in the orchestra. (*L.D.*). It was burned down in 1868. Ref. *The London of Dickens.*

SWAN INN, Hungerford Stairs. The original of the little, dirty, tumble-down public-house where Mr. Micawber and his family were lodged just before their departure for Australia. The " Swan " was exactly on the spot described, and was in existence when Dickens worked, as a boy, in the blacking factory, close by. Ref. *Dickensian Inns and Taverns.*

SWAN HOTEL, West Malling. Suggested as the original of the " Blue Lion " at Muggleton (*P.P.*), but until the vexed question of which town was Muggleton is settled, the identification cannot be fully accepted. Ref. *Inns and Taverns of Pickwick.*

If Town Malling be Muggleton, however, it is by no means certain that the " Swan " was the original of the inn where the Pickwickians were deposited by the Muggleton Telegraph. Another hotel, in the main street, seems to more nearly fit the description.

See Bear Hotel, Malling.

SWEEDLEPIPE (POL.). (*M.C.*). The original of this character has been claimed to be the father of Willie Clarkson, the wig-maker, but the evidence does not appear to be very strong. Ref. *John o' London's Weekly*, Jan. 20, 1923.

The name " Pol " was taken from a fellow-worker at the blacking warehouse named Paul (Pol) Green, but of course Pol Green was not the original of Pol Sweedlepipe in any other respect.

SWINTON STREET, Grays Inn Road. See Acton Street.

T., J.P. See Staple Inn.

TALFOURD (Judge). According to Edwin Pugh, the original of Tommy Traddles. (*D.C.*). Sergeant Talfourd was a friend of Dickens, and the *Pickwick Papers* were dedicated to him.

TAPPERTIT (SIMON). (*B.R.*). See Mitton (Thos.).

TAVERN IN THE MINT. (*On duty with Inspector Field*). See Bull Inn, Birdcage Alley.

TAVISTOCK HOTEL. See Piazza Hotel.

TAYLOR (Mr.). See Goldsmith (Oliver).

TAYLOR (PRESIDENT JAMES). See Staple Inn.

TELLSON'S BANK. (*T.T.C.*). See Child's Bank.

TEMPLAR (SALLY). Suggested by G. W. Hilburn as the original of Miss Flite (*B.H.*). Sally Templar was found, as an infant, abandoned on the steps of one of the Inns of Court, and was supported by the various Inns. She was a constant visitor at the Courts, but not at all mad. Ref. *Daily News*, Aug., 1906.

TENTERDEN. See Muggleton.

TERRETT'S PLACE, Islington. Suggested as the place where Tom Pinch and his sister had lodgings. (*M.C.*). Terrett's Place is, or was, close to No. 146 (formerly 102), Upper Street, where Upcott lived. Dickens visited him in 1830. Ref. *Dickensian* XX., 159.

THEATRE. (*L.D.*). See Surrey Theatre.

THIEVES' KITCHEN. (*R.P. On duty with Inspector Field*). See Fox Court.

THIRSTY WOMAN OF TUTBURY. (*N.N.*). See Moore (Ann).

THOMAS (JESSE). According to Mr. Edwin Harris, the original of Mr. Sapsea, the pompous Mayor of Cloisterham. (*E.D.*). Thomas was Mayor of Rochester in 1857, and was an auctioneer in High Street, Chatham. He had a distinctly clerical appearance, which he cultivated, and always wore a silk hat, or a round clerical one, and a black frock coat. In *Edwin Drood*, Dickens described the wooden effigy of an auctioneer as being over the door of Mr. Sapsea's house. This effigy really existed and was as real as the wooden Midshipman of Leadenhall Street, but it was fixed outside the sale-room of John Batten, an auctioneer at St. Margaret's Banks, whilst Mr. Sapsea's house was over against the Nun's house in Eastgate, Rochester. Batten's sale-room is now a Savings Bank.

THOMAS STREET, Portsmouth. No. 78 has been identified as the house of the Pilot, where Mr. and Mrs. Crummles lodged during their stay in Portsmouth. Thomas Street runs parallel with the High Street, where the Theatre was. (*N.N.*). Ref. *The Dickens Atlas.*

THREE JOLLY BARGEMEN. (*G.E.*). See Old Chequers Inn, Lower Higham.

THREE PIGEONS, Brentford. The original of the " Three Magpies," where Mr. Boffin's equipage was left, while the Secretary and Bella Wilfer went in search of the orphan. (*O.M.F.*). The " Three Pigeons " was closed in 1916. Ref. *Dickensian* XII., 32, 67.

TICE (HARRIET LUCY). Born at the Old Curiosity Shop, in Compton Street, in 1827, and said to be the original of Little Nell (*O.C.S.*). She was the daughter of John Pepperill, an inveterate gambler, as a consequence of which vice father and daughter had to take to a roving life not unlike that depicted in the *Old Curiosity Shop.* Ref. *Daily Chronicle*, Mar. 12, 1914.

In *The Dickens Originals* Pugh says the original of Little Nell was Dickens's sister-in-law Mary Hogarth. On the other hand Forster stated that Little Nell was a purely imaginary character, which is probably true.

TILTED WAGON. (*E.D.*). See Coach and Horses, Strood Hill.

TINSLEY. According to the writer of " *Sixty-seven Years in the Temple*," the original of Sampson Brass (*O.C.S.*) was an attorney named Tinsley, who lived in Rolls Buildings. Sally Brass was Mrs. Tinsley, who assisted her husband and always appeared at the door with a pen behind her ear. Ref. *Daily News*, Aug. 8, 1906.

TITBULL'S ALMSHOUSES. (*U.T.*). See Vintner's Almshouses.

TODD (THOMAS). Said to be the orignal of John Browdie. (*N.N.*). Todd was a native of Bowes, the village where Dotheboys Hall was situated, and was a big, bluff, hearty Yorkshireman, locally recognised as the prototype of John Browdie. He died in June, 1885. Ref. *Dickensian* VII., 11.
See also Barnes (Richard).

TOM-ALL-ALONES. (*B.H.*). A region of slums where the new part of York Street, Covent Garden, now is. In Dickens's boyhood it is said there was a place at the back of Chatham lines belonging to a man named Thomas Clarke, who used to cry "Tom's all alone" as he went home at night, and the place thus came to be known as Tom-all-alones. Possibly Dickens adopted from this the name of the rookery near Covent Garden. Ref. *Dickensian* I., 202.

TOM'S COFFEE HOUSE. Suggested as the noted coffee house where Mr. Chester had an interview with Hugh. (*B.R.*). Other people say Curtriss's coffee house was the place.

TONG CHURCH. Shifnal, Salop. Generally agreed to be the church where Little Nell died. (*O.C.S.*). The church, which has a remarkable tower, was built in 1510, and dedicated to St. Mary the Virgin and St. Bartholomew. Dickens himself told the late Archdeacon Lloyd that Tong was the church he was thinking of, when he wrote the closing scenes of the *Old Curiosity Shop*. Ref. *Dickensian* III., 273.
See also London to Tong.

TOODLE (POLLY). (*D. & S.*). See Hayes (Mrs.).

TOOK'S COURT, Cursitor Street. Original of Cook's Court, Cursitor Street. (*B.H.*). Some of the old houses in the street remained until recent years, and one of them was the house and shop of Mr. Snagsby, law stationer, where he and his little woman received the Rev. and Mrs. Chadband on a certain occasion. The district is still largely occupied by law stationers and retains the atmosphere of *Bleak House*.

TOPE (Mr.). (*E.D.*). See Miles (William)

TOWER DOCK, No. 6. See Tower Hill.

TOWER HILL. No. 2, Tower Hill (formerly No. 6, Tower Dock) was identified as the original of Quilp's house. (*O.C.S.*). It was demolished about a dozen years since. Tower Dock was part of the west side of Tower Hill, between Great Tower Street and Lower Thames Street. In 1811, No. 6 was a tavern with the sign of the "Three Tuns." Quilp's Wharf was on the Surrey side of the river, close to the present Tower Bridge. Ref. *Dickensian* X., 95.

TOWN (SMALL). (*B.R.*). See Luton.

TRADDLES (TOMMY). (*D.C.*). See Talfourd (Judge).

TRAVELLERS' TWOPENNY. (*E.D.*). See White Duck, Rochester.

TROOD (EDWIN). See Originals founded on names.

TROTWOOD (BETSEY). (*D.C.*). See Strong (Mary).

TUBBY, A SHOWMAN. Said to be the original of Harris and of Short, Punch and Judy showmen. (*O.C.S.*). The statement is of no value.

TULKINGHORN (Mr.). House of. (*B.H.*). See Lincoln's Inn Fields.

TUPMAN (TRACY). (*P.P.*). See Chapman (Lacey).

TURK'S HEAD, Exeter. See Budden.

TURNPIKE GATE. (*G.E.*). This was at Strood, at the junction of the High Street and the Cliffe Road, on the direct way to the village of Lower Higham. The gate, which was erected in 1768 and demolished in 1876, stood across the High Street, or Watling Street, and its little gate-house with the lamp that appeared to Pip to be quite out of its usual place, one foggy night, adjoined the old "Angel" Inn, on the same site as the present "Angel." Ref. *Dickensian* XXII., 238.

TURVEYDROP (Prince). See Dickens (Fanny).

TURVEYDROP'S DANCING ACADEMY. (*B.H.*) See Newman Street.

TWIST (OLIVER). (*O.T.*). See Originals founded upon names.

UNION ROAD (formerly Horsemonger Lane), Southwark. No. 5 has been identified as the shop of John Chivery, at one time turnkey at the Marshalsea Debtors' Prison. (*L.D.*). Dickens described the shop as "a rural establishment, one story high, situate round the corner in Horsemonger Lane, which had the benefit of the air from the yards of Horsemonger Lane jail, and the advantage of a retired walk under the walls of that establishment." The small house has now a modern brick front, but is remembered to have been a tobacconist's shop years ago, with a small Highlander on a bracket at the door. Ref. *Dickensian* V., 10.

UPPER THAMES STREET. The business house of Mrs. Clennam, and her partner Mr. Flintwinch (*L.D.*), was somewhere in this neighbourhood, for Arthur Clennam crossed by St. Paul's and went down at a long angle, almost to the water's edge, through some of the crooked and descending streets between the river and Cheapside. Sprigwiffin's Wharf, where Mrs. and Miss Nickleby were lodged by the latter's uncle Ralph, was a large, old, dingy house in Thames Street. Ref. *Dickensian* XVIII., 198.

VALE (SAM). See Weller (Sam).

VENUS (Mr.). (*O.M.F.*). See Willis (J.).

VILLAGE MAID, Lound. The original of the inn where Barkis the carrier made his first halt to deliver a bedstead. The "Village Maid" at Lound may also have suggested the name of the Inn, the "Willing Mind," where Daniel Peggotty sometimes went for relaxation. There is no inn of that name at Yarmouth. Ref. *Dickensian Inns and Tavens.*

VILLAGE ON THE MARSHES. (*G.E.*). See Lower Higham.

VINES (THE), Rochester. The Monk's vineyard of *Edwin Drood.* Dickens here gave it its true name, for it was at one time the vineyard belonging to the Priory of St. Andrew. It is also the Priory Garden mentioned in *Great Expectations.* The Vines are now leased to the Corporation, and laid out as gardens.

VINTNER'S ALMSHOUSES, Mile End Road. The almshouses referred to in the *Uncommercial Traveller,* chap. 29. Dickens described these as Titbull's Almshouses, in the East of London, in a great highway. in a poor, busy, and thronged neighbourhood; and as having a little paved courtyard in front, enclosed by iron railings. It has been suggested that Dickens meant the Almshouses at Cobham, but there is obviously no justification for this. A more reasonable suggestion would be the little Almshouses with a paved courtyard and iron railings in Chatham High Street, but as the Vintner's Almshouses in Mile End Road are where Dickens said Titbull's were, and they conform to the picture, there is no need to look elsewhere.

It has also been suggested that Titbull's Almshouses are "reminiscent" of Almshouses on the east side of Bayham Street, Camden Town, although Dickens distinctly placed them in the East End of London.

WAINWRIGHT (THOMAS GRIFFITHS). Said to be the original of Blandois, *alias* Rigaud. (*L.D.*). Also of Jonas Chuzzlewit (*M.C.*), and Julius Slinkton (*Hunted Down*).

Wainwright was born in 1794, of good family, but was criminally inclined. Under the cloak of a dilettante in art and literature he became a forger, and secret poisoner of relatives to obtain insurance money. Dickens saw him in Newgate about 1838 or 1839, and was struck with the shabby-genteel felon. While in Newgate, Wainwright is said to have made the following speech, which has its counterpart in *Little Dorrit*: "I have always been a gentleman, always lived like a gentleman, and I am a gentleman still. Yes sir, even in Newgate, I am a gentleman. The prison regulations are that we should, each in turn, sweep the yard. There are a barber and a sweep here besides myself. They sweep the yard; but, sir, they have never offered me the broom." Ref. *Dickensian* II., 291.

Compare the above speech with those of Monsieur Rigaud, *alias* Lagnier, *alias* Blandois in chapters I. and XI. of *Little Dorrit*: "Ha-ha! you are right! a gentleman I am, a gentleman I'll live, and a gentleman I'll die. Its my intent to be a gentleman. It's my game. Death of my soul, I play it out wherever I go." "Cavaletto! give me your hand. You know Lagnier the gentleman. Touch the hand of a gentleman."

WAITER (THE FRIENDLY). (*D.C.*). See Duke's Head, Yarmouth.

WAGON AND HORSES, Beckhampton. Original of the inn described in the bagman's story. (*P.P.*). B. W. Matz accepted this inn as the scene, and Mr. Dexter gives it as "said to be the inn," in *Mr. Pickwick's Pilgrimages.* The "Wagon and Horses," Beckhampton, certainly bears out the book description in its outward appearance. It was identified as the original by C. G. Harper (*The Old Inns of Old England*).

Another inn suggested is the "Marquis of Ailsbury" at Clatford.

See also Shepherd's Shore.

WARD of Chas. Dickens. See Elton Esther.

WARDLE (Mr.). (*P.P.*). See Spong (W.).

WARDOUR (Richard). See Allen (Gordon).

WARMINGTON. 5 miles from Banbury, on the Warwick road. Probably the village where the kind school-master befriended the travellers. (*O.C.S*). Ref. *The England of Dickens.*

WARREN (The) (*B.R.*). See Loughton Hall.

WARWICK. Suggested by Mr. Dexter as the town where Little Nell exhibited the wax figures. (*O.C.S.*) Ref. *The England of Dickens.*

WARREN'S BLACKING FACTORY. See Blacking Factory.

WATSON (ROBERT), Secretary to Lord Gordon at the time of the No Popery Riots in 1780. Said to be the original of Gashford (*B.R.*). Robert Watson was born in 1746 and had a remarkable career, committing suicide in 1838. Whether Dickens had Lord George Gordon's real secretary in mind when depicting Gashford is difficult to decide, but there are points of similarity in the two characters and the latter was made to commit suicide as did the former. Each died, by his own hand, at an inn. Ref. *Dickensian* II., 39 ; XXI., 43.

WATTS' CHARITY. See High Street, Rochester.

WATSON (Hon. Mrs.). Dickens's hostess at Rockingham Castle. Said to be the original of Lady Dedlock. (*B.H.*). The authority for this is not known, but anyone more unlike the character of Lady Dedlock it is difficult to imagine.

WEGG (SILAS). (*O.M.F.*). The original of this character is stated to be a well-known character who, for many years, kept a ballad and gingerbread stall near Cavendish Square. Ref. *The Dickens Encyclopaedia*.

WELBECK STREET, Cavendish Square. No. 64 is said to be the house where Lord George Gordon lived. (*B.R.*).

WELLER (MARY). Dickens's early nurse, who afterwards married Mr. Gibson, a shipwright in Chatham Dockyard, is stated to have been the original of Sam Weller's sweetheart, housemaid to Mr. Nupkins of Ipswich. (*P.P.*). Mrs. Gibson died in 1888. She has also been said to be the original of Peggotty (*D.C.*), which seems reasonably likely.

WELLER (SAM). (*P.P.*). It has been commonly stated that the original of this character was Sam Vale, the actor, but Vale only acted a part and spoke the words written for him by someone else. He was no more the original of Sam Weller than he was the original of any other Dickens character. Wellerisms were a common form of wit in the early part of the nineteenth century. Scott employed it in Rob Roy (1818) ; and Longfellow adopted it again in *The Spanish Student*, in 1840, after *Pickwick* had appeared. In depicting Sam Weller Dickens employed the popular form of wit of the time, and made him a topical as well as a typical Cockney, but the character did not consist of witty sayings only. According to Marcus Stone, the artist, Dickens admitted to him that a fruiterer in Chatham market was more or less the immortal man. The name, and possibly some characteristics, might have been taken from Weller of Chatham, but Sam himself had no one prototype. Dickens's early nurse was named Mary Weller. Another suggested original was Joe Baldwin, buried in Rainham Churchyard. Ref. *Dickensian* IV., 193 ; VI., 63 ; VIII., 317 ; *The Dickens Originals*.

WELLER (THOMAS). See Weller (Tony).

WELLER (TONY). (*P.P.*). Various originals have been claimed for the elder Mr. Weller. Mrs. Lynn Linton (from whom Dickens purchased Gadshill Place), and other people in Rochester confidently recognised in Tony Weller the old coachman Chumley, who drove the Rochester coach to and from London daily. According to the *Dickens Originals*, Tony Weller was in real life a certain Cole, driver of the Ipswich coach ; and Mr. E. Harris has suggested Thomas Weller, who kept the " Granby Head " inn at Chatham, where Barnard's music hall now stands. The probability is that Tony Weller is merely a typical stage-coach driver, founded on Dickens's extensive acquaintance with coachmen.

WELLINGTON HOUSE ACADEMY, Mornington Place, Hampstead Road. Probably the original of " Our School." (*R.P.*). The school-room and part of the house, were sliced away when the London-Birmingham railway was built, about 1835. Ref. *The London of Dickens*.

The Birmingham railway was opened to traffic on the 17th of September, 1838. Wellington House is also suggested as the original of Salem House School. (*D.C.*).

WEMMICK. (*G.E.*). See Mitton (Thos.).

WEMMICK, MARRIAGE OF. (*G.E.*). See St. Giles', Camberwell.

WESTGATE HOUSE, Bury St. Edmunds. (*P.P.*). The scene of Mr. Pickwick's adventure at the Ladies' School has been variously stated to be (1) Southgate House, (2) Pageant House, Bury St. Edmunds, (3) The High School at Bury, and (4) Eastgate House, Rochester. Possibly Dickens had the latter chiefly in mind when he described the place in *Pickwick*, but the question cannot be said to be settled.

WHITE DUCK, Rochester. Original of the " Traveller's Twopenny." (*E.D.*). It was a somewhat disreputable public-house in Maidstone Road, or Crow Lane, as it was then. It was also known as Kit's lodging house, and Mr. E. Harris says it was locally designated " The Traveller's Threepenny " in his young days. In the original manuscript of *Edwin Drood*, Dickens wrote " Travellers' Threepenny," but altered the last word to " Twopenny " in the proof-sheets.

WHITE HART, Greenhithe. A study of chapter 54 of *Great Expectations*, in conjunction with the set of the tides and currents from London Bridge to

Gravesend, makes it possible to locate the little riverside inn where the boat-party got ashore to buy some bottles of beer. The writer has in this way located the inn as the "White Hart" at Greenhithe, a village some five miles above Gravesend. Sir John Franklin slept at this inn the night before he sailed on his last and fatal voyage to the Arctic seas, in May, 1845.

WHITE HART, St. John Street, Salisbury. Said to be the hotel where John Westlock entertained Martin Chuzzlewit and Tom Pinch to dinner. Ref. *Dickensian Inns and Taverns.*

WHITE HART, Southwark. (*P.P.*). This well-known coaching inn at 61, High Street, in the Borough, was the inn where Sam Weller was first encountered by Mr. Pickwick. It was pulled down in 1889. Several writers have stated that the George Inn, near by, and which still remains, was the one Dickens meant, but this is quite wrong. The "George" was a similar inn to the "White Hart," and serves to show what the latter was like, but it was not the inn Dickens described. Ref. *Dickensian* XVI., 222; *Inns and Taverns of Pickwick.*

WHITE HART, Stevenage. Identified by F. C. Kitton as the original of the "Peal o' Bells" Inn mentioned in *Tom Tiddler's Ground.*
See also Lucas (James).

WHITECHAPEL WORKHOUSE. It was at the entrance to the casual ward of this Institution, in Thomas Street, that Dickens saw on a dark, muddy and rainy night, in November, 1855, what he described as "five bundles of rags"—dumb, wet, silent horrors. These were all wretched girls or young women shut out of the already full casual ward, and designing to spend the whole of the wet night on the steps. Dickens gave each of them a shilling with which to purchase a night's lodging but received no thanks. The five bundles got up and went away without a word, one after the other. Ref. *M.P.*, *A night scene in London.*

WICK HOUSE, Brighton. See Chichester House.

WICKFIELD (AGNES). (*D.C.*).
See Hogarth (Mary).
Hogarth (Georgina).

WICKFIELD (Mr.), HOUSE OF. (*D.C.*). See St. Dunstan's Street, Canterbury.

WIGMORE STREET. It is stated, on very doubtful evidence, that No. 11 was the establishment of Madam Mantalini. (*N.N.*). Ref. *Dickens Encyclopaedia.*

WILFER (Mrs.). (*O.M.F.*). See Dickens (Mrs. John).

WILLIS (J.) Stated by Percy Fitzgerald to be the original of Mr. Venus, the despondent articulator of human warious in *Our Mutual Friend.* Willis had a shop at 42, St. Andrew's Street, Seven Dials, and Fitzgerald asserted that Dickens admitted to him the correctness of the identification.

WILLIS (TOM). A showman, said to be the original of Codlin, senior partner in the firm of Codlin and Short, Punch and Judy showmen. (*O.C.S.*). The original statement has not been found.

WILKINS (Mr.). A well-known lawyer in Dickens's time is suggested as "very likely" to have sat for Mr. Skimpin, the junior counsel who appeared, under the leadership of Sergt. Buzfuz, for the plaintiff in Bardell *v.* Pickwick. (*P.P.*). Ref. *The Dickens Originals.*

WILLING MIND TAVERN. (*D.C.*). See Village Maid, Lound.

WINTER (Mr.). See Chapman (Lacey).

WINTER (Mrs. HENRY). See Beadnell (Maria).

WOOD, IN WHICH JONAS MURDERED TIGG. (*M.C.*). See Clarendon Park.

WOOD (Mrs. SOMERVILLE). See Monckton (Hon. Miss).

WOODEN MIDSHIPMAN. (*D. & S.*). The little wooden Midshipman that once stood at the door of Solomon Gills's instrument shop in Leadenhall Street, can still be seen inside the shop of Messrs. Ismay, Laurie, Norie and Wilson, 123 Minories. Dickens said the wooden Midshipman had his right leg thrust foremost, but as a matter of fact it is the left leg which is advanced, while the Midshipman takes a sight through that "most offensively disproportionate piece of machinery"—his sextant.

WORK-HOUSE GIRL. See Marchioness.

WREN (JENNY). (*O.M.F.*).
See Mitford (Mary).
Church Street, Millbank.

WRIGHT'S HOTEL. See Crown Inn, Rochester.

YORK HOUSE, Bath. The present York House in George Street, was the Royal Hotel described in *Pickwick.* Queen Victoria stayed there in 1830. Ref. *The Pickwick Pilgrimages.*

YORK STREET, Covent Gardens. See Tom-all-alones.

ZOAR CHAPEL. Great Alie Street, Goodman's Fields (now a warehouse), claimed by local tradition to be the original of the Little Bethel which Mrs. Nubbles attended. (*O.C.S.*). Zoar Chapel, however, could not be described as "a particularly little Bethel," but was a good-sized specimen of a seventeenth-century conventicle, built for Elias Keach, a popular preacher, in 1698. Ref. *Dickensian* IX., 233.
See also Orange Street Chapel.

List of Abbreviations.

Abbreviation.	Title.
A. N.	*American Notes.*
B. H.	*Bleak House.*
B. R.	*Barnaby Rudge.*
C. B., B. of L.	*Christmas Books, Battle of Life.*
C. B., C.	*Christmas Books, Chimes.*
C. B., C. C.	*Christmas Books, Christmas Carol.*
C. B., C. o. H.	*Christmas Books, Cricket on the Hearth.*
C. S., D. M. P.	*Christmas Stories, Dr. Marigold's Prescription.*
C. S., H. H.	*Christmas Stories, Haunted House.*
C. S., H. T.	*Christmas Stories, Holly Tree.*
C. S., H. to L.	*Christmas Stories, House to Let.*
C. S., M. f. S.	*Christmas Stories, Message from the Sea.*
C. S., M. J.	*Christmas Stories, Mugby Junction.*
C. S., M. L. L.	*Christmas Stories, Mrs. Lirriper's Legacy.*
C. S., M. L. Lo.	*Christmas Stories, Mrs. Lirriper's Lodgings.*
C. S., N. T.	*Christmas Stories, No Thoroughfare.*
C. S., P. o. C. E. P.	*Christmas Stories, Perils of Certain English Prisoners.*
C. S., S. L.	*Christmas Stories, Somebody's Luggage.*
C. S., S. P. T.	*Christmas Stories, Seven Poor Travellers.*
C. S., T. T. G.	*Christmas Stories, Tom Tiddler's Ground.*
C. S., W. o. G. M.	*Christmas Stories, Wreck of the "Golden Mary."*
D. and S.	*Dombey and Son.*
D. C.	*History of David Copperfield.*
E. D.	*Mystery of Edwin Drood.*
G. E.	*Great Expectations.*
G. S. E.	*George Silverman's Explanation.*
H. D.	*Hunted Down.*
H. R.	*Holiday Romance.*
H. T.	*Hard Times.*
L. D.	*Little Dorrit.*
L. T.	*Lazy Tour of two Idle Apprentices.*
M. C.	*Life and Adventures of Martin Chuzzlewit.*
M. H. C.	*Master Humphrey's Clock.*
M. P., A. A. P.	*Miscellaneous Papers, Adelaide Anne Procter.*
M. P., A. in E.	*Miscellaneous Papers, American in Europe.*
M. P., A. in H. W.	*Miscellaneous Papers, Address (Announcement) in "Household Words."*
M. P., A. J. B.	*Miscellaneous Papers, Crisis in the Affairs of Mr. John Bull.*
M. P., A. o. P.	*Miscellaneous Papers, Amusements of the People.*
M. P., A. P.	*Miscellaneous Papers, American Panorama.*
M. P., A. Y. R.	*Miscellaneous Papers, Address, . . . in the twentieth volume . . . of "All the Year Round."*
M. P., Ag. Int.	*Miscellaneous Papers, Agricultural Interest.*
M. P., B.	*Miscellaneous Papers, Blacksmith.*
M. P., B. A.	*Miscellaneous Papers, Best Authority.*
M. P., B. L.	*Miscellaneous Papers, British Lion.*
M. P., B. S.	*Miscellaneous Papers, Betting Shops.*
M. P., C.	*Miscellaneous Papers, Chips.*

ABBREVIATION.	TITLE.
M. P., C. C. ...	*Miscellaneous Papers, Court Ceremonies.*
M. P., C. E. ...	*Miscellaneous Papers, Crime and Education.*
M. P., C. H. ...	*Miscellaneous Papers, Child's Hymn.*
M. P., C. H. T. ...	*Miscellaneous Papers, Chauncy Hare Townshend.*
M. P., C. J. ...	*Miscellaneous Papers, Chinese Junk.*
M. P., C. M. B. ...	*Miscellaneous Papers, Card from Mr. Booley.*
M. P., C. P. ...	*Miscellaneous Papers, Capital Punishment.*
M. P., C. Pat. ...	*Miscellaneous Papers, Cheap Patriotism.*
M. P., D. M. ...	*Miscellaneous Papers, Demeanour of Murderers.*
M. P., D. V. ...	*Miscellaneous Papers, December Vision.*
M. P., D. C. ...	*Miscellaneous Papers, Cruikshank's Drunkard's Children*
M. P., E. A. S. ...	*Miscellaneous Papers, Edinburgh Apprentice School Association.*
M. P., E. C. ...	*Miscellaneous Papers, Enlightened Clergyman.*
M. P., E. S. ...	*Miscellaneous Papers, Narrative of Extraordinary Suffering.*
M. P., E. T. ...	*Miscellaneous Papers, Some Account of an Extraordinary Traveller.*
M. P., F. and S.	*Miscellaneous Papers, Fire and Snow.*
M. P., F. C. ...	*Miscellaneous Papers, Few Conventionalities.*
M. P., F. F. ...	*Miscellaneous Papers, Frauds on the Fairies.*
M. P., F. L. ...	*Miscellaneous Papers, Fast and Loose.*
M. P., F. O. E. G.	*Miscellaneous Papers, Fine Old English Gentleman.*
M. P., F. of the L.	*Miscellaneous Papers, The Friend of the Lions.*
M. P., F. N. P. ...	*Miscellaneous Papers, Five New Points of Criminal Law*
M. P., F. S. ...	*Miscellaneous Papers, Finishing Schoolmaster.*
M. P., G. A. ...	*Miscellaneous Papers, Gone Astray.*
M. P., G. B. ...	*Miscellaneous Papers, Great Baby.*
M. P., G. D. ...	*Miscellaneous Papers, Gone to the Dogs.*
M. P., G. F. ...	*Miscellaneous Papers, Gaslight Fairies.*
M. P., G. H. ...	*Miscellaneous Papers "Good" Hippopotamus.*
M. P., G. L. A.	*Miscellaneous Papers, Guild of Literature and Art.*
M. P., H. H. ...	*Miscellaneous Papers, Haunted House.*
M. P., H.H.W.	*Miscellaneous Papers, Home for Homeless Women.*
M. P., I. ...	*Miscellaneous Papers, Insularities.*
M. P., I. and C. ...	*Miscellaneous Papers, Ignorance and Crime.*
M. P., I. C. ...	*Miscellaneous Papers, International Copyright.*
M. P., I. M. ...	*Miscellaneous Papers, Idea of Mine.*
M. P., I. M. T. ...	*Miscellaneous Papers, In Memoriam: W. M. Thackeray*
M. P., I. S. H. W.	*Miscellaneous Papers, Is She His Wife?*
M. P., I. W. M. ...	*Miscellaneous Papers, Great International Walking Match.*
M. P., J. G. ...	*Miscellaneous Papers, Joseph Grimaldi.*
M. P., J. O. ...	*Miscellaneous Papers, John Overs.*
M. P., J. S. P. ...	*Miscellaneous Papers, Judical Special Pleading.*
M. P., J. T. ...	*Miscellaneous Papers, Late Mr. Justice Talfourd.*
M. P., L. ...	*Miscellaneous Papers, Lamplighter.*
M. P., L. A. V. ...	*Miscellaneous Papers, Lost Arctic Voyagers.*
M. P., L. E. J.	*Miscellaneous Papers, Legal and Equitable Jokes.*
M. P., L. H. ...	*Miscellaneous Papers, Leigh Hunt, A Remonstrance.*
M. P., L. L. ...	*Miscellaneous Papers, Landor's Life.*
M. P., L. S. ...	*Miscellaneous Papers, Late Mr. Stanfield.*

ABBREVIATION.	TITLE.
M. P., L. T. ...	*Miscellaneous Papers, Lively Turtle.*
M. P., L. W. O. Y.	*Miscellaneous Papers, Last Woods of the Old Year.*
M. P., M. B. ...	*Miscellaneous Papers, Macready as "Benedick."*
M. P., M. B. S.	*Miscellaneous Papers, Mr. Bull, Somnambulist.*
M. P., M. B. V. ...	*Miscellaneous Papers, Mr. Booley's View of the Last Lord Mayor's Show.*
M. P., M. E. ...	*Miscellaneous Papers, Murderous Extremes.*
M. P., M. E. R.	*Miscellaneous Papers, Curious Misprint in the Edinburgh Review.*
M. P., M. M. ...	*Miscellaneous Papers. Martyr Medium.*
M. P., M. N. D. ...	*Miscellaneous Papers, M. Nightingale's Diary.*
M. P., M. P. ...	*Miscellaneous Papers, Murdered Person.*
M. P., N. E. ...	*Miscellaneous Papers, Niger Expedition.*
M. P., N. G. K.	*Miscellaneous Papers, It is not generally known.*
M. P., N. S. ...	*Miscellaneous Papers, New Song.*
M. P., N. S. E. ...	*Miscellaneous Papers, Nobody, Somebody, Everybody.*
M. P., N. S. L. ...	*Miscellaneous Papers, Nightly Scene in London.*
M. P., N. T.	*Miscellaneous Papers, No Thoroughfare.*
M. P., N. Y. D. ...	*Miscellaneous Papers, New Year's Day.*
M. P., O. C. ...	*Miscellaneous Papers, Our Commission.*
M. P., O. F. A. ...	*Miscellaneous Papers, On Mr. Fletchers' Acting.*
M. P., O. L. N. O.	*Miscellaneous Papers, Old Lamps for New Ones*
M. P., O. S. ...	*Miscellaneous Papers, On Strike.*
M. P., Ox. C. ...	*Miscellaneous Papers, Report of the Commissioners, Oxford*
M. P., P. A. P. ...	*Miscellaneous Papers, Proposals for Amusing Posterity.*
M. P., P. F. ...	*Miscellaneous Papers, Perfect Felicity.*
M. P., P. F. D.	*Miscellaneous Papers, Prologue to "The Frozen Deep."*
M.P ., P. L. U. ...	*Miscellaneous Papers, Please to Leave your Umbrella.*
M. P., P. M. B. ...	*Miscellaneous Papers, Poor man and his Beer.*
M. P., P. N. J. B.	*Miscellaneous Papers, Proposals for a National Jest-Book*
M. P., P. P. ...	*Miscellaneous Papers, Pet Prisoners.*
M. P., P. P. D. ...	*Miscellaneous Papers, Prologue to "The Patrician's Daughter.*
M. P., P. S. ...	*Miscellaneous Papers, Poetry of Science.*
M. P., P. T. ...	*Miscellaneous Papers, Paradise at Tooting.*
M. P., Q. D. P. ...	*Miscellaneous Papers, Quack Doctor's Proclamations.*
M. P., R. D. ...	*Miscellaneous Papers, Railway Dreaming.*
M. P., R. G. ...	*Miscellaneous Papers, Leech's "The Rising Generation.*
M. P., R. H. F. ...	*Miscellaneous Papers, From the Raven in the Happy Family."*
M. P., R. L. M. ...	*Miscellaneous Papers, Reflections of a Lord Mayor.*
M. P., R. S. ...	*Miscellaneous Papers, Railway Strikes.*
M. P., R. S. D. ...	*Miscellaneous Papers, Rather a Strong Dose.*
M. P., R. S. L.	*Miscellaneous Papers, Restoration of Shakespeare's "Lear."*
M. P., R. T. ...	*Miscellaneous Papers, Red Tape.*
M. P., S.	*Miscellaneous Papers, Supposing!*
M. P;, S. B. ...	*Miscellaneous Papers, Spirit Business.*
M. P., S. C. ...	*Miscellaneous Papers, Spirit of Chivalry.*
M. P., S. D. C.	*Miscellaneous Papers, Slight Depreciation of the Currency.*

Abbreviation.	Title.
M. P., S. F. A. ...	*Miscellaneous Papers, Stories for the First of April.*
M. P., S. G. ...	*Miscellaneous Papers, Strange Gentleman.*
M. P., S. O. W. ...	*Miscellaneous Papers, " Song of the Wreck."*
M. P. ,S. for P. ...	*Miscellaneous Papers, Subjects for Painters.*
M. P., S. P. ...	*Miscellaneous Papers, Scott and his Publishers.*
M. P., S. Pigs. ...	*Miscellaneous Papers, Sucking Pigs.*
M. P., S. Q. F. ...	*Miscellaneous Papers, Slight Question of Fact.*
M. P., S. R. ...	*Miscellaneous Papers, Smuggled Relations.*
M. P., S. S. ...	*Miscellaneous Papers, Sunday Screw.*
M. P., S. S. U.	*Miscellaneous Papers, Sleep to Startle us.*
M. P., T. B. ...	*Miscellaneous Papers, Tattlesnivell Bleater.*
M. P., T. D. ...	*Miscellaneous Papers, Trading in Death.*
M. P., T. F. ...	*Miscellaneous Papers, Tooting Farm.*
M. P., T. L. ...	*Miscellaneous Papers, The Lighthouse.*
M. P., T. O. H. ...	*Miscellaneous Papers, Thousand and One Humbugs.*
M. P., T. O. P.	*Miscellaneous Papers, That other Public.*
M. P., T. T. ...	*Miscellaneous Papers, Toady Tree.*
M. P., T. T. C. D.	*Miscellaneous Papers, Things that cannot be done.*
M. P., T. W. M....	*Miscellaneous Papers, To Working Men.*
M. P., Th. Let. ...	*Miscellaneous Papers, Threatening Letter to Thomas Hood.*
M. P., U. N. ...	*Miscellaneous Papers, Unsettled Neighbourhood.*
M. P., V. and B. S.	*Miscellaneous Papers, Virginie and Black-eyed Susan*
M. P., V. C. ...	*Miscellaneous Papers, Village Coquettes.*
M. P., V. D. ...	*Miscellaneous Papers, Verdict for Drouet.*
M. P., W. ...	*Miscellaneous Papers, Why?*
M. P., W. A. R.	*Miscellaneous Papers, Well-authenticated Rappings.*
M. P., W. H. ...	*Miscellaneous Papers, Whole Hogs.*
M.P., W. L. ...	*Miscellaneous Pieces, Hymn of the Wiltshire Labourers.*
M. P., W. M. ...	*Miscellaneous Papers, Worthy Magistrate.*
M. P., W. S. ...	*Miscellaneous Papers, Word in Season.*
M. P., W. S. G. ...	*Miscellaneous Papers, Where we Stopped Growing.*
M. P., Y. M. C. ...	*Miscellaneous Papers, Young Man from the Country.*
Mud. Pap. ...	*Mudfog Papers.*
N. N. ...	*Life and Adventures of Nicholas Nickleby.*
O. C. S. ...	*Old Curiosity Shop.*
O. M. F. ...	*Our Mutual Friend.*
O. T.	*Adventures of Oliver Twist.*
P. P.	*Posthumous Papers of the Pickwick Club.*
P. F. I.	*Pictures from Italy.*
P. N. P.	*Pic-nic Papers.*
R. P., B. L. W. ...	*Reprinted Pieces, Begging Letter Writer.*
R. P., B. M. S. ...	*Reprinted Pieces, Births, Mrs. Meek, of a Son.*
R. P., B. S. ...	*Reprinted Pieces, Bill Sticking.*
R. P., C. D. S. ...	*Reprinted Pieces, Child's Dream of a Star.*
R. P., C. S. ...	*Reprinted Pieces, Child's Story.*
R. P., C. T., ...	*Reprinted Pieces, Christmas Tree.*
R. P., D. P. ...	*Reprinted Pieces, Detective Police.*
R. P., D. W. T. T.	*Reprinted Pieces, Down with the Tide.*
R. P., F.	*Reprinted Pieces, Flight.*
R. P., G. A. ...	*Reprinted Pieces, Ghost of Art.*
R. P., L. A. ...	*Reprinted Pieces, Lying Awake.*

ABBREVIATION.	TITLE.
R. P., L. V., ...	*Reprinted Pieces, Long Voyages.*
R. P., M. F. F.	*Reprinted Pieces, Monument of French Folly.*
R. P., N. Sa. ...	*Reprinted Pieces, Noble Savage.*
R. P., N. S. ...	*Reprinted Pieces, Nobody's Story.*
R. P., O. B. ...	*Reprinted Pieces, Our Bore.*
R. P., D. W. I. F.	*Reprinted Pieces, On Duty with Inspector Field.*
R. P.. O. E. W. P.	*Reprinted Pieces, Our English Watering Place.*
R. P., O. H. F. ...	*Reprinted Pieces, Our Honourable Friend.*
R. P., O. o. T. ...	*Reprinted Pieces, Out of Town.*
R. P., O. of the S.	*Reprinted Pieces, Out of the Season.*
R. P., O. S. ...	*Reprinted Pieces, Our School*
R. P., O. V. ...	*Reprinted Pieces, Our Vestry.*
R. P., P. A. ...	*Reprinted Pieces. Plated Article.*
R. P., P. B.,	*Reprinted Pieces, Prince Bull.*
R. P., P. M. T. P.	*Reprinted Pieces, Poor Man's Tale of a Patent.*
R. P., P. R. S. ...	*Reprinted Pieces, Poor Relation's Story.*
R. P., S. S. ...	*Reprinted Pieces, Schoolboy's Story.*
R. P., T. D. A. ...	*Reprinted Pieces, Three Detective Anecdotes.*
R. P., W. W. ...	*Reprinted Pieces, Walk in the Workhouse.*
S. B. B., Char. ...	*Sketches by Boz, Characters.*
S. B. B., O. P. ...	*Sketches by Boz, Our Parish.*
S. B. B., Scenes ...	*Sketches by Boz, Scenes.*
S. B. B., Tales. ...	*Sketches by Boz, Tales.*
S. U. T. H. ...	*Sunday under Three Heads.*
S. Y. C.	*Sketches of Young Couples.*
S. Y. G.	*Sketches of Young Gentlemen.*
T. T. C.	*Tale of Two Cites.*
U. T.	*Uncommercial Traveller.*